Presented to

John Thomason

Best Actor in a One Act

1981~1982

Herb, "I Ought to be in Pictures"

Ten Great Musicals of the American Theatre

Ten Great Musicals of the American Theatre

Edited, with an introduction and notes on the plays, authors and composers, by

STANLEY RICHARDS

Chilton Book Company
Radnor, Pennsylvania

Published in Radnor, Pa., by Chilton Book Company
and simultaneously in Ontario, Canada
by Thomas Nelson & Sons, Ltd.

Manufactured in the United States of America

for the

authors, lyricists and composers

of the

American Musical Theatre

CONTENTS

INTRODUCTION

Although it had its antecedents, *The Black Crook* generally is regarded as the progenitor of the American musical. Opening on September 12, 1866, at Niblo's Garden, it became the sensation of New York where it ran for 475 performances and grossed an unprecedented one million dollars. Curiously enough, however, its origin came about by accident. A large ballet troupe and a profusion of novel scenic effects had been imported from abroad to perform at the Academy of Music but the theatre burned down before the opening. Meanwhile, William Wheatley, the enterprising manager of Niblo's Garden had announced a melodrama without music, *The Black Crook*. A showman as well as visionary, he conceived the idea of grafting the displaced ballet performers and scenic equipment onto the Charles M. Barras melodrama. As it has been encyclopedically recorded: "Niblo retired in 1861, and under the management of Wheatley was produced *The Black Crook* with which the name of Niblo's is indissolubly linked. This was a fantastic mixture of drama and spectacle, with wonderful scenery and transformations, for which the entire stage was remodeled, and with an amazing ballet of scantily clad dancers—it has been called New York's first 'leg-show'."

There is little reason to disagree with the contention that *The Black Crook* was directly responsible for making the musical extravaganza an extremely popular form of theatre during the succeeding decades and well into the twentieth century. With its emphasis on elaborate staging, lavish ensemble numbers and sumptuous production accouterments welded to a dramatic plot line, it is easy to discern why this innovative presentation is described as America's progenitive musical for it indeed heralded various theatrical components that henceforth were to be utilized in the development of this indigenous art form.

While it may be said with considerable justification that in the early part of this century our musical theatre also was significantly influenced by European styles (particularly operetta and comic opera, which in turn were based on the Italian *opera buffa* and the French *opéra bouffe*) it eventually evolved a style distinctively its own and became our most creative and potent form of theatrical expression, one acknowledged and admired throughout the world.

The evolution did not come about swiftly, rather it inched its way somewhat cautiously. For at least three decades, the musical theatre largely was populated by highly romanticized operettas (many derived from foreign sources), lush extravaganzas with their acres of feminine pulchritude, and light-hearted musical comedies. With perhaps just a few exceptions, the latter harbored stereotype and banal books between song and dance cues and most only are recalled today for the many memorable songs they contributed to America's musical lexicon.

It wasn't until 1927 that a major indication of a change in style and treatment was to appear. The event was the opening of *Show Boat* which pointedly demonstrated the value of integrating music with characters and story. The real breakthrough, however, came in 1931 with *Of Thee I Sing.* As recounted elsewhere in this volume, it was the very first musical to be recognized by the Pulitzer Prize committee for its inherent merits as "a biting and true satire on American politics."

With this eminent recognition musical comedy took on a new and distinguished status and the days of the slapdash librettos with their interjected songs seemed to be numbered. But not quite, for it wasn't until 1935 that another musical, *Porgy and Bess,* would again resoundingly demonstrate the potential power of the musical stage, an area of entertainment that markedly continued its development into the 1940s when the musical play permanently evolved with its stress on a strong book and the full integration of music and dance to characterize and enhance the progression of the plot. To celebrate this notable advancement, its creators, by and large, dropped the "comedy" connotation of the term and billed their productions either as "musical plays" or simply as "musicals."

Not only do the ten works contained in this volume represent some of the finest achievements of our musical theatre, but they also have won enormous popularity with audiences both here and abroad. Collectively, they tallied 9,371 performances in their original New York engagements, an eloquent testimony to their copious entertainment values and an unquestionable manifestation of public approbation, which, in the final analysis, is the most significant critical factor of all.

Now for the omissions. It must be explained that publication rights for certain properties were unavailable at the time of compiling this volume. But on the credit side of the ledger, let me add that *Porgy and Bess* is here being published for the very first time, while six other of the plays (*Of Thee I Sing; One Touch of Venus; Brigadoon; Kiss Me, Kate; West Side Story* and *Gypsy*) have all been out of print until their appearance in this book.

It was the hope of the editor, therefore, to present a work that encompassed and perpetuated in print a comprehensive and valuable collection of outstanding musicals, all of which added in some way to the distinction and glory of the American musical theatre—indisputably, the world's finest.

Stanley Richards

Ten Great Musicals of the American Theatre

OF THEE I SING

Book by George S. Kaufman *and* Morrie Ryskind
Music by George Gershwin
Lyrics by Ira Gershwin

Production Notes

Of Thee I Sing was first presented by Sam H. Harris at the Music Box Theatre, New York, on December 26, 1931. The cast was as follows:

Louis Lippman, *Sam Mann*
Francis X. Gilhooley, *Harold Moffet*
Maid, *Vivian Barry*
Matthew Arnold Fulton, *Dudley Clements*
Senator Robert E. Lyons, *George E. Mack*
Senator Carver Jones, *Edward H. Robins*
Alexander Throttlebottom, *Victor Moore*
John P. Wintergreen, *William Gaxton*
Sam Jenkins, *George Murphy*
Diana Devereaux, *Grace Brinkley*
Mary Turner, *Lois Moran*
Miss Benson, *June O'Dea*
Vladimir Vidovitch, *Tom Draak*
Yussef Yussevitch, *Sulo Hevonpaa*
The Chief Justice, *Ralph Riggs*
The Scrubwoman, *Leslie Bingham*
The French Ambassador, *Florenz Ames*
Senate Clerk, *Martin Leroy*
Guide, *Ralph Riggs*
Photographers, Policemen, Supreme Court Justices, Secretaries, Sightseers, Newspapermen, Senators, Flunkeys, Guests, Etc.

Directed by *George S. Kaufman*
Dances staged by *Georgie Hale*
Settings by *Jo Mielziner*
Costumes by *Charles LeMaire*
Orchestrations by *Russell Bennett* and *William Daly*
Musical Director: *Charles Previn*

Act One

Scene 1: Main Street.
Scene 2: A hotel room.
Scene 3: Atlantic City.
Scene 4: A hotel suite.
Scene 5: Outside Madison Square Garden.
Scene 6: Inside Madison Square Garden.
Scene 7: Election night.
Scene 8: Washington.

Act Two

Scene 1: The White House.
Scene 2: The Capitol.

Scene 3: The Senate.
Scene 4: Again the White House.
Scene 5: The Yellow Room.

Musical Numbers

Act One

Scene 1:
Wintergreen for President — Ensemble
Scene 3:
Who Is the Lucky Girl to Be? — Diana Devereaux and Ensemble
The Dimple on My Knee — Diana Devereaux, Jenkins and Ensemble
Because, Because — Diana Devereaux, Jenkins and Ensemble
Finaletto:
Scene 4:
Never Was There a Girl So Fair — Company
Some Girls Can Bake a Pie — Wintergreen and Company
Scene 5:
Love Is Sweeping the Country — Jenkins, Miss Benson and Ensemble
Scene 6:
Of Thee I Sing — Wintergreen, Mary and Company
Scene 8:
Finale:
Entrance of Supreme Court Justices
Here's a Kiss for Cinderella — Wintergreen and Ensemble
I Was the Most Beautiful Blossom — Diana Devereaux

Act Two

Scene 1:
Hello, Good Morning — Jenkins, Miss Benson and Secretaries
Who Cares? — Wintergreen, Mary and Reporters
Finaletto:
Garçon, S'il Vous Plaît — French Soldiers
Entrance of French Ambassador
The Illegitimate Daughter — The French Ambassador
Scene 3:
The Roll Call — Alexander Throttlebottom
Finaletto:
Jilted — Diana Devereaux and Company
Who Could Ask for Anything More? — Mary and Company
Posterity — Wintergreen and Company

Scene 5:
Trumpeter, Blow Your Horn
Finale

ACT ONE

SCENE 1

A campaign parade. The background is a street drop, and across it is flung a huge election banner. It reads: "For President, John P. Wintergreen. For Vice-President, Alexander Throttlebottom." *The bottom of the banner is so wrinkled, however, that the name* THROTTLEBOTTOM *is not legible. Huge, out-of-focus pictures of the two candidates are also on the banner. It is night, and the paraders carry flares, red lights and noise-making machines. Each second or third person carries a sign—probably of the box variety, and lit from the inside so that the lettering may be easily read. The signs read as follows:*

"Even Your Dog Likes John P. Wintergreen"
"The People's Candidate"
"Don't Waste Your Vote"
"Turn the Reformers Out"
"Hawaii Wants Wintergreen"
"He's Good Enough for Me"
"Vote for Prosperity and See What You Get"
"Wintergreen—A Man's Man's Man"
"The Full Dinner Jacket"
"Wintergreen Loves You"
"He Kept Us Out of Jail"
"Next Stop the White House"
"Wintergreen—The Flavor Lasts"
"A Vote for Wintergreen Is a Vote for Wintergreen"
"Win With Wintergreen"
"Wintergreen for President"

There are about fifty in the parade. They march around three times, stopping the third time and facing the audience. The music is "Wintergreen for President"—a song which includes bits of old campaign tunes. They march off and the lights black out.

SCENE 2

A hotel bedroom.

Ingredients for drinks on a table—glasses, White Rock, whiskey. Lolling on the bed, shirt-sleeved and reading a newspaper, LOUIS LIPPMAN; *sitting at the table, leisurely playing solitaire, is* FRANCIS X. GILHOOLEY.

GILHOOLEY *finishes his game, leans back in his chair, repeats the last phrase of the parade music.* LIPPMAN *puts down his paper; sings. A knock on the door.*

CHAMBERMAID: (*Enters, carrying towels. Crossing to bathroom*) I brought you some towels. (*Phone rings. To* GILHOOLEY, *as she passes him*) I'm just going to the bathroom.

GILHOOLEY: First door to the left. (MAID *disappears into bathroom as* LIPPMAN *answers phone*)

LIPPMAN: So what? Who? What's his name? Throttle *what?* Must have the wrong room. This is the National Committee. I say this is the National Campaign Committee. (*Hangs up*) Some fellow downstairs. (CHAMBERMAID *re-enters*)

GILHOOLEY: Did you find it?

CHAMBERMAID: Shall I turn the bed down now?

LIPPMAN: Sure. Go ahead.

CHAMBERMAID: I can't turn it down unless you get off it.

LIPPMAN: Oh, then the hell with it!

CHAMBERMAID: Yes, sir. (*Crossing to door*) Shall I come back later?

LIPPMAN: Why not?

CHAMBERMAID: Yes, sir. (*Exits*)

LIPPMAN: Nice girl.

GILHOOLEY: (*Rising and stretching*) Ho-hum! Certainly is great to take it easy for a while.

LIPPMAN: Yep. It was a tough convention, all right.

GILHOOLEY: I'll say it was tough. Sixty-three ballots.

LIPPMAN: But we put the ticket over. That's the big thing.

GILHOOLEY: Well, there's still the election. I don't mind telling you I'm a little bit worried.

LIPPMAN: Say, we never lost an election yet, and we've had a lot worse candidates.

GILHOOLEY: It ain't just the candidates—it's the whole party.

LIPPMAN: What do you mean the whole party?

GILHOOLEY: Mm. I think maybe they're kind of getting wise to us.

LIPPMAN: Say! If they haven't got wise to us in forty years, they'll never get wise.

GILHOOLEY: Yah, but I don't like the way they've been acting lately. You know, we never should have sold Rhode Island.

LIPPMAN: What are you worrying about? We've got a great ticket, haven't we? For President: John P. Wintergreen. He even *sounds* like a President.

GILHOOLEY: That's why we picked him.

LIPPMAN: Yes—and for Vice-President— (*Hesitates*) Say—what's the name of that fellow we nominated for Vice-President?

GILHOOLEY: Ah—Pitts, wasn't it?

LIPPMAN: No, no—it was a longer name.

GILHOOLEY: Barbinelli?

LIPPMAN: No.

GILHOOLEY: Well, that's longer.

LIPPMAN: You're a hell of a National Committeeman. Don't even know the name of the Vice-President we nominated.

(MATTHEW ARNOLD FULTON *enters. The others greet him*)

FULTON: Hello, Louis; hello, Frank.

LIPPMAN: Hey, Fulton, to decide a bet: What's the name of that fellow we nominated for Vice-President?

FULTON: What? Oh—Schaeffer, wasn't it?

GILHOOLEY: That's right.

LIPPMAN: No, no! Schaeffer turned it down.

GILHOOLEY: Wait a minute! Wait a minute! Are you sure we nominated a Vice-President?

FULTON: Of course. Didn't I make the nominating speech? What was his name again?

GILHOOLEY: (*Simultaneously with* LIPPMAN) Well, think a minute. How did you come to nominate him?

LIPPMAN: (*Simultaneously with* GILHOOLEY) Who introduced him to you?

FULTON: Nobody introduced him. I picked his name out of a hat. We put a lot of names in a hat, and this fellow lost.

(*Phone rings*)

LIPPMAN: (*At phone*) Hello. No, no, you've got the wrong room. What's his name again? Gotabottle? Oh, Throttlebottom. Wait a minute. (*To others*) Guy named Bottle-throttle says he has an appointment with somebody here.

FULTON: (*Sitting*) Never heard of him.

GILHOOLEY: Not me.

LIPPMAN: (*Into phone*) Must have the wrong room. Tell him this is the National Committee. Well, then, tell him it isn't the National Committee. Hello. And give me Room Service, will you?

GILHOOLEY: (*Lighting a cigar*) What do you know, Matty?

FULTON: (*Crossing to table*) I know I'm thirsty.

GILHOOLEY: Got just the ticket. (*Getting bottle from under table*)

FULTON: Had it analyzed?

GILHOOLEY: Had it psycho-analyzed. (*At table with drink*)

LIPPMAN: Room Service? This is four hundred and thirteen. Listen–send up a half a dozen bottles of White Rock, a couple of ginger ales– (*To others*) Who's paying for this?

GILHOOLEY: General party expense.

LIPPMAN: (*Into phone*) Make that a dozen ginger ales. And some dill pickles. (*Hangs up*) Well, Matty, how's the newspaper king?

FULTON: Well, if you want to know, a little bit worried.

LIPPMAN: What's the matter?

FULTON: Well, I've just been over to the office doing some long-distance phoning. Called up about twenty of my editors all over the country, and it's not going to be the cinch we figured on.

GILHOOLEY: (*To* LIPPMAN, *and simultaneously with his question*) What did I tell *you?*

LIPPMAN: What did you find out?

FULTON: Just that. It isn't going to be the cinch we–

(SENATORS CARVER JONES *and* ROBERT E. LYONS *enter.* SENATOR JONES *is from the West, and* SENATOR LYONS *is from the South.* LYONS *shakes hands with* GILHOOLEY)

JONES: (*Oratorical in manner*) Ah, gentlemen, good evening!

LYONS: Good evening, gentlemen!

GILHOOLEY: Hello, Senator!

LIPPMAN: Senator!

FULTON: How about Wintergreen? Is he coming over?

JONES: My friends, I am informed on excellent authority that John P. Wintergreen will shortly honor us with his presence. (*He sits*)

FULTON: Fine! Gentlemen, you probably wonder why I asked you over here.

LYONS: (*Sighting the liquor and pouring a drink*) Something about a drink, wasn't it?

FULTON: Senator Jones–

JONES: (*Rises; at once the orator*) My friends–

FULTON: Senator Jones–

JONES: My good friends–

FULTON: You're a man that keeps his ear close to the ground. What do they think about the ticket in the West?

JONES: My very good friends– (*Clearing his throat*) John P. Wintergreen is a great man–one of the greatest that the party has nominated since Alexander Franklin–

LYONS: And Robert E. Lee–

JONES: Unfortunately, however, while the people of the West admire our party, and love our party, and respect our party, they do not trust our party. And so, gentlemen, in the name of those gallant boys who fought overseas, and the brave mothers who sent them, we must not, we can not, we dare not allow Russian Bolshevism to dump cheap Chinese labor on these free American shores! Gentlemen, I thank you. (*Finishes his drink, hands glass to* LIPPMAN *for refilling, sits on trunk rack*)

FULTON: Thank *you,* sir. And now, Senator Lyons, tell us about the South.

LYONS: (*Puts glass on table*) Gentlemen, you ask me about the South. It is the land of romance, of roses and honeysuckle, of Southern chivalry and hospitality, fried chicken and waffles, salad and coffee.

LIPPMAN: No dessert?

(LYONS *reacts–goes to table and takes drink*)

FULTON: Thank you, gentlemen. That just about confirms what my editors have been telling me. The people of this country demand John P. Wintergreen for President, and they're going to get him whether they like it or not. And, between you and me, gentlemen, I don't think they like it. (*A knock on door*) Come in.

(*Door is slowly opened.* ALEXANDER THROTTLEBOTTOM *enters–hopefully and timidly smiling*)

THROTTLEBOTTOM: Good evening, gentlemen.

FULTON: Yes, sir. What can we do for you?

THROTTLEBOTTOM: Good evening–Mr. Fulton.

FULTON: (*All rise*) I'm afraid I don't quite place you. Your face is familiar, but—

THROTTLEBOTTOM: I'm Throttlebottom.

FULTON: What?

THROTTLEBOTTOM: Alexander Throttlebottom.

JONES: (*All pushing him out backwards*) We're very busy, my good man. If you'll just—

THROTTLEBOTTOM: But I'm Throttlebottom.

FULTON: I understand, Mr. Teitelbaum, but just at present—

GILHOOLEY: You come back later on.

LIPPMAN: After we're gone.

THROTTLEBOTTOM: But I'm Throttlebottom. I'm the candidate for Vice-President.

(*General ad lib. greeting*)

FULTON: That's the fellow!

GILHOOLEY: Of course!

LIPPMAN: (*Shakes hands with* THROTTLEBOTTOM) Sure.

(WAITER *enters with White Rock, etc. Places them on table by bed, and comes to* LIPPMAN)

FULTON: What's your name again?

THROTTLEBOTTOM: Alexander—

FULTON: Of course! I nominated you! Alexander! Boys, this is— What's your first name, Mr. Alexander?

THROTTLEBOTTOM: That's my first name. Alexander.

FULTON: Alexander Alexander.

GILHOOLEY: Well, that certainly is a coincidence.

(WAITER *taps* LIPPMAN *on arm.* LYONS *goes to table—takes cigar*)

THROTTLEBOTTOM: But that isn't my last name. It's Throttlebottom.

GILHOOLEY: Oh, well, that's different.

LIPPMAN: (*As the* WAITER *hands him the check*) Throttle what?

THROTTLEBOTTOM: Bottom.

LIPPMAN: How do you spell it?

THROTTLEBOTTOM: (*As he starts to spell,* LIPPMAN *takes the check from the* WAITER *and writes*) "T-h-r-o-t-t-l-e-b-o-t-t-o-m."

LIPPMAN: Right! And thank you very much. (WAITER *exits with check, pushed out by* LIPPMAN)

FULTON: Well, sir, we're very glad, indeed, to see you, and very proud to have you on our ticket. Won't you sit down?

(*All sit, leaving no place for* THROTTLEBOTTOM)

THROTTLEBOTTOM: (*After a good look around*) Thanks. I won't sit. I'm only going to stay a minute. There's something I came up to see you about.

FULTON: What's that?

THROTTLEBOTTOM: Being Vice-President. I want to know if you won't let me off.

FULTON: (*Rises, and together with* GILHOOLEY) What?

GILHOOLEY: (*Rises*) What do you mean?

THROTTLEBOTTOM: I don't want to be Vice-President. I want to resign.

FULTON: Why, you can't do that!

JONES: (*Rises*) That's treason!

LYONS: Absurd, suh!

LIPPMAN: (*Rises*) Why don't you want to be Vice-President? That's a good job.

THROTTLEBOTTOM: It's—it's on account of my mother. Suppose she found out?

FULTON: You've got a mother?

GILHOOLEY: (*To others*) Boys, he's got a mother.

(JONES *and* GILHOOLEY *take off hats*)

LIPPMAN: This is a fine time to tell us.

FULTON: Yes, why didn't you tell us? You can't back out now. Everything's printed.

GILHOOLEY: Listen, she'll never hear about it.

JONES: Of course not.

THROTTLEBOTTOM: But maybe she will. Somebody may tell her.

LIPPMAN: Who'll tell her?

FULTON: Why, nobody'll know.

(LYONS *pours drink*)

GILHOOLEY: (*Gets drink from table*) You'll forget it yourself in three months.

FULTON: Of course.

LIPPMAN: Besides, suppose something should happen to the President?

THROTTLEBOTTOM: What?

LIPPMAN: Suppose something should happen to the President? Then you become President.

THROTTLEBOTTOM: Me?

LIPPMAN: Sure.

THROTTLEBOTTOM: President! Say!

LIPPMAN: Let's drink to that! (*To* LYONS) Bob! To our next President!

(LYONS *passes the glass to* LIPPMAN, *right under* THROTTLEBOTTOM'S *nose, as* THROTTLEBOTTOM *makes a futile pass for it.* JONES *passes a glass to* FULTON)

GILHOOLEY: Our next President!

JONES: (*By door*) Our next President!

(WINTERGREEN *enters as this line is being spoken, and simultaneously* THROTTLEBOTTOM, *seeing that there is no glass for him, makes a dash for the bathroom, from which he emerges with a green bathroom glass, a moment later*)

WINTERGREEN: I'll drink to that! (*Takes the glass in the extended arm of* JONES *and drinks. There is an ad lib. greeting from all. Hands back glass and crosses to* THROTTLEBOTTOM)

LIPPMAN: Well, how's the candidate?

WINTERGREEN: Thirsty. Say, doesn't a fellow get a drink? (*He sees the drink* THROTTLEBOTTOM *has just poured for himself, and takes it from his hand*) Ah! Thank you, waiter. And get me one of those dill pickles, will you?

THROTTLEBOTTOM: But I'm not—

WINTERGREEN: There they are—right over there. (THROTTLEBOTTOM *obediently goes for the pickle at bed table*) Well, gentlemen, it certainly was a great convention. I never expected to get the nomination. Didn't *want* the nomination. Never was so surprised as when my name came up. (*Takes pickle from* THROTTLEBOTTOM, *and gives him the empty glass.* THROTTLEBOTTOM *goes back to table and pours another drink*)

GILHOOLEY: Say, who brought it up, anyhow?

FULTON: Yah. Who was that in the back calling "Wintergreen!"

WINTERGREEN: That was me. Most spontaneous thing you ever saw. So here I am, gentlemen—nominated by the people, absolutely my own master, and ready to do any dirty work the committee suggests.

(*In one movement he takes the full glass* THROTTLEBOTTOM *has finally succeeded in getting for himself, and replaces it with the pickle he has been holding in his own hand.* THROTTLEBOTTOM *returns pickle to table*)

LYONS: *Mister* President—

WINTERGREEN: I'll drink to that, too! Anything else, gentlemen? Anything at all! What's the matter, Fulton? Something wrong? You're not sober, are you?

FULTON: (*His tone belying the words*) No, no! I'm all right.

WINTERGREEN: Must be something up. (*A look at the others as he puts down his glass*) What's the matter?

LIPPMAN: (*Deprecatingly*) A lot of schmoos.

FULTON: Well, it's this way. Begins to look as though there may be a little trouble ahead.

WINTERGREEN: Trouble?

FULTON: I don't think people are quite satisfied with the party record.

WINTERGREEN: Who said they were?

FULTON: Well, you know what Lincoln said.

WINTERGREEN: Who?

FULTON: Lincoln.

GILHOOLEY: What did he say?

WINTERGREEN: Was it funny?

FULTON: "You can fool some of the people all the time, and you can fool all of the people some of the time, but you can't fool all of the people all of the time."

THROTTLEBOTTOM: (*His lips start moving as* FULTON *speaks, and at the last half of the speech he is unable to keep silent, so with great assurance he comes in on*) "–but you can't fool all of the people some– (*Corrects himself*) –all of the time."

WINTERGREEN: Was that Lincoln?

THROTTLEBOTTOM: Abraham J. Lincoln.

WINTERGREEN: It's different nowadays. People are bigger suckers.

GILHOOLEY: Yes, but we made one bad mistake. Never should have sold Rhode Island.

WINTERGREEN: Rhode Island! Nobody missed it! (*A gesture indicating its size*) H'm. Where is Rhode Island now? Anybody know?

THROTTLEBOTTOM: It's in Providence.

FULTON: Wall Street, some place. Never get it back.

WINTERGREEN: (*A slap of the hands*) I'll tell you what! We'll leave it out of the campaign–not mention it! (*There is a chorus of approval.* JONES: *"Say, that might do it!"* LYONS: *"That's great, suh!"* LIPPMAN: *"Sure it would!"* GILHOOLEY: *"That's the idea!"* FULTON: *"Swell."*) Yes, sir, that's the idea –we won't mention it!

THROTTLEBOTTOM: But suppose somebody else brings it up?

WINTERGREEN: Don't answer 'em! It takes two to make an

argument. (*Notices, but does not recognize* THROTTLEBOTTOM. *Crosses to* FULTON. THROTTLEBOTTOM *backs away*) I thought this was a closed meeting.

FULTON: Sure it is. Why?

WINTERGREEN: (*Gesturing and whispering*) Who's that?

FULTON: (*Also whispering*) Vice-President.

WINTERGREEN: (*Whispers*) What? (*Shrugs his shoulders*)

FULTON: Oh—this is Mr. Wintergreen. Mr.—ah—ah—

THROTTLEBOTTOM: (*Taking a moment to remember*) Ah—ah—Throttlebottom.

(*They shake hands—an exchange of "How do you do's"*)

WINTERGREEN: Haven't I seen you before some place?

THROTTLEBOTTOM: I gave you that dill pickle.

WINTERGREEN: Of course.

FULTON: But, look here, Mr. President—it's not only Rhode Island. There've been a whole lot of things the last four years.

GILHOOLEY: How about the four years before that?

WINTERGREEN: I'll tell you what—let's stick to the party record of Seventeen Hundred and Seventy-Six. That was a good year.

LIPPMAN: What's the matter with Fourteen Ninety-Two?

WINTERGREEN: We can use that year, too. We won't mention anything before Fourteen Ninety-Two, or after Seventeen Seventy-Six. That gives us pretty nearly three hundred years.

FULTON: Say, that's great!

LYONS: (*Rises*) But, just a minute, suh! Down South the people want to hear about the Civil War.

WINTERGREEN: What year was that?

LYONS: (*Searching pocket*) Well, I haven't got the exact figures with me, but it was around Eighteen Hundred and Twelve.

THROTTLEBOTTOM: What year was Eighteen Twelve?

WINTERGREEN: Well, how about putting the Civil War back to Seventeen Seventy-Six? I think it's safer.

LYONS: (*Together with* JONES) Perfectly satisfactory, suh. Perfectly satisfactory.

JONES: Eminently fair.

FULTON: Yah, but it isn't enough.

GILHOOLEY: No! What we need is a good live issue!

FULTON: Yes! That's what we need—an issue. Something that everybody is interested in, and that doesn't matter a damn. Something the party can stand on.

2

THROTTLEBOTTOM: Excuse me, gentlemen, but what party are we?

WINTERGREEN: We've got plenty of time for that. The important thing is to get elected.

JONES: You see, we're Republicans in most states.

LYONS: (*Rises*) But the South is Democratic. (*Sits*)

JONES: Oh, sure. We're Democrats down there.

THROTTLEBOTTOM: (*To* WINTERGREEN) I had a dog that was bitten by a Democrat.

WINTERGREEN: (*Whispers to* JONES) Who is that?

JONES: (*Whispers*) Vice-President.

(*The* CHAMBERMAID *enters*)

CHAMBERMAID: Excuse me. (*Crosses back of group and exits into bathroom*)

FULTON: Boys, I tell you this is serious. We've got to get something that'll take hold of the popular imagination—sweep the country.

LIPPMAN: The country could stand a good sweeping.

JONES: Mr. Fulton is quite correct.

CHAMBERMAID: (*Re-enters from bathroom*) Can I turn the bed down now?

FULTON: What?

CHAMBERMAID: Can I turn the bed down now?

FULTON: Say—come here a minute. (*The* MAID *and* THROTTLEBOTTOM *both start toward* FULTON. *To* THROTTLEBOTTOM) No, not you. (*To* CHAMBERMAID) You're an American citizen?

CHAMBERMAID: Yes, sir.

FULTON: Ever vote?

CHAMBERMAID: Oh, *no*, sir.

FULTON: What do you care more about than anything else in the world?

CHAMBERMAID: I don't know. Money, I guess.

GILHOOLEY: That's no good.

WINTERGREEN: It brings up Rhode Island.

JONES: That's right.

CHAMBERMAID: (*Looking at* THROTTLEBOTTOM) What?

THROTTLEBOTTOM: I didn't say anything—

FULTON: Of course, money. We all want money. But there must be something else, isn't there?

CHAMBERMAID: (*Thinks*) No—I like money.

FULTON: But after money, what?

CHAMBERMAID: Well, maybe love.
FULTON: Love?
CHAMBERMAID: Yeh. You know, to meet a nice young fellow that's crazy about you, and you're crazy about him, and you get engaged, and then you get married, and–*you* know–(*To* THROTTLEBOTTOM) –love.
THROTTLEBOTTOM: Sure.
FULTON: Oh, yes, all right. Thank you. Thank you very much.
CHAMBERMAID: Shall I turn the bed down now, sir?
FULTON: Not now. Come back later on.
CHAMBERMAID: Yes, sir. (*Starts to go*)
FULTON: Ah–here you are. (*Gives her a coin.* THROTTLEBOTTOM *reaches for it*) No, not you.
CHAMBERMAID: Thank you, sir. (*Exits*)
LIPPMAN: Well, you got a lot out of that.
WINTERGREEN: Put women into politics and that's what you get. Love.
GILHOOLEY: Love!
FULTON: What's the matter with love?
WINTERGREEN: (*Disgustedly*) A-ah!
THROTTLEBOTTOM: I like love!
FULTON: People *do* care more about love than anything else. Why, they steal for it; they even kill for it.
WINTERGREEN: But will they vote for it?
FULTON: You bet they will! If we could find some way to put it over–why, we could get every vote in the country! Everybody loves a lover; the whole world loves a– (*Stops as he gets an idea; looks fixedly at* WINTERGREEN)
WINTERGREEN: What's the matter?
FULTON: I've got it!
THROTTLEBOTTOM: (*To others*) He's got it.
WINTERGREEN: Got what?
FULTON: You've got to fall in love!
WINTERGREEN: You're crazy!
FULTON: You've got to fall in love with a typical American girl.
WINTERGREEN: Huh?
LIPPMAN: What good's that?
GILHOOLEY: What are you talking about?
JONES: What for?
FULTON: Wait a minute! You make love to her from now till Election Day as no girl was ever made love to before.
WINTERGREEN: What's the gag?

GILHOOLEY: Yah!

LIPPMAN: So what?

FULTON: (*Crossing to* WINTERGREEN) My God, are you blind? You do this right and you'll get elected by the greatest majority that the American people ever gave a candidate! You'll get every vote!

WINTERGREEN: But wait a minute—

GILHOOLEY: I think there's something in it.

JONES: It sounds good.

LYONS: Certainly does!

LIPPMAN: Say!

FULTON: I tell you it's great!

WINTERGREEN: But just a minute—

FULTON: You'll go down in history as the greatest lover this country has ever known! You'll be the romantic ideal of every man, woman and child in America!

WINTERGREEN: Oh, no! I don't want anything like that!

FULTON: But, man, it's the biggest thing in the world! A hundred million hearts will beat as one; they'll follow your courtship in every State in the Union! You meet the girl, you fall in love with her, you propose, you're accepted, and you're swept into the White House on a tidal wave of love!

WINTERGREEN: But there's nobody I'm in love with! I'm not in love with anybody!

FULTON: We'll get a girl. That'll be easy.

LIPPMAN: My wife's sister!

FULTON: I've got the idea! We'll have a contest—a nationwide contest to select Miss White House—choose the most beautiful girl from every State—get them all together at Atlantic City, pick the winner, and you fall in love with her!

WINTERGREEN: But suppose I *don't* fall in love with her?

THROTTLEBOTTOM: Then *I* get her!

(*All to table for drinks except* FULTON)

FULTON: (*Goes to phone*) You can't *help* falling in love with her! The most beautiful girl in America! I tell you this is wonderful! (*Into the telephone*) Give me Beekman five thousand.

WINTERGREEN: (*Through* FULTON'S *phone conversation*) Give me another drink!

LIPPMAN: Let's all have another drink! Scotch or rye, Jack?

WINTERGREEN: Both!

FULTON: (*At phone*) Give me Jenkins! Hello!

LIPPMAN: (*With bottle*) Say when!

FULTON: That's what I said–Jenkins!

WINTERGREEN: (*Stopping* LIPPMAN; *there is hardly anything in the glass*) That's enough! (*Takes the bottle instead of the glass*)

FULTON: Jenkins? Fulton! Stop the presses! John P. Wintergreen will run for President on a one-word platform: "Love!" National beauty contest in Atlantic City to select Miss White House! Now, listen! I want a love cartoon on the front page of every one of my papers from now till Election Day! Right! And call up Al Smith and tell him I want a thousand words on love tomorrow morning!

Blackout

SCENE 3

The boardwalk in Atlantic City.

DIANA *enters left, followed by* TWELVE GIRLS. *At the same time* TWELVE *more* GIRLS *enter right. They parade on, in showgirl fashion, singing. All are in bathing suits.*

GIRLS:

Who is the lucky girl to be?
Ruler of Washington, D.C.?
Who is to be the blushing bride?
Who will sleep at the President's side?
Strike up the cymbals, drum and fife!
One of us is the President's future wife!

EIGHT GIRLS:

We're in Atlantic City
To meet with the committee,

EIGHT OTHERS:

And when they've made their mind up
The winner will be signed up.

EIGHT SHOWGIRLS:

The prize is consequential–
Presidential!
Our bodies will bear witness
To our fitness.

ALL:

If a girl is sexy
She may be Mrs. Prexy!

One of us is the President's future wife!

(*The two melodies are repeated together, the* SHOWGIRLS *singing the first verse, the* DANCERS *the other. At its conclusion, the* PHOTOGRAPHERS, *led by* JENKINS, *enter*)

PHOTOGRAPHERS:

More important than a photograph of Parliament,
Or a shipwreck on the sea—
What'll raise the circulation
Of our paper through the nation
Is the dimple on your knee.

More important than a photograph of Parliament,
Or a Western spelling bee,
Or the latest thing in science,
For our pleasure loving clients
Is the dimple on your knee.

(SHOWGIRLS *exit*)

PHOTOGRAPHERS:

What our readers love to see
Is the dimple on your knee,
What our readers love to see
Is the dimple on your knee.

GIRLS:

More important than a photograph of Parliament
Is the dimple on my knee.
But supposing I am losing
When the judges are a-choosing—
What will my poor future be?

Do I have to go back to the cafeteria
With my lovely dimpled knee?
Does a girl who's so ambitious
Have to work at washing dishes?
I'm afraid that worries me.

PHOTOGRAPHERS:

Don't worry, little girl,
For even if you lose the prize—
Don't worry, little girl,
Myself, I can't resist your eyes.

GIRLS:

I'll worry, little boy,
Until you tell what's on your mind.

(DIANA *exits*)

PHOTOGRAPHERS:

Don't worry, little girl,
I've asked my heart and this is what I find—
Don't worry, little girl;
Don't worry, little girl.

GIRLS:

Why shouldn't we worry?

PHOTOGRAPHERS:

Because, because, because, because,
Because you're in the money
With a smile that's sweet and sunny—
I could fall for you myself.
Because, because, because, because
Your looks are so appealing
They have given me a feeling,
I could fall for you myself.

The thrills you're sending through me
Are doing something to me!
The opposite of gloomy—
If *they* don't want you, *I* want you!
Because, because, because, because,
Because your ways are simple,
And your knee can show a dimple,
I could fall for you myself.

Blackout

SCENE 4

Parlor of an Atlantic City hotel suite.

EIGHT GIRLS *in bathing suits are on stage.* MARY TURNER, *distinguished from the others by the fact that she wears a dress, is seated at the desk. From the moment of the rise, other girls in bathing suits stream on from the entrance at left, to make a total of twenty-four.*

As the lights come on, FULTON *and* GILHOOLEY *enter, followed by* FOUR MEN *with movie cameras, which are set up down right.*

GILHOOLEY: (*To* MOVIEMEN) Come on, boys! Set 'em up right here—that'll give you a good angle! Hello, ladies!

FULTON: (*Speaking through* GILHOOLEY'S *speech*) Well, well! What a crowd! How are you, ladies? This certainly is a big day, all right! Must be ten thousand people outside this hotel! Never saw so much excitement in all my life!

GIRL: Say! What does a President's wife have to do, anyhow?

GILHOOLEY: That depends on the President.

MARY: (*Coming to* FULTON) Good morning, Mr. Fulton.

FULTON: Well, Miss Turner! Having quite a day, huh?

MARY: Quite a day, Mr. Fulton.

FULTON: Heard some very nice things about the way you've been handling this. Afraid I'll have to give you a raise.

MARY: Well, I'm afraid I'll have to take it. (*Goes to desk, then exits*)

(LYONS *and* JONES *enter*)

LYONS: Afternoon, gentlemen! Ladies!

FULTON: Ah, here's some of the committee now! Good afternoon, gentlemen!

JONES: Mr. Fulton! Good afternoon, ladies! Good afternoon! Well! Quite a battery you have here—quite a battery!

LYONS: Gentlemen of the press!

JONES: Very glad to see you, gentlemen. Always glad to meet the newspaper boys.

(JENKINS *enters, followed by* TWO BOYS)

JENKINS: (*To* FULTON) Good morning, Chief!

FULTON: Oh, hello, Jenkins!

JONES: Hello, there! I've met you before. Never forget a face! Just tell me—we've met before? Am I right?

JENKINS: Right you are, Senator!

JONES: Right! Where was it?

JENKINS: San Francisco. That opium joint on Fourth Street.

JONES: Well, I guess I got the wrong man. Remarkable resemblance, though; remarkable resemblance.

(*The* GIRLS *have laughed at* JONES' *discomfiture*)

THROTTLEBOTTOM: (*Enters*) Hello, everybody! Hello, Mr. Fulton!

GILHOOLEY: Hello, there!

JONES: How are you?

LYONS: Good morning, suh!

FULTON: Who is that guy?

GILHOOLEY: Vice-President.

FULTON: Oh, yes. Hello! How are you?

THROTTLEBOTTOM: Are these the girls? I'm Mr. Throttlebottom. (*To a* GIRL) Hello! How are you?

GIRL: Fine!

THROTTLEBOTTOM: Is your mother down here with you?

GIRL: Yes, sir.

THROTTLEBOTTOM: Oh! Well! Never mind! (*He turns to another* GIRL)

FULTON: (*Goes to* THROTTLEBOTTOM) Say, look here a minute. You know, Vice-Presidents don't usually go around in public. They're not supposed to be seen.

THROTTLEBOTTOM: But I'm not Vice-President yet. Couldn't I go around a little longer?

GILHOOLEY: That isn't the point. If you're going to be Vice-President you've got to practice up for it. You've got to go in hiding.

THROTTLEBOTTOM: But I came up the back way.

FULTON: You shouldn't have come at all. Suppose somebody sees you?

GILHOOLEY: We'd lose the election.

THROTTLEBOTTOM: You mean you want me to hide from everybody?

JONES: (*Simultaneously with* FULTON) That's it!

FULTON: Right!

THROTTLEBOTTOM: I could go back to my old business.

FULTON: What's that?

THROTTLEBOTTOM: I used to be a hermit.

FULTON: (*Together with* GILHOOLEY) Great!

GILHOOLEY: That's the idea!

THROTTLEBOTTOM: But I thought you might want me to make some speeches.

FULTON: No, no!

GILHOOLEY: You just go and sit in your cave.

THROTTLEBOTTOM: Well—I could go back to the cave and write my speeches there.

FULTON: (*Together with* JONES) That's the idea!

JONES: Perfect!

GILHOOLEY: And make 'em there, too!

JONES: Don't let anybody find you—don't let anybody see you.

THROTTLEBOTTOM: I won't—I won't even come out in February to cast my shadow. (*Exits*)

DIANA: (*Enters*) Mo'nin', Senator Lyons.

LYONS: Well, Miss Devereaux! And how is the fairest flower of the South?

DIANA: (*Thick Southern accent*) Senator Lyons, that's the prettiest thing been said to me since I left Louisiana. I sure been gettin' pow'ful homesick.

GIRL: She sure is getting pow'ful Southern.

LYONS: You're just a breath of the old Southland.

DIANA: You keep on sayin' sweet things like that and I'm just going to throw my arms right around your neck.

FULTON: You never made me an offer like that, Miss Devereaux.

DIANA: Why, Mr. Fulton!

FULTON: Yes, sir; when I look around I'm sorry I didn't run for President myself.

DIANA: You'd make a mighty fine consolation prize. Wouldn't he, girls? (*The* GIRLS *assent*)

FULTON: Now, now! Matter of fact, we're getting up some consolation prizes. Got that list, Jenkins?

JENKINS: (*Crossing to* FULTON) Here you are, sir.

FULTON: Of course, the first prize, as you all know, is Mr. Wintergreen himself. The second prize is a season pass to Coney Island. And the third prize is an autographed photograph of Clara Bow, or ten cents in gold. (*A murmur of excitement from the* GIRLS. *Enter* WINTERGREEN *and* LIPPMAN. *There is a buzz at their entrance*) Well, well! The candidate himself! Hello, Jack!

WINTERGREEN: Hello, there!

FULTON: Ladies, permit me to introduce your future husband, John P. Wintergreen! (*The* GIRLS *greet him*) Here they are, Jack. How do you like 'em?

WINTERGREEN: Why, they're wonderful. Hello. (*The* GIRLS *respond*) How are you? (*Another response. Having done his duty, he crosses back to* FULTON)

FULTON: Say something to them.

WINTERGREEN: Well, ladies, this certainly is a pleasure. All I can say is I love you, and you are the only girls I have ever loved. (GILHOOLEY, *who is standing in the line with the* GIRLS, *giggles*) Say, you're not one of them, are you? (GILHOOLEY, *affronted, moves out of line*) And after we're married, I hope you'll all be happy, and— (*Back to* FULTON) Listen, Fulton, I can't go through with this.

FULTON: You've got to go through with it.

WINTERGREEN: But I don't know any of these girls! How can I marry them? If it was only somebody I knew, like—Lippman —whatever became of your wife's sister?

LIPPMAN: (*With a shake of the head*) Not in a bathing suit.

FULTON: By the way, I want you to meet Miss Diana Devereaux.

LYONS: Miss Devereaux, may I have the honor—

DIANA: (*Cutting through his speech as she crosses to him*) Mr. President, I'm mighty happy to meet you! I hope we're going to see a lot of each other.

WINTERGREEN: Any hope of yours, Miss Devereaux, is a hope of mine—I hope.

DIANA: You keep on saying sweet things like that and I'm just going to throw my arms right around your neck.

(*The remaining* TWENTY-THREE GIRLS *chime in when she is halfway through the sentence and finish it with her, Southern accent and all*)

WINTERGREEN: Seems to be quite an echo here.

DIANA: (*Playing with his lapel*) Mr. Wintergreen—have you-all got a fraternity pin?

WINTERGREEN: Well, would a safety pin do?

DIANA: Mr. Wintergreen, you've got the grandest sense of humor. (*Still working the lapel.* MARY *re-enters*) Oh—Mr. Wintergreen—

MARY: All right, Mr. Fulton. (*Goes to desk*)

FULTON: And now, ladies—attention, please! The time has come for the final test. (*The* GIRLS *start a general primping and there is an excited buzz*) It has been a grueling contest—you have been under a great strain. And we of the committee want to thank you—and through you the three million others who took part in this contest, only ninety-eight percent of whom had to be sent home for misbehavior. And, now, ladies, the judges await you. And may the best girl win.

(COMMITTEE *forms up center. Music*)

GIRLS:

Who is the lucky girl to be—
Ruler of Washington, D.C.?

DIANA: (*Pulling* WINTERGREEN *to center*)

Bye-bye, Mr. President—I'm a-prayin'
I'm the little lady they're okayin'.

(DIANA *starts*)

GIRLS: (*Exiting, followed by* DIANA)
Strike up the cymbals, drum and fife!
One of us is the President's future wife!

COMMITTEE:
We'll get you, Mrs. Wintergreen.

WINTERGREEN:
Oh-o-o-o-o-o-o.

COMMITTEE:
We'll get you, Mrs. Wintergreen.

WINTERGREEN:
Oh-o-o-o-o-o-o-o-o-o.

COMMITTEE:
We'll present you with a bride!
She will be the Nation's pride!
Ta-Ta-Ta-Ta-Ta-Ta.

(*They exit on musical ending.* WINTERGREEN *is left on stage with* MARY. WINTERGREEN, *calling "good-bye," watches them exit. Looks after them thoughtfully a moment, then starts to pace up and down. He pulls out handkerchief and mops his brow.* MARY *takes papers from desk, starts toward balcony*)

WINTERGREEN: (*As he sees her*) Oh! Say! (*She stops*) You haven't got a drink on you, have you?

MARY: Why, no. I'm sorry.

WINTERGREEN: Oh, that's all right. Didn't want it anyhow. (*Pacing*)

MARY: Little bit nervous?

WINTERGREEN: (*Whirling*) Who? Me? What have I got to be nervous about?

MARY: That's what I was wondering. Twenty-four of the most beautiful girls in the country—and you get the winner. Lots of men would like to be in your shoes.

WINTERGREEN: (*Crossing to her*) Yeah, but it's my bedroom slippers I'm worrying about. Say, you've been watching them —who do you think it's going to be?

MARY: Oh, I couldn't say. Likely to be any one of them.

WINTERGREEN: That's what I was afraid of. Which one? What's your guess?

MARY: (*Sits*) Well, don't hold me to it, but I shouldn't be surprised if it were Miss Devereaux.

WINTERGREEN: Devereaux! I thought so! Is that the—ah—the one with the Southern exposure? (*Indicating the figure*)

MARY: That's Miss Devereaux. She's a good-looking girl, don't you think?

WINTERGREEN: (*Doubtfully*) Yes, she's a good-looking girl, all right.

MARY: (*In broad Southern accent*) Don't you-all like good-looking girls?

WINTERGREEN: Down Carolina way we're all a-crazy about good-looking girls. But we-all don't like 'em talking that-a-way.

MARY: How do you-all like 'em to talk, sure enough?

WINTERGREEN: We-all like them-all to let us-all do the talking. (*Abandons the dialect*) Say, that's terrible, isn't it? If she wins would I have to listen to that all the time?

MARY: But she does it charmingly. And she's very beautiful.

WINTERGREEN: Beautiful, yeah—I like a beautiful girl—they're all right—(*He stumbles*)—but when a fellow gets married he wants a home, a mother for his children.

MARY: (*Rises*) You've got children?

WINTERGREEN: (*Down to her*) No, no; I mean if I was married. You see, when you're married—well, *you* know.

MARY: Well, I think Miss Devereaux might listen to reason. And she'd make a very beautiful mother for your children.

WINTERGREEN: Beautiful! I don't know anything about these girls—whether they can sew, or make a bed, or cook. They don't look as though they'd ever had a skillet in their hands. Say, what *is* a skillet?

MARY: You wouldn't have to worry about that in the White House. They have plenty of servants there.

WINTERGREEN: Yeah, but some day we'll have to move out of the White House. Then what? The Old Presidents' Home? There'll be no servants there. She'll *have* to cook; then what?

MARY: Then she'll cook. And like it.

WINTERGREEN: But will *I* like it? Why, the average girl today can't cook—she can't even broil an egg.

MARY: Nonsense! Every girl can cook.

WINTERGREEN: (*Scornfully*) Every girl can cook—can *you?*

MARY: I certainly can.

WINTERGREEN: Then what are you doing here?

MARY: (*Right back at him*) I'm holding down a job! (*Crossing to him*) And I can cook, and sew, and make lace curtains, and bake the best darned corn muffins you ever ate. And what do you know about that?

WINTERGREEN: Corn muffins? Did you say corn muffins?

MARY: Yes, corn muffins!

WINTERGREEN: Corn muffins! You haven't got one on you, have you?

MARY: (*Crossing*) I haven't far to go.

WINTERGREEN: I'm crazy about corn muffins. I eat them all the time.

MARY: (*Gets lunch box from table*) It's lunch, but you can have it.

WINTERGREEN: Oh, I couldn't do that! (*He fumbles in box, looking at her*)

MARY: Please! The second from the left is a corn muffin. That's an apple.

WINTERGREEN: Oh, that's an apple. (*Picking up a muffin*) Well! You must let me take *you* to lunch some day. Mmm! Delicious! (*Samples it*) Why–it melts in the mouth!

MARY: (*Putting the box back on table*) And I'm the only person in the world who can make them without corn.

WINTERGREEN: Without–say, do you know I don't even know your name.

MARY: That's right–you don't.

WINTERGREEN: Mine's Wintergreen.

MARY: *I* know. Mine's Turner.

WINTERGREEN: Just Turner?

MARY: Mary Turner.

WINTERGREEN: (*Suddenly*) Say, why in God's name didn't you get into this contest?

MARY: One of the three million?

WINTERGREEN: Well, you know what the first prize is?

MARY: Yeah, can you imagine?

WINTERGREEN: And you get your picture in the paper.

MARY: Having tea on the lawn with the Filipino delegation. And you throwing the medicine ball at the cabinet.

WINTERGREEN: Oh, do we have to have a cabinet?

MARY: What would you throw the medicine ball at? Me?

WINTERGREEN: (*Suddenly sobered*) Gosh, it'd be fun with you. We could have a grand time.

MARY: (*The Southern accent*) Why, Mr. Wintergreen–

WINTERGREEN: No, I mean it. (*Noise offstage*) Listen–I've only got a minute–maybe less than that! I love you! I know it's awful sudden, but in a minute it'll be too late! Let's elope–let's get out of here! (*Pulls her away*)

MARY: But–but wait a minute. You don't know me. (*Pulls him back*)

WINTERGREEN: I know you better than those girls! (*A gesture*) You can make corn muffins, and–you're darned cute-looking, and–I love you! (*Pulls her away*)

MARY: But I don't know *you!* (*Stops him*)

WINTERGREEN: What's there to know? I'm young, I'm a swell conversationalist, and I've got a chance to be President! And, besides that–you love me!

MARY: But it's absurd. Why, you can't–

WINTERGREEN: The hell I can't! (*He seizes her and starts kissing her*) It's fate, Mary, that's what it is–fate! (*Kisses her again*) Why, we were meant for each other–you and me!

MARY: You and *I!*

WINTERGREEN: All right, you and I! (*Continues kissing her*)

(*The sound of talking off.* MARY *and* WINTERGREEN *go down right. The committee*–FULTON, GILHOOLEY, LYONS, LIPPMAN *and* JONES–*enter*)

FULTON:

As the chairman of the committee
I announce we've made our choice;
Ev'ry lover from Dubuque to Jersey City
Should rejoice!

COMMITTEE:

We rejoice.

(*Eight* CONTEST JUDGES, *in cutaways, enter singing*)

JUDGES and COMMITTEE:

When the angels up there designed her,
They designed a thoroughbred;
And on March the Fourth the President will find her
Worthy of his board and bed.

(*Music changes to waltz,* FULTON *speaking through it*)

FULTON: And now it thrills me to introduce the rarest of American beauties, the future first lady of the land–a fit consort for the ruler of our country–gentlemen–Miss Diana Devereaux! (*Crosses to escort* DIANA)

(DIANA *appears with a golden crown on her head, followed by all the other* GIRLS, *still in bathing suits.* ALL *sing as she parades close to where* WINTERGREEN *and* MARY *are standing*)

ALL: (*As* DIANA *makes circle of* COMMITTEE)

How beautiful, beautiful, beautiful,
How utterly, utterly so!
The charming, the gracious, the dutiful
Diana Devereaux.

FULTON: (*Spoken*) The committee will now tell why she was chosen—with music!

ALL:

Never was there a girl so fair!
Never was there a form so rare!

DIANA: (*Spoken*) Ah could throw mah arms right around your neck!

ALL:

A voice so lyrical
Is given few;
Her eyes a miracle
Of Prussian blue;
Ruby lips and a foot so small;
As for hips—she has none at all!

GILHOOLEY:

Did you ever see such footsies,
Or a more enticing limb?

LIPPMAN:

And the ankles of her tootsies
Are so slim!

LYONS and JUDGES:

What a charming epiglottis!
What a lovely coat of tan!
Oh, the man who isn't hot is
Not a man!

ALL:

She's a bargain to whom she's wed;
More than worthy his board and bed!

FULTON:

Says the chairman of the committee,
Let the newsmen now come in.

(*Crosses to* DIANA)
For the sound reels you must look your best, my pretty.
Have the interviews begin!

GILHOOLEY and LYONS: (*Starting*)
We shall go and bring them in!

WINTERGREEN:
Stop! No!
Though this may be a blow
I simply cannot marry
Diana Devereaux!

ALL:
What's this? What's this?
He says he cannot marry
Diana Devereaux!

COMMITTEE and JUDGES:
You mean you will not marry
Diana Devereaux!

WINTERGREEN:
Please understand—it isn't that I would jilt or spurn 'er:
It's just that I love someone else—

ALL:
Who?

WINTERGREEN: (*Correcting them*)
Whom! (*Crosses to* MARY)
Mary Turner.

ALL:
The man is mad!
Or else a cad!
He'll have to take her—
He can't forsake her!

DIANA: (*Crossing to him*)
This jilting me,
It cannot be!
This lousy action
Calls for retraction!

COMMITTEE and JUDGES:
We must know why
You should prefer

(*Pointing to* DIANA)
Instead of Di
(*Pointing to* MARY)
A girl like her.

GIRLS: (*Same gestures*)
Yes, tell us why
You should prefer
Instead of Di
A girl like her.

WINTERGREEN:
All that I can say of Mary Turner
Is that I love Mary Turner.

COMMITTEE and JUDGES:
What's to be done?
Though she has won,
(*Indicating* DIANA)
Though she is signed up,
He's made his mind up!
His love he'd ruther
(*Indicating* MARY)
Give to the other.
What shall we do now?
What is our cue now?

DIANA: (*To* COMMITTEE)
He will do nothing of the sort.
First we'll settle this thing in court.
(*To* WINTERGREEN)
You seem to think Miss Turner hits the spot;
But what has she got that I haven't got?

ALL:
Yes, what has *she* got that *she* hasn't got!

WINTERGREEN: (*To* DIANA)
My Mary makes corn muffins—
Can *you* make corn muffins?

DIANA:
I can't make corn muffins!

ALL: (*Sorrowfully*)
She can't make corn muffins!

WINTERGREEN:

Some girls can bake a pie
Made up of prunes and quinces;
Some make an oyster fry–
Others are good at blintzes.
(*Crossing to table*)
Some lovely girls have done
Wonders with turkey stuffin's,
(*Gets muffins; passes them around*)
But I have found the one
Who can really make corn muffins.

DIANA:

Who cares about corn muffins?
All I demand is justice!
(WINTERGREEN *repeats his verse,* MARY, DANCERS *joining in, the* COMMITTEE, JUDGES *singing an obligato, while* DIANA *and the* SHOWGIRLS *sing another counter-melody*)

COMMITTEE and JUDGES:

Corn muffins–
Though other girls are good at turkey stuffin's
She takes the cake–for she can bake–corn muffins,
Corn muffins–
He's not to blame for falling if she's able
To serve them at his table.
(WINTERGREEN *crosses with box.* COMMITTEE *samples muffins*)
They should be happy night and day;
They'll make a couple so delightful;
When two agree on corn muffins
Their marriage is only rightful.

DIANA and SHOWGIRLS: (*Simultaneously, to the* COMMITTEE)

Don't surrender!
Don't be tender!
I'm (she's) the winner!
She is a little sinner!
Come! Make your mind up.
I (she) not she–am (is) the one who's really signed up!
(DIANA *starts*)

ALL:

Great, great!
It really must be fate!

COMMITTEE and JUDGES:
We must declare these muffins
The best we ever ate!

GIRLS: (*Singing with* COMMITTEE)
There's none but Mary Turner
Could ever be his mate!
(DIANA *exits*)

BOYS: (*Singing with* COMMITTEE *and* GIRLS)
She can make corn muffins!
She can make corn muffins!

(*These couplets are repeated eight times, then all form a picture for the last line*)

ALL:
Let's all rejoice!

Curtain

SCENE 5

Outside Madison Square Garden.

In the center of the drop are double doors leading into the Garden, and through them is seen the corridor. Above the entrance is a large banner bearing pictures of WINTERGREEN *and* MARY, *and the inscriptions,* "WOO WITH WINTERGREEN" *and* "LOVERS! VOTE FOR JOHN AND MARY."

BAND *enters, followed by* EIGHT MEN (DANCERS). *They play one chorus of "Wintergreen for President," and then a chorus of "Love Is Sweeping the Country," on which* JENKINS *and* MISS BENSON *enter.*

(JENKINS *and* BENSON *sing verse and chorus of "Love Is Sweeping the Country," at conclusion of which* BAND *exits*)

JENKINS and BENSON:
Why are people gay
All the night and day,
Feeling as they never felt before?

BENSON:
What is this thing

JENKINS:
That makes them sing?
Rich man, poor man, thief,
Doctor, lawyer, chief—

JENKINS and BENSON:

Feel a feeling that they can't ignore:
It plays a part
In ev'ry heart
And ev'ry heart is shouting "Encore!"

Refrain

Love is sweeping the country;
Waves are hugging the shore;
All the sexes
From Maine to Texas
Have never known such love before.
See them billing and cooing
Like the birdies above.
Each girl and boy alike,
Sharing joy alike
Feels that passion'll
Soon be national.
Love is sweeping the country—
There never was so much love.

Blackout

SCENE 6

Inside Madison Square Garden.

The lights reveal the interior of the Garden. A speakers' platform, four feet high, stands about ten feet upstage. Leading up to it, both right and left, are little flights of stairs. On the platform itself, at the back, is a row of seven chairs. The two center chairs are empty; those who occupy the others are LIPPMAN, GILHOOLEY, JONES *and* LYONS. *The space between the platform and the footlights is bare. The seats in which spectators sit are at right and left against walls. Two rows of seats are visible on each side, and one gets the feeling that they extend far off on both sides. As far as the eye can see, of course, they are filled.*

The scene is in full blast when the curtains open.

FULTON: (*At the rostrum, in the middle of a speech and the middle of a sentence*)—Seventeen Hundred and Seventy-Six, Eighteen Hundred and Twelve, Eighteen Hundred and Sixty-One, Eighteen Hundred and Ninety-Eight, and Nineteen Hundred and Seventeen! (*There is loud applause as he stops*) And so, my friends, on Tuesday next yours is a great privilege.

You will cast your ballots for the greatest cause and the greatest emotion known to the heart of mankind! Love! (*Applause*) Yes, my good friends, for love! For love and for the greatest of all lovers! John P. Wintergreen! (*He sits down to great applause*)

LOUDSPEAKER: (*Through the cluster of megaphones that hangs overhead*) Attention, please! Next Wednesday night: Jack Sharkey, American champion of the world, versus Max Schmeling, German champion of the world, in their annual battle for the championship of the world! (*Applause*)

FULTON: (*Again to his feet*) And, my friends, as a good American, I believe that Jack Sharkey will win! (*Applause. He sits*)

LOUDSPEAKER: Attention, please! Message for Doctor Hugo Kristmacher! Doctor Kristmacher! Your wife has just telephoned the box-office and says not to come home tonight. (*Applause*)

FULTON: (*Rises.* JONES *covers face with hand*) And now, my good people, it is my great pleasure and privilege to introduce a man who has served his country long and gloriously, a man who has for many years waged a great and single-handed fight for what he considered his own interests—the silver-tongued orator of the golden West, Senator Carver Crockett Jones! (*Applause*)

(JONES *comes forward; shakes hands with the* COMMITTEE. ATTENDANTS *enter, spread mat center, then stand left and right of it*)

LOUDSPEAKER: Attention, please! While Senator Jones is speaking you will be entertained by the world's greatest wrestlers, Vladimir Vidovitch—(*He enters left*)—the Harlem Heaver, and Yussef Yussevitch—(*He enters right*)—the Terrible Turk, in a match for the world's championship.

(*Applause after "Vidovitch" and "Yussevitch." There is the sound of a gong. Simultaneously the* WRESTLERS *go into action and* SENATOR JONES *starts his speech.* ATTENDANTS *exit with bathrobes*)

JONES: My friends! We have arrived at a great moment in our history. Magnificent though our past has been, it dwindles into utter insignificance beside the brilliance of our future destiny. Gaze into that future, my friends, and what do you see? What do you see? (*At this moment what one chiefly sees is the rear elevation of* VIDOVITCH *which is being stared at with something akin to admiration by* YUSSEVITCH. *Gradually they draw all eyes, with* LIPPMAN *and* GILHOOLEY *trying discreetly to peer over the edge. They break, and resume wrestling as* JONES *resumes talking*) Not for us the entangling alliances of Europe, not for us the allying entanglances of Asia. (*A burst of applause. The* WRESTLERS, *at the moment, have a complicated double scissors hold on each other but their arms are free. Pausing in their labors, they join in the applause*) Here, then, we stand, alone in our strength, solitary in our splendor, the greatest, the most glorious country that God Almighty put upon earth—the United States of *America!!!* (*The* WRESTLERS, *relinquishing a complicated hold, jump to their feet and salute. The* CROWD *bursts into applause*) And so, my friends—

(*One of the* WRESTLERS *makes a sensational dive for the other's legs, throwing him to the mat with a crash. The* CROWD *rises and sets up a cheering and yelling, egging on the* WRESTLERS. *The* COMMITTEEMEN *sitting behind* JONES *crowd to the edge of the rail to look on. The whole* CROWD *is on its feet.* JONES *tries bravely to talk against this for a moment, but his own interest in the* WRESTLERS *finally gets the better of him. He joins the cheerers. The match now turns into real wrestling, with the* CROWD *on high all the time. It comes to a climax as one of the* WRESTLERS *finally gets the other down. The gong sounds seven or eight times. Cheers. Applause. Bows. The* WRESTLERS *exit. The* ATTENDANTS *roll up the mat and exit. The* CROWD *settles back*)

FULTON: (*Is on his feet, ready to speak. There is a hullabaloo offstage—sound of a scuffle, voices, etc. The* CROWD *gets to its feet as the noise mounts. Enter* THROTTLEBOTTOM, *trying to fight off* FOUR POLICEMEN. *As he comes into view it is seen that he is practically in tatters, his coat off, his collar askew. He struggles to the foot of the platform stairs*) Here, here, here! What's all this? Who is this man? Stop that noise! What is this? (*The noise quiets down. The* POLICEMEN *stand holding tightly onto* THROTTLEBOTTOM, *two to each arm*) What is all this? What do you want here?

THROTTLEBOTTOM: (*At the foot of the steps*) But, wait, wait! I'm Throttlebottom! I'm the Vice-President. Here—look! I'm Throttlebottom! (*Takes a banner from his pocket and unrolls it. It bears his picture and reads:* "For Vice-President: ALEXANDER THROTTLEBOTTOM")

FULTON: Oh, yes! Yes! It's all right, officers. This man is all right! (THROTTLEBOTTOM *gets up on the platform, is trying to get his clothes together, stuffing his shirt into his trousers, getting his collar back on*) Well, what happened to you?

THROTTLEBOTTOM: They wouldn't let me in.

FULTON: Why didn't you tell 'em who you were?

THROTTLEBOTTOM: I did.

FULTON: Well–?

THROTTLEBOTTOM: That's when they tried to throw me out.

FULTON: (*At the rostrum, reluctantly*) My friends, we have an unexpected surprise for you. It is your great and rare privilege to hear a few words from–(THROTTLEBOTTOM *prompts him*) –Alexander Throttle-something–(*He pronounces the name with great care*)–candidate for–what's it? (THROTTLEBOTTOM *prompts him again, first looking at the banner himself*) Vice-President–(*Then, as an afterthought*)–of the United States of America. (*Sits*)

(*The* CROWD *is silent.* THROTTLEBOTTOM *shows* CROWD *his banner, hands hat to* FULTON, *who passes it to* GILHOOLEY, *who passes it to* LIPPMAN, *who throws it off the platform.* THROTTLEBOTTOM *advances to the rostrum; takes his speech from his pocket. It unrolls all the way to the ground and proves to be about ten feet long. A pleased expression spreads over his face; recognition is his at last*)

LOUDSPEAKER: (*Just as* THROTTLEBOTTOM *opens his mouth to speak*) Attention, please! (THROTTLEBOTTOM'S *eyes go up to the megaphone*) At the end of the first period in Montreal: Boston Bruins, 3; Chicago White Sox, 1. (*The machine clanks off.* THROTTLEBOTTOM *again gets ready to speak. Once more a slow smile comes over his face; once more he is just about to speak*) Attention, please! There will now be an intermission of fifteen minutes. (*There is a great pushing back of chairs;* EVERYBODY *gets up and starts to leave*)

THROTTLEBOTTOM: No, no, no! No!

(*The various noises on stage merge into a greater and growing noise offstage. Cries of "Wintergreen!" "Here comes Wintergreen!" Those on stage pick the cry up. Enter* WINTERGREEN *and* MARY TURNER, *preceded by the* POLICEMEN. *To the accompaniment of cheers and handshaking they advance to the platform and go up the stairs. There is a great shaking of hands with the* COMMITTEEMEN. THROTTLEBOTTOM, *as the presidential procession gets up onto the platform, is simply pushed right out of the way by the* POLICEMEN *and practically falls down the stairs on the right side. Here he is met again by the* POLICEMEN, *and is ignominiously dragged out, kicking and protesting. Meanwhile, as the noise subsides,* WINTERGREEN *and* MARY *take the two center seats that have been left empty for them, and* FULTON *advances to the rostrum to introduce them*)

FULTON: (*Stilling the tumult with upraised hand*) No need to tell you who the next speakers will be. They are the most beloved couple in America today, the most beloved couple that have ever run for the highest office in the gift of the American people. There have been many great lovers in history. But Romeo never loved Juliet, Dante never loved Beatrice, Damon never loved Pythias, as John P. Wintergreen loves Mary Turner. (*Applause*) My friends, the issue of this campaign is a simple one. We do not talk to you about war debts or wheat or immigration—we appeal to your hearts; not your intelligence. It is the old, old story, yet ever new—the sweetest story ever told. John P. Wintergreen, candidate for President of the United States, loves Mary Turner. Mary Turner, the most beautiful, the loveliest example of typical American womanhood—and I defy our opponents to say otherwise—(*Glares at audience*)—loves John P. Wintergreen. He has proposed to her in forty-seven States of the Union, and in forty-seven States she has accepted him. Tonight she will give him her answer in the great Empire State of New York! John and Mary, stand up! (*They do so. Applause*) Can you look at them and not be thrilled by their youth, their charm, their passion? Ladies and gentlemen, I give you John P. Wintergreen and Mary Turner!

(FULTON *sits down as pandemonium breaks loose.* WINTERGREEN *and* MARY *come forward; the tumult slowly dies*)

WINTERGREEN: (*The orator*) My friends, I come before you in this final rally of the campaign, not as John P. Wintergreen the candidate, not as John P. Wintergreen the statesman, but as a simple man in love. So I beg you to bear with me for a moment, while I ask the girl of my dreams if she will be my heart's delight. (*There is applause as he turns to* MARY, *still the orator*) Miss Turner, there has been something on my mind for a long, long time.

MARY: (*Looks away from him*) Yes, Mr. Wintergreen?

WINTERGREEN: (*The hesitant lover*) May I not call you—Mary?

MARY: I wish you would—John.

3

WINTERGREEN: Do you remember that night we first walked together, on the boardwalk in Atlantic City?

MARY: With the moon shining overhead?

WINTERGREEN: (*Puts arm around her*) And the lights rippling on the water. Do you remember what I said to you, Mary, as I took your dear hand in mine?

MARY: Ah, yes—(*She drops her eyes*)

WINTERGREEN: And in the cornfields of Kansas, on the plains of Arizona, in the mountains of Nebraska, I whispered to you how much you were beginning to mean to me.

MARY: Our friendship has been a wonderful thing to me.

WINTERGREEN: And in the cave in Kentucky—(TWO MEN *come on, one with camera, other with flash.* WINTERGREEN *stops, and he and* MARY *pose till flash goes off and until picture is taken*)—when you were frightened of the darkness, I put my arm around your trembling shoulder and drew you to me.

MARY: (*To him*) You were so brave, so strong.

WINTERGREEN: Mary, I can conceal it from you no longer. Look at me. (*She pays no attention—he nudges her*) Look at me! I love you. (*The* CROWD *breaks into great cheers and applause.* WINTERGREEN *stops them with a gesture*) Yes, Mary, I love you. (*Stops applause, which has not come*)

MARY: Why, John! I hardly know what to say.

WINTERGREEN: Say that you love me, Mary, and that you will be mine.

MARY: I do love you, John. (*Applause*)

WINTERGREEN: (*Again checks them*) And if I am elected President, you will marry me?

MARY: (*With simple determination*) I will.

WINTERGREEN: (*Turns quickly to the* CROWD, *his arm still around* MARY) Citizens, it is up to you! Can you let this glorious romance end unhappily?

MARY: Can you tear asunder two loving hearts whom God hath joined together?

WINTERGREEN: I put my faith and trust in the American people! Go, then, to the polls on Tuesday and show the whole world that the United States of America stands first, last and always for Love! Are you with me?

ALL: (*On their feet*) *Yes!*

FULTON: Sing 'em the campaign song, Jack! Sing the campaign love song!

(*Another burst of applause. The lights on stage dim, leaving only the ring light on, and a spot on* WINTERGREEN)

WINTERGREEN:

Of thee I sing, baby,
Summer, autumn, winter, spring, baby;
You're my silver lining,
You're my sky of blue;
There's a love light shining,
All because of you.
Of thee I sing, baby;
You have got that certain thing, baby;
Shining star and inspiration,
Worthy of a mighty nation—
Of thee I sing!

MARY:

Of thee I sing, baby,
Summer, autumn, winter, spring, baby!
You're my silver lining,
You're my sky of blue,
There's a love light shining,

ALL:

All because of you!
Of thee I sing, baby;
You have got that certain thing, baby!

WINTERGREEN:

Shining star and inspiration,
Worthy of a mighty nation—
Of thee I—

ALL:

Of thee I sing, baby,
Summer, autumn, winter, spring, baby!
Shining star and inspiration,
Worthy of a mighty nation—
Of thee I sing!

Curtain

SCENE 7

A motion picture screen. Election night—the returns. There is a steady blast of cheering and shouting that accompanies the picture from beginning to end. There is also, of course, a musical accompaniment.

As the scene progresses the various items follow each other in quicker and quicker succession, so that a climax is built to and a real pitch of excitement achieved.

Herewith the sequence:

WHITESIDE, VERMONT.

Indications are that WINTERGREEN *has swept the town by a plurality of* 154.

WATERVILLE, MASS.

Early returns show WINTERGREEN *well ahead. First election district gives:*

WINTERGREEN	12
Scattering	1

JOHN P. WINTERGREEN (*Picture*)

MARY TURNER (*Picture*)

ATLANTA, GA.

16 *election districts out of* 184 *give:*

WINTERGREEN	12,736
JEFFERSON DAVIS	1,653

NEW YORK, N.Y.

126 *election districts report:*

WINTERGREEN	72,639
BRYAN	128
Absent	4
Late	2

MARY TURNER (*Picture*)

JOHN P. WINTERGREEN (*Picture*)

GEORGE WASHINGTON (*Picture*)

LANDSLIDE, NEB.

JOHN P. WINTERGREEN	12,538
A Man Named WILKINS	1

PATRICK HENRY (*Picture*)

HOLLYWOOD, CAL.

WINTERGREEN	160,000
MICKEY MOUSE	159,000
GLORIA SWANSON'S FIRST HUSBAND	84,638

Caption: Candidate JOHN P. WINTERGREEN *casting Ballot No.* 8 *at Public School* 63 *at* 6:05 *o'clock this morning. Picture of* WINTERGREEN *casting ballot.*

Same picture of WINTERGREEN *casting ballot.*
Caption: Candidate JOHN P. WINTERGREEN *casting Ballot No.* 168 *at Public School* 145 *at* 8:10 *o'clock this morning and* 2:25 *this afternoon.*

NEW YORK, N.Y.

ALEXANDER THROTTLEBOTTOM, *Vice-Presidential candidate, gets his shoes shined preparatory to entering election booth. (Picture of a pair of hands shining a pair of shoes. The candidate is not visible above the knees)*

THE WHITE HOUSE *(Picture)*

JOHN P. WINTERGREEN *(Picture)*

J. P. WINTERGREEN *at the age of* 5 *years (Picture)*

DEAL, N.J.

Returns from Contract Bridge Tournament give:

WINTERGREEN	1,500
CULBERTSON	Double
LENZ	Redouble
THROTTLEBOTTOM	Pass

BENJAMIN FRANKLIN *(Picture)*

BABE RUTH *(Picture)*

NEW YORK, N.Y.

41 *Election Districts give:*

WINTERGREEN	46,572
WALTER HAMPDEN	136
MAE WEST	82

LEXINGTON, KENTUCKY.

WINTERGREEN	27,637
LIGHT WINES AND BEER	14
STRAIGHT WHISKEY	1,850,827

JOHN P. WINTERGREEN *(Picture)*

PATRICK HENRY *(Picture)*

JACK DEMPSEY *(Picture)*

MAN O' WAR *(Picture)*

MANCHESTER, ENGLAND.

WINTERGREEN	14,653
KING GEORGE	3

QUEEN MARY	1
ALSO RAN	NURMI

ROME, ITALY.

127 Election Districts give:

WINTERGREEN	0
MUSSOLINI	828,638

NEW YORK.

Empire State gives WINTERGREEN *plurality of* 1,627,535, *with only three counties missing.*

DETROIT, MICH.

New eight-cylinder Ford gives WINTERGREEN *huge plurality with only two cylinders missing.*

TOLEDO, OHIO.

Twelfth National Bank gives WINTERGREEN *plurality with all its cashiers missing.*

GEORGE WASHINGTON (*Picture*)

THE MARX BROTHERS (*Picture*)

NEW YORK, N.Y.

First returns from Wall Street give:

WINTERGREEN	192,000
RADIO	5¾
GOLDMAN, SACHS	2⅛

THE WHITE HOUSE (*Picture*)

THE CAPITOL (*Picture*)

THE ROXY (*Picture*)

ROXY HIMSELF (*Picture*)

A FRIEND OF ROXY'S (*Picture*)

AN UNIDENTIFIED MAN (*Picture of* THROTTLEBOTTOM)

MACY'S BASEMENT.

WINTERGREEN	97¢

Only One to a Customer

RICHMOND, VA.

WINTERGREEN	98,728
MASON	499
DIXON	1
MASON & DIXON	500

All returns indicate that WINTERGREEN *is sweeping country!*

WINTERGREEN *lacks only four votes*
to win!
WINTERGREEN CASTS LAST FOUR VOTES
WINTERGREEN
ELECTED!

OUR NEXT PRESIDENT (*Picture*)
OUR NEXT FIRST LADY (*Picture*)

BULLETIN: *At a late hour tonight the defeated candidate sent the following telegram to* JOHN P. WINTERGREEN, *the winner: "Heartily congratulate you on your splendid victory and charge fraud in Indiana, Illinois, Nebraska, Montana, Washington, Ohio and Massachusetts."*

BULLETIN: *At midnight tonight* ALEXANDER THROTTLEBOTTOM *refused to concede his election as Vice-President.*

Next Week:
NORMA SHEARER
(*Picture*)
in
"THE LOVE GIRL"

Flash of Metro-Goldwyn-Mayer lion.
It opens its mouth. It crows.

CURTAIN

SCENE 8

The steps of the Capitol. Inauguration Day. The steps begin as close to the footlights as possible. Three steps up there is a platform about six feet deep, with space for entrances right and left. There are twelve steps above this, with another platform, rather narrow, at the top of these. Where the steps end the idea of steps is carried out by a painted back drop, which also shows the Capitol building itself and its great dome. At right and left downstage are huge pillars. Upstage, wings right and left and borders above are painted to represent flags and bunting. Ground rows right and left show an immense crowd, of which nothing can be seen but masses of umbrellas.

SIXTEEN GIRLS *enter right and left in red uniforms, with tall, feather headdresses. They are followed by* SIXTEEN BOYS *in blue and white military uniforms. All carry silvered batons. They go through a short drill to the music of "Wintergreen for President," and finish on the upper steps in fan-shaped formation.*

The NINE SUPREME COURT JUSTICES *enter, come to the center of the platform, and sing, the* CHIEF JUSTICE *in the center.*

JUSTICES:

We're the one, two, three, four, five, six, seven, eight, nine
Supreme Court Judges;
As the Super Solomons of this great nation;
We will supervise today's Inauguration,
And we'll sup'rintend the wedding celebration
In a manner official and judicial.

ALL:

One, two, three, four, five, six, seven, eight, nine Supreme
Court Judges!

JUSTICES:

We have powers that are positively regal;
Only we can take a law and make it legal.

ALL:

They're (we're) the A.K.'s who give the O.K.'s!
One, two, three, four, five, six, seven, eight, nine Supreme
Court Judges!
(*Another fanfare*)

ALL:

Hail, hail, the mighty ruler of love!
Hail, hail, the man who made us love love!
Hip, hip, hooray,
For his Inaugural and wedding day—
Hurray!
(*Cheers from all. Enter* WINTERGREEN, *followed by* COMMITTEE *and* JENKINS)

CHIEF JUSTICE: And, now, Mr. President, if you don't mind, we'd like your Inaugural address.

WINTERGREEN:

I have definite ideas about the Philippines
And the herring situation up in Bismarck;
I have notions on the salaries of movie queens,
And the men who sign their signatures with *this* mark!
(*Makes cross*)

ALL:

He has definite ideas about the Philippines
And the herring situation up in Bismarck;

He has notions on the salaries of movie queens,
And the men who sign their signatures with this mark!
(*Make cross*)

WINTERGREEN:
But on this glorious day I find
I'm sentimentally inclined,
And so—
I sing this to the girls I used to know:
Here's a kiss for Cinderella,
And a parting kiss for May;
Toodle-oo, goodbye! This is my wedding day!
Here's a parting glance for Della,
And the lady known as Lou;
Toodle-oo, goodbye! With bach'lor days I'm through!
Though I really never knew them,
It's a rule I must obey;
I am singing goodbye to them
In the customary way.
My regards to Arabella,
And to Emmaline and Kay;
Toodle-oo, dear girls, goodbye! This is my wedding day!
(*He repeats the first six lines, the* COMMITTEE *joining in—all others sing the counter melody*)

ALL:
He is toodle-ooing all his lady loves,
All the girls he didn't know so well;
All the innocent and all the shady loves—
Oh, dinga donga dell!
Bride and groom! Their future should be glorious!
What a happy story they will tell!
Let the welkin now become uproarious—
Oh, dinga donga, dinga donga dell!
(ALL *turn to greet* MARY, *who appears at top of steps*)

ALL:
Clear the way!
Hail the bride!
Sweet and gay—
Here comes the bride!

MARY: (*Coming down steps*)
Is it true or am I dreaming?

Do I go to Heav'n to stay?
Never was a girl so happy on her wedding day!

(MARY *and* WINTERGREEN *now are on lower platform. Music continues*)

CHIEF JUSTICE: Do you, John P. Wintergreen, solemnly swear to uphold the Constitution of the United States of America and to love, honor and cherish this woman so long as you two shall live?

WINTERGREEN: I do.

CHIEF JUSTICE: Do you, Mary Turner, promise to love, honor and cherish this man as long as you two shall live?

MARY: I do.

CHIEF JUSTICE: Therefore, by virtue of the power that is vested in me as Chief Justice, I hereby pronounce you President of the United States, man and wife.

WINTERGREEN: Mary!

MARY: John! (*They embrace*)

ALL: Hurray!

BOTH:
Is it true or am I dreaming?
Do I go to Heav'n to stay?
Never was a girl (man) so happy on her (his) wedding—

(*Discord in orchestra.* DIANA *appears*)

DIANA: Stop! Halt! Pause! Wait!

ALL:
Who is this intruder?
There's no one could be ruder!

ALL: (*To* DIANA)
What's your silly notion
In causing this commotion?

DIANA: (*Recitative*) I was the most beautiful blossom in all the Southland. I was sent up North to enter the contest, with the understanding that the winner was to be the President's wife. The Committee examined me. My lily white body fascinated them. I was chosen. It was the happiest moment of my life.

ALL: (*Excepting, of course,* MARY, JOHN *and* COMMITTEE) Yes, yes, go on! Yes, yes, go on!

DIANA: Suddenly the sky fell—suddenly for no reason at all, no reason at all, this man rejected me. All my castles came tumbling down. And so I am serving him with a summons—for breach of promise!

ALL:

What! What!
The water's getting hot!
She says he made a promise—
A promise he forgot!

DIANA:

It's true! It's true!

CHIEF JUSTICE:

The day he's getting married
You put him on the spot!

ALL:

It's dirty work of Russia—
A communistic plot!

WINTERGREEN:

Please understand. It wasn't that I would jilt or spurn 'er;
It's just that there was someone else—

ALL:

Whom?

WINTERGREEN:

Who! Mary Turner!

CHIEF JUSTICE:

We're having fits!

ALL:

They're having fits!

CHIEF JUSTICE:

The man admits

ALL:

The man admits

CHIEF JUSTICE:

This little sinner

ALL:

This little sinner

CHIEF JUSTICE:

Was really winner!

ALL:
Was really winner!

DIANA:
I couldn't see

ALL:
She couldn't see

DIANA:
His jilting me,

ALL:
His jilting she,

DIANA:
And so I'm doing

ALL:
And so she's doing

DIANA:
A bit of suing.

ALL:
A bit of suing.

MEN:
And if it's true she has a claim,
You should be called a dirty name!

GIRLS:
Yes, if it's true she has a claim,
Then you're a dirty, dirty name!

MARY:
John, no matter what they do to hurt you,
The one you love won't desert you.

DIANA:
I'm a queen who lost her king;
Why should she wear the wedding ring?

WINTERGREEN:
Some girls can bake a pie,
Made up of prunes and quinces,
Some make an oyster fry—
Others are good at blintzes.
Some lovely girls have done
Wonders with turkey stuffin's,

But I have found the one
Who can really make corn muffins!

ALL:
Yes, he has found the one
Who can really make corn muffins.

DIANA:
Who cares about corn muffins?
All I demand is justice.

WINTERGREEN and MARY: (*To* JUSTICES)
Which is more important—corn muffins or justice?

ALL:
Which is more important—corn muffins or justice?

CHIEF JUSTICE: (*Speaks*) If you will wait a moment—you'll have our decision. Forty—seven—eleven—

(*The* JUSTICES *leap into a football huddle. Music agitato. After a moment they resume positions*)

CHIEF JUSTICE: The decision of the Supreme Court is—Corn Muffins!

ALL:
Great! Great!
It's written on the slate!
There's none but Mary Turner
Could ever be his mate!

DIANA:
It's I, not Mary Turner,
Who should have been his mate;
I'm off to tell my story
In ev'ry single state! (*Exits*)

CHIEF JUSTICE: (*Chasing* DIANA *off*)
Be off with you, young woman,
He's married to his mate!
Be off with you, young woman,
He's married to his mate!

ALL:
There's none but Mary Turner
Could ever be his mate!
There's none but Mary Turner
Could ever be his mate!

WINTERGREEN:

Of thee I sing, baby,

ALL:

Summer, autumn, winter, spring, baby—
Shining star and inspiration,
Worthy of a mighty nation,
Of thee I sing!

Curtain

ACT TWO

SCENE 1

It is the President's office, in the White House. Not only is it the office of the President, however, but it is also the office of the First Lady, and the room reflects the fact that it is a joint affair. The Presidential desk, for example, is divided into two parts: one left piled high with various state papers, the other right lined with perfumes, powders and other perquisites of femininity. MARY'S *half of the desk is really a dressing table, and stands on gracefully curved legs, whereas the President's half is a solid piece of office furniture.*

The door at left leads to the outer offices, and through it come all visitors. Another door, at the right, leads to the more private portions of the White House. At the rear is a window through which can be seen the Capitol and Washington Monument.

The desk is set at an angle and there are various comfortable chairs for possible visitors.

The scene opens with a number, done by twelve PRESIDENTIAL SECRETARIES (BOYS) *and twelve of* MARY'S SECRETARIES (GIRLS, *of course*). *Each group is led by a* CHIEF SECRETARY—*a man and a woman—who turn out to be* JENKINS *and* MISS BENSON.

(BOY SECRETARIES *enter left,* GIRL SECRETARIES *enter right, whistling*)

BOYS:

Hello, good morning—

GIRLS:

Good morning, hello.

BOYS:

How are you this very lovely day?

GIRLS:

I feel very well, sir.

BOYS:

And I'm feeling swell.

BOTH:

It's great to be alive,
And work from nine to five—
(*Enter* JENKINS *and* MISS BENSON)

JENKINS and BENSON:

Hello, good morning—

GIRLS and BOYS:

Good morning, hello.
Isn't this a morning that's divine?

JENKINS and BENSON:

I see it's almost nine.

ALL:

And we only have one minute more to say:
Hello, good morning,
Isn't this a lovely day?
Isn't this a lovely day?

ALL:

Oh, it's great to be a secret'ry
In the White House, D. C.
You get inside information on Algeria;
You know ev'ry move they're making in Liberia.
You learn what's what and what is not
In the land of the free.
Ev'ry corner that you turn you meet a notable
With a statement that is eminently quotable—
Oh, it's great to be a secret'ry
In the White House, D. C.

(JENKINS *and* BENSON *dance,* BOYS *and* GIRLS *gesture. At conclusion of dance* BOYS *and* GIRLS *and* JENKINS *and* BENSON *exit, arm in arm, singing:*)

So long, good morning;
Wasn't this a lovely day?
Wasn't this a lovely day?

(*They whistle as they exit*)

(*As the* SECRETARIES *exit the left door opens and a* GUIDE *enters, followed by a crowd of ten* SIGHTSEERS. *The* SIGHTSEERS *are plainly from the country, with loosely wrapped umbrellas, women with waistlines not in the right place, and perhaps a terrible child or two. The voice of the* GUIDE *is heard as the door opens*)

GUIDE: And this, ladies and gentlemen, is the executive office. This is the room in which the President discharges his official duties, and has been occupied by every President since Hoover. On your right stands the famous double desk used by the President and Mrs. Wintergreen in administering the affairs of the country. During the 1912 coal shortage this room was used as a garage. Right this way, please. (*Opens door at right*) We are now entering the room from which, on a historic occasion, the Spanish Ambassador jumped out of the window, in the very nick of time. (*Going through door, with* CROWD *following. The phone rings.* JENKINS *enters; crosses to desk*) Here the diplomatic corps gathers once a month to pay its formal respects to the Chief Executive, and here, too, the cabinet assembles when– (*The last* SIGHTSEER *is through the door. It closes*)

JENKINS: (*At phone*) Hello. Who? No, the Coolidges don't live here any more! (MISS BENSON *enters*) Gosh, I can't do these dances every morning.

MISS BENSON: (*Holding a perfume bottle up to the light*) Mrs. Wintergreen is running low on Chanel Number Five.

JENKINS: (*Consulting paper*) Looks like a pretty full day. (*Reads*) Delegation from South America–

MISS BENSON: What's eating them?

JENKINS: Usual thing. Want Hollywood cleaned up. (*Looking at list*) Delegation of Camisole Indians–they want scalping restored. Committee of cotton manufacturers–that's for Mrs. Wintergreen. They want her to bring back cotton stockings.

MISS BENSON: Oh, they do, eh?

JENKINS: (*Consulting schedule*) Mayors of fourteen American cities– (SECOND SECRETARY *enters with newspaper clippings*) Well?

SECOND SECRETARY: Morning editorials. (*Hands over clippings; goes.* JENKINS *looks the clippings over; shakes his head*)

MISS BENSON: What's the matter?

JENKINS: Same thing. They're still harping on it.

MISS BENSON: You mean Devereaux?

JENKINS: (*As he reads*) Mm.

MISS BENSON: What's it say?

JENKINS: Nothing new. They just think she got a raw deal.

MISS BENSON: A lot of people think that.

JENKINS: (*Crumpling a clipping*) Just as well if he doesn't see this one. You know, it wouldn't surprise me a bit– (THIRD SECRETARY *enters*)

THIRD SECRETARY: Mr. Jenkins–

JENKINS: Yes?

THIRD SECRETARY: Those people are here now. Can you see them?

JENKINS: Show them into the Blue Room.

THIRD SECRETARY: Yes, sir. (*Goes*)

JENKINS: Delegation from the Virgin Islands. Want to come along?

MISS BENSON: Well, well! And what are they after?

JENKINS: Want their name changed. They claim it's hurting business.

(MISS BENSON *exits, followed by* JENKINS. GUIDE *enters left again, leading another sightseeing party. It is the same sort of group as the first, except that included in it, although not visible in the beginning, is* ALEXANDER THROTTLEBOTTOM)

GUIDE: Right this way, please–follow me. This, ladies and gentlemen, is the executive office. You will probably find this the most interesting room in your entire tour of the White House. It is in this room that the President signs the many laws that govern your everyday life, and from which he controls the various departmental activities. (THROTTLEBOTTOM, *all eyes, emerges a bit from the crowd. He is gaping at the room, taking in every detail*) Here come the various heads of government for daily consultation with the Executive, and to receive from him the benefit of his wide experience. It is in this room– (*To* THROTTLEBOTTOM, *who has strayed about ten feet from the group*) I beg your pardon, sir, but would you please stay over there? You see, we're personally responsible if anything's stolen.

THROTTLEBOTTOM: (*Meekly rejoining the group*) Yes, sir.

GUIDE: Thank you. (*Resuming his formal tone*) Now, are there any questions?

FIRST SIGHTSEER: Does the President live here all year round?

GUIDE: All year round. Except when Congress is in session.

FIRST SIGHTSEER: Where does the Vice-President live?

GUIDE: Who?

FIRST SIGHTSEER: The Vice-President. Where does he live?

GUIDE: (*Taking a little red book out of his pocket*) Just one moment, please. Vice-regent, viceroy, vice societies– I'm sorry, but he doesn't seem to be in here.

THROTTLEBOTTOM: I can tell you about that.

GUIDE: What?

THROTTLEBOTTOM: I know where the Vice-President lives.

GUIDE: Where?

THROTTLEBOTTOM: He lives at fourteen forty-eight Z Street. (*To the* SIGHTSEER) It's the next to the last house, 'way down at the other end of Z Street.

GUIDE: Well, that's very interesting. He has a house there, has he?

THROTTLEBOTTOM: Well, he lives there.

GUIDE: All by himself?

THROTTLEBOTTOM: No, with the other boarders. It's an awfully nice place. Mrs. Spiegelbaum's. It's a great place, if you like Kosher cooking.

GUIDE: Think of your knowing all that! Are you a Washingtonian?

THROTTLEBOTTOM: Well, I've been here since March fourth. I came down for the Inauguration, but I lost the ticket.

GUIDE: You don't say? Well! First time you've been to the White House?

THROTTLEBOTTOM: (*Nods*) I didn't know people were allowed in.

GUIDE: You seem to know the Vice-President pretty well. What kind of fellow is he?

THROTTLEBOTTOM: He's all right. He's a nice fellow when you get to know him, but nobody wants to know him.

GUIDE: What's the matter with him?

THROTTLEBOTTOM: There's nothing the matter with him. Nothing. He's just Vice-President.

GUIDE: Well, what does he do all the time?

THROTTLEBOTTOM: He sits around in the parks, and feeds the pigeons, and takes walks, and goes to the movies. And the other day he was going to join the library, but he had to have two references, so he couldn't get in.

GUIDE: But when does he do all his work?

THROTTLEBOTTOM: What work?
FIRST SIGHTSEER: Doesn't he preside over the Senate?
THROTTLEBOTTOM: What?
GUIDE: Sure he does! That's the Vice-President's job!
THROTTLEBOTTOM: What is?
GUIDE: To preside over the Senate.
THROTTLEBOTTOM: Over what?
GUIDE: The Senate. You know what Senators are, don't you?
THROTTLEBOTTOM: Sure.—I saw them play yesterday.
GUIDE: No, no! The Vice-President presides over the Senate. It meets in the Capitol.
THROTTLEBOTTOM: When does it?
GUIDE: Right now! It's going on now!
THROTTLEBOTTOM: (*Frenzied*) How do you get there?
GUIDE: The Capitol?
THROTTLEBOTTOM: Yeah!
GUIDE: Street car at the door—right up Pennsylvania Avenue.
THROTTLEBOTTOM: (*Hurrying off*) Street car at the door—right up Pennsyl— (*Turns back*)—What's the name of that place?
GUIDE: The Senate!

(THROTTLEBOTTOM *dashes off*)

GUIDE: (*Going right*) Right this way, please. (*Opens door. As the* SIGHTSEERS *reach center there is a fanfare in the orchestra*) Here the diplomatic corps gathers monthly to pay its formal respects to the Chief Executive, and here, too, the cabinet assembles upon the occasion of its weekly meetings. (*The* SIGHTSEERS *and the* GUIDE *are off*)

(JENKINS *and* MISS BENSON *have entered.* MISS BENSON *first —on the fanfare. At its conclusion and as the last of the* SIGHTSEERS *exit,* WINTERGREEN *and* MARY *enter.* JENKINS *and* MISS BENSON *are standing at attention at their respective chairs*)

WINTERGREEN and MARY: Good morning!
JENKINS and MISS BENSON: Good morning!

(*As* WINTERGREEN *reaches his chair, the phone rings; he answers it*)

WINTERGREEN: (*In phone*) Hello—no—no—no. (*Hangs up. To* JENKINS) Make a note of that.
JENKINS: Yes, sir.

(MARY *is seated at her desk, going through letters.* WINTERGREEN *looks out the window, through which is visible the panorama of Washington, with the Washington Monument prominent in the foreground*)

WINTERGREEN: What a country—what a country! Jenkins, what monument is that?

JENKINS: (*Disgustedly*) Grant's Tomb.

WINTERGREEN: Oh, yes. Well, what's on the schedule this morning? Ah, here we are! (*Takes up some letters, paces up and down*) Tell the Secretary of the Navy to scrap two battleships.

JENKINS: What?

WINTERGREEN: Tell him to scrap two battleships. Scrap two and build four. Disarmament.

JENKINS: Oh, yes, sir.

WINTERGREEN: Cablegram to the President of San Domingo: "Congratulations on beginning your second day in office. That's five dollars I owe you, and will bet you double or nothing on tomorrow."

JENKINS: Yes, sir.

WINTERGREEN: Tell the Secretary of War to stand ready to collect that bet.

JENKINS: Yes, sir.

WINTERGREEN: Letter to the Friars' Club, Forty-eighth Street, New York City. "Dear Brother Friars: Regret very much I cannot take part in this year's minstrel show. Owing to conditions in the South, I do not think it would be wise for me to black up." (*Goes to the desk, looks through mail*) I get the lousiest mail for a President!

MARY: Emily—take a letter to the A. and P. "Atlantic and Pacific Tea Stores, ladies and gentlemen: I have your bill for eighty-two sixty-three for eggs, for the month of April. One of the eggs delivered on April fifteenth arrived in bad condition and has shown no improvement since that date. I must refuse to pay this bill until you send a new egg, or have the old one attended to." That's all. (BENSON *exits. To* WINTERGREEN) They're not going to put anything over on me.

WINTERGREEN: That's telling 'em. Jenkins!

JENKINS: Yes, sir.

WINTERGREEN: Take a memo to the Secretary of State: "Referring to last Tuesday night's poker game, please note that the Liberian minister's check for twelve dollars and forty-five cents has been returned for lack of funds. Kindly get a new minister for next Tuesday night's game, and add twelve dollars and forty-five cents to the Liberian National Debt."

JENKINS: Yes, sir.

WINTERGREEN: (*Takes* JENKINS *out of earshot of* MARY) Get

the Governor of Maryland on the phone and ask him what horse he likes in the fourth race at Pimlico.

JENKINS: Yes, sir.

WINTERGREEN: (*Brandishing a telephone bill*) And tell the telephone company that this is not my bill. (*Hands it to* JENKINS) That long-distance call was March third.

JENKINS: Yes, sir.

WINTERGREEN: (*As* JENKINS *starts to go*) Oh, anybody in the ante-room?

JENKINS: Yes, sir. Secretary of the Navy, Secretary of Agriculture, and four zebras.

WINTERGREEN: Zebras?

JENKINS: There's a man who wants to give them to you.

WINTERGREEN: Not unless they're housebroken.

(*A* SECRETARY *enters with a wooden board, about two feet square, covered with electric buttons. A long wire is attached to the board, and stretches across the stage as the* SECRETARY *advances to* JENKINS)

JENKINS: All ready, Mr. President. (*Takes the board. The* SECRETARY *exits*) Time to press a button. Opening of the International Corn Growing Exposition in Dubuque, Iowa. Button Number One.

WINTERGREEN: (*Presses button, then laughs*) Say, Jenkins, I never will forget the time I reopened the Bank of United States by mistake. (BOTH *laugh boisterously;* WINTERGREEN *slaps* JENKINS *on the back;* JENKINS, *a moment later, returns the slap considerably harder.* WINTERGREEN *straightens, freezes;* JENKINS *beats a hasty retreat. The phone rings*) Hello— (*Annoyed, hands instrument to* MARY) For you!

MARY: Who is it?

WINTERGREEN: The butcher!

MARY: Hello! Oh, good morning, Mr. Schneidermann. Fine, thank you. Now, let me see. What have you got that's good? Well, we had lamb chops yesterday. They are? Well, wait a minute. (*To* WINTERGREEN) John, who's coming to dinner tonight?

WINTERGREEN: What? Let me see—the Chief Justice, the Attorney General, Jackie Cooper, and those three judges that got paroled. That's six.

MARY: (*As she returns to phone*) That's eight with us. Hello, Mr. Schneidermann. Make it sixteen lamb chops—

WINTERGREEN: Wait a minute! What about that moving picture train from Hollywood.

MARY: That what?

WINTERGREEN: That moving picture train from Hollywood. If that gets in we've got to have *them.*

MARY: Oh, dear! How many are there?

WINTERGREEN: Ah—sixty-four motion picture stars—there may be two actors among them. That's sixty-six.

MARY: That's seventy-four in all.

WINTERGREEN: But they may not get here.

MARY: But when'll we know? Just a minute, Mr. Schneidermann. (*Back to* WINTERGREEN, *pretty testily*) I've got to know whether they're going to get here.

WINTERGREEN: How do I know? Take a chance! You can always use lamb chops.

MARY: (*Back to phone, wearily*) Listen, Mr. Schneidermann. A hundred and forty-eight lamb chops. That's right. Now, how is your asparagus? Well, make it a carload of asparagus, and about seventy-five loaves of rye bread. That's all, thank you. (*Hangs up*)

JENKINS: (*Enters*) Beg pardon, sir. Time to press another button.

WINTERGREEN: What's this? Button Number Two. Opening of a new speakeasy on Fifty-second Street, New York. (*Presses button*) Wait a minute, Jenkins— Didn't I open that yesterday?

JENKINS: Yes, sir. This is the reopening. It was closed last night. (*Exits*)

MARY: (*Coming to* WINTERGREEN *with a stack of bills in her hand*) John, look at these grocery bills!

WINTERGREEN: Well, what about it?

MARY: I've simply got to have a bigger allowance.

WINTERGREEN: Again! For God's sake, Mary!

MARY: Well, I can't help it. Fifty people to dinner every night. And Senators to breakfast every morning. It mounts up.

WINTERGREEN: I've got to have them. It's business.

MARY: Then you've got to give me enough to feed them.

WINTERGREEN: Where am I going to get it from?

MARY: Get it from! If you had any gumption you'd ask Congress for a raise.

WINTERGREEN: Ask Congress for a raise! I'm lucky they don't lay me off!

JENKINS: (*Enters*) I beg your pardon. The Secretary of Agriculture and the Secretary of the Navy are still waiting.

WINTERGREEN: I forgot. Have them come in.

JENKINS: The Secretary of Agriculture! (*Enter* LIPPMAN)

LIPPMAN: (*Together with* WINTERGREEN *and* JENKINS) Hello, Jack! Hello, Mary!

WINTERGREEN: Hello, Secretary!

JENKINS: The Secretary of the Navy!
(*Enter* GILHOOLEY. JENKINS *withdraws*)

GILHOOLEY: Mr. President! And Mary!

MARY: Mr. Secretary!

WINTERGREEN: Sit down, boys. Sorry I kept you waiting.

LIPPMAN: That's all right.

GILHOOLEY: O.K., Chief.

WINTERGREEN: Well, what's on your mind, Louis? How's agriculture?

LIPPMAN: That's what I came to talk to you about. Listen, Jack! I don't know anything about agriculture. I told you I wanted the Treasury.

WINTERGREEN: What's the matter with agriculture?

LIPPMAN: Agriculture's all right– It's those farmers. Wheat, wheat! All they know is raise wheat! And then they raise hell with me because nobody wants it.

WINTERGREEN: Why do you let them raise so much?

LIPPMAN: How can you stop 'em? I did all I could. I invited the seven-year locusts, but they didn't come. Even the locusts don't want their lousy wheat. And they're always complaining about being in one place all the time.– They want to travel.

GILHOOLEY: You call that trouble? How'd you like to have a lot of sailors on your neck?

WINTERGREEN: What do *they* want–*two* wives in every port?

GILHOOLEY: Yeah. And any port in a storm. And no more storms. And another thing–they won't stand for those bells any more. They want to know what time it is the same as anybody else. But that's not the big thing.

WINTERGREEN: Well?

GILHOOLEY: It's the ocean. They don't like the ocean.

WINTERGREEN: (*Rises*) Which ocean don't they like?

GILHOOLEY: All of them. They say it's a nice place to visit, but they don't want to live there. It's no place to bring up a family.

WINTERGREEN: The farmers want to travel and the sailors want to settle down. I've got it! Have them change places!

LIPPMAN: What?

WINTERGREEN: It'll solve the whole problem. Sailors don't know anything about farming—in two years there won't *be* any wheat. You'll have a wheat shortage.

LIPPMAN: And I'll get hell again.

WINTERGREEN: And look what it does for business. You get the farmers on the boats; the traveling salesmen will come back to the farmhouses—you know, to stay over night. Why, I haven't heard a good story in years.

GILHOOLEY: Say, Louis, I wouldn't be surprised if he's got hold of something. That's not a bad idea, Mr. President; not a bad idea at all. That's pretty darned good.

LIPPMAN: The farmers won't like it. I tell you, you don't know those boys. You know what I think of them?

WINTERGREEN: Just bring your troubles to me, boys; I'll fix them up! Anything else, boys? Anything at all.

MARY: John, I think that's the most wonderful idea I ever heard!

(*A* SECRETARY *enters*)

SECRETARY: The Secretary of State!

(FULTON *strides in; the* SECRETARY *withdraws. They all greet him. "Hello, Matty!" "Hi, Sec!"*)

FULTON: Hello, boys. Everybody.

WINTERGREEN: How are you, Matty?

FULTON: (*Preoccupied*) What are you doing, Jack? Important?

WINTERGREEN: Just chinning.

FULTON: (*A look toward the doors*) Can you keep the room clear for a little while?

WINTERGREEN: Sure. What's up?

FULTON: (*Starts toward door*) Shall I tell 'em?

WINTERGREEN: No, here we are. (*Presses a buzzer*)

LIPPMAN: (*Starting off*) See you later.

(JENKINS *enters*)

FULTON: No, no. Want you fellows to stay.

WINTERGREEN: I don't want to be disturbed for a little while.

JENKINS: Yes, sir.

FULTON: Just a minute. When Senators Jones and Lyons get here, bring 'em in.

JENKINS: Yes, sir.

FULTON: And nobody else.

JENKINS: Yes, sir. What shall I do about the press conference?

FULTON: Have 'em wait! (JENKINS *exits.* FULTON *waits for the*

President John P. Wintergreen (William Gaxton) and his Vice-President Alexander Throttlebottom (Victor Moore) in their formal best. *Theatre Collection, New York Public Library*

(Above) An anxious moment in the President's Office in the White House. (June O'Dea, Lois Moran, William Gaxton, George Murphy) *Theatre Collection, New York Public Library*. *(Right)* The First Lady presents her husband—and the nation—with twins. (William Gaxton, Lois Moran, Victor Moore and Company) *Theatre Collection, New York Public Library*

Political Campaigners and wrestlers vying for equal time at Madison Square Garden. On center platform: John P. Wintergreen (William Gaxton) and Mary Turner (Lois Moran) surrounded by their supporters. *Theatre Collection, New York Public Library*

Porgy and Bess

"Bess, You Is My Woman Now." (Todd Duncan, Anne Brown) *Theatre Collection, New York Public Library*

(*Above, left*) Porgy (Todd Duncan) in his goat cart being greeted by residents of Catfish Row. (*Below, left*) Sportin' Life (John W. Bubbles) advising the picnickers on Kittiwah Island that "It Ain't Necessarily So." (*This Page*) Catfish Row and Summertime. *Pictures, Theatre Collection, New York Public Library*

doors to close and crosses to WINTERGREEN) There's hell to pay!

WINTERGREEN: What's the matter?

FULTON: Devereaux!

MARY: John!

WINTERGREEN: (*He puts an arm around her*) What about her?

FULTON: (*To* LIPPMAN *and* GILHOOLEY) The thing has been growing for weeks—you know that, boys—

WINTERGREEN: What has?

FULTON: Well, you know there's always been a certain bunch that said Devereaux didn't get a square deal.

WINTERGREEN: A handful of Southerners.

FULTON: At the beginning. And now it's spreading all over the country!

WINTERGREEN: What do you mean?

MARY: What's happened?

FULTON: I'll tell you what I mean. Yesterday the Federation of New Jersey Women's Clubs came out solid for Devereaux.

MARY: John!

(*A sob from her.* GILHOOLEY *whistles*)

FULTON: And this morning I get a petition from the Kansas City Elks—demanding Devereaux! And the same thing'll happen with the Moose and the Shriners!

(*Enter* SENATORS JONES *and* LYONS)

JONES: Mr. President! Good morning, Mary.

LYONS: Good morning, suh!—and Mary!

(*A nod or two from the others*)

FULTON: Good! I've just been telling the President how things stand!

JONES: Mr. President, I cannot overstate the case. The West is up in arms.

LYONS: The South, suh, is on fire!

JONES: Nebraska has just declared martial law! A posse has been formed!

LYONS: In Louisiana you have been hanged in effigy!

WINTERGREEN: (*Defiant*) How do the Philippines feel about it?

MARY: It's all my fault.

WINTERGREEN: I'd rather have you than Nebraska.

FULTON: It doesn't matter whose fault it is. We've got to do something. We've got to do something to counteract this Devereaux propaganda.

WINTERGREEN: I'll tell you what we'll do! (*Presses a buzzer*)

We carried forty-eight states in the campaign, didn't we? Mary and I?

FULTON: Yeah.

WINTERGREEN: And there was Devereaux propaganda then. But we licked it before, and we can do it again.

JENKINS: (*Enters*) Yes, sir.

WINTERGREEN: Those newspaper men still out there?

JENKINS: Yes, sir.

WINTERGREEN: Bring 'em in when I ring.

JENKINS: Yes, sir. (*Exits*)

WINTERGREEN: The trouble with you boys is you're yellow.

FULTON: Now, look here!

WINTERGREEN: One sock and you're ready to quit. We've got to fight, that's all. I'm as good as I ever was. And so's Mary. And we still love each other. (*Turning to her*) Don't we?

MARY: (*With spirit*) You bet we do.

WINTERGREEN: (*Swinging back onto the men*) There you are! We're not through. We haven't begun to fight. By God, we can tour again if we have to. I can still sing. Once a trouper, always a trouper. (MARY *is freshening the lipstick through all this*) What do you say, boys? Are you with me?

ALL: Yes.

(WINTERGREEN *presses the buzzer*)

FULTON: You got to put it over, Jack.

WINTERGREEN: I'll put it over. I'll give them the best performance since Richard Mansfield. Are you ready, Mary?

MARY: (*Finishing the makeup job*) Ready!

WINTERGREEN: (*As a* SECRETARY *enters*) Bring in those damn newspaper men.

(*Music strikes up. Enter twelve* NEWSPAPER MEN)

WINTERGREEN: Well, gentlemen, what's on your mind?

REPORTERS:

We don't want to know about the moratorium,
Or how near we are to beer,
Or about the League of Nations,
Or the seventeen vacations,
You have had since you've been here.
Here's the one thing that the people of America
Are beside themselves to know:
They would like to know what's doing
On the lady who is suing

You–Diana Devereaux?
Ev'rybody wants to know:
What about Miss Devereaux?
From the highest to the low:
What about Miss Devereaux?

WINTERGREEN:
It's a pleasant day–
That's all I can say!

MARY:
Here's the one thing we'll announce:
Love's the only thing that counts!

REPORTERS:
People want to know:
What of Devereaux?

WINTERGREEN:
When the one you love is near
Nothing else can interfere.

ALL:
When the one you love is near
Nothing else can interfere.

WINTERGREEN:
Here's some information
I will gladly give the nation:
I am for the true love;
Here's the only girl I do love.

MARY:
I love him and he loves me,
And that's how it will always be,
So what care we about Miss Devereaux?

BOTH:
Who cares what the public chatters,
Love's the only thing that matters.

WINTERGREEN:
Who cares
If the sky cares to fall in the sea?
Who cares what banks fail in Yonkers–
Long as you've got a kiss that conquers.
Why should I care?
Life is one long jubilee,

So long as I care for you
And you care for me.

(*All repeat chorus twice,* WINTERGREEN *and* MARY *dancing.* REPORTERS *exit at end of second chorus. As* REPORTERS *leave, there is a chorus of approval from the* COMMITTEE)

WINTERGREEN: Nothing at all, boys! I owe it all to the little woman.

MARY: You were grand, John.

FULTON: I never heard you in better voice.

WINTERGREEN: Did you hear that F sharp I gave them?

GILHOOLEY: Great!

WINTERGREEN: (*Letting his voice loose for a second in a snatch of operatic aria*) Do you know what I'll do? I'll go on the radio every night! Mary and I!

FULTON: National Biscuit Company! They've been after you.

JONES: National Biscuit! That's a very popular hour in the West.

WINTERGREEN: A new song every night! I'll even get a megaphone.

MARY: And we can make records.

WINTERGREEN: They don't sell any more.

FULTON: Well, every little helps.

MARY: And I can still bake.

WINTERGREEN: What!

MARY: Corn muffins! Corn muffins for the unemployed!

WINTERGREEN: That's my girl. You feed 'em and I'll sing to them. We'll get the country back. Give us a week and they'll forget that Devereaux ever lived. (*A chorus of approval from the* COMMITTEE) And you fellows wanted to quit! Why, we haven't begun to fight! This is a cinch! What would you do if a *real* fight came along! (*Four bars of "Garçon, S'il Vous Plaît" from the orchestra. Six* GIRL SECRETARIES *enter, line up along wall, downstage*) What's this?

GIRL SECRETARIES: The French Ambassador!

WINTERGREEN: I can't see him! (*Four bars of "Garçon" repeated as six* BOY SECRETARIES *enter, line up across stage*) And what's this?

BOY SECRETARIES: The French Ambassador!

WINTERGREEN: I can't see him! (*Six* FRENCH SOLDIERS *enter, march downstage in exaggerated goose-step*) And what's this? (FRENCH SOLDIERS *go into song*)

SOLDIERS:

Garçon, s'il vous plaît,
Encore Chevrolet Coupe;
Papah, pooh, pooh, pooh!
A vous toot dir veh, a vous?
Garçon, q'est-ce que c'est?
Tra la, Maurice Chevalier!
J'adore crêpes Suzette
Et aussi Lafayette!

And now we give the meaning of this song:
We're six of the fifty million and we can't be wrong!

SECRETARIES:

They're six of the fifty million and they can't be wrong.

(FRENCH AMBASSADOR *enters*)

FRENCH SOLDIERS: Ze French Ambassador!

WINTERGREEN: I still can't see him.

FRENCH AMBASSADOR: I am the Ambassador of France—

WINTERGREEN: Europe?

FRENCH AMBASSADOR: And I have come to see a grievous wrong righted. My country is deeply hurt. Not since the days of Louis the Seventh, the Eighth, the Ninth, the Tenth, and possibly the Eleventh has such a thing happened!

WINTERGREEN: What's troubling you?

FRENCH AMBASSADOR: You have done a great injustice to a French descendant—a lovely girl, whose rights have been trampled in the dust!

WINTERGREEN, MARY and COMMITTEE: Who is she? What's her name?

FRENCH AMBASSADOR: Her name is Diana Devereaux.

WINTERGREEN, MARY and COMMITTEE: Diana Devereaux! Diana Devereaux! Since when is she of French descent?

FRENCH AMBASSADOR:

I've been looking up her family tree
And I have found a most important pedigree!
She's the illegitimate daughter of an illegitimate son—
Of an illegitimate nephew of Napoleon!

ALL: (*Awed*) Napoleon!

FRENCH AMBASSADOR:

She offers aristocracy
To this bizarre democracy

Where naught is sacred but the old simoleon!
I must know why
You crucify
My native country
With this effront'ry
To the illegitimate daughter of an illegitimate son
Of an illegitimate nephew of Napoleon!

ALL:
To the illegitimate daughter of an illegitimate son
Of an illegitimate nephew of Napoleon!

ALL: (*To* WINTERGREEN)
You so-and-so!
We didn't know
She had a tie-up
So very high up.
She's the illegitimate daughter of an illegitimate son
Of an illegitimate nephew of Napoleon!

DIANA: (*Off*) Oh– (*Enters*) I was the most beautiful blossom in all the Southland. I–

MARY and WINTERGREEN: We know all that.

FRENCH AMBASSADOR: You know all that–but you *don't* know the misery of this poor little girl who has suffered because–

COMMITTEE: Because–?

MARY and WINTERGREEN: Because–?

FRENCH AMBASSADOR: Because– (*Motioning to* DIANA *to go ahead*)

DIANA:
Because, because, because, because
I won the competition
But I got no recognition,
And because he broke my heart!
(*Indicating* WINTERGREEN)
Because, because, because, because
The man who ought to love me
Tried to make a monkey of me;
Double-crossing from the start!
I might have been First Lady,
But now my past is shady–
Oh, pity this poor maidie!

FRENCH AMBASSADOR and DIANA:
And there's the man who ought to pay!

ALL:
Because, because, because, because
She won the prize for beauty
And he didn't do his duty
He has broken her poor heart!

FRENCH AMBASSADOR: (*To* WINTERGREEN) You see how this poor child has suffered. And so, on behalf of France, I demand that your marriage be annulled and that you marry Diana.

WINTERGREEN: Never! Never!

FRENCH AMBASSADOR: Then you will arouse the anger of France and you must be prepared to face the consequences.

(SOLDIERS *line up with* AMBASSADOR *and* DIANA. *They march off singing first four lines, "Garçon, S'il Vous Plaît"*)

FULTON: Jack, you've got to do something about this.

WINTERGREEN: Leave Mary? Never!

FULTON:
We are all in this together;
We are birdies of a feather;
And if you don't change your thesis
Then our party goes to pieces!

LYONS:
All our jobs you'll be destroying
With your attitude annoying.

GILHOOLEY:
You will get us all in trouble!
And in spades, sir, which is double!

WINTERGREEN:
I will never leave my Mary!

LYONS:
Since he's acting so contrary
Send him off on a vacation!

GILHOOLEY:
I suggest his resignation!

WINTERGREEN:
Resignation?

ALL:

Resignation!

FULTON:

You've got to face it—this is a crisis!
To leave your Mary you may decline,
But to save us, my good advice is
You resign!

ALL:

Yes, resign!

WINTERGREEN:

I assure you—though it's a crisis,
To leave my Mary I must decline,
And I don't care what your advice is,
I decline to resign!

MARY:

We decline to resign!

COMMITTEE: (*To each other*)

He is stubborn—we must teach him;
I'm afraid we must impeach him!

ALL:

He is stubborn—we must teach him;
He has forced us to impeach him!
You decline to resign,
(*They start backing out in tempo*)
So we'll teach you!
We'll impeach you!
(ALL *start to exit*)
You decline to resign,
We don't envy you at all!
You decline to resign,
So we'll teach you,
We'll impeach you!
You decline to resign—
Humpty Dumpty has to fall!
(*And off*)

WINTERGREEN and MARY:

Who cares
If the sky cares to fall in the sea?

WINTERGREEN:
We two together can win out.
Just remember to stick your chin out.

MARY:
Why should we care?
Life is one long jubilee—

BOTH:
So long as I care for you
And you care for me!

Blackout

SCENE 2

A corridor in the Capitol, immediately outside the Senate. The doors to the Senate are at center—two swinging doors, not unlike those found in our more elegant movie palaces. In neat letters above the doors are the words: "UNITED STATES SENATE."

A PAGE *enters; goes through the doors.*

Immediately the Committee, FULTON, GILHOOLEY, LYONS, JONES *and* LIPPMAN, *enter, talking as they enter.*

FULTON: Say, I'm just as sorry as anybody. I like Jack as much as you do, and I'd give my shirt not to have to do this.

JONES: We can't be sentimental at a time like this.

GILHOOLEY: Say! Wait a minute!

FULTON: Yah!

(THROTTLEBOTTOM *enters, just as he had left the White House*)

GILHOOLEY: If he's put out of office who becomes the President?

JONES: Why, the Vice-President, of course.

FULTON: (*As it dawns on him*) We haven't got a Vice-President.

GILHOOLEY: Sure we have! He came up to the room.

FULTON: (*Suddenly remembering*) Pitts! I nominated him.

(*A chorus of dissent.* LIPPMAN: *"No, that wasn't his name!"* JONES: *"It was Schaeffer!"* LYONS: *"No, not Pitts!"* GILHOOLEY: *"No, it was a longer name—Barbinelli!"*)

THROTTLEBOTTOM: (*Who has been listening to all this in full expectation of imminent discovery, now comes over to them*) Hello, gentlemen! (*In a knot, the other five continue the argument, repeating their original statements*)

FULTON: It was Alexander Something.

GILHOOLEY: Yah, that's it!

THROTTLEBOTTOM: Throttlebottom.

GILHOOLEY: That's right!

(*A chorus from the others: "Yes, that's right!" "What's his name?"*)

FULTON: (*Realizing that it is a stranger who has spoken*) Oh! Thank you. (*Hands him a cigar*)

THROTTLEBOTTOM: Oh, thank you, Mr. Fulton.

FULTON: (*Looking at him*) Haven't I seen you before some place?

THROTTLEBOTTOM: I'm Throttlebottom.

FULTON: Huh?

THROTTLEBOTTOM: Throttlebottom. The Vice-President. That's how I knew the name.

(*A chorus of greetings. "Well, hello!" "Where have you been?" "Well, for God's sake!" "Here! Have a light!"*)

FULTON: Well, for heaven's sake! Just the fellow we were looking for!

GILHOOLEY: Yes, sir!

FULTON: We want to talk to you!

THROTTLEBOTTOM: Me?

LYONS: That's what!

FULTON: We've got a surprise for you!

THROTTLEBOTTOM: (*Covering his eyes*) A surprise?

LIPPMAN: Sure! Remember I told you you had a chance to be President?

THROTTLEBOTTOM: Yeah!

FULTON: Well, we've been thinking it over and we're going to make you President!

GILHOOLEY: That's what we are!

THROTTLEBOTTOM: President! Say! You mean of the United States?

JONES: That's what we do!

THROTTLEBOTTOM: But what was the matter with the other fellow?

FULTON: We're going to impeach him!

GILHOOLEY: He wouldn't play ball with us.

THROTTLEBOTTOM: Well, *I* don't play very good—

FULTON: Come on! Let's get started! (*Starting for the door*)

GILHOOLEY: Yeah, we've got work to do!

THROTTLEBOTTOM: You really mean it? I'm not Vice-President any more?

JONES: Not if we impeach the President! (*Starts for door*)

THROTTLEBOTTOM: Well, when do we do that?

JONES: Right now! Come on!

FULTON: You've got to preside over the Senate.

(LIPPMAN, FULTON *and* GILHOOLEY *exit*)

THROTTLEBOTTOM: And after that I'll be President?

LYONS: That's what you will!

(LYONS *and* JONES *exit*. SCRUBWOMAN *enters*)

THROTTLEBOTTOM: President! Say! How will that sound? President Alexander Bottlethrottom. (*Corrects himself*) Throttlebottom.

SCRUBWOMAN: Huh?

THROTTLEBOTTOM: (*He dances up to her*) I'm going to be President!

SCRUBWOMAN: I'd rather have this job. It's steady. (*Exits*)

(*Enter* WINTERGREEN *and* JENKINS)

JENKINS: Well, it's a dirty trick, Chief. That's all I've got to say.

WINTERGREEN: Well, it's politics. They've got to eat, too.

JENKINS: Want me to go in with you?

WINTERGREEN: No. I want to handle this alone.

JENKINS: More power to you, Chief. (*Takes his hand; holds it during following speech*) And I want you to know that, if the worst comes to the worst, and they fire you out—

WINTERGREEN: I know—if they fire me out you want a job with the next President.

JENKINS: Right! (*Exits*)

(WINTERGREEN *starts for door*)

THROTTLEBOTTOM: Hello, Mr. President.

WINTERGREEN: (*Not recognizing* THROTTLEBOTTOM) How do you do?

THROTTLEBOTTOM: I'll bet you don't remember me, do you?

WINTERGREEN: (*After a moment's thought*) You're the fellow that gave me that dill pickle.

THROTTLEBOTTOM: That's right.

WINTERGREEN: What are you doing now?

THROTTLEBOTTOM: I'm Vice-President.

WINTERGREEN: You don't say? Lost your other job, huh?

THROTTLEBOTTOM: Well, I'm going to have a good job now, because I'm going to be President.

WINTERGREEN: (*Realizing it*) Say, that's right! If they kick me out that makes you President. (*Looks at him*) The country certainly *is* in a hole.

THROTTLEBOTTOM: Say, I wonder if you'd mind doing me a favor?

WINTERGREEN: Sure!

THROTTLEBOTTOM: You see, I don't know anything about being President. I just found out today how to be Vice-President.

WINTERGREEN: Well, that's something.

THROTTLEBOTTOM: Isn't there some book I could read?

WINTERGREEN: Sure—I'm writing one. *"What Every Young President Ought To Know."*

THROTTLEBOTTOM: Has it got pictures?

WINTERGREEN: It's got everything. Tells you just what to do. Of course the first four years are easy. You don't do anything except try to get re-elected.

THROTTLEBOTTOM: That's pretty hard these days.

WINTERGREEN: The next four years you wonder why the hell you wanted to be re-elected. Then you go fishing.

THROTTLEBOTTOM: Well, couldn't I save a lot of time and go fishing right now?

WINTERGREEN: No, you got to wait until an important matter comes up and then you go fishing.

THROTTLEBOTTOM: Well, do you ever catch any fish?

WINTERGREEN: Well, I'm the President.

THROTTLEBOTTOM: Yeah, but it's a pretty hard job being President. You've got to keep on writing those Thanksgiving proclamations, no matter what—and then there's that other bunch, Congress— I guess there isn't anything you can really do about Congress, is there?

WINTERGREEN: Well, you could keep them out of Washington.

THROTTLEBOTTOM: Can you do that?

WINTERGREEN: Saint Patrick did it—keep them out—quarantine the place. Get the measles.

THROTTLEBOTTOM: I had measles once.

WINTERGREEN: Yeah, but you never had Congress. That's worse.

THROTTLEBOTTOM: Oh! What about those messages that the President is always sending to Congress—who reads those, anyway?

WINTERGREEN: The fellow who prints 'em.

THROTTLEBOTTOM: Well, wouldn't everybody read them if you made 'em funnier?

WINTERGREEN: Some of them have been pretty funny.

THROTTLEBOTTOM: Couldn't you make a speech instead? Then they'd have to listen.

WINTERGREEN: No, no! You've got to be careful about speeches. You only make a speech when you want the stock market to go down.

THROTTLEBOTTOM: What do you do when you want the stock market to go up?

WINTERGREEN: Oh, boy! Wouldn't I like to know! (*A big handshake*)

Blackout

SCENE 3

The Senate Chamber. In the center of the right wall is a platform about five feet high, on which are the desk and chair of the presiding officer. The desk is reached by two stairs, one upstage and one down, both curving into the room. The senatorial desks are set in a semi-circle at stage left, facing the platform, in three rows, the last of which is partly offstage. There are chairs for eighteen SENATORS. *In the back wall center are large double doors. They are up on a platform three steps high.*

THROTTLEBOTTOM, *the* CHIEF CLERK, *and the* SENATORS, *most of them heavily bearded, are in their places. They are humming and swaying back and forth rhythmically.*

THROTTLEBOTTOM: The Senator from North Dakota?

SENATOR: Present!

THROTTLEBOTTOM: Check! The Senator from Minnesota?

SENATOR: Present!

THROTTLEBOTTOM: Check! The Senator from Lou'siana?

LYONS: Present!

THROTTLEBOTTOM: Check! The Senator who's from Montana?

SENATOR: Present!

THROTTLEBOTTOM: Check! The Senator who's from Alaska?

SENATOR: Present!

THROTTLEBOTTOM: Check! The Senator who's from Nebraska?

SENATOR: Present!

THROTTLEBOTTOM: Check!

The Senators from other states will have to bide their time,
For I simply can't be bothered when the names don't rhyme!

ALL:

He simply can't be bothered when the names don't rhyme.

The Senators from other states will have to bide their time,
For he simply can't be bothered when the names don't rhyme!

ALL:
Ha ha ha ha ha ha ha ha ha ha ha ha ha!

(*All the* SENATORS *fall sound asleep*)

CLERK: (*At finish of the number*) It is now twelve o'clock noon and the Senate of the United States is hereby declared in session. (*Hands gavel up to* THROTTLEBOTTOM)

THROTTLEBOTTOM: Gentlemen, when you hear the musical note it will be exactly twelve o'clock noon. (*Brings gavel down with a resounding bang. It lands right on the watch which he has just taken from his pocket and laid on the desk, completely splintering it. Shakes the watch, then puts it back in his pocket. The* SENATORS *are awakened by the gavel*) Well, gentlemen, I'm glad to meet you all. You'll have to excuse me for not knowing much about this job. I see I made one mistake already—I went and got shaved. Now let's get at things. I'm only going to be with you one day, so let's make it a pip. Now what have we got to take up?

CLERK: (*Announcing*) The first thing before the Senate is unfinished business.

THROTTLEBOTTOM: Unfinished business—is that still going on? But aren't we going to impeach the President?

CLERK: That comes later. (*Announcing*) Unfinished business!

SENATOR FROM MASSACHUSETTS: (*Rises*) Mr. Chairman! Mr. Chairman!

CLERK: (*To* THROTTLEBOTTOM) That's you.

THROTTLEBOTTOM: Oh, I thought I was just Vice-President.

CLERK: You must recognize the Senator from Massachusetts.

THROTTLEBOTTOM: Oh, hello! How's everything in Massachusetts?

SENATOR FROM MASSACHUSETTS: Mr. Chairman! I rise to protest against a great injustice! In Seventeen Hundred and Seventy-Five Paul Revere made the famous ride that saved this country from the greedy clutch of England.

THROTTLEBOTTOM: That's right—I read about that. "Listen, my children—" (*Informally, to the* CLERK) He went from one house to another, and he knocked on the door, but by the time they came out he was at the next house. (*A glare from the* SENATOR) Well, you want to make anything out of it?

SENATOR FROM MASSACHUSETTS: Because of this great exploit,

Paul Revere's name has been given the affectionate tribute of a great people. But what of that gallant figure who is even more responsible? Gentlemen, what about Jenny, Paul Revere's horse? (*Applause*) Surely, gentlemen, Jenny is entitled to the protection of a governmental pension. A bill providing such a pension was introduced into this body in the year Eighteen Hundred and Four, and came up for its first reading in Eighteen Hundred and Fifty-Two.

THROTTLEBOTTOM: I wasn't here then. That fellow there might know something about it. (*Pointing to bearded* SENATOR)

SENATOR FROM MASSACHUSETTS: Gentlemen, in these hundred and forty-five years Jenny has not been getting any younger. I ask you, gentlemen, what are we going to do about Jenny?

THROTTLEBOTTOM: Well, that's unfinished business if I ever heard it.

JONES: May I point out to the Senator from Massachusetts that Jenny is dead?

THROTTLEBOTTOM: She is? What do you think of that? Good old Jenny! When did she die?

JONES: She died in Eighteen Hundred and Five.

THROTTLEBOTTOM: The Senate will rise for one minute in silent tribute to the departed horse from Massachusetts. (*They rise. He bangs the gavel*) Well, that finishes Jenny. (*The* SENATOR *angrily returns to his seat*) Is there any other unfinished business?

LYONS: Mr. Chairman! Gentlemen! I crave the indulgence of this august body while I say a few words in honor of my wife's birthday. (*Applause*) And I move you, Mr. Chairman, that the Senate appropriate five thousand dollars for flowers to be sent her on this historic occasion.

SENATOR FROM NORTH DAKOTA: Second the motion!

THROTTLEBOTTOM: All in favor say "Aye"! (*A full-throated "Aye" from the assemblage*) Motion carried! (*To the* CLERK) Put in my card.

(LYONS *indignantly goes to his chair and sits*)

THROTTLEBOTTOM: Now, what comes next? How about impeaching the President?

CLERK: (*Handing him a sheet of paper*) Mr. Vice-President—

THROTTLEBOTTOM: What's this?

CLERK: (*Indicating the paper*) The following committees are ready to report.

THROTTLEBOTTOM: (*Consulting the paper*) Oh, what a lot of

committees! I don't know which– (*Closes his eyes, one finger suspended over the paper*) Eenie, meenie, minie, mo. Catch a committee by the toe. If they holler give 'em dough; eenie, meenie, minie, mo. (*Places his finger on the paper; looks to see what committee he has selected. Announces*) Committee on Unemployment.

JONES: (*Rising*) The Committee on Unemployment is gratified to report that due to its unremitting efforts there is now more unemployment in the United States than ever before. (*Sits*)

THROTTLEBOTTOM: Now we're getting some place. Now let's impeach the President.

SENATOR FROM MASSACHUSETTS: (*Rising*) Mr. Chairman: I would like to call the attention of the Senate to a matter that has been puzzling me for some time. It has to do with a very interesting bridge hand, in which the cards were distributed as follows: East held the four aces, West the four kings, North the four queens, and South–ah–nothing of any importance.

LYONS: (*Rising indignantly*) Mr. Chairman! (*Faces the* SENATOR FROM MASSACHUSETTS) The South will never stand for a hand like that! (*After a glare they both sit*)

CLERK: (*Recitative*) The next business before the Senate is the resolution on the impeachment of the President.

(*A fanfare of trumpets.* TWO PAGES *enter, take their places at either side of door*)

PAGES: (*Announcing*) The President of the United States!

THROTTLEBOTTOM: Who?

CLERK: The President of the United States!

(WINTERGREEN *enters; comes down to below* THROTTLEBOTTOM'S *desk*)

THROTTLEBOTTOM: Oh, Mr. President, won't you sit down while we kick you out?

(WINTERGREEN *sits in chair under rostrum. Enter* FULTON, LIPPMAN, GILHOOLEY. *They are joined by* LYONS)

FULTON, LIPPMAN, GILHOOLEY: (*A trio*) Whereas–

LYONS: (*As others close eyes*) At a meeting of the Senate at which a quorum was present a motion was made and it was proposed that–

SENATORS: Whereas–

LYONS: John P. Wintergreen has undertaken to marry the winner of a contest held at Atlantic City–

SENATORS: Whereas–

LYONS: His subsequent refusal to marry the winner, Miss Diana Devereaux, will lead to dire international complications—

SENATORS: Whereas—

LYONS: Now, therefore, be it resolved that President John P. Wintergreen be, and he hereby is, impeached from the said office of President of these United States.

JONES: I second the resolution.

FULTON: Our first witness—the French Ambassador.

(*Enter the* SIX FRENCH SOLDIERS *as in Act 2, Scene 1*)

FRENCH SOLDIERS:

Garçon, s'il vous plaît,
Encore, Chevrolet Coupe;
Papah, pooh, pooh, pooh!
A vous toot dir vay a vous?

SENATORS:

We say how de do,
Which means that we welcome you;
We're glad of the chance
To say hello to France.

(FRENCH SOLDIERS *march upstage as* FRENCH AMBASSADOR *enters*)

FRENCH AMBASSADOR:

You've dealt a lovely maid
A blow that is injurious;
A very dirty trick was played,
And France is simply furious!

SENATORS:

He says a lovely maid
Was dealt a blow injurious;
He says a dirty trick was played,
And France is simply furious.

FULTON: (*To* AMBASSADOR) Ambassador, please explain why France should be concerned about the plaintiff.

FRENCH AMBASSADOR:

She's the illegitimate daughter of an illegitimate son
Of an illegitimate nephew of Napoleon!

ALL: Napoleon!

FRENCH AMBASSADOR:

She's contemplating suicide
Because that man he threw aside

A lady with the blue blood of Napoleon.
What sort of man
Is this who can
Insult my country
With this effront'ry?

ALL:
To the illegitimate daughter of an illegitimate son
Of an illegitimate nephew of Napoleon!

FRENCH AMBASSADOR: The Atlantic City witnesses—(*Eight* SHOWGIRLS, *in white bathing suits, with red, white and blue scarves, march on*)—and Miss Diana Devereaux.
(DIANA *enters*)

DIANA: I have come all ze way from France to bring ze greetings.
(WINTERGREEN *rises*)

FRENCH AMBASSADOR: Tell your story, little one. Commencez, s'il vous plaît.
(GIRLS *close in semi-circle behind her*)

DIANA: (*All swaying*)
Jilted, jilted,
I'm a flow'r that's wilted;
Blighted, blighted,
Till the wrong is righted;
Broken, broken,
By a man soft-spoken;
Faded, faded,
Heaven knows why.
When men are deceivers, I'm afraid
'Tis sad to be a trusting maid.
Jilted, jilted, jilted am I,
Oh, what is there left but to die?

ALL:
Jilted, jilted,
She's a flow'r that's wilted!
Blighted, blighted,
Till the wrong is righted;
Broken, broken,
By a man soft-spoken;
Faded, faded,
Heaven knows why.

DIANA:
Just as in the Frankie and Johnny song,

THROTTLEBOTTOM:
He done her wrong!

ALL:
He done her wrong!
Jilted, jilted, jilted is she,
Oh, what is there left but—to dee?
Boo-hoo, boo-hoo, boo-hoo-o-o-o.
(SENATE *is visibly affected; all are crying into handkerchiefs*)

THROTTLEBOTTOM: And, now, Mr. President, what have you to say for yourself?

WINTERGREEN:
Impeach me! Fine me! Jail me! Sue me!
My Mary's love means much more to me!

THROTTLEBOTTOM:
Enough, enough! We want no preachment!
It's time to vote on his impeachment!

ALL:
It's time to vote on his impeachment!

THROTTLEBOTTOM:
The Senator from Minnesota?

SENATOR:
Guilty!

THROTTLEBOTTOM:
Check! The Senator from North Dakota?

SENATOR:
Guilty!

THROTTLEBOTTOM:
Check! The Senator from Lou'siana?

SENATOR:
Guilty!

THROTTLEBOTTOM:
Check! The Senator who's from Montana?

MARY: (*Breaks into room. Recitative*) Stop! Stop! Stop!
WINTERGREEN: Mary!

MARY:
Before you go any further—with your permission,
I must tell you of my husband's delicate condition.

ALL:

Delicate condition! What do you mean?

MARY:

I'm about to be a mother;
He's about to be a father;
We're about to have a baby;
(WINTERGREEN *is congratulated by the* COMMITTEE)

MARY:

I must tell it,
These doings compel it!
Oh, I'm about to be a mother;
He's about to be a father;
We're about to have a baby.

ALL:

A baby!

MARY:

A baby to love and adore–
Who could ask for anything more?

ALL:

She's about to be a mother;
He's about to be a father;
They're about to have a baby.
We can't bother
A budding young father!

(*Music continues;* SENATORS *swaying in time.* MARY *is pirouetting in a dance. The* SENATOR FROM MASSACHUSETTS *is doing a cartwheel; all the* SENATORS *are dancing joyously*)

WINTERGREEN: Mary, is it true? Am I to have a baby?

MARY: It's true, John; it's true.

WINTERGREEN: It's wonderful, it's wonderful–water!–water! (*He faints.* CLERK *catches him. A laugh and a cheer from* SENATORS)

ALL: (*Picking up song again*)

They're about to have a baby–a baby–

DIANA: (*Breaking in*) It eez a fine countree–I am compromised and she has ze babee!

THROTTLEBOTTOM: Gentlemen, gentlemen–this country has never yet impeached an expectant father. What do you say?

SENATORS: Not guilty!

THROTTLEBOTTOM: (*To* WINTERGREEN) You can still be President and I'll go back to Vice!

FRENCH AMBASSADOR: (*Crossing to* WINTERGREEN)
Sacré! I go to the telegraph office to cable my report;
This is American trickery of the most reprehensible sort!
(*He starts to exit and is stopped by* DIANA'S *singing*)

DIANA:
I was the most beautiful blossom—
(FRENCH AMBASSADOR *takes her by the hand; leads her off*)

DIANA:
In all the Southland.

GIRLS: (*As they exit*)
Strike up the cymbals, drum and fife,
One of us was to be the President's wife.

SENATOR FROM MASSACHUSETTS: Great work, Jack; you'll be reinstated in the hearts of the American people.

JONES: You're doing your duty by posterity.

WINTERGREEN: Posterity? Why, posterity is just around the corner.
(SENATORS *and* COMMITTEE *come downstage, surrounding* WINTERGREEN *and* MARY)

WINTERGREEN:
Posterity is just around the corner;
(SENATORS *bring out tambourines*)

ALL:
Posterity is just around the corner!

MARY:
It really doesn't pay to be a mourner.

ALL:
Posterity is just around the corner!

WINTERGREEN:
Posterity is here—I don't mean maybe!

ALL:
There's nothing guarantees it like a baby!

MARY:
Posterity is here and will continue!

ALL:
We really didn't know you had it in you!

Posterity
Is in its infancy!

WINTERGREEN:
I sing to ev'ry citizen and fore'gner:

ALL:
Posterity is just around the corner!

(THROTTLEBOTTOM, *with a bass drum, is leading a march around the stage, followed by* MARY, *dancing, and* WINTERGREEN, *borne on the shoulders of two of the* SENATORS. *The drum bears the legend "Wintergreen for President," but the "Wintergreen" is crossed out and "Throttlebottom" is substituted*)

ALL:
We'll soon be pulling plums, like Jackie Horner!
Posterity is just around the—
Oomp-osterity, oomp-osterity, oompah, oompah, oomp-osterity.
Oomp-osterity, oomp-osterity, oompah, oompah, oomp-osterity is just around the corner!
Around the corner!

Blackout

SCENE 4

A corridor in the White House.

Enter JENKINS *and* MISS BENSON. *They are singing "Posterity" as they come on.*

JENKINS: It'll certainly be great to have a baby in the White House. I wonder when it'll be born.

MISS BENSON: Let's see—they were married March fourth, weren't they?

JENKINS: That's right.

MISS BENSON: (*Counting on her fingers*) April, May, June, July, August, September, October, November, *December!* It'll be born in December.

JENKINS: How do you know?

MISS BENSON: Well, it won't be born *before* December.

JENKINS: How do you know?

MISS BENSON: Oh, the President wouldn't do a thing like that. He'd never be re-elected.

JENKINS: You can't tell. Might be the very thing that would re-elect him. What a platform!

MISS BENSON: It's certainly wonderful the way this has lined people up behind the President.

JENKINS: Yeah, but we don't know what France is going to do. She's still liable to make trouble.

MISS BENSON: My, you'd think a woman could have a baby without France butting in.

JENKINS: Well, fifty million Frenchmen—they've got to do something.

MISS BENSON: Let 'em do it in Paris. Why should they come over here and—

WINTERGREEN: (*Singing as he enters*) "Somebody's coming to our house; somebody's coming to stay—" Oh, hello.

JENKINS: Hi, Chief!

MISS BENSON: Good morning, Mr. President. And how is Mrs. Wintergreen this morning?

WINTERGREEN: (*Vaguely*) Who? Mrs. Wintergreen? (*Realizes that there is such a person*) Oh, she's fine! Fine! Yes, sir! (*Tapping his own chest*) Should have seen the breakfast I ate!

MISS BENSON: Tell me, Mr. President. Ah—(*Hesitantly*)—when is the baby expected?

WINTERGREEN: Well, of course, you can't tell about such things, but we think some time in November. (JENKINS *gives* BENSON *a slap that says, "What did I tell you?"* WINTERGREEN *catches it, does some quick counting on his fingers, corrects himself*) December.

MISS BENSON: (*Slaps* JENKINS *in triumph*) Oh, December.

WINTERGREEN: Yes, we sort of thought December would be a very nice month. End the old year right and all that sort of thing. Have a cigar? Oh, pardon me, the baby isn't born yet.

FULTON: (*Enters*) Hello, Jack!

WINTERGREEN: Hello, there! Should have seen the breakfast I ate. (*To the* SECRETARIES) See you later.

MISS BENSON: (*To* JENKINS) I told you December.

JENKINS: Yeah—well, I'd still like to make a bet on it. (*He and* BENSON *exit*)

FULTON: Well, Jack, how are you? And how's the wife?

WINTERGREEN: Fine, fine! Never felt better.

FULTON: Mighty smart girl, Mary. She certainly saved the day for us.

WINTERGREEN: *She* saved the day? I suppose I was just an innocent bystander?

FULTON: I don't mean that, but I thought it sort of came as a surprise to you.

WINTERGREEN: Surprise? Why, I planned the whole thing. I foresaw the situation months ago.

FULTON: Anyway, it settled France. They're still yelling, but there's nothing they can do about it. The American people are behind you to a man. How'd you ever get the idea, Jack?

WINTERGREEN: Why, it wasn't anything. Nothing at all. Anybody in my place would have done the same.

FULTON: Yes, sir, it'll be a wonderful thing to have a baby in the White House.

WINTERGREEN: You mean instead of the President?

FULTON: No, no, Jack—I mean it. I tell you, there's something about the patter of baby feet, trickling down the stairs—

(*Enter the* FRENCH AMBASSADOR)

FRENCH AMBASSADOR: Gentlemen!

FULTON: (*With a bow*) Monsieur! (*To* WINTERGREEN) The French Ambassador.

FRENCH AMBASSADOR: (*With an elaborate bow*) Monsieur President.

WINTERGREEN: You all alone?

FRENCH AMBASSADOR: But yes.

WINTERGREEN: Where are those six guys with the trailing arbutus who used to march in ahead of you— (*His gesture carries out the idea of crossed bayonets, and even goes a bit further by bringing thumb and nose into close juxtaposition*)

FRENCH AMBASSADOR: They could not come today. They have dancing lesson.

WINTERGREEN: You look kind of naked without them.

FRENCH AMBASSADOR: (*Acknowledges this with a bow*) You will pardon this intrusion, Monsieur, but I have received another note from my country.

WINTERGREEN: That's all right. We've got a lot of notes from your country, and some of them were due ten years ago.

FRENCH AMBASSADOR: But this is not a promise to pay—this is serious.

WINTERGREEN: O-oh!

FRENCH AMBASSADOR: (*Bows*) Monsieur, I have good news for you. France consents to your having the baby.

FULTON: Ah!

WINTERGREEN: France consents?

FRENCH AMBASSADOR: Freely.

WINTERGREEN: Why, that's wonderful of her. Good old France! Do you mind if I tell my wife, so she can go ahead? (AMBASSADOR *bows*) You've no idea how this will please her. Will December be all right for France? (*Starts to go, then stops*) Won't take me a minute—I'll be right back.

FRENCH AMBASSADOR: But one moment, Monsieur. (WINTERGREEN *pauses*) France consents, but on one condition.

WINTERGREEN: Yeah?

FRENCH AMBASSADOR: France must have the baby.

FULTON and WINTERGREEN: *What?*

FRENCH AMBASSADOR: Do not be hasty, Monsieur. You must understand the desperate situation of my country. For fifty years the birth rate of France has been declining, declining, declining.

WINTERGREEN: What's that got to do with me?

FRENCH AMBASSADOR: You must see, Monsieur. If you had married Mademoiselle Devereaux, as you have promise, the baby she is French. But now you have taken away from France one baby, and she demand replacement.

WINTERGREEN: Never!

FULTON: I should say not!

FRENCH AMBASSADOR: It is the old law, Monsieur; an eye for an eye, a tooth for a tooth, and a baby for a baby.

WINTERGREEN: You'll get no tooth from my baby.

FRENCH AMBASSADOR: The tooth, the whole tooth, and nothing but the tooth!

WINTERGREEN: Not one tooth!

FRENCH AMBASSADOR: That is your final word?

WINTERGREEN: It is! Good day, Monsieur!

FRENCH AMBASSADOR: Good day! (*Clicks his heels; salutes; turns and starts out*) Lafayette, we are coming! (*Exits*)

FULTON: What do you think France'll do?

WINTERGREEN: What's the worst she can do? Sue us for what she owes us?

FULTON: But that other thing! France is awful touchy about her birth rate!

WINTERGREEN: What are you worrying about? I fixed *this* up, didn't I?

FULTON: What?

WINTERGREEN: Well, Mary's going to have a baby, isn't she?

FULTON: Yes!

WINTERGREEN: Well! Next year I make a tour of France! Lafayette! (*He salutes*)

Blackout

SCENE 5

The Yellow Room of the White House. A great crystal chandelier. A series of columns as far as the eye can see, giving the effect of an enormous ballroom. Entrances on each side.

It is a magnificent room, and is made more so by the striking clothes of the women and the uniforms of the men. Those men who are not in full dress uniform wear evening clothes, with bands across their shirt fronts, and hung with medals and insignia.

The stage is almost filled—various groups are gathered together, chatting. Stretched across the stage, from one archway to the other, is a line of four gorgeously dressed FLUNKEYS. *Guests are still arriving, and each one, as he enters, brings a baby carriage with him as a gift. The carriage is accepted by the* FIRST FLUNKEY *and is then passed down the line until it is shot offstage at the other side. When the curtain rises each* FLUNKEY *is handing a baby carriage to the next one, and at the entrance new guests are bringing new carriages.*

As the FLUNKEYS *pass on the carriages they repeat the line that has been spoken as the gift arrived: "Compliments of Ecuador," "Compliments of Bolivia," etc.*

There is an undercurrent of music throughout the scene.

CHIEF FLUNKEY: (*As another couple enter*) The Minister from Turkey!

MINISTER FROM TURKEY: (*Handing over baby carriage*) Compliments of Turkey.

CHIEF FLUNKEY: The Ambassador from Spain!

AMBASSADOR FROM SPAIN: (*Handing over his carriage*) Compliments of Spain.

CHIEF FLUNKEY: The Minister from Montenegro!

MINISTER FROM MONTENEGRO: (*With carriage*) Compliments of Montenegro!

CHIEF FLUNKEY: The Minister from Lithuania!

MINISTER FROM LITHUANIA: (*With carriage*) Compliments of Lithuania!

MINISTER FROM SCOTLAND: (*Presenting a very small carriage*) Compliments of Scotland!

(*Music.* COUPLES *come forward.* FLUNKEYS *stand at attention behind them*)

ALL:

Oh, trumpeter, trumpeter, blow your golden horn!
Oh, trumpeter, trumpeter, blow your golden horn!
A White House baby will very soon be born;
A White House baby will very soon be born!
Blow your horn!

ALL:

With a hey, nonny nonny, and a ha cha cha!
With a hey, nonny nonny, and a ha cha cha!
There's something glorious happening today
For all the citizens of the U. S. A.
A White House baby will very soon be born!
Oh, trumpeter, blow your horn,
Oh, trumpeter, blow your horn,
Oh, trumpeter, blow your horn,
Your golden horn, your golden horn!
(DOCTOR *enters followed by two* NURSES)

ALL:

Oh, Doctor, Doctor, what's the news, we pray,
We've waited for your bulletin all day.

DOCTOR:

The baby of the President and frau
Will be here almost any minute now.

ALL:

With a hey, nonny nonny, and a ha cha cha!
With a hey, nonny nonny, and a ha cha cha!
Oh, Doctor, here is the one thing we must know.
We're all of us anxious and we've got to know:
The baby, is it to be a girl or boy?
A baby girl or boy?
A nation's pride and joy!
We must know whether it's a girl or boy—a girl or boy?

DOCTOR:

On that matter no one budges,
For all cases of the sort
Are decided by the judges
Of the Supreme Court.

CHIEF FLUNKEY: The *Su*preme Court!
(SUPREME COURT JUSTICES *enter*)

JUSTICES:
We're the one, two, three, four, five, six, seven, eight, nine
Supreme Court Judges.

ALL:
With a hey, nonny nonny, and a ha cha cha!
With a hey, nonny nonny, and a ha cha cha!
(DOCTOR *and* NURSES *exit*)

ALL:
About the baby—will it be
A boy or girl—a he or she?

JUSTICES:
On that matter no one budges
For all cases of the sort
Are decided by the judges
Of the *Su*preme Court!

ALL:
Are decided by the judges
Of the *Su*preme Court!

CHIEF FLUNKEY: The Secretary of Agriculture!
(*Enter* LIPPMAN)

LIPPMAN:
Oh—the farmers in the dell,
The farmers in the dell,
They all keep a-asking me:
A boy or a gel?

JUSTICES:
On that matter no one budges
For all cases of the sort
Are decided by the judges
Of the *Su*preme Court!

ALL:
Are decided by the judges
Of the *Su*preme Court!

CHIEF FLUNKEY: The Secretary of the Navy!
(*Enter* GILHOOLEY)

GILHOOLEY:

All the sailors in the Navy
Of these great United States,
Do not eat their bowls of gravy,
Nor the captains, nor the mates.
They refuse to jib an anchor,
Strike a boom or heave a sail,
Till you've satisfied their hanker:
Is it female or a male?

JUSTICES:

On that matter no one budges
For all cases of the sort
Are decided by the judges
Of the *Su*preme Court!

ALL:

Are decided by the judges
Of the *Su*preme Court!

CHIEF FLUNKEY: Senator Carver Jones!
(*Enter* JONES)

JONES:

Out on the prairie,
The cowboys all keep asking of me:
He or a she–
She or a he?
Out on the prairie,
For baby boy or girl they are keen,
But they want nothing in between.

JUSTICES:

On that matter no one budges,
For all cases of the sort
Are decided by the judges
Of the *Su*preme Court!

ALL:

Are decided by the judges
Of the *Su*preme Court!

CHIEF FLUNKEY: Senator Robert E. Lyons!
(*Enter* LYONS)

LYONS:

Way down upon the Swanee River
Folks are filled with joy,

But they want to know what will the stork deliver?
Will it be a girl or boy?

ALL:

There's something glorious happening today;
A baby will be born,
A baby will be born.
Oh, trumpeter, trumpeter, blow your golden horn!

(*At the end of the number,* WINTERGREEN, *followed by* FULTON *and* JENKINS, *enter*)

FULTON: Take it easy, Jack! Nothing can happen to her.

WINTERGREEN: I know, but at a time like this–Mary in there alone– (*A chorus of greeting from all*) Oh! Hello! God, I'm nervous! I'm–anybody got a drink? (*Every man brings out a flask.* WINTERGREEN *takes* FULTON'S) Thanks. When I think of Mary in there alone– (*Takes a drink*) Well, I guess it's not going to be so hard for her.

GILHOOLEY: How is Mary?

WINTERGREEN: Oh! Her! Finest little woman in the world! When I think of what she's got to–anybody got a drink? (*The flasks come out again*) Well, I guess I'd better not mix them. (*Drinks again from* FULTON'S)

MISS BENSON: (*Enters*) Oh, Mr. Wintergreen!

WINTERGREEN: (*Wheeling*) Any news?

MISS BENSON: The baby will be here at any moment.
(*An excited buzz from the crowd*)

WINTERGREEN: Tell 'em I'm ready. (MISS BENSON *exits*) My God! You hear that? What do I do now? Anybody got a drink?

CHIEF JUSTICE: Gentlemen, duty calls. The baby is now being born. We must decide the sex.

WINTERGREEN: You decide?

CHIEF JUSTICE: We do, sir.

JUSTICES:

On that matter no one budges,
For all cases of the sort
Are decided by the judges
Of the *Su*preme Court!
(*They exit*)

ALL:

Are decided by the judges
Of the *Su*preme Court!

WINTERGREEN: I shouldn't be drinking at a time like this. (*To* JENKINS *and the* COMMITTEE) Here! Take it away! (JENKINS *reaches for the flask;* WINTERGREEN *pulls it away*) Oh, no, you don't. My wife's the finest little woman in the world! And I can lick anybody that says she ain't!

FLUNKEYS: (*Announcing*) The French Ambassador!

WINTERGREEN: Bring him in!

FRENCH AMBASSADOR: (*Entering*) Your Excellency! I have another message from France.

WINTERGREEN: Not another nickel!

FRENCH AMBASSADOR: Will you surrender the baby?

(*Reaction from the crowd*)

WINTERGREEN: Never! Give my baby to France and have it eat snails and get ptomaine poisoning! Never!

FRENCH AMBASSADOR: Then, sir, I am instructed to say that with the birth of the child France severs diplomatic relations.

(*Another reaction from the crowd*)

WINTERGREEN: Hurray!

FRENCH AMBASSADOR: And that is not all, sir. I wish furthermore to report—(*Two* FLUNKEYS *enter and blow a fanfare on their trumpets. The* SUPREME COURT JUSTICES *re-enter, to the music of "On That Matter."* WINTERGREEN *returns flask to* FULTON)

JUSTICES: Whereas—

CHIEF JUSTICE: A child has been born to the President of the United States and his consort—

JUSTICES: Whereas—

CHIEF JUSTICE: The Supreme Court of the United States has been called upon to determine the sex of the aforesaid infant—

JUSTICES: Whereas—

CHIEF JUSTICE: By a strict party vote it has been decided that—

JUSTICES: It's a boy!

(JUSTICES *exit to reprise of "On That Matter." The* COMMITTEE *and guests press around* WINTERGREEN *to congratulate him*)

WINTERGREEN: A boy! That makes me a father! Well, thank you. Thank you very much! I certainly am a lucky man! Boy, the cigars! Smoke up, everybody! Here you are! Have a cigar, Frenchy!

FRENCH AMBASSADOR: My thanks, Monsieur. On behalf of France, permit me to offer my felicitations.

WINTERGREEN: Attaboy! Let bygones be bygones! Have another cigar!

FRENCH AMBASSADOR: And permit me also to inform you that France hereby severs diplomatic relations! (*He reaches for the cigar*)

(*There is a reaction from all*)

WINTERGREEN: (*Closes the humidor with a bang*) Then the hell with you!

(*A buzz in the crowd*)

FRENCH AMBASSADOR: You understand what this means, Monsieur?

WINTERGREEN: I do! It means no smoke! (*Takes back cigar; puts it in the humidor*)

FRENCH AMBASSADOR: Precisely. And where there is no smoke there's fire. I am instructed to say, Monsieur, that this means that the French government will—

(*The* FLUNKEYS *re-enter. Another fanfare. The* JUSTICES *re-enter, to music as before*)

JUSTICES: Whereas—

CHIEF JUSTICE: A child has been born to the President of the United States and his consort—

WINTERGREEN: We had that.

CHIEF JUSTICE: But you are having it again, sir. This one is a girl.

(*All crowd around* WINTERGREEN *to congratulate him again. Music: reprise of "On That Matter," on which* FLUNKEYS *exit*)

WINTERGREEN: A girl! That makes me a father *and* a mother. Well, thanks very much, but I don't know about this! Twins! That's a little more than I counted on!

JENKINS: Cigars, sir?

WINTERGREEN: No, the cigarettes this time! A boy *and* a girl! Well!

FRENCH AMBASSADOR:

Oh, I can stand no more,
My temper's getting gingery;
This certainly will lead to war!
This insult added to injury!

ALL:

Oh, he can stand no more,
His temper's getting gingery;

He says that this will lead to war!
This insult added to injury!

FRENCH AMBASSADOR: You realize what you have done, sir? You have taken away from France not one baby, but two! What you have done to Mademoiselle Devereaux! That poor little girl! Where is she? What is she doing?

(*Offstage* DIANA *is heard singing "I Was the Most Beautiful Blossom"*)

WINTERGREEN: She's still singing.

(DIANA *enters*)

FRENCH AMBASSADOR: My poor motherless one! My sweet blossom of the Souseland!

FLUNKEY: (*Enters; announcing*) The Vice-President of the United States! (*Exits*)

THROTTLEBOTTOM: (*Enters, knitting a baby's sweater*) Is the baby born yet? I just got this finished!

WINTERGREEN: Only one? Where's the other one?

THROTTLEBOTTOM: (*Pulls out second sweater*) I thought something like that might happen.

FRENCH AMBASSADOR: Once and for all, Monsieur, what are you going to do? What are you going to do about Mademoiselle Devereaux and her babies?

WINTERGREEN: Well, she can have her own babies.

DIANA: But I am not married, Monsieur.

WINTERGREEN: What's that got to do with it?

FRENCH AMBASSADOR: Everything. The family has been illegitimate long enough.

WINTERGREEN: Then let her get married!

FRENCH AMBASSADOR: Exactly! But it was agreed, Monsieur, that she was to marry the President of the United States.

WINTERGREEN: But she can't have me. I'm married.

FRENCH AMBASSADOR: Then it is war, sir (*Reaction from crowd*) When the President of the United States fails to fulfil his duty—

WINTERGREEN: That's it! I've got it!

THE COMMITTEE: Got what?

WINTERGREEN: It's in the Constitution! When the President of the United States is unable to fulfil his duties, his obligations are assumed by—

THROTTLEBOTTOM: (*Clapping his hands gleefully*) The Vice-President! I get her!

CHIEF JUSTICE: Article Twelve!

FRENCH AMBASSADOR: Monsieur, you are a genius!

THROTTLEBOTTOM: (*To* WINTERGREEN) I could throw my arms right around your neck!

WINTERGREEN: Oh, no, you don't! Hers!

(WINTERGREEN *passes* DIANA *over to* THROTTLEBOTTOM. *Music.* TRUMPETERS *re-enter. Fanfare*)

WINTERGREEN: Oh, my God!!

CHIEF JUSTICE: It's all right. The boys are merely practicing.

(*From up left a huge canopied bed enters, preceded by* MISS BENSON, *who is carrying two baby blankets, and propelled by two* FLUNKEYS, *with a* NURSE *riding on each side of the bed, and* MARY, *propped up on pillows—with a baby in each arm*)

WINTERGREEN:

Of thee I sing, baby,
Summer, autumn, winter, spring, baby,
You're my silver lining,
You're my sky of blue;
There's a love light shining,
All because of you.

ALL:

Of thee I sing, baby,
You have got that certain thing, baby;
Shining star and inspiration,
Worthy of a mighty nation,
Of thee I sing!

Curtain

PORGY & BESS

Music by George Gershwin
Libretto by DuBose Heyward
Lyrics by DuBose Heyward *and* Ira Gershwin

(Based on the play *Porgy*
by Dorothy and DuBose Heyward)

Production Notes

Porgy and Bess was first presented by the Theatre Guild at the Alvin Theatre, New York, on October 10, 1935. The cast was as follows:

Mingo, *Ford L. Buck*
Clara, *Abbie Mitchell*
Sportin' Life, *John W. Bubbles*
Jake, *Edward Matthews*
Maria, *Georgette Harvey*
Annie, *Olive Ball*
Lily, *Helen Dowdy*
Serena, *Ruby Elzy*
Robbins, *Henry Davis*
Jim, *Jack Carr*
Peter, *Gus Simons*
Porgy, *Todd Duncan*
Crown, *Warren Coleman*
Bess, *Anne Brown*
Detective, *Alexander Campbell*
Two Policemen, *Harold Woolf, Burton McEvilly*
Undertaker, *John Garth*
Frazier, *J. Rosamond Johnson*
Mr. Archdale, *George Lessey*
Nelson, *Ray Yeates*
Strawberry Woman, *Helen Dowdy*
Crab Man, *Ray Yeates*
Coroner, *George Carleton*

Directed by *Rouben Mamoulian*
Settings by *Sergei Soudeikine*
Musical Director: *Alexander Smallens*
Choral Director: *Eva Jessye*

Act One

Scene 1: Catfish Row. A summer evening.
Scene 2: Catfish Row. The following night.
Scene 3: Catfish Row. A month later.

Act Two

Scene 1: Kittiwah Island. Evening of the same day.
Scene 2: Catfish Row. Before dawn. A week later.
Scene 3: Serena's room. Dawn of the following day.

Act Three

Scene 1: Catfish Row. The next night.
Scene 2: Catfish Row. The following morning.
Scene 3: Catfish Row. A week later. Afternoon.

Place: Charleston, South Carolina.
Time: The Past.

Musical Numbers

Act One

Scene 1:

Lullaby, *Summertime* — Clara

A Woman Is a Sometime Thing — Jim, Jake, Sportin' Life and Ensemble

Entrance of Porgy: *They Pass By Singing* — Porgy

Crap Game Fugue

Scene 2:

Gone, Gone, Gone — Ensemble

Overflow — Ensemble

Arioso: *My Man's Gone Now* — Serena and Ensemble

Train Song: *Leavin' fo' de Promis' Lan'* — Bess and Ensemble

Scene 3:

Rowing Song: *It Takes a Long Pull* — Jim, Jake and Ensemble

I Got Plenty o' Nuttin' — Porgy

Divorce Scene: *Woman to Lady* — Porgy, Bess, Frazier, Ensemble

Duet: *Bess, You Is My Woman Now* — Porgy and Bess

Picnic Song: *Oh, I Can't Sit Down* — Ensemble

Act Two

Scene 1:

I Ain't Got No Shame — Sportin' Life and Ensemble

It Ain't Necessarily So — Sportin' Life and Ensemble

Duet: *What You Want With Bess?* — Crown and Bess

Scene 2:

Time and Time Again — Serena and Ensemble

Street Cries — Strawberry Woman, Crab Man

Duet: *I Loves You, Porgy* — Porgy and Bess

Scene 3:

Oh de Lawd Shake de Heaven — Ensemble

A Red Headed Woman — Crown and Ensemble

Act Three

Scene 1:

Clara, Don't You Be Downhearted — Ensemble

Scene 2:

There's a Boat That's Leavin' Soon for New York — Sportin' Life and Bess

Scene 3:

Buzzard — Porgy

Where's My Bess? — Porgy

I'm On My Way — Porgy and Ensemble

NOTE: Since *Porgy and Bess* is a folk opera, much of what is written as dialogue generally is sung in production.

ACT ONE

SCENE 1

Catfish Row is quiet, except for SPORTIN' LIFE *and a half a dozen couples dancing in a slow, almost hypnotic rhythm.* SPORTIN' LIFE *is sounding off a rhythmic chant, and the dancers join in lazily.*

GROUP: Da-doo-da. Da-doo-da. (*As a rhythmic chant*)

Wa, wa, wa, wa. Da-doo-da. Da-doo-da.
Wa, wa, doo-da–o wa-de-wa. Wa, wa, doo-da o wa-de-wa
Wa, wa, doo-da–o wa-de-wa. Wa, wa, doo-da o wa-de-wa
Wa, wa, doo-da–o wa-de-wa. Wa, wa, doo-da o wa-de-wa
Wa, wa, doo-da

(*Lights come up on another group on stage, in the center of which* CLARA *sits with her baby in her arms, rocking it back and forth*)

CLARA:

Summertime and the livin' is easy,
Fish are jumpin', and the cotton is high.
Oh your daddy's rich, and your ma is good lookin',
So hush, little baby, don' yo' cry.

One of these mornin's you goin' to rise up singin',
Then you'll spread yo' wings an' you'll take to the sky.
But till that mornin', there's a-nothin' can harm you
With Daddy and Mammy standin' by.

(*Lights come up on still another group, this time a crap game*)

MINGO: Oh, nobody knows when de Lawd is goin' to call.

MEN: Roll dem bones, roll.

SPORTIN' LIFE: It may be in the summertime and maybe in the fall.

MEN: Roll dem bones, roll.

SPORTIN' LIFE: But you got to leave yo' baby and yo' home an' all, So–

MEN: Roll dem bones, oh, my brudder, oh, my brudder, oh, my brudder Roll dem bones, roll dem bones, roll, roll.

(*The stage grows lighter and* CATFISH ROW *takes up its normal life; children pass, couples walk about, the crap game continues.* ROBBINS *is on his way to join men in game*)

SERENA: (*To* ROBBINS) Honey boy!

JAKE: Come on down, Robbins, we're waiting for you.

SERENA: Honey, don't play tonight. Do like I say.

ROBBINS: (*To* SERENA) I been sweatin' all day. Night time is man's time. He got a right to forget his troubles. He got a right to play.

GROUP: A man's got a right to play.

ROBBINS: Yes, sir, that's right. That ole lady of mine is hell on savin' money to join the buryin' lodge.

MINGO: What did you tell her?

ROBBINS: I says spend it while you is still alive and kickin'. (*He picks up dice and throws them with a grunt*)

JIM: (*Enters*) Lord, I is tired this night. I'm done with cotton.

JAKE: Better come along with me on the *Seagull*. I got room for another fisherman.

JIM: That suit me. This cotton hook done swing its las' bale of cotton. Here, who wants a cotton hook? (*He throws cotton hook to the ground: children dive for it; scramble*)

CLARA: (*Walking with baby*)
Summertime and the livin' is easy.

(*Simultaneously with "Summertime," Crapshooters Song*)

CRAPSHOOTERS: Seven come, seven come to pappy! Throw that beautiful number! Come seven to me! Yeah, man! I'll bet yo' wrong. I'll bet he's right! Gettin' hot!

CLARA:
. . . Oh, yo' daddy's rich and yo' ma is good lookin' . . .

CRAPSHOOTERS: Come, seven! Shoot! Made it! He made it!

CLARA:
So hush, little baby, don't yo' cry!

CRAPSHOOTERS: Ol' man seven come down from heaven!

JAKE: (*To* CLARA) What, that chile ain't asleep yet? Give him to me. I'll fix him for you. (JAKE *takes the baby from* CLARA)

Lissen to yo' daddy warn you,
'Fore you starts a-travelling,
Woman may born you, love you and mourn you,
But a woman is a sometime thing,
Yes, a woman is a sometime thing.

MINGO:
Oh, a woman is a sometime thing.

JIM:

Yo' mammy is the first to name you,
Then she'll tie you to her apron string,
Then she'll shame you and she'll blame you till yo' woman comes to claim you,
'Cause a woman is a sometime thing,
Yes, a woman is a sometime thing.

SPORTIN' LIFE:

Oh, a woman is a sometime thing.

Don't you never let a woman grieve you
Jus' cause she got yo' weddin' ring.
She'll love you and deceive you, take yo' clothes and leave you
'Cause a woman is a sometime thing.

ALL:

Yes, a woman is a sometime thing.
Yes, a woman is a sometime thing.
Yes, a woman is a sometime thing.

JAKE: There now, what I tells you; he's asleep already. (BABY *wails.* MEN *at crap game laugh*)

CLARA: He got better sense than to listen to that nonsense. (*She carries baby out*)

ROBBINS: Come back, Jake, you make a better crapshooter.

PETER: Here comes de honey man. Yes mam, dis de honey man. You got honey in de comb? Yes mam, I got honey in de comb. An' is yo' honey cheap? Yes mam, my honey very cheap. Here comes de honey man.

ALL: Hello, Peter.

LILY: Well, here come my ol' man. (*Takes tray from his head*) Now gimme the money! Now go sit and rest.

MARIA: You, Scipio! Here come Porgy. Open the gate for him. (SCIPIO *stops playing the harmonica and opens one side of the iron gate.* PORGY *enters in goat cart; crowd greets him*)

JAKE: Here's the ol' crap shark!

MINGO: Now we'll have a game!

PORGY: Evenin' ladies, hello, boys! Luck been ridin' high with Porgy today. I got a pocket full of the Buckra money, and it's goin' to any man what got the guts to shoot it off me.

MINGO: Get it down, son, we'll take it.

SPORTIN' LIFE: Lay it down.

ROBBINS: All right, mens, roll 'em. We done wait long enough.

JIM: (*Coming from gate*) You bes' wait for Crown. I see him comin', takin' the whole sidewalk.

CRAPSHOOTER: And he looks like he ain't gonna stand no foolin'.

PORGY: Is Bess with him?

JAKE: Lissen to Porgy. I think he's sof' on Crown's Bess. (MEN *laugh*)

PORGY: I ain't nebber swap two words with Bess.

MARIA: Porgy got too good sense to look twice at that liquor guzzlin' slut.

SERENA: That gal Bess ain't fit for Gawd fearin' ladies to 'sociate with.

PORGY: Can't you keep yo' mouth off Bess! Between the Gawd fearin' ladies and the Gawd damnin' men that gal ain't got a chance.

JAKE: Ain' I tells you Porgy sof' on her?

PORGY: No, no, brudder, Porgy ain't sof' on no woman; they pass by singing, they pass by crying, always looking. They look in my do' and they keep on movin'. When Gawd make cripple, He mean him to be lonely. Night time, day time, he got to trabble dat lonesome road. Night time, day time, he got to trabble dat lonesome road.

(CROWN *shouts offstage; a moment later he appears with* BESS)

MINGO: Here comes Big Boy!

SPORTIN' LIFE: 'Lo, Bess.

JAKE: 'Lo, Crown.

JIM: 'Lo, Bess.

(*General greetings*)

CROWN: Hi, boys! All right, Sportin' Life, give me a pint and make it damn quick.

(SPORTIN' LIFE *pulls out a flask and hands it to* CROWN *who takes a long drink*)

CROWN: Pay him, Bess.

JAKE: Drunk again!

PORGY: He sure love his liquor, but some day she's gonna throw him down.

ANNIE: Put your skirt down, gal.

CROWN: That damn whiskey jus' as weak as water. (*Passes bottle to* BESS)

SPORTIN' LIFE: Thirty-five percent!

SERENA: See that hussy drinkin' like any man!

BESS: (*Offers bottle to* ROBBINS) Here, Robbins, have one to the Gawd fearin' ladies. There's nothin' like 'em, thank Gawd. (ROBBINS *drinks*)

CROWN: Oh, no, you don't. Nobody ain't drinkin' none of my licker. (*Throws down money*) All right, mens, I'm talkin' to you. Anybody answerin' me?
(*All throw down money*)

MINGO: Yeah, I'm answering you.

ROBBINS: (*Throwing*) Boxcars again.

MINGO: Cover 'em, brother, cover 'em.

ROBBINS: Cover hell! I goin' to pass 'em along and see if I can break my luck.

MINGO: Robbins' ole lady ain't allow him but fifty cent and he can't take no chances with bad luck.

BESS: That's all right, honey boy, I'll stake you when yo' four bits done gone.

SERENA: Go ahead an' play. You don't need no charity off no she-devils.

BESS: See what I get for you. Yo' woman is easy when you know the way.

JAKE: (*Throws*) Crapped out!

PORGY: (*To* ROBBINS)
Don't you ever let a woman grieve you
'Cause she got yo' wedding ring.

BESS:
'Cause she got yo' wedding ring.

PORGY and ALL:
She'll love you and deceive you, take yo' clothes and leave you
'Cause–

PORGY:
A woman is a sometime thing.

ALL:
Yes–a–wo-man–is–a–some-time–thi-ing.

CROWN: Shut yo' damn mouth and throw!

MINGO:
Yo' mammy's gone and yo' daddy's happy.
Come home little bones, come hope to pappy.
Four to make. Come four!
(*Throws*)

PORGY: Crapped out!

MINGO: Here, Crown!

CROWN: I passes 'em. I ain't drunk enough to read 'em! Dis licker ain't no damn good. Give me a pinch of happy dust, Sportin' Life. (SPORTIN' LIFE *produces a small paper from hat band*)

BESS: Don't give him that stuff, Sportin' Life. He's ugly drunk already.

CROWN: Pay him an' shut up. (*He takes paper from* SPORTIN' LIFE *and inhales.* BESS *pays* SPORTIN' LIFE)

SPORTIN' LIFE: Huh, seven! Huh, seven! Huh, seven! 'Leven come home, Fido! I'm just a lucky cat, that's all. (*Whistles, pulls pot in. All ante*)

CROWN: God damn it, I ain't read 'em yet.

MEN:

Crown cockeyed drunk, he can't tell dice from a watermelon;
Crown cockeyed drunk, he can't tell dice from a wa–

CROWN: Shut up!

SPORTIN' LIFE: Six to make! (*Shoots again*)

PORGY: Seven!

JAKE: Seven, seven, Porgy shoots now.

MINGO: Crapped out!

PORGY:

Oh, little stars, little stars,
Roll, roll, roll me some light,
'Leven little stars, come home, come home,
Roll dis poor beggar a sun an' a moon,
A sun an' a moon.
(*Shoots*)

MINGO: Li'l Joe.

JAKE: Little Joe.

PORGY: Oh, no, my brother, that ain't Little Joe.

MINGO: What is it then?

PORGY: They is the mornin' and the evenin' stars. An' just you watch 'em rise and shine for this poor beggar. (CROWN *grabs his arm*) Turn me loose. (*Shoots*)

MINGO: Made 'em!

CROWN: Roll up that bastard's sleeve. (PORGY *pulls in pot, laughs, rolls up sleeve*) Well, you got them damn dice, conjer them.

PORGY: Boy, boy, boy, I'm a crap shootin' idiot. (*Rolls*)

SPORTIN' LIFE and JAKE: Crapped out.

MINGO: Rolled out!

ROBBINS: (*Takes up dice*) Nine to make, come nine! (*Shoots*) Read 'em. Nine spot! Nine right! (*He sweeps up money.* CROWN *seizes his wrist*)

CROWN: Touch that money an' meet yo' Gawd!

ROBBINS: Take yo' hand off me, you lousy houn'. Han' me that brick behin' you. (*He pulls himself free of* CROWN'S *grasp*)

CROWN: Nobody's gettin' away with Crown's money. I'm goin' kill dat bastard! (*He lunges at* ROBBINS)

BESS: Someone will surely get hurt–so stop!–won't somebody stop them? Come on, Crown, stop it! Oh! I'm so afraid–make 'em cut it out!

ALL: (*Simultaneously with* BESS) Oh, stop them! Don' let them fight! I warned him, oh! Won't somebody stop them now–won't somebody stop them now!

WOMEN: Oh, stop them–someone will get hurt! Why must people fight? Crown is a bad, bad man when he's drunk.

MEN:

Crown is drunk.
Robbins' got no chance!
Oh! Robbins' got no chance.
Crown is a bad bad man when he's drunk.

(*Suddenly* CROWN *stabs* ROBBINS *with a cotton hook.* ROBBINS *falls dead.* SERENA *screams*)

MINGO: Jesus, he killed him!

(SERENA *flings herself upon* ROBBINS' *body*)

BESS: Wake up an' hit it out. You ain't got no time to lose.

CROWN: What the matter?

BESS: You done kill Robbins and the police will be comin'. (*She shakes him to his senses*)

CROWN: Police! (*The entire crowd disperses in various directions.* CROWN *and* BESS *start for the gate*) Where you goin' hide? They know you an' I pulls together.

BESS: Some man always willin' to take care of Bess.

CROWN: Well, get this: whoever he is, he's temporary. I'm comin' back when the hell dies down.

BESS: All right, only get out now. Here, take this. (*She takes money from her stocking and gives it to him. He disappears.* BESS *runs–senses* SPORTIN' LIFE *behind her*) That you, Sportin' Life?

SPORTIN' LIFE: Sure, and I's the only friend you got left.

BESS: For Gawd's sake, give me a touch of happy dust. I shakin' so I can hardly stand. (*He gives her powder*)

SPORTIN' LIFE: Listen, I'll be goin' to New York soon. I'll hide you out and take you with me. Why you an' me will make a swell team.

BESS: I ain't come to that yet.

MARIA: Get out before de police come!

SPORTIN' LIFE: Well, the cops ain't goin' find me here for no woman.

(*He slinks out.* BESS *looks for shelter, knocks at doors. They are locked or slammed in her face*)

LILY: Get away from here!

ANNIE: Get out–Git!

MARIA: Didn't I say to get out before the police come!

BESS: You wouldn't have a heart and let me in?

MARIA: Not till hell freeze!

BESS: Who live over there?

MARIA: That's Porgy, he ain't no use to your kind, he's a cripple and a beggar.

(BESS *moves toward the gate. As she reaches it, a police whistle sends her rushing back, frightened.* PORGY'S *door opens.* PORGY *stretches out his hand to her. Shuddering, she moves quickly away from* SERENA *and* ROBBINS' *body and goes to* PORGY'S *door.* PORGY *reaches for* BESS' *hand. She enters his room*)

Curtain

SCENE 2

Chanting begins.

Funeral procession of mourners move ROBBINS' *body*

WOMAN:

Where is brudder Robbins?

ALL:

He's a-gone, gone, gone, gone, gone, gone, gone.

WOMAN:

I seen him in de mornin' wid his work clo'es on

ALL:

But he's gone, gone, gone, gone, gone, gone, gone.

MAN:

An' I seen him in the noontime straight and tall,
But death come a-walkin' in the evenin' fall,

ALL:

An' he's gone, gone, gone, gone, gone, gone, gone.

WOMAN:

An' death touched Robbins wid a silver knife

ALL:

An' he's gone, gone, gone, gone, gone, gone, gone.

MAN:

An' he's sittin' in de garden by de tree of life.

ALL:

An' he's gone, gone, gone, gone, gone, gone, gone.
Robbins is gone.

(PORGY *and* BESS *enter.* BESS *advances toward bier, money in hand*)

SERENA: I don't need yo' money for to bury my man.

BESS: Dis ain't Crown's money. Porgy give me my money now.

SERENA: All right, then, you can put it in the saucer.

WOMAN:

Come on, sister, come on, brother,
Fill up the saucer till it overflow, overflow, overflow.

GROUP:

Fill up de saucer till it overflow.

PORGY:

Yes, my Jesus, overflow.

1st WOMAN:

'Cause de Lawd will meet you,

2nd WOMAN:

Yes, de Lawd will meet you at the court-house door—

ALL:

Court-house door, court-house door, de Lawd will meet you at the court-house door.

PORGY:

Yes, my Jesus, court-house door.
How de saucer stand now, my sister?

SERENA:

Fourteen dollars an' fifty cents.

MARIA:

Dat's a-comin' on, sister, you can bury him soon.

SERENA:

What am I goin' to do if we ain' got the money?

PORGY:

Gawd got plenty of money for de saucer.

ALL:

Bless de Lord.

PORGY:

An' He goin' to soffen dese people heart for to fill de saucer till he spill all over.

ALL:

Amen, my Jesus.

PORGY:

De Lawd will provide a grave for His chillun.

ALL:

Bless the Lord!

PORGY:

An' He got comfort for de widder.

ALL:

Oh, my Jesus.

PORGY:

An' He goin' feed his fadderless chillun.

ALL:

Yes Lawd, Truth Lawd.

PORGY:

An' He goin' raise dis poor sinner up out of de grave.

ALL:

'Allelujah.

PORGY:

An' set him in de shinin' seat ob de righteous.

SERENA:

Amen, my Jesus.

ALL:

Overflow, overflow, oh, fill up de saucer till it overflow,
Everybody helpin' now—sendin' our brudder to heaven,
Lawd, Oh Lawd, send down your blessing!
Robbins is rising to heaven!

PORGY: (*Simultaneously with group*) Oh, sufferin' Jesus! You knows right from wrong. You knows Robbins was a good man, an' now he's weary an' he's goin' home. Reach down yo' lovin' hands an' take our brudder to yo' bosom. Thank you, Lawd, Bless you, Lawd.

ALL: (*Simultaneously with* PORGY)
Overflow, overflow, Oh Lawd will fill de saucer,
Lawd will fill de saucer–

(*Whistle–scream–singing cuts off abruptly.* DETECTIVE *enters*)

DETECTIVE: Um! A saucer-burial setup, I see. You're his widow?

SERENA: Yes, suh.

DETECTIVE: He didn't leave any burial insurance?

SERENA: No, boss, he didn't leave nuttin'.

DETECTIVE: Well, see to it he's buried tomorrow. (*To* PETER) You killed Robbins an' I'm going to make you hang for it!

LILY: He ain't done um!

PETER: What he say?

LILY: He say you kill Robbins.

PETER: 'Fore Gawd, boss, I ain't never done um.

DETECTIVE: Who did it, then? You heard me, who did it?

PETER: Crown done it, boss. I done see him do it.

DETECTIVE: You're sure you saw him?

PETER: I swear to Gawd, boss, I was right there beside him.

DETECTIVE: (*Laughs*) That's easy. I thought as much. (*To* PORGY) You. You saw it, too. Look at me, you damn cripple.

PORGY: I don't know nuttin' 'bout it, boss.

DETECTIVE: That's your room in the corner, ain't it?

PORGY: Yes, boss, dat's my room.

DETECTIVE: The door opens on the court, don't it?

PORGY: Yes, boss, my door opens on the court.

DETECTIVE: An' yet you didn't see or hear anything?

PORGY: I don't know nuttin' 'bout it, boss. I been asleep inside, and my door been closed.

DETECTIVE: You're a damn liar. (*Indicating* PETER) He saw the killing; take him along and lock him up as a material witness.

POLICEMAN: Come along.

PETER: I ain't done it, boss.

LILY: How long you goin' lock him up for?

DETECTIVE: Till we catch Crown.

PORGY: I reckon Crown done loose now in de palmetto thickets, an' dere ain' a rope long enough to reach him.

DETECTIVE: Then the old man's out of luck. Remember, you've got to bury that body tomorrow or the board of health will take him an' turn him over to the medical students. Come on, get the old man in the wagon.
(*Music resumes*)

PETER: I ain' done it, boss, I ain't done it. (POLICEMAN *drags him off*) I swear to Gawd I ain't done nothing.

PORGY: I can't puzzle this thing out. Peter was a good man, but dat lousy Crown was a killer and forever gettin' into trouble.

JAKE: That's the truth, brother.

PORGY: But there go Peter to be lock up like a thief.

JAKE: Like a thief.

PORGY: An' here be Robbins with his wife and his fadderless chillun, an' Crown done gone his ways drinkin'—

ANNIE: Yeah!

PORGY:—gamblin'—

ANNIE: Yeah!

PORGY:—swearin'—

ANNIE: Yeah!

PORGY:—to do the same thing over and over somewheres else.

ALL:

Gone, gone, gone, gone, gone, gone.

SERENA:

My man's gone now,
Ain't no use a-listenin'
For his tired foot-steps
Climbin' up de stairs. Ah—
Ole Man Sorrow's
Come to keep me comp'ny,
Whisperin' beside me
When I say my prayers. Ah—
Ain't dat I mind workin',
Work an' me is travellers,
Journeyin' together
To de promise land.
But Ole Man Sorrow's
Marchin' all de way wid me

Tellin' me I'm ole now
Since I lose my man.

ALL:
Since she lose her man.

SERENA:
Since I lose my man.

ALL:
Ah!

SERENA:
Ole Man Sorrow sittin' by de fireplace,
Lyin' all night long by me in de bed.
Tellin' me de same thing mornin', noon an' eb'nin',
That I'm all alone now since my man is dead. Ah—
Since my man is dead!

ALL:
Ah—

SERENA:
Ah—

UNDERTAKER: (*Entering*) How de saucer stan' now, my sister?

SERENA: There ain't but fifteen dollar.

UNDERTAKER: Hum! Can't bury him for fifteen dollar.

JAKE: He got to be buried tomorrow or the board of health will take him and give him to the medical students.

UNDERTAKER: (*Kindly*) Life is hard, brudder, but we all got to live. It cos' money for to bury a grown man.

SERENA: Oh, for Gawd sake, bury him in the graveyard! Don't let the students take him to cut up an' scatter. I goin' to work on Monday, an' I swear to Gawd, I gon' pay you ev'ry cent. (*They all plead with* UNDERTAKER)

PORGY: Please! Brother!

ALL: Please, Mr. Undertaker, help 'em. Be kind, etc.

UNDERTAKER: All right, sister, with the box and one carriage, it'll cost me more'n twenty-five, but I'll see you through.

ALL: Bless you—brudder! Jesus bless you, my brudder.

UNDERTAKER: You can all be ready tomorrow mornin'. It's a long trip to the cemetery. (*He leaves*)

ALL: Hallelujah—praise de Lawd, you are kind.

BESS:
Oh, the train is at the station

An' you better get on board
'Cause it's leavin' today,

ALL:
Leavin' today, leavin' today.

BESS:
Oh, the train is at the station
An' you better get on board,
'Cause it's leavin' today,

ALL:
An' it's headin' for the Promise' Lan'.

BESS:
Oh, we're leavin' for the Promise' Lan',
Leavin' for the Promise' Lan'.

BESS and ALL:
Keep that drivin' wheel a-rollin', rollin', rollin', rollin', rollin', rollin', let it roll!
Until we meet our brudder in the Promise' Lan'.
In the Promise' Lan'!

GROUP:
Oh, he's gone, gone, gone, gone, gone, gone, gone

MAN:
And he's sittin' in the garden by the tree of life

ALL:
And he's gone, gone, gone, gone, gone, gone, gone
Oh he's gone, Robbins is gone
Ah, ah, ah, ah, ah, ah, ah ah.

(*Wails of the mourners fade and segues into bell sounds heralding morning*)

Curtain

SCENE 3

Fishermen enter, carrying net, examine it, repair net and sway to rhythm of song.

JAKE:
Oh, I'm a-goin' out to the Blackfish banks
No matter what de wedder say,
An' when I say I'm goin' I means goin'
An' I'm leavin' at de break o' day.

JIM and MEN:

It take a long pull to get there, huh!
It take a long pull to get there, huh!
It take a long pull to get there,
But I'll anchor in the Promise' Lan',
In de Promise' Lan'.

JAKE:

I got a blister on my settin' down place
I got a blister in my han'
But I'm goin' row dis little boat, trust me Gawd,
Till I anchor in de Promise' Lan'.

JIM and MEN:

It takes a long pull to get there, huh!
It takes a long pull to get there, huh!
It takes a long pull to get there, huh!
But I'll anchor in de Promise' Lan'!

ANNIE: Mus' be you mens forgot about de picnic. Ain't you knows dat de p'rade start up de block at ten o'clock?

JAKE: That's right, mens. Turn out tomorrow mornin' an' we'll push de *Seagull* clean to de Blackfish banks 'fore we wet de anchor.

CLARA: Jake, you ain't plannin' to take de *Seagull* to de Blackfish banks, is you? It's time for de September storms.

JAKE: How you think dat boy goin' get a college education, if I don' work hard an' make money?–Mornin', Porgy.

PORGY: (*At window, laughing*)

Oh, I got plenty o' nuttin',
An' nuttin's plenty for me.
I got no car, got no mule, got no misery.
De folks wid plenty o' plenty
Got a lock on dey door.
'Fraid somebody's a-goin' to rob 'em
While dey's out a-makin' more.
What for?

WOMAN:

He got no lock on de door,

PORGY:

Dat's no way to be.

2nd WOMAN:

Dey can steal de rug from his floor.

PORGY:

Dat's okay wid me,
'Cause de things dat I prize
Like de stars in de skies
All are free.
Oh, I got plenty o' nuttin',
An' nuttin's plenty for me,
I got my gal, got my song, got Hebben de whole day long!
No use complainin'!
Got my gal, got my Lawd, got my song.

WOMEN: Porgy change since dat woman come to live with he.

SERENA: How he change!

ALL: He ain't cross with chillun no more, an' ain't you hear how he an' Bess all de time singin' in their room?

MARIA: I tells you he's happy now.

ALL: Happy!

PORGY:

I got plenty o' nuttin',
An' nuttin's plenty fo' me.
I got de sun, got de moon, got de deep blue sea.

MAN:

De folks wid plenty o' plenty,
Got to pray all de day.

2nd MAN:

Seems wid plenty you sure got to worry
How to keep de debble away, away.

PORGY:

I ain't a-frettin' 'bout hell
Till de time arrive.
Never worry long as I'm well,
Never one to strive to be good, to be bad,
What de hell, I is glad I's alive.

Oh, I got plenty o' nuttin',
An' nuttin's plenty for me.
I got my gal, got my song,
Got Hebben de whole day long.
No use complainin',
Got my gal, got my Lawd, got my song!

(LAWYER FRAZIER *enters.* MARIA *sees him and follows after him*)

MARIA: Mornin', Lawyer, lookin' for somebody?

FRAZIER: Porgy live here, don't he?

MARIA: Hey, Porgy, here's Lawyer Frazier come to see you.

FRAZIER: Mornin', Porgy.

PORGY: Mornin', Lawyer.

FRAZIER: Ain't that Crown's Bess in yo' room?

PORGY: No, sir, she ain't. She's Porgy's Bess.

MARIA: She's *anybody's* Bess!

FRAZIER: Ah ha, ah ha, Porgy's Bess, eh? Den I guess she'll be wantin' divorce.

PORGY: Huh?

LILY: What's a divorce?

FRAZIER: If de woman livin' wid you now, she got to have divorce from Crown or else it ain't legal. (*He takes document and shows it to* PORGY)

PORGY: How much dat t'ing cost?

FRAZIER: One dollar. Dat is, if there ain' no complications.

PORGY: Bess, you likes to have divorce?

BESS: What you think, Porgy?

PORGY: I'm goin' to buy you a divorce. (*He hands* FRAZIER *money*)

FRAZIER: Wait a minute, it ain't legal yet. Yo' name.

ALL: Bess!

FRAZIER: Your age?

BESS: Twenty year.

ALL: Lord, Lord, listen what she say.

MARIA: Dat girl's thirty if she's a day!

FRAZIER: You desire to be divorce from dat man Crown?

ALL: Sho' she do, sho' she do. Yes suh, yes suh, sho' she do!

FRAZIER: I'm askin' you.

BESS: Yes, boss, dat's true.

FRAZIER: Address the court as "Yo' honor."

ALL: Yes, yo' honor. Yes, yo' honor. Yes, yo' honor. Yes, yo' honor.

MINGO: Yes, yo' honor!

FRAZIER: When was you an' Crown marry?

BESS: I don't rightly remember, yo' honor.

FRAZIER: One yeah, five yeah, ten yeah, huh?

LILY: Dat gal ain' never marry!

FRAZIER: Ah, dat's a complication!

ALL: Dat's a complication. Dat's a complication, Lord, Lord—

MARIA: Dat *is* a complication.

PORGY: You can't sell her divorce, gimme back my dollah!
(*Everybody laughs*)

FRAZIER: 'Course I sells divorce. You got no right to laugh, but it takes expert to divorce a woman what ain't marry, an' it cos' you, ahem, a dollar an' a half.

BESS: It ain't worth it, Porgy.

FRAZIER: All right, go on livin' in sin. (PORGY *counts out money and gives it to* FRAZIER, *who signs and seals paper and hands it to* BESS) Good day to you, Missis Porgy. Only dollar an' a half to change woman to lady.

ALL: Woman to lady, woman to lady, Lord, Lord, woman to lady!

ANNIE: Ain't you gonna get dressed for the picnic?

WOMAN: I sure am.

2nd WOMAN: I'm gonna wear my red dress.
(*All move off to their various rooms, leaving* BESS *alone.* SPORTIN' LIFE *enters, sneaks up to* BESS)

SPORTIN' LIFE: 'Lo, Bess. Goin' to picnic?

BESS: No, guess I'll stay home.

SPORTIN' LIFE: Picnics is all right for these small town suckers, but we is use to the high life, you know. You an' me, we understand each other. I can't see for the life of me what you is hangin' roun' this place for; why, with your looks, Bess, an' your way with the boys, there's big money for you, an' me, in New York.

BESS: I can't remember ever meetin' a nothin' what I likes less than I does you.

SPORTIN' LIFE: Oh, come on, now, how about a little touch of happy dus' for old time sake?

BESS: I's through with that stuff!

SPORTIN' LIFE: Come on, give me yo' han'.

BESS: I tells you, I's through!

SPORTIN' LIFE: Just a pinch, not enough to hurt a flea.

BESS: No, no, I done give up dope.

SPORTIN' LIFE: Tell that to somebody else, nobody ever gave up happy dus'. (PORGY *opens shutters and seizes* SPORTIN' LIFE'S *wrist*) Leggo, you damn cripple! Gawd, what a grip for a piece of a man!

PORGY: Sportin' Life, you keep away from my woman, or I'll break yo' damn neck!

SPORTIN' LIFE: I'd like to see a lousy cripple, like you, break my neck.

PORGY: If I get my hands on you once more, you'll see quick enough.

BESS: (*Simultaneously with* PORGY) Go 'long now.

SPORTIN' LIFE: All right, yo' men frien's come an' they go, but remember Ole Sportin' Life an' de happy dus' here all along.

PORGY: (*Threatening* SPORTIN' LIFE) Get out, you rat, you louse, you buzzard!

(SPORTIN' LIFE *scuttles off.* JAKE *and* CLARA *appear, dressing and preparing for the picnic*)

JAKE: Honey, we sure goin' strut our stuff today!

CLARA: We is that!

JAKE: (*Calling*) Bess! Be sure to come 'long to de picnic!

(*They go back into room*)

PORGY: Dere! You see dey all ask you to go along to de picnic.

BESS: Plenty of de mens ask me. But I don't hear none of de ladies say nuttin'!

PORGY: Bess, you can put on my lodge sash an' be as good as any woman in dat crowd.

BESS: Yo' an' me know it take more'n sash.

PORGY:

Bess, you is my woman now, you is, you is!
An' you mus' laugh and sing an' dance for two instead of one.
Want no wrinkle on yo' brow, no how,
Because de sorrow of de past is all done, done.
Oh, Bess, my Bess,
The real happiness is jes' begun.

BESS:

Porgy, I's yo' woman now, I is, I is!
An' I ain' never goin' nowhere 'less you shares de fun.
Dere's no wrinkle on my brow, no how,
But I ain' goin'! You hear me sayin',
If you ain' goin', wid you I'm stayin'.
Porgy, I's yo' woman now, I's yours forever,
Mornin' time and evenin' time and summer time an' winter time.

PORGY:

Mornin' time and evenin' time and summer time an' winter time,
Bess, you got yo' man.

PORGY: (*Simultaneously with* BESS)

Bess, you is my woman now an' forever.

Dis life is jes' begun.
Bess, we two is one now and forever.
Oh, Bess, don't min' dose women.
You got yo' Porgy, you loves yo' Porgy
I knows you means it, I seen it in yo' eyes, Bess.
We'll go swingin' through de years a-singin'
Hmmm . . . Mornin' time and evenin' time and summer time and winter time.
My Bess, my Bess, from dis minute I'm tellin' you, I keep dis vow;
Oh, my Bessie, we's happy now,
We is one now.

BESS: (*Simultaneously with* PORGY)
Porgy, I's yo' woman now, I is, I is,
An' I ain't never goin' nowhere
'Less you shares de fun.
Dere's no wrinkle on my brow, no how
But I ain' goin', you hear me sayin'
If you ain' goin', wid you I'm stayin'.
Porgy, I's yo' woman now! I's yours forever,
Mornin' time and evenin' time and summer time and winter time, hmmmmmm.
Oh, my Porgy, my man Porgy,
From dis minute I'm tellin' you, I keep dis vow;
Porgy, I's yo' woman now.
(*They embrace*)

(*Buzz of picnic preparations.* MARIA *comes out with basket*)

MARIA: What's de matter wid you, sister? Ain't you know you goin' be late for de picnic?

BESS: I stayin' with Porgy.

MARIA: Sho' you goin'. Everybody goin'. You got to help me wid my basket. Come now, where's yo' hat? (*She gets her hat from* PORGY'S *room*)

PORGY: Bess, I want yo' to go.

MARIA: What's dis talk about stayin' home when everybody goin' to de picnic?

BESS: Porgy, I hates to go an' leave you all alone.

PORGY: Bess, my honey, I so glad to have you go. I been wantin' you to be so happy here in Catfish Row.

BESS: Yes, Porgy, I know.

PORGY: Go, chile, go.

MARIA: Come on, chile! You stay roun' here an' you'll die of de lonesome blues!

(SPORTIN' LIFE *dances out. Some of crowd attired in lodge regalia start coming out.* SPORTIN' LIFE *sings "Oh, I Can't Sit Down!" One by one the various sections of Catfish Row join in the song as they pour out into the court—until they are all singing it as they prance and dance off*)

SPORTIN' LIFE:

Oh, I can't sit down!
Got to keep a-goin' like de flowin' of a song.
Oh, I can't sit down!
Guess I'll take my honey and her sunny smile 'long.
Today I is gay and I's free,
Jes' a-bubblin', nothin' troublin' me.
Oh, I's gwine to town,
I can't sit down.

ALL:

Oh, I can't sit down.
Got to keep a-goin' like de flowin' of a song.
Oh, I can't sit down,
Guess I'll take my honey and her sunny smile 'long.
Today I is gay and I's free
Jes' a-bubblin', nothin' troublin' me
Oh, I's gwine to town,
I can't sit down.

Happy feelin', in my bones a-stealin',
No concealin' dat it's picnic day.
Sho' is dandy, got de licker handy.
Me an' Mandy, we is on de way
'Cause dis is picnic day.
Oh, I can't sit down,
Got to keep a-jumpin' to de thumpin' of de drum!
Oh, I can't sit down.
Full of locomotion like an ocean full of rum!
Today I is gay and I's free.
Jes' a-bubblin', nothin' troublin' me!
Oh, I's gwine to town,
I can't, jes' can't, sit down!

(*Crowd leaves.* MARIA *goes to* BESS)

MARIA: Come on, now, hurry up. We'll be late for dat boat.

BESS: Goodbye, Porgy.

PORGY: Goodbye, honey.

BESS: Goodbye, Porgy, goodbye. (MARIA *and* BESS *leave*)

PORGY:

Oh, I got plenty o' nuttin',
An' nuttin's plenty for me,
I got my gal, got my Lawd, got Hebben de whole day long.
Got my gal, got my Lawd, got my song!

Curtain

ACT TWO

SCENE 1

Kittiwah Island. General gaiety. All well-fed—some few well-liquored. Some dancing. They are humming *melody: "I Ain't Got No Shame."* SPORTIN' LIFE *darts up on mound and sings to them.*

SPORTIN' LIFE:

I ain't got no shame doin' what I like to do!
I ain't got no shame doin' what I like to do!
Sun ain't got no shame; moon ain't got no shame.
So *I* ain't got no shame, doin' what I like to do!

(*This "charges" the group. They sing—as rhythm of dance and movement intensifies*)

ALL:

I ain't got no shame doin' what I like to do!
I ain't got no shame doin' what I like to do!
Sun ain't got no shame; moon ain't got no shame.
So *I* ain't got no shame, doin' what I like to do!!
So *I* ain't got no shame, doin' what I like to do!!

(*Laughter, hollering, etc.* MARIA *storms over to stump—yelling the crowd down*)

MARIA: Shame!—Shame on all you sinners! You call yourselves church members, you goes on a decent picnic of "The Sons and Daughters of Repent Ye Says the Lord" and you start behaving like Sodom and Gomorrah!

ANNIE: It's a Gawd's wonder de Lord don't send His living fire to burn you offen the face of the earth!

(SPORTIN' LIFE *dances over to* ANNIE)

SPORTIN' LIFE:

It ain't necessarily so,
De t'ings dat yo' li'ble
To read in de Bible,
It ain't necessarily so.
Li'l David was small, but oh my!
Li'l David was small, but oh my!
He fought big Goliath
Who lay down an' dieth,
Li'l David was small, but oh my!
Wa-doo–Zim bam boodle-oo,
Hoodle ah da wa da–Scatty wah. Yeah!
Oh, Jonah, he lived in a whale,
Oh, Jonah, he lived in a whale
Fo' he made his home in
Dat fish's abdomen.
Oh, Jonah, he lived in a whale.
Li'l Moses was found in a stream,
Li'l Moses was found in a stream,
He floated on water
Till Ole Pharaoh's daughter
She fished him, she says from dat stream.
Wa-doo–Zim bam boodle-oo,
Hoodle ah da wa–Scatty wah. Yeah!
It ain't necessarily so,
It ain't necessarily so,
Dey tell all you chillun
De debble's a villun
But 'tain't necessarily so.
To get into Hebben,
Don't snap for a sebben!
Live clean, don' have no fault.
Oh, I takes dat gospel
Whenever it's pos'ble
But wid a grain of salt.
Methuselah lived nine hundred years,
Methuselah lived nine hundred years,
Say, but what good is livin'
When no gal'll give in
To no man what's nine hundred years?
I'm preachin' dis sermon to show
It ain't nessa, ain't nessa, ain't nessa, ain't nessa,

Ain't necessarily so.
I'm preachin' dis sermon to show
It ain't nessa, ain't nessa, ain't nessa, ain't nessa,
Ain't necessarily so.

ALL:

Ha-da-ha–ha-da-da–Ha da da da da da da da da
Ha——Ha da da——Ha da da da da da da da da da–
Ha da da da da da da da da da da da——Ha da da da da da
Ha da da da da–Ha da da–Ha da da da da da–
Ha da da–Ah——

(MARIA *stomps in and shouts*)

MARIA: Tell me, when did you start working fer de devil?!
(*Boat whistle*)

MINGO: The boat!

MARIA: Take them baskets an' git–all you wicked chillun of de devil!!
(*Another whistle. People gather baskets, hats, paraphernalia, and leave. Several quick toots of whistle*)

MARIA: Hurry up, Bess, dat boat's got de whooping cough!
(MARIA *exits with others*)

GIRL: Come on, Bess!

ANOTHER GIRL: Hurry–we'll miss the boat! (*Exits*)

BESS: Oh, Maria–my basket! (BESS *runs to pick up basket.* CROWN'S *arm shoots out from behind a tree and whirls* BESS *back*) Crown!

CROWN: You know very well dis Crown; I seen you lan' an' I been waitin' all day for you. I mos' dead on this damn island. Lor'! I'se glad you come! (*He pulls her to him. Boat whistle*)

BESS: I can't stay, Crown, or de boat'll go widout me.

CROWN: Damn dat boat! Got any happy dus' wid you?

BESS: No! No, I ain'. I done gib up dope. (CROWN *laughs*) Dat's de Gawd's trut'! Crown! I got something to tell you. (*Boat whistle.* CROWN *grunts and holds her*)

CROWN: What dat?

BESS: I–I livin' with Porgy now, an' I livin' decent.

CROWN: (*Wheels her around*) You hear what I tol' you–I say in a couple ob weeks I'm comin' for you, an' you is goin' play fair, lessen you wants to meet yo' Gawd. Yo' gets dat? (*He seizes her*)

BESS: I tells yo' I mean what I says! Porgy my man now!

CROWN: Yo' tellin' me dat yo' radder hab dat cripple dan Crown?

BESS: It's like dis, Crown, I's the only woman Porgy ever had, an' I'se thinkin' now, how it's goin' to be tonight when all the others go back to Catfish Row. He'll be sittin' an' watchin' the big front gate, a-countin' 'em off, waitin' for Bess. An' when the las' woman goes home to her man an' I ain't there . . . . (CROWN *laughs*) Lemme go, Crown! You can get plenty other women.

CROWN: What I wants wid other women? I got a woman an' dat's you, see!

BESS:

Oh, what you want wid Bess?
She's gettin' ole now;
Take a fine young gal
For to satisfy Crown.
Look at this chest
An' look at these arms you got.
You know how it always been with me,
These five years I been yo' woman,
You could kick me in the street,
Then when you wanted me back,
You could whistle, an' there I was
Back again, lickin' yo' hand.
There's plenty better lookin' gal than Bess.
(*Simultaneously with* CROWN)
Can' you see I'm with Porgy
Now and forever
I am his woman, he would die without me,
Oh, Crown, won't you let me go to my man, to my man.
He is a cripple an' needs my love, all my love.
What you want wid Bess? Oh, let me go to my man, what you want with Bess?

CROWN: (*Simultaneously with* BESS)
What I wants wid other woman,
I gots a woman, yes,
An' dat is you, yes, dat is you, yes,
I need you now an' you're mine jus' as long as I want you.
No cripple goin' take my woman from me.
You got a man tonight and that is Crown, yes, Crown, yes Crown.
You're my woman, Bess, I'm tellin' you, now I'm your man.

BESS: Lemme go, Crown, de boat it's goin' without me.

CROWN: (*Pressing her very close*) You ain't goin' nowhere!

BESS: Take yo' hands off me, I say, yo' hands, yo' hands, yo' hands . . .

CROWN: I knows you ain' change—wid you and me it always be the same. Come on up here!

(CROWN *scoops her up in his arms*)

Curtain

SCENE 2

Catfish Row. The court before dawn. Bells herald the new day. FISHERMEN *loll about sleepily.*

JAKE: Honey, dat's all de breakfast I got time for. It's gettin' late, the weather's fine. I'm on my way. Come on, you fishermen, it's time to trabble.

NELSON: All right, Jake.

JIM: All ready, Jake, we bes' be off.

MARIA: Goodbye, boys.

JIM: Goodbye, Maria. It looks to me like it goin' storm today.

CLARA: What?!

JAKE: Don't you know dat ain' de way to talk 'fore my woman. So long, Clara, gangway for de *Seagull*. (*He kisses* CLARA)

JIM and MEN:

It take a long pull to get there, huh!
It take a long pull to get there, huh!
It take a long pull to get there, but
I'll anchor in de Promise' Lan',
In de Promise' Lan'.

(GROUP *continues singing as they go off*)

BESS: (*Deliriously . . . in* PORGY'S *room*) Take yo' han's off me, I say. Yo' han's, yo' han's, yo' han's!

PORGY: (*Inside—soothingly*) Das all right, Bess. Yo' here wid Porgy now.

CLARA: Ain't Bess no better this morning?

SERENA: She still out of her head.

BESS: Eighteen mile to Kittiwah! Lawd, what a long road, ain' nobody to help me! Ain' nobody to help me!

MARIA: She no better—She still got de fever.

PETER: (*Enters*) Honeyman—honeyman—

SERENA: Daddy Peter!

MARIA: Hello, Peter!

PETER: Good mornin', Maria—Serena.

MARIA: How come they let you out?

PETER: De white folks put me in, an' de white folks take me out, an' I ain' know yet what I done, what I done, done, done.

BESS: Oh, there's a rattlesnake in dem bushes. Oh, Lord, ain' nobody to help me!

PORGY: Yo' right here with Porgy—an' nuttin' can hurt yo'—

PETER: What's de matter?

MARIA: Porgy woman very sick more'n a week now; she gone to the picnic an' get los' in de jungle. She ain' come home for two day.

PORGY: (*Comes out*) I think dat maybe she goin' to sleep now; a whole week gone now an' she ain' no better. Hello, Peter, welcome back home, ole frien'.

PETER: Hello, Porgy. Son, I advise you to send her to de white folks' hospital.

SERENA: Hospital!

PORGY: Oh, Gawd, don't let 'em take Bess to the hospital!

SERENA: Hospital! Mus' be you is all forget how I pray Clara' baby out of the convulsions. There ain't never been a sick person or corpse in Catfish Row dat I has refused my prayers.

PORGY: Dat's right, sistuh, you pray over her.

SERENA:

Oh, Doctor Jesus, who done trouble de water in de Sea of
Gallerie.

PORGY:

Amen!

SERENA:

An' likewise who don' cas' de devil out of the afflicted time
an' time again.

PORGY:

Time an' time again.

PETER:

Oh, my Jesus!

SERENA:

Oh, Doctor Jesus, what make you ain' lay yo' han' on dis po'
sister's head?

PORGY:

Oh, my Father!

SERENA:
An' chase de devil out of her down a steep place into de sea like you used to do time an' time again.

PORGY:
Time an' time again. Oh, my Jesus!

SERENA:
Lif' dis po' cripple up out of de dus'!

(*Various residents of Catfish Row join the prayer with "Amen," "Hallelujah," etc.*)

PORGY:
'Allelujah!

SERENA:
An' lif' up his woman an' make her well time an' time again, an' save us all for Jesus' sake, Amen.

PORGY and PETER:
Amen. Amen.

SERENA: All right, now, Porgy, Doctor Jesus done take de case.
By five o'clock your woman's goin' be well.
(*All exit except* PORGY)

STRAWBERRY WOMAN: (*Enters*)
Oh dey's so fresh an' fine,
An' dey's jus' off de vine.
Strawberry, strawberry, strawberry,
Oh, dey's so fresh an' fine
An' dey's just off de vine,
Strawberry, strawberry, strawberry!

(*Cry is interrupted by* WOMEN *calling, beckoning* STRAWBERRY WOMAN. *"Uh huh." "How much are they?" "I don't want none." "Not today." Etc.*)

CRAB MAN: (*Enters*)
I'm talkin' about devil crabs,
I'm talkin' about devil crabs,
I'm talkin' about de food I sells,
She crab, she crab.

PORGY: On yo' way, brother.

CRAB MAN:
Devil crab!

MARIA: Hey, crab man!

CRAB MAN:

I'm talkin' about de food I sell.
I'm talkin' about de food I sell.
Now what is *I* talkin' about? Now *what* is I talkin' about?

MARIA: Who the hell yo' hollerin' at?!

CRAB MAN:

I'm talkin' about devil crab.
Now I's talkin' about yo' pocketbook, yo' pocketbook
I'm talkin' about devil crabs, she crab, she crab,
Devil crabs, I'm talkin' about de food I sells.

(*He exits.* MARIA *follows, then returns. Bell chimes five times.* SERENA *enters quickly on her balcony—looks at* PORGY)

PORGY: Now de time, oh Gawd, now de time.

(*Some shutters open—heads pop out—slight dead pause*)

BESS: (*Within the shanty*) Porgy, Porgy, dat you there, ain't it?

PORGY: Thank God, thank God!

(SERENA *nods and smiles at* PORGY *and exits.* MARIA *motions to Catfish Row residents to withdraw. They do.* BESS *appears in the doorway*)

BESS: I lonesome here all by myself, it's hot in there, let me sit here with you in the cool.

PORGY: Oh, Bess! Bess!

BESS: I been sick, ain't I?

PORGY: You been very sick. But now I got you back, Bess.

BESS: How long I been sick?

PORGY: Over a week now. You come back from Kittiwah with eye like fireball, an' Maria get you into bed, an' you ain' know me. (*She sobs*) What de matter, Bess?

BESS: I guess I ain' know nuttin' wid de fever, or I ain' come back at all.

PORGY: Dat's all right, don't you worry, Honey, I know you been with Crown.

BESS: (*Kneeling*) How you know?

PORGY: Gawd give cripple to understand many things he ain' give strong men.

BESS: You ain' want me to go 'way?

PORGY: No, no, I ain' want you to go. How things stan' between you an' Crown?

BESS: He's comin' for me when de cotton come to town.

PORGY: You goin'? You goin'?

BESS: I tell 'im, yes. (PORGY *grabs* BESS' *arm—she winces*)

Porgy—! Gawd, man!! Don't do dat—You make me scared! (BESS *pulls away*)

PORGY: I ain't tryin' to keep no woman that don't want to stay. If you want to go to Crown—that's for you to say.

BESS: I wants to stay here, but I ain't worthy. You is too decent to understand. For when I see him he hypnotize me. When he take hold of me with his hot hands. Someday I know he's coming back to call me. He's going to handle me and hold me so. It's going to be like dying, Porgy—Deep inside me—But when he calls, I know I have to go.

PORGY: If dere warn't no Crown, Bess, if dere was only jus' you an' Porgy, what den?

BESS: I loves you, Porgy, don' let him take me, don' let him handle me an' drive me mad. If you kin keep me, I wants to stay here wid you forever, an' I'd be glad.

PORGY: There, there, Bess, you don' need to be afraid no mo', you's picked up happiness and laid yo' worries down. You goin' to live easy, you goin' to live high. You goin' to outshine every woman in dis town. An' remember, when Crown come, that's my business, Bess!

BESS: (*Simultaneously with* PORGY)
I loves you, Porgy,
Don't let him take me,
Don't let him handle me
With his hot han'
If you kin keep me
I wants to stay here wid you forever.
I got my man.

PORGY: (*Simultaneously with* BESS)
What you think I is, anyway,
To let another feller steal my woman?
If you wants to stay wid Porgy, you goin' stay,
You got a home now, Honey, an' you got love.
So no mo' cryin', can't you understan'?
You goin' to go about yo' business, singin' 'cause
You got Porgy, you got a man.

PORGY: You and me, Bess—we share a little something after all.

MARIA: What yo' stan' dere watchin' fo', Clara?

CLARA: Somet'ing in my head keep a-listenin' for dat *hurricane bell*—

MARIA: Hurricane bell! Lawd, chile, dere ain' goin' be no hurricane! I's gettin' ole now an' I ain' hear dat bell but *fo' time* in my life!

CLARA: I got a feelin'—

MARIA: (*To* CLARA—*who has been on balcony staring out through gateway*) Clara, you got no cause to worry about yo' man and his boat. Go along wid de baby and quiet down—

CLARA: I never see de water look so black. It sit there waitin', holdin' his breath, listenin' for dat hurricane bell.

(*The wind rises. Heads appear at windows and faces show terror. People pass, shouting warnings. The deep ominous clang of a bell is heard. It keeps striking. Wind increases—clouds deepen—People from court move about in terror.*

A slowly rising wail commences.

The raging hurricane manifests itself in various ways—a banging shutter, a leaning pillar, a tree starts to quiver, fish sign starts swaying, etc.

Voices of men and women are heard in individual prayer as the hurricane violence increases)

Curtain

SCENE 3

SERENA'S *room. Storm. Antiphonal singing of "Oh Heavenly Father"—"Doctor Jesus"—etc. Prayers. A fear-stricken group is huddled, singing in* SERENA'S *room.*

ALL:

Oh, de Lawd shake de Heavens an' de Lawd rock de groun'
Ah——An' where you goin' stand, my brudder an' my sister,
When de sky come a tumblin' down.
Oh, de sun goin'—to rise in de wes'

MINGO:

My Jesus.

ALL:

An' de moon goin' to set in de sea—

WOMAN:

My Saviour.

ALL:

An' de stars goin' to bow befo' my Lawd, bow down befo'
My Lawd who died on Calvarie.
(*Repeat*)

PORGY: (*Simultaneously with the repeat*) Clara, come sing wid us, sister, ain' you know, song make you forget yo' trouble. An' lif' up dat burden of sorrow offen yo' heart.

CLARA: How can you sing dat same song over an' over since daylight yesterday?

SERENA: We got to be ready singin' praises to de Lawd when Gabriel soun' dat trumpet an' de graveyards spew up de dead.

MINGO: We had storm befo', I ain't so sure this is Judgment Day.

SERENA: Well, anyhow, it ain' no time fo' takin' no chances.

CLARA:

Summertime and the livin' is easy,
Fish are jumpin' and the cotton is high–
Oh yo' daddy's rich, and yo' ma is good lookin'
So hush, little baby–don't you cry–

(CLARA *sobs*)

(*There is a sudden burst of wind, lightning and thunder*)

ALL: Lawd have mercy on our souls–

PORGY: You ain' afraid, is you, Honey?

BESS: I jus' thinkin' an' you know what I's thinkin' about.

PORGY: Ain' nobody–not even Crown–could live on dat island in a storm like dis.

BESS: I guess you got me for keeps, Porgy.

(*Lightning flash and the roar of storm drown out singing. There is fearful screaming and shouting*)

ALL:

Oh, dere's somebody knockin' at de do',
Oh, dere's somebody knockin' at de do',
Oh, Mary, Oh, Marta, dere's somebody knockin' at de do'.

PETER: I hear Death knockin' at de do'.

LILY: What you say, Daddy Peter?

PETER: I hear Death knockin' at de do'.

LILY: It mus' be Death if Peter can hear 'im. He can't hear no livin' pusson.

MINGO: He ain't hear nuttin', ain' nobody knocking at dat door.

PETER: Death knockin' at de do'.

LILY: Yes, dey is somebody dere!

MARIA: Open de do', Mingo, an' show Peter dere ain' nobody dere.

MINGO: Open um up yo'self.

MARIA: All right, I'll show you.

(*Suddenly—several sharp knocks on door. Terror. Cries. More knocks. Door shakes violently. Men lean against it*)

WOMAN: Dat ain' no use, if he's Death, he comin' in anyway.

MARIA: Oh, Gawd, Gawd, don't let 'im in.

(*The door slowly gives way inward, pushing men back. Wind, shrieks, prayers. Men fall back.* CROWN *enters*)

CROWN: You is a nice pa'cel of Christians! Shut a friend out in a storm like dis!

SERENA: Who' frien' is you?

CROWN: I's yo' frien', Sister. (*Spies* BESS) Oh, here's de woman I's lookin' fo'. Why you ain' come an' say hello to yo' man?

BESS: You ain't my man!

CROWN: It's sho' time I was comin' back for you, sweet Bess! You ain't done much for yo'self while I been gone. Ain' dere no whole one left?

BESS: You keep yo' mouth off Porgy.

CROWN: Woman, do you want to meet yo' Gawd? Come here!

BESS: Porgy my man now!

CROWN: (*Laughs*) Well, for Gawd sake, do you call dat a man? Well, don' you min', I got de forgivin' nature an' I goin' take you back.

(*He grabs* BESS. PORGY *rises to defend her, but* CROWN *throws him back to the floor*)

PORGY: Turn dat woman loose!

BESS: Keep yo' han' off me.

SERENA: You bes' behave yo'self in dis storm! Don' you know, Gawd might strike you dead!

CROWN: If Gawd want to kill me, He had plenty of time 'tween here an' Kittiwah Island. Me an' Him havin' it out all de way from Kittiwah, firs' Him on top, den me on top. There ain' nothin' He likes better den a scrap wid a man. Gawd an' me is frien'! (*Thunder*) Hear dat? Gawd's laughin' at you!

LILY: (*On knees*)

Oh, de Lawd shake de Heavens an' de Lawd rock de groun'

ALL:

Ah, ah, ah
An' where you goin' stan' my brudder an' my sister,
When de sky come a-tumblin' down.

CROWN: (*Simultaneously with group*) Here, cut dat out! Stop it! I didn't come all the way from Kittiwah to sit up wid no corpses! Hear dat—Gawd's laughin' at you. (*He laughs—thunder follows*) Dat's right, drown 'em out, don' let 'em sing. (*Laughs*)

How 'bout dis one, Big Frien'?
A red-headed woman makes a choochoo jump its track,
A red-headed woman, she can make it jump right back.

ANNIE: (*Shrieks*) Lord—strike him down!

CROWN:

Oh, she's jus' nature's child,
She's got somethin' dat drives men wild.
A red-headed woman's gonna take you wedder you're white, yellow or black.

ALL:

Lawd, Lawd, save us, don't listen to dat Crown, Lawd,
Jesus, oh, pay no min' to dat Crown.
Oh, Lawd, strike him down, strike him down.
Oh, Lawd, don't listen to dat Crown.

CROWN: (*Simultaneously with group*)

Oh, show me the redhead that can make a fool of me,
Oh, she ain't existin' on the land or on the sea.
Oh, you can knock me down if they don't fall for brother Crown.
Oh, show me de redhead dat can make a goddam fool of,
I said a fool out o' me!

(*Suddenly the wind and storm stop. Silence*)

MARIA: Mus' be de storm ober—

MINGO: He jus' takin' a res'.

CROWN: Ain' I tell yo' Gawd like um? He *quiet* now fo' listen.
(CLARA, *at the window, screams and falls back*)

CLARA: Jake! Jake!
(BESS *runs to look out of window*)

BESS: Jake's boat in de river, upside down!
(CLARA *reels*)

CLARA: (*Turns to* BESS) Bess, keep my baby for me till I get back! (BESS *reaches out for baby.* CLARA *rushes out*) Jake! Jake!
(*People try to stop* CLARA *from going out into storm*)

BESS: Clara! Won't somebody go to Clara? Ain't dere no man here?!

CROWN: Yeah, where is a man? Porgy, what you sittin' dere

for? Ain't you hear yo' woman callin' for a man? Looks to me like dere ain' only one man 'roun' here! All right, I'm goin' out to get Clara, then I'm comin' back to get you.

PORGY: No, you don't!

CROWN: All right, Big Frien', we're on for another bout!

(CROWN *opens door and plunges out. Roar of wind—men slam door shut. Moment of near-quiet.* MINGO *is at window looking out*)

MINGO: Dat man t'ink he goin' find Clara *alibe!*

WOMAN: I hope he do!

WOMAN: Jake's boat's in the river upside down—

(*Moan from people*)

PETER: (*As he turns away*) Gawd hab mercy on de souls ob Jake and Clara.

(BESS *looks down at baby through her tears*)

BESS:

One of dese mornings
You goin' to rise up singing—

(*Clap of thunder. Moans and wails pierce the noise of the hurricane intensity, which builds to a crescendo*)

Curtain

ACT THREE

SCENE 1

Late night. The courtyard is dark. Slow mournful chant is heard.

ALL:

Clara, Clara, don't you be downhearted
Clara, Clara, don't you be sad and lonesome
Jesus is walking on the waters
Rise up and follow him home—

Jake, Jake, don't you be downhearted
Jake, Jake, don't you be sad and lonesome
Jesus is walking on the waters
Rise up and follow him home—

(*Women wend their way homeward after the chant—carrying lanterns to light their way—they go in groups—stop and bid each other adieu and continue homeward.*

SERENA *leaves a group of women and crosses toward her room —sees light coming from* MARIA'S *door—pauses—calls out*)

SERENA: Yo' still up, Maria? (MARIA *enters*) How come yo' ain't sing wid de women fo' de dead in de storm? Dey singin' for Clara now.

MARIA: Oh Lawd, it break my heart to hear dese womans mournin' fo' de mens, it break my heart.

(PORGY'S *shutter slams*)

SERENA: What's dat?

MARIA: Jus' Porgy watchin' at de window.

SERENA: What's he watchin' for?

MARIA: Crown dead, ain't he? Mus' be he t'inks Crown's ghost is a-comin' for trouble Bess. Dere she is now.

(BESS, *baby in arms, enters. She hesitates at foot of stairs and looks up toward the room listening. Then she moves toward her door*)

SERENA: What we all goin' to do with dat poor mudderless baby? Somebody ought to make sure de poor child gets a proper Christian raisin'.

BESS: (*Wheels around*) Clara ain't said nuttin' to me 'bout no *we* an' until she do I goin' to stand on her las' libbin' word an' keep the baby till she do come back. (*Looking at the baby*) He t'ink already dat I his ma. Ain' yo' see, Serena, how he scroogin' down? Dis baby know already dat Bess make him a good ma.

(*She holds baby for* SERENA *to look at.* SERENA *looks to* MARIA *who gestures back*)

SERENA: Yes, I reckon yo' gots a good ma now. (*As* BESS *turns to go*) Good night, sistuh.

BESS: Good night, sistuh. Sistuh. Sistuh.

(BESS *exits.* SERENA *exits. Several women with lanterns come out of* CLARA'S *room, go to their own doors.*

SPORTIN' LIFE *enters, laughs*)

MARIA: You low-lived skunk, ain' you got no shame, laughin' at those po' womens' what's singin' for their mens los' in the storm?!

SPORTIN' LIFE: I ain't see no sense in makin' such a fuss over a man when he's dead; when a gal loses her man dere's plenty o' men still livin' what likes good lookin' gals.

MARIA: I know it ain' dem gals you is after, ain' you see Bess got no use for you, ain' you see she got a man?

(PORGY *is listening behind half-closed shutter*)

SPORTIN' LIFE: I see more'n dat, Auntie, I see she got *two* men.

MARIA: What you mean by dat? Bess got two men. Crown dead, ain' he?

SPORTIN' LIFE: (*Laughs*) I ain' tellin' you nothin', but a woman who got jus' one man, maybe she got him for keeps, but when she got two mens, there's mighty apt to be a carvin', den the cops comes in an' takes de leavin'. An' pretty soon she ain't got none.

(MARIA *enters shop.* SPORTIN' LIFE *goes off.*

BESS, *at window with baby, hums "Summertime." During lullaby, several more women come out, each carrying a lantern. There are low-voiced words: "Good night," "Gawd comfort you, sistuh," as they drift off to their several rooms. Two women are crying softly. After lullaby,* BESS *leaves window.*

SPORTIN' LIFE *returns, stops to light cigarette.* CROWN *appears in gateway.*

SPORTIN' LIFE *sees* CROWN*—quickly blows out match and sneaks into his door.* CROWN *stealthily draws knife. A woman exits from* CLARA'S *room, hurries down steps.* CROWN *hides in shadows, then goes to* PORGY'S *window—pauses and listens. He crouches down as he hears noise.* SPORTIN' LIFE *opens his door slightly. As* CROWN *looks away,* PORGY *emerges and grabs* CROWN'S *right wrist—raises it high—and plunges* CROWN'S *own knife into* CROWN'S *midriff.* CROWN *twists around—*PORGY *clutches at* CROWN. *With a bull's rush forward* CROWN *drags* PORGY *out of doorway with him, then shakes off* PORGY*—and with a spasmodic struggle falls dead.* PORGY *laughs as* BESS *comes to doorway*)

PORGY: Bess. Bess, yo' got a man now! Yo' got Porgy!!

(*Lights start fading as* BESS *bends over and helps* PORGY *into house. Heads appear in windows.* MINGO *motions to everyone to return inside. All disappear as four men silently and swiftly carry the body of* CROWN *elsewhere*)

Curtain

SCENE 2

Catfish Row. Next morning. SERENA, LILY *and* ANNIE *very conspicuously scrub and clean area where* CROWN *was killed.*

MAN: Good mornin', sister.

WOMAN: Good mornin', brudder.

MAN: Good mornin', sister.

WOMAN: Good mornin', brudder.

ALL: How are you dis very lovely mornin'? How are you dis very lovely mornin'?

(*A group of girls play Ring Around Rosy*)

GIRLS:

La, la, la, la, la, la, la. Sure to go to Heaven,
Yes, you bound to go to Heaven, sure to go to Heaven,
If yo' good to yo' mammy an' yo' pappy, wash yo'
Face an' make dem happy. Den you'll be St. Peter's
Lovable chile. La, la, la, la, la, la, la, la.

ALL:

How are you dis mornin'?
Feelin' fine an' dandy
Tell me how are you dis mornin'?
Feelin' fine an' dandy
Tell me how are you dis mornin'?
Feelin' fine an' dandy.
Tell me how are you on dis lovely
Mornin'—How are you this lovely day?

(*A boy runs down in through gate—gesticulates and calls "Police"—which is repeated by others as it spreads around the court. The song cuts off sharply—and the court is emptied as they all go quickly to their rooms. The court is deserted and still. Enter* DETECTIVE, CORONER *and* POLICEMAN)

DETECTIVE: (*To* POLICEMAN) Bring the wagon around the corner, Al, and wait for us there.

(POLICEMAN *exits.* DETECTIVE *and* CORONER *look around court*)

DETECTIVE: This is the joint.

CORONER: Looks pretty dead to me—

DETECTIVE: Dead, hell! If you was on the police force, 'stead of sittin' around in that Coroner's office, *you'd* know!

CORONER: Well—all I need is a witness to identify the body at the inquest— (*Starts to go*) Bring one along when you come.

DETECTIVE: Like hell I will! You stay here and get your own witness!

CORONER: But what makes you think that Buck Crown was killed here?

DETECTIVE: Found right out there.

CORONER: So . . . ?

DETECTIVE: Oh! A hell of a lot you know about these people . . .

CORONER: (*Looking around*) I don't know . . . mighty *quiet* around here.

(*Just then two children run across like a flash screaming bloody murder. As they pass all shutters suddenly open and occupants yell and gesticulate at children. When children disappear shutters close quickly–dead silence again.* DETECTIVE *and* CORONER *exchange looks*)

DETECTIVE: Come on, I'll show you– (*Yells up at* SERENA'S *door*) Come on down, Serena Robbins, and make it damn quick!

(*Slight pause. Then shutter pops open*)

ANNIE: (*At the window*) Huh! Serena been very sick in her bed three day an' I been here with her all de time. (*She pops back in–closes shutters*)

DETECTIVE: The hell she has. Tell her if she don't come down I'll get the wagon and run her in. (DETECTIVE *blows whistle*)

CORONER: Take it easy!

DETECTIVE: I know what I'm doin'.

(SERENA *appears at the window*)

SERENA: Mercy . . .

DETECTIVE: Where were you last night, Serena Robbins?

SERENA: I been sick in dis bed three day an' three nights.

LILY: An' we been nursin' her all dat time.

ANNIE: Dat's de Gawd's truth.

CORONER: Would you swear to that?

ALL: Yes, boss, we swear to that.

CORONER: There you are, a air-tight alibi.

DETECTIVE: Just two months ago right here Crown killed your husband, didn't he? (*Pause*) Answer me, either talk here or in jail. Did Crown kill your husband, yes or no?

WOMEN: We swear to dat, boss.

DETECTIVE: And last night Crown got his right here, didn't he?

ANNIE: (*Laughs*) Go 'long, boss, ain' dat gentleman say we is a "alibi?"

DETECTIVE: (*Shouting with rage*) Was Crown killed here–yes or no?

SERENA, ANNIE and WOMAN: We ain' seen nuttin', boss. We been in dis room three days and nights an' de window been closed.

DETECTIVE: Look at me, Serena Robbins. Do you mean to tell me that the man who killed your husband was bumped off under your window and you didn't know it?

SERENA, ANNIE and WOMAN: We ain' seen nuttin', boss. We been in dis room three days and nights an' de window been closed. (*They close shutters*)

DETECTIVE: (*Exasperated*) Three days and three nights! (*Shutters start to open*) You needn't do that one again! (*Pacing*) Oh hell! You might as well argue with a parrot, you'll never break their story. (*Giggles from behind a closed window*) By God, I'll get you a witness for your inquest. Where's that cripple Porgy? You wait here, I'll find him. (DETECTIVE *exits*) (*Woman and man enter carrying packages.* CORONER *approaches the two*)

CORONER: Can you tell me where I can find a man named Porgy?

WOMAN: Porgy—no boss, I neber heah ob nobody 'round these parts named Porgy. Anybody here know a man named Porgy? (*Crowd opens shutters*)

CROWD: Porgy? Uh uh. (*All slam their shutters closed*)

CORONER: Please! I'm trying to help him. I'll be his friend and help him, if he'll help me.

MARIA: Go along and call Porgy. Can't you tell *folks* when you see 'um?

ROSS: Oh, you mean Porgy—Yes, Porgy!—I ain't understood what name you say, boss.
(*Shutters open. "Oh—Porgy!" They point*)

ROSS: Just right over here—Porgy, a white genmun come to see you.
(PORGY *comes out with* BESS. CORONER *crosses over to them*)

CORONER: What's your name?

PORGY: Jus' Porgy. You knows me, boss.

CORONER: Oh, yes, of course, you're the *goat* man. I didn't recognize you. I'm the Coroner, I'm not a policeman.
(*A sigh from all—as shutters open and they all listen*)

CORONER: Now this dead man Crown, you knew him by sight, didn't you? I mean you'd know him if you saw him again?
(DETECTIVE *enters, listens*)

PORGY: Yes, boss, seems like I remember him, when he used to come 'round here long time ago. (DETECTIVE *steps down close to* PORGY) But I don't care none 'bout seein' him.

DETECTIVE: Well, you've got to anyway, come along.

CORONER: Wait a minute, let me handle this.

DETECTIVE: All right, I'll get the wagon. (*He blows whistle; exits*)

CORONER: Now, you don't need to be afraid. All you've got to do, is look at the body, as a witness, and tell us who it is.

PORGY: I gots to look at Crown's face?!

CORONER: Yes, that's all—(*Exits*)

(PORGY *turns to* BESS)

PORGY: Oh, Gawd, what I goin' to do? I can't look on Crown's face?

BESS: You've got to go, Porgy. I'll tell you, maybe you can just make like you lookin' at him, and keep yo' eyes shut.

MARIA: You're goin' to be alright, Porgy. You're just goin' to be a witness.

SPORTIN' LIFE: (*Who has been enjoying it*) Witness, I ain't so sure about dat! All I know is, dat when de man dat kill Crown go in dat room—an' look at him—Crown's wounds begin to bleed!!

PORGY: (*Terror-stricken*) Oh—what I goin' do!

SPORTIN' LIFE: Dat's one way de cops got ob tellin' who done um!

PORGY: Oh—Lawd!!

(DETECTIVE *and* POLICEMAN *enter—start dragging* PORGY *off*)

PORGY: Turn me loose, turn me loose—you can't make me look on his face! Ain' nobody can make me look on Crown's face!! (*He is dragged out*)

BESS: Oh, Gawd! They goin' make him look on Crown's face!

SPORTIN' LIFE: (*Laughs*) Sister, that Porgy ain' goin' be no witness now. They goin' lock him up in jail—

BESS: Lock him up? Not for long, Sportin' Life?!

SPORTIN' LIFE: Not for long. Maybe one year, maybe two year, maybe—just like I tol' you, ain' nobody home now but Bess and ole Sportin' Life. (*He takes her hand*) But cheer up, sistuh, ole Sportin' Life givin' you de stuff for to scare away dem lonesome blues.

BESS: Happy dus'! I ain' want none of dat stuff, I tells you. Take dat stuff away, hophead! (*She suddenly yields and claps her hand over her mouth*)

SPORTIN' LIFE: That's the thing, ain' it? An' 'membuh there's plenty more where that come from. Listen:

There's a boat that's leavin' soon for New York.
Come with me, dat's where we belong, sister.
You an' me kin live dat high life in New York.
Come wid me, dere we can't go wrong, sister.
I'll buy you de swellest mansion
Up on upper Fifth Avenue,

An' through Harlem we'll go struttin',
We'll go a-struttin',
An' dere'll be nuttin'
Too good for you.
I'll dress you in silks and satins,
In de latest Paris styles.
All your blues you'll be forgettin',
You'll be forgettin',
There'll be no frettin',
Just nothin' but smiles.
Come along wid me, dat's de place,
Don't be a fool, come along, come along.
There's a boat dat's leavin' soon for New York.
Come wid me, dat's where we belong, sister,
Dat's where we belong! Come on, Bess!

BESS: You low, crawlin' hound! Get away from my door, I tells you, leave it, you rattlesnake. Dat's what you is, rattlesnake.

(SPORTIN' LIFE *hands her a second paper. She knocks it out of his hand and runs to her door and inside*)

SPORTIN' LIFE: Don't want take a second shot, eh! All right, I'll leave it here. Maybe you'll change yo' mind.

(*He tosses the paper of dope on the doorstep where she can reach it. She moves suddenly, snatches it up–sniffs it, then starts to strut out with* SPORTIN' LIFE. *She hesitates for a moment while she looks back at* PORGY'S *shack. Then she struts off with* SPORTIN' LIFE)

Curtain

SCENE 3

Catfish Row. A week later–afternoon. Quiet–lazy–some sleeping in court.

MINGO, LILY, ANNIE *are sitting at* MARIA'S *table.*

WOMAN *comes out of* PORGY'S *shanty*–SERENA *follows carrying baby.*

HONEY MAN *is heard off. "Here Comes de* HONEY MAN." *Suddenly he comes trotting in–chanting–"Here comes de* PORGY *man!"*

MINGO: Porgy's comin'.

(*This galvanizes the court into action. They whoop and run toward gate–then stop and look at each other–slowly they turn in their individual directions and scatter.*

PORGY *enters. The children are with him—all carrying bundles*)

PORGY: Thank Gawd I's home again!

ALL: Welcome home, Porgy, we're all so glad you is back again. (PORGY *crosses over near* MARIA'S *place*)

MINGO: How come dey let you out, Porgy?

PORGY: Dem white folks sho' ain't puttin' anything over on dis cripple.

MINGO: Sho' 'nuff—

PORGY: Shh, don' nobody let on yet dat I's home again. I got a surprise for Bess, an' I ain't wants her to know till I gots everyt'ing ready. (*Removes packages and hands harmonica to* SCIPIO) Here, boy. T'row away dat ole mout' organ you gots an' start in on dis one. See, he gots picture ob brass band on um. Work on dat, an' fusting yo' know yo'll be playin' wid de orphans' band.

(SCIPIO, *sad and embarrassed, runs to gate. Few others leave quietly.* PORGY *is too jubilant to notice.* PORGY *laughs*)

PORGY: Porgy's luck riding high now—ain' nuthin' can stop um! I reckon I'se the first baby what go to jail po'—an' leabe dere rich. (*Laughs—grabs another package—calls. Turns to* LILY) Lily! Lily Holmes! Where is dat gal? (LILY *crosses to him*) Here gal, hol' up yo' head. Now smile. Dat's right. I nebber did like dem ole funeral bonnet Peter buy fo' yo'. (*Unwraps a hat and gives it to her; she puts it on as everyone "oh's" and "ah's". Then to* ANNIE) Here now, git under that—you'll make all the blue jays jealous.

(LILY *and* ANNIE *preen, showing off their hats—dance, etc. Suddenly—there is an ugly flapping sound from above—a shadow runs across the court. The shadow runs over again—all rush for objects to show bird*)

MINGO: Look out—dat's a buzzard!

ALL: Aah, aah, aah, aah, aah, aah—

PORGY: Lawd! dat bird mean trouble. Once de buzzard fold his wings and light over yo' house, all yo' happiness, done dead. (MINGO *whistles*)

PORGY: Trouble, is dat you over yonder lookin' lean an' hungry? Don't you let dat buzzard keep you hangin' round my do'.

ALL:

Ain' you heard de news this mornin'?

PORGY:

Step out, brudder, hit de gravel;
Porgy, who you used to feed on, don' live here no mo'.

ALL:

Buzzard, on yo' way!

PORGY:

Ole age, what is you, anyhow?
Nuttin' but bein' lonely.
Pack yo' things and fly from here,
Carry grief and pain.
Dere's two folks livin' in dis shelter,
Eatin', sleepin', singin', prayin',
Ain' no such thing as loneliness,
An' Porgy's home again.

ALL:

Buzzard, keep on flyin', never come again! (*Several run to* PORGY*—embrace him*)

PORGY: Now bring me dat box over dere. (*Unwraps dress*) Now dat's de style for Bess. She is one gal what always did look good in red. (*Throws dress over shoulder*) Just you wait till dat gal see me. Oh, Bess—

(*Silence—pause—as all move away in various directions.* PORGY *looks around—surprised*)

PORGY: Here Lily, Peter, Mingo, where you all goin'? What de hell kin' ob welcome dis fo' a man what bin in jail—an' fo' contempt ob court, too!

(SERENA *enters with baby.* PORGY *stops her*)

PORGY: Why, hello! If dere ain' Serena! Yo' sho work fast, sistuh! I ain't been gone a week an' yo' gots a new baby already.

(SERENA *starts away, but* PORGY *stops her again*)

PORGY: Here, hold on. Let me see dat chile. Dat's Bess' baby, ain't it? Where yo' got um? Where Bess anyhow? She ain't answer me. Bess—Maria, Maria, where's Bess? Tell me quick, where's my Bess, tell me quick, where's Bess?

MARIA: Dat buzzard Sportin' Life make believe you lock up forever. He tol' her dat you be gone fo' de rest ob your days!

SERENA: She gone back to de happy dus' and to de red eye. She done t'row Jesus out ob her heart!

MARIA: Ain' we tell yo' all a-long, Porgy—dat woman ain' fit fo' you?!

PORGY: I ain't axin' yo' opinion! (PORGY *looks about helplessly,* BESS' *dress in his arms*) Oh, Bess, oh, where's my Bess, won't somebody tell me where? I ain' care what she say, I ain' care what she done, won't somebody tell me where's my Bess? Bess, oh Gawd, (*Simultaneously with* SERENA *and* LILY) in Yo' big Heav'n, please show me where I mus' go,—oh, give me de strength, show me de way! Tell me de truth, where is she, where is my gal, where is my Bess! Where Bess gone?

SERENA: (*Simultaneously with* PORGY *and* LILY)
She worse than dead, Porgy
She gone back to the happy dust
She gone back to the red eye with him
And she's headin' for hell.
Thank God she's out of your way
Try forget about Bess.

LILY: (*Simultaneously with* PORGY *and* SERENA)
Man, don't you let it break your heart
About dat gal.
We told you all along—
That woman ain't worthy of you.
She was no good, Porgy—or she'd never go away
Try forget—about Bess.

MARIA: Noo York, Porgy.

PORGY: I hear you say Noo York. Where dat?

MARIA: A thousand mile from here. It's way up North, pas' de custom house, Porgy.

PORGY: Bring my goat!

(MINGO *and* SCIPIO *go for goat*)

MARIA: What you wants wid goat, Porgy? You bes' not go any place.

PORGY: Bring my goat!

ALL: Where you goin', Porgy?

PORGY: Ain't you say Bess gone to Noo York? Dat's where I goin'. I got to be wid Bess. Gawd help me to fin' her.

(MINGO *leads goat and cart over.* PORGY *is helped into cart*)

PORGY:
I'm on my way.
(*As the cart is led out*)

Oh, Lawd, I'm on my way

(PORGY *and* ALL)

I'm on my way to a Heav'nly Lan', I'll ride–dat long, long road. If you are there to guide my han'.

(PORGY *puts* BESS' *dress over his shoulder*)

Oh, Lawd, I'm on my way. I'm on my way to a Heav'nly Lan'–

Oh, Lawd, it's a long, long way, but You'll be there to take my han'.

(PORGY *starts off. The residents of Catfish Row wave as* PORGY *departs and slowly each person returns to his own life*)

Curtain

ONE TOUCH OF VENUS

Book by S. J. Perelman *and* Ogden Nash
Music by Kurt Weill
Lyrics by Ogden Nash

(Suggested by
F. Anstey's story, "The Tinted Venus")

Production Notes

One Touch of Venus was first presented by Cheryl Crawford, in association with John Wildberg, at the Imperial Theatre, New York, on October 7, 1943. The cast was as follows:

Whitelaw Savory, *John Boles*
Molly Grant, *Paula Laurence*
Taxi Black, *Teddy Hart*
Stanley, *Harry Clark*
Rodney Hatch, *Kenny Baker*
Venus, *Mary Martin*
Mrs. Moats, *Florence Dunlap*
Store Manager, *Sam Bonnell*
Bus Starter, *Lou Wills, Jr.*
Sam, *Zachary A. Charles*
Mrs. Kramer, *Helen Raymond*
Gloria Kramer, *Ruth Bond*
Police Lieutenant, *Bert Freed*
Rose, *Jane Hoffman*
Zuvetli, *Harold J. Stone*
Dr. Rook, *Johnny Stearns*
Anatolians, *Sam Bonnell, Matthew Farrar*
Première Danseuse, *Sono Osato*
Singers, *Misses Jane Davies, Beatrice Hudson, Rose Marie Elliot, Julie Jefferson, Willa Rollins, Betty Spain. Messrs. Lynn Alden, Arthur Davies, Matthew Farrar, Jeffrey Warren.*
Dancers, *Nelle Fisher, Ruth Harte, Jinx Heffelfinger, Jean Houloose, Ann Hutchinson, Pearl Lang, Allyn Ann McLerie, Lavina Nielsen, Ginee Richardson, Patricia Schaeffer, Kirsten Valbor, Carle Erbele, Robert Pageant, Peter Birch, William Garrett, Ralph Linn, Duncan Nobl, Kevin Smith, William Weber, Lou Wills, Jr., Parker Wilson.*

Directed by *Elia Kazan*
Choreography by *Agnes de Mille*
Settings by *Howard Bay*
Costumes by *Paul du Pont, Kermit Love* and *Mainbocher*
Musical Director: *Maurice Abravanel*

Act One

Scene 1: Main Gallery of the Whitelaw Savory Foundation of Modern Art.
Scene 2: Rodney's room.
Scene 3: Radio City Plaza.
Scene 4: Arcade of N.B.C. Building, Radio City.
Scene 5: Waiting room of Mid-City Bus Terminal.
Scene 6: The roof garden of the Foundation.
Scene 7: Rodney's barbershop.
Scene 8: The roof garden of the Foundation.

Act Two

Scene 1: Savory's bedroom.
Scene 2: The Tombs.
Scene 3: The sitting room of a de luxe suite.
Scene 4: Main Gallery of the Foundation.

Musical Numbers

Act One

New Art Is True Art	Savory and Chorus
One Touch of Venus	Molly and Girls
How Much I Love You	Rodney
I'm a Stranger Here Myself	Venus
Forty Minutes for Lunch Ballet	
West Wind	Savory
Way Out West in Jersey	Mrs. Kramer, Gloria and Rodney
Foolish Heart	Venus
The Trouble with Women	Rodney, Savory, Taxi and Stanley
Speak Low	Venus and Rodney
Dr. Crippen	Savory and Dancers

Act Two

Very, Very, Very	Molly
Reprise: *Speak Low*	Rodney and Venus
Catch Hatch	Savory, Molly et al.
That's Him	Venus
Wooden Wedding	Rodney
Venus in Ozone Heights Ballet	
Finale	Rodney

ACT ONE

SCENE 1

Main Gallery of the Whitelaw Savory Foundation of Modern Art. A spacious, beautifully lit room, designed to display at their best an impressive group of the modern masters—Cézanne, Van Gogh, Gauguin, Picasso, Matisse, etc. At rear center, a semicircular alcove containing a pedestal. Arched openings rear left and right lead to adjoining exhibition rooms.

Five o'clock of a spring afternoon.

The STUDENTS *of the Foundation, girls and boys, are seated cross-legged on the floor in a rough semicircle.* WHITELAW SAVORY *surveys them malignantly, hands on hips. In his late thirties, decidedly an original,* SAVORY *is dynamic, egotistic, dogmatic. Rich enough to ignore the opinion of others, he devotes his time and fortune to the dissemination of his own unorthodox theories.*

SAVORY and STUDENTS: (*Opening Chorus*)

New art is true art
The old masters slew art;
They all learned how to draw,
But they painted what they thought they saw,
Instead of what they saw they thought,
As a liberated artist ought.
How are they to be trusted?
They must have been maladjusted.
Giotto and Watteau
Were obviously blotto;
Rubens and Goya,
Their trouble was paranoia;
Velásquez and El Greco,
They mimicked nature like an echo.

Old art is cold art,
The new art is bold art;
The best of ancient Greece,
It was centuries behind Matisse,
Who has carried us beyond Renoir,
Till our bosoms are tri-an-gu-lar.
Cézanne and Modigliani
De-glamorized the human fanny;
Rivera, Orozco,
They made it look like Moscow,
Since Tchelitcheff and Gropper
The nude is brutal, not improper—
Was Gauguin really in love with a rhinoceros?
That's prepocerous!

Was Van Dyck as good as Watkins, only different?
Confidentially, the question is odoriferant!
What is your verdict on Gainsborough and Romney?
Wrong Anno Domini!
Kindly unlearn your Romneys and your Rembrandts;
Only the recent is worthy of your remembrance!

New art is true art,
Forget Gilbert Stuart!
Greuze and Millais, as a duo,
Shine the shoes of Shahn and Rouault.
Titian and a couple of other fellows
Simply tinted Gross and Bellows.
Every Renaissance New Dealer
Stole from Chirico and Sheeler.
Lastly, but vastly,
Tradition is ghastly,
We're immune to classical knavery,
We're disciples of Whitelaw Savory!

SAVORY: (*With deceptive sweetness*) Now, you all understand what I've been saying?

STUDENTS: (*Dutifully*) Yes, Mr. Savory.

SAVORY: You comprehend it fully? You've digested it? You realize its implications?

STUDENTS: Yes, Mr. Savory.

SAVORY: Aha. Well, you're a pack of mealy-mouthed, pusillanimous toadies. In the nine years since I had the sublime misfortune to endow the Whitelaw Savory Foundation of Modern Art, I can't recall one student who had the faintest inkling of what I was saying. And don't think you're any better than the rest!

STUDENTS: (*Chanting*) No, Mr. Savory.

SAVORY: (*Hollowly*) "No, Mr. Savory!" "Yes, Mr. Savory!" That's right; mock me, deride me, beat me, stone me! What am I? A mumbling, toothless old crackpot, a prophet without a people, a visionary windbag begging you to take Art out of your museums and put it into your lives. (*Quickly*) But don't think I've surrendered! I still fight on, gallant Don Quixote that I am, though my buckler be dented and my blade shattered—(*Fencing spiritedly*) *En garde!* Thrust! Parry! Riposte! Nor shall I cry enough until the hydra-headed monster of bad taste lies dead on the doily of every tea shoppe in the land!

(MOLLY GRANT, SAVORY'S *secretary, enters hurriedly at left. She is a girl in her late twenties, knowing, uninhibited, attractive in a cynical and disillusioned way*)

MOLLY: (*Signaling to* SAVORY *over heads of* STUDENTS) P-s-s-t! —P-s-s-t! Hey, *Mahatma!*

SAVORY: (*Roaring*) Well, what is it, what is it?

MOLLY: He's here!

SAVORY: Who?

MOLLY: That shabby bloodhound you sent to Asia Minor for the statue.

SAVORY: (*Joyfully*) Not Taxi Black!

MOLLY: Yep! Came through the customs without a mark on him.

SAVORY: Capital! (*Indicating* STUDENTS) Clear them out! Clear them out!

MOLLY: Okay, squabs—I'll call you when the oracle's in the mood. (*She shoos* STUDENTS *off*)

SAVORY: Get out your pencil.

MOLLY: (*Opening notebook*) What's this? Another blast at the Metropolitan Museum?

SAVORY: The Memoirs.

MOLLY: Here we are—*The Life and Times of Whitelaw Savory.* (*Thumbing through notebook*) I was born in the cloakroom during the Bachelors' Cotillion . . . My brain, which is now in the Harvard Medical School—

SAVORY: Enough of that, you trollop! Where'd we leave off?

MOLLY: End of Chapter Eight. You'd just been thrown out of Oxford.

SAVORY: Right! (*Dictating*) "It was in 1926 that Whitelaw Savory first heard the legend of the famous Venus of Anatolia. This exquisite statue, which had passed from hand to hand during the course of three thousand years, was described to him by one Kristakos, a shady importer in Istanbul."

MOLLY: Who was found murdered in his bed the following day.

SAVORY: No, somebody else's bed.

MOLLY: Oh, *that's* why he was murdered.

SAVORY: "From then on, the great collector never rested. Tirelessly, courageously, regardless of personal risk—"

MOLLY: Look, puss, that's okay for posterity, but tell me something. What's this statue got that any other Venus hasn't got?

SAVORY: Well, if you must know, it reminds me of a girl—the girl who got away. (*Thoughtfully*) That's quite a tragedy for a collector, Molly. I lost the girl but at least I've got the statue —(*Brusquely*) that is, if those web-footed truckmen of yours ever get it here in one piece!

(TAXI BLACK *enters right, followed by* STANLEY, *his assistant.* TAXI *is small, nervous, romantic; a private dick who sees a Fu Manchu in every laundryman. He affects rainbow-colored shirts and ties, wears a black hat raked over one eye.* STANLEY *is a lubberly, wooden-faced lout, a man of few but slow reactions*)

TAXI: Greetings all!

SAVORY: (*Delightedly*) Taxi, *mon brave!* Where's the statue?

TAXI: Coming up!

SAVORY: Is it safe?

TAXI: Lock, stock and buttock, Mr. Savory. Hiya, Miss Grant?

MOLLY: (*With a glance at* STANLEY, *who has relapsed into coma*) Land sakes alive! Is this the statue?

TAXI: (*With disgust*) Nah, that's Stanley, my wife's brother. Ain't he brutal?

SAVORY: The statue! Where's the statue?

TAXI: They're loadin' her on the elevator. And brother, am I glad to get rid of her! I never closed an eye after that snake-charmer handed her over in Smyrna.

SAVORY: What happened?

TAXI: Everything. We ain't on the boat ten minutes when a big box of dates falls on Stanley's knob. Show 'em, Stanley. (STANLEY *stolidly removes his derby, exhibits a plaster on crest of skull*) We lay over in Alexandria, a hit-and-run camel knocked him down. (STANLEY *daintily lifts his trouser leg to reveal a bandaged shinbone*) We're standin' on the wharf at Algeciras when these two Arabs start to slug it out. Next thing you know, Stanley's got a dagger in the behind!

MOLLY: (*Quickly*) Never mind, Stanley.

SAVORY: (*Eyes glistening*) You think these accidents were deliberate?

TAXI: Listen, Mr. Savory, I've been a private dick twenty-five years. *Somebody ain't happy about that statue.*

(*There is a spectacular jarring crash off, mingled with the screech of nails being yanked from wood.* ALL *except* STANLEY *react*)

SAVORY: Oh, my God! The statue!

MOLLY: You better get a dustpan!

TAXI: (*Smiting his forehead*) Jeez, the minute I turn my back.

(SAVORY *runs out, followed by* TAXI *and* STANLEY. *The Girl* STUDENTS, *chattering, come on, attracted by the noise. They gather about* MOLLY)

1ST STUDENT: Is that the Venus he was telling you about?

MOLLY: Why, little pitcher, what big ears you have!

2ND STUDENT: A classical statue's going to look pretty wacky against this modern stuff!

MOLLY: Look, kids—forget that routine Savory's been dishing out. If you've got what Venus had, you're all set!

MOLLY: (*"One Touch of Venus"*)

Some girls have a touch of Venus,
It can help a girl a lot,
Why describe a touch of Venus?
You either have it or not.
If you have a touch of Venus,
Men will all react the same,
With a little touch of Venus, one little touch of Venus,
A lady can beat the game.

The world belongs to men and women,
But the banks belong to men.
The world is just a green persimmon
If you're an average hen.
Venus found she was a goddess
In a world controlled by gods,
So she opened up her bodice, she opened up her bodice,
And equalized the odds.

If you have a touch of Venus,
Men of Iron turn to clay.
Confidentially, between us,
They are suckers in the hay.
Look what Beatrice did to Dante,
What du Barry did to France,
Venus showed them that the pantie
Is mightier than the pants.

Some girls have a touch of Venus,
They get diamonds every night.
If she has a touch of Venus,
When a girl does wrong she does it right.
I could use a touch of Venus,

It comes in handy in a pinch,
Mix a little touch of goddess, a little touch of damsel,
And life is just a goddess damsel cinch.

(*The* GIRLS *and* MOLLY *exit. A* TRUCKMAN *enters*)

TRUCKMAN: Take it easy through the door, boys!

(*Two other* TRUCKMEN *maneuver a dolly on stage, on which rests a burlap-covered box*)

SAVORY: (*Following them*) *Doucement–doucement*–you're not handling coal!

TAXI: (*Entering*) Well, Mr. Savory–she's your responsibility from here in. (*To* MOLLY, *who has entered*) Say, Miss G.–can I use your phone?

MOLLY: In the office, right through there.

TAXI: (*Exiting*) The wife don't even know I'm home yet.

1ST TRUCKMAN: (*Examining the Picasso nudes at rear*) Hey, boys, get a load of the red-hot mommas!

2ND TRUCKMAN: Ah–I seen them in *Esquire*.

SAVORY: Come on–get that statue up and out of there!

2ND TRUCKMAN: Keep your girdle on, pal.

3RD TRUCKMAN: We're taxpayers, too!

SAVORY: (*As they lift statue onto pedestal*) Easy, you blockhead, she's not your wife!

1ST TRUCKMAN: He's right, Frankie–her mouth is shut.

2ND TRUCKMAN: That okay now, mister?

SAVORY: Clear this stuff out of here.

1ST TRUCKMAN: (*Exiting with dolly*) Yes, sir–we'll pick up every itsy-bitsy wisp.

3RD TRUCKMAN: Maybe he'd like us to wax the floor.

(TRUCKMEN *exit*)

MOLLY: (*As* SAVORY *regards the statue*) Satisfied?

SAVORY: She's come back to me forever.

MOLLY: She's very beautiful.

SAVORY: I told you so, didn't I?

MOLLY: You're a tyrant, Savory, but you've got flair.

SAVORY: I had it when I knew that girl.

MOLLY: (*Briskly*) Well, two's company–I'll get back to my knitting . . .

(RODNEY HATCH *enters. He is diffident, undistinguished, likable. His manner is that of a small tradesman. He carries a black satchel, wears a barber's white jacket.* MOLLY *stops as she sees him*)

MOLLY: Hello, where'd you come from?

RODNEY: I'm Rodney Hatch.

MOLLY: Is that good?

RODNEY: (*Helpfully*) You don't understand. Tony's in bed with sciatica.

MOLLY: Why tell me? Tell Mr. Sciatica.

RODNEY: (*Harassed*) No, no, I'm here to shave Savory instead of Mr. Tony—I mean I—

MOLLY: Oh, you're the *barber*. You'll have to wait.

RODNEY: I have to get back to my shop!

MOLLY: (*Indicating bench*) There, there—just relax. (*With a bright smile*) You're next!

(*Exit* MOLLY. RODNEY *sits for a moment, then, overcome by curiosity, approaches alcove and peers past* SAVORY'S *shoulder at statue*)

RODNEY: (*Tentatively*) Pretty, isn't it? . . . It's real lifelike. (SAVORY *ignores him*) Sort of classical—but it's tasty . . .

SAVORY: (*Automatically*) They haven't equaled it in three thousand years.

RODNEY: Oh. Is that so? (*Encouraged*) What's it supposed to represent, Venus or something?

SAVORY: (*Suddenly aware of him*) What are *you* yammering about?

RODNEY: I just said it was a nice statue.

SAVORY: (*Snarling*) Nice? Why, you chowderheaded earwig, do you realize you're standing before the most beautiful woman ever conceived by the mind of man?

RODNEY: Oh, I don't know . . .

SAVORY: Where would you find a girl today with such proportions? Look at the delicacy and grace of those fingers!

RODNEY: (*With dignity*) I happen to be engaged to a certain party's fingers would make 'em look like Bill Dickey.

SAVORY: (*Dangerously*) Oho! So we're an expert on feminine beauty, are we?

RODNEY: (*Stoutly*) Well, I know the size of Gloria's fingers, and I'll show you the ring to prove it. (*He fumbles in pocket, produces ring*)

MOLLY: (*From doorway*) Customs House calling, Mr. Savory. Something about the duty.

SAVORY: Oh, those nitwits—(*Starts out, suddenly turns on* RODNEY) Say, who are you anyhow? What the hell are you doing here?

RODNEY: I'm the barber; I'm pinch-hitting for Tony.
SAVORY: Oh. Well, I'll be with you in a minute . . .

(SAVORY *exits.* RODNEY *eyes the statue, tosses the ring speculatively in the air. He approaches the statue and eyes it disparagingly. Then, with a quick look to make sure he is unobserved, he slips the ring on its outstretched finger.*

There is a sudden restless stirring of wind in the room, followed by a low, ominous roll of thunder. RODNEY *takes an involuntary backward step. The lights flicker sharply as the thunder rolls closer and then go out. They flash back on sharply, and* RODNEY, *blinking, stares up at the statue. Its hands have changed position, its eyes are open and gaze on him with grave interest. Breaking the silence of thirty centuries,* VENUS *addresses* RODNEY HATCH)

VENUS: (*Softly*) Who are you?
RODNEY: Wh-wh-what?
VENUS: What have you done to me?
RODNEY: (*In terror*) I didn't do anything to you, lady. I'm only the barber.
VENUS: Come closer. (*He advances as if hypnotized*) Let me look at you.
RODNEY: Please—er—lady, that ring is mine—I mean I need it!
VENUS: The ring . . . (*With sudden joyful understanding*) Of course! This is what they said would make me a woman again!
RODNEY: (*Desperately*) You can't have it! I'm saving it for someone!
VENUS: (*Coldly*) Do not deny me, barber. I have been waiting three thousand years!
RODNEY: Look here, I'm not joking! Give me back that ring!
VENUS: And turn this flesh to stone again? Ah, no!
RODNEY: What kind of a woman *are* you, anyway?
VENUS: One you have awakened with your ring. Why do you evade me? You are my lover.
RODNEY: I'm not your lover, Madam, honest I'm not! (*Suddenly brightening*) Maybe you got me confused with the regular barber—with Tony.
VENUS: No, no, it's you. Here—release me.
RODNEY: (*Backing off*) What do you think I am? I'm in enough trouble already!
VENUS: Ah, barber, release me!
RODNEY: (*Panting*) I—I've got to get out of here! (*He runs out*)
VENUS: (*Calling after him*) Come back, barber! Come back!

(*There is no answer; she stares at the door incredulously for a moment; then, outraged, draws herself up, makes an imperious gesture. A blinding flash of lightning and a terrific thunderclap. Blackout. A pause, then a mounting hubbub of voices offstage.* FIGURES *swarm on, some with electric torches*)

VOICES: (*Ad lib*) What happened? . . . The generator blew out . . . No, it was lightning . . . Must have struck the main fuse . . . Find the janitor!

SAVORY'S VOICE: Molly–Molly–Where are you?

MOLLY'S VOICE: Here I am!

SAVORY'S VOICE: Where's Taxi?

MOLLY'S VOICE: Taxi! Taxi!

TAXI'S VOICE: Here I am! Stanley–Stanley–where are you?

STANLEY: (*As the lights come on, revealed on the pedestal*) I'm up here!

MOLLY: Where's the statue?

STANLEY: It's gone!

SAVORY: (*To* TAXI) Find the statue!

TAXI: Where's the barber?

STANLEY: He's gone!

TAXI: Find the barber!

SAVORY: (*To* MOLLY) Sound the alarm!

(*As burglar alarms mingle with shouting voices . . .*)

Curtain

SCENE 2

RODNEY'S *room. A small room containing a Morris chair; a a bureau dominated by a large framed picture of* GLORIA; *a table holding a bottle of milk and a box of crackers.*

Seven o'clock the same evening.

RODNEY *in trousers and undershirt, discovered on telephone, obviously agitated.*

RODNEY: Fifty dollars down? Gee, Mr. Adler, I can't afford that much for a new ring–I made thirty-nine payments on the other one . . . Huh? I don't know what happened to it, I tell you–it disappeared . . . A statue stole it from me . . . A STATUE stole it from me! . . . Oh, skip it! (*Hangs up*) Fifty dollars down! Darn old skinflint! Why, that's over onc hundred haircuts! (*He picks up* GLORIA'S *picture and admires it*) Yes, Mr. Know-it-all Savory! We *are* an expert on feminine beauty, and you can put that in your pipe and smoke it!

RODNEY: (*"How Much I Love You"*)

More than a catbird hates a cat,
Or a criminal hates a clue,
Or the Axis hates the United States,
That's how much I love you.
As a sailor's sweetheart hates the sea,
Or a juggler hates a shove,
As a wife detests unexpected guests,
That's how much you I love.

I love you more than a wasp can sting,
And more than a hangnail hurts,
I love you more than commercials are a bore,
And more than a grapefruit squirts.
I swear to you by the stars above,
And below if such there be,
As a bride would resent a blessed event,
That's how you are loved by me.

More than a waiter hates to wait,
Or a lioness hates the zoo,
Or a batter dislikes those called third strikes,
That's how much I love you.
As much as a lifeguard hates to swim
Or a writer hates to read,
Or the Hays office frowns on low-cut gowns,
That's how much you I need.

I love you more than a hive can itch,
And more than a chilblain chills,
I yearn for you in an ivy-clad igloo
As a liver yearns for pills.
I swear to you, by the earth below,
And above, if such there be,
As a dachshund abhors revolving doors,
That's how you are loved by me.

(*Finishing the number,* RODNEY *goes to wall mirror, tests the straight razor on a hair from his head; then, placing the straight razor on the shelf, he brings forth an electric razor from the drawer and proceeds to shave himself. The lights dim and roses appear in the washbasin.* VENUS *slowly enters.* RODNEY *turns and sees her*)

RODNEY: Oh my God! What are you doing here?

VENUS: Did you think I wouldn't find you?

RODNEY: Take off that nightgown! (VENUS *starts to do so*) I mean, put something over it!

VENUS: I've come to stay with you.

RODNEY: You can't do that—it's against the law!

VENUS: What law?

RODNEY: The—the law against men and women rooming together.

VENUS: You mean to say they've got around to regulating *that?*

RODNEY: Have you been running around the streets in nothing but this—this petticoat?

VENUS: Certainly, why not?

RODNEY: (*Closing the door hurriedly*) Did anyone see you come in?

VENUS: Tell me, barber—where do you sleep?

RODNEY: Sleep? I never sleep—I never get a chance to sleep—I mean my landlady won't let me!

VENUS: She must be very lively—your landlady.

RODNEY: Listen, Miss, you've got to get out of here!

VENUS: (*Picking up* GLORIA'S *picture*) Who is this? (*She rests a hand on bureau, inadvertently presses button. A Murphy bed swings into view*) Oh, *there* it is! Aren't you going to ask me to lie down? (RODNEY *gasps. She sits on bed, then swings her feet up on it*) Thank you.

RODNEY: Please, Madam, I was going along minding my own business—

VENUS: (*Indicating picture in her hand*) Is that your landlady?

RODNEY: Of course not!

VENUS: What's she angry about?

RODNEY: That's my girl friend.

VENUS: Does *she* sleep here?

RODNEY: I tell you nobody sleeps here! I sleep all alone—by myself!

VENUS: Poor boy—no *wonder* you're so nervous.

RODNEY: (*Ejecting her from the bed*) You leave me alone now! (*Pushing bed back into bureau*) I'll have you know that I'm an engaged man!

VENUS: Then why did you give me this ring?

RODNEY: I didn't give it to you—you ran away with it.

VENUS: But we're pledged to each other. I'm your bride. You can't escape your destiny! (*She draws very close to him*) Am I such a frightful destiny?

RODNEY: Don't do that. You're practically naked! I can see your *—form!*

VENUS: Don't you like my—form?

RODNEY: (*Taking a step back from her*) You shouldn't bring up questions like that! (*Querulously*) Why can't you dress like other girls? People will think you're some kind of a strip-tease.

VENUS: Oh, then it isn't my body you object to—simply my clothes!

RODNEY: That's it! That's it! They give me the heebie-jeebies! (*Picks up military brushes on end table and brushes his hair*)

VENUS: (*Repeats thoughtfully*) The heebie-jeebies . . .

RODNEY: (*Still brushing his hair*) Why don't you get yourself something decent to wear?

(*The telephone rings*)

VENUS: What's the matter? What's that sound?

RODNEY: (*Agitated*) The telephone!

VENUS: I don't like it.

RODNEY: (*Taking up telephone*) Hello? . . . Yes, this is Rodney Hatch.

VENUS: (*Thoughtfully testing the words*) Rodney—Hatch . . . *Venus* Hatch. (*She loves the sound of it*)

RODNEY: Hello, Gloria—how's Spring Lake? . . . Sure I was thinking about you . . .

VENUS: (*Peering over* RODNEY'S *shoulder*) There's somebody inside! Who is it?

RODNEY: (*To* VENUS) Get away—get away! (*In phone*) Are you having a good ti—? . . . What? . . . There's nobody here . . . How's your mother? . . .

VENUS: Is someone punishing you? (*Suddenly comprehending*) Oh! It's an instrument of torture!

RODNEY: Oh, the ring . . . (VENUS *admires the ring on her finger*) Yes, dear—I've got it, but there's going to be a little Hatch—I mean, a little hitch! (*He looks imploringly at* VENUS) The bus station—three-thirty tomorrow. (*There is a knock on the door*) Yes, dear—I'll be there.

VOICE OFFSTAGE: Mr. Hatch! (*Another knock*) Mr. Hatch!

VENUS: (*Brightly*) Somebody wants to come in.

RODNEY: (*Frantic—to* VENUS) Don't open it!

VOICE: Mr. Hatch—Open this door!

RODNEY: (*In phone*) Good-by, dear!

(*He hangs up, just too late to prevent* VENUS *from opening door.* MRS. MOATS, *the landlady, enters*)

MRS. MOATS: (*Looks* VENUS *up and down, arms folded*) Mr. Hatch–did I hear a woman's voice?

RODNEY: (*Agonized*) Mrs. Moats–listen to me–it's not what you think!

VENUS: Is *this* your girl friend?

MRS. MOATS: (*Furiously–to* VENUS) Get out of this house–you . . . you common creature! (VENUS *eyes her impassively*) I said get . . .

RODNEY: (*Shrilly*) Mrs. Moats!

(VENUS *raises her arm and* MRS. MOATS *falls like a column to the floor*)

VENUS: (*Smiles sweetly at* RODNEY, *steps over* MRS. MOATS) There, you see? Don't meddle with destiny, darling! (*As she exits*)

Curtain

SCENE 3

RADIO CITY PLAZA. *Before the curtain.*

VENUS, *still in classic costume, enters.*

VENUS: (*"I'm a Stranger Here Myself"*)

Tell me, is love still a popular suggestion,
Or merely an obsolete art?
Forgive me for asking this simple question,
I'm unfamiliar with his heart,
I'm a stranger here myself.
Why is it wrong to murmur I adore him
When it's shamefully obvious I do?
Does love embarrass him or does it bore him?
I'm only waiting for my cue,
I'm a stranger here myself.
I dream of a day, a gay warm day,
With my face between his hands;
Have I missed the path, have I gone astray?
I ask, and no one understands.
Love me or leave me, that seems to be the question,
I don't know the tactics to use,
But if he should offer a personal suggestion,
How could I possibly refuse,
When I'm a stranger here myself?
Please tell me, tell a stranger,
By curiosity goaded,

Is there really any danger
That love is now outmoded?
I'm interested especially
In knowing why you waste it,
True romance is so fleshly—
With what have you replaced it?
What is your latest foible?
Is gin rummy more exquisite?
Is skiing more enjoy'ble?
For heaven's sake, what is it?
I can't believe that love has lost its glamor,
That passion is really passé;
If gender is just a term in grammar
How can I ever find my way,
When I'm a stranger here myself?
How can he ignore my available condition?
Why these Victorian views?
You perceive before you a woman with a mission,
This is a case for a woman's intuition,
I must discover the key to his ignition,
Then if he should make a diplomatic proposition,
How could I possibly refuse,
When I am a stranger here myself?

(*As she finishes the song, the curtain rises behind* VENUS. *She turns in wonder*)

SCENE 4

Arcade of the N.B.C. Building in Radio City. Its most prominent feature is a couturier's shop window at rear, featuring a wax mannequin and a folding screen.

Two dozen office workers have erupted from the building and swirl mechanically about, their faces strained and abstracted. VENUS *joins them, is swept into their midst as their nervous pressure mounts into a series of formalized dance patterns parodying the tension of metropolitan life.*

BALLET: ("*Forty Minutes For Lunch*")

(*As the ballet develops,* VENUS *summons forth one of their number, a* GIRL, *and projects her into a romantic interlude with a* FREE FRENCH SAILOR. *The two share a moment's happiness, and though forced to part, their gratitude to* VENUS *is unmistakable. The dancers leave. A moment later, a* SALESGIRL *enters the couturier's window carrying a lady's suit, which she drapes over the screen. As she exits,* VENUS, *interested, snaps her fingers. The façade moves down to her; with a gesture, she brusquely dissolves the glass, enters the window, and proceeds to clothe herself. Suddenly the* MANAGER *of the shop plummets out of the door, followed by the* SALESGIRL)

MANAGER: I heard some kind of a noise– (*Sees* VENUS *in window*) Hey, you! What are you up to? Come out of there!

SALESGIRL: She's an exhibitionist!

MANAGER: Get a guard–find a policeman!

(*Two* MEN *enter*)

1ST MAN: Maybe it's "Truth or Consequences."

2ND MAN: Nah, it's a plug for brassieres! (*A* CROWD *begins to gather.* POLICEMAN *enters*)

SALESGIRL: (*To* POLICEMAN) It's a drunk!

MANAGER: She broke my window; who's going to pay for my window?

(SAVORY *and* MOLLY, *his secretary, enter from the elevators at right*)

SAVORY: What are you defending Taxi for? If he can't uncover something in twenty-four hours I– (POLICEMAN *blows whistle.* SAVORY *turns and sees* VENUS *in the window*) Good God!

MOLLY: What is it?

SAVORY: Where'd that girl come from?

MANAGER: That's what I want to know!

SAVORY: Shut up, you! (*To* POLICEMAN) Officer, clear these people out of here.

POLICEMAN: Oh yeah? Who do you think *you* are, Mr. Big?

MOLLY: This is Mr. Whitelaw Savory, officer.

POLICEMAN: Oh, pleased to meet you, Mr. Savory. Lady a friend of yours?

SAVORY: (*Roaring*) Of course she is, you bottlenosed idiot! What do you suppose I'm doing here?

POLICEMAN: Yessir . . . (*Turning to* CROWD) Come on now, break it up, break it up!

MANAGER: (*Shrilly, as* CROWD *disperses*) Just a minute, Mr. Savory, who's going to pay–

SAVORY: (*Curtly*) Molly. (*He turns toward window*)

MOLLY: (*Drawing* MANAGER *away and exiting with him*) Wipe the oatmeal off your bib, honey. You've hit the jackpot.

SAVORY: (*To* VENUS) Will you come out–or shall I come in?

(VENUS, *smiling her thanks, extends a hand to his, steps down gracefully.* SAVORY *studies her incredulously*) You're so much like her . . .

VENUS: Who?

SAVORY: A girl I knew years ago—a girl I thought I'd never see again . . . Who are you?

VENUS: A stranger.

SAVORY: Not to me. I feel as if we were meeting again . . . after a long journey.

VENUS: (*Dryly*) In love with a memory? You're not very practical, are you?

SAVORY: Why? What do you mean?

VENUS: You can't play beanbag with a memory on a rainy afternoon!

SAVORY: Well, I must say you're a bit prosaic.

VENUS: No, simply realistic. Is there anything more tiresome than languishing sighs and moon-drenched partings and broken hearts? Love isn't the dying moan of a distant violin—it's the triumphant twang of a bedspring.

SAVORY: (*Approaching her*) My word, we're getting along famously, aren't we?

VENUS: Don't misunderstand me. That was an opinion, not an invitation.

SAVORY: It's an opinion I'd like to discuss with you in a more secluded setting. Why don't we slip into something comfortable (*Offering her his arm*) like my den?

VENUS: No, no—you're already too much at home right here. But thank you anyway. I'd wondered of late whether my so-called charm hadn't deserted me.

SAVORY: God forgive me for feeding a woman's vanity, but you've no reason to worry. You're ravishing.

VENUS: I don't give *you* the . . . er . . . heebie-jeebies, do I?

SAVORY: May I tell you what you do to me?

VENUS: No, my friend—I am not a policeman to be bullied or a shopkeeper to be bought.

SAVORY: All right, but I warn you—I'll get you when you least expect it. I'll use any weapon—I'll lie, cheat, steal, blackmail! When can I see you again?

VENUS: (*Moving away*) I don't know—perhaps very soon . . .

SAVORY: Until that day, if I can do anything—if you want a rival poisoned, or a magic carpet woven—you *will* call on me, won't you?

VENUS: Instantly. (*Giving him her hand*) Good-by.

SAVORY: Wait a moment—you haven't even told me your name!

VENUS: (*Provocatively*) I haven't, have I?

SAVORY: (*Calling after her*) You don't even know where to find me!

VENUS: I'll find you—(*She goes out*)

SAVORY: (*"West Wind"*)

I had a love, and my love was fair,
Fair as a summer's dawn.
I lost my love, I never knew where,
Suddenly she was gone.
The West Wind stirred the meadow
The night she slipped away,
And I seem to glimpse her shadow
When the West Wind brushes the day.

West Wind, can you waken my true love?
West Wind, can your whisper renew love?
Speak to her softly of the dream we lost,
The theme we lost,
The gleam we lost.
West Wind, can you call back an old love?
West Wind, can you kindle a cold love?
West Wind, can the magic of then
Become ours once again?
Breathe on the embers,
If by chance she remembers,
Then some day at last,
We can recapture the past.

Curtain

SCENE 5

Waiting room of Mid-City Bus Terminal. At right is a row of lockers; behind them, swinging doors to the bus platform.

At center is a lunch counter—five revolving stools without backs are below the counter. Near by is a small round table with a chair.

TAXI BLACK *stands by the lockers.* STANLEY, *in soda dispenser's hat and white coat, is behind the counter.*

A BUS STARTER *is seated on high stool in front of swinging doors.*

Two GIRLS *and a* SOLDIER *exchange embraces, pressing against* RODNEY, *who is seated at the table. He betrays annoyance.*

BUS STARTER: Manasquam–Long Branch–Elizabeth–Rahway–Perth Amboy–Matawan–Red Bank–Asbury Park–Little Egg Harbor–All aboard!

SOLDIER: (*Giving* GIRL *last kiss*) Good-by, darling–look up my wife, won't you?

(SOLDIER *goes out through the swinging doors.* STANLEY *comes from behind the counter, wipes table with a cloth as he picks up a Coca-Cola glass from table*)

STANLEY: (*To* RODNEY) You've been waiting a long time, bud–expecting somebody?

RODNEY: Yes–my girl.

STANLEY: (*Places glass on counter–quickly crosses to* TAXI) Did you hear that, Taxi? He's waiting for a dame.

TAXI: (*Galvanized*) What's he up to?

STANLEY: He's jumpy–he's had five cokes already!

TAXI: Now write everything down! Mr. Savory expects a full report! (*A* WOMAN WELDER, *dressed in rough work clothes, heavy gloves and a welder's helmet tipped back on her head, enters, goes to lockers*)

WOMAN WELDER: One side, gentlemen. (*She opens a locker, takes out a baby, and dandles it in her arms*) There, there, darling. Mamma will feed you right away. (*She carries baby out*)

RODNEY: (*Rising–to* BUS STARTER) Oh, er . . . pardon me–is the Spring Lake bus on time?

BUS STARTER: (*Wearily*) Listen, Jack–I told you three times already–it's due any minute!

(RODNEY *starts back toward the table, almost bumps into* VENUS, *who has just entered. He reacts violently*)

RODNEY: (*To* VENUS) Oh . . . I didn't recognize you with your clothes on.

VENUS: Do you like me better with my clothes on?

RODNEY: Yes, I do. It's a big improvement!

VENUS: That's refreshing–most men are so vice versa. (*Sits at table*) Have we long to wait?

RODNEY: For what?

VENUS: Your girl friend–we must tell her.

RODNEY: (*Pallidly*) Tell her what?

VENUS: That she's–out.

RODNEY: Well, I like your nerve! I've been engaged to Gloria Kramer for five years. This is a free country–and if I want to marry a *hyena* nobody's going to stop me!

VENUS: I know—but if you ever got tired of the hyena, it would be nice to have a good-looking woman around.

TAXI: Hey, droopy, here's your Spring Lake bus!

RODNEY: (*Starts out—stops quickly*) Oh, it's them! They're here —look, please—give me a break—just for five minutes!

VENUS: (*Relenting*) Well, if you two are still vertical after five years, five minutes more won't make any difference.

(*She exits to street as* SAM *backs in from bus platform, laden with bags. He is sleek, sharp, and unctuous, a Flatbush version of George Raft*)

SAM: (*With oily deference*) Careful of the door, Mrs. Kramer!

(MRS. KRAMER *and* GLORIA *follow him on.* MRS. KRAMER *is large, noisy, vindictive.* GLORIA *is young, aggressive, attractive in a tasteless way. Her clothes just miss being chic. Her skirt is too short, her hat too extravagant*)

MRS. KRAMER: I've never sat through such torture in my whole life! (*Seeing* RODNEY) And you—I thought you were going to help us with the bags!

RODNEY: (*Making an abortive lunge toward the bags*) I got tied up—er—

SAM: (*Sweeping the bags away from* RODNEY'S *reach*) Save your strength, Buster—let a man handle 'em.

GLORIA: Well, I must say, Rodney, this is a fine time to show up! For all you care, Mother and I could have broken our backs!

(MRS. KRAMER *flops into a chair, breathing hard.* SAM *stands over her attentively*)

RODNEY: (*Placatingly*) Gee, Gloria, it's good to see you again.

GLORIA: I don't know what we'd have done without Sam! (*To* SAM) Sam, you were simply marvelous!

SAM: Well, when your boy friend is otherwise occupied, someone has to take over, eh, Mrs. Kramer? (*He pats* MRS. KRAMER'S *hand*)

GLORIA: (*Chanting*) Sam was a perfect gentleman. Sam just couldn't do enough for us. Sam made all the arrangements for the bus and procured the sandwiches. This is Sam.

RODNEY: Pleased to meet you. (*Extends his hand to* SAM)

SAM: *Hm.* I must say I got a more romantic picture from Glory. (*Shaking hands*) Hiya, sport—what's new in the shampoo division?

RODNEY: I'm doing all right.

SAM: (*After a glance at* GLORIA) That's what you think. Well, if there's nothing more I can do for you ladies, I better run along. Business before business, you know.

MRS. KRAMER: Don't forget. I'm going to come in and try on a pair of those Eezi-Tred Oxfords.

SAM: You do that little thing. (*Turning to* RODNEY) And it wouldn't hurt you to stop in for a foot consultation, brother. We got an elevator model that'll build you up two inches.

RODNEY: Oh, is that so?

SAM: (*Flicks* RODNEY's *nose with his index finger*) Abadaba! (*To* GLORIA, *with a meaning leer*) You'll be hearing from me any minute, little lady. Goom-by! (*He goes out*)

MRS. KRAMER: Now, that's what I call a gentleman of the old school.

RODNEY: (*Eager to ingratiate himself*) Well, Mother Kramer, I see you developed a real nice tan.

MRS. KRAMER: Tan? It's probably jaundice. I never slept a wink the whole time I was gone. I am positively exhausted!

GLORIA: And the hoi polloi at that hotel were simply a scream, my dear. When Sam came in with his tuxedo, they thought he was a waiter.

MRS. KRAMER: Well, what can you expect from New Jersey? I always say the minute you cross the Hudson River you're in the Wild West!

RODNEY: You're right, Mother Kramer!

MRS. KRAMER: (*Rising—brushing* RODNEY *aside*) Yahoo!

MRS. KRAMER: (*"Way Out West In Jersey"*)

Yippi-Yi, away out West in Jersey
I declare these are the thoughts I thunk—
Yippi-Yi, if Jersey looks like this to me,
Either Jersey or me is drunk.
By the time I reached Weehawken,
With my banjo on my knee,
Yippi-Yi, I heard the natives talkin',
And I knowed that it wasn't me.

RODNEY, GLORIA and MRS. KRAMER:

Oh, New Jersey—Oh, New Jersey—
It's a land we proudly hail—All hail!
No matter what the weather's you'll enjoy the tar and feathers
When you're riding through New Jersey on a rail.

GLORIA:

Yippi-Yi, the cowboys in Hohokus

Haven't seen a woman in a year,
Yippi-Yi, when their minds begin to focus,
They have got only one idea.
Oh, I met with one in Rahway,
He said courtin' was sublime,
But I found that his way wasn't mah way,
Yippi-Yi, and I shot him just in time.

RODNEY, GLORIA and MRS. KRAMER:
Oh, New Jersey–Oh, New Jersey–
It's a land we proudly hail–All hail!
You'll enjoy the friendly tussle with the cactus in your bustle
When you're riding through New Jersey on a rail.

RODNEY:
Yippi-Yi, across the Jersey border
At the bar, the politicians are a plague.
Yippi-Yi, whatever drink you order
It turns out to be Hague and Hague.
Oh, a buckaroo from Texas
Ran for Marshal of Passaic,
So much lead landed in his solar plexus
Now he rattles just like a snaic.

RODNEY, GLORIA and MRS. KRAMER:
Oh, New Jersey–Oh, New Jersey–
It's a land we proudly hail–All hail!
You will bellow like an oxen for a shot of antitoxin
When you're riding . . .
When you're riding . . .
When you're riding through New Jersey on a rail.

RODNEY:
Yippi-Yi, from Neptune up to Nutley,
From Cape May to Deal and Hackensack,
Yippi-Yi, the Jersey cowgirls woo you subtly,
But there's something they seem to lack.
Oh, the sheriff, he went a-swimmin'
One fine evening after dark,
Yippi-Yi, before he got one limb in
He'd been chosen Miss Asbury Park.

RODNEY, GLORIA and MRS. KRAMER:
Oh, New Jersey–Oh, New Jersey–
It's a land we proudly hail–

Fire your Flit-gun at the varmints
That investigate your garmints
When you're riding . . .
When you're riding . . .
When you're riding through New Jersey on a rail.

BUS STARTER: (*Announcing, as song ends*) Elizabeth–Rahway –Perth Amboy–Pompton Lakes–and Peapack!

MRS. KRAMER: Gloria, I just know I'm coming down with something. I ought to be home in bed right this minute.

GLORIA: Well, Rodney–at least you could get Mother a cab!

RODNEY: Oh, sure–sure.

(*He goes out, followed by* BUS STARTER. MRS. KRAMER *is bending down–fixing the lock on one of the handbags*)

TAXI: (*Crosses to* MRS. KRAMER, *bends down, looking directly at her rear*) I beg your pardon, Madam, but I am addressing Mrs. T. Blessington Kramer?

MRS. KRAMER: (*Slowly rises to a standing position, very much the* grande dame) Why no–I'm Mrs. Florabelle Kramer.

TAXI: I knew I was right! (*Presenting card*) Black. Julius E. Black. (*Sotto voce*) I have some information that may interest you strangely.

MRS. KRAMER: Really?

TAXI: I'd rather not discuss it here. Allow me. (*He picks up handbags*)

MRS. KRAMER: Thank you. (*To* GLORIA) Now, Gloria–remember what I told you about Rodney. Be firm! (*She exits after* TAXI)

RODNEY: (*Entering through swinging doors*) There's nothing but busses out there–where's your mother?

GLORIA: She got tired of waiting. (*Seating herself, motions him to her*) Come here, dear!

(RODNEY *sits beside her.* STANLEY, *behind counter, eavesdrops on their conversation and makes notes in little black book*)

RODNEY: I sure missed you, honey.

GLORIA: Like fun you did! Who was that in your room when I phoned you?

RODNEY: Oh–oh that must have been the landlady. She–er . . . she was doing a little housecleaning.

GLORIA: Well, let me tell you, Mr. Rodney, I'm not in the habit of people hanging up on me! If I didn't have such an easy-going disposition, I'd never speak to you again!

RODNEY: Aw, honey—that's no way for us to be talking! (*Brightly*) I tell you what—let's go out someplace tonight and have a quick bite and take in a good show.

GLORIA: Well—I half-promised Sam—

(VENUS *enters, approaches* RODNEY)

—I'd drop in at the Twenty-One Club with him.

RODNEY: Hey! Who are you engaged to, anyhow?

(VENUS *lightly taps* RODNEY *on the left shoulder; he stares at her in panic*)

GLORIA: That's just what I was going to ask you! It seems to me I remember something about a ring. (*She suddenly looks up, sees* VENUS)

VENUS: (*Smiling*) Hmm, nice . . . (*She sits beside* GLORIA)

GLORIA: Well, of all the nerve! (*Deliberately turning her shoulder on* VENUS) Go on, I'm listening.

RODNEY: (*Perspiring*) Gloria—I don't know how to tell you this—

GLORIA: You haven't got my ring!

RODNEY: I have, too—I mean I know where it is—

GLORIA: (*Grimly*) All right, where is it?

RODNEY: I'm trying to tell you! Did you ever hear of a statue that turned into a real person?

GLORIA: Rodney Hatch, *what have you done with my ring?*

RODNEY: I'm trying to tell you what—

GLORIA: Mother was right, she said even if you did manage to pay for it you'd probably lose it before—

RODNEY: (*Rising*) All right, I lost it! (*Wildly*) I hocked it! I threw it away! (*Frenziedly*) I don't know what happened to the God-damn thing!

GLORIA: (*Gasping*) Oh!—What did you say?

RODNEY: You heard me! You understand English!

GLORIA: (*Rising*) Swearing at me! So that's the kind of a husband you're going to be!

RODNEY: (*Uncomfortably*) You started it! (*To* VENUS, *automatically*) Didn't she?

VENUS: (*Emphatically*) She certainly *did!*

RODNEY: (*Triumphantly to* GLORIA) You see?

GLORIA: (*Wallowing in self-pity*) When I think of the offers I've had—(*She stops abruptly, conscious of* VENUS) What did she say? Who is this woman?

VENUS: (*Simply*) I'm Venus.

GLORIA: Rodney! Do you know her? Answer me!

RODNEY: (*Shouting*) Of course I know her. Didn't I give her the ring?

GLORIA: Now you listen to me, Mr. Smarty-pants, you're not going to get away with it! I'll give you twenty-four hours to come through with my ring, or the engagement is off! (*She flounces out*)

RODNEY: (*Trembling*) Your ring, eh? Well, let's get this straight once and for all! It's *my* ring and I'll give it to whoever I damn well want! And how do you like those little green apples?

VENUS: (*Approvingly*) I love those little green apples.

RODNEY: She's got a crust, bawling me out! Who does she think she is—the Queen of Sheba?

VENUS: Oh now, aren't you being a bit ungenerous?

RODNEY: That tongue of hers'll get her into real trouble some day!

VENUS: It's a physical thing. I shouldn't wonder if you opened her up you'd find a spleen as big as a summer squash.

RODNEY: Nothing I do satisfies her. If we go to a cheap restaurant, I'm stingy; if we go to an expensive one, I'm throwing our money away.

VENUS: She's a perfectionist; you can tell that from her prim little mouth.

RODNEY: I've been pushed around long enough!

VENUS: Too long!

RODNEY: She can take her Sam and her Twenty-One Club—

VENUS: —And her mother—

RODNEY: —And jump in the lake! See if I care!

VENUS: That's the kind of language a woman understands. What a pity she can't hear you!

RODNEY: (*Shouting after* GLORIA) You're not going to wipe your feet on me!

VENUS: Spoken like a man.

RODNEY: You can't lead me around by the nose!

VENUS: A man's nose is his castle.

RODNEY: I'll show you who's going to wear the pants in this family!

VENUS: With a figure like hers, I hope it's you.

RODNEY: Why, I ought to . . . (*He turns in indignation*) Say, who gave you the right to talk that way about my intended?

VENUS: Why, the girl's as mean as a horsefly and we both know it. Don't we?

RODNEY: I consider that a dirty dig!

VENUS: Well, speaking purely as your future roommate, I'd say you were well out of it.

RODNEY: I'm not out of anything! If I make up my mind to marry Gloria, I'll marry her, and if I don't, I won't! No woman's going to tell me what to do—you, or Gloria, or anybody else! Women, women, women—I'm sick of 'em! (*With low intensity*) And that goes for you, too! (*He stalks out*)

STANLEY: (*Sidling up to* VENUS, *his pencil poised over his notebook*) What were those last few words he said?

VENUS: I don't know, my friend—but whatever they were, he'll eat them.

Curtain

SCENE 6

The roof garden of the Foundation. Several Etruscan statues contrast strongly with the functional architecture of the building. At rear a parapet, the distant sky beyond.

An art class is in session.

The STUDENTS *sketch from a living model, whose head and bare shoulders are visible above an antique screen.* SAVORY *is examining the work of his pupils.*

SAVORY: (*Taking sketch from* STUDENT) Look here, that's no abstraction. It makes me want to pinch it.

MOLLY: (*Entering, notebook in hand*) Hail, moon of my delight! What's the matter? Why the puss vinaigrette?

SAVORY: Bah!

MOLLY: Oh, snap out of it. Grab yourself one of these goslings. A girl on the couch is worth two on the mind!

SAVORY: I'm sulking on my own time, aren't I?

ANOTHER STUDENT: (*Displaying drawing*) Excuse me, Mr. Savory—would you look at this?

SAVORY: That's a very interesting fixation you have, my boy. I'd like to meet your mother. (*To* MOLLY—*indicating notebook in her hand*) Anything important?

MOLLY: Well, 20th Century Fox would like two dozen Gauguins for a fashion short—

SAVORY: Telegram 39A, collect, the one that begins "You can take the motion picture business"—

MOLLY: Some babe from *PM* called up—they want to take pictures tonight of the Students' Ball.

SAVORY: Out. No photographers.

MOLLY: They're willing to co-feature us next Sunday with a big poultry exposé.

SAVORY: No!

MOLLY: Oh, the kids only have one big binge a year!

SAVORY: Who's running this foundation—you or me?

MOLLY: Sorry. If anyone wants me, I'll be around the corner having my tongue torn out.

(TAXI *dashes in excitedly*)

TAXI: I've got it! I've got the statue!

SAVORY: (*Rising*) You haven't!

TAXI: No, I haven't—but I know where it is!

SAVORY: You don't!

TAXI: No, I don't—but wait'll I tell you!

(MRS. KRAMER *enters, carrying two suitcases*)

MRS. KRAMER: How do you do? How do you do?

SAVORY: Who the hell is that?

TAXI: Allow me. Madam Kramer, may I present Whitelaw Savory, the connoisseur?

MRS. KRAMER: (*Very elegant*) Likewise. (*Looks about*) What a charming old-world atmosphere!

TAXI: Never mind the chicken fat! Tell your story!

MRS. KRAMER: (*Explosively*) I've suspected him from the first. There's something sneaky about him!

SAVORY: Who, for Pete's sake?

TAXI: The barber!

SAVORY: Oh. (*To* MRS. KRAMER) What do *you* know about him?

MRS. KRAMER: Plenty! He may tell you he's a barber—but there's more goes on inside that shop than hair-cutting!

SAVORY: Aha! You WERE right, Taxi.

MRS. KRAMER: He's one of those quiet ones. You never know what he's thinking. And he's always puttering around the cellar. If you ask me, he's some kind of a radical.

SAVORY: By God, Taxi, that clinches it! That damned barber stole my statue!

TAXI: I'll call Headquarters. (*He starts out*)

SAVORY: No, you won't! This is a private matter. I'm going to search that barbershop in person!

TAXI: Wait a minute, Mr. Savory—we can't do that!

SAVORY: Why not?

TAXI: We got no warrant! He can have us up for mayhem, disorderly conduct, and God knows all!

SAVORY: I've dealt with rascals of his kidney before! (*Indicating*

MRS. KRAMER) Here, take this good lady down to the kitchen and give her a cool glass of beer. I want to think.

TAXI: (*Picking up two suitcases*) I gotcha.

MRS. KRAMER: (*Graciously to* SAVORY) I just adore your little nook. It's a veritable Shangri-La. (*She follows* TAXI *out*)

MOLLY: Are you going down to that barbershop?

SAVORY: Why not?

MOLLY: Listen, lad—you're an eccentric millionaire, not Huckleberry Finn!

SAVORY: What are you talking about? It's my statue, isn't it? (*He breaks off suddenly as* VENUS *enters*)

MOLLY: Well, here's a quick return on your investment!

SAVORY: My dear—I can't believe it!

VENUS: (*Smiling*) I told you I'd find you.

MOLLY: (*Meaningly*) So did I! (*To* STUDENTS) Okay, fellow workers—back to the salt mines. (*The* STUDENTS *and the* MODEL *collect their paraphernalia and exit*)

SAVORY: Look at her, Molly! She's like a hawthorn in flower!

MOLLY: (*Dead pan*) How do you do, Miss Hawthorn?

SAVORY: This ill-favored shrew is Molly Grant, my secretary.

VENUS: She seems a faithful little thing.

MOLLY: Oh, I'd put my arm in the fire up to there for Mr. Savory.

VENUS: That's rather specialized work, isn't it?

MOLLY: (*A duelist who has met her equal*) She'll do, Savory.

SAVORY: Er . . . Molly, I think your cake is burning.

MOLLY: That's not my cake, brother. That's your cookie. (*She exits*)

VENUS: You told me if I ever needed help, I could come to you.

SAVORY: I'm delighted you did. We can take up just where we left off.

VENUS: (*"Foolish Heart"*)

Will you tell me how these things happen?
Have I trusted in love too much?
When did the magic vanish?
Have I somehow lost my touch?
How gay the world could be
Could I love you, could he love me.
Love shouldn't be serious, should it?
You meet, perhaps you kiss, you start.
I fancied that I understood it;
I forgot my foolish heart.

Love can't be illogical, can it?
You kiss, perhaps you smile, you part.
It happens the way that you plan it,
If you hush your foolish heart.
Poor foolish heart,
Crying for one who ignores you!
Poor foolish heart,
Flying from one who adores you!
Ah, love used to touch me so lightly,
Why will my heart betray me so?
I could dance with a new lover nightly,
But my foolish heart says No.

(*Music continues under the scene*)

SAVORY: You're in love with someone. Who is he?

VENUS: I don't think you'd know him. He's not powerful like you. He's just an obscure little barber.

SAVORY: What's his name?

VENUS: Rodney Hatch.

SAVORY: Oh.

VENUS: Do you know him?

SAVORY: No . . . No.

VENUS: I'm sure he's in love with me—but he's afraid to say so. (*Sings*)

Poor foolish heart,
Crying for one who . . .

SAVORY: Then he's in love with another girl?

VENUS: He's been tied to her apron-strings for years.

SAVORY: (*Taking her in his arms*) I could help you forget him.

VENUS: (*Breaks away*) No. (*Sings*)

Love shouldn't be serious, should it?
You meet, perhaps you kiss, you start . . .

SAVORY: I've always gone on the principle that direct action is least painful. Isn't it better to have two people happy than three miserable?

VENUS: You're right.

SAVORY: I'd say the thing to do . . . is to eliminate the rival.

VENUS: (*Looking at him*) Eliminate the rival?

SAVORY: (*Returning her look*) And quickly.

VENUS: You don't think that's a bit too drastic?

SAVORY: Do you—under the circumstances?

VENUS: I don't know how to thank you.

SAVORY: Oh, yes you do.

VENUS: You're far too generous.

SAVORY: Don't overrate my generosity.

VENUS: (*Sings*)

Poor foolish heart,
Crying for one who ignores you,
Poor foolish heart,
Flying from one who adores you!
Ah, love used to touch me so lightly,
Why will my heart betray me so?
I could dance with a new lover nightly,
But my foolish heart says No.

(*She goes out swiftly*)

Curtain

SCENE 7

RODNEY'S *barbershop. It is a small, one-chair shop definitely old-fashioned in feeling. The street door has a bell that tinkles to announce customers. Two other doors lead respectively to* RODNEY'S *room and the cellar.*

STANLEY *is brandishing a prospectus at* RODNEY.

STANLEY: What do you mean, you don't need the *Book of Knowledge?*

RODNEY: Well, I haven't got room—

STANLEY: Do you think you know everything already?

RODNEY: I didn't say that, I—

STANLEY: Don't you want the true facts about spontaneous combustion? Don't you want to learn how to stuff a buffalo?

RODNEY: I haven't got time to read.

STANLEY: (*Cunningly*) Ah, what do you do in your spare time—hang out in art galleries?

(SAVORY *enters warily*)

SAVORY: (*As he passes his hat to* RODNEY) Shave—not too close.

RODNEY: Yes, sir. (*As he hangs up the hat and coat,* TAXI *enters. He and* SAVORY *exchange a furtive nod.* RODNEY *turns*) Have a chair—I'll be with you in a minute.

(SAVORY *sits in barber chair,* TAXI *and* STANLEY *sit by the table*)

TAXI: What's that sign you got outside—"Four Barbers No Waiting?"

RODNEY: (*Draping a towel about* SAVORY) Some fellow sold it to me; he said it would boost business. I guess he meant his business.

TAXI: Very funny.

STANLEY: (*Picking up a* Police Gazette) Boy, get a load of this pair of elbows!

TAXI: (*Glancing at magazine*) You sure pick 'em, barber!

RODNEY: Oh, I never look at those things.

TAXI: (*Rising*) What's the matter—afraid of dames?

RODNEY: They're nothing but a great big headache, if you ask me.

TAXI: They've been a lot of trouble to me, too!

TAXI, STANLEY, SAVORY and RODNEY: (*"The Trouble with Women"*)

TAXI:

I once loved a girl out in Flatbush,
A picture of beauty and grace;
But she thought kittens came from a catbush,
And she never had heard of first base.
I travel no longer to Flatbush,
Though the girl is both wealthy and pure,
For whenever I tried my desires to confide
Her mind was upon her coiffure.

TAXI, STANLEY, SAVORY and RODNEY:

Oh, the trouble, the trouble with women,
They soften your heart till it melts,
And then at the critical moment
They are thinking about something else.

SAVORY:

As a student my life was Parisian,
I languished, a captive of sex.
When specks interfered with my vision
They were lovely, voluptuous specks.
I toiled on a farm tilling soybeans,
In a struggle to chasten my brain,
But the girl beans got in with the boy beans,
And I never struggled again.

TAXI, STANLEY, SAVORY and RODNEY:

Oh, the trouble, the trouble with women,
You think you have left them behind,

You frolic in physical freedom,
And then they turn up on your mind.

STANLEY:

The reason each day I grow frailer,
Is that I'm trapped in a one-way romance
With a lady who lives in a trailer,
With some devil-may-care debutantes.
Her love for her kin is exquisite,
She entertains uncles galore;
But whenever I pay her a visit
Them uncles won't open the door.

TAXI, STANLEY, SAVORY and RODNEY:

Oh, the trouble, the trouble with women,
I fear that their life is a lie,
While they stall you with maidenly murmurs
They are romping with some other guy.

RODNEY:

When I drove in my glamorous Chevvy
I would park in a suitable spot,
Then I'd turn to the girls like a heavy,
And inquire if they would, or would not.
I always implied that they had to,
But, oh Jimminies, was I perplexed,
On the night that one said she'd be glad to—
I didn't know what to do next.

TAXI, STANLEY, SAVORY and RODNEY:

Oh, the trouble, the trouble with women
They are either too cold or too warm.
Yes, they're either in flight or insatiable.
Oh, God give me strength to ignor'm.

RODNEY:

One weekend I rented a Packard
For a maiden of whom I was fond.
Her lips and her toenails were lacquered
And I think she was technically blond.
Her defenses had started to crumble,
I was bursting with masculine pride,
When up spoke a voice from the rumble—
Her mother had stolen a ride.

SAVORY:

Oh, the trouble, the trouble with women,
They are constantly one jump ahead.
You touch what you think is a bosom,
And you find it's an eight-ball instead.

STANLEY:

The reason I moan in my slumber
Is that I'm subject to female rebuffs,
Or if I make a note of a number,
The laundry erases my cuffs.
If I droop like a lily in sadness,
The diagnosis is easy to see,
Every woman has moments of madness,
But never, no never with me.

RODNEY, SAVORY, STANLEY and TAXI:

Oh, the trouble, the trouble with women,
I repeat it again and again,
From Kalamazoo to Kamchatka
The trouble with women is men.

(*As song ends,* TAXI *quickly unscrews the handle of the valve under the washbasin, tosses it to* STANLEY)

SAVORY: See here, this lather's too cold!

RODNEY: I'll get some fresh. (*He crosses to washbasin*)

(STANLEY *shows the handle of the valve to* SAVORY *and then places it in his pocket.* RODNEY *turns the faucets vainly*)

TAXI: What's the matter, bud? Pipe busted?

RODNEY: (*Puzzled*) It was all right a minute ago. (*Bends down to look underneath the basin*)

TAXI: Your trouble's in the cellar! Your Bemis valve is clogged, brother. The frogging is scored on your lynch-pin and that bandles the bushing!

SAVORY: Hey, are you a plumber?

TAXI: Been working with drips all my life! (*Looks at* STANLEY *and pushes* RODNEY *to the cellar door*) Here, stupid, go down the cellar with the man.

RODNEY: Oh, I don't need any help!

TAXI: No trouble at all.

STANLEY: (*Herding* RODNEY *out the door*) Glad to help you! (*Exits after* RODNEY)

RODNEY: (*Offstage*) I hate to impose on you—

TAXI: (*Closing door*) How's that, Mr. Savory?

SAVORY: (*Rising*) Great, Taxi! Now look, that statue might be anywhere.

TAXI: You go through the closets—

SAVORY: You search his room upstairs!

TAXI: We gotta move fast!

(*He runs out. The doorbell tinkles and* GLORIA *enters*)

GLORIA: (*Hesitatingly*) Oh—isn't Mr. Hatch here?

SAVORY: Who?

GLORIA: Mr. Hatch—the proprietor.

SAVORY: Oh, is he a close friend of yours?

GLORIA: (*Sitting in barber chair*) We have an understanding.

SAVORY: That's nice. He'll be back in a few minutes. Great fellow, Hatch. Got an amazing mind.

GLORIA: Are you kidding?

SAVORY: (*Cunningly*) I understand he's quite a connoisseur of art. Statues and things like that?

GLORIA: That's the first I heard of it.

SAVORY: (*Suddenly a Humphrey Bogart*) Listen, puss, cut the act. Let's you and I work together.

GLORIA: (*Bewildered*) Come again?

SAVORY: I'm Flashy John from Cicero. I specialize in hot statuary.

GLORIA: (*Starts to rise*) I forgot something—I'll be back later.

SAVORY: (*Holding her in barber chair*) Stick with me, Feathers, and I'll cover you with diamonds!

GLORIA: (*Terrified*) I don't want to be covered with diamonds!

SAVORY: What do you want?

GLORIA: I want to get out of here!

SAVORY: Where's the statue?

GLORIA: You let me go!

SAVORY: Shut up, you little fool!

(*She screams—*SAVORY *whips a towel around her head.* TAXI *enters*)

TAXI: Tie her up! Make a loop knot . . . sailor knot, any kind of a knot! (*They knot apron around her middle*)

SAVORY: (*Exultant*) We've got her!

TAXI: We've got her! (*They crow and shake hands across* GLORIA) Who is she?

SAVORY: (*Crestfallen*) I don't know.

(STANLEY *enters from cellar*)

STANLEY: No dice. They must have hid it somewheres else!

TAXI: Where's the barber?

STANLEY: (*Pleased with himself*) He got tough. I had to slug him.

TAXI: (*In horror*) We'll lay in jail for ninety-nine years! That's what I get for working with amateurs! (*The doorbell sounds*) Someone's coming—we've got to lam outta here and fix up an alibi! Out the back—out the back!

(*He rushes off, followed by* STANLEY *and* SAVORY. *As the back door closes behind them,* VENUS *enters from the street*)

VENUS: (*Sees* GLORIA *tied in barber chair*) Oh! What happened? (*Untying* GLORIA) What have they done to you? Are you all right?

GLORIA: (*Gasping*) That gangster! He tried to kill me!

VENUS: Where's Rodney? Isn't he here?

GLORIA: Oh—I think I'm going to faint!

VENUS: (*Sweetly*) You do that. You'll feel much better.

GLORIA: (*Recognizing her*) You! Why, you brazen thing! The *gall* of you marching in here as if you owned the place! I knew he was two-timing me!

VENUS: You know, I can hear you as plainly as though you were in the next room.

GLORIA: You led Rodney on! He never had any nerve until you showed up!

VENUS: Why, that's the nicest thing anyone ever said to me.

GLORIA: I'm going to sue that little weasel for breach of promise —and name you!

VENUS: Be careful, dear. You're not appealing to my better nature!

GLORIA: (*Advancing on* VENUS) I'll scratch your eyes out!

VENUS: (*Almost maternally*) Now, lambie, you're overtired. You're just a bundle of nerves. I'm going to send you on a nice long trip to the moon, or would you prefer something closer, like the North Pole?

GLORIA: You're a cheap, no-good, gold-digging tart!

VENUS: Have a nice trip, dear—and be careful of drafts!

(*She extends her arm. There is a crash of music, and the lights black out. When they come on again,* VENUS *is alone. The barber chair is spinning slowly, and on the seat is* GLORIA'S *compact.* VENUS *picks it up*)

VENUS: Why, she forgot her compact. (*Opening it and looking at herself*) Oh, she's going to arrive there with a shiny nose! (RODNEY *stumbles groggily through the cellar door*)

VENUS: (*Anxiously*) Darling, what's the matter? Are you hurt?

RODNEY: (*Tottering to barber chair*) No—I'm all right . . . I'm all right.

VENUS: You look pale!

RODNEY: Something hit me.

VENUS: Where does it hurt? Show me.

RODNEY: (*Clasping his jaw*) Right here. (*Faintly*) I can't remember. I was in the cellar—

VENUS: Don't try to talk. Just let yourself go. (*She leans over him and strokes his face*) There . . .

RODNEY: Oh, this is wonderful. It's just what I needed.

VENUS: It's doing me a world of good, too.

RODNEY: You're so nice to touch.

VENUS: Does it make you happy?

RODNEY: I—I never felt like this before.

VENUS: It's been a long time since anyone has.

VENUS: (*"Speak Low"*)

Speak low when you speak love,
Our summer day
Withers away
Too soon, too soon.
Speak low when you speak love;
Our moment is swift,
Like ships adrift,
We're swept apart too soon.
Speak low, darling, speak low,
Love is a spark,
Lost in the dark,
Too soon, too soon.
I feel, wherever I go,
That tomorrow is near,
Tomorrow is here,
And always too soon.
Time is so old, and love so brief,
Love is pure gold, and time a thief.
We're late, darling, we're late,
The curtain descends,
Everything ends,
Too soon, too soon.
I wait, darling, I wait—
Will you speak low to me,
Speak love to me,
And soon?

(*She finishes the song, and* RODNEY, *rising, takes it up. As he concludes, they are in each other's arms*)

RODNEY: (*Exuberantly*) Well, the shop'll have to take care of itself today! You and I are going to *celebrate!*

VENUS: (*Smiling*) Have you anything special in mind?

RODNEY: Yes, I tell you what let's do! (*With a deep breath*) Let's go down to Sheepshead Bay and have a big shore dinner! (*He automatically reaches for the coat hanging on the wall hook and starts to put it on*) Hey! Whose coat is this? (*Extracting letter from coat pocket*) Why, it's Mr. Savory's! Look at this! It's from a detective! It says I stole a statue. They say I'm a criminal—they've been following me!

VENUS: (*Thoughtfully*) Following you! We can't have that! You know, I think it's about time we had a few words with Mr. Savory.

RODNEY: Nobody's going to push me around!

VENUS: Spoken like a man!

RODNEY: He's not going to call me a thief!

VENUS: What a pity he can't hear you!

RODNEY: I'll show him who stole his old statue!

VENUS: With a statue like me, I'm glad it's you!

(*As they kiss . . .*)

Curtain

SCENE 8

The roof garden of the Foundation. Midnight of the same day.

The STUDENTS, *dressed in the period of 1910, are dancing a variation of the Cancan.* SAVORY *and* MOLLY *stand watching the dancers. The music stops and* VENUS *enters with* RODNEY.

SAVORY: (*Sotto voce, to* MOLLY) Molly, we've got them here. Now watch me. (*To* RODNEY) Oh, hello! I got your telephone call. Delighted you could come!

VENUS: What a charming party!

SAVORY: My students like to kick up their heels once in a while.

RODNEY: Mr. Savory, I found this letter in your coat quite by accident. It says here that I stole your statue!

SAVORY: Not a word, old man, till we've all had a drink. Let's sit down. We all know each other, don't we?

MOLLY: Sure. How are you, Miss Hawthorn?

RODNEY: Hello.

(SAVORY *conducts* VENUS *to a table*)

RODNEY: (*Anxiously*) Oh, Mr. Savory—about the statue—

SAVORY: Plenty of time to discuss that later, old man. Our entertainment is just about to begin. (*A small portable stage is rolled on, its curtain down*) Now, I want you all to watch this closely; it's pretty special. You in particular, Hatch—I'll be interested in your reaction.

RODNEY: (*Persisting*) But the statue—

SAVORY: After you've seen this, the statue'll be the least of your troubles. . . . Ladies and gentlemen—everybody loves a good murder. The one you are about to witness is a classic—the dark and horrid crime that led Dr. Crippen to the scaffold. Here you will see reenacted the sinister events that petrified London in 1910. Let me recall the central figures of the tragedy: Dr. Hawley Harvey Crippen—Belle Elmore, the wife of whom he wearied—and Ethel Le Neve, his pretty little typist. (*Turning toward* RODNEY) Before we begin, Hatch, I have just received a piece of startling news—or is it news to you? Gloria Kramer, your fiancée, has disappeared, and the police . . . suspect . . . foul . . . play.

(*As* RODNEY *rises in alarm,* SAVORY *launches immediately into "Doctor Crippen." During the song, the curtain of the small stage rises to reveal a series of tableaux in which the actors portray the drama of Dr. Crippen, Belle Elmore, and Ethel Le Neve*)

SAVORY: ("*Doctor Crippen*")
Passion is not a laughing matter,
And in love you must not fall,
Unless for the sake of a woman
You are ready to give your all.
Let me tell you about a lover
Who made the sacrifice,
Let me tell you about a lover
Who never loved but twice.

Here's to Doctor Crippen,
Hawley Harvey Crippen,
Lying in a felon's grave.
When they tried him in court
He had one retort,
It was all for Ethel Le Neve.

Harvey Crippen was a doctor,
Who would be unknown to fame

If he hadn't met an actress,
Belle Elmore was her name.
She had promised if he'd wed her
She'd be the best of wives—
An unfortunate proposal,
Since it cost them both their lives.

Here's to Doctor Crippen,
Hawley Harvey Crippen,
Lying in a felon's grave.
But he told the guard
In the prison yard,
It was all for Ethel Le Neve.

Belle Elmore was a vixen,
Belle Elmore was a shrew,
Nobody knows the embarrassment
She subjected Doctor Crippen to.
He hired a secretary,
Ethel Le Neve by name,
If she had gone to work for somebody else
She'd be unknown to fame.

Here's to Doctor Crippen,
Hawley Harvey Crippen,
Lying in a felon's grave.
But as he swung
He proudly sung
It was all for Ethel Le Neve.

Doctor Crippen liked her typing,
Her ladylike self-control,
She had an understandable figure,
And an understanding soul.
He prescribed for Belle a tonic,
Dug a hole in the cellar floor,
And then he packed in quicklime
What was left of Belle Elmore.

Here's to Doctor Crippen,
Hawley Harvey Crippen,
Lying in a felon's grave.
But he didn't mope
When they cut the rope,
It was all for Ethel Le Neve.

(MRS. KRAMER *has entered.* RODNEY *rises in puzzled alarm. A* POLICE LIEUTENANT *and a* DETECTIVE *emerge from the crowd, start toward him*)

He put boy's clothes on his sweetheart,
They fled to a country far,
But the law identified Belle Elmore
Through an old abdominal scar.
He would never have been suspected,
Of the police he would have made fools,
But Ethel was observed at a party
Wearing Belle Elmore's jewels . . .

(VENUS *has drawn out the compact she took from* GLORIA *in the barbershop, begins to powder her nose*)

MRS. KRAMER: (*Snatches compact from* VENUS' *hand*) That's my daughter's compact! He did it! He killed her!

POLICE LIEUTENANT: (*Grasping* RODNEY) You're under arrest!

RODNEY: (*Thunderstruck*) Wha–what for?

LIEUTENANT: The murder of Gloria Kramer.

RODNEY: You're crazy! I don't know what you're talking about!

MRS. KRAMER: (*Hysterically*) What have you done with my baby, you fiend, you?

RODNEY: I haven't seen Gloria since she got off the bus!

TAXI: (*Appearing from among the guests*) We happen to know different!

VENUS: (*Rising, to* MRS. KRAMER) This is fantastic. Rodney never touched your daughter.

MRS. KRAMER: (*Viciously*) She's back of the whole thing! Gloria told me how they were carrying on! They're like two bugs in a rug!

SAVORY: This lady has no connection with the matter.

LIEUTENANT: (*Dubiously*) Maybe the D.A. ought to decide that, Mr. Savory.

SAVORY: (*Flatly*) She's a friend of mine. I'll vouch for her personally. Take him away.

VENUS: (*To* LIEUTENANT) Just a moment. Where are you taking him?

SAVORY: (*With grim satisfaction*) To a snug little room where he won't be disturbed for a long, long time.

VENUS: (*Moving to* RODNEY'S *side*) In that case I'm going with him.

SAVORY: That's absurd. You're not involved in this.

VENUS: (*Blandly*) Oh, but I am. I managed the whole thing.

RODNEY: Don't listen to her, she's only trying to take the blame for me!

VENUS: No, really I did. The girl was becoming impossible. I dissolved her.

MRS. KRAMER: You *what?*

VENUS: I dissolved her.

LIEUTENANT: (*Perplexed*) Well, I don't know whether it's Haig and Haig or nose-candy, but you're coming downtown, too.

SAVORY: (*Angrily*) Over my dead body she is!

VENUS: (*Dangerously*) Don't tempt me–I'm just in the mood to oblige you. (*To* RODNEY) Cheer up, darling, don't look so glum! This is our honeymoon!

(*The* POLICE *lead* VENUS *and* RODNEY *out*)

MOLLY: (*In* SAVORY'S *ear*) Well, Cupid, you certainly loused that up!

ENTIRE ENSEMBLE:

Here's to Doctor Crippen,
Hawley Harvey Crippen,
Lying in a felon's grave . . .

(*The curtain on small stage opens to reveal* DR. CRIPPEN *hanging by the neck*)

DR. CRIPPEN: (*Sings, as he dances briskly*)

I gave not only my life
But that of my wife
For the love of Ethel Le Neve!

ENTIRE ENSEMBLE:

He gave not only his life
But that of his wife
For the love of Ethel Le Neve . . .

Curtain

ACT TWO

SCENE 1

SAVORY'S *bedroom. An elaborately paneled room containing a canopy bed. Beside the bed is a table with a telephone; on the wall, a bellpull.*

SAVORY *lies in bed, asleep, an ice-pack on his head.* MOLLY *enters, straightens up.* ROSE, *the maid, enters. She carries an easel, which she sets up at the foot of the bed, facing* SAVORY.

MOLLY: Morning, Rose.

ROSE: Mornin', Miss Molly. Faith, an' yez puts me in moind of a darlint shamrock, indade yez do.

MOLLY: Listen, Rose, that brogue of yours is a pain in the . . . macushla. Where are you from, anyway?

ROSE: Council Bluffs, Iowa, but the employment agency recommends a touch of dialect. (*She goes out*)

MOLLY: Well, we'll stick to the local patois, if you don't mind. What's today's special?

ROSE: (*Re-entering with framed painting*) It's a young girl leaning on some watermelons—that is, I *think* they're watermelons.

MOLLY: O.K. Give us the sound effects.

(ROSE *exits, returns striking a melodious Chinese gong, backs out*)

SAVORY: (*Stirs, opens his eyes, and stares incredulously at painting*) Did I pay twelve thousand dollars for *those?*

MOLLY: And we've got the stubs to prove it.

SAVORY: No wonder they call me the shrewdest collector in America. I could sell 'em tomorrow for twenty-five.

MOLLY: (*Picking up* SAVORY'S *dressing gown*) That hiss you hear is the sound of escaping esteem.

(SAVORY *swings his feet over edge of bed into his slippers*)

SAVORY: (*Groaning*) What was I drinking last night—*fine* or Mickey *Fine?*

MOLLY: When I went to bed you had just invented the Shostakovitch Special—malted mare's milk and vodka.

SAVORY: Where's my breakfast? (*Pulling bell cord*) Hathaway!

MOLLY: Hathaway's losing his grip. I told him half an hour ago.

SAVORY: Any word from George Dreamy? What about that bail?

MOLLY: He's been out of his office all morning. I'll try him again. (*She picks up phone, and dials*)

SAVORY: (*Sitting at dressing table, gazes into mirror*) *God,* I feel awful! All my teeth have little sweaters on them.

MOLLY: (*In phone*) Hello, Drexel, Van Wagonen, Languorous and Dreamy? Mr. Dreamy, please . . . Oh, hello, Miss Conquest—Mr. Savory calling Mr. Dreamy . . . (*Not to be outsmarted*) Oh, no—you put Mr. Dreamy on first . . . Oh, no, I won't! Mr. Savory got on first the last time! . . . (*Sweetly*) Is that you, Mr. Dreamy? (SAVORY *rises*) Here's Mr. Savory.

SAVORY: (*In phone*) Well, George, did you get her out? . . .

What? She won't leave jail? . . . But she's got to! . . . How should I know? That's what I'm paying you for! (*Slumps on bed*) Damnedest thing I ever heard!

MOLLY: Complications?

SAVORY: She's locked her cell from the inside and won't come out!

MOLLY: She's no fool. God knows there are times when I could do with a short stretch in solitary.

SAVORY: I'm beginning to feel like a scrambled egg! (*Impatiently*) What the Sam Hill's holding up my breakfast?

MOLLY: I'll tiptoe down and light a fire under Hathaway. (*A man enters, his back to them. He carries a breakfast tray*) Oh, here he is now . . . (*Starting out*) By the way, there was a note there from Clare Luce. I swallowed it. (*She exits*)

SAVORY: Don't stand there, Hathaway!

(*The man sets down the breakfast tray and turns. He wears a vaguely Oriental costume–jeweled tunic, baggy trousers, and slippers that curl at the toes. This is* ZUVETLI, *a thoroughly unreconstructed Anatolian. He whips out an Oriental dagger and kneels across the bed, the dagger at* SAVORY'S *throat*)

ZUVETLI: Do not move, Effendi. I would not wish to harm you. (SAVORY *yanks at the bellpull; it comes away in his hand.* ZUVETLI *laughs;* SAVORY *reaches in panic for the phone*) Equally useless, my dear sir. The service has been discontinued.

SAVORY: Damn your eyes, what romantic nonsense is this?

ZUVETLI: (*Rapidly*) Be good enough to hear me out–my time is limited. The Cytherean brotherhood has marked you down. In thirty centuries none has ever profaned our goddess and lived. You know your crime and you know the penalty. The statue returns to us before the old moon wanes, or by the beard of my father, you will never greet the new one!

SAVORY: (*Cringing*) I haven't got the statue! Hatch stole it!

ZUVETLI: Hatch? What is this Hatch?

SAVORY: Rodney Hatch, the barber! Present address, Cell 39, the Tombs.

ZUVETLI: (*Slowly withdrawing dagger, across* SAVORY'S *throat*) Oh–pardon the intrusion. (*He picks up breakfast tray, places it on* SAVORY'S *lap.*) Your breakfast, Effendi–(*Picks up napkin–snaps it open and tosses it on* SAVORY'S *stomach*)–and good appetite to you! (*He vanishes through a panel in the wall beside bed*)

MOLLY: (*Entering, breathless*) Hey, what do you think? Hathaway's down in the coalbin with a black eye!

SAVORY: Tell him to move over. I'll be down as soon as I can find my strait jacket. (*Pulls covers over his head*)

MOLLY: Oh, you and your Taj Mahal, your town house, your country house—your fabulous collection of modern paintings —and your thirty-nine million dollars in the Corn Exchange Bank! I should have your troubles!

MOLLY: (*"Very, Very, Very"*)

One way to be very wealthy
Is to be very, very, very rich.
You can pile up mink and ermine
Like a hermit accumulates vermin
If you occupy the proper financial niche.
One way to be very happy
Is to be very, very, very rich.
There are kinds of human pleasure
That are not to be purchased with treasure,
But I can't remember exactly which.
I've heard my gilded friends complain
There are troubles money cannot cure,
But a trouble is a trouble is a trouble, and it's twice
The trouble when a person is poor.
In the carefree kingdom of the wealthy
You will never see an eyebrow twitch.
It's a minor peccadillo
To patronize the wrong pillow,
When you're very, very, very rich.

Sit down, my dear, I'll have the soup on
As soon as I clip this coupon,
Last year I paid for the maid's appendix,
Now she's taken a job with Bendix.
It's weeks since I heard a word of gossip,
What's the latest from Jane and Ossip?
She's a girl that dozens are the beau of—
She's been faithful to him twice that I know of.
Damn Uncle Pierpont!
He left me a packet,
And moved me into a higher bracket.
Since Sally ran off with her obstetrician,
Her hair's turned red and she looks like a Titian;

Of course, I'd hate to swear in court
What kind of Titian: beaut—or mort—.
Have you paid your platina fur tax?
I am up to my neck in surtax!
One way to never spend a penny
Is to be very, very, very rich.
If you live along Park Avenue
You've dandy credit havenue?
So why pay your grocery bills and sich?
In the dreamy night life of the wealthy
True love unwinds without a hitch.
You just engage Menuhin
To fiddle her to her ruin
When you're very, very, very, very rich.

One way to be very wedded
Is to be very, very, very prosperous.
You can sublimate your passion on a Balkan or Circassian,
And then toss them legally in the Bosporus.
In the costly dotage of the wealthy
You resurrect that bygone itch,
You huddle with your memoirs, and *boy!* what memoirs them was!
When you're very, very, very rich.

Curtain

SCENE 2

The Tombs. Two cells, separated by the width of the stage. The doors of the cells face each other. In each is a small stool, and in front of each, a bench.

VENUS, *in one cell, extends her hand longingly to* RODNEY, *in the other. The* POLICE LIEUTENANT, *followed by* DR. ROOK, *the prison psychiatrist, and a* MATRON, *enters, stops outside* RODNEY'S *cell.*

LIEUTENANT: Come on, Hatch, stop moping over that beetle. Dr. Rook wants to talk to you. (*He unlocks the door and* RODNEY *emerges*)

DR. ROOK: (*Sits down; motions* RODNEY *to sit beside him*) Now, Rodney, nobody's going to hurt you. I'm only here to help you.

LIEUTENANT: That's right. You answer polite or I'll beat your brains out.

ROOK: No, no, Lieutenant–that's the wrong approach. (*To* RODNEY) Now, this statement of yours. You say you brought a statue of Venus to life and she followed you home? (*Suddenly hits* RODNEY'S *crossed knee with a small hammer.* RODNEY *twitches*) Aha. Typical Gauss-Honeywell reaction. (*Reflectively*) I wonder what that means. (*Shrugging his shoulders*) Oh, well . . . Now tell me, Rodney–you frequently hear voices when nobody's around, don't you?

RODNEY: Why, no, I–

ROOK: (*Rises and jabs a pencil flashlight at* RODNEY'S *eyes.* RODNEY *flinches*) Aha! Adolescent reflex!

RODNEY: Yes, sir . . .

ROOK: How often do you get the sensation of frying–I mean, of flying? (*Laughs deprecatingly*) I'm getting ahead of myself.

RODNEY: I never said that.

LIEUTENANT: Don't contradict the doctor, you little squirt!

ROOK: No, no–give him enough rope, Lieutenant! Now, Rodney, you read a great many fairy tales, don't you?

RODNEY: You must have got the wrong statement, Doctor!

ROOK: (*Tolerantly*) Aha–obvious desire to shift responsibility.

LIEUTENANT: (*Starting for* RODNEY) Aarh!

ROOK: (*Rising*) No–no–I don't think this poor fellow's in your department–clear psychiatric case.

LIEUTENANT: (*Taking* RODNEY'S *arm*) Come on, Hatch–back in the incubator. (*He locks* RODNEY *in the cell*)

RODNEY: (*To* DR. ROOK) I'm not the loony one–you are!

ROOK: (*Crossing to* VENUS' *cell*) That's what they all say. (*To* MATRON) Bring her out, please.

VENUS: Well? (*Emerging from cell*)

ROOK: Won't you sit down? (*He joins her on the bench*) I'd like to ask you a few questions. (*Notebook and pencil in hand*) Who were your parents?

VENUS: The Mediterranean.

ROOK: (*With pencil poised*) I beg your pardon?

VENUS: I was born of the sea-foam.

ROOK: Ah, yes, yes. Your occupation?

VENUS: Delightful.

ROOK: (*Doubtfully*) "Delightful." You have no previous record, I suppose?

VENUS: Indeed I have! As a matter of fact, it makes fascinating reading.

ROOK: How old are you?

VENUS: Well, there's some doubt. Homer says one thing—Vergil says another.

ROOK: How can I contact these people?

VENUS: (*After a thoughtful pause—answering him with sweet helpfulness*) Go to Hell.

ROOK: (*Rising indignantly*) This is impossible. (*As he exits*) I wash my hands of the entire case.

MATRON: (*Calling*) All right, miss, you can have your five minutes now.

(MOLLY *enters, smiles at* VENUS)

MOLLY: Hiya, Hawthorn.

VENUS: How nice of you to come down.

MOLLY: (*Sitting beside her on bench*) Oh well, things have been pretty dull around the Foundation since you left. Savory's eating his heart out. I don't get it—why do you moon around this place when there's a bubble bath and a dry Martini waiting for you up at the house?

VENUS: I like it here.

MOLLY: You realize, of course, that when your bail's posted, you're supposed to get out.

VENUS: No—I won't leave until Rodney does.

MOLLY: You'd better straighten it out with the Warden, because come noon he's going to heave you out on that beautiful can of yours. Say, you haven't anything against Savory, have you?

VENUS: Oh, don't misunderstand me—I find him extremely attractive at times.

MOLLY: Of course, he's got the ethics of a burglar and the temper of a short-order cook, but why boggle? Whatever he is, he's not dull. Say, let me be your diary for a minute. (*Indicating* RODNEY) What's the big attraction about that little citizen?

VENUS: I don't know. Maybe it's something that's happened to me. All my other men have been such heroic figures. I want somebody nobody's ever heard of.

MOLLY: Well, that certainly is a reasonable facsimile of Rodney Hatch.

VENUS: I'm in a very bad way. I want to choose his neckties for him, part his hair on the opposite side—

MOLLY: In other words, having found exactly what you want, you can't wait to change it.

VENUS: Naturally. I'm in love with him.

MOLLY: I hope he can take it.

VENUS: Why?

MOLLY: (*Glancing at* VENUS' *figure*) Hmmm. Because . . . Look, I never said this to anyone before, but you're Venus, aren't you?

VENUS: Of course.

MOLLY: That's what I figured—it didn't make sense any other way. I mean the statue and the barber and the statue and—(*Rising*) Oh, do you mind if I go home and lie down for a week or two?

VENUS: You're a very thoughtful person.

MOLLY: And you're a very nice one. In fact, you're the nicest goddess I've ever met.

VENUS: Thank you.

MOLLY: Keep 'em guessing!

(*She goes out. The* MATRON *locks* VENUS *in cell, and follows* MOLLY *off.* ZUVETLI *appears from the shadows*)

ZUVETLI: (*Abasing himself outside cell*) Majesty . . . Gracious Deity, grant me one moment's audience.

VENUS: Oh . . . What do you want?

ZUVETLI: (*Rising*) Why hast thou deserted us, O radiant one? The virtue has gone out of us. The earth in your homeland is parched; the grain withers on the stalk—the lizard and the locust invade your sacred temple. Your people are stricken. Return to us, we entreat you.

VENUS: (*Rising*) No. There is one who has greater need of me than you.

ZUVETLI: (*Turning menacingly toward* RODNEY) Is it this infidel whose ring you wear?

VENUS: Wait! (ZUVETLI *stops*) I have given him my pledge. I will not leave him.

ZUVETLI: Think well, O Goddess!

VENUS: Do you dare threaten me?

ZUVETLI: We are sworn to destroy all who profane thee!

VENUS: Go—before I lose patience with you! (ZUVETLI *bows and withdraws*) Rodney—can you hear me?

RODNEY: (*Anxiously*) Are you all right?

VENUS: They want to take me away from you.

RODNEY: I won't let 'em. We're getting out of here! (*In a low, rapid voice*) I've got it all figured out! When the man brings my dinner I'm going to tie him up with my belt and take away his keys.

VENUS: (*Worried*) No, no, he'll hurt you—he's bigger than you.

RODNEY: I don't care how big he is! If he gets between you and me I'll kill him!

VENUS: Then they'd never let you go!

RODNEY: (*Sings*)

Speak low when you speak love,
Our summer day
Withers away
Too soon, too soon,
Speak low when you speak love,
Our moment is swift,
Like ships adrift,
We're swept apart too soon.
Speak low, darling, speak low,
Love is a spark,
Lost in the dark,
Too soon, too soon.
I feel, wherever I go
That tomorrow is near,
Tomorrow is here,
And always too soon.

(VENUS *makes a sudden joyful gesture, and the cell doors swing open.* VENUS *and* RODNEY *hasten toward each other*)

VENUS and RODNEY:

We're late, darling, we're late,
The curtain descends
Everything ends
Too soon, too soon.
I wait, darling, I wait.
Will you speak low,
When you speak love to me . . .

(RODNEY *takes her hand and they go off. The stage is empty for a moment, then* SAVORY *and* MOLLY *rush on, followed by the rest of the cast, brandishing weapons*)

ALL: (*"Catch Hatch"*)

SAVORY and MOLLY:

Bring bloodhounds for the barber!
The killer runs amuck!
Blockade the lower harbor!
Search every Macy truck!

One battle cry will spark us!
Bring on the barber's carcass!

TAXI and STANLEY:
The barber took a powder!
We'll grab him while he scrams!
We'll chop him into chowder!
And feed him to the clams!
Upon his track we'll park us!
Bring on the barber's carcass!

MRS. KRAMER and SAM:
Roll out the torture engines!
The barber flew the coop!
The victim shrieks for vengeance!
Avengers, allez-oop!
A mother's cries are raucous!
Bring on the barber's carcass!

ZUVETLI and his ANATOLIANS:
Our sacred shrine is pompless!
Unbearable our loss!
The barber's the accomplice!
But Savory's the boss!
And lynch law is the right law
For Rodney and for Whitelaw!

ALL:
Avengers, allez-oop!
Avengers, allez-oop!

Curtain

SCENE 3

The sitting room of a de luxe suite. One door leads to the bedroom, another opens into a clothes closet. Against the wall, a chaise longue.

VENUS, *clad in negligee, reclines on the chaise longue.* RODNEY *stands before a mirror, arranging his necktie.*

RODNEY: Do you like this one better?

VENUS: Come here. (RODNEY *crosses to her*) Love me?

RODNEY: Uh-huh. (*He kisses her on the forehead*)

VENUS: Rodney—come here! (*She kisses him—a lingering embrace*)

RODNEY: (*Rising ecstatically*) Oh God! Is it all right for anybody to feel as good as I do?

VENUS: Don't be so humble, darling.

RODNEY: (*Sitting by her*) I can't help it. I keep wondering why anyone as wonderful as you would waste their time on me.

VENUS: If you ever change, I'll leave your bed and board. (*Her arm goes around his shoulder*) Rodney, may I confess something? . . . This ring only brought us together. It had no power to make me love you. (RODNEY *kisses her fingertips*) Oh, that tie's not nearly gay enough. You look so somber. Like–like a notary public whose term is about to expire.

RODNEY: (*Rising*) How about the yellow one–with the little horses' heads? That's pretty keen! It's in the bedroom.

VENUS: And while you're away, remember I love you. (*She throws him a kiss as he goes out*) And Rodney–part your hair on the other side.

VENUS: (*"That's Him"*)

You know the way you feel when there is autumn in the air?
That's him . . . That's him . . .
The way you feel when Antoine has finished with your hair?
That's him . . . That's him . . .
You know the way you feel when you smell bread baking,
The way you feel when suddenly a tooth stops aching?
Wonderful world, wonderful you,
That's him . . . That's him . . .
He's simple as a swim in summer,
Not arty, not actory,
He's like a plumber when you need a plumber,
He's satisfactory.
You know the way you feel when you want to knock on wood,
The way you feel when your heart is gone for good?
Wonderful world, wonderful you,
That's him.

You could shuffle him with millions,
Soldiers and civilians,
I'd pick him out.
In the darkest caves and hallways
I would know him always
Beyond a doubt.

Identification comes easily to me
Because—that's he.

You know the way you feel about the *Rhapsody in Blue?*
That's him . . . That's him . . .
The way you feel about a hat created just for you?
That's him . . . That's him . . .
You know the way you feel when the fireflies glimmer,
The way you feel when overnight your hips grow slimmer?
Wonderful world, wonderful you,
That's him . . . That's him . . .

He's like a book directly from the printer:
You look at him—he's so commenceable,
He's comforting as woolens in the winter,
He's indispensable.
You know the way you feel that you know you should conceal,
The way you feel that you really shouldn't feel?
Wonderful world, wonderful you,
That's him.

(*As the song ends* RODNEY *emerges from bedroom. His face is worried*)

VENUS: What's the matter?

RODNEY: Uh . . . Nothing . . . (*With a bright effort*) You know, I was just thinking—this time every morning I'm just about halfway down Mr. Frisbie's chin. (*Grinning*) Oh, ish-ka-bibble—let him grow a beard.

VENUS: (*Rising*) What would you like me to wear today, darling?

RODNEY: Oh, I don't know—Have you got anything kind of summery? With dots. I like dots.

VENUS: Wouldn't it be fun to take a walk in the woods? We could even have a picnic! (*Noting his hesitation*) Don't you like picnics?

RODNEY: Oh, sure—I guess we could go to Central Park . . . (*Driven to facing facts*) Look, it's no good. I can't go anywhere. I can't even leave this room!

VENUS: What's the matter? Are you ill?

RODNEY: They're still after me for Gloria! We'd never get by the first policeman!

VENUS: Oh, bother the first policeman!

RODNEY: I'm not joking! We're in a heck of a spot until Gloria turns up!

VENUS: Well, if that's all that's worrying you, step back a little. (*She raises her arm. The closet door flies open and* GLORIA *ricochets out, wild-eyed and disheveled, just as we last saw her in the barbershop*)

RODNEY: My God—has she been in here all night!

GLORIA: (*Babbling to empty air*) You give me back my ring! I'll show that little stinker he can't two-time me!

RODNEY: That's Gloria, all right! (*Tentatively*) Honey, are you okay?

VENUS: (*Sitting back on sofa*) Honey's as fit as a fiddle. She'll live to bury us both!

RODNEY: Gloria! Snap out of it!

GLORIA: (*Emerging from the fog*) Where am I? (*Staring around*) Where's the barbershop? (*Sees* VENUS) Oooh! (*Confronts* RODNEY) What are you doing with that woman in here?

VENUS: (*Nodding toward other room*) We got tired of it in there.

GLORIA: Rodney Hatch! You—in a hotel room—with an actress!

RODNEY: I know it looks bad . . . but it's good!

GLORIA: Don't come near me . . . I never want to see you again! Wait till I tell my mother! You utter, utter cad! (*Turning to* VENUS) And you . . . you libido! (*She stalks out*)

VENUS: *Sic transit* Gloria Kramer.

RODNEY: (*Slowly staring after* GLORIA) To think I've been taking that for five years, and if it wasn't for you, I'd be taking it for the rest of my life. (*Sitting beside* VENUS) I'm so afraid of losing you.

VENUS: (*Arms around him*) You'll never be alone again, Rodney, I promise you.

RODNEY: Just think of the fun we're going to have! Did you ever hear of Ozone Heights?

VENUS: No, what are they?

RODNEY: It's a great big new real estate development over on Staten Island. Every bungalow's just the same. They got an electric incinerator and a radio that looks like a fireplace—

VENUS: And a fireplace that looks like a radio?

RODNEY: Yes. And when you sign the lease, you get a year's subscription to the *Reader's Digest!* And I almost forgot the most important thing of all—a dandy big yard for the kiddies when they start to come along.

VENUS: (*Wryly*) You'd better look for something with a lake. With me, you might get swans.

RODNEY: Jeepers Creepers, if I love you this much now, just think how I'll love you in five years!

RODNEY: ("*Wooden Wedding*")

Waiting for our wooden wedding,
Golly, how the time will fly!
Stealing kisses in the kitchen,
Holding hands while the dishes dry.
Waiting for our wooden wedding,
Golly, how the sun will shine!
We will linger o'er the laundry,
I'll wash yours and you'll wash mine.
Payday will be a magic casement
Opening on something peachy,
Maybe a trip to Gimbel's basement,
Or a double feature with Don Ameche.
Waiting for our wooden wedding,
Golly, what a trail we'll leave!
Sipping Coca-Cola at the pianola
On our wooden wedding eve.

Waiting for our wooden wedding,
Golly, how the birds will sing!
While we whistle in the garden,
Planting onions in the spring.
Waiting for our wooden wedding,
Golly, how the bees will buzz!
Spreading pollen o'er the flowers—
We can do what a bee can does.
You shall have on every anniversary
A present we can pay for later;
Maybe a tenant for the nursery,
Or a self-adjusting incinerator.
Waiting for our wooden wedding,
Golly, what a spell we'll weave;
You can cook a biscuit, maybe I can risk it
On our wooden wedding eve.

VENUS: (*Her face troubled*) Rodney, I hope I'll be the right kind of wife for you.

RODNEY: Why shouldn't you be?

VENUS: I can't sew, or weave, or milk a goat.

RODNEY: When I get through with you, you'll be an A Number One homebody! (*Pushing her gently to bedroom door*) Hurry up and dress now—I want to walk down Fifth Avenue and show you off to everybody!

VENUS: (*As she exits*) Darling!

RODNEY: Yes?

VENUS: (*From bedroom*) What will it be like—you and I—in five years?

RODNEY: (*Taking his jacket out of closet*) Why, we'll be an old married couple—like Blondie and Dagwood in the funny papers. Say, that reminds me—I missed reading them for two whole days now.

VENUS: We'll know what to expect every minute, won't we?

RODNEY: (*Surveying himself in mirror*) Sure, you won't have to worry about a thing. You won't have time—before you know, it'll be seven o'clock and hubby'll be coming up the stoop . . .

VENUS: Won't you ever be late, or early?

RODNEY: (*Taking his hat from closet*) No siree! I'm as punctual as clockwork! I like everything on the dot.

VENUS: I'm nervous. I might get restless.

RODNEY: Oh, you'll settle down, after the second set of twins arrive.

VENUS: How do you know you won't take me for granted?

RODNEY: I know Rodney Hatch.

VENUS: Do you think I'll be able to compete with the evening paper?

RODNEY: After Dick Tracy—you'll come first.

VENUS: I keep wondering, darling—if you see me every day, will you want to see me every night?

RODNEY: Sure, married people are all the same, aren't they?

VENUS: I've never been able to *be* like everybody else.

RODNEY: Don't worry. Ozone Heights will change all that . . .

(*The lights fade, the hotel room disappears. As the lights come on again, we see three identical suburban doorways.* VENUS, *in housewifely garments, is seated in front of the center doorway, caught in her own conception of domesticity*)

BALLET: (*"Venus In Ozone Heights"*)

(*The life of Ozone Heights closes in on her—the neighbors, the children;* RODNEY *dividing his attention between the lawnmower and the comics. Stealthily, the creatures of her magic world invade the scene. She resists them, but they will not be resisted; now Ancient Greece is real, and Ozone Heights the myth.* RODNEY *vanishes, the humdrum houses vanish, only the vast open sky remains.* VENUS, *once again the goddess, returns to her people*)

Curtain

SCENE 4

The Main Gallery of the Foundation, the same as Act One, Scene 1, except that the pedestal in the niche is empty.

SAVORY *is seated, his hands bound behind his back.* ZUVETLI *stands over him, eyeing him impatiently.*

ZUVETLI: Come, come, Mr. Savory. Must I spatter you all over this charming museum of yours? I had supposed you a civilized person, a man of the world. Either you will tell me the whereabouts of the goddess—(*Indicating silk scarf in his hands*)—or I shall be forced to cut off your supply of oxygen.

SAVORY: I tell you again, I don't know!

ZUVETLI: Oh dear, oh dear, why must you make it so difficult for both of us? Surely you don't think I look forward to seeing your face turn black and your eyeballs leap from your head! (*Two* ANATOLIANS *force* RODNEY *on and thrust him down beside* SAVORY) Well, where did you find him?

FIRST ANATOLIAN: At the hotel—he was alone.

ZUVETLI: (*To* RODNEY) Where is she?

RODNEY: If I knew, do you think I'd tell you?

ZUVETLI: Hold your tongue, you dog! Your master merely stole our goddess—you have sullied her! Your punishment is long overdue! Pin his arms, Zorab!

(*As the man grips* RODNEY'S *arms and* ZUVETLI *raises his dagger to strike, there is a clap of thunder and the lights black out. A moment of darkness and the lights return.* ZUVETLI *and his followers are gone—and standing on the pedestal is the statue of* VENUS. RODNEY *and* SAVORY *stagger to their feet, look about in bewilderment*)

SAVORY: Where are they?

RODNEY: They're gone!

(*He turns, stands transfixed as he sees the statue.* SAVORY'S *eyes follow his*)

SAVORY: (*Regarding the statue reverently*) It's a masterpiece, Hatch—but it doesn't do her justice.

RODNEY: (*Bitterly*) She never even said good-by to me.

SAVORY: Don't feel badly. We were both very lucky that she stayed as long as she did.

RODNEY: Thanks for saying it, Mr. Savory–but–but–that's a lot of applesauce.

(MOLLY, *clad in bathrobe and slippers, appears in doorway, dabbing her eyes with a towel*)

MOLLY: Mercy me! Can't a girl even take a bath in this foolish place without being struck in the tub by lightning?

SAVORY: Take a firm grip on the floor. We've got a surprise for you.

MOLLY: After five years with you, Butch, nothing could surprise me. (SAVORY *points to statue*) Oh!–(*To* RODNEY *with genuine sympathy*) She was the nicest goddess I ever met.

SAVORY: (*Drops a friendly arm about* RODNEY'S *shoulder*) Come along, old man. You're going to drink a bottle of brandy while I eat crow.

RODNEY: I . . . I'll be along in a minute . . . (SAVORY *and* MOLLY *exit*) Why did you leave? You said I'd never be alone again . . . (*He sings*)

Speak low, darling, speak low,
Love is a spark,
Lost in the dark,
Too soon, too soon.
I wait, darling, I wait–

(*A* GIRL *enters. Her clothes are simple, and she has an attractive, awkward grace; she might be* VENUS' *country cousin. She carries a straw suitcase*)

GIRL: Oh–excuse me. Can you tell me where I register for the Art Course?

RODNEY: (*Looks at statue–then at* GIRL) Why–sure . . . Where do you come from?

GIRL: Ozone Heights.

RODNEY: Do you like it there?

GIRL: I wouldn't think of living any place else.

RODNEY: My name is Rodney Hatch.

GIRL: Mine is–

RODNEY: (*Going quickly to her*) You don't have to tell me. I know.

(*He takes suitcase from her and offers her his arm. She takes his arm, their eyes never leaving each other, and as they start off . . .*)

Curtain

One Touch of Venus

(*Opposite*) Venus (Mary Martin) sings "That's Him." (*This page, above*) Venus (Mary Martin) is about to temporarily liquidate Gloria (Ruth Bond) in Rodney's barbershop. (*Left*) Venus (Mary Martin) and Rodney Hatch (Kenny Baker) speak low and lovingly. *Pictures, Theatre Collection, New York Public Library*

Venus (Mary Martin) and Company in the "Forty Minutes for Lunch" Ballet.
Theatre Collection, New York Public Library

Brigadoon

"The Heather on the Hill" (David Brooks, Marion Bell).
Theatre Collection, New York Public Library

(*Left*) Mr. Lundie (William Hansen) welcomes Tommy (David Brooks) back to Brigadoon as Jeff (George Keane) looks on. *Theatre Collection, New York Public Library*. (*Below*) Fiona (Marion Bell), Tommy (David Brooks) and Jeff (George Keane) listen as Mr. Lundie (William Hansen) relates the miracle of Brigadoon. *Theatre Collection, New York Public Library*

The Wedding Dance celebrating the nuptials of Jean MacLaren (Virginia Bosler) and Charlie Dalrymple (Lee Sullivan). *Theatre Collection, New York Public Library*

(*This page, above*) Bianca (Lisa Kirk) and Lucentio (Harold Lang). *Graphic House*. (*Opposite, top*) Lilli Vanessi (Patricia Morison) and Fred Graham (Alfred Drake) are the center of attention as they portray Katherine and Petruchio in a musicalized "Taming of the Shrew." *Theatre Collection, New York Public Library*. (*Opposite, below*) Katherine gets the paddling of her life from Petruchio. (Alfred Drake, Patricia Morison and "The Taming of the Shrew" Company). *Graphic House*

Kiss Me, Kate

Lilli Vanessi (Patricia Morison) and Fred Graham (Alfred Drake) recall "Wunderbar." *Graphic House*

BRIGADOON

Book and Lyrics by Alan Jay Lerner
Music by Frederick Loewe

Production Notes

Brigadoon was first presented by Cheryl Crawford at the Ziegfeld Theatre, New York, on March 13, 1947. The cast was as follows:

Tommy Albright, *David Brooks*
Jeff Douglas, *George Keane*
Archie Beaton, *Elliott Sullivan*
Harry Beaton, *James Mitchell*
Fishmonger, *Bunty Kelley*
Angus MacGuffie, *Walter Scheff*
Sandy Dean, *Hayes Gordon*
Andrew MacLaren, *Edward Cullen*
Fiona MacLaren, *Marion Bell*
Jean MacLaren, *Virginia Bosler*
Meg Brockie, *Pamela Britton*
Charlie Dalrymple, *Lee Sullivan*
Maggie Anderson, *Lidija Franklin*
Mr. Lundie, *William Hansen*
Sword Dancers, *Roland Guerard, George Drake*
Frank, *John Paul*
Jane Ashton, *Frances Charles*
Bagpipers, *James MacFadden, Arthur Horn*
Stuart Dalrymple, *Delbert Anderson*
MacGregor, *Earl Redding*

Townsfolk of Brigadoon

Directed by *Robert Lewis*
Choreography by *Agnes de Mille*
Scenery by *Oliver Smith*
Costumes by *David Ffolkes*
Lighting by *Peggy Clark*
Orchestrations by *Ted Royal*
Musical Director: *Franz Allers*

Act One

Scene 1: A forest in the Scottish Highlands.
About five on a May in the morning.
Interlude: A road in the town of Brigadoon.
A few minutes later.
Scene 2: The square of Brigadoon–MacConnachy Square.
Later that morning.
Scene 3: The Brockie open shed.
Just past noon.
Scene 4: The MacLaren house.
Midafternoon.
Scene 5: Outside the house of Mr. Lundie.
Immediately following.
Scene 6: Outside the kirk of Brigadoon.
Dusk.

Act Two

Scene 1: A forest inside Brigadoon.
Later that night.
Scene 2: On the way from the forest.
A few minutes later.
Scene 3: The glen.
Soon after.
Scene 4: A bar in New York City.
Four months later.
Scene 5: The forest (same as Act One, Scene 1).
Three nights later.

Musical Numbers

Prologue

Once in the Highlands	Chorus
Act One	
Scene 1:	
Brigadoon	Chorus
Scene 2:	
Down on MacConnachy Square	Sandy, Meg, and Townsfolk
Waitin' for My Dearie	Fiona and Girls
I'll Go Home with Bonnie Jean	Charlie and Townsfolk
Dance	Maggie, Harry, and Dancers
The Heather on the Hill	Tommy and Fiona
Down on MacConnachy Square	Townsfolk (*Reprise*)
Scene 3:	
The Love of My Life	Meg
Scene 4:	
Jeannie's Packin' Up	Girls
Come to Me, Bend to Me	Charlie
Dance	Jean and Dancers
Almost Like Being in Love	Tommy and Fiona
Wedding Dance	Jean, Charlie, and Dancers
Sword Dance	Harry and Dancers
Act Two	
Scene 1:	
The Chase	Men of Brigadoon
Scene 2:	
There but for You Go I	Tommy

Scene 3:

My Mother's Weddin' Day	Meg and Townsfolk
Funeral Dance	Maggie
From This Day On	Tommy and Fiona
Brigadoon	Chorus (*Reprise*)

Scene 4:

Come to Me, Bend to Me	Fiona (*Reprise*)
The Heather on the Hill	Fiona (*Reprise*)
I'll Go Home with Bonnie Jean	Charlie and Townsfolk (*Reprise*)
From This Day On	Fiona and Tommy (*Reprise*)
Down on MacConnachy Square	Townsfolk (*Reprise*)

Scene 5:

Finale

PROLOGUE

Near the end of the overture, when the house curtain is up, the music fades down and a singing chorus is heard.

CHORUS:

Once in the Highlands, the Highlands of Scotland,
Deep in the night on a murky brae;
There in the Highlands, the Highlands of Scotland,
Two weary hunters lost their way.
And this is what happened,
The strange thing that happened
To two weary hunters who lost their way.

(*The music fades gradually out and the play begins.*)

ACT ONE

SCENE 1

A forest in the Highlands of Scotland.
About five in the morning.

The forest is dipped in the deep gray that comes between night and morning. As the scene progresses, the gray lightens in shade.

TOMMY ALBRIGHT *and* JEFF DOUGLAS *are discovered on stage.* TOMMY *is about thirty. He is of medium height, virile looking, with an attractive but sensitive face. He is dressed in tweeds.*

JEFF *is about the same age. He is retiring, and good-natured primarily because he doesn't care. He is in gray flannels and a tweed jacket.*

At this moment, JEFF *is seated on what appears to be a rucksack sort of affair. Next to him are lying two rifles.* JEFF *is lookat a map.*

TOMMY: (*Taking the map*) Here! Let me see that map. (*Points to a spot on the map*) Here's Auchintoul.

JEFF: As I remember, that should be on the left, and I don't remember.

TOMMY: It is. (*Points to another spot*) And here's Braemore.

JEFF: Should be on the right.

TOMMY: It is. Now where the hell are we?

JEFF: What's in the middle?

TOMMY: Nothing.

JEFF: That's where we are.

TOMMY: In nothing?

JEFF: Yes. And for a fellow with my potentialities, this is an ideal location. We'll find our way out when the sun comes up.

TOMMY: (*Putting the map in his pocket*) A fine couple of game hunters we are. We come all the way over here from New York, and the first night out we get lost.

JEFF: Maybe we took the high road instead of the low road. (*Taking a flask from his inside pocket*) Would you like a drink?

TOMMY: No, thanks.

JEFF: Good. That leaves more for me. (*He unscrews the top*)

TOMMY: Didn't you tell me you were going to cut down on that stuff?

JEFF: Yes, I did. But I'm a terrible liar. Besides, it doesn't pay. I remember one time I was going with a wonderful girl and she used to plead with me and plead with me to give it up. So one day I did. Then we discovered we had nothing more to talk about so we broke up.

TOMMY: (*Not really listening to him*) There's something about this forest that gives me the feeling of being in a cathedral.

JEFF: If we were, I'd know where the exit was.

TOMMY: You don't believe in anything, do you?

JEFF: Of course I do.

TOMMY: Really? What?

JEFF: Practically anything I can understand; you know—anything that's real to me. Like things I can touch, taste, hear, see, smell, and . . . (*Indicates the flask*) . . . swallow. (*He takes a swig*)

TOMMY: What about the things you don't understand?

JEFF: I dismiss them.

TOMMY: That makes everything very easy, doesn't it?

JEFF: Comfortable is the word. (*He puts the flask on the ground*)

TOMMY: I envy you.

JEFF: Why?

TOMMY: You seem to be very satisfied.

JEFF: I am. Aren't you?

TOMMY: No, I'm not.

JEFF: That's the silliest thing I've ever heard. You've got a fine job and you're engaged to a fine girl, and you're lost in a fine forest. What more do you want?

TOMMY: I don't know. But something seems wrong, especially about Jane and me. And that makes everything seem wrong. Look how I postpone getting married. I just can't get myself to that altar.

JEFF: I don't know what could be wrong about it. She's young, attractive, fits smack into your niche in life; and on top of that she loves you. And just the proper amount, too.

TOMMY: What's the proper amount?

JEFF: Enough to make you happy and not enough to embarrass your friends.

TOMMY: It looks ideal, doesn't it? But why don't I see it? I must be lacking somewhere.

JEFF: Now don't start talking yourself into an inferiority. You don't deserve it.

TOMMY: What do you mean?

JEFF: Well, most of my friends who have inferiority complexes are absolutely right. They're *not* as good as everyone else. But someone like you who . . .

(*At this moment the distant hum of voices is heard offstage. They are humming "Brigadoon"*)

TOMMY: Wait a minute. (JEFF *is silent*) Do you hear that?

JEFF: Uh-huh!

TOMMY: Ssh!

(*The offstage voices slowly, very slowly become more audible. They are heard under the following sequence:*)

CHORUS:

Brigadoon, Brigadoon,
Blooming under sable skies,
Brigadoon, Brigadoon,
There my heart forever lies.
Let the world grow cold around us;
Let the heavens cry above!
Brigadoon, Brigadoon,
In thy valley there'll be love.

TOMMY: (*Pointing out*) Look over there!

JEFF: It looks like a village.

TOMMY: It is.

JEFF: But I thought you said there were no towns listed on the map around here.

TOMMY: I did. (*Points*) Look. See where that village is? There's a peculiar heavy fog all around it.

JEFF: And there's no other mist in the valley.

TOMMY: Only around that village. Let's walk over to it. It can't be very far from here. Come on!

(JEFF *runs back for his flask and then moves to follow* TOMMY *off*)

JEFF: Wait till Rand McNally hears about this!

Curtain

INTERLUDE

The scene is a road in the town of Brigadoon. The gray of dawn is gradually changing into day. Figures are seen coming along the road. They are in simple Scottish peasant garb. Some are carrying baskets, some of them have jugs of ale on their shoulders, some have long sticks with meat and/or fish hanging from them. The music continues under.

MAN: (*Entering–calling off*)

Come all to the square!

GIRL:

The market square!

GIRL 2:
The market fair!

MAN 2: (*Carrying meat*)
Salted meat I'm sellin' there!
At the fair, laddie!

MAN 3:
Come ye to the fair!

MAN 4:
Ale for sale or barter there!
At the fair, laddie!
(GIRL 3 *joins him in this*)

GIRL 4:
Come all ye down!

GIRL 5:
Ye in the town!

MAN:
Come ye from the hills!

MAN 5:
Wool 'n' cloth I'm sellin' there!
At the square, laddie!

MAN:
Come ye from the mills!

GIRL:
Come all ye there!

GIRL 2:
Come all ye there!

MAN:
Come ye to the fair!

ALL:
Come ye, all ye ev'rywhere
To the fair!

The Lights Dim Out

SCENE 2

The Square of Brigadoon—MacConnachy Square.

Physically, this is an eighteenth-century-looking community. It was the custom in Scotland then for a fair to be held once a week. At these fairs the townsfolk engaged in mutual buying, selling, and bartering. This, then, is the activity of the moment. In the rear is a series of low huts. Painted high on the center hut is the name "MacConnachy Square." The buying, however, is done from a series of booths and carts. The booths are not unlike contest booths at our amusement parks. The carts are the usual thing but with a square rigging over which is hung the merchandise.

Downstage right is a milk and cream booth presided over by a middle-thirtied Scot named ANGUS MAC GUFFIE. *In front of the booth downstage right is a wooden bench. In the center upstage is a candy booth run by another young Scot,* SANDY DEAN. *Downstage left is a weaving cart covered with wools, plaids, and the like. This cart is operated by a kind-looking Scot about fifty, named* ARCHIE BEATON. *There is a straight wooden chair next to the cart. Standing next to it with a book under his arm is Archie's son,* HARRY BEATON. HARRY *is about twenty-four. He is a slender, extremely sensitive-looking lad.*

The time is about nine in the morning.

Groups of three and four are filling the stage. Most of the women carry baskets. All are singing. As the song continues, the stage fills till it becomes a beehive of activity.

TOWNSFOLK: (*Sing*) (*"Down on MacConnachy Square"*)

Come ye from the hills!
Come ye from the mills!
Come ye in the glen,
Come ye, bairn,
Come ye, men!
Come ye from the loom!
Come from pail an' broom!
Hear ye ev'rywhere:
Don't ye ken
There's a fair
Down on MacConnachy Square?

(*Through the bustle of the crowd a young lass,* MAGGIE ANDERSON, *skips flirtatiously near* HARRY BEATON, *trying to catch his eye.* HARRY *looks at her disdainfully and then sits on a stool next to his father's booth and opens his book.* MAGGIE *skips away into the crowd.*

On the other side of the square ANGUS MAC GUFFIE'S *assistant,* MEG BROCKIE, *appears carrying jugs and milk pails.* MEG *is a brash, buxom girl in her mid-twenties*)

MEG: (*Sings*)

I'm sellin' a bit o' milk an' cream.
Come sip it an' ye will vow
That this is the finest milk an' cream
That ever came out a cow.
Though finest it is, the price is small.
With milk an' the cream, alack,
There's nothin' to do but sell it all.
The cow winna take it back.

SANDY: (*Sings*)

Now all of ye come to Sandy here,
Come over to Sandy's booth.
I'm sellin' the sweetest candy here
That ever shook loose a tooth.
I eat it myself an' there's no doubt
'Tis creamy an' good an' thick.
So, laddies, I hope ye'll buy me out—
'Tis makin' me kind o' sick.

TOWNSFOLK: (*Sing*)

Come ye from the loom!
Come from pail an' broom!
Hear ye ev'rywhere:
Don't ye ken
There's a fair
Down on MacConnachy Square?

(*Now the full chorus sings. Half sing the melody sung by* SANDY *and* MEG. *The rest sing the main theme*)

HALF:

Come all ye down from in the hills,
An' all of ye in the glen!
Come all of ye down from in the mills,
An' all of ye bairns an' men!
Come all of ye from the weavin' loom!
Come all of ye to the square!
Come all of ye from your pail an' broom!
Come all of ye to the fair!

HALF:

Come ye from the hills!
Come ye from the mills!
Come ye in the glen,

Come ye, bairn,
Come ye, men!

ALL THE TOWNSFOLK:
Come ye from the loom!
Come from pail an' broom!
Hear ye ev'rywhere:
Don't ye ken
There's a fair
Down on MacConnachy Square?

(*At the conclusion, the* TOWNSFOLK *sing the chorus again. Now the stage empties a bit. The rest continue their shopping. A few shoppers gather around* ARCHIE'S *cart as* ARCHIE *calls:*)

ARCHIE: Woolens! Come, Harry! Plaids! (*To* HARRY) Come, Harry. Put down your book an' help your father. (HARRY *looks up and sullenly closes the book*) Ye may even get to like the weavin' business.

HARRY: (*Rising and standing next to him*) I'll never like the weavin' business, Father. An' ye know it well.

ARCHIE: Try, lad. Tell Angus MacGuffie we need some eggs. I'll give 'im enough wool for a pair of trousers for enough eggs for our dinner.

(HARRY, *who has picked up a piece of cloth to show, throws it down and walks across the stage to* ANGUS' *milk and cream booth.* ARCHIE *addresses one of the women around the cart.*

MR. ANDREW MAC LAREN *and his two daughters,* FIONA *and* JEAN, *enter upstage left and move down toward* ARCHIE'S *cart.* MR. MAC LAREN *is a hardy soul in his late fifties. He is a bit pompous and has a loud and gruff voice.* FIONA *is about twenty-two or -three. As we become acquainted with her we discover she is bright, has a gentle sense of humor, and is completely frank and direct, to a point that is often quite disarming. She is graceful and altogether lovely.* JEAN *is about eighteen. She is also attractive but obviously shy and diffident. She seldom stands alone. She is either clinging to her father or* FIONA. *As they make their way through the shoppers, they nod good morning, to which the* TOWNSFOLK *nod and bid them good morning in response.* FIONA *is carrying a basket,* MR. MAC LAREN *a large piece of parchment*)

ARCHIE: Good mornin' to ye, Mr. MacLaren.

MR. MAC LAREN: Good day, Archie. (*He stands for a moment looking over the parchment*)

ARCHIE: An' good mornin' to your two bonnie daughters.

FIONA: (*Beginning to rummage through the cloth on the cart*) Good mornin', Mr. Beaton.

JEAN: Good mornin', Mr. Beaton.

ARCHIE: What would ye be lookin' for, Miss Fiona?

FIONA: A waistcoat for my father for the weddin'.

ARCHIE: (*He looks over at his son,* HARRY) Why, of course! Ye an' young Charlie Dalrymple are gettin' married this evenin', aren't ye, Miss Jean?

JEAN: (*Sighing*) Aye, Mr. Beaton.

ARCHIE: Well, if ye had to choose someone other than my son, Harry, I'm glad 'tis a lad as fine as Charlie.

JEAN: Aye, Mr. Beaton.

ARCHIE: Ye mus' be happy as a lark in the glen.

JEAN: Aye, Mr. Beaton.

FIONA: (*Smiling*) As ye see, Mr. Beaton, Jean is a wee bit short of words today.

MR. MAC LAREN: (*Looking up from the parchment*) An' 'tis just as well ye dinna talk too much. When a lass gets married, she mus' get used to listenin' an' not talkin'.

ARCHIE: I dinna think Charlie'll have trouble with Miss Jean, here. She's a good maiden.

MR. MAC LAREN: Archie, *all* maidens are good. So then tell me where all the bad wives come from. (*He walks center.* FIONA *and* JEAN *go back to rummaging*) Friends! (*Everyone turns his attention to* MR. MAC LAREN) Mr. Lundie has written upon this parchment a few reminders. He asked me to hang it in the public square where ye all can see it . . . an' be reminded.

TOWNSFOLK: Aye!

MR. MAC LAREN: This is the second day of our blessing. An' this is to remind ye of the obligations we have so gratefully accepted.

TOWNSFOLK: Aye!

MR. MAC LAREN: An' so I shall hang it in the square . . . as I told Mr. Lundie I would.

(*He walks upstage and high on one of the huts tacks the parchment. A few gather around and read it. He pauses and engages in quiet conversation as* FIONA *turns back to the cart*)

ARCHIE: (*Good-humoredly*) Your father likes to take charge o' things, doesn't he, Miss Fiona?

FIONA: (*Smiling*) Aye! Especially after everythin's been done.

(*She picks up a swatch of cloth*) Would ye have a waistcoat of this that would fit 'im?

ARCHIE: I think so, Miss Fiona.

(*He starts to look through the cart.* HARRY *crosses back to the cart*)

JEAN: Hello, Harry.

HARRY: Hello, Jean.

JEAN: (*A little self-consciously*) How are ye today?

HARRY: How do ye expect me to be? This is your weddin' day, isn't it?

JEAN: (*Putting her hand on* HARRY'S *arm*) I'm truly sorry, Harry.

HARRY: (*Pulling his arm away*) Well, dinna be. If anybody's goin' to pity me, let it be me; trapped forever without ye in this peasant village.

ARCHIE: What did Angus say, Harry?

HARRY: I forgot.

FIONA: Hello, Harry.

HARRY: Hello, Fiona. (*To* JEAN) It jus' isn't fair for Charlie Dalrymple to be weddin' ye, Jean. He got everythin': school in Edinburgh an' now ye. An' I got nothin'.

ARCHIE: Harry, take this material to the house an' see if there's a waistcoat of it there.

HARRY: (*Indicating his father, who is holding out the material*) Nothin' but to be doin' this all my life.

ARCHIE: An' why dinna ye pay attention to Maggie Anderson? Ye know she has a yearnin' fer ye.

HARRY: Aye, Father! (*He exits left.* JEAN *turns to* FIONA *almost in tears*)

JEAN: Oh, Fiona, I feel so sorry for 'im.

FIONA: I know, darlin'.

JEAN: Mr. Beaton, ye dinna hate me for not lovin' Harry, do ye?

ARCHIE: No, Miss Jean. 'Tis not your fault. I sometimes think that the only woman that could have loved Harry an' helped 'im was his mother, rest her soul.

MR. MAC LAREN: (*Coming down*) Come, Jean. Ye stay with your father today. (JEAN *takes his arm*) An', Fiona, ye'll be certain to buy everythin' that's needed for the weddin' supper.

FIONA: I will, Father.

MR. MAC LAREN: Remember, jus' what's needed. My aim on this

occasion is to be hospitable—not philanthropic. (JEAN *and* MR. MAC LAREN *exit up left*)

FIONA: (*Calling over to* ARCHIE) Ye'll send the waistcoat to the house, Mr. Beaton?

ARCHIE: Aye, Miss Fiona.

(FIONA *is heading toward the milk and cream booth*)

MEG: Good mornin', Fiona.

FIONA: Hello, Meg. A jug o' cream, please.

(*During the following* MEG *hands her the jug,* FIONA *puts it in her basket and hands* MEG *a coin*)

MEG: Mr. MacGuffie will be pleased 'tis a lass buyin' for a change.

FIONA: Why?

MEG: When the lads come shoppin', they look so braw I dinna like to ask 'em for money.

FIONA: But ye'll never make a profit doin' that!

MEG: Aye! But I make a lot o' friends. (MEG *starts leaving the booth and coming around to* FIONA) Is this for the weddin' tonight?

FIONA: Aye.

MEG: Fiona, when are ye goin' to think about marriage for yourself?

FIONA: Oh, when I find someone who makes me think of it.

MEG: An' ye've never found anyone up till now who made ye think of it?

FIONA: No. Ye see, I dinna want to jus' get married.

(*The music begins under*)

FIONA: I think ye should only do it when ye an' your lad want to stay together fiercely an' gettin' married is the only way ye can do it that's proper.

MEG: That's an unusual idea, Fiona.

(FIONA *seats herself on a stool near the center and explains*)

FIONA: (*Sings "Waitin' for My Dearie"*)

Many a lassie as everyone knows 'll
Try to be married before twenty-five.
So she'll agree to 'most any proposal,
All he mus' be is a man an' alive.

I hold a dream an' there's no compromisin';
I know there's one certain laddie for me.
One day he'll come walkin' o'er the horizon;
But should he not, then an old maid I'll be.

Foolish ye may say.
Foolish I will stay.
Waitin' for my dearie
An' happy am I
To hold my heart till he comes strollin' by.

When he comes, my dearie,
One look an' I'll know
That he's the dearie I've been wantin' so.

Though I'll live forty lives
Till the day he arrives
I'll not ever, ever grieve.
For my hopes will be high
That he'll come strollin' by;
For ye see, I believe

That there's a laddie weary
An' wanderin' free
Who's waitin' for his dearie:
Me!

(EIGHT GIRLS *have surrounded* FIONA *and now sing with her as she repeats the chorus*)

GIRLS:
What do ye do while ye're waitin' around
For your lad to come your way?

FIONA:
Well, when no one is lookin' ye kneel on the ground
An' ye pray an' pray an' pray!

GIRLS:
But when lassies sit an' have no men,
Oh, how long becomes the night!

FIONA:
But I fear the night is longer when
The lad's not right.
Waitin' for my dearie
Is sweeter to me
Than wooin' any laddie on the lea.

FIONA and GIRLS:
Dreamin' of your dearie
An' idlin' the day

FIONA:

That's how I am an' how I'll ever stay.

Though I'll live forty lives
Till the day he arrives
I'll not ever, ever grieve.
For my hopes will be high
That he'll come strollin' by;
For ye see, I believe

That

FIONA and GIRLS:

There's a laddie weary
An' wanderin' free
Who's waitin' for his dearie:

FIONA:

Me!

(*At the conclusion of the song the orchestra reaches a climax and then continues under softly for a few seconds as* FIONA *picks up her basket to get along. Then the music stops abruptly as* TOMMY *and* JEFF *enter from upstage left. They walk downstage center slowly looking at everyone and everything in amazement and curiosity. Everyone stares back at them. There is an awkward moment of silence. Then—*)

TOMMY: Hello! (*A few murmur a reserved hello in response*)

JEFF: (*After another pause*) Could you tell us where we are?

ARCHIE: Of course we can tell ye. Ye're in Brigadoon.

TOMMY: Brigadoon?

ARCHIE: Aye.

TOMMY: That's funny. There's no town called Brigadoon on the map.

ARCHIE: I shouldna be surprised.

JEFF: You mean you know it isn't on the map?

ARCHIE: Aye.

JEFF: It's a little snobbish of you, don't you think?

TOMMY: Why isn't it on the map?

ARCHIE: For good an' sound reasons.

JEFF: (*To* MEG) What are you all dressed up for? Is this the day you take pictures for postcards?

MEG: We're not dressed up.

JEFF: You mean you always walk around with all these clothes on?

MEG: No!

TOMMY: (*A little impatiently*) Now come on. Somebody. What's going on here? What is this?

MEG: We're havin' a fair.

TOMMY: Oh! (*Seeing the cream booth*) Is that milk you're selling there?

ANGUS: Aye.

TOMMY: Can I buy some? I'm thirsty. We've been walking all night.

ANGUS: I'll have to see your money first.

TOMMY: What?

(*He stops, then shrugs and tosses* ANGUS *a coin.* ANGUS *takes it, and before* TOMMY *can move any nearer the booth, a group gathers quickly around* ANGUS *examining the coin. Exclamations of "Oh" and "Ah" and "Look at the date" and "Nineteen hundred and—" come from the group*)

JEFF: (*As he and* TOMMY *look at each other in amazement*) What did you give him, a hunk of uranium?

TOMMY: Just a shilling. What a loony layout this is!

ANGUS: (*Handing* TOMMY *the coin*) 'Tis very interestin', sir, but it does me no good.

TOMMY: (*A little irritated*) What do you mean it does you no good? Sell me something and it will.

ANGUS: I'm sorry, but I canna sell you anythin'. However, if ye're thirsty I'll *give* ye some milk.

TOMMY: Never mind. I don't want any favors.

MEG: (*To* TOMMY) I see from the coin ye're from England.

TOMMY: No, we're from America.

MEG: Ye're Americans?

JEFF: (*Takes* TOMMY *by the arm*) I am. He's from Georgia. Come on, boy. We're out of our element.

FIONA: (*Coming to them quickly*) No! Wait! Please! (TOMMY *and* JEFF *turn to her*) We dinna mean to act so strangely. We're jus' a wee bit taken back. People dinna come here very often.

TOMMY: I can understand why. You people stare at us as if we'd just dropped in from another world. (*At this* MEG *begins to giggle.* TOMMY *looks at her*) Does that amuse you?

MEG: (*Still giggling*) Aye. Very much.

FIONA: Quiet, Meg.

JEFF: (*Indicating* MEG) Obviously the daughter of two first cousins.

FIONA: If ye've been walkin' all night, ye mus' be tired an' hungry. Winna ye like somethin' to eat an' perhaps a place to lie down afore ye start back?

TOMMY: That's very nice of you. Thank you.

FIONA: Good! Oh! (*She holds out her hand to* TOMMY) My name is Fiona MacLaren.

TOMMY: (*Taking her hand*) Mine is Tommy Albright. (*They look at each other for a moment*) And this is Jeff Douglas.

FIONA: (*Withdrawing her hand*) How do ye do, sir?

MEG: (*Enthusiastically*) I'm Meg Brockie!

JEFF: I'm glad you're happy about it.

FIONA: There's a little tavern on the next street where ye can get some food.

MEG: (*Quickly taking* JEFF'S *arm*) I'll take ye to it.

TOMMY: Go ahead. I'll be along in a minute. I want to call the inn first. (*He looks around him as* JEFF *and* MEG *start off left*)

ARCHIE: (*As they pass his cart*) Is Miss Meg going to take care of ye, sir?

JEFF: I think so. Why?

ARCHIE: Well, I have some plaid trousers here, an' after ye leave the tavern if Miss Meg should take ye someplace to rest an' ye should happen to rip your own on a thistle, I'd be more than pleased to replace them for ye.

JEFF: Thanks, old man, but I don't expect to get stuck.

ARCHIE: (*Chuckling*) Laddie, ye dinna know it, but ye're stuck now.

MEG: Ye tend to your sellin', Mr. Beaton.

(*She and* JEFF *exit left.* TOMMY, *who has been roaming around, returns to* FIONA)

TOMMY: What a place! Is there a phone around here?

FIONA: A phone?

TOMMY: Yes.

FIONA: I dinna think we have one.

TOMMY: No phone?

FIONA: No, sir.

TOMMY: Tell me. What's so strange about this place?

(CHARLIE DALRYMPLE *enters upstage right. He is a sandy-haired youth in his early twenties. He greets the few around him as he comes on*)

FIONA: Nothin', sir. Ye're the one who's . . .

ANGUS: (*Calling upstage to* CHARLIE) Charlie! Here's a bottle o' claret. Have a dram o' good luck with me.

FIONA: Well, the merry bridegroom himself!

TOMMY: Bridegroom?

FIONA: Aye.

CHARLIE: Good mornin', darlin'. (*Kisses her on the forehead*)

FIONA: He's marryin' my sister this evenin'.

TOMMY: Oh!

CHARLIE: (*To* TOMMY) Good mornin', sir.

TOMMY: Good morning.

FIONA: Charlie, this is Tommy Albright. He jus' happened in a little while ago.

CHARLIE: What? Oh! Why, of course. Welcome to ye, sir.

TOMMY: Thanks. Welcome to you.

(ANGUS *walks around with a jug and a couple of glasses and hands one to* CHARLIE)

ANGUS: Here's your dram, Charlie.

CHARLIE: Thank ye, Angus.

ANGUS: (*To* TOMMY) An' how about ye, sir? Some claret?

TOMMY: Thanks. (*He takes the offered cup*)

CHARLIE: I think I'll drink this one to Mr. Forsythe. I jus' hope he knows how grateful I am to 'im for postponin' the miracle for me.

TOMMY: (*To* FIONA) The what?

FIONA: Ssh!

CHARLIE: An' may God bless me this evenin' as much as I would bless Him if I were He an' He were Charles Dalrymple.

TOMMY: What did you say about postponin' a miracle?

CHARLIE: Oh! 'Tis a toast we have here.

FIONA: Take it down. I'll explain it to ye sometime.

TOMMY: (*Drinks*) Say, that's wonderful. (*To* ANGUS) May I have another?

ANGUS: That was a weddin' gesture, sir. From now on, 'tis for sale only.

FIONA: I mus' buy some claret for the supper. Come with me an' ye can have some more.

TOMMY: Fine.

(FIONA *moves to exit right and* TOMMY *follows.* ARCHIE *calls to him*)

ARCHIE: Woolens! Plaids!

(TOMMY *and* FIONA *exit*)

ANGUS: He's an odd lad, isn't he?

CHARLIE: Aye. He has a peculiar accent.

ANGUS: I wonder what American women mus' be like.

CHARLIE: I dinna wonder about women any more, Angus. I'm not allowed to.

ANGUS: Why, that's right, Charlie. Ye're through with the lasses for good, aren't ye?

(*The music begins softly*)

CHARLIE: (*Sings "I'll Go Home with Bonnie Jean"*)

I used to be a rovin' lad.
A rovin' an' wanderin' life I had.
On any lass I'd frown
Who would try to tie me down,
But then one day I saw a maid
Who held out her hand an' I stayed an' stayed.
An' now, across the green,
I'll go home with bonnie Jean.

CHARLIE and TOWNSFOLK:

Go home, go home, go home with bonnie Jean!
Go home, go home, I'll go home with bonnie Jean!

CHARLIE:

I used to have a hundred friends;
But when ye are wedded the friendship ends.
They never come to call,
So farewell to one an' all.
Farewell to all the lads I knew;
I'll see them again when they're married too.
For soon, across the green,
I'll go home with bonnie Jean.

CHARLIE and TOWNSFOLK:

Go home, go home, go home with bonnie Jean!
Go home, go home, I'll go home with bonnie Jean!

CHARLIE:

In Aberdeen I used to know
A lass with an air an' her name was Jo;
An' ev'ry night at ten
I would meet her in the glen.
But now I'll not see her again;
Especially not in the glen at ten.
For now across the green,
I'll go home with bonnie Jean.

CHARLIE and TOWNSFOLK:

Go home, go home, go home with bonnie Jean!
Go home, go home, I'll go home with bonnie Jean!

CHARLIE:

Hello to married men I've known.
I'll soon have a wife an' leave yours alone,
A bonnie wife indeed,
An' she'll be all I'll ever need.

With bonnie Jean my days will fly,
An' love her I will till the day I die.
That's why, across the green,
I'll go home with bonnie Jean.

CHARLIE and TOWNSFOLK:

Go home, go home, go home with bonnie Jean!
Go home, go home, I'll go home with bonnie Jean!

(*The music reaches a climax and stops.*
FIONA *and* TOMMY *enter*)

FIONA: Charlie, ye winna forget to come over this afternoon an' sign the family Bible?

CHARLIE: No, I'll be over. (*To* TOMMY) I hope, sir, ye'll stay for the weddin' supper.

TOMMY: Thanks, but I won't be here that long.

CHARLIE: 'Tis a pity.

FIONA: (*As* CHARLIE *moves to go*) What are ye goin' to do all day, Charlie?

CHARLIE: Rest, dearie, rest.

(CHARLIE *exits. The stage begins to empty, leaving a few upstage who continue their shopping quietly. The attention falls on* TOMMY *and* FIONA)

TOMMY: (*Smiling*) He's a nice kid.

FIONA: Aye. He is that.

TOMMY: It's wonderfully refreshing to see a fellow so enthusiastic about getting married.

FIONA: Is it so unusual?

TOMMY: I think it is. Look at me. I'm not bubbling over like Charlie. And next month I'm facing the minister.

FIONA: Ye're gettin' married?

TOMMY: Yes.

FIONA: Oh!

TOMMY: Oh—what?

FIONA: I'm very surprised. Somehow ye dinna look like the sort of lad who would want to settle down.

TOMMY: I didn't say that. I just said I was getting married.

FIONA: If ye feel that way, why are ye?

TOMMY: Because the girl wants to.

FIONA: Is that reason enough?

TOMMY: Sure. I don't know how it is in the Highlands, but in my neighborhood if you've been going with a woman for a while and she decides she wants to get married, you'd better agree right away and save yourself a lot of trouble.

FIONA: Why?

TOMMY: Because if you don't, she'll either torment you so you'll marry her for relief, or she'll be so sweet about it you'll feel guilty and your conscience will make you do it.

FIONA: I mus' say it dinna sound like ye love her very much.

TOMMY: It doesn't, does it?

FIONA: An' it also sounds like a very peculiar land ye come from.

TOMMY: Well, believe me, lass, this isn't the usual hamlet off the highway either. What was that business about Charlie and the man who postponed the miracle?

FIONA: Oh, that. (*Thinks a moment*) I'm sorry. I canna say.

TOMMY: But you said you'd tell me later.

FIONA: I know. But I canna say.

TOMMY: That's fine. You know, if I hang around this town very long I'll probably discover that everybody in it is slightly nutty. Is that possible?

FIONA: I canna say.

TOMMY: Why not?

FIONA: I dinna know what "nutty" means.

TOMMY: It means slightly insane.

FIONA: (*Turning on him suddenly*) Well, then I can assure ye we're all far from insane. We're a most blessed group of people. An' I never realize how fortunate we are until I meet someone from the outside—I mean, a stranger to Brigadoon. I dinna know anythin' about ye, but from the little ye've said I'm quite certain that everythin' ye think I think differently about, an' I'm also quite certain that what I think is much more . . . (*She begins to calm down*) . . . well . . . pleasant. An' now I'm sorry I said all that, but ye angered me when ye called us insane.

TOMMY: (*Quite surprised and a bit sheepish at the outburst*) Hey, you don't like me very much, do you?

FIONA: That's the odd part. I like ye very much. I jus' dinna like anythin' ye say.

TOMMY: (*After a moment*) Fiona . . .

FIONA: Aye?

TOMMY: If I stuck around here today, would you take me to the wedding this evening?

FIONA: Why do ye suddenly want to go?

TOMMY: (*Imitating her*) I canna say.

FIONA: Well, I'll take ye. An' I'll be highly pleased ye'll be there.

TOMMY: You will? Why?

FIONA: Because of what I jus' told ye. I like ye very much.

TOMMY: (*Amused and a little bewildered*) That's right. You did say that, didn't you?

FIONA: Now I'll show ye some place where ye can lie down an' rest.

TOMMY: What are you going to do?

FIONA: Gather some heather for the weddin'.

TOMMY: Where do you do that?

FIONA: On the hill—where the heather is.

TOMMY: May I go with you?

FIONA: No. I'll do it much faster alone.

TOMMY: (*Coming close to her*) I won't bother you. Really. Maybe I'm the one who's slightly nutty, but . . .

(FIONA *walks away from him. The music begins*)

TOMMY: (*Sings "The Heather On The Hill"*)

Can't we two go walkin' together,
Out beyond the valley of trees,
Out where there's a hillside of heather
Curtseyin' gently in the breeze?
That's what I'd like to do:
See the heather—but with you.

The mist of May is in the gloamin',
And all the clouds are holdin' still,
So take my hand and let's go roamin'
Through the heather on the hill.

The mornin' dew is blinkin' yonder;
There's lazy music in the rill;
And all I want to do is wander
Through the heather on the hill.

There may be other days as rich and rare.
There may be other springs as full and fair.
But they won't be the same—they'll come and go;
For this I know:

That when the mist is in the gloamin',
And all the clouds are holdin' still,
If you're not there I won't go roamin'
Through the heather on the hill;
The heather on the hill.
(*The music continues under*)

FIONA: (*A little disconcerted*) Ye see. Ye can say nice things when ye want to.

TOMMY: It almost sounded like I was making love to you, didn't it?

FIONA: Oh! There's a difference between makin' love an' jus' bein' sentimental because ye're tired.

TOMMY: Is that what I'm being—sentimental because I'm tired?

FIONA: I believe so. But 'tis very agreeable.

(*Sings*)
The mist of May is in the gloamin',
An' all the clouds are holdin' still,
So take my hand an' we'll go roamin'
Through the heather on the hill.

The mornin' dew is blinkin' yonder;
There's lazy music in the rill;
An' 'tis a lovely time to wander
Through the heather on the hill.

There may be other days as rich an' rare.
There may be other springs as full an' fair.
But they won't be the same—they'll come an' go.

TOMMY and FIONA:

For this I know:
That when the mist is in the gloamin',
And all the clouds are holdin' still,
If you're not there I won't go roamin'
Through the heather on the hill;
The heather on the hill.

(*The music stops and* TOMMY *and* FIONA *stand looking at each other. Then suddenly thunder is heard and the blink of lightning is seen in the distance. This is a signal for renewed activity on stage as the* TOWNSFOLK *start closing up the booths and carts. The music is heard under playing "Down on MacConnachy Square")*

TOMMY: (*Still staring at her*) What's that?

FIONA: (*Looking up at him*) We have a storm here every now an' then.

(TOMMY *leans forward as if to kiss her, but she draws away from him*)

FIONA: I'll get my basket and we'll be off.

(FIONA *crosses to get her basket and returns to* TOMMY. *Arm in arm, rather dreamily, they walk slowly off. Around them, in contrast, the* TOWNSFOLK *are rushing to escape the rain. A group huddles under an umbrella and sings*)

TOWNSFOLK:

Go back to the hills!
Go back to the mills!

(*Suddenly as the thunder was heard, so suddenly does the sky brighten and the sun shine through. They come out from under the umbrella, and they all start setting up their booths again*)

TOWNSFOLK:

Come ye in the glen!
Come ye, bairn,
Come ye, men!

Come ye from the loom!
Come from pail an' broom!
Come ye everywhere!
'Tis the end
Of the fair
Down on MacConnachy Square.

Curtain

SCENE 3

The Brockie open shed. It is a small inset in the center of the stage with the countryside painted on the surrounding drop. There is a rather peculiar-looking cot upstage, peculiar in that it looks like a rectangular mound. It is draped to the floor. Downstage there is a simple, wooden armless rocking chair.

Just past noon.

JEFF *and* MEG *are discovered on stage.* JEFF *is standing looking straight out in front of him.* MEG *is standing near him.*

JEFF: It's a very picturesque view of the glen.

MEG: Thank ye.

JEFF: What for?

MEG: Why, for likin' where I've brought ye. It makes me very happy.

JEFF: You get happy very easily, don't you?

MEG: Aye.

JEFF: (*After giving her a quizzical look*) I haven't been in an open shed like this since I was a boy; which at this point seems a good two thousand years ago.

MEG: Ye mean ye're tired?

JEFF: Aye, lassie. I'm tired. That's why you brought me here, isn't it? So I could take a nap.

MEG: I shouldna think a long walk would fatigue a young lad like ye.

JEFF: A young lad?

MEG: Aye! Ye're very young.

JEFF: That is either a deliberate lie or wishful thinking. I am ancient, decrepit, and disintegrating rapidly.

MEG: Aye! (JEFF *walks up and sits on the cot. It is hard. He tries to bounce but it doesn't give*)

JEFF: What's under here—a rock garden?

MEG: My father used to sleep on it.

JEFF: That was his second mistake.

MEG: He an' my mother met in this shed. Ye see, my mother was a gypsy. An' one day she was walking past this shed an' she saw my father asleep on the cot. She liked his looks an' she was a wee bit tired anyhow, so she took off her shoes, sat in the rockin' chair, an' waited for 'im to wake up. An' it wasn't long after that that I was born.

JEFF: That's one of the sweetest bedtime stories I've ever heard. (*He lies back*)

MEG: Ye're sure ye're comfortable?

JEFF: Very.

(MEG *comes over and stares down at him. There is a moment of silence. Then* JEFF *looks up and sees her*)

JEFF: Thank you very much. You've been more than kind. And now if you want to round out your generosity, buzz off.

MEG: (*Staring down at him*) Ye're a braw an' handsome lad.

JEFF: (*Still reclining*) You should see me when I'm rested. I'm almost robust.

MEG: I jus' hate to leave ye.

JEFF: You'd better. When I sleep I make all sorts of odd noises.

MEG: Who told ye? Do ye have a wife?

JEFF: (*Raising himself on his elbows*) No, but I was engaged once.

MEG: (*Quickly*) What happened to the lass ye were engaged to?

JEFF: She fell in love with a Russian.

MEG: A Russian?

JEFF: Yes.

MEG: Russia is in Europe, isn't it?

JEFF: Yes, more and more.

MEG: (*Mystified*) Oh!

JEFF: It's not far from here. You just cross the Channel and turn left. (*He lies back*)

MEG: (*Staring at him for a moment*) Aye, ye're a winnin' lad. A right winnin' lad.

JEFF: (*Sitting up and swinging his feet over the side*) Now, look, lass. I'm not sure what you're after; but I don't want to. I want to go to sleep.

MEG: But dinna ye see? I'm highly attracted to ye.

JEFF: Thank you very much. When I wake up we'll discuss the whole problem. And believe me, you have a problem.

MEG: An' when I look at ye lying on the cot I feel little tadpoles jumpin' on my spine.

JEFF: That's about as repulsive an idea as I've heard in years. You know, if sex were a hobby you'd be a collector's item.

MEG: But I've been waitin' so long . . .

JEFF: (*Firmly but politely*) Go!

MEG: (*Rising and walking away*) Oh, ye men are all alike!

JEFF: I should certainly hope so.

MEG: Ye're all brutes. Ye get what ye want from a lass an' then 'tis farewell.

JEFF: Get what I want? I can't even get you to go away.

MEG: That's what I'm referrin' to. I thought ye were interested in me an' that's why ye let me take ye here! Ye misled me!

JEFF: You certainly have one hell of an imagination. Can you think of one good reason why I, a strange man, should be interested in you, a strange woman, and at this hour of the day?

MEG: Of course I can. Because ye're a lad an' I'm a lass.

JEFF: With that philosophy, you must have had a provocative career. (*The music begins under*)

MEG: Aye, I've had a great many heartbreaks.

JEFF: I don't doubt it at all. (*He sits back on the cot*)

MEG: (*Sings "The Love of My Life"*)

At sixteen years I was blue an' sad.
Then Father said I should find a lad.
So I set out to become a wife,
An' found the real love of my life.
His name it was Chris an' the last was MacGill.
I met him one night pickin' flow'rs on the hill.
He had lots of charm an' a certain kind o' touch,
An' a certain kind of eagerness that pleased me very much.
So there 'neath the moon, where romance often springs,
I gave him my heart—and a few other things.
I don't know how long that I stayed up on the hill,
But the moon had disappeared an' so had Christopher MacGill.

So I went home an' I thought I'd die;
Till Father said: Make another try.
So out I went to become a wife,
An' found the real love of my life.
He came from the Lowlands, the Lowlands said he;
I saw him an' knew he was perfect for me.
Jus' one thing that puzzled me an' it always will,
Was he told me he had heard about me from his friend MacGill.
We quick fell in love an' went down by the creek;
The next day he said he'd be back in a week.
An' I thought he would, for now how was I to know
That of all the Lowland laddies there was never one as low!

I told my Father the awful truth.
He said: What difference? Ye've got your youth.
So out I went, mad to be a wife,
An' found the real love of my life.

Oh, he was a poet, a rhymer was he.
He read me some verse he had written for me.
He said they would move me, these poems from his pen;
An' how right he was, because they moved me right into the glen.

We stayed till the dawn came an' lighted the sky.
Then I shook his hand an' I bid him good-by.
I never went back, for what I had heard was true:
That a poet only writes about the things he cannot do.

My Pa said: Look out for men who think.
Ye'll be more certain with men who drink.
So out I went to become a wife,
An' found the real love of my life.

Oh, he was a soldier, a fine Highland son.
He told me about all the battles he'd won.
He wasted his time tellin' me about his might,
For one look at him decided me to not put up a fight.
We skirmished for hours that night in the glen,
An' I found the sword has more might than the pen.
But when I was drowsin' I snored to my dismay,
An' he thought it was a bugle an' got up and marched away.

Now Pa said: Daughter, there must be one,
Someone who's true or too old to run.
So I'm still lookin' to be a wife,
An' find the real love of my life.

(*The music reaches a climax, stops, and then begins the same melody over again.* MEG *turns around to* JEFF. *She walks over and looks down at him. He is obviously asleep. She pushes him a bit but he doesn't stir. She stands looking at him for a moment, then walks downstage a bit, takes off her shoes, sits in the rocking chair, and begins to rock with a smile on her face*)

Curtain

SCENE 4

The MacLaren house. It is a sparsely furnished living room. Off right center on the rear wall is a large window through which can be seen the surrounding countryside. Next to the window center is the front door. Downstage left is a door presumably leading to another room. The door is raised and there are two steps leading up to it. Upstage right is another door leading to another room. Upstage left against the wall is a rectangular, wooden table with a few chairs placed against it. Downstage right is a large, open, wooden crate, almost like a crude trunk. There are fixtures for candles on the wall.

About four in the afternoon.

The music is playing and several girls are lined up across the stage from the door left to the packing crate. They are passing bits of feminine Scottish clothing from the room left, down the line, to the girl next to the crate, who then deposits said bits in the crate. In other words, they are packing the hard way. As they pass, they sing.

GIRLS:

Jeannie's packin' up!
Jeannie's movin' out!
Jeannie's packin' up!
Jeannie's movin' out!
Pack all her clothes;
Tonight away she goes!
Jeannie's packin' up!
Jeannie's movin' out!
Jeannie's packin' up!
Jeannie's movin' out!
The town all knows
Tonight away she goes!

What with all the clothes,
All the these an' those,
Why do ye suppose
Jeannie never froze?
Hankies for her nose!
Ribbons for her bows!
Cotton for her hose!
Slippers for her toes!
Pack all her clothes,
Tonight away she goes!

(*They continue packing till* CHARLIE *appears at the door*)

CHARLIE: Hy!

GIRLS: Charlie!

CHARLIE: (*Entering*) Aye! Charles MacPherson Dalrymple! Tonight the founder of a new clan. Where's Jean?

GIRL: Upstairs.

(CHARLIE *moves to door left.* MR. MAC LAREN *enters from the right carrying a large Bible*)

MR. MAC LAREN: Aye, now, Charlie, ye're not supposed to see Jeannie afore the weddin'. It brings bad luck.

CHARLIE: Really, sir?

MR. MAC LAREN: My quill is at my desk in the other room. Here is the Bible. Take it an' sign it right under the name of my dear departed wife.

(CHARLIE *takes the Bible and exits right as* HARRY BEATON *is seen coming up the road. There is a knock at the door*)

MR. MAC LAREN: Come in.

(*The door opens and* HARRY *enters carrying a waistcoat. He hands it to* MR. MAC LAREN)

HARRY: Here, Mr. MacLaren. I've . . . I've brought your waistcoat. (*He hands it to* MR. MAC LAREN)

MR. MAC LAREN: Thank ye, Harry. 'Tis good to see ye. (*He holds out his hand for* HARRY *to shake.* HARRY *stands for a moment looking over the room, then looks at* MR. MACLAREN'S *outstretched hand, doesn't take it, and turns to go*) Wait a minute, lad.

HARRY: (*Turning back*) What for?

MR. MAC LAREN: Why dinna ye take my hand? I'm not your enemy.

HARRY: Ye . . . ye may not mean to be, but ye are. An' so is everybody in this town! (*He moves again to go*)

MR. MAC LAREN: (*Holding him lightly by the arm*) What is it, lad? Why do ye hate everybody?

HARRY: (*Not bitterly at first, but almost pathetically*) I couldna get through this day of seein' her marry someone else if I dinna. What can I do? What could anyone do but hate when ye realize your life dinna mean a damn? I canna leave here . . . I canna go to the university an' make somethin' of myself . . . an' I canna have Jean. So there's nothin' left to do but hate everythin' an' everybody in this cursed town.

MR. MAC LAREN: Ye'll never find any peace by hatin', lad. It only shuts ye off more from the world. An' this is only a cursed town if ye make it so. To the rest of us, this is a blessed place.

HARRY: Well, ye can keep it.

(*He exits.* CHARLIE *returns from the room right carrying the Bible. As he speaks, he leaves it open on top of the crate*)

CHARLIE: Well, all done! Who was that?

MR. MAC LAREN: (*Simply*) My waistcoat came.

CHARLIE: Oh!

JEAN: (*Offstage*) Charlie, please go away. I want to come out.

MR. MAC LAREN: Dinna obey her, lad. Ye'll spoil her.

(*He exits right.* CHARLIE *turns to go and then pauses under the balcony and calls up to* JEAN)

CHARLIE: Jeannie!

(*The music starts under*)

JEAN: (*Offstage*) Charlie, are ye still there?

CHARLIE: (*Sings "Come to Me, Bend to Me"*)

Because they told me
I can't behold ye
Till weddin' music starts playin',
To ease my longin'
There's nothing wrong in
Me standin' out here an' sayin':

Come to me, bend to me, kiss me good day!
Darlin', my darlin', 'tis all I can say.
Jus' come to me, bend to me, kiss me good day!
Gie me your lips an' don't take them away!

JEAN: (*A little more pleadingly*) Charlie, please go away.

CHARLIE: (*He crosses to the steps, puts one foot on them, and sings softly:*)

Come, dearie, near me
So ye can hear me,
I've got to whisper this softly.
For though I'm burnin'
To shout my yearnin',
The words come tiptoein' off me.

Come to me, bend to me, kiss me good day!
Darlin', my darlin', 'tis all I can say.
Jus' come to me, bend to me, kiss me good day!
Gie me your lips an' don't take them away!

JEAN: (*Almost pathetic now*) Charlie, please go away. (*He starts for the door*)

CHARLIE: (*Through the window*)

Gie me your lips an' don't take them away!

(*He exits down the road.* JEAN *enters and looks around to make certain he's gone. The music continues. There is a dance between* JEAN *and the girls. At the conclusion, the girls exit out the door. As* JEAN *is about to exit left,* TOMMY *and* FIONA *are seen coming past the window and then entering the house. They are laughing and talking.* FIONA *is carrying an armful of heather*)

FIONA: Aren't ye goin' to greet our guest?

JEAN: Greetin's! Fiona, where have ye been? Ye know I canna dress without ye.

FIONA: (*Putting the heather on the table*) Ye mean 'tis time for ye to dress?

JEAN: Aye! So, come! (*She exits left*)

FIONA: Ye see, I knew we were out far too long.

TOMMY: I know, but I'm not sorry.

FIONA: Wait for me. I shan't be but a few minutes. (*She starts to exit left*)

TOMMY: Fiona!

(FIONA *stops and turns. He crosses and without saying a word takes her in his arms and kisses her. She exits left. Then* JEFF *is seen coming to the window. He looks in*)

JEFF: Good morning, laddie.

TOMMY: Hi! Where've you been?

JEFF: (*Looking around appraisingly*) This is very nice. You should have seen the apartment I got—complete with a built-in lassie.

TOMMY: Come on in. (JEFF *enters. He is sporting a new pair of trousers. Not brilliant plaid, but obviously new*) What kind of a day did you . . . ? (*He looks at the trousers*) What the hell happened to you?

JEFF: Thistles.

TOMMY: What?

JEFF: Never mind. It's a *professional* secret. Mine will be ready before we leave. (*He takes one of the chairs from against the table, moves it out in the room a bit, and sits down*) And another thing, disregard all that rubbish about Scottish frugality. Their generosity is overpowering.

TOMMY: Well, how do you *feel?*

JEFF: (*As if the thought just dawned on him*) Surprisingly well! How about you?

TOMMY: (*With incredible enthusiasm*) I never felt better in my life!

JEFF: (*Eying him with sudden interest*) You, too?

TOMMY: (*Sings "Almost Like Being in Love"*)

Maybe the sun gave me the pow'r,
For I could swim Loch Lomond
And be home in
Half an hour.

Maybe the air gave me the drive,
For I'm all aglow and alive!

What a day this has been!
What a rare mood I'm in!
Why, it's . . . almost like being in love!

There's a smile on my face
For the whole human race!
Why, it's . . . almost like being in love!

All the music of life seems to be
Like a bell that is ringin' for me!

And from the way that I feel
When that bell starts to peal,
I would swear I was falling,
I could swear I was falling,
It's almost like being in love.

When we walked up the brae

FIONA: (*Enters singing*)
Not a word did we say.
It was . . . almost like bein' in love.
(*She walks over to him*)

But your arm linked in mine
Made the world kind o' fine.

TOMMY:
It was . . . almost like being in love.

FIONA:
All the music of life seems to be

TOMMY:
Like a bell that is ringin' for me!

FIONA and TOMMY:
And from the way that I feel
When that bell starts to peal,

FIONA:
I would swear I was falling,

TOMMY:
I could swear I was falling,

FIONA and TOMMY:
It's almost like being in love!

(*The music stops*)

FIONA: Hand me that bundle of heather, Tommy?

TOMMY: Right, darling.

JEFF: Darling? (TOMMY *crosses and hands it to her*)

FIONA: Thank ye, dearie. (*She takes it and exits*)

JEFF: (*Rising*) Well, when do we start back?

TOMMY: (*Crossing to the trunk*) There's no hurry. Let's stay for the wedding. After all, how often do you . . .

(*He stops himself as his eyes fall on the open Bible that is lying on the crate. He picks it up and looks at it. He looks at* JEFF *quickly in bewilderment and then looks back at the Bible again*)

JEFF: What's the matter?

TOMMY: I must be a little touched. Listen to this. "Married: Elizabeth Lang to Andrew MacLaren. July second, 1719."

JEFF: What's so amazing? People used to get married then.

TOMMY: Wait a minute! (*Reading*) "Children: Fiona, born October tenth, 1722. Jean, born April eighth, 1728."

JEFF: Well?

TOMMY: (*Tensely*) But Fiona is twenty-four, and she's got a sister six years younger named Jean.

JEFF: Well?

TOMMY: But those are the two sisters in this Bible.

JEFF: Ridiculous. They're probably just named after them.

TOMMY: Jean's getting married today. Did you know that?

JEFF: Yes . . .

TOMMY: Do you know the name of the guy she's marrying?

JEFF: They told me at the tavern. Someone named Dalrymple.

TOMMY: Well, get this. (*Reading*) "Married: Jean MacLaren to Charles MacPherson Dalrymple, May twenty-fourth, 1746." (*Neither says a word for a moment*) Now what do you say?

JEFF: Congratulations!

TOMMY: Wait! (*Piecing it together*) No Brigadoon on the map. No phones in the whole town. Thanks to Mr. Dumfaddle for doing something about a miracle. And three or four other things that I passed over when I was out with Fiona this afternoon.

JEFF: That hyperthyroid I was with never heard of Haig and Haig.

TOMMY: What do you make of it?

JEFF: I don't know.

TOMMY: I don't understand it. I'm beginning to feel a little like a damn fool.

JEFF: What are you getting so worked up about? If it makes them happy to disregard two hundred years of human bing-bang, let 'em.

TOMMY: But I've just spent the most wonderful day of my life; and now I run into something like this. It doesn't make sense to me.

JEFF: It does to me. It just means that batty people relax you.

TOMMY: She is not. She can't be! (*Calls off*) Fiona! (*To* JEFF) There must be a logical explanation. Even logical enough for you.

JEFF: They don't have to explain anything to me. I don't care.

TOMMY: (*Calls*) Fiona!

FIONA: (*Entering*) What, Tommy?

TOMMY: Come here.

FIONA: Tommy, what is it?

TOMMY: (*Showing her the Bible*) Is this your name here in this Bible?

FIONA: Aye! An' why . . . ? (*She stops herself. Then, thoughtfully:*) Oh!

JEFF: Someone seems to have loused up your books.

TOMMY: Well, come on. What does it all mean? Is there any explanation or isn't there?

FIONA: Aye, there is. But *I* canna tell ye.

TOMMY: Well, is there anybody who can? I'd like to know.

FIONA: Ye mus' talk with the dominie.

TOMMY: The who?

FIONA: Our schoolmaster, Mr. Lundie.

TOMMY: Where does he live?

JEFF: Down the road, in a tree.

FIONA: He doesn't live in a tree, Mr. Douglas. Mr. Lundie is a great man. (*To* TOMMY) All right, Tommy. I'll take ye to 'im. I hadna wanted to 'cause I was hopin' we could have this day together.

TOMMY: What's that got to do with it?

FIONA: 'Tis goin' to be so hard for ye to believe what ye'll hear. Ye'll think there is somethin' wrong with us an' ye'll leave. I know it.

TOMMY: Maybe I will and maybe I won't. Come on, Jeff.

JEFF: Is it informal, or should I wear my three-cornered hat?

TOMMY: Come on, I said!

(*The music swells as they start for the door*)

Curtain

SCENE 5

Outside the house of MR. LUNDIE.
Immediately following.

MR. LUNDIE *is seated on the porch reading.* MR. LUNDIE *is a quaint Scottish schoolmaster in his late fifties. Though his eyes have a genuine kindness and his manner is entirely benign, he speaks with little trace of emotion. He wears metal-framed glasses.*

FIONA, TOMMY, *and* JEFF *enter and walk toward the house.*

FIONA: Good day, Mr. Lundie.

MR. LUNDIE: (*Rising*) Why, hello, Fiona. What a pleasant surprise!

FIONA: Mr. Lundie, I'd like ye to meet Mr. Tommy Albright and Mr. Jeff Douglas.

MR. LUNDIE: (*Holding out his hand*) Good afternoon, gentlemen. (*He studies them both carefully*)

TOMMY: (*Trying to be polite*) How do you do, sir? (*He shakes his hand*)

JEFF: (*Also taking his hand*) Good afternoon.

MR. LUNDIE: (*After a moment of looking at them*) Where do ye gentlemen come from?

TOMMY: We're from New York.

MR. LUNDIE: (*As if to himself but saying it distinctly*) We're from New York.

JEFF: Uh-huh!

TOMMY: Yes. New York.

MR. LUNDIE: (*Simply*) I heard ye.

FIONA: Mr. Lundie, I was wonderin' if ye'd be good enough to tell these gentlemen about Brigadoon. They've heard an' seen a good deal an' they're very perplexed indeed.

TOMMY: Perplexed is right.

FIONA: I would very much like him, I mean them, to know.

MR. LUNDIE: (*Stating his echo*) I would very much like him, I mean them, to know.

FIONA: Aye, sir.

MR. LUNDIE: (*After a moment*) Winna ye be seated, gentlemen?

TOMMY: Thank you. (*They all do*)

MR. LUNDIE: Are ye stayin', Fiona?

FIONA: If I may, sir. I'd love to hear it all again.

TOMMY: From what I gather, nobody can talk about anything around here but you. Is that right?

MR. LUNDIE: No, that's wrong. Mr. Forsythe could have told ye.

TOMMY: Forsythe. I've heard about him. But I didn't meet him.

MR. LUNDIE: Likely not. I think he's dead.

JEFF: That would stand in the way, I suppose.

MR. LUNDIE: Let me warn ye afore I begin that what I'm goin' to tell ye ye winna believe.

TOMMY: It's all right. I've already been warned. Why won't I believe it?

MR. LUNDIE: Because what happened in Brigadoon was a miracle an' most folk dinna believe in miracles. Miracles require faith, an' faith seems to be as dead as . . . er . . .

JEFF: Mr. Forsythe?

MR. LUNDIE: Aye. Now, if an outsider who chanced to come to Brigadoon were to hear the tale from the lips of someone in the town, he'd think the lass or lad was daft. An' that would lead to many unpleasant an' humiliatin' things for the poor lass or laddie. Now, wouldna it?

TOMMY: I suppose so.

MR. LUNDIE: I suppose so. So, only I can talk about the miracle to strangers.

JEFF: (*With a touch of sarcasm*) And you don't imagine anybody would think you're crazy?

MR. LUNDIE: Ye might very well. But it winna hurt me. I'd jus' pity ye. Now, this miracle happened . . . let's see . . . what's today?

FIONA: Friday.

MR. LUNDIE: Friday. That means it happened exactly two hundred years ago. Two hundred years ago the Highlands of Scotland were plagued with witches; wicked sorcerers who were takin' the Scottish folk away from the teachin's of God an' puttin' the devil in their souls. They were indeed horrible destructive women. I dinna suppose ye have such women in your world.

TOMMY: Witches?

JEFF: Yes, we still have them. We pronounce it differently.

MR. LUNDIE: Uh-huh! It dinna matter they were not *real* sorcerers, because ye an' I know there is no such thing. But their influence was very real indeed. Now, here in Brigadoon we had an old minister of the kirk named Mr. Forsythe. An' a good man he was.

FIONA: The kindest man in Scotland.

MR. LUNDIE: I believe he was. No man ever loved his parish as did Mr. Forsythe. But he was growin' old, an' it grieved him that one day soon he would leave all those so dear to him. But most of all, he worried about the witches. They hadna visited Brigadoon yet, but he knew there was a band of them comin' our way. So he began to wonder if there wasn't somethin' he could do to protect the folk of his parish not only from them, but from all the evils that might come to Brigadoon from the outside world after he died.

FIONA: What a kind man!

MR. LUNDIE: He spent days walkin' through the glen, thinkin'. An' if ye had passed his house any hour of the night, ye would have seen the candles lit an' Mr. Forsythe sittin' in his chair, thinkin'. Then one day he came to me an' told me he had decided to ask God for a miracle.

FIONA: (*Touching her eye*) This part is so nice I cry thinkin' about it.

MR. LUNDIE: He consulted with me about it because he knew I had a highly logical mind, an' he figured as long as he was goin' to ask for a miracle, it might as well be a well-organized miracle. So for many days I walked through the glen with him, an' for many nights I sat with him by candlelight. Finally Mr. Forsythe decided what he was goin' to pray for. An' on an early Wednesday morn, right after midnight, Mr. Forsythe went out to a hill beyond Brigadoon an' made his prayer to God. There in the hush of a sleepin' world, he asked God that night to make Brigadoon an' all the people in it vanish into the Highland mist. Vanish, but not for always. It would all return jus' as it was for one day every hundred years. The people would go on leadin' their customary lives; but each day when they awakened it would be a hundred years later. An' when we awoke the next day, it was a hundred years later.

TOMMY: (*Half whispering*) My God!

MR. LUNDIE: Ye see, in this way Mr. Forsythe figured there would be no change in the lives of the people. They jus' wouldna be in any century long enough to be touched by it.

TOMMY: (*Quite shaken*) You mean . . . you mean you go to

bed at night and when you get up the next day it's a hundred years later?

MR. LUNDIE: Aye.

TOMMY: Then every day is a hundred years later?

MR. LUNDIE: Aye.

JEFF: What happened to the minister?

MR. LUNDIE: We never saw him again. Ye see, he realized that to ask for such a miracle, some sacrifice would have to be made, an' he wanted to be the one to make it. Now, what would be the greatest sacrifice he could offer? It was to be separated afore his time from the ones he loved. So that's why he went out to a hill *beyond* Brigadoon. Were the miracle granted, he would never see Brigadoon again.

TOMMY: And all this happened two hundred years ago.

MR. LUNDIE: Aye, lad. Which, ye see, is only two days ago to us. He had intended to ask for the miracle on Tuesday. But Charlie Dalrymple was in school in Edinburgh an' was not expected back till Tuesday late. Mr. Forsythe, not wantin' anythin' to go wrong with the weddin', postponed prayin' till Charlie got back.

FIONA: Wasn't that sweet of him?

TOMMY: Let me ask you something. Suppose somebody around here gets fed up and wants to leave. Then what?

MR. LUNDIE: Oh, he canna leave.

JEFF: You mean *I've* got to stay here now?

MR. LUNDIE: No, no, lad. But accordin' to Mr. Forsythe's contract with God, if anyone *of* Brigadoon leaves, the enchantment is broken for all.

TOMMY: And . . . ?

MR. LUNDIE: That night when the people go to sleep, Brigadoon will disappear forever.

TOMMY: (*After a moment*) Look, I'm not saying I believe all this, but just for argument's sake, suppose a stranger like . . . well . . . me came to Brigadoon and wanted to stay. Could he?

MR. LUNDIE: Aye, he could. Mr. Forsythe provided for that.

JEFF: He didn't miss a trick, did he?

MR. LUNDIE: No, lad, he dinna. A stranger can stay if he loves someone here—not jus' Brigadoon, mind ye—but someone in Brigadoon enough to want to give up everythin' an' stay with that person. Which is how it should be. 'Cause after all, lad, if ye love someone deeply, anythin' is possible.

FIONA: I think I like that part the best.

MR. LUNDIE: Shouldna ye be thinkin' about changin' for the weddin'?

FIONA: (*Jumping up*) Aye, I had. (*To* TOMMY, *a little fearfully*) Tommy, will I see ye later?

TOMMY: (*Looks at her a moment, then pauses, then:*) Yes. I'll be there.

FIONA: (*Expressively*) Thank ye, Tommy.

TOMMY: I think I want to stick around and see if this place evaporates like you say.

FIONA: I mus' hurry now. Good-by, Mr. Lundie. (*She exits*)

MR. LUNDIE: She's a dear lass.

TOMMY: I'm finding that out. Tell me, Mr. Lundie, you're all perfectly happy living here in this little town?

(*A distant choir is heard*)

MR. LUNDIE: Of course, lad. After all, sunshine can peep through a small hole.

TOMMY: But at night when you go to sleep; what's it like?

MR. LUNDIE: Well, for me, 'tis like bein' carried on shadowy arms to some far-off cloud an' there I float till mornin'. An' yet, sometimes I think I hear strange voices.

TOMMY: Voices?

MR. LUNDIE: Aye. They say no words I can remember. But they're voices filled with a fearful longin'; an' often they seem to be callin' me back. I've pondered it when I'm awake; an' I think—I have a feelin' I'm hearin' the outside world. There mus' be lots of folk out there who'd like a Brigadoon.

(*The choir swells and then chimes are heard*)

MR. LUNDIE: Oh! 'Tis the weddin' time.

(*The chimes and choir grow louder.* TOMMY *and* JEFF *in mixed awe and bewilderment rise and move slowly to leave*)

Curtain

SCENE 6

Outside the kirk of Brigadoon. On the left veering toward center is the façade of the kirk. There are practical steps leading up to it. The kirkyard would seem to be in the middle of some ancient Gothic ruins.

Dusk of that day.

Music is playing a rousing theme representing the meeting of the clans. In the center is standing a group of MacLarens all dressed in their family plaid. One by one the clans arrive, marching in proudly and taking their places around the kirkyard. As they enter the leader of each group announces the name of the family to the MacLarens. Among those represented are the MacLeods, the MacGuffies, the Dalrymples, and the Beatons. When they are all present, the MacLarens announce themselves, bow courteously to their guests, and stand back. MR. LUNDIE *appears and stands before the kirk. As the others see him they become suddenly still as* MR. LUNDIE *says:*

MR. LUNDIE: There's goin' to be a weddin'.

(*The music of "Brigadoon" is played softly under.* CHARLIE *and his best man enter and stand left of* MR. LUNDIE. *Simultaneously with* CHARLIE'S *entrance,* FIONA *appears dressed in her wedding finery and stands in the clearing not far from* MR. LUNDIE. TOMMY *and* JEFF *enter quietly from the side and stand at the edge of the crowd. Now* MR. MAC LAREN *and* JEAN *enter from the kirk, and* JEAN, *after first giving her wedding bouquet to* FIONA, *takes her place on* MR. LUNDIE'S *right*)

MR. LUNDIE: We have no minister in Brigadoon now. In most villages this would be a calamitous thing. But we know 'tis a blessin'. When there is no minister present it is perfectly proper accordin' to the laws of Scotland for two people to be wed by sincere mutual consent. There need be nothin' in writin'. All that's necessary is the promise of love as long as ye both are on earth. (*He pauses for a moment*) Go ahead, lad.

CHARLIE: (*Awkwardly, as he slips a ring on* JEAN'S *finger*) I shall love ye till I die. An' I'll make *all* effort to be a good husband to ye.

JEAN: An' . . . an' so much will I try . . . to be a fine . . . an' . . . an' lovin' wife.

(*They look at each other uncomfortably*)

MR. LUNDIE: Well, kiss her, lad. (*They kiss gingerly*) Mr. Forsythe, I know, would have liked to be here. But if ye'll both be good an' true to each other, then ye canna help but live in the grace of God. An' Mr. Forsythe could have asked no more than that.

CHARLIE: (*After a slight pause*) Are we married now, Mr. Lundie?

MR. LUNDIE: Are we married now, Mr. Lundie? Aye, lad. Ye're married.

(*The* TOWNSFOLK *gather quickly around them, shaking hands, kissing, etc. All done quietly, of course.* FIONA *crosses quickly down to* TOMMY *at left.* TOMMY *has been so completely moved by the ceremony that it almost looks as if a tear had come to his eye. When* FIONA *comes to him, she is almost in tears herself and comes right into his arms*)

FIONA: It was a nice weddin', wasn't it?

(*Suddenly the wedding music starts and* CHARLIE *and* JEAN *begin the wedding dance. Everybody joins in and* TOMMY *is circled. He steps back with* FIONA *to watch.*

The wedding dance is interrupted then by the appearance of HARRY BEATON, *who comes holding two swords high. He places them on the ground and the music changes to the tempo of a Sword Dance.* HARRY *dances this, and then turns to ask* JEAN *to dance, which she does. They twirl, then* HARRY *suddenly stops and kisses her violently. The crowd parts and* JEAN *is seen lying on the floor sobbing with* HARRY *hovering over her. She slowly rises and runs to* CHARLIE. *A fight starts between* HARRY *and one of the men.* HARRY *picks up the sword with one hand and pulls his dirk from his stocking with the other and moves around toward the crowd menacingly.* TOMMY *comes forward with a shawl wrapped around his arm, and as one of the men knocks the sword from* HARRY'S *hand,* TOMMY *successfully wrenches the dirk from him and knocks* HARRY *on the ground.* TOMMY *kicks the dirk away, and as he goes quickly to pick it up,* FIONA *runs to him*)

FIONA: Tommy! Tommy! (TOMMY, *his eyes fixed on* HARRY, *doesn't turn to reply to her.* HARRY *slowly rises and looks over at* JEAN)

HARRY: All I've done is to want ye too much. (*He walks slowly to the side of the stage and then suddenly turns back to the crowd. They all hold their positions as if not knowing what he is going to do next*) I'm leavin' Brigadoon an' 'tis the end of all of us. The miracle's over!

(*He runs off. There is a sudden stunned moment. Then everyone realizes the import of his leaving and springs into action. Cries of "we mus' stop 'im" fill the stage. All the men surge forward to run after him, including* TOMMY, *who motions to* JEFF *to follow*)

Curtain

ACT TWO

SCENE 1

A forest near the borders of Brigadoon. By now the sun has fallen and a mist beclouds the dark woody green of the forest.

This scene is the chase through the forest of the men of Brigadoon after HARRY BEATON. *Under it all a strong pulsating rhythm is played in the orchestra. Offstage an all-male chorus intermittently sings. The action on stage other than the one or two singing soloists is done entirely in pantomime.*

Immediately following.

HARRY BEATON *runs on, stops in the center, and looks from side to side wildly as if he doesn't know which way to go. The chorus is heard softly.*

CHORUS: (*Sings*)
Harry Beaton!

(HARRY *looks around him hysterically*)

CHORUS:
Harry Beaton!

(*He looks again and then runs off right. The chorus sings again, growing louder and louder until it reaches full voice. As it sings, a few men run on from the left and in pantomime divide themselves up and take off in different directions*)

CHORUS:
Run an' get 'im!
Run an' get 'im!
Run, ye men, or ye
will never see
another mornin'!

Go an' stop 'im!
Go an' stop 'im!
Run, ye Highland men,
or ye won't ken
another day!

(SANDY, STUART DALRYMPLE, *a member of Charlie's family,* ANGUS, *and two or three others enter swiftly from the left. They pause in the center and look around. The music continues under*)

ANGUS: (*Sings*)
Beaton sure came this way,

An' we canna be too far behind 'im, laddie.
(*To one of the men*)
Ye, there, head for the brae!
Keep your eye ope' or ye winna find 'im, laddie!
(*The man exits off right*)

STUART DALRYMPLE: (*Sings*)
I'll go down to the creek,
An', by God, if I see 'im I'll throw 'im in it!
(*He exits swiftly*)

ANGUS: (*To* SANDY)
Search the hill to the peak!
(*To the rest*)
Find 'im, lads, or tomorrow will never, never come!

(*All exit off right. The chorus sings again. More men enter and illustrate the chase in pantomime*)

CHORUS:
Run an' get 'im!
Run an' get 'im!
Run an' get 'im now
or ye won't plough
another meadow!

Go an' stop 'im!
Go an' stop 'im!
Run, ye Highland men,
or ye won't ken
another day!

(TOMMY *and* JEFF *enter from the left*)

TOMMY: Let's separate. You go right and I'll go left. He can't be too far from here.

(*Sings*)
If he comes into sight
Hold him fast! Many lives are depending on it!
This must not end tonight!
They must know that tomorrow is really gonna come!

(TOMMY *exits downstage right.* JEFF *upstage right. Chorus and pantomime again*)

CHORUS:
Run an' get 'im!
Run an' get 'im!

Spread your human net
but don't forget
that time's agin ye!

Go an' stop 'im!
Go an' stop 'im!
Run, ye Highland men,
or ye won't ken
another day!

Run an' get 'im!
Run an' get 'im!

(*At this point there is a sudden discord in the orchestra and then silence. It lasts a few seconds. The music begins under.* SANDY, STUART, TOMMY, ANGUS, *and the others enter from the right.* SANDY *and* ANGUS *are dragging the body of* HARRY BEATON. ANGUS *kneels down over the body, looks up at the others, and sings:*)

ANGUS:

Lads, say a prayer, I'm afraid Harry Beaton is dead!

TOMMY: (*Looking down*)

Looks like he fell on a rock and it crushed in his head.

STUART:

Nobody wanted for Harry to be smitten down!
All that we wished was to keep 'im from leavin' the town.

ANGUS:

Look ye, I understand!
There's no sense for us all to be sad about it!
This was clear God's own hand,
An' we all should be grateful an' glad about it!

STUART: (*Pleadingly*)

Though it may be very true what the lad here has said,
Don't tell the rest till tomorrow that Harry is dead!
They'll find he's dead tomorrow!
Tell them all is right!
There should be no more sorrow
On this weddin' night!

ALL: (*Speaking, and nodding understandingly*) Aye!

(SANDY *and* ANGUS *pick* HARRY *up and all start off left as the chorus sings*)

CHORUS:

Thanks to heaven!
Thanks to heaven!
Thank the pow'rs that be,
ye all will see
another mornin'!

Thanks to heaven!
Thanks to heaven!
Thank an' thank again,
ye'll ken
another day!

Blackout

SCENE 2

On the way from the forest. A few minutes later. FIONA, *a girl, and then four of the girls enter left.*

FIONA: I thought I heard a cry from over there! (*Indicates off right*)

(MR. MAC LAREN, ANGUS, *and five of the men enter from the right. There is a moment of silence, then* FIONA *goes fearfully to her father*)

FIONA: Well, Father?

MR. MAC LAREN: 'Tis all right now. He was stopped.

(*The women sigh "Thank God" and "Thank heaven" and run to the men*)

FIONA: (*To her father*) Was he hurt bad?

(ARCHIE BEATON *enters left*)

MR. MAC LAREN: No, dearie. Jus' scratched a bit. There's no need for grievin' now. We mus' go on with the weddin' supper!

(ARCHIE *goes quickly to* MR. MAC LAREN. FIONA *leaves him and moves across toward the right as if searching. When she reaches the extreme right, she waits and keeps looking off*)

ARCHIE: He dinna get away, Mr. MacLaren?

MR. MAC LAREN: No, Archie.

ARCHIE: Then where is my son? I want to see 'im! I thank God ye stopped 'im from his terrible intention, but I want to see 'im.

MR. MAC LAREN: He's all right, Archie. He's in good hands. 'Tis better he be left alone for a while. Come join us for a bit o' supper.

ARCHIE: I'm too ashamed for 'im, Mr. MacLaren. I canna join ye. (*He moves toward the right*)

MR. MAC LAREN: But, Archie . . . ! (*But* ARCHIE *exits right.* MR. MAC LAREN *turns to the others*) Come, everybody. Back to the glen for some food an' ale. The alarm is over!

(*They all start moving to exit left.* FIONA *turns to* ANGUS)

FIONA: Angus! Have ye seen Tommy?

ANGUS: The American? Why, no, I dinna think he came back with us.

FIONA: Oh, dear.

(*She turns and looks off right again. By this time most of the people have exited.* MR. MAC LAREN *calls over to her*)

MR. MAC LAREN: Come, Fiona.

(*He exits.* FIONA *turns and starts to cross the stage, then stops and looks back as* TOMMY *enters*)

TOMMY: Fiona!

FIONA: (*Running to him*) Tommy! I thought ye might have gone.

TOMMY: No, I didn't go. I couldn't.

FIONA: An' ye're all right?

TOMMY: Of course I'm all right.

FIONA: I'd have died if anythin' had happened to ye. (*Going into his arms*) I love ye so.

TOMMY: You . . . ?

FIONA: Aye!

TOMMY: But how can you be sure of that after one day?

FIONA: I dinna know. 'Tis jus' when a lass falls in or out of love she knows it right away.

TOMMY: I wish it were that clear to me.

FIONA: Why?

TOMMY: Because I have the peculiar sensation I'm hearing my own secret being told.

FIONA: Ye mean—ye think ye're in love with me?

TOMMY: Think? What good does thinking do? If I thought about it, it wouldn't make any more sense than the miracle. (*The music starts under*) But what I feel is something else.

FIONA: What do ye feel, then, Tommy?

TOMMY: (*Sings "There but for You Go I"*)

This is hard to say,
but as I wandered through the lea
I felt for just a fleeing moment

that I suddenly was free
of being lonely;
then I closed my eyes and saw
the very reason why.
I saw a man with his head bowed low.
His heart had no place to go.
I looked and I thought to myself with a sigh:
There but for you go I.

I saw a man walking by the sea.
Alone with the tide was he.
I looked and I thought as I watched him go by:
There but for you go I.
Lonely men around me,
Trying not to cry.
Till the day you found me
There among them was I.

I saw a man who had never known
A love that was all his own.
I thought as I thanked all the stars in the sky:
There but for you go I.
(*The music continues*)

FIONA: (*Holding him close*) Oh, Tommy! Tommy, darlin'!

TOMMY: I love you, Fiona. I guess that's all there is to it.

FIONA: I've wanted to hear ye say it. Even though it be at the last minute like this.

TOMMY: (*Holding her away from him*) The last minute?

FIONA: Aye. Soon now 'tis the end of our day.

TOMMY: And then you . . . you . . . ? (*He motions with his hand.* FIONA *nods*) But, Fiona, I can't leave you. Not now I can't. (*Pauses–then with hesitant excitement*) Didn't Lundie say someone could stay if he loved someone enough?

FIONA: Aye.

TOMMY: Well, that's for me! Where do I go? Who do I talk to? Where do I get a passport to disappear?

FIONA: (*In his arms again*) Tommy! Tommy! (*They kiss*)

TOMMY: I don't want to be without you ever again. I'd be afraid to be.
(*Sings*)

I saw a man who had never known
A love that was all his own.

I thought as I thanked all the stars in the sky:
There but for you go I.
(*The music swells*)

Curtain

SCENE 3

The glen. A short while later.

The wedding supper is on! There is music under as the scene begins. CHARLIE *and* JEAN *are upstage on a rock. The* TOWNSFOLK *are engaged in a Country Dance. After a reasonable amount of time of this sort of thing, the people stand back and* MEG *appears.*

MEG: (*Sings "My Mother's Weddin' Day"*)
Now if ye think this weddin' day went jus' a bit amiss,
Then I will tell ye 'bout a weddin' far more daft than this.
The lad involved turned out to be no other but my pa,
An' by the strangest bit o' luck, the woman was my ma!

MacGregor, MacKenna, MacGowan, MacGraw,
MacVitie, MacNeil, an' MacRae;
Aye, all of the folk in the village were there
At my mother's weddin' day.

For Pa had asked his friend MacPhee,
An' Mac had come with May MacGee,
An' May invited ninety-three
To my mother's weddin' day.
Then up the road came Ed MacKeen
With half the town of Aberdeen.

CHORUS:
Aye, ev'ryone was on the scene
At her mother's weddin' day.

MEG:
At quarter to five everybody was there,
A-waitin' around in the room.
MacVicker, MacDougall, MacDuff, an' MacCoy,
Everybody but the groom.
An' as the hours turtled by
The men got feelin' kind o' dry
An' thought they'd take a nip o' rye
While a-waitin' for the groom.

An' while the men were dippin' in
The ladies started on the gin.

CHORUS:

An' soon the room began to spin
At her mother's weddin' day.

MEG:

Then all of a sudden the liquor was gone;
The gin an' the whisky an' all.
An' all of a sudden the weddin' affair
Had become a bonnie brawl.

For Pete MacGraw an' Joe MacPhee
Began to fight for May MacGee,
While May MacGee an' Sam MacKee
Were a-wooin' in the hall.
So cold an' stiff was John MacVay
They used 'im for a servin' tray.

CHORUS:

For ev'ryone was blithe an' gay
At her mother's weddin' day.

MEG:

MacDuff an' MacVitie were playin' a game
An' usin' MacCoy for the ball.
MacKenna was eatin' the bridal bouquet
An' MacNeil hung on the wall.
When finally my father came,
His eyes were red, his nose aflame;
He dinna even know his name;
He was drunkest of them all.

The people were lyin' all over the room,
A-lookin' as if they were dead.
But Mother uncovered the minister quick,
An' she told 'im: Go ahead.
So Pa kneeled down on Bill MacRae,
An' Mother kneeled on Jock MacKay;
The preacher stood on John MacVay;
An' that's how my ma was wed.
It was a sight beyond compare.
I ought to know, for I was there.

MEG and CHORUS:
There never was a day as rare
As my (her) mother's weddin' day!

(*The music comes to a stop and then begins again. The people prepare themselves to go back into the Country Dance. As they are doing so,* CHARLIE *and* JEAN *steal silently off, waving good-by to a few as they go.* MEG *exits after her song. The* TOWNSFOLK *start to dance again, but by now they are all a wee bit tight, and so the dance is done in that spirit.*

Then, suddenly the dance is interrupted by the sound of the pipes. Two BAGPIPERS *enter followed by* ARCHIE BEATON, *who is carrying the body of* HARRY. *Everyone starts back in horror.*

The BAGPIPERS *play a funeral dirge and a funeral takes place. During the funeral* JEFF *enters quietly and stands watching in a group on stage left and* TOMMY *enters and stands in a group stage right. At the end of the ceremony,* HARRY'S *body is carried off and all the* TOWNSFOLK *exit.* TOMMY *and* JEFF *then turn and discover each other*)

JEFF: Hi!

TOMMY: Jeff, I'm not going back with you!

JEFF: Just for the record, what are you talking about?

TOMMY: I'm staying here!

JEFF: You're pulling my bonnie leg, aren't you?

TOMMY: No! I've never been more serious in my life. I tell you, Jeff, in one day I feel more a part of her and all this than I ever felt about Jane or anybody or anything back home.

JEFF: My dear boy, that's because it is one day. But don't you realize if you stay here it's for always?

TOMMY: I know.

JEFF: And do you know how long always is around here? It's one hell of a long time.

TOMMY: I know.

JEFF: This can't be a trial marriage, because you can't change your mind after trying it out for six or seven hundred years.

TOMMY: I won't ever want to.

JEFF: You're absolutely positive that there'll never come a time when you'll miss your family, your friends, the life you belong to? How can you know that now?

TOMMY: Because—well, here's where I know you'll think I'm crazy—because I believe in her. And what's more, I believe in this place.

JEFF: You do not. You just want to. This Highland voodoo town makes no more sense to you than it does to me. So how can you believe in it when you don't understand it? When you leave here, in a few weeks or even a few days you'll forget all about it. You won't feel a thing. That's the way a dream is.

TOMMY: What do you mean–dream?

JEFF: That's what this is: a dream. Why, even now you're not really moved by it. You just think you are.

TOMMY: How do you know?

JEFF: Because I do. (*Pauses a moment*) Did you see that funeral here a moment ago?

TOMMY: Yes. Why?

JEFF: I'm responsible for it.

TOMMY: What do you mean?

JEFF: Harry Beaton. I killed him.

TOMMY: You did what?

JEFF: I killed him. Accidentally, of course, but nevertheless I killed him. Out in the forest tonight I suddenly saw him rushing past me from behind a bush. Without even thinking what I was doing, I stuck out my foot and down he went. And I heard his head hit a rock with a very nasty thud.

TOMMY: My God, Jeff. I'm so sorry.

JEFF: What in the world for?

TOMMY: You must feel half dead inside.

JEFF: On the contrary, I don't feel a thing.

TOMMY: You actually don't feel anything?

JEFF: Nothing. Except like going home.

TOMMY: But why don't you?

JEFF: Because this is a dream. A good one for you and a bad one for . . .

TOMMY: Wait a minute, will you?

JEFF: You see, I've confused you, haven't I?

TOMMY: Yes, you have.

JEFF: And if you really believe as much as you think you do, I couldn't do that.

(MR. LUNDIE *and* FIONA *enter from the right*)

JEFF: I'll wait for you outside the town. (*He exits left*)

FIONA: Tommy, what did he mean by that?

MR. LUNDIE: Fiona tells me ye want to stay, lad.

FIONA: Tommy, what is it?

TOMMY: It's no good, Fiona. I'm leaving. And it isn't because I don't love you. I think I do. But I guess I don't trust my own feelings.

FIONA: Ye mean ye're not sure ye can accept everythin'?

TOMMY: That's about it.

MR. LUNDIE: Ye better hurry, Fiona. There's not much time left. (*He turns to exit and then stops*) Dinna feel ashamed of yourself, Tommy. 'Tis the hardest thing in the world to give up everythin'; even though 'tis usually the only way to get everythin'. (*He exits left. The music begins under*)

TOMMY: Do you understand at all?

FIONA: (*Looks at him, then sings*)
Dinna ye know, Tommy,
That ye're all I'm livin' for?
So how can ye go, Tommy,
When I'll need ye more and more?

TOMMY: (*Kindly*) No, Fiona. You won't remember that way. And neither will I

(*Sings "From This Day On"*)
You and the world we knew
Will glow till my life is through;
For you're part of me
From this day on.

And
Someday if I should love,
It's you I'll be dreaming of;
For you're all I'll see
From this day on.

These hurried hours were all the life we could share.
Still I will go with not a tear, just a prayer

That
When we are far apart
You'll find something from your heart
Has gone! Gone with me
From this day on.
(*The music continues*)
(*He speaks*) You see? We mustn't be sorry about anything.

FIONA: I'm not. In fact, I shouldna be surprised if I'll be less lonely now than I was afore ye came. I think real loneliness is not bein' in love in vain, but not bein' in love at all.

TOMMY: But it'll fade in time.

FIONA: No. It winna do that.

(*Sings*)

Through all the years to come
An' through all the tears to come
I know I'll be yours
From this day on.

(*The lights begin to dim and the chorus is heard singing offstage*)

CHORUS:

Brigadoon, Brigadoon,
Blooming under sable skies.
Brigadoon, Brigadoon,
There my heart forever lies.
Let the world grow cold around us;
Let the heavens cry above!
Brigadoon, Brigadoon,
In the valley there'll be love.

(*The song grows softer and softer. Over the fading song and dimming lights and the mist that slowly seems to be engulfing the glen,* TOMMY *and* FIONA *speak*)

FIONA: Oh, Tommy! 'Tis the end of our day!

TOMMY: I'm sorry, Fiona. To stay I had to have no fears and no doubts. And . . . well . . . (*He puts his arms around her*) . . . good-by.

(*They kiss. The voices are quite soft now. The lights are quite dim. As* FIONA *speaks she moves slowly away from him, her voice becoming softer as she becomes cloudy in the darkening mist*)

FIONA: Good-by, Tommy . . . An' dinna forget . . . any day . . . any night . . . that always an' always . . . I love ye . . . I love ye . . . I love ye . . . I love ye . . . I love ye . . .

(*Darkness! Silence! Then for but a moment, the lights come up a bit.* FIONA *is no longer there. The hazy distant view of the houses is gone. The stage is filled with a misty gray-yellow light.* TOMMY *looks at it for a moment. Then he turns and exits slowly right*)

Curtain

SCENE 4

A bar in New York City. This is a small inset placed downstage right. It is like the end of an elliptical-shaped bar so that one gets the feeling the rest of the bar is offstage right. There are two or three stools in front. The rest of the stage is blacked out.

Late afternoon, four months later.

A piano is heard offstage playing "cocktail music." It fades as the scene begins. JEFF *is seated on a stool. Although not incoherent, he is quite obviously "pickled." Behind the bar stands Frank, the bartender, looking like a bartender.*

JEFF: (*Taking a sip from a glass*) Ugh! What is this, Frank? D.D.T.?

FRANK: The usual, bourbon.

JEFF: Why do you say "the usual?" Have I been drinking it long?

FRANK: Continuously since you got back from Scotland four months ago.

JEFF: Well, I just decided I don't like it. It's not near as good as the whisky Mother used to make. Give me some gin.

FRANK: What'll you have with it, sir?

JEFF: A little bourbon.

FRANK: Yes, sir.

JEFF: (*Shakes his watch*) What time is it, Frank? I think my watch has stopped.

FRANK: (*Looking at his wrist watch*) Six-ten, sir.

JEFF: Hmph! I'd better be getting home. (FRANK *hands him his drink*) Give me another one to take with me, Frank. I like to drink portal to portal.

FRANK: (*Fixing it*) It's just about time for Miss Ashton to call, sir.

JEFF: Who?

FRANK: Jane Ashton, Mr. Albright's fiancée. Don't tell me you don't remember her?

JEFF: All right, I won't. What about her?

FRANK: Well, just about this time every day she either calls or comes in or both, looking for Mr. Albright.

JEFF: She does, eh?

(FRANK *takes out a cigarette,* JEFF *lights it, then takes it out out of his mouth and smokes it*)

FRANK: Yes, sir. From what I gather, she can't find him.

JEFF: I'm glad you warned me. I'll drink up and get out of here.

FRANK: Don't you like Miss Ashton, sir?

JEFF: Oh, very much. But not when she's stalking Mr. Albright. (*He drinks*) I tell you, Frank, scratch the surfacc of any woman . . . and she'll enjoy it.

FRANK: But where is Mr. Albright, sir?

JEFF: I don't know, Frank. He quit his job about a month ago, picked up his parcels, and vanished like . . . Brigadoon.

FRANK: Like who?

JEFF: That was the name of my brother who ran away. (TOMMY *enters*)

TOMMY: Hi!

FRANK: Hello, Mr. Albright.

JEFF: (*Going to him*) Tommy! My old friend Tommy. (*He throws his arms around* TOMMY)

TOMMY: How are you, Jeff?

JEFF: (*To* FRANK) It's my old friend Tommy. He's back.

TOMMY: Hello, Frank.

JEFF: Where've you been all month, Tommy?

TOMMY: Up on a farm in New Hampshire.

JEFF: A farm. Messing around in all that dirty dirt and everything. What were you doing there?

TOMMY: Enjoying myself. A rye and soda, please, Frank.

JEFF: Well, if that's what you like, when you get married why don't you buy one?

TOMMY: I wonder if I want to get married, Jeff.

JEFF: Why?

TOMMY: Because, my dear tank, I'm in love with someone else. And I "canna" get over it.

JEFF: Oh!

TOMMY: And the trouble is, because I can't be with her I can't be with anyone else. That's why I went away. So many things remind me of her. When I'm with people and they're talking to me, they might say one little word that opens the door to a memory for me and suddenly I don't hear them talking anymore. I'm a few thousand miles away with . . . well, you know. Then slowly I come back to the conversation, they ask me a question and I don't know what the hell they're talking about, I haven't heard a word.

JEFF: You must be fascinating company.

TOMMY: When I'm alone, it's easier.

(JANE ASHTON *enters. She is in her late twenties, chic, very attractive, though perhaps a little severe*)

JANE: Tommy!

(*Both men rise and she walks past* JEFF *into* TOMMY'S *arms*)

TOMMY: Hello, Jane.

JANE: What a wonderful surprise!

JEFF: Hello, Jane.

JANE: When did you get back?

JEFF: Hello, Jeff.

TOMMY: A little while ago.

JEFF: How are you, Jane?

JANE: (*Ignoring him*) I've been worried half to death about you.

JEFF: Fine, Jeff, how are you?

JANE: Let me look at you.

JEFF: I've had a little cold, but other than that . . .

JANE: I must say you do look well.

TOMMY: So do you.

JEFF: Well, I don't want to eat and run. I think I'll go up to my room and have a drink.

TOMMY: I'll see you, Jeff.

JANE: (*Half turning*) Hello.

JEFF: Good-by! Put it on the bill, Frank.

FRANK: Your bill, sir, is awfully high.

JEFF: So am I. (*He exits*)

JANE: Tommy, why didn't you write me?

TOMMY: Nothing to say, I guess. Drink?

JANE: Old Fashioned, please. (FRANK *gets busy*) And why didn't you wire me you were coming in? After all, darling, I did think the minute you'd get in town you'd call me . . . or come to me . . . or in fact, why didn't you . . .

(*The instant she says the words "come to me,"* FIONA'S *voice is heard upstage singing.* TOMMY *turns from the bar and looks off dreamily. The lights come up behind the bar revealing* FIONA *against a misty Scottish background. As* FIONA *sings,* JANE *continues talking, but in pantomime. Her mouth is moving, but no sound is forthcoming. She takes her cocktail from* FRANK *and says something to him. But no words are heard. Then she returns to* TOMMY. *Occasionally as her mouth is moving he nods to her*)

FIONA: (*Sings*)

Come to me, bend to me, kiss me good day!

Darlin', my darlin', 'tis all I can say.
Jus' come to me, bend to me, kiss me good day!
Gie me your lips an' don't take them away.

(*She exits and the lights dim completely out. The music fades out and the lights come up at the bar. We hear* JANE *speaking. The first part of her sentence is barely audible and then she reaches full speaking voice*)

JANE: . . . (and I didn't think) you'd want to do that, would you?

TOMMY: Oh! Why–er–maybe.

JANE: You mean you'd even consider it?

TOMMY: What?

JANE: Commuting from sixty miles out of New York?

TOMMY: Oh, no! I don't want to do that.

JANE: I didn't think so. And I told Mr. Jackson.

TOMMY: Who?

JANE: Herbert Jackson.

TOMMY: (*As if he knows*) Oh! (*Then*–) Who's he?

JANE: I just told you. He's the real estate man I've been working with. I told him you'd call him.

TOMMY: I can hardly wait.

JANE: Please do. I'm trying so hard to arrange everything. Do you still want Jeff to stand up for you?

TOMMY: Yes, if he can. Why?

JANE: Nothing. It's just that he's so impossible these days. Everybody is bored to death with him.

TOMMY: I'm not interested in everybody, especially the everybody we know.

JANE: You've certainly been antisocial since you returned from Scotland. If you really *want* to avoid everybody, why don't we take Mr. Jackson's house? It's far away and right on the top of a high, beautiful hill . . .

(*Same business again.* FIONA *is heard, then seen singing. Only this time she is nearer*)

FIONA: (*Sings*)

. . . Through the heather on the hill.
But when the mist is in the gloamin',
An' all the clouds are holdin' still,
If ye're not here I won't go roamin'
Through the heather on the hill;
The heather on the . . .

(TOMMY *turns sharply to* JANE. *The moment he speaks, the half lights come up at the bar and blackout on the full stage*)

TOMMY: No, Jane! No!

JANE: No, what?

TOMMY: I can't go through with it! There's going to be no wedding next month.

JANE: Do you mean you're postponing it again?

TOMMY: No, I am not postponing it. I'm calling it off for good!

JANE: Calling it off!

TOMMY: I can't do it! Ever.

JANE: You have a nerve! After all this time I've waited for you and tried to be patient and put up with your idiotic whims and temperament?

TOMMY: I'm sorry. It's not your fault. You've been wonderfully kind to me. But something strange happened a few months ago that I can't explain, and now I don't fit here any more.

JANE: I think you're going clean out of your mind. But I refuse to stand here and argue with you in this bar! Let's go home and . . .

(*Same business.* CHARLIE *and several of the* TOWNSFOLK *are seen all around behind him as the lights come slowly up on them*)

CHARLIE and TOWNSFOLK: (*Sing*)

Go home, go home, go home with bonnie Jean!
Go home, go home, I'll go home with bonnie Jean!

(*The music continues and they seem to be walking away from him into the night. We hear* JANE *say:*)

JANE: And if you think anyone else is going to put up with your nonsense, you're raving mad. So think that over, Mr. Albright, when you're all alone!

(*She exits.* TOMMY *stands and looks out front.* FIONA *appears again, this time very near him*)

FIONA: I think real loneliness is not bein' in love in vain, but not bein' in love at all.

TOMMY: You understood, Fiona–I didn't.

FIONA: (*Sings "From This Day On"*)

You walkin' through the heather
When we were there together,
That's all I'll see
From this day on.

TOMMY: You were right. It never faded.

(*Sings*)
These hurried hours were all the life we could share.
Still I will go with not a tear, just a prayer
That—

FIONA:
Through all the years to come
An' through all the tears to come

FIONA and TOMMY:
I know I'll be yours
From this day on.

(*She begins to walk back as the chorus is heard upstage singing*)

CHORUS:
Come ye from the hills!
Come ye from the mills!
Come ye in the glen!
Come ye, bairn,
Come ye, men! . . .

(*They reach full voice. Bagpipers are heard. It all swells and swells as* TOMMY *turns to the bar and hurriedly picks up the telephone. Then:*)

TOMMY: (*On the phone—over chorus*) Hello? Room 732, please! . . . Jeff? Are you sober? . . . I want to go back to Scotland . . . Never mind what for! . . . Do you want to come with me? . . . Well, get plane reservations right away! . . . I know it isn't there, but I want to see where it was . . . Who cares if it doesn't make sense? . . . I want to go . . . (*The voices are fortissimo*) I want to go, do you hear? . . . I want to go!

Blackout

SCENE 5

The forest. This is the same as Act One, Scene 1. Three nights later. TOMMY *and* JEFF *walk on from the right. They look around them for a moment in silence.*

TOMMY: It's unbelievable! Awful and unbelievable!

JEFF: (*Quite drunk*) What is awful and unbelievable?

TOMMY: To think that somewhere out there—between the mist

and the stars—there's somebody I want so terribly. She's not dead. She's only asleep. And yet I'll never see her again.

JEFF: Did you come all the way over here just to say that? You could have told me that on the phone in New York for a nickel.

TOMMY: No. I'll tell you why. She became so alive to me that I had to come back and see for myself that the place really wasn't here.

JEFF: It didn't work that way for me. It's so much like a dream now that I'd have to work hard to convince myself it happened at all.

TOMMY: There's the big difference between us.

JEFF: Tell me about it.

TOMMY: I found that sometimes what you believe in becomes more real to you than all the things you can explain away or understand. (*He looks around for a moment*) God! Why do people have to lose things to find out what they mean?

JEFF: Well, take a last look and let's start walking. I got lost around here once.

(*He turns to move to exit, when suddenly singing is heard softly in the distance. It is the chorus singing*)

CHORUS:

Brigadoon, Brigadoon,
Blooming under sable skies.
Brigadoon, Brigadoon,
There my heart forever lies,
Let the world grow cold around us;
Let the heavens cry above!
Brigadoon, Brigadoon,
In thy valley there'll be love!

(*The singing continues under the following sequence. When it first starts,* TOMMY *and* JEFF *look at each other in bewilderment. Then suddenly* MR. LUNDIE *appears from the left. He is very sleepy. He walks half over to* TOMMY, *then stops and peers at him*)

MR. LUNDIE: Tommy, lad! Ye! My, my! Ye mus' really love her! Ye woke me up! (TOMMY *and* JEFF *just stare at him in astonishment*) Come, lad. (*He holds out his hand.* TOMMY *walks toward it as one in a trance*) Ye shouldna be too surprised, lad. I told ye when ye love someone deeply anythin' is possible. (*They start to walk off right.* MR. LUNDIE *stops and looks up at him*) Even miracles.

(*Just before they exit,* TOMMY *turns and looks back at* JEFF, *who stands looking at them in bewilderment. The chorus swells and* TOMMY *and* MR. LUNDIE *exit*)

Curtain

KISS ME, KATE

Book by Samuel *and* Bella Spewack
Music and Lyrics by Cole Porter

Production Notes

Kiss Me, Kate was first presented by Saint Subber and Lemuel Ayers at the New Century Theatre, New York, on December 30, 1948. The cast was as follows:

Fred Graham, *Alfred Drake*
Harry Trevor, *Thomas Hoier*
Lois Lane, *Lisa Kirk*
Ralph (*Stage Manager*), *Don Mayo*
Lilli Vanessi, *Patricia Morison*
Hattie, *Annabelle Hill*
Paul, *Lorenzo Fuller*
Bill Calhoun, *Harold Lang*
First Man, *Harry Clark*
Second Man, *Jack Diamond*
Stage Doorman, *Dan Brennan*
Harrison Howell, *Denis Green*
Specialty Dancers, *Fred Davis, Eddie Sledge*

"TAMING OF THE SHREW" PLAYERS

Bianca (*Lois Lane*), *Lisa Kirk*
Baptista (*Harry Trevor*), *Thomas Hoier*
Gremio (*First Suitor*), *Noel Gordon*
Hortensio (*Second Suitor*), *Charles Wood*
Lucentio (*Bill Calhoun*), *Harold Lang*
Katharine (*Lilli Vanessi*), *Patricia Morison*
Petruchio (*Fred Graham*), *Alfred Drake*
Haberdasher, *John Castello*

Singing Ensemble, *Peggy Ferris, Christine Matsios, Joan Kibrig, Gay Laurence, Ethel Madsen, Helen Rice, Matilda Strazza, Tom Bole, George Cassidy, Herb Fields, Edwin Clay, Allan Lowell, Stan Rose, Charles Wood.*

Dancers, *Janet Gaylord, Jean Houloose, Doreen Oswald, Cynthia Riseley, Ingrid Secretan, Gissela Svetlik, Jean Haas, Harry Asmus, Marc Breaux, John Castello, Victor Duntiere, Tom Hansen, Glen Tetley, Rudy Tone.*

Directed by *John C. Wilson*
Choreography by *Hanya Holm*
Settings and Costumes by *Lemuel Ayers*
Orchestrations by *Robert Russell Bennett*
Musical Director: *Pembroke Davenport*

Act One

Scene 1: Stage of Ford's Theatre, Baltimore.
Scene 2: The corridor backstage.

Scene 3: Dressing rooms, Fred Graham and Lilli Vanessi.
Scene 4: Padua.
Scene 5: Street scene, Padua.
Scene 6: Backstage.
Scene 7: Fred's and Lilli's dressing rooms.
Scene 8: Before the curtain.
Scene 9: Exterior church.

Act Two

Scene 1: Theatre alley.
Scene 2: Before the curtain.
Scene 3: Petruchio's house.
Scene 4: The corridor backstage.
Scene 5: Lilli's dressing room.
Scene 6: The corridor backstage.
Scene 7: Before the asbestos curtain.
Scene 8: Baptista's home.

Musical Numbers

Act One

Scene 1:
Another Op'nin', Another Show — Hattie and Singing Ensemble
Danced by Dancing Ensemble

Scene 2:
Why Can't You Behave? — Lois Lane

Scene 3:
Wunderbar — Lilli and Fred
So in Love — Lilli

Scene 4:
We Open in Venice — Petruchio, Katharine, Bianca, Lucentio

Scene 5:
Dance — By Dancing Ensemble
Tom, Dick, or Harry — Bianca, Lucentio, and the Two Suitors
Specialty Dance — Lucentio
I've Come To Wive It Wealthily in Padua — Petruchio and Singing Ensemble
I Hate Men — Katharine
Were Thine That Special Face — Petruchio
Danced by Janet Gaylord and Dancing Girls

Scene 8:
I Sing of Love — Bianca, Lucentio, and Singing Ensemble

Scene 9:

Tarantella — Danced by Bianca, Lucentio, and Dancing Ensemble

Finale: *Kiss Me Kate* — Katharine, Petruchio, and Singing Ensemble

Act Two

Scene 1:

Too Darn Hot — Paul, Fred Davis, and Eddie Sledge
Danced by Fred Davis, Eddie Sledge, Bill Calhoun and Dancing Ensemble

Scene 3:

Where Is The Life That Late I Led? — Petruchio

Scene 4:

Always True To You in My Fashion — Lois

Scene 6:

Bianca — Bill Calhoun and Singing Girls
Danced by Bill Calhoun and Dancing Girls

Reprise: *So in Love* — Fred

Scene 7:

Brush Up Your Shakespeare — First Man and Second Man

Scene 8:

Pavane — By Dancing Ensemble

I Am Ashamed That Women Are So Simple — Katharine

Finale: — Petruchio, Katharine, and Company

ACT ONE

SCENE 1

The bare stage of Ford's Theatre in Baltimore, the land of Mencken and nod. It's hot. It's sticky. It's late afternoon. It's June. Numbered flats of the painted sets lean against the rear brick wall. Stagehands move leisurely in and out of the wings. The bright glare of a single bulb known in the theatre as a pilot light sharpens the faces of the actors and dancers within its orbit. They have just finished a run-through rehearsal of the musical version of The Taming of the Shrew, *and are standing around in their street clothes in groups of two and three, presumably all ears for last-minute directorial criticism. What they're really thinking about is food and if they'll have time to eat before the show starts. Actors have to eat even if it's the opening night of a tryout.*

FREDERICK GRAHAM, *writer, director, actor, and superman, is out in the empty theatre listening to the overture as he wants it played.* LILLI VANESSI, *motion picture star and once married to* GRAHAM, *is seated on a chair on stage right, obviously seething.* LOIS LANE *is standing, talking to* RALPH, *the stage manager, on stage left.*

CONDUCTOR: (*At the end of the overture*) Is that all right, Mr. Graham?

FRED: (*Enters from theatre*) Yes, the cut's good, leave it in. (*Reading through notes on clipboard*) Baptista. (HARRY TREVOR, *an elderly actor, steps forward.* HATTIE, LILLI'S *Negro maid, enters, crosses to* LILLI *with glass of water, then exits*) Harry, be sure and shake off Gremio and Hortensio in that entrance in the street scene.

HARRY: *Si, signor*. Mr. Graham is it all right if—

FRED: In a minute, Harry—Bianca—

(LOIS LANE *turns to* FRED)

LOIS: (*Coyly*) Yes, Fred. I mean, Mr. Graham.

FRED: I realize, Lois, that in night club work you don't have to cheat—(*Theatrical expression to cover actor's appearing to play scene with another actor but actually aiming his lines out to the audience*)

LOIS: (*Interrupting*) Oh, don't you though?

FRED: You don't have to cheat front, Miss Lane, but on stage when you're playing scenes with other people, you do. This is your first show and I know it's hard for you.

(LILLI *says nothing, but glares*)

LOIS: (*Almost baby-wise*) Do you mean thus—(*Of course she turns wrong*) or thus?

FRED: We'll thus it later.

(LOIS *retreats.* FRED *crosses to* RALPH)

HARRY: (*Crosses to* FRED) Mr. Graham, is it all right if I leave now? I can just make the dentist. Upper plate wobble.

FRED: In a minute, Harry. All right, let's set the curtain calls. First call all principals. (*Principals step forward*) Miss Vanessi care to join us? (LILLI *does so*) Thank you! Leave room for me. Baptista, change places with Gremio. (*They change places*) That's right. Looks like somebody's missing—Lucentio—where the hell's Lucentio?

RALPH: (*Looking offstage left and right, yelling*) Bill Calhoun! Bill Calhoun!

VOICE OFFSTAGE: Bill Calhoun!

RALPH: He *was* here.

FRED: Give a Broadway hoofer a chance to play Shakespeare and what happens? He isn't even here.

LOIS: (*Who has been trying to attract their attention*) I think he went to the chiropodist.

FRED: Second call—Harry, run along to your dentist.

HARRY: Much obliged, old man . . . (*Exits left*)

FRED: Second call, Bianca and Suitors—thank you, that looks all right. (*Hands* RALPH *clipboard and moves toward center*) Third call—myself and Miss Vanessi. (LILLI VANESSI *steps forward*) Excuse me—(*Turns from her*) Lois!

LOIS: (*Stops when* FRED *calls*) Did thou call me, honey? (*She moves toward him.* LILLI *glares*)

FRED: (*Puts his arm on her shoulder*) I'd rather you didn't leave the theatre between now and opening.

LOIS: (*Very much gal with man*) Whatever thou say, Fred.

FRED: I want you to rest and relax, and let your mind go blank. Blank!

LOIS: How blank can it get? Honest—those *thee's* and *thou's*—I hope I don't louse you up. (*She exits*)

(*Stagehands exit with ladders.* FRED *turns toward* LILLI, *who's been waiting with suppressed anger*)

FRED: Now. Sorry to have kept you waiting, Miss Vanessi. (*To* RALPH) Now watch it, Ralph—call it!

RALPH: Third call!

(FRED *and* LILLI *bow to each other and the audience*)

FRED: No, I think it would look better if we came down together—and then bowed to each other. (*They walk upstage.* FRED *takes* LILLI'S *hand, walks downstage with her. They bow to audience, then to each other.* FRED *pauses in middle of bow. To* LILLI) Now, how about a smile, Miss Vanessi? Ready? (*She smiles, curtsies*)

LILLI: (*Still curtsying and smiling, looking straight at* FRED, *as he bows*) You bastard!

(LILLI *stalks offstage right.* FRED, *startled, looks after her. Music starts*)

FRED: (*Turning back angrily*) Call them on, Ralph.

RALPH: On stage everybody!

(SINGERS, DANCERS, *and* HATTIE *enter*)

FRED: I want to thank each and every one of you for the fine spirit you've shown all through rehearsals. There'll be a gang down from New York, don't let that worry you. This is a tryout and I know we're going to make a helluva show out of *The Shrew*. After all, we owe it to Shakespeare, not to mention the six other fellows who've been sitting up nights rewriting him. That's all. Thank you. (*Exits angrily right. Stagehand strikes* LILLI'S *chair, right, during speech*)

(TWO SINGING GIRLS *bring* HATTIE *down center.* HATTIE *begins:*)

HATTIE: ("*Another Op'nin', Another Show*")

Another op'nin', another show
In Philly, Boston, or Baltimo'e,
A chance for stage-folks to say "Hello,"
Another op'nin' of another show,
Another job that you hope, at last,
Will make your future forget your past,
Another pain where the ulcers grow,
Another op'nin' of another show.
Four weeks, you rehearse and rehearse,
Three weeks, and it couldn't be worse,
One week, will it ever be right?
Then out o' the hat, it's that big first night!
The overture is about to start,
You cross your fingers and hold your heart,
It's curtain time and away we go,
Another op'nin',
Of another show.

HATTIE and ENSEMBLE:

Another op'nin', another show
In Philly, Boston, or Baltimo'e,
A chance for stage-folks to say "Hello,"
Another op'nin' of another show,
Another job that you hope, at last,
Will make your future forget your past,
Another pain where the ulcers grow,
Another op'nin' of another show.
Four weeks, you rehearse and rehearse,
Three weeks, and it couldn't be worse,
One week, will it ever be right?
Then out o' the hat, it's that big first night!

The overture is about to start,
You cross your fingers and hold your heart,
It's curtain time and away we go,
Another op'nin' of another show.

(*As* HATTIE *and* SINGERS *exit,* DANCERS *in practice costumes enter in twos and threes and go through routines of ballet exercises, waltz and jazz movements. Electricians checking on lights bathe the dancers in alternate floods of pink, blue, and amber. As the dance finishes,* HATTIE *and* SINGERS *come back on stage to join* DANCERS *in the final chorus of "Another Op'nin', Another Show"*)

HATTIE:
Four weeks, you rehearse and rehearse,
Three weeks, and it couldn't be worse.
One week, will it ever be right?
Then out o' the hat, it's that big first night!

ALL:
The overture is about to start,
You cross your fingers and hold your heart,
It's curtain time and away we go,

FINAL ENDING:
Another op'nin',
Just another op'nin', of another show.

Blackout

SCENE 2

Corridor backstage. Spiral staircase stage right. DOORMAN'S *booth stage left. Coin box telephone attached to upstage corner of booth. Backdrop depicts corridor of theatre.*

BOYS *and* GIRLS *separate, some exit left. Others move briskly to iron staircase and exit.* LOIS *is at telephone.* DOORMAN *in his booth.*

LOIS: (*On phone*) Hello! Hello! Is Bill Calhoun there? I said Bill Calhoun! Well, you don't have to be so fresh about it! (*Hangs up*) Pop, let me know the minute Mr. Calhoun comes in. (*She moves toward staircase*)

PAUL: (*Bearing* FRED'S *first act costume.* PAUL *is* FRED'S *Negro dresser*) Miss Lane, you got two dollars?

LOIS: What do you want two dollars for?

PAUL: It ain't for me. It's for Mr. Calhoun.
LOIS: Where is he?
(DOORMAN *leaves booth, stands by phone*)
PAUL: He's a prisoner of the Yellow Cab Company.
(BILL *enters from door with* CAB DRIVER, *smoking cigarette. He whistles first three notes of "Bianca"*)
LOIS: Bill!
BILL: Hiya, Sarah Bernhardt!
CAB DRIVER: I want my fare.
(HARRY *enters stage right*)
BILL: (*Shaking dice*) Shoot you for it—double or nothing!
(CAB DRIVER *shakes his head*)
PAUL: (*Calling* LOIS'S *attention to* HARRY) Psst! Psst!
LOIS: Harry, you got two dollars?
HARRY: Child, if I had two dollars, I'd retire and never do a lick of work again! (*Exits*)
LOIS: Paul, do you suppose Mr. Graham's got two dollars?
PAUL: Mr. Graham? Not him! He's a producer! (*Exits*)
LOIS: (*To* CAB DRIVER) Can you wait until Saturday night?
(DRIVER *shakes head, "No"*)
DOORMAN: (*Steps forward*) All right, Miss Lane. I'll lay it out! That'll make sixteen dollars.
(CAB DRIVER *exits, followed by* DOORMAN. DOORMAN *returns to his stool in booth and reads racing form*)
LOIS: Bill, you've been gambling again. And I told Mr. Graham you went to the chiropodist's.
BILL: I went to the cleaner's. (*Turning out empty trouser pockets*)
LOIS: How much did you lose this time?
BILL: Ten G's. Ten thousand fast little bucks!
LOIS: Ten G's? Did you sign an IOU again?
BILL: Uhuh!
LOIS: Whose name did you sign this time?
BILL: Frederick Graham! (*Writes the name in the air*)
LOIS: Mr. Graham! Oh, Bill! This is our big chance. Do you want to play night clubs all your life?
BILL: We were doing all right, weren't we?
LOIS: Yeah, it's as Mr. Graham said: "Give a Broadway hoofer a chance to play Shakespeare and . . ."
BILL: Mr. Graham—your hero!
LOIS: Mr. Graham is a great actor, a scholar, and a gentleman.

He's just culturing me—but there's nothing wrong between him and I—I mean he and I.

BILL: (*Crosses to staircase*) I know . . . Art!

LOIS: I'll never forgive you, Bill, if anything happens to Mr. Graham before I'm a star on Broadway. (*Crosses onto stairs*)

BILL: (*At foot of stairs*) Gee, honey, I'm sorry.

LOIS: If you only meant it!

(*And* LOIS *sings*)

LOIS: (*"Why Can't You Behave?"*)

Why can't you behave?
(BILL *sits on platform*)
Oh, why can't you behave?
After all the things you told me
And the promises that you gave,
Oh, why can't you behave?

Why can't you be good?
And do just as you should?
Won't you turn that new leaf over
So your baby can be your slave?
Oh, why can't you behave?

There's a farm I know near my old home town
Where two can go and try settlin' down,
There I'll care for you forever,
Well at least till you dig my grave,
(BILL *rises*)
Oh, why can't you behave?
(*Takes off hat*)

BILL:

Gee, I need yuh, kid.

LOIS:

I always knew you did
But why can't you behave?

(Lights Fade Out)

SCENE 3

Dressing rooms, with FRED'S *room right and* LILLI'S *room left. A connecting door between the rooms is open.* LILLI'S *room is elaborate, with a chaise longue, poufs, dressing table with mirror and chair, rug on floor, and phone on table left. Elaborate screen. Dressing table holds make-up mirror and make-up of all kinds. Also a jewel case and a small photo of a nude baby. Suitcase handy.*

FRED'S *room is drab, with steam pipes showing on ceiling. Sink in upper right corner; dressing table with make-up mirror and make-up box downstage, waste basket, old towel. An old wardrobe trunk open revealing a couple of garments. Screen and a suitcase and hatbox on a shelf, plain chair in front of table.*

FRED: (*Shouting angrily toward* LILLI'S *room*) Calling me a bastard and on stage.

LILLI: (*From her room*) I didn't say it—I just indicated it.

(RALPH *knocks at* LILLI'S *door*)

RALPH: Half-hour.

LILLI: Thank you, Ralph. Oh, this heat.

RALPH: (*Moving to* FRED'S *room*) You know Baltimore!

FRED: How's the house?

RALPH: You know Baltimore!

FRED: I know. There'll be deer running around the balcony. Next time I open a show here, I'll bring my shotgun and eat.

(RALPH *exits, calling*)

RALPH: (*Offstage*) Half-hour.

FRED: (*Entering* LILLI'S *room*) Hah! So much for a Hollywood name. Your fans must have heard you were appearing in person. (*Phone rings*) Go on, pick it up—it's probably Harrison.

LILLI: (*Picks up phone*) Hello, hello, Harrison darling. I thought you'd be here by now. (*Puts part down on dressing table*) Oh, you're still at the White House? He is? He's taking your advice? He's getting a player piano? What? The President wants to talk to me? To unimportant little me? . . . But what'll I say? Good evening, Mr. President.

FRED: (*Grabbing phone and speaking into it*) Is it true, Mr. President, you're serving borscht at the White House?

LILLI: (*Pulls phone away from* FRED) How dare you! Mr. President, I apologize. I beg your pardon? . . . With sour cream.

FRED: What did I tell you?

LILLI: Thank you, Mr. President . . . Hello, Harrison . . . I wish you'd come tonight, angel, after all, it's your show . . . Yes, angel . . . I understand . . . yes, darling . . . yes, love. I'm blowing you two kisses. (*Two kisses into phone*)

(FRED *blows two kisses at same time* LILLI *does.* HATTIE *enters with vase of roses*)

FRED: (*Sneezing*) Roses! Get those damn roses out of here—

you know I'm allergic to roses. I'll break out in a rash again and you know where.

LILLI: Hattie! Take these roses to Miss Lane's dressing room with my compliments! (HATTIE *exits with roses.* LILLI *displays resplendent ring for* FRED'S *benefit*)

FRED: I see it! I see it! What is it? The Hope Diamond or Aly Khan's emerald?

LILLI: Did I show you the star sapphire Harrison sent me? It was his mother's engagement ring.

FRED: His mother must have worn it on her big toe.

LILLI: (*Beaming pridefully*) And now it's mine! (*Sits on couch*)

FRED: Congratulations!

LILLI: Do you know what day this is, Fred? Our anniversary, and you forgot.

FRED: What anniversary?

LILLI: (*Sweetly*) The first anniversary of our divorce.

FRED: If you must know, I was thinking of sending you a cactus. But, no money. I know you're rolling in it.

LILLI: Every night before I go to bed, that's exactly what I do. Roll in my money. Wonderful for the hips. (*She pats one and moves to sit at dressing table*)

FRED: (*Bitterly*) Hollywood–swimming pool–avocado ranches. While I–I put every penny I could scrape, borrow, or steal into my *Cyrano* in Paris. My magnum opus! But I was a huge success.

LILLI: (*Looking into mirror*) And you closed on Saturday? Four glorious performances!

FRED: I'll have you know, there was a general strike!

LILLI: (*With mock sympathy and looking right at* FRED) Oh, you couldn't have been that bad!

FRED: Same old Lilli! (*Picks up photo on dresser*) Who's this little monster? Harrison Howell?

LILLI: That's you at the age of two–bottoms up!

FRED: Cute little fellow. Mind if I keep it?

LILLI: No. And you can have this, too. (*Holding up cork and rising*)

FRED: What's this? A cork?

LILLI: Our first bottle of champagne.

FRED: Our wedding breakfast?

LILLI: Yes, in my apartment.

FRED: You mean that one room of yours over the Armenian bakery?

LILLI: You're a fine one to complain. You didn't even have a room.

FRED: Why do you think I married you? (*Sits on couch*)

LILLI: (*Thinking back*) That was the season we played the Barter Theatre in Virginia and they gave you a ham.

FRED: (*Stung*) Well, we lived on that all winter, you forget!

LILLI: *You* forget I got a job reading tea leaves in a Gypsy tea room opposite Macy's. (*Sits on couch beside him*)

FRED: And *you* forget *I* demonstrated shaving soap in Woolworth's.

LILLI: (*Suddenly remembering*) That's right. That's how I spent my honeymoon—at Woolworth's. Watching you shave.

FRED: We weren't married then?

LILLI: (*Nodding*) Oh yes, dear, we were. Mother was coming to stay with us. It was right after we closed on the road in a little British makeshift of a Viennese operetta that for some reason was laid in Switzerland. But the costumes were Dutch.

FRED: And so were those salaries. I could have sworn it was right after that flop revival of the *Prince of Potsdam*. Yes, I was understudying the lead. I was the youngest understudy in the business.

LILLI: No, dear. We were both in the chorus. (*Music starts*) There was a waltz in it. Remember? Something about a bar. (*She starts to hum*)

FRED: (*Rises*) *Ja!* Madame, you are ravishing tonight . . . You have made me the happiest of men.

LILLI: (*Rising, goes to* FRED) Your Highness. (*Both suddenly remember and speak*)

FRED: *Wunderbar!*

LILLI: *Wunderbar!*

FRED and LILLI: (*"Wunderbar"*)

SHE:

Wunderbar.

HE:

Wunderbar!

SHE:

There's our fav'rite star above.

HE:

What a bright-shining star!

BOTH:

Like our love, it's *wunderbar!*

(FRED, *back of lounge.* LILLI *sits on lounge*)
(*Verse*)

HE:

Gazing down on the Jungfrau

SHE:

From our secret chalet for two,

HE:

Let us drink, *Liebchen mein,*

SHE:

In the moonlight benign,

BOTH:

To the joy of our dream come true.

(*Refrain*)

BOTH:

Wunderbar, wunderbar!
(*He takes her hand*)

HE:

What a perfect night for love,

SHE:

Here am I, here you are,
(*Rises*)

HE:

Why, it's truly *wunderbar!*

BOTH:

Wunderbar, wunderbar!

HE:

We're alone and hand in glove,

SHE:

Not a cloud near or far,

HE:

Why, it's more than *wunderbar!*

SHE:

Say you care, dear,

HE:

For you madly.

SHE:
Say you long, dear,

HE:
For your kiss.

SHE:
Do you swear, dear?
(*Turns and takes his hand*)

HE:
Darling, gladly,

SHE:
Life's divine, dear,

HE:
And you're mine, dear!
(*Embrace*)

BOTH:
Wunderbar, wunderbar!

HE:
There's our fav'rite star above,

SHE:
What a bright-shining star!

BOTH:
Like our love, it's *wunderbar!*
(*They waltz a bit*)

HE:
And you're mine, dear!
(*Embrace*)

BOTH:
Wunderbar, wunderbar!
(*Sway*)

HE:
There's our fav'rite star above,

BOTH:
What a bright-shining star!
Like our love, it's *wunderbar!*

(*They kiss at end of song.* RALPH *knocks, opens door, speaks from doorway, closes door as he leaves*)

RALPH: Fifteen minutes.

LILLI: Whose fault was it?

FRED: It could have been your temper.

LILLI: Could have been your ego.

FRED: Let's get dressed. (*Goes into his room. Closes door*)

(*Lights fade out in* LILLI'S *room but remain on in* FRED'S *room.* FRED *sits at dressing table.* TWO MEN *enter. They are well dressed. Too much so—from their expensive pearl-gray felt hats, and neat, hand-sewn blue suits to their over-polished shoes. They look like gunmen. They are. The soft-spoken kind. They're obviously embarrassed at being backstage and in the presence of the great* FREDERICK GRAHAM)

FIRST MAN: Hello.

FRED: (*Staring*) Who are you? What are you doing backstage?

FIRST MAN: Fine-looking fella.

SECOND MAN: Clean cut.

FIRST MAN: What a figger!

SECOND MAN: What a profile!

FRED: (*Crosses to gunmen*) Gentlemen, I'm deeply touched by your admiration and devotion.

FIRST MAN: What diction!

SECOND MAN: Very elocutionary.

FIRST MAN: And he does not spit when he talks.

SECOND MAN: (*Looks*) High-type fella.

FRED: As I was saying, this is all very flattering, but I receive the public *after* the performance, not before. (*Crosses to dressing table*)

FIRST MAN: Oh, what grace!

SECOND MAN: If I hadda do something to him, I'd cry like a baby.

FRED: Gentlemen, come back *after* the show. I'll be very happy to present you with my autograph.

FIRST MAN: (*Crosses to* FRED) We got your autograph. That's why we're here.

FRED: What?

FIRST MAN: A little matter of an IOU. Here it is— (*Shows it*) Ten G's. Mr. Hogan—that's our employer—regards this as a debt of honor. How's about it, Mr. Graham?

FRED: You're mad. Paul! Paul! (SECOND MAN *makes certain door is securely shut and both cross to* FRED) Let's see that. (*Grabs for IOU.* FIRST MAN *stops him. He looks*) Why, that's not even my signature!

FIRST MAN: They all say that. I'm surprised at you, Mr. Graham. You signed it only this afternoon after quite a little game down at the hotel. We wasn't there, of course. Mr. Hogan says he plied you plenty with good liquor, too.

FRED: You're really mad! I've been in this theatre since eight this morning. (*Sits and begins to apply make-up*)

FIRST MAN: He forgot.

SECOND MAN: Yeah. That's human nature for you. (FRED *continues making up*)

FIRST MAN: The minute a man signs an IOU everything goes dark.

SECOND MAN: The doctors call it magnesia.

FIRST MAN: We cure it.

SECOND MAN: I'd cry like a baby, if I hadda do something to such a high-type fella. Last week–remember that high-type fella–I used up three handkerchiefs.

FIRST MAN: (*Looking in mirror*) I don't like my face. Do you?

SECOND MAN: No!

FRED: Gentlemen, would you mind leaving?

FIRST MAN: Ain't he virile? We now wish to express all best wishes for a magnificent opening and the success your brilliant talents deserve! I copied that out of Western Union.

SECOND MAN: (*Hat in hand*) Heartiest felicitations! I made that up myself!

FIRST MAN: Mr. Graham, try and jostle your memory. (*Only, he pronounces it* jostill)

SECOND MAN: We'll be back.

(*They exit.* FRED *looks after them in amazement, shrugs, and goes on with his dressing. Lights dim in* FRED'S *room. Lights up in* LILLI'S *room.* PAUL *knocks on* LILLI'S *door, opens it, and waits there*)

HATTIE: (*Turns to door*) Hello, Paul.

PAUL: Hiya, beautiful. (PAUL *gives* HATTIE *a box of flowers, and exits*)

HATTIE: Here's some flowers. Paul gave them to me. They must be from Mr. Fred. (LILLI *lifts lid of box–sees bouquet*)

LILLI: Snowdrops and pansies and rosemary. My wedding bouquet! Oh, Hattie, he didn't forget.

HATTIE: (*Cooing*) Of course not, honey. Now, I'll get you some coffee. (*Exits*)

(*Lights dim as* LILLI *regards the bouquet in her lap and begins to sing*)

LILLI: (*"So in Love"*)

Strange, dear, but true, dear,
When I'm close to you, dear,
The stars fill the sky,
So in love with you am I.
(*Puts box down*)
Even without you
My arms fold about you,
You know, darling, why,
So in love with you am I.
In love with the night mysterious,
The night when you first were there,
In love with my joy delirious
When I knew that you could care.
So taunt me and hurt me,
Deceive me, desert me,
I'm yours till I die,
So in love,
So in love,
So in love with you, my love, am I.

(*Music continues as she takes flower box to dressing table and returns to couch with bouquet. A rather sad* LILLI, *a defenseless* LILLI, *finishes with:*)

LILLI:

So taunt me and hurt me,
Deceive me, desert me,
I'm yours till I die,
So in love,
So in love,
So in love with you, my love, am I.

(*Lights go up in* FRED'S *dressing room.* PAUL *enters, starts helping* FRED *into his costume*)

FRED: Paul, what the devil do you mean letting a couple of raving maniacs in here, five minutes before curtain?

PAUL: There was no one in here when I left.

FRED: Tell Ralph next time no one's to be admitted into my dressing room without a psychoanalyst's certificate! Of course, they may have been just overwhelmed at meeting me!

PAUL: I'm sure that's it, sir! Everybody feels the magnetism of your personality, sir, off stage and on.

FRED: You know, Paul, you're not only the finest dresser I've ever had but a true connoisseur of the theatre.

PAUL: Thank you, Mr. Graham.

FRED: (*Sits at dressing table*) Did you–uh–deliver my flowers?

PAUL: Yes, sir.

FRED: Did you put the note in?

PAUL: Yes, sir.

FRED: Good. You gave them to Miss Lane personally, of course?

PAUL: Miss Lane? I thought they were for Miss Vanessi, sir.

FRED: Miss Vanessi. Don't tell me you . . . you driveling idiot!

PAUL: I'm sorry, sir. I haven't been myself since Blue Blood was scratched in the third race! (*Exits hastily*)

FRED: Moron!

(FRED *enters* LILLI'S *dressing room*)

LILLI: (*Tremulous and loving*) Fred, you darling . . . You didn't forget . . . (*Holding up bouquet*)

FRED: (*Quick to pick up a cue*) You didn't think I would?

(RALPH *opens door, sticks his head in. Overture music can be heard*)

RALPH: (*Bawling*) On stage! Good luck! (*Leaves door open*)

FRED: (*Snapping his fingers nervously*) Come on, let's go.

LILLI: I can't. My hands are freezing. (*Sits on lounge*)

FRED: (*Begins rubbing her hands*) Now, Lilli, you're not going to whoops?

LILLI: (*Nervously*) Do you think they'll like me? After all, I've been away from the theatre almost . . .

FRED: (*Shouting*) They'll love you! (*As* FRED *grabs* LILLI *by the hand,* HATTIE *holds up envelope containing card*)

HATTIE: I found it, Miss Lilli. Here's the card that came with the flowers!

LILLI: Quick, Hattie, give it to me! (HATTIE *does so, beaming, and exits, closing the door.* LILLI *is about to read the card*)

FRED: (*Taking both her hands–aghast*) You're not going to read that now! . . . Look, I'll tell you what I wrote: "To Lilli, the only woman I've ever loved, the only artist I've ever worshipped!" Now give me the card and you can read it after the show!

LILLI: Oh, Fred, did you really mean that? (*Rises, throws arms around* FRED)

FRED: (*Plenty nervous, tries to get card*) With all my heart!

LILLI: Then–that's where it's going. (*She slips card into her bosom*) Right next to mine. I'm not nervous—I'm not going to whoops and I'll never call you a bastard—Fred dear, never!

FRED: (*In grim resignation*) You will, my sweet, you will!

(Blackout)

(*And now we go into the musical version of* The Taming of the Shrew)

SCENE 4

Before the curtain, a lovely confection of yellow and pink purporting to be a map of Italy with its principal towns.

TWO BOYS *carrying* Taming of the Shrew *banner start parade of* DANCERS *and* SINGERS, *followed by* KATHARINE, PETRUCHIO, BIANCA, LUCENTIO. *They sing:*

ALL: ("*We Open in Venice*")

(*Verse*)

ALL:

A troupe of strolling players are we,

LILLI:

Not stars like L. B. Mayer's are we

ALL:

But just a simple band
Who roams about the land
Dispensing fol-de-rol frivolitee.
Mere folk who give distraction are we,

FRED:

No Theatre Guild attraction are we

ALL:

But just a crazy group
That never ceases to troupe
Around the map of little Italee.

(*1st Refrain*)

ALL:

We open in Venice,
We next play Verona,
Then on to Cremona,

LILLI:

Lotsa laughs in Cremona.

ALL:

Our next jump is Parma,

That dopey, mopey menace,
Then Mantua, then Padua,
Then we open again, where?

(*2nd Refrain*)

ALL:
We open in Venice,
We next play Verona,
Then on to Cremona,

BILL:
Lotsa bars in Cremona.

ALL:
The next jump is Parma,
That beerless, cheerless menace,
Then Mantua, then Padua,
Then we open again, where?

(*3rd Refrain*)

ALL:
We open in Venice,
We next play Verona,
Then on to Cremona,

LOIS:
Lotsa dough in Cremona.

ALL:
Our next jump is Parma,
That stingy, dingy menace,
Then Mantua, then Padua,
Then we open again, where?

(*4th Refrain*)

ALL:
We open in Venice,
We next play Verona,
Then on to Cremona,

FRED:
Lotsa quail in Cremona.

ALL:
Our next jump is Parma,
That heartless, tartless menace,
Then Mantua, then Padua,

Then we open again, where?
In Venice.

(*All exit right*)

SCENE 5

Piazza in Padua. To one side is the entrance and façade of BAPTISTA'S *house with a balcony over the door. On the other side the entrance to the inn with a shallow striped awning over it. Back of that is a platform with drawn curtains where the mummers perform.*

Market Day. Peddlers hawk their wares from trays. As lights come up, dance is in progress. During dance, BIANCA *sidles forth, carrying a red rose, followed by* GREMIO *and* HORTENSIO *carrying nothing.* LUCENTIO *tags along carrying books.* BIANCA, *the little flirt, exits into house, leaving three disconsolate suitors at the door. After the mummers finish their dance and go offstage,* BIANCA *re-enters with* BAPTISTA, *her father.*

BIANCA: (*Eyes cast down, rose in hand*) Father, to your pleasure, humbly I subscribe, my books and my instruments shall be my company on them to look and practice by myself. (*She eyes* LUCENTIO)

BAPTISTA: Poor child.

GREMIO and HORTENSIO: (*Taking* BAPTISTA *by each arm*) Signor Baptista.

GREMIO: Why will you let Bianca bear the penance of Katharine's tongue?

BAPTISTA: (*Shaking off suitors*)
Gentlemen, importune me no farther.
For how firmly I am resolved, you know,
That is, not to bestow my youngest daughter
(*Indicating* BIANCA)
Before I have a husband for the elder;
Now, if either of you love Katharine

(KATHARINE *appears on balcony with watering-can. She has been watering the potted plants. She listens*)

BAPTISTA:
Leave shall you have to court her at your pleasure.

GREMIO:
To cart her rather: she's too rough for me.

BAPTISTA: (*Very confidentially*)
If you Hortensio, or Signor Gremio,

If either of you can find a husband,
I would be most liberal.

HORTENSIO:
A husband? A devil.

KATHARINE: (*From balcony*)
Indeed!

(*Throws three geranium pots at* HORTENSIO. *One-two-three! One is a dead hit*)

HORTENSIO: (*Holding head*)
Thinkst thou, sir, though you be very rich,
Any man be so very a fool to be married to hell?

KATHARINE: (*From balcony*)
Comb thy noddle with a three-legged stool.
(*She hurls a stool. . . . All duck*)

GREMIO:
I'd as lief take her dowry with this condition,
To be whipped at the high-cross every morning.

(KATHARINE *throws watering-can from balcony. Suitors back away. All look up*)

KATHARINE:
So, father, is it your will to make a stale of me amongst those males?
(*She disappears*)

BAPTISTA: (*Picking up the wreckage*)
Oh! If I could only find a man that would thoroughly woo
Her, wed her, and bed her and rid my house of her.
(*Totters into house*)

BIANCA: (*Sighing*)
Ah, me!

(GREMIO, HORTENSIO, *and* LUCENTIO *seek to assuage her grief with song:*)

THREE SUITORS: (*"Tom, Dick, or Harry"*)
(*Verse*)

GREMIO:
I've made a haul in all the leading rackets
From which rip-roarin' rich I happen to be
And if thou wouldst attain the upper brackets,
Marry me, marry me, marry me.

LUCENTIO:

My purse has yet to know a silver lining,
Still lifeless is my wifeless family tree
(*Kneels*)
But if for love unending thou are pining,
Marry me, marry me, marry me.

HORTENSIO:

I come to thee, a thoroughbred patrician
Still spraying my decaying family tree,
To give a social goose to thy position,
Marry me, marry me, marry me
Marry me.

GREMIO and LUCENTIO:

Marry me!

HORTENSIO:

Marry me!

GREMIO and HORTENSIO:

Marry me!

LUCENTIO:

Marry me!

GREMIO:

Marry me!

THREE SUITORS:

Marry me!
(*1st Refrain*)

BIANCA:

I'm a maid who would marry
And will take with no qualm
Any Tom, Dick, or Harry,
Any Harry, Dick, or Tom.
I'm a maid mad to marry
And will take double-quick
Any Tom, Dick, or Harry,
Any Tom, Harry, or Dick.

(*2nd Refrain*)

GREMIO:

I'm the man thou shouldst marry.

BIANCA:
Howdy, Pop!

GREMIO:
Howdy, Mom.

LUCENTIO:
I'm the man thou shouldst marry.

BIANCA:
Art thou Harry, Dick, or Tom?

HORTENSIO:
I'm the man thou shouldst marry.

BIANCA:
Howdy, pal!

HORTENSIO:
Howdy, chick!

BIANCA:
Art thou Tom, Dick, or Harry?

HORTENSIO:
Call me Tom, Harry, or Dick.

(*3rd Refrain*)

(LUCENTIO *and* HORTENSIO *kneel on one knee to form a seat for* BIANCA. *She sits*)

BIANCA:
I'm a maid who would marry

SUITORS:
She's a maid who would marry

BOTH:
And would no longer tarry

BIANCA:
I'm a maid who would marry,

SUITORS:
She's a maid who would marry,

BIANCA:
May my hopes not miscarry!
I'm a maid mad to marry

SUITORS:
She's a maid mad to marry

BOTH:

And will take double-quick
Any Tom, Dick or Harry,
Any Tom, Harry, or Dick,

BIANCA:

A-dicka dick,
A-dicka dick,
A-dicka dick,
A-dicka dick,
A-dicka dick,
A-dicka dick!

(*Encore 3rd refrain in swing time*)

BIANCA:

I'm a maid who would marry

SUITORS:

She's a maid who would marry

BOTH:

And would no longer tarry,

BIANCA:

I'm a maid who would marry,

SUITORS:

She's a maid who would marry,

BIANCA:

May my hopes not miscarry!
I'm a maid mad to marry

SUITORS:

She's a maid mad to marry

BIANCA:

And will take double-quick
Any Tom, Dick, or Harry,
Any Tom, Harry, or Dick,
A-dicka dick,
A-dicka dick,
A-dicka dick,
A-dicka dick,
A-dicka dick,
A-dicka dick!

(GREMIO *and* HORTENSIO *exit.* LUCENTIO *follows* BIANCA *to door of house, where she exits. She re-enters, throws him a rose, and exits*)

LUCENTIO: (*Looking at rose*) Sweet Bianca, she sings as sweetly as a nightingale. She looks as clean as morning roses newly washed with dew. Sweet Bianca.

(*He dances divinely with the rose, representing the fair* BIANCA. *Innkeeper and waiter tactfully wait until he finishes his balletic rhapsody before they place a table in position with pewter mug and trays. To* LUCENTIO'S *surprise,* GREMIO *and* HORTENSIO *enter menacingly, followed by some of their "friends"*)

GREMIO: (*Threateningly*) Are you a suitor to the maid you talk of?

(PETRUCHIO *enters through arch, unseen by others*)

LUCENTIO: And if I be, sir, is it of any offense?

GREMIO: (*Angrily*) No, if without more words, you will get you hence.

(*During this altercation, local Paduans gather round hopefully for a fight.* LUCENTIO *sees he's vastly outnumbered, when* PETRUCHIO *advances, and pushes* GREMIO *aside*)

PETRUCHIO: Why, sir, I pray are not the streets as free for him as for you?

LUCENTIO: Petruchio!

PETRUCHIO: Lucentio!

(*They all but embrace*)

LUCENTIO: What happy wind blows you to Padua from old Verona?

PETRUCHIO: Such wind as scatters young men through the world to seek their fortunes farther than at home. And you?

LUCENTIO: I came to study.

PETRUCHIO: (*Puts arm around* LUCENTIO)

I am glad that you thus
Combine your resolve
To suck the sweets of
Sweet philosophy,
The mathematics and the
Botany.

(*Indicates rose.* LUCENTIO, *embarrassed, ostentatiously tosses rose on table; that finishes the rose*)

Fall to them as your
Stomach serves.

No profit grows where
Is no pleasure taken.
(*Removes hat and cape, along with riding crop, places them on table*)
In brief, sir–study–
As for me:

PETRUCHIO and MALE CHORUS: (*"I've Come to Wive It Wealthily in Padua"*)

(*1st Refrain*)

PETRUCHIO:
I've come to wive it wealthily in Padua,
If wealthily then happily in Padua.
If my wife has a bag of gold
Do I care if the bag is old?
I've come to wive it wealthily in Padua.

(*2nd Refrain*)

MEN OF PADUA:
He's come to wive it wealthily in Padua.

PETRUCHIO:
I heard you mutter: "Zounds, a loathsome lad you are."
I shall not be disturbed a bit
If she be but a quarter-wit,
If she only can talk of clo'es
While she powders her God-damned nose,
I've come to wive it wealthily in Padua.

(*3rd Refrain*)

MEN OF PADUA:
He's come to wive it wealthily in Padua.

PETRUCHIO:
I heard you say: "Gadzooks, completely mad you are!"
'Twouldn't give me the slightest shock
If her knees, now and then, should knock,
If her eyes were a wee bit crossed,
Were she wearing the hair she'd lost,
Still the damsel I'll make my dame,
In the dark they are all the same,
I've come to wive it wealthily in Padua.

(*4th Refrain*)

MEN OF PADUA:

He's come to wive it wealthily in Padua.

PETRUCHIO:

I heard you say: "Good gad but what a cad you are!"
Do I mind if she fret and fuss,
If she fume like Vesuvius,
If she roar like a winter breeze
On the rough Adriatic seas,
If she scream like a teething brat,
If she scratch like a tiger cat,
If she fight like a raging boar,
I have oft stuck a pig before,
I've come to wive it wealthily in Padua.

(*Coda*)

MEN OF PADUA:

With a hunny, nunny, nunny,
(*All move forward*)
And a hey, hey, hey,

PETRUCHIO:

Not to mention money, money
(*Stops them with a gesture*)
For a rainy day,
I've come to wive it wealthily in Padua.

MEN OF PADUA:

He's come to wive it wealthily in Padua.

GREMIO: (*Digging* HORTENSIO *with elbow*)

This gentleman is happily arrived!

LUCENTIO:

Petruchio, thou'rt too much my friend . . .
(*To the others*)
I cannot wish him to a shrewd, ill-tempered wife.

HORTENSIO:

But she is rich!

GREMIO:

And young and beauteous.

LUCENTIO:

But shrewd and forward so beyond all measure

That were my state far poorer than it is
I would not wed her for a mine of gold.

PETRUCHIO: (*The cynic*) Peace! Lucentio, thou know'st not gold's effects. And therefore, if thou know one rich enough to be Petruchio's wife, tell me her father's name and 'tis enough.

GREMIO:
Her father is Baptista Minola. Her name Katharine—
Elder sister of the fair Bianca.

(*Shrieks are heard from the house*)

LUCENTIO:
That is she! An irksome, brawling scold.

PETRUCHIO:
Think you a little din can daunt mine ears?
Have I not in my time heard lions roar?
Have I not heard great ordnance in the field
And Heaven's artillery thunder in the skies?
And do you tell me of a woman's tongue
That give not half so great a blow to hear
As will a chestnut in a farmer's fire?

HORTENSIO:
Then you will woo this wildcat?

PETRUCHIO:
Will I live?

GREMIO:
I promise we will be contributors
And bear your charge of wooing, whatsoe'er.

PETRUCHIO:
Done!

GREMIO:
Let's quaff carouses to this gentleman!

(*As they exit to inn, waiter picks up hat, cloak, riding crop, and rose from table, and exits. One can't take chances even in a university town. Incidentally, this really finishes the rose*)

PETRUCHIO:
For all this, much thanks—

GREMIO:
Provided that you win her

PETRUCHIO:

Go you to old Baptista and say:
"I have a husband for Katharine."

(*All exit into inn*)

LUCENTIO: (*Stops* PETRUCHIO) Katharine, the curst!

PETRUCHIO: Katharine the curst! A title for a maid of all titles the worst!

(*Exits into inn. Door flies open and* BIANCA, *pursued by* KATHARINE *and* BAPTISTA, *runs past* LUCENTIO *standing near door*)

BIANCA: (*Weeping*) Sister—sister—sister, content you in my discontent.

(*Exits left*)

BAPTISTA: Katharine, Katharine—for shame, thou hilding of a devilish spirit . . . Poor child, she weeps!

KATHARINE: She is your treasure; she must have a husband; I must dance barefoot on her wedding day—and for your love to her, lead apes in hell.

BAPTISTA: Oh, oh! Was ever a father thus grieved as I?

LUCENTIO: (*Timidly*) A word with you, kind sir.

BAPTISTA: (*Going into his old spiel*) Importune me no farther, good sir . . .
For how firmly am I resolved, you know . . . (LUCENTIO *whispers to* BAPTISTA)

BAPTISTA: Eh? Whisper louder . . . (LUCENTIO *whispers some more into other ear.* BAPTISTA *brightens*) That is indeed news, good news! Come in, Lucentio. (*They exit left*)

KATHARINE: (*As they exit*) Lucentio, thou meacock wretch. (*She strides to table, sits on the stool. Alone, surly and unhappy, she sings:*)

KATHARINE: ("*I Hate Men*")

(*1st Refrain*)

I hate men.

(*Bangs pewter mug on table*)

I can't abide 'em even now and then,
Than ever marry one of them, I'd rest a virgin rather,
For husbands are a boring lot and only give you bother.
Of course, I'm awf'lly glad that Mother had to marry Father
But, I hate men.
Of all the types I've ever met within our democracy,
I hate the most, the athlete with his manner bold and brassy,

He may have hair upon his chest but, sister, so has Lassie,
Oh, I hate men!
(*Picks up cup and bangs upon table*)

(*2nd Refrain*)

I hate men.
(*Bangs cup*)
Their worth upon this earth I dinna ken.
Avoid the trav'ling salesman though a tempting Tom he may be,
From China he will bring you jade and perfume from Araby
But don't forget 'tis he who'll have the fun and thee the baby,
Oh, I hate men.
If thou shouldst wed a bus'nessman, be wary, oh be wary.
(*Crosses to table*)
He'll tell you he's detained in town on bus'ness necessary,
His bus'ness is the bus'ness which he gives his secretary,
Oh, I hate men!
(*Bangs pewter mug*)

(BAPTISTA *enters and beats a hasty retreat as* KATHARINE *goes into:*)

(*3rd Refrain*)

I hate men.
(*Bangs cup*)
Though roosters they, I will not play the hen.
(*Crosses to center*)
If you espouse an older man through girlish optimism,
He'll always stay at home at night and make no criticism,
Though you may call it "love," the doctors call it "rheumatism."
Oh, I hate men.
From all I've read, alone in bed, from A to Zed, about 'em,
Since love is blind, then from the mind, all womankind should rout 'em.
But ladies, you must answer too, what would we do without 'em?
Oh still, I hate men!
(*Bangs cup, crosses to center, bows*)
(*Enter* BAPTISTA *and crosses to* KATHARINE)

BAPTISTA: Katharine! Wonder of wonders!
KATHARINE: (*Belligerently*) What?

BAPTISTA: (*Panting*) A gentleman from Verona–desires you–in marriage.

KATHARINE: (*Picks up the mug and throws it, but misses her father*) Then he best go back there. (*She exits*)

BAPTISTA: Heavens!

(PETRUCHIO *emerges from inn and approaches* BAPTISTA. *The ever-watchful waiter now removes mugs and trays from table and floor. Also takes stool. Unless it's nailed down, he'll take anything. He also sings tenor*)

PETRUCHIO: Greetings, good sir. I hear, sir, you have a daughter call'd Katharine, fair and virtuous.

BAPTISTA: I have a daughter, sir, called Katharine.

PETRUCHIO: I am a gentleman from Verona, sir, that hearing of her beauty and her wit, her affability and bashful modesty; her wondrous qualities and mild behavior–(*Shriek is heard offstage.* PETRUCHIO *pauses for a second with a glance toward balcony, but plows on*) uh–mild behavior, am bold to make myself a forward guest within your house to make mine eye the witness of that report. Signor Baptista, my business asketh haste, and every day, I cannot come to woo.

BAPTISTA: I am afraid my daughter Katharine is not for your turn, the more my grief.

PETRUCHIO: I see you do not mean to part with her.

BAPTISTA: (*Follows* PETRUCHIO) Mistake me not, sir–

PETRUCHIO: Or else you like not of my company–

BAPTISTA: You are more than welcome–

PETRUCHIO: (*Sits on table*) Well, then–what dowry shall I have with her to wife?

BAPTISTA: After my death, the one half of my lands.

PETRUCHIO: The fertile part?

BAPTISTA: So be it!

PETRUCHIO: And in possession?

BAPTISTA: Twenty thousand crowns!

PETRUCHIO: Thirty!

(BAPTISTA *turns away,* PETRUCHIO *rises as if to go*)

BAPTISTA: (*Turns back hastily*) Thirty!

PETRUCHIO: Father! (*They embrace*) And for that dowry I'll assure her of her widowhood–be it that she survive me. Let specialties be therefore drawn between us, that covenants may be kept on either hand. Go, get thee to a notary.

4

(BAPTISTA *exits through arch. Waiter takes table off*)

KATHARINE: (*On balcony*) Aye, when that special thing is well obtained. That is, my love—or is that all in all?

PETRUCHIO: (*Looking up to balcony*) Could I but see thy face?

KATHARINE: Why, sir! 'Tis but a face like any other . . .

PETRUCHIO: Aye—there's the rub.

(KATHARINE *watches from balcony*)

(*And he sings:*)

PETRUCHIO: (*"Were Thine That Special Face"*)

(*Refrain*)

Were thine that special face,
The face which fills my dreaming,
Were thine the rhythm'd grace,
Were thine the form so lithe and slender,
Were thine the arms so warm, so tender,
Were thine the kiss divine,
(*Looks at balcony*)
Were thine the love for me,
The love which fills my dreaming,
When all these charms are thine
Then you'll be mine, all mine.

(KATHARINE *exits angrily as* DANCERS *in black rustling gowns carrying fans swish on*)

(*Verse*)

PETRUCHIO:

I wrote a poem
In classic style,
I wrote it with my tongue
In my cheek
And my lips in a smile
But of late my poem
Has a meaning so new
For to my surprise
It suddenly applies to my darling, to you.

(*Looks to balcony.* KATHARINE *is gone.* PETRUCHIO *shrugs and sings to* DANCERS)

(*Refrain repeats*)

Were thine that special face,
The face which fills my dreaming,
Were thine the rhythm'd grace,
Were thine the form so lithe and slender,

Were thine the arms so warm, so tender,
Were thine the kiss divine,
Were thine the love for me,
The love which fills my dreaming,
When all these charms are thine
Then you'll be mine, all mine.
When all these charms are thine
Then you'll be mine, all mine.

(*Lights up at end of number. Waiter moves table on stage on applause*)

BAPTISTA: (*Enters*) 'Twas not to her liking.

PETRUCHIO: But that is nothing. For I tell you, father, I am as peremptory as she proud-minded. And where two raging fires meet together, they do consume the thing that feeds their fury.

I will attend her here and woo her with some spirit when she comes. If she do bid me pack—I'll give her thanks—

KATHARINE: (*Enters angrily from house. She holds bouquet in hand, as if it were a stiletto*) I bid thee pack! (*This is obviously not her cue for entrance and* FRED, *as* PETRUCHIO, *is a little off guard. The others obviously sense something wrong*) Were thine that special face! Hah!

(LILLI *tosses bouquet at* FRED. *He barely catches it. Reaction*)

FRED: (*Ad-libbing*) Grazia, signorina. (*He bows*)

BAPTISTA: (*A little nonplused, but plowing on*) And now, Petruchio, speak! (*He exits into house*)

KATHARINE: (*Extracting card from bosom*) Speak, Petruchio . . . Though thy message is not meant for me. (*She tears up card, throws it in* PETRUCHIO'S *face*) You bas—

PETRUCHIO: (*Hastily breaking in*) Good morrow, Kate. (*In aside. Grabs her hand*) We're on stage, now, Lilli . . .

Good morrow, Kate, for that's your name, I hear.

KATHARINE:

Well have you heard, but somewhat hard of hearing;
They call me Katharine that do speak of me.
(*Crosses down center*)

PETRUCHIO:

You lie, in faith; for you are called plain Kate,
And bonny Kate, and sometimes Kate the curst;
(*Throws flowers away*)

But Kate, the prettiest Kate in Christendom;
And therefore, Kate, take this of me, Kate of my consolation;
Hearing thy mildness prais'd in every town,
Thy virtues spoke of, and thy beauty sounded,
Yet not so deeply as to thee belongs—
(*She hits him in stomach*)
Myself am moved to woo thee for my wife.

KATHARINE:
Hah! Mov'd in good time: let him that mov'd you hither
Remove you hence; I knew you at the first, you were a movable.

PETRUCHIO:
Why, what's a movable?

KATHARINE:
A joint stool.

PETRUCHIO:
Thou hast hit it. Come, sit on me.
(*Slaps knee*)

KATHARINE:
Asses are made to bear, and so are you.

PETRUCHIO:
Women are made to bear, and so are you.

KATHARINE:
No such jade as bear you, if me you mean.
(*She bites his hand*)

PETRUCHIO: (*Nursing his hand*)
Come, come, you wasp; i' faith, you are too angry.

KATHARINE:
If I be too waspish, best beware my sting.
(*Slaps* PETRUCHIO)

PETRUCHIO:
My remedy is then to pluck it out.

KATHARINE:
Aye, if the fool could find it where it lies.

PETRUCHIO:
Who knows not where a wasp does wear his sting? In his tail.

(KATHARINE *slaps him again.* PETRUCHIO *grabs her, bends her back over his knee*)

PETRUCHIO:

I swear I'll cuff you, if you strike again! (*Aside*) You keep on acting just the way you've been doing, Miss Vanessi, and I will give you the paddling of your life and right on stage.

KATHARINE: (*Breaking away*) You wouldn't dare!

PETRUCHIO: (*Laughs–a forced stage-laugh*) No?

KATHARINE: If you strike me you are no gentleman. What is your crest–a coxcomb? (*Holds up her hand*)

PETRUCHIO:

A combless cock, so Kate will be my hen.
(*Grabs* KATE'S *raised hand*)
Come, give me thy hands.

KATHARINE: No! No!

(PETRUCHIO *slaps her behind, propelling her to table. From other side of table he grabs her hands and holds them down*)

PETRUCHIO:

Come.
Setting all this chat aside,
Thus in plain terms; your father has consented
That you shall be my wife;
And will you, nill you, I will marry you.
Now, Kate, I am a husband for your turn
For by this light, whereby I see thy beauty–
Thy beauty that doth make me like thee well–
Thou must be married to no man but me.
(*Brings* KATE *around in front of table*)
For I am he, am born to tame you, Kate;
And bring you from a wild Kate to a Kate
Conformable as other household Kates.

KATHARINE: You devil! Father! (*Struggles to remove her hands*)

(BAPTISTA *enters quickly and suitors enter from upstage right*)

BAPTISTA: And now, Signor Petruchio, how speed you with my daughter?

PETRUCHIO: How but well! How, but well. It were impossible I should speed amiss. We have 'greed so well together that upon Sunday is the wedding day.

BAPTISTA: (*Puts his hands over theirs*) God give you joy, son! 'Tis a match!
(*Withdraws hands quickly*)

SUITORS: Amen, say we!

PETRUCHIO:
Father and wife and gentlemen, adieu:
(*Swings her away from him; enter crowd*)
I will unto Venice
(*She kicks him*)
—I'm warning you!—to buy apparel, against the wedding day.
Sunday comes apace
And we will have rings and things and fine array and
Kiss me, Kate.
(*She slaps him*)
All right, Miss Vanessi—you asked for this and you're going to get it! (*He takes her across his knee. He begins paddling her*)

KATHARINE: *Oh!* (*He paddles her harder*) Fred, what are you doing? *Oh! . . . Oh! . . . Oh! . . .*
(*She screams. He paddles her harder. Screams from crowd*)

(Blackout)

SCENE 6

Backstage—on stage performance of The Shrew *is still going on, but unseen and unheard. The stagehands move about with ladders and pieces of scenery as* LILLI *enters.*

LILLI: (*Really angry*) Hattie! Hattie! Darn that girl! (FRED *enters, grinning. She turns on him*) That's the last time you'll ever lay your hands on me, Mr. Graham!

FRED: (*Laconically*) You asked for it. May I remind you, Miss Vanessi, the name of this piece is *The Taming of the Shrew,* not *He Who Gets Slapped.*

LILLI: I am a realistic actress.

FRED: Huh! Your latest picture is still in the can where it belongs.

LILLI: Cuddling up to that Copa canary!

FRED: You're jealous—that's what's the matter with you.

LILLI: Sending my wedding bouquet to that little tramp.

FRED: That's no excuse for ad-libbing! None!

LILLI: "Let my lovely Lois shine through Bianca tonight, and there'll be a new star in the heavens." Thou jerk!

FRED: All right, all right! I sent the child some flowers—I sent her a card with the flowers. May I point out that I'm free, male, and thirty-one!

LILLI: (*Derisively*) Thirty-one—hah!

FRED: All right, thirty-two. What the hell has my age got to do with this? They were full, rich years and I'm proud of them. Every minute of them. Show me an actor who's done all I've done—my Peer Gynt in London—

LILLI: You never got to London.

FRED: My Hamlet in Dublin—

LILLI: You got paid in potatoes. Mashed!

FRED: That's all you ever think of—money—money—money. Miss Vanessi, you have no soul! And what the hell do you mean by poking me in the ribs?

LILLI: It's in the script!

FRED: The hell it is! I couldn't teach you manners as a wife, but by God I'll teach you manners as an actress!

LILLI: Not in this production, my pet.

FRED: What did you say?

LILLI: You heard me! And here's something to remember me by. (*Slaps him*)

FRED: What are you trying to do? Kill me? Ralph! Ralph! Paul! (FRED *limps across, holding his cheek. Touches his cheek*) Good God, I'm bleeding!

RALPH: Yes, Mr. Graham?

FRED: Get me some alcohol.

RALPH: Yes, sir.

FRED: (*Shouting*) There's a law against attempted murder—even in Baltimore. (*He feels his side*) God, my rib—I think she broke a rib. Ralph, how can you tell if you have a broken rib?

RALPH: X-ray.

FRED: Where am I going to get an X-ray?

RALPH: All I've got is alcohol.

FRED: That monstrous female. Literally a vampire. Am I bleeding heavily, Ralph?

RALPH: I don't see any blood.

FRED: Here—what do you call that? (*Looks at his hand*) Max Factor Number Two? Oh, I thought it was blood. Skin's bruised though, isn't it?

RALPH: I don't see anything.

FRED: Discolored?

RALPH: I don't see anything.

FRED: That's all I need. A blind stage manager!

(Blackout)

SCENE 7

FRED'S *and* LILLI'S *dressing rooms. Both rooms lit.* LILLI *is on phone in* Shrew *costume.*

LILLI: (*Holding phone in one hand and rubbing her posterior with the other*) Harrison, I'll marry you tonight. You don't know what that villain's done to me. I can't sit down! I said: "I can't sit down!" I'm through with the theatre. Send a car for me. Better still, send an ambulance! I want to go where no one will ever find me. I'll go to Washington! I adore you, Harrison. Yes, dear . . . yes, love. (HATTIE *enters*) Hattie, pack my things! I'll wear that blue suit. Yes, Harrison . . . He beat me! I'm black-and-blue!

FRED: (*Enters his room, overhears her plaint and crosses into hers*) I'm a realistic actor!

LILLI: I'm quitting right now. (*Hangs up phone*)

FRED: You don't think you can walk out of a show in the middle of a performance?

LILLI: Oh, no?

FRED: I'll have you up on charges at Equity!

LILLI: Hah! I'll be glad—glad to appear before Equity! I shall bring photographs (*Indicates backside*) of what you have done to me. In Technicolor!

FRED: And I'll bring my X-rays! (*Goes to his room*)

LILLI: Nothing you can say or do will stop me. Harrison's coming for me.

FRED: (*Coming back into* LILLI'S *room*) Do you think he'd let you quit? That imbecile's got two hundred thousand dollars in this show.

LILLI: He'll take it off his tax!

FRED: You don't really mean you would . . .

(*She turns to him quickly, facing him squarely, belligerently. What* FRED *reads in her eyes frightens him. He remembers that look from the old connubial days*)

FRED: Yes, I guess you do.

LILLI: You bet I do.

(*The* TWO GUNMEN *quietly enter* FRED'S *room. They've been out front and are pleased*)

FRED: You'll never play the theatre again!
LILLI: Who wants to?
FRED: You're out of your mind.
LILLI: (*Picking up an object*) Get out! Get out!

(*He opens door to his room. She follows him, threatening, and* FRED *shuts door between them*)

LILLI: Get out!

(*We leave* LILLI *for the moment and stay with* FRED. FRED, *now in his room, sees the two men*)

FRED: (*Aghast*) Oh, for heaven's sake!
FIRST MAN: What a performance.
SECOND MAN: What unction!
FIRST MAN: You think the audience is getting it? It's way over their heads.
SECOND MAN: Bunch of lowbrows.
FRED: Look here–
FIRST MAN: We just want to check with you to see if you jostled your memory.
FRED: I told you I never signed anything . . . (*Suddenly inspired*) Well, as a matter of fact, I did sign that IOU.
FIRST MAN: He remembers.
SECOND MAN: What a relief.
FIRST MAN: When are you gonna pay this debt of honor to one of America's most respectable floating crap games?
FRED: That's just it. I haven't got it. I would have, at the end of the week, if the show could run.
FIRST MAN: It'll run. It's entertaining, vivacious, and calculated to please the discriminating theatregoer. You can quote me.
FRED: Unfortunately, Miss Vanessi, my co-star, is quitting.
FIRST MAN: Quitting?
FRED: As of right now. Temperament. Didn't like the way I played a little scene. She's dressing to leave the theatre. I'll have to return whatever money there is in the box office.
FIRST MAN: She can't do that!
FRED: Perhaps if you talked to her, heart to heart.
FIRST MAN: That's our specialty.

(FRED *opens the door to* LILLI'S *dressing room*)

FRED: (*Small-voiced and affable, entering* LILLI'S *room*) Lilli! Oh, Lilli!
LILLI: (*Without turning to look at him*) There's no use trying to persuade me to stay.

FRED: Some very ardent admirers of yours. Come in, gentlemen. (*The two men enter.* LILLI *turns around to meet them*)

LILLI: (*Graciously*) How do you do? (*Indicates couch*)

(GUNMEN *sit rather gingerly, remove hats.* LILLI *sits on pouf*)

FIRST MAN: Miss Vanessi, you been my ideal for years. I married my wife because in a certain light, when it's kinda dark, she might pass for your sister.

LILLI: How sweet.

FIRST MAN: Your glorious voice has been a inspiration to me in my work.

SECOND MAN: What a trouper!

FIRST MAN: What a personality!

SECOND MAN: Is it true, Miss Vanessi, that you're contemplating quitting this high-type entertainment?

LILLI: I am.

FIRST MAN: Now, you know, Miss Vanessi, the show must go on. (*Takes gun from shoulder holster, puts it in coat pocket*) I'm just transferring the weight offa one side and onto the other. We've got a financial interest in the success of this show, as well as personal. And Miss Vanessi, you gotta play this show out tonight, and at least to the end of the week, when Mr. Graham pays his debt of honor.

LILLI: (*Rising, incensed–she's a brave girl*) Are you threatening me?

(*Both men rise*)

FIRST MAN: Now, Miss Vanessi, let's talk it over. (*He moves toward her, hand in gun pocket*)

LILLI: (*Backing away, frightened*) Fred!

FRED: (*Leaning unconcernedly against the door and looking off into space*) This is an outrage!

(Blackout)

SCENE 8

Front of Shrew *curtain, a thing of colorful diamond-shaped pattern.* BIANCA, LUCENTIO, *and* SINGERS.

SINGERS *enter in couples.* BIANCA *and* LUCENTIO *dance on from left and right. This number gives us time to change to the next scene.*

ALL: (Song: "*I Sing of Love*")

We sing of love,
We sing only of love,

Ye gods above,
May we never sing of anything but love
For love is the joy
Of ev'ry girl and boy
As love, later on,
Keeps 'em going till they're gone,
Yes, love is the theme
Of all people who dream
So love, let's confess,
(GIRLS *sit on* BOYS' *knees*)
Is ev'rybody's business.
Oh ye gods above,
May we never sing of anything but love,
Sweet love.

(*1st Patter*)

BOY:
I won't sing a song about battle,

GIRL:
I won't sing of babies who prattle,

BOY:
I get no glee
From songs about the sea
Or cowboys' songs about cattle.

GIRL:
I won't waste a note of my patters
On socially significant matters,

ALL:
We sing of one thing and we adore it
Thank Heaven for it!
We sing of love,
We sing only of love,
Ye gods above,
May we never sing of anything but love

BIANCA:
For love is the joy
Of ev'ry girl and boy
As love, later on,
Keeps 'em going till they're gone,

LUCENTIO:

Yes, love is the theme
Of all people who dream
So love, let's confess,

ALL:

Is ev'rybody's business.
Oh ye gods above,
May we never sing of anything but love,
Sweet love.

SCENE 9

Exterior church, seven arches covered with greenery, with oranges and white flowers showing through.

DANCING ENSEMBLE *begins tarantella, joined by* BIANCA *and* LUCENTIO. *At end of dance church bells ring. The ceremony within is over. Wedding guests enter, some laughing, others puzzled and disapproving.*

BAPTISTA *comes out of church, dismayed, followed by* BIANCA, LUCENTIO.

BAPTISTA: Such a marriage never was before! The man is mad.

LUCENTIO: And so madly mated.

BIANCA: And in such garb! An old jerkin! And a pair of breeches thrice turned!

LUCENTIO: A pair of boots that have been candle cases and not even mates! One buckled! Another laced!

(PETRUCHIO *emerges from church, carrying whip*)

PETRUCHIO: Come, my bonny Kate—(*After pause, roars*) I said, come!

(*Cracks whip*)

(KATHARINE *emerges in real, sullen anger, flanked by both* GUNMEN *in* Shrew *costumes*)

PETRUCHIO: Oh Kate, content thee, I prithee be not angry.

(*As* GUNMEN *enter with* KATHARINE, LUCENTIO *whispers to* BIANCA *his fear and rushes for exit.* BIANCA *catches him and drags him back*)

KATHARINE: (*Moving to* PETRUCHIO. GUNMEN *move after her. Sullenly*) I will be angry. What has thou to do? (*Waves toward the house*) Forward to the bridal dinner. I see a woman may be made a fool of, if she has not spirit to resist!

PETRUCHIO: Obey the bride, you that attend on her. Go to the feast and revel and domineer.

(PETRUCHIO *whirls first gangster downstage left, returns to center*)

PETRUCHIO: Carouse full measure to her maidenhead. Be mad, be merry, or go hang yourselves!

(*Shoves second gangster downstage right. They assume positions of guards and case the house. Snaps whip at* SECOND GUNMAN *to bring both* GUNMEN'S *attention to stage.* SECOND GUNMAN *pulls gun from belt, then reassured, puts it back*)

PETRUCHIO: But for my bonny Kate, she must with me! . . . Nay, look not big, nor stamp, nor stare, nor fret—I will be master of what is mine own. She is my goods, my chattels, my horse, my ox, my ass, my anything—touch her whoever dare! I'll bring mine action on the proudest he that dares to stop my way in Padua.

(*As* KATE *attempts to run upstage, he catches her with whip*)

(*Begins*)

PETRUCHIO, KATHARINE, BIANCA, LUCENTIO, and COMPANY:
("*Kiss Me, Kate*")

PETRUCHIO:
So kiss me, Kate,
Thou lovely loon,
Ere we start
On our honeymoon,
Oh, kiss me, Kate
Darling devil divine
For now thou shall ever be mine.

KATE:
I'll never be thine.

PETRUCHIO:
So kiss me, Kate,

ALL OTHER PRINCIPALS, and SINGERS:
So kiss him, Kate,

KATE:
No!

PETRUCHIO and OTHERS:
Thou lovely loon,

KATE:
Go!

PETRUCHIO:
Ere we start

OTHERS:
Ere you start

KATE:
Nay!

PETRUCHIO:
On our honeymoon

OTHERS:
On your honeymoon

KATE:
Away!

PETRUCHIO:
Oh, kiss me, Kate,

OTHERS:
Oh, kiss him, Kate,

KATE:
Fred!

PETRUCHIO and OTHERS:
Darling devil divine,

KATE:
Kindly drop dead!

PETRUCHIO: (*Solo*)
For now thou shall ever be

KATE:
Now I shall never be

PETRUCHIO and MEN:
Now thou shall ever be

KATE:
Now I shall never be thine

GIRLS:
Now thou shall never be

PETRUCHIO:
Yes, mine.

KATE:
Not thine.

PETRUCHIO:
Yes, mine.

KATE:
You swine.

PETRUCHIO:
Yes, mine.

KATE:
You swine.

PETRUCHIO and SINGERS:
She called

PETRUCHIO:
Yes, mine

PETRUCHIO and SINGERS:
Him a swine.

PETRUCHIO:
So kiss me, Kate

KATE:
I'll crack your pate.

PETRUCHIO:
Oh, please don't pout.

KATE:
I'll knock you out.

PETRUCHIO:
My priceless prize!

KATE:
I'll black your eyes.

PETRUCHIO:
Oh kiss me quick!

KATE:
Your rump I'll kick.

PETRUCHIO:
Oh, kiss me!

OTHERS:
Oh, kiss him!

KATE:
Bounder!

OTHERS:
He's not her dish, he's not her dish.

PETRUCHIO:
Oh, kiss me!

OTHERS:
Oh, kiss him!

KATE:
Flounder!

OTHERS:
A type of fish she would not wish,

PETRUCHIO:
Oh, kiss me!

OTHERS:
Oh, kiss him!

KATE:
Dastard!

OTHERS:
What's that we heard, what's that we heard?

PETRUCHIO:
Oh, kiss me!

OTHERS:
Oh, kiss him!

KATE:
Bastard!

OTHERS:
Oh! Katie! That's a naughty word.

PETRUCHIO:
Oh, kiss me.

GIRLS:
Oh, kiss him.

MEN and GIRLS:
Kiss him.

PETRUCHIO:
Kiss me.

GIRLS:
Kiss him.

MEN and GIRLS:
Kiss him.

PETRUCHIO:
Kiss me.

GIRLS and BASSES:
Kiss him.

MEN and GIRLS:
Kiss him.

KATE: (*In a paroxysm of coloratura*)
Never! Never—never—never . . .

(*As* KATHARINE *starts coloratura, a girl enters carrying a bird. At end of coloratura bird goes up in air.* FIRST GUNMAN *shoots at bird. Bird drops to stage, generally on* BAPTISTA'S *hat*)

PETRUCHIO:
Kiss me, Kiss me, Kate, Kiss me

OTHERS:
Kiss him, Kiss him, Kate, Kiss him

PETRUCHIO:
Kiss me, Kate, Kiss me

OTHERS:
Kiss him, Kate, Kiss him

PETRUCHIO:
Kiss me, Kate, Kiss me

OTHERS:
Kiss him, Kate, Kiss him

PETRUCHIO:
Kiss me, Kate, Kiss me

OTHERS:
Kiss him, Kate, Kiss him

PETRUCHIO:
Kiss me, Kate, Kiss me

OTHERS:
Kiss him, Kate, Kiss him

PETRUCHIO:
Kiss me, Kate

OTHERS:
Kiss him, Kate

PETRUCHIO:
Kiss me, Kate

OTHERS:
Kiss him, Kate

PETRUCHIO:
Kiss me, Kate

OTHERS:
Kiss him, Kate

PETRUCHIO:
Kiss me, Kate

OTHERS:
Kiss him, Kate

PETRUCHIO:
Kiss me, Kate

OTHERS:
Kiss him, Kate

(*Two girls unwind silken ropes to hold the wedding guests back. The* DANCERS, *now perched on top of arches, throw streamers and confetti*)

PETRUCHIO:
Kiss me, Kate

OTHERS:
Kiss him, Kate

PETRUCHIO:
Kiss me, Kate

OTHERS:
Kiss him, Kate

PETRUCHIO and OTHERS:
Kiss . . .

(*Streamers fall from cradle above*)

PETRUCHIO:
me

OTHERS:
him

GANGSTERS: (*Spoken*)
Aw–kiss him.

PETRUCHIO and OTHERS:
Kate!

(PETRUCHIO *picks up* KATHARINE *and throws her over his shoulder, carries her out, kicking and pummeling him in wild, useless protest as:*)

The Curtain Falls

ACT TWO

SCENE 1

INTERMISSION (*from the professional side*). *Music: "Too Darn Hot," softly underneath.*

The dimly lit alley fronting the smudgy, red-brick rear of the theatre. A single bulb over the stage door barely illuminates the black lettering on it. Through the small open windows that break the monotony of the wall, you can make out the faces of the performers in their cubicles as they give in to the heat of of the night. In back, an electric-light sign indicates a distant street corner. On stage, two Negro friends of PAUL, FRED'S *dresser, are seated on an empty packing-case playing cards in desultory fashion. They're waiting to make a "touch." A working* PAUL *is legitimate prey.*

PAUL *enters, leaving stage door open. Sees his friends and we go into the number: "Too Darn Hot."*

During this number, the DANCERS *and* SINGERS *saunter out in twos and threes, drinking pop and Cokes out of bottles and lighting an occasional cigarette. They are all in* Shrew *costumes, but the men have opened up their jackets, and the women have tucked their purple-and-cerise chiffon skirts into their waistbands as high as they'll go. They fan themselves with Woolworth fans and pieces of newspaper.*

At a certain point of the number, BILL *comes out for a quiet smoke, tosses cigarette away, and joins* PAUL *and his two friends in a spirited jazz session into which the* DANCERS *throw themselves with Bacchanalian zest. We must assume that it's never too hot to dance.*

And so PAUL *and his two pals sing:*

PAUL and BOYS: (*"Too Darn Hot"*)

(*1st Verse*)

PAUL:

It's too darn hot,
It's too darn hot.
I'd like to sup with my baby tonight
And play the pup with my baby tonight,
I'd like to sup with my baby tonight
And play the pup with my baby tonight
But I ain't up to my baby tonight
'Cause it's too darn hot.

BOYS:

It's too darn hot,
It's too darn hot.

PAUL:

I'd like to stop for my baby tonight
And blow my top with my baby tonight,
I'd like to stop for my baby tonight
Blow my top with my baby tonight
But I'd be a flop with my baby tonight
'Cause it's too darn hot.

BOYS:

It's too darn hot,
It's too darn hot.

PAUL:

I'd like to fool with my baby tonight,
Break ev'ry rule with my baby tonight,

TRIO:

I'd like to fool with my baby tonight,
Break ev'ry rule with my baby tonight
But pillow, you'll be my baby tonight
'Cause it's too darn hot.

(*1st Refrain*)

TRIO:

According to the Kinsey report
Ev'ry average man you know
Much prefers to play his favorite sport
When the temperature is low
But when the thermometer goes 'way up
And the weather is sizzling hot

PAUL:

Mister Adam
For his madam,
Is not.

TRIO:

'Cause it's too, too,
Too darn hot,
It's too darn hot.
It's too darn hot.

(2nd Verse)

BOYS:

It's too darn hot,
It's too darn hot.

PAUL:

I'd like to call on my baby tonight
And give my all to my baby tonight,

TRIO:

I'd like to call on my baby tonight
And give my all to my baby tonight

PAUL:

But I can't play ball with my baby tonight
'Cause it's too darn hot.

TRIO:

It's too, too darn hot,
It's too, too darn hot.

PAUL:

I'd like to meet with my baby tonight,
Get off my feet with my baby tonight,
I'd like to meet with my baby tonight,
Get off my feet with my baby tonight
But no repeat with my baby tonight
'Cause it's too darn hot.

BOYS:

It's too darn hot,
It's too darn hot.

PAUL:

I'd like to coo to my baby tonight
And pitch some woo with my baby tonight,

I'd like to coo to my baby tonight
And pitch some woo with my baby tonight
But, brother, you bite my baby tonight
'Cause it's too darn hot.

(*2nd Refrain*)

TRIO:

According to the Kinsey report
Ev'ry average man you know
Much prefers to play his favorite sport
When the temperature is low
But when the thermometer goes 'way up
And the weather is sizzling hot
Mister Gob
For his squab,
A marine
For his queen,
A G.I.
For his cutie-pie
Is not
'Cause it's too, too,
Too darn hot.
It's too darn hot,
It's too, too, too, too darn hot.

(*End of dance, blackout leaving on lights in stage door.* RALPH *enters through door*)

RALPH: On stage everybody!

(BILL *and* DANCERS *exit through stage door*)

(Blackout)

SCENE 2

On stage again. Intermission is over. The diamond-patterned Shrew *curtain is in place, but the stage is empty. After a second or two,* FRED GRAHAM, *in his* PETRUCHIO *costume, comes quickly through the break in the curtain. Conductor in pit senses something amiss and taps baton on stand for musicians to stop playing.*

FRED: Ladies and Gentlemen, due to unavoidable circumstances, the scene which was to have opened the second part of *The Shrew* will have to be omitted this evening. It's the scene on the mule where I, Petruchio, take Katharine, my wife, to Verona. We have a slight accident where my wife rolls off the mule into the mud and then proceeds to revile me. Miss Vanessi is unable to ride the mule this evening. We are, therefore, continuing with the next scene, which takes place in Petruchio's house. Thank you. (*Indicates to orchestra conductor to carry on, and retreats*)

SCENE 3

Curtain parts to disclose main room in PETRUCHIO'S *house. It is barely furnished. A door leads to* PETRUCHIO'S *bedroom. Long table with bowl of fruit and large vase and a low chair on either side of table comprise the furnishings.*

PETRUCHIO: (*Offstage*) What–no man at the door to hold my stirrup nor to take my horse? (*He enters before servants can get there*) Where be these knaves?

(*We now see* KATHARINE *grimly following* PETRUCHIO *in. She is disheveled, her wedding gown torn, her hair streaming down her back in sweet disorder*)

PETRUCHIO: Where is Nathaniel?

NATHANIEL: (*Entering*) Here, sir.

PETRUCHIO: Gregory.

GREGORY: (*Entering*) Here, sir.

PETRUCHIO: Phillip.

PHILLIP: (*Entering*) Here, sir.

PETRUCHIO: You logger-headed and unpolish'd grooms! (*Pushes* NATHANIEL *over to other two servants*)

(GUNMEN *enter. They're still in their ill-fitting* Shrew *costumes and street shoes*)

PETRUCHIO: What? No attendance? No regard? No duty? (*Removes cape and hat and throws them to servants*) Go, rascals, go, and fetch my supper in. (*Servants exit. To* GUNMEN) Kind strangers, thou angels in disguise who did help me in my hour of need, 'twere well you rested from your travels in yon chamber. (*Indicates door right.* GUNMEN, *puzzled, look in direction indicated, but don't budge*) Get ye hence. Go to, go to–(*Indicates for them to scram*)

FIRST MAN: (*Getting it, nudges his colleague*) Come to, come to–(*They exit*)

PETRUCHIO: Food! Food! Food! Where are those . . . (*Glances at* KATHARINE *carelessly*) Sit down, Kate. . . .

KATHARINE: (*Glumly*) Thou knowest full well that I cannot.

PETRUCHIO: Well, then, stand and be merry! (*Sits at table*) Some water, here; what, ho! Where's my spaniel Troilus?

Shall I have some water? (*A servant enters with jug and cup.* PETRUCHIO *trips him*) Come, Kate, and wash, and welcome heartily. You whoreson villain, will you let it fall? (*Picks up servant and as he runs off, kicks at him. Other servants enter with food and a chair cushion*)

KATHARINE: Patience, I pray you, 'twas a fault unwilling.

PETRUCHIO: A whoreson beetle-headed, flap-ear'd knave! Come, Kate, sit down; I know you have a stomach. (*Places cushion on chair. As* KATE *goes to sit down he snatches cushion, as she almost sits on it, and gives it to servant*) Will you give thanks, sweet Kate, or else shall I? What's this? Mutton?

NATHANIEL: Aye.

PETRUCHIO: (*Taking it from her*) Who brought it?

PHILLIP: (*Stepping forward*) I.

(KATHARINE *tries to take some*)

PETRUCHIO:

'Tis burnt, and so is all the meat,
What dogs are these? Where is the rascal cook?
How durst you, villains, bring it from the dresser,
And serve it thus to me that love it not?
Here, take it 'way, trenchers, cups, and all.

(PETRUCHIO *throws cups and plates off stage and servants scatter.* KATHARINE, *her back to* PETRUCHIO, *stuffs string of sausages down front of dress*)

KATHARINE:

I pray you, husband, be not so disquiet,
The meat was well, if you were so contented.

PETRUCHIO:

I tell thee, Kate, 'twas burnt and dried away
And I expressly am forbid to touch it,
For it engenders choler, planteth anger, and
(*Takes sausages out of* KATE'S *dress*)
Better 'twere that both of us did fast
Since of ourselves, ourselves are choleric
Than feed it with such over-roasted flesh.

KATHARINE:

Did you marry me to famish me?

PETRUCHIO:

Tomorrow shall you eat, my honey love,
When we return unto thy father's house

And revel it as bravely as the best with silken coats.
And caps and golden rings,
With ruffs and cuffs and farthingales and things . . .

(*Enter* HABERDASHER *with cap and mirror upstage left*)

PETRUCHIO:
Come, let us see these ornaments.
(*To* HABERDASHER)
And what news with you, sir?

HABERDASHER:
The cap your worship did bespeak.

PETRUCHIO:
Aha! 'Tis for thee, Kate.
(HABERDASHER *holds up cap*)

PETRUCHIO:
Why this was molded on a porringer,
A velvet dish—
(*Puts on cap and looks in mirror*)
—fie!—'tis lewd and filthy,
'Tis a cockle or a walnut shell.
Come! Let me have a bigger.

KATHARINE: (*Rising, takes hat*)
I'll have no bigger, this doth fit the time,
And gentlewomen wear such caps as these.

PETRUCHIO:
When you are gentle, you shall have one, too
And not till then.
(*Takes hat from* KATE)

KATHARINE: (*In anger*)
I am no child, no babe;
Your betters have endur'd me say my mind,
And if you cannot, best you stop your ears.
My tongue will tell the anger of my heart.
Or else my heart concealing it, will break.
(*Grabs hat from* PETRUCHIO *and puts it on*)

PETRUCHIO:
Why, thou say'st true, it is a paltry cap,
I love thee well in that thou lik'st it not.
(*Takes hat from* KATE)
Begone! Take it hence!

(*Throws hat to* HABERDASHER. HABERDASHER *exits. Assuming gentleness*)

PETRUCHIO:

Well, my Kate; tomorrow we will unto your father's,
(*Slaps her on shoulder*)
Even in these honest mean habiliments:
Our purses shall be proud, our garments poor;
For 'tis the mind that makes the body rich:
What,
(*Slap*)
Is the jay more precious than the lark,
Because his feathers are more beautiful?
Or is the adder better than the eel,
Because his painted skin contents the eye?
(*Slaps her again*)
Oh, no, good Kate; neither art thou the worse
For this poor furniture and mean array.
Come, come, I will bring thee to thy bridal chamber.
(*Takes her to bedroom door*)

KATHARINE: (*In tears*) I'm hungry.

PETRUCHIO: How canst thou think of food at such a time?

(*Helps* KATHARINE *through door. Slams it shut, triumphantly. To audience*)

PETRUCHIO:

Thus have I politically begun my reign,
And 'tis my hope to end it successfully.
My falcon now is sharp, and passing empty,
And, till she stoop, she must not be full-gorged,
She ate no meat today, nor none shall eat;
Last night she slept not, nor tonight she shall not;
As with the meat, some undeserved fault
I'll find about the making of the bed,
And here I'll fling the pillow, there the bolster,
This way the coverlet, another way the sheets;
Aye, and amid this hurly I intend
That all is done in reverent care of her,
And, in conclusion, she shall watch the night,
And if she chance to nod, I'll rail and brawl,
And with the clamor keep her still awake;
This is a way to kill a wife with kindness,
And thus I'll curb her mad and headstrong humor.

(*Turns upstage to door*)

He that knows better how to tame a shrew,
Now let him speak, 'tis charity to show.

(*He goes to bedroom door. Softly*)
Kate—

(*No answer. Louder*)
My bonny Kate—

(*No answer. Bawling*)
My winsome Kate—

(*No answer. He tries door in anger. It is locked*)
I' faith, the woman's shot her bolt!
She has performed
While I did act the dolt!

PETRUCHIO: ("*Where Is the Life that Late I Led?*")
(*Verse*)

Since I reached the charming age of puberty
And began to finger feminine curls,
Like a show that's typically Shuberty
(*Kicks leg*)
I have always had a multitude of girls,
But now that a married man, at last, am I,
How aware of my dear, departed past am I.

(*1st Refrain*)

Where is the life that late I led?
Where is it now? Totally dead.
Where is the fun I used to find?
Where has it gone? Gone with the wind.
A married life may all be well,
But raising an heir
Could never compare
With raising a bit of hell.
So I repeat what first I said,
Where is the life that late I—
(*Takes address book from waistband, consults it*)

(*1st Patter*)

In dear Milano, where are you, Momo,
Still selling those pictures of the scriptures in the Duomo?
And Carolina, where are you, Lina,

Still peddling your pizza in the streets o' Taormina?
And in Firenze, where are you, Alice,
Still there in your pretty, itty-bitty Pitti palace?
And sweet Lucretia, so young and gay-ee?
What scandalous doin's in the ruins of Pompeii!

(*2nd Refrain*)

Where is the life that late I led?
Where is it now? Totally dead.
Where is the fun I used to find?
Where has it gone? Gone with the wind.
The marriage game is quite all right,
Yes, during the day
It's easy to play,
But oh what a bore at night.
So I repeat what first I said,
Where is the life that late I—
(*Looks in book again*)

(*2nd Patter*)

Where is Rebecca, my Becki-weckio,
Could still she be cruising that amusing Ponte Vecchio?
Where is Fedora, the wild virago?
It's lucky I missed her gangster sister from Chicago.
Where is Venetia who loved to chat so,
Could still she be drinkin' in her stinkin', pink palazzo?
And lovely Lisa, where are you, Lisa?
You gave a new meaning to the leaning tow'r of Pisa.

(*3rd Refrain*)

Where is the life that late I led?
Where is it now? Totally dead.
Where is the fun I used to find?
Where has it gone? Gone with the wind.
I've oft been told of nuptial bliss
But what do you do,
A quarter to two,
With only a shrew to kiss?
So I repeat what first I said,
Where is the life that late I led?

(*At the end of song,* PETRUCHIO *bows and backs into door. It opens. He winks, throws black address book away, and exits through door*)

(*Note: Carolina is pronounced* Caroleena; *Lina is pronounced* Leena; *pizza is pronounced* peetsa; *Lisa is pronounced* Leeza.)

SCENE 4

Corridor backstage. Same setting as Act One, Scene 2. An ambulance siren, first heard faintly, then real loud and stopping as if ambulance has drawn up outside.

DOORMAN *comes through stage door as* RALPH *enters from opposite direction.*

RALPH: Who's making all that noise? What's that siren?

DOORMAN: There's an ambulance out there for Miss Vanessi, and a gentleman by the name of Harrison Howell–

RALPH: What?

DOORMAN: He's raising a helluva rumpus.

(HOWELL *enters, followed by a doctor and two nurses. He's a dignified gentleman–not bad-looking, but a little stuffy*)

HOWELL: I demand . . . Where is Miss Vanessi?

RALPH: Are you Mr. Harrison Howell?

HOWELL: Of course I'm Harrison Howell. Where's Miss Vanessi? How is she?

RALPH: She's doing fine.

HOWELL: Where is she?

RALPH: On stage.

HOWELL: On stage? How can she be on stage? She's ill.

RALPH: Not that I know of.

HOWELL: Of course she's ill! She told me so herself. She's been assaulted by that brute, dammit.

(FRED *enters right, followed by* TWO GUNMEN)

FRED: Quiet, dammit!

HOWELL: Look here, Graham!

FIRST GUNMAN: He said quiet, dammit.

SECOND GUNMAN: Shhh . . .

FIRST GUNMAN: (*Softly*) Ain't you got no appreciation of the finer things of life?

SECOND GUNMAN: (*As softly*) Man cannot live by bread alone.

HOWELL: What?

FRED: (*To* GUNMEN, *very quietly*) Be tolerant, gentlemen. Remember Mr. Howell didn't have your advantages–eight years in the prison library in Atlanta!

HOWELL: What?

FRED: However, Mr. Howell is a very distinguished man. He's the only Republican who didn't run for the nomination.

HOWELL: How dare you assault my fiancée?

FRED: She hit me first!

HOWELL: I don't understand this. She asked me to bring an ambulance.

FRED: My dear Howell. You fail to take into consideration the caprices of women of talent and beauty. She may even say to you tonight: "Harrison, I am playing this show under duress. Call the F.B.I."

FIRST GUNMAN: A very efficient organization.

SECOND GUNMAN: Admirable co-ordination.

HOWELL: But why should she want the F.B.I.?

FRED: Why should she want an ambulance? My dear Howell, your fiancée may ask for chewing gum, a miniature of the Empire State in pale ivory, or a fifth of Chanel Number Five.

RALPH: On stage, Mr. Graham.

(LOIS *starts down stairs*)

FRED: Why how now, Kate? I hope thou art not mad. This is a man—old—wrinkled—faded and withered. (*Clears his throat noisily and exits reciting same line*)

LOIS: (*At bottom of staircase*) Harold! . . . Why, Harold Murgatroyd!

HOWELL: All right, Doctor, nurses—I shan't need you. (*They exit*)

LOIS: (*Crossing to* HOWELL *center*) Harold! Harold!

HOWELL: My name is not Harold! I am Harrison Howell!

LOIS: Harold, don't you remember? In front of the Harvard Club. (*He looks about guiltily*) I had something in my eye, and you took me to Atlantic City to take it out?

HOWELL: Look here, my child—

LOIS: Harold, I've still got that diamond bracelet with the rubies. I think of you all the time when I go down to my safe deposit box.

(BILL *enters, unseen by* LOIS)

HOWELL: Very touching . . . Very touching . . . (*Looks about*) But you must understand—

LOIS: I understand—

HOWELL: I rely on your discretion. I'm marrying Miss Vanessi, you know—

LOIS: Oh, I understand—

HOWELL: After all, I was just sowing my wild oats. Let me see —I was quite a young man at the time—barely forty-five.

LOIS: And now you're a big man in Washington!

HOWELL: Well, I have achieved a certain distinction. I'm the minority elder statesman. I have my own park bench.

RALPH: This way, Mr. Howell.

HOWELL: Thank you. (*To* LOIS) Excuse me. (*Starts to go*)

LOIS: One thing I've always wanted to know—what do you do about the pigeons?

HOWELL: Duck, my dear. Just duck. (*Exits*)

BILL: (*Whistling first three notes of "Bianca"*) When did you initiate him?

LOIS: (*Caught, therefore indignant*) What a thing to say! And about a man I haven't seen in years! I assure you there was nothing between he and I. Just because a girl is goodhearted and normal—and wants to get along—with her fellow man! (*She goes into:*)

LOIS: (*"Always True to You in My Fashion"*)
(*Verse*)

Oh, Bill,
Why can't you behave?
Why can't you behave?
How in hell can you be jealous
When you know, baby, I'm your slave?
(BILL *shrugs and exits*)
I'm just mad for you,
And I'll always be
But naturally.

(*1st Refrain*)

If a custom-tailored vet
Asks me out for something wet,
When the vet begins to pet, I cry "Hooray!"
But I'm always true to you, darlin', in my fashion,
Yes, I'm always true to you, darlin', in my way.
I enjoy a tender pass
By the boss of Boston, Mass.
Though his pass is middle-class and notta Backa Bay,
But I'm always true to you, darlin', in my fashion,
Yes, I'm always true to you, darlin', in my way.
There's a madman known as "Mack"

Who is planning to attack,
If his mad attack means a Cadillac, okay!
But I'm always true to you, darlin', in my fashion,
Yes, I'm always true to you, darlin', in my way.

(*2nd Refrain*)

I've been asked to have a meal
By a big tycoon in steel,
If the meal includes a deal, accept I may,
But I'm always true to you, darlin', in my fashion,
Yes, I'm always true to you, darlin', in my way.
I could never curl my lip
To a dazzlin' diamond clip
Though the clip meant "let 'er rip," I'd not say "Nay!"
But I'm always true to you, darlin', in my fashion,
Yes, I'm always true to you, darlin', in my way.
There's an oil man known as "Tex"
Who is keen to give me checks
And his checks, I fear, mean that sex is here to stay!
But I'm always true to you, darlin', in my fashion,
Yes, I'm always true to you, darlin', in my way.

(*3rd Refrain*)

There's a wealthy Hindu priest
Who's a wolf, to say the least,
When the priest goes too far east, I also stray,
But I'm always true to you, darlin', in my fashion,
Yes, I'm always true to you, darlin', in my way.
There's a lush from Portland, Ore.
Who is rich but sich a bore
When the bore falls on the floor, I let him lay,
But I'm always true to you, darlin', in my fashion,
Yes, I'm always true to you, darlin', in my way.
Mr. Harris, plutocrat,
Wants to give my cheek a pat,
If the Harris pat
Means a Paris hat
Bé-bé
Oo-la-la
Mais je suis toujours fidèle,
Darlin' in my fashion,

Oui, je suis toujours fidèle,
Darlin' in my way.

(*4th Refrain*)

From Ohio Mister Thorne
Calls me up from night till morn,
Mister Thorne once cornered corn and that ain't hay, ha, ha, ha,
But I'm always true to you, darlin', in my fashion,
Yes, I'm always true to you, darlin', in my way.
From Milwaukee, Mister Fritz
Often moves me to the Ritz,
Mister Fritz is full of Schlitz and full of play,
But I'm always true to you, darlin', in my fashion,
Yes, I'm always true to you, darlin', in my way.
Mister Gable, I mean Clark,
Wants me on his boat to park,
If the Gable boat
Means a sable coat,
Anchors aweigh!
But I'm always true to you, darlin', in my fashion,
Yes, I'm always true to you, darlin', in my way.

(Blackout)

SCENE 5

LILLI'S *dressing room.* HARRISON HOWELL *is on the telephone at dressing table.*

HOWELL: This is Harrison Howell. Give me my secretary—Timothy? I'm waiting here for Miss Vanessi, and I thought I'd jot down my wedding itinerary . . . Ready? We'll be married in St. Thomas's, 2:30. Got that? (*Consults notes*) Wedding reception at the Waldorf, 4:15. Got that? Press conference, 5:38. Arrive La Guardia, 6:25. Depart, 6:30. Got that?

(FRED *enters, in dressing gown over costume, and sits on couch*)

HOWELL: Arrive Washington, 9:35. Arrive White House, 9:55. Got that? Conference with President and honeymoon with wife.

FRED: It's a good trick if you can do it.

(LILLI *enters in* Shrew *outfit, followed by the* TWO GUNMEN, *also in* Shrew *costumes, who post themselves back of lounge*)

LILLI: Harrison! They told me you were here!

HOWELL: That's all, Timothy.

LILLI: Don't hang up, Harrison. I'm playing this show under duress. Call the F.B.I.

(HARRISON *looks at* FRED. *That's what he said she'd say*)

FRED: What did I tell you?

HOWELL: (*Hanging up phone*) Now, my dear—I don't mind bringing an ambulance and a doctor and two nurses. They're on my payroll. But the F.B.I. is not. I'm perfectly willing—in fact I enjoy humoring the caprices of a beautiful woman whom I happen to adore—

LILLI: Caprices? These thugs threatened me!

HOWELL: What?

LILLI: They're making me play at the point of a gun. They won't let me leave the theatre.

(HOWELL *looks at* FRED. FRED *shrugs*)

HOWELL: Now, my dear—

LILLI: Can't you see they're gangsters?

FIRST GUNMAN: I guess it shows.

FRED: (*Rising and going toward* TWO GUNMEN) Are you referring to two of the most promising graduates of the Group? Not to mention the Guild Theatre, Inc., the Civic Repertory, and Miss Pennyfeather's School of Charm, whose faculty they grace!

LILLI: And you're in cahoots with them!

HOWELL: What?

FRED: What can one say to libel?

FIRST GUNMAN: Should I say something?

FRED: No.

SECOND GUNMAN: Discretion is the better part of valor.

FIRST GUNMAN: "Famous Sayings" . . . Top shelf, under Non-Fiction, right-hand corner, Atlanta . . . No talking . . . No smoking.

HOWELL: (*A little dazed*) Obviously, my dear, judging by their costumes, and their speech, these men are not what you say they are.

LILLI: Harrison, darling, I tell you—

FRED: (*Interrupting*) Do you realize what it means to blast a reputation? Of course not. You think nothing of dragging Harrison down here—and an entire Medical Corps—for a whim!

HOWELL: Now, my dear, I'd like to go over my wedding itinerary—I just dictated it to Timothy. Now, I thought we'd be married a week from Monday. At 2:30, St. Thomas's. That'll give you just enough time to assemble a trousseau.

LILLI: Harrison darling, listen to me. I can't get out of this theatre!

HOWELL: Why not?

LILLI: These thugs won't let me.

FRED: Why don't you try it?

LILLI: What?

FRED: Go! . . . Of course you can leave the theatre. That's what you want, and I can't say I blame you. After all, what is there in the theatre to hold you? It's so tawdry–the dreary business of creating a part–the dull routine of watching a character come to life. The meaningless excitement of opening night. The boring thundering applause of the crowd–the pictures in the papers–the parties–the idiotic men and women who stare and whisper: "There goes Lilli Vanessi!" Dreadful! I don't blame you for leaving all that–when you've a chance for happiness–real happiness–with Harrison.

HOWELL: Thank you, Graham. I think I can make the little woman happy.

LILLI: I never want to see the theatre again! (*To* FRED) Or you again!

FRED: I envy you, Harrison. Never has a man acquired a woman with more sweetness of disposition, who's more even-tempered, has more poise, more gentleness, more sheer unadulterated goodness. Yum, yum, yum . . . Yes, Lilli Vanessi is the wife for you. Get Lilli Vanessi today! This is N.B.C.!

LILLI: I hope you're enjoying yourself.

FRED: Enormously . . . And envying *you*.

LILLI: Me?

FRED: The life you're going to lead with Harrison. So different than the one you had with me.

LILLI: I'll see to that.

FRED: No quarrels–no bickering . . .

LILLI: I want peace!

FRED: And you shall have it–peace–quiet–stability.

HOWELL: I've got a place down in Georgia–thirty thousand acres. Ride for days, and not see a soul, except my tenant farmers!

FRED: You won't have to talk to a soul.

LILLI: I shall adore it!

FRED: Of course you will.

HOWELL: Wonderful life.

FRED: What do you call the place: *Solitude?*

HOWELL: No. *Contentment.*

FRED: Ah! *Contentment.* Just think. No cocktail parties. No malicious gossip. No backbiting friends. In fact, no friends at all, except an occasional mongoose who'll drop in for dinner.

LILLI: Go on! Go on!

HOWELL: We'll see all the people we want to see in Washington.

FRED: Certainly. Just think of those intimate little dinner parties for the sparkling Supreme Court. Just think of the privilege of sitting next to one of the Great Judicial Brains while he tells you the inside story of his sciatica.

HOWELL: (*Indicating his back*) It always hits me here . . .

FRED: Oh, it'll be a mad whirl—

LILLI: I'll still love it.

HOWELL: I always rest up in my place in Aiken. Got a dining room there can seat a hundred.

FRED: Marvelous!

FIRST GUNMAN: Eight years I et in a dining room that could seat twelve hundred.

LILLI: Where did you say this was?

FRED: (*Quickly, crossing to left end of lounge*) The commissary at M.G.M.

HOWELL: Got my own projection room in Aiken. Got the finest collection of Mickey Mouses in the country.

FIRST GUNMAN: Where's your grammar? Mickey Mice.

SECOND GUNMAN: Don't be a purist.

HOWELL: Mickey Mice?

(*The* GUNMEN *exit, satisfied. They've corrected a millionaire*)

FRED: Yes, I can just see life at Aiken. Morning. Harrison rises —with the aid of a valet—

HOWELL: Been with me thirty years—

FRED: Into his riding clothes. You into yours. A brisk canter.

LILLI: I'm mad about horses.

FRED: And eventually you'll stop falling off . . . It's yoicks and away . . . Back to the castle. A brisk shower. A massage. An injection of Vitamin B_1.

HOWELL: Making a new man out of me.

FRED: And then—Harrison takes a nap.

HOWELL: Oh, no. Breakfast first.

FRED: Ah, yes, breakfast. You sit at one end of the long, long table. Harrison at the other. You pick up your telescope and watch fondly as Harrison slops his Wheaties.

HOWELL: Wheaties are good eatin'! There's nothing finer.

FRED: And then the nap!

HOWELL: Twenty minutes. Rests the brain.

FRED: Then up. You dress. You contemplate the luxurious swamps. You toy with your toilette. Harrison wakes. You discuss this and that, topics of the day. Will Big Frost escape Dick Tracy?

HOWELL: I very much doubt it!

FRED: Time for another nap.

HOWELL: Lunch first.

FRED: Correction accepted. Lunch first.

HOWELL: Got the finest chef in the country. But I've got to watch my diet. Stick to the yolk of an egg, shredded raw carrot, and a glass of milk. Done wonders for me.

FRED: As you'll be able to see through your telescope. And then —a nice, soothing, refreshing nap!

HOWELL: (*Lying back*) Thirty minutes. Rests the brain.

FRED: You, too, will nap, Miss Vanessi. Thirty minutes. Rests the brain. Then up. Dress. Walk in the formal gardens. Time for tea. High tea.

HOWELL: Always refreshes me.

FRED: Time for a nap—before dinner.

HOWELL: Fifteen minutes.

FRED: A quickie . . . Rested, you rise. (HOWELL *starts to sit up.* FRED *pushes him back*) You dress for dinner. You dine in that cozy little hundred-seater. Then a brisk game of dominoes.

HOWELL: Wonderful game.

FRED: (*By* HOWELL'S *head*) The mockingbird sings . . . The air is still . . . You feel drowsy . . . You yawn deliciously . . . (*And* HARRISON *yawns*) Time for the final nap of the day—the long one . . . You stretch out . . . (HARRISON *does so*) Your eyes close . . . (HARRISON'S *do so*)

LILLI: (*Whispering fiercely*) Get out!

FRED: Sh! . . . And so the little Momma bear said to the Poppa bear: "*You bore me . . .*"

(HARRISON *lets out a deafening snore*)

(Blackout)

SCENE 6

Corridor, same as Act Two, Scene 4.

At opening of scene, FOUR DANCING GIRLS *are grouped on stage.* DOORMAN *is standing left center stage.* BILL CALHOUN *stage right.* FOUR SINGING GIRLS *are on staircase.*

MESSENGER *enters from* DOORMAN'S *booth carrying an exaggerated hatbox. He walks to* DOORMAN.

MESSENGER: Package for Miss Lois Lane.

(DOORMAN *indicates right.* MESSENGER *exits with box*)

SINGING GIRLS: (*"Bianca"*)

For your Bianca!
Ha, ha, ha, ha, ha.

MESSENGER: (*Same business. He carries box from furrier's*) Package for Miss Lois Lane.

(DOORMAN *directs. He exits*)

SINGING GIRLS: For your Bianca!
Ha, ha, ha, ha, ha.

CHAUFFEUR: (*Same business. He carries bottle of champagne*) Package for Miss Lois Lane.

(DOORMAN *directs. He exits right*)

BANKER: (*Same business. He carries two bags of money*) Package for Miss Lois Lane.

(DOORMAN *directs. He exits*)

TRUCKMAN: (*Same business. Enters from back of booth with a barrel of Schlitz*) Package for Miss Lois Lane.

(DOORMAN *directs him and follows him off*)

SINGING GIRLS:

Ha, ha, ha, ha, ha, ha, ha. Ha, ha, ha, ha, ha, ha, ha.
Your Bianca.
Ha!

BILL: (*Stops them, goes to center, and sings:*)

Sweet Bianca,
While rehearsing with Bianca
She's the darling I adore
Off stage I found,
She's been around,
But I still love her more and more.
So I've written her a love song
Though I'm just an amateur,
I'll sing it through

For all of you
To see if it's worthy of her.
Are you list'nin'?

(*Refrain*)

(BILL *sings chorus.* SINGING GIRLS *whistle.* DANCERS *dance. What else can they do?*)

(*1st Chorus*)

Bianca, Bianca,
Oh, baby, will you be mine?
Bianca, Bianca,
You better answer yes
Or Poppa spanka.
To win you, Bianca,
There's nothing I would not do.
I would gladly give up
Coffee for Sanka,
Even Sanka, Bianca,
For you.

(*2nd Chorus*)

(BILL *sings while he and* DANCERS *go into tap routine.* SINGING GIRLS *sing from stairs*)

(*3rd Chorus*)

(BILL *and* DANCERS *doing routine.* SINGING GIRLS *on stairs. Exit at finish. One girl ascending stairs, other three exit right.* BILL *and* FOUR DANCING GIRLS *exit, with the traditional high kick of the bygone musical show.*

The TWO GUNMEN *enter, in* Shrew *outfits, and go to coin phone box*)

FIRST GUNMAN: (*Puts in dime and dials number*) Hello. Hello, Gumpy. I want to talk to Mr. Hogan. Well, I want to report in, Gumpy. Mr. Hogan likes me to report in, Gumpy. Why should I call you *Mister* Gumpy? Where's Mr. Hogan? Oh, I see . . . Yeah . . . I see . . . Well, certainly, we'll pay you a visit, Mr. Gumpy.

(FRED *enters, still in dressing gown*)

FIRST GUNMAN: All right, Mr. Gumpy. (*Hangs up. Points up*) Gumpy! (*Then down*) Hogan.

SECOND GUNMAN: You mean it?

FRED: Who's Mr. Gumpy?

FIRST GUNMAN: Mr. Graham—(*Takes out IOU*) I guess this is the end of our very pleasant association.

SECOND GUNMAN: I guess so.

FRED: What's this?

FIRST GUNMAN: I guess we got to declare a moratorium. You see, Mr. Gumpy declared a moratorium on Mr. Hogan. His unidentified remains will be found floating in the bay tomorrow morning.

SECOND GUNMAN: Rest his soul.

(GUNMEN *remove hats and bow heads*)

FIRST GUNMAN: So that lets you out . . . And we must part.

FRED: Do you think Mr. Gumpy has the executive ability, the enterprise, the initiative, and the imagination for the post?

FIRST GUNMAN: (*Astutely*) No, but he's got the post.

(LILLI *enters with* HATTIE, *carrying suitcase and jewel box. Both in street attire*)

SECOND GUNMAN: (*Bows in grand manner*) We want to say au revoir, Miss Vanessi.

LILLI: What?

FIRST GUNMAN: (*Same bow*) It's been a delightful experience.

SECOND GUNMAN: Very educational.

FIRST GUNMAN: We'll always think of you.

SECOND GUNMAN: Should old acquaintance be forgot?

FRED: What they're trying to tell you is—you're free to go. You don't have to finish the show.

SECOND GUNMAN: Au revoir. (*Bows*)

FIRST GUNMAN: Au revoir. (*Bows*) (*They exit.* FIRST GUNMAN *takes dime from phone slot on way out*)

LILLI: Run along, Hattie.

(HATTIE *exits to street*)

FRED: Aren't you taking Sleeping Beauty with you?

LILLI: Let him sleep.

FRED: Don't tell me the bloom is off—the rose?

LILLI: (*On the verge of tears*) You are not Louella Parsons and I don't care to discuss my personal life with you.

FRED: Same old Lilli . . . And I thought I detected a note—a new note of softness—a new humility—even a spark of affection—a glimmer of love . . . (*Close to her*)

LILLI: (*Hesitates—then pulls away*) You're not going to hypnotize me, Svengali.

FRED: Lilli, you can't walk out on me now.

LILLI: You walked out on me once.

FRED: But I came back.

(LILLI *hesitates*)

DOORMAN: (*From his cubbyhole*) Your cab's waiting, Miss Vanessi!

(LILLI *leaves.* FRED, *alone, reprises:*)

FRED: (*"So in Love"*)

Strange, dear, but true, dear,
When I'm close to you, dear,
The stars fill the sky,
So in love with you am I.
Even without you
My arms fold about you,
You know darling why,
So in love with you am I.
In love with the night mysterious
The night when you first were there,
In love with my joy delirious
When I knew that you could care,
So taunt me and hurt me,
Deceive me, desert me,
I'm yours till I die,
So in love,
So in love,
So in love with you, my love, am I.

(*Goes off as lights dim*)

(Blackout)

SCENE 7

Safety asbestos curtain with two rather Rabelaisian cherubs painted on either side. Underneath, softly, music of "Brush Up Your Shakespeare." The TWO GUNMEN, *in their hand-sewn blue suits, make their way clumsily through opening in curtain. They carry straw hats.*

FIRST GUNMAN: (*As he comes through curtain*) Hey! How do we get out of here?

SECOND GUNMAN: (*Following him*) How'd we get in here?

FIRST GUNMAN: I don't know–on that side–no . . . (*Sees backdrop*) Hey, look! . . .

SECOND GUNMAN: (*Regarding cherub*) It's a boy!

(*And off they go into:*)

TWO GUNMEN: (*"Brush Up Your Shakespeare," with an intermittent soft-shoe dance*)
(*Verse*)

The girls today in society
Go for classical poetry,
So to win their hearts, one must quote with ease
Aeschylus and Euripides,
One must know Homer, and, b'lieve me, bo,
Sophocles—also Sappho-Ho,
Unless you know Shelley and Keats and Pope,
Dainty debbies will call you a dope.
But the poet of them all
Who will start 'em simply ravin'
Is the poet people call
(*Take hats off to Shakespeare*)
"The Bard of Stratford-on-Avon"

(*1st Refrain*)

BOTH:
Brush up your Shakespeare,
Start quoting him now,
Brush up your Shakespeare
And the women you will wow.

SECOND GUNMAN:
Just declaim a few lines from *Othella*
And they'll think you're a helluva fella,

FIRST GUNMAN:
If your blonde won't respond when you flatter 'er
Tell her what Tony told Cleopaterer.

SECOND GUNMAN:
If she fights when her clothes you are mussing,

BOTH:
What are clothes? *Much Ado About Nussing*.
Brush up your Shakespeare
And they'll all kowtow.

(*2nd Refrain*)

BOTH:
Brush up your Shakespeare,
Start quoting him now,

Brush up your Shakespeare
And the women you will wow.

FIRST GUNMAN:
With the wife of the British Embessida
Try a crack out of *Troilus and Cressida*

SECOND GUNMAN:
If she says she won't buy it or tike it
Make her tike it, what's more, *As You Like It*.

BOTH:
If she says your behavior is heinous
Kick her right in the *Coriolanus*.
Brush up your Shakespeare
And they'll all kowtow.

(*3rd Refrain*)

BOTH:
Brush up your Shakespeare,
Start quoting him now,
Brush up your Shakespeare
And the women you will wow.

SECOND GUNMAN:
If you can't be a ham and do *Hamlet*
They will not give a damn or a damnlet,

FIRST GUNMAN:
Just recite an occasional sonnet
And your lap'll have "Honey" upon it.

SECOND GUNMAN:
When your baby is pleading for pleasure

BOTH:
Let her sample your *Measure for Measure*.
Brush up your Shakespeare
And they'll all kowtow
Forsooth,
I' Faith.

(*4th Refrain*)

BOTH:
Brush up your Shakespeare,
Start quoting him now,

Brush up your Shakespeare
And the women you will wow.

FIRST GUNMAN:
Better mention *The Merchant of Venice*
When her sweet pound o' flesh you would menace.

SECOND GUNMAN:
If her virtue, at first, she defends—well,
Just remind her that *All's Well That Ends Well,*

FIRST GUNMAN:
And if still she won't give you a bonus,

BOTH:
You know what Venus got from Adonis!
Brush up your Shakespeare
And they'll all kowtow.
Thinks thou
Odds—bodkins.

(*5th Refrain*)

BOTH:
Brush up your Shakespeare,
Start quoting him now,
Brush up your Shakespeare

SECOND GUNMAN:
And the women you will wow.
If your goil is a Washington Heights dream
Treat the kid to *A Midsummer Night's Dream.*

FIRST GUNMAN:
If she then wants an all-by-herself night
Let her rest ev'ry 'leventh or *Twelf' Night,*

BOTH:
If because of your heat she gets huffy,
Simply play on and "Lay on, Macduffy!"
Brush up your Shakespeare
And they'll all kowtow.
We trow,
We vow.

(Blackout)

SCENE 8

A splendid room in BAPTISTA'S *house, beautifully painted in black and white with touches of yellow. There's a large arch at rear on platform with three steps leading down to stage level. Full stage of wedding guests watching the dancers in a pavane based on the thematic melody of "Why Can't You Behave?"* BIANCA *and* LUCENTIO, *in dazzling white of bride and groom, come down steps, as guests applaud softly. End of pavane.* PETRUCHIO *enters, down steps.*

BAPTISTA:

My dear Bianca, and her new-found spouse—
(*Sees* PETRUCHIO)
Brother Petruchio—daughter Katharine—
Feast with the best and welcome to my house.
(*Then stalling*)
. . . But where is Katharine?
(*To* PETRUCHIO)
Where is she?
(*To one of the dancers*)
Sirrah, go you to Mistress Katharine.
Say I command her to come to me.

(NATHANIEL *exits*)

PETRUCHIO:

I know she will not come.
The fouler fortune mine and there an end.

(*Enter* KATHARINE. *Startled sighs from guests, also relief*)

KATHARINE: (*Going right into part as if she'd never quit the show*)
What is your will, sir?

PETRUCHIO: (*Really moved, forgetting Shakespeare*) Darling—
(*Then, as actor, picking up play again*)
Katharine, that cap of yours becomes you not;
Off with that bauble, throw it underfoot.
(*She does so*)

BIANCA:

Fie! What a foolish duty call you this?

PETRUCHIO:

Kate, I charge thee, tell these headstrong women what duty they do owe their lords and husbands.

(KATHARINE *does so, with Shakespeare's lyrics and Porter's music*)

KATHARINE: (*"I Am Ashamed That Women Are So Simple," moves downstage, gestures to crowd.* SIX GIRL SINGERS *cross to stage left*)
I am ashamed that women are so simple
To offer war where they should kneel for peace,
Or seek for rule, supremacy, and sway,
When they are bound to serve, love, and obey.
Why are our bodies soft and weak and smooth
Unapt to toil and trouble in the world
But that our soft conditions and our hearts
Should well agree with our external parts?
So wife, hold your temper and meekly put
Your hand 'neath the sole of your husband's foot.
In token of which duty, if he please
(*Extends hand*)
My hand is ready; ready—may it do him ease.

PETRUCHIO: (*Taking hand and drawing her to him*)
Why! There's a wench! Come on and kiss me, Kate. (*They kiss as* FRED *and* LILLI)

FULL COMPANY: (Shrew *Finale*)

PETRUCHIO:
So kiss me, Kate,

KATE:
Caro!

PETRUCHIO:
And twice and thrice,

KATE:
Carissimo!

PETRUCHIO:
Ere we start

KATE:
Bello!

PETRUCHIO:
Living in Paradise.

KATE:
Bellissimo!

PETRUCHIO:
Oh, Kiss me, Kate,

OTHERS:
Oh, Kiss him, Kate,

KATE:
Presto!

PETRUCHIO and OTHERS:
Darling angel, divine!

KATE:
Prestissimo!

PETRUCHIO:
For now thou shall ever be

KATE:
Now thou shall ever be

PETRUCHIO and MEN:
Now thou shall ever be

KATE and GIRLS:
Now thou shall ever be

PETRUCHIO:
Mine,

KATE:
Mine,

PETRUCHIO and KATE:
Darling mine,

KATE and PETRUCHIO:
And I am thine, and I am thine,

OTHERS:
And she is thine, and she is thine

ALL:
All Thine!

(*The* DANCERS *start a criss-cross routine that reveals the principals in the center, in the bows rehearsed in opening scene of the play. As the curtain falls to rise again on the first note of "Brush Up Your Shakespeare," the entire company is doing a waltz clog while singing:*)

ALL:
Brush up your Shakespeare.

Start quoting him now,
Brush up your Shakespeare
And the women you will wow.

PETRUCHIO and KATE:

So tonight just recite to your matey
Kiss me, Kate, Kiss me, Kate, Kiss me, Katey.

ALL:

Brush up your Shakespeare
And they'll all kowtow.

Curtain

WEST SIDE STORY

Book by Arthur Laurents
Music by Leonard Bernstein
Lyrics by Stephen Sondheim

(Based on a conception of Jerome Robbins)

Production Notes

West Side Story was first presented by Robert E. Griffith and Harold Prince (by arrangement with Roger L. Stevens) at the Winter Garden Theatre, New York, on September 26, 1957. The cast was as follows:

THE JETS

Riff (*The Leader*), *Mickey Calin*
Tony (*His Friend*), *Larry Kert*
Action, *Eddie Roll*
A-rab, *Tony Mordente*
Baby John, *David Winters*
Snowboy, *Grover Dale*
Big Deal, *Martin Charnin*
Diesel, *Hank Brunjes*
Gee-Tar, *Tommy Abbott*
Mouthpiece, *Frank Green*
Tiger, *Lowell Harris*

THEIR GIRLS

Graziella, *Wilma Curley*
Velma, *Carole D'Andrea*
Minnie, *Nanette Rosen*
Clarice, *Marilyn D'Honau*
Pauline, *Julie Oser*
Anybodys, *Lee Becker*

THE SHARKS

Bernardo (*The Leader*), *Ken Le Roy*
Maria (*His Sister*), *Carol Lawrence*
Anita (*His Girl*), *Chita Rivera*
Chino (*His Friend*), *Jamie Sanchez*
Pepe, *George Marcy*
Indio, *Noel Schwartz*
Luis, *Al De Sio*
Anxious, *Gene Gavin*
Nibbles, *Ronnie Lee*
Juano, *Jay Norman*
Toro, *Erne Castaldo*
Moose, *Jack Murray*

THEIR GIRLS

Rosalia, *Marilyn Cooper*
Consuelo, *Reri Grist*
Teresita, *Carmen Guiterrez*
Francisca, *Elizabeth Taylor*
Estella, *Lynn Ross*
Margarita, *Liane Plane*

THE ADULTS

Doc, *Art Smith*
Schrank, *Arch Johnson*
Krupke, *William Bramley*
Glad Hand, *John Harkins*

Entire production directed and choreographed by *Jerome Robbins*
Scenic production by *Oliver Smith*
Costumes designed by *Irene Sharaff*
Lighting by *Jean Rosenthal*
Musical direction by *Max Goberman*
Orchestrations by *Leonard Bernstein*, with *Sid Ramin* and *Irwin Kostal*

Co-choreographer: *Peter Gennaro*
Production Associate: *Sylvia Drulie*

Act One

Prologue: The Months Before

5:00 P.M.	The Street
5:30 P.M.	A Back Yard
6:00 P.M.	A Bridal Shop
10:00 P.M.	The Gym
11:00 P.M.	A Back Alley
Midnight	The Drugstore

The Next Day

5:30 P.M.	The Bridal Shop
6:00 to 9:00 P.M.	The Neighborhood
9:00 P.M.	Under the Highway

Act Two

9:15 P.M.	A Bedroom
10:00 P.M.	Another Alley
11:30 P.M.	The Bedroom
11:40 P.M.	The Drugstore
11:50 P.M.	The Cellar
Midnight	The Street

Place: The West Side of New York City
Time: The Last Days of Summer

Musical Numbers

Act One

Prologue	Danced by Jets and Sharks
Jet Song	Riff and Jets
Something's Coming	Tony
The Dance at the Gym	Jets and Sharks
Maria	Tony
Tonight	Tony and Maria
America	Anita, Rosalia, and Shark Girls
Cool	Riff and Jets
One Hand, One Heart	Tony and Maria

Tonight (Quintet and Chorus)	Company
The Rumble	Riff, Bernardo, Jets and Sharks

Act Two

I Feel Pretty	Maria, Rosalia, Teresita, Francisca
Somewhere	Danced by Company; Sung by Consuelo
Gee, Officer Krupke	Action, Snowboy, and Jets
A Boy Like That	Anita and Maria
I Have a Love	Anita and Maria
Taunting	Anita and the Jets
Finale	Company

ACT ONE

SCENE 1

5:00 P.M. The street.

A suggestion of city streets and alleyways; a brick wall.

The opening is musical: half-danced, half-mimed, with occasional phrases of dialogue. It is primarily a condensation of the growing rivalry between two teen-age gangs, the Jets and the Sharks, each of which has its own prideful uniform. The boys—sideburned, long-haired—are vital, restless, sardonic; the Sharks are Puerto Ricans, the Jets an anthology of what is called American.

The action begins with the Jets in possession of the area: owning, enjoying, loving their "home." Their leader is RIFF: *glowing, driving, intelligent, slightly whacky. His lieutenant is* DIESEL: *big, slow, steady, nice. The youngest member of the gang is* BABY JOHN: *awed at everything, including that he is a Jet, trying to act the big man. His buddy is* A-RAB: *an explosive little ferret who enjoys everything and understands the seriousness of nothing. The most aggressive is* ACTION: *a catlike ball of fury. We will get to know these boys better later, as well as* SNOWBOY: *a bespectacled self-styled expert.*

The first interruption of the Jets' sunny mood is the sharply punctuated entrance of the leader of the Sharks, BERNARDO: *handsome, proud, fluid, a chip on his sardonic shoulder. The*

Jets, by far in the majority, flick him off. He returns with other Sharks: they, too, are flicked off. But the numerical supremacy, the strength of the Jets, is gradually being threatened. The beginnings of warfare are mild at first: a boy being tripped up, or being sandbagged with a flour sack or even being spit on—all with overly elaborate apologies.

Finally, A-RAB *comes across the suddenly deserted area, pretending to be an airplane. There is no sound as he zooms along in fancied flight. Then over the wall drops* BERNARDO. *Another Shark, another and another appear, blocking* A-RAB'S *panicky efforts at escape. They close in, grab him, pummel him, as a Shark on top of the wall is stationed as lookout. Finally,* BERNARDO *bends over* A-RAB *and makes a gesture (piercing his ear); the lookout whistles; Jets tear on, Sharks tear on, and a free-for-all breaks out.* RIFF *goes at once to* A-RAB, *like a protective father. The fight is stopped by a police whistle, louder and louder, and the arrival of a big goonlike cop,* KRUPKE, *and a plain-clothes man,* SCHRANK. SCHRANK *is strong, always in command; he has a charming, pleasant manner, which he often employs to cover his venom and his fear.*

KRUPKE: Knock it off! Settle down.

SCHRANK: All right: *kill each other!* . . . But not on my beat.

RIFF: (*Such innocence*) Why if it isn't Lieutenant Schrank!

SEVERAL JETS: (*Dancing-class manners*) Top of the day, Lieutenant Schrank.

BERNARDO: (*One with Riff*) And Officer Krupke!

SEVERAL SHARKS: Top of the day, Officer Krupke.

SCHRANK: Boy, what you Puerto Ricans have done to this neighborhood. Which one of 'em clobbered ya, A-rab?

(A-RAB *looks to* RIFF, *who takes over with great helpful seriousness*)

RIFF: As a matter of factuality, sir, we suspicion the job was done by a cop.

SNOWBOY: Two cops.

A-RAB: Oh, at least!

KRUPKE: Impossible!

SCHRANK: Didn't nobody tell ya there's a difference between bein' a stool pigeon and co-operatin' with the law?

RIFF: You told us the difference, sir. And we all chipped in for a prize for the first guy who can figure it out.

ACTION: (*Indicating* SCHRANK) Maybe buddy boy should get the prize.

SCHRANK: Don't buddy boy me, Action! I got a hot surprise for you: you hoodlums don't own the streets. There's been too much raiding between you and the PRs. All right, Bernardo, get your trash outa here. (*Mock charm*) Please.

BERNARDO: Let's go, Sharks.

(*They exit*)

SCHRANK: (*To the* JETS) If I don't put down the roughhouse, I get put down—on a traffic corner. Your friend don't like traffic corners. So you buddy boys are gonna play ball with me. I gotta put up with them and so do you. *You're gonna make nice with them PRs from now on.* Because otherwise I'm gonna beat the crap outa every one of ya and *then* run ya in. Say good-bye to the nice boys, Krupke.

KRUPKE: Good-bye, boys. (*He follows* SCHRANK *out*)

SNOWBOY: (*Imitating* KRUPKE) Good-bye, boys.

A-RAB: They make a very nice couple.

ACTION: (*Bitterly*) "You hoodlums don't own the streets."

SNOWBOY: Go play in the park!

ACTION: Keep off the grass!

BABY JOHN: Get outa the house!

ACTION: Keep off the block!

A-RAB: Get outa *here!*

ACTION: Keep off the world! A gang that don't own a street is nuthin'!

RIFF: WE DO OWN IT! Jets—square off! Acemen: (DIESEL, ACTION *and* SNOWBOY *line up at attention*) Rocketmen: (*Three others line up*) Rank-and-file: (*Sheepishly,* A-RAB *trudges into position,* BABY JOHN *behind him*)

BABY JOHN: (*Shocked, to* A-RAB) Gee, your ear's got blood on it!

A-RAB: (*Proudly*) I'm a casual, Baby John.

BABY JOHN: (*Examining the ear*) Them PRs! They branded you!

SNOWBOY: That makes you a Puerto Rican tomato. Cha-cha-cha, señorita?

RIFF: Cut the frabbajabba. Which one of the Sharks did it?

A-RAB: Bernardo. 'Cause I heard him say: "Thees ees for stink-bombin' my old man's store." (*He makes the same gesture* BERNARDO *made when he pierced his ear*)

BABY JOHN: Ouch!

ACTION: You shoulda done worse. Them PRs're the reason my old man's gone bust.

RIFF: Who says?

ACTION: My old man says.

BABY JOHN: (*To* A-RAB) My old man says his old man woulda gone bust anyway.

ACTION: Your old man says what?

BABY JOHN: My old man says them Puerto Ricans is ruinin' free ennaprise.

ACTION: And what're we doin' about it?

(*Pushing through the gang comes a scrawny teen-age girl, dressed in an outfit that is a pathetic attempt to imitate that of the Jets. Perhaps we have glimpsed her in the fracas before the police came in. Her name is* ANYBODYS)

ANYBODYS: Gassin', crabbin'—

ACTION: You still around?

ANYBODYS: Listen, I was a smash in that fight. Oh, Riff, Riff, I was murder!

RIFF: Come on, Anybodys—

ANYBODYS: Riff, how about me gettin' in the gang now?

A-RAB: How about the gang gettin' in—ahhh, who'd wanta!

ANYBODYS: You cheap beast! (*She lunges for* A-RAB, *but* RIFF *pulls her off and pushes her out*)

RIFF: The road, little lady, the road. (*In a moment of bravado, just before she goes,* ANYBODYS *spits—but cautiously*) Round out! (*This is* RIFF'S *summoning of the gang, and they surround him*) We fought hard for this territory and it's ours. But with those cops servin' as cover, the PRs can move in right under our noses and take it away. *Unless* we speed fast and clean 'em up in one all-out fight!

ACTION: (*Eagerly*) A rumble! (*A jabbing gesture*) Chung! Chung!

RIFF: Cool, Action boy. The Sharks want a place, too, and *they are tough.* They might ask for bottles or knives or zip guns.

BABY JOHN: Zip guns . . . Gee!

RIFF: I'm not finalizin' and sayin' they will: I'm only sayin' they might and we gotta be prepared. Now, what's your mood?

ACTION: I say go, go!!

SNOWBOY: But if they say knives or guns—

BABY JOHN: I say let's forget the whole thing.

DIESEL: What do you say, Riff?

RIFF: I say this turf is small, *but it's all we got.* I wanna hold it like we always held it: with skin! But if they say switchblades, I'll get a switchblade. I say I want the Jets to be Number One, to sail, to hold the sky!

DIESEL: Then rev us off. (*A punching gesture*) Voom-va voom!

ACTION: Chung chung!

A-RAB: Cracko, jacko!

SNOWBOY: Riga diga dum!

BABY JOHN: Pam pam!

RIFF: O.K., buddy boys, we rumble! (*General glee*) Now protocality calls for a war council to decide on weapons. I'll make the challenge to Bernardo.

SNOWBOY: You gotta take a lieutenant.

ACTION: That's me!

RIFF: That's Tony.

ACTION: Who needs Tony? (*Music starts*)

RIFF: Against the Sharks we need every man we got.

ACTION: Tony don't belong any more.

RIFF: Cut it, Action boy. I and Tony started the Jets.

ACTION: Well, he acts like he don't wanna belong.

BABY JOHN: Who wouldn't wanna belong to the Jets!

ACTION: Tony ain't been with us for over a month.

SNOWBOY: What about the day we clobbered the Emeralds?

A-RAB: Which we couldn't have done without Tony.

BABY JOHN: He saved my ever lovin' neck.

RIFF: Right. He's always come through for us and he will now.

(*He sings*)
When you're a Jet,
You're a Jet all the way
From your first cigarette
To your last dyin' day.
When you're a Jet,
If the spit hits the fan,
You got brothers around,
You're a family man!
You're never alone,
You're never disconnected!
You're home with your own—
When company's expected,
You're well protected!
Then you are set
With a capital J,
Which you'll never forget

Till they cart you away.
When you're a Jet,
You stay
A Jet!

(*He speaks*)
I know Tony like I know me. I guarantee you can count him in.

ACTION: In, out, let's get crackin'.

A-RAB: Where you gonna find Bernardo?

RIFF: At the dance tonight at the gym.

BIG DEAL: But the gym's neutral territory.

RIFF: (*Sweet innocence*) I'm gonna make nice there! I'm only gonna challenge him.

A-RAB: Great, Daddy-o!

RIFF: So everybody dress up sweet and sharp. Meet Tony and me at ten. And walk tall! (*He runs off*)

A-RAB: We always walk tall!

BABY JOHN: We're Jets!

ACTION: The greatest!

(*He sings with* BABY JOHN)
When you're a Jet,
You're the top cat in town,
You're the gold-medal kid
With the heavyweight crown!

A-RAB, ACTION, BIG DEAL:
When you're a Jet,
You're the swingin'est thing.
Little boy, you're a man;
Little boy, you're a king!

ALL:
The Jets are in gear,
Our cylinders are clickin'!
The Sharks'll steer clear
'Cause every Puerto Rican
'S a lousy chicken!

Here come the Jets
Like a bat out of hell—
Someone gets in our way,
Someone don't feel so well!
Here come the Jets:

Little world, step aside!
Better go underground,
Better run, better hide!
We're drawin' the line,
So keep your noses hidden!
We're hangin' a sign
Says "visitors forbidden"–
And we ain't kiddin'!
Here come the Jets,
Yeah! And we're gonna beat
Every last buggin' gang
On the whole buggin' street!

DIESEL and ACTION:
On the whole!

ALL:
Ever–!
Mother–!
Lovin'–!
Street!

The Lights Black Out

SCENE 2

5:30 P.M. A back yard.

On a small ladder, a good-looking sandy-haired boy is painting a vertical sign that will say: Doc's. Below, RIFF *is haranguing.*

RIFF: Riga tiga tum tum. Why not? . . . You can't say ya won't, Tony boy, without sayin' why not?

TONY: (*Grins*) Why not?

RIFF: Because it's me askin': Riff. Womb to tomb!

TONY: Sperm to worm! (*Surveying the sign*) You sure this looks like sky-writin'?

RIFF: It's brilliant.

TONY: Twenty-seven years the boss has had that drugstore. I wanna surprise him with a new sign.

RIFF: (*Shaking the ladder*) Tony, this is important!

TONY: Very important: Acemen, Rocketmen.

RIFF: What's with you? Four and one-half years I live with a buddy and his family. Four and one-half years I think I know a man's character. Buddy boy, I am a victim of disappointment in you.

TONY: End your sufferin', little man. Why don't you pack up your gear and clear out?

RIFF: 'Cause your ma's hot for me. (TONY *grabs his arm and twists it*) No! 'Cause I hate livin' with my buggin' uncle uncle UNCLE! (TONY *releases him and climbs back up the ladder*)

TONY: Now go play nice with the Jets.

RIFF: The Jets are the greatest!

TONY: Were.

RIFF: Are. You found somethin' better?

TONY: No. But–

RIFF: But what?

TONY: You won't dig it.

RIFF: Try me.

TONY: O.K. . . . Every single damn night for the last month, I wake up–and I'm reachin' out.

RIFF: For what?

TONY: I don't know. It's right outside the door, around the corner. But it's comin'!

RIFF: *What* is? Tell me!

TONY: I don't know! It's–like the kick I used to get from bein' a Jet.

RIFF: (*Quietly*) . . . Or from bein' buddies.

TONY: We're still buddies.

RIFF: The kick comes from people, buddy boy.

TONY: Yeah, but not from being a Jet.

RIFF: No? Without a gang you're an orphan. With a gang you walk in two's, three's, four's. And when your gang is the best, when you're a Jet, buddy boy, you're out in the sun and home free home!

TONY: Riff, I've had it. (*Pause*)

RIFF: Tony, the trouble is large: the Sharks bite hard! We got to stop them now, and we need *you!* (*Pause. Quietly*) I never asked the time of day from a clock, but I'm askin' you: Come to the dance tonight . . . (TONY *turns away*) . . . I already told the gang you'd be there.

TONY: (*After a moment, turns to him with a grin*) What time?

RIFF: Ten?

TONY: Ten it is.

RIFF: Womb to tomb!

TONY: Sperm to worm! And I'll live to regret this.

RIFF: Who knows? Maybe what you're waitin' for'll be twitchin' at the dance! (*He runs off*)

TONY: Who knows?

(*Music starts and he sings*)
Could be! . . .
Who knows? . . .
There's something due any day;
I will know right away
Soon as it shows.
It may come cannonballin' down through the sky,
Gleam in its eye,
Bright as a rose!
Who knows? . . .
It's only just out of reach,
Down the block, on a beach,
Under a tree.
I got a feeling there's a miracle due,
Gonna come true,
Coming to me!

Could it be? Yes, it could.
Something's coming, something good,
If I can wait!
Something's coming, I don't know what it is
But it is
Gonna be great!

With a click, with a shock,
Phone'll jingle, door'll knock,
Open the latch!
Something's coming, don't know when, but it's soon—
Catch the moon,
One-handed catch!

Around the corner,
Or whistling down the river,
Come on—deliver
To me!
Will it be? Yes, it will.
Maybe just by holding still
It'll be there!
Come on, something, come on in, don't be shy,
Meet a guy,
Pull up a chair!

The air is humming,
And something great is coming!
Who knows?
It's only just out of reach,
Down the block, on a beach . . .
Maybe tonight . . .

The Lights Dim

SCENE 3

6:00 P.M. A bridal shop.

A small section, enough to include a table with sewing machine, a chair or two.

ANITA, *a Puerto Rican girl with loose hair and slightly flashy clothes, is finishing remaking what was a white communion dress into a party dress for an extremely lovely, extremely young girl:* MARIA. ANITA *is knowing, sexual, sharp.* MARIA *is an excited, enthusiastic, obedient child, with the temper, stubborn strength and awareness of a woman.*

MARIA: (*Holding out scissors*) *Por favor,* Anita. Make the neck lower!

ANITA: Stop it, Maria.

MARIA: One inch. How much can one little inch do?

ANITA: Too much.

MARIA: (*Exasperated*) Anita, it is now to be a dress for dancing, no longer for kneeling in front of an altar.

ANITA: With those boys you can start in dancing and end up kneeling.

MARIA: *Querida,* one little inch; *una poca poca—*

ANITA: Bernardo made me promise—

MARIA: *Ai!* Bernardo! One month have I been in this country —do I ever even touch excitement? I sew all day, I sit all night. For what did my fine brother bring me here?

ANITA: To marry Chino.

MARIA: When I look at Chino, nothing happens.

ANITA: What do you expect to happen?

MARIA: I don't know: something. What happens when you look at Bernardo?

ANITA: It's when I don't look that it happens.

MARIA: I think I will tell Mama and Papa about you and 'Nardo in the balcony of the movies.

ANITA: I'll rip this to shreds!

MARIA: No. But if you perhaps could manage to lower the neck—

ANITA: Next year.

MARIA: Next year I will be married and no one will care if it is down to here!

ANITA: Down to where?

MARIA: Down to here. (*Indicates her waist*) I hate this dress!

ANITA: Then don't wear it and don't come with us to the dance.

MARIA: (*Shocked*) Don't come! (*Grabs the dress*) Could we not dye it red, at least?

ANITA: No, we could not. (*She starts to help* MARIA *into the dress*)

MARIA: White is for babies. I will be the only one there in a white—

ANITA: Well???

MARIA: Ahhhh—*sí!* It is a beautiful dress: I love you!

(*As she hugs* ANITA, BERNARDO *enters, followed by a shy, gentle sweet-faced boy:* CHINO)

BERNARDO: Are you ready?

MARIA: Come in, 'Nardo. (*Whirls in the dress*) Is it not beautiful?

BERNARDO: (*Looking only at* MARIA'S *face*) Yes. (*Kisses her*) Very.

ANITA: I didn't quite hear . . .

BERNARDO: (*Kissing* ANITA *quite differently*) Very beautiful.

MARIA: (*Watches them a second, then turns to* CHINO) Come in, Chino. Do not be afraid.

CHINO: But this is a shop for ladies.

BERNARDO: Our ladies!

MARIA: 'Nardo, it is most important that I have a wonderful time at the dancing tonight.

BERNARDO: (*As* ANITA *hooks up* MARIA) Why?

MARIA: Because tonight is the real beginning of my life as a young lady of America!

(*She begins to whirl in the dress as the shop slides off and a flood of gaily colored streamers pours down. As* MARIA *begins to turn and turn, going offstage, Shark girls, dressed for the dance whirl on, followed by Jet girls, by boys from both gangs. The streamers fly up again for the next scene*)

SCENE 4

10:00 P.M. The gym.

Actually, a converted gymnasium of a settlement house, at

the moment being used as a dance hall, disguised for the occasion with streamers and bunting.

Both gangs are jitterbugging wildly with their bodies, but their faces, although they are enjoying themselves, remain cool, almost detached. The line between the two gangs is sharply defined by the colors they wear: the Jets, girls as well as boys, reflecting the colors of the Jet jackets; the same is true of the Sharks. The dancing is a physical and emotional release for these kids.

MARIA *enters with* CHINO, BERNARDO *and* ANITA. *As she looks around, delighted, thrilled by this, her first dance, the Jets catch sight of* BERNARDO, *who is being greeted by* PEPE, *his lieutenant, and other Sharks. As the music peters away, the Jets withdraw to one side of the hall, around* RIFF. *The Sharks, seeing this, draw to their side, around* BERNARDO. *A brief consultation, and* RIFF *starts across—with lieutenants—to make his challenge to* BERNARDO, *who starts—with his lieutenants—to meet him. The moment is brief but it would be disastrous if a smiling, overly cheerful young man of about thirty did not hurry forward. He is called* GLAD HAND, *and he is a "square."*

GLAD HAND: (*Beaming*) All right, boys and girls! Attention, please! (*Hum of talk*) Attention! (KRUPKE *appears behind* GLAD HAND: *the talk stops*) Thank you. It sure is a fine turnout tonight. (*Ad libs from the kids*) We want you to make friends here, so we're going to have a few get-together dances. (*Ad libs: "Oh, ginger peachy," etc.*) You form two circles: boys on the outside, girls on the inside.

SNOWBOY: Where are you?

GLAD HAND: (*Tries to laugh at this*) All right. Now when the music stops, each boy dances with whichever girl is opposite. O.K.? O.K. Two circles, kids. (*The* KIDS *clap their hands back at him and ad lib: "Two circles, kids," etc., but do not move*) Well, it won't hurt you to try.

SNOWBOY: (*Limping forward*) Oh, it hurts; it hurts; it—

(KRUPKE *steps forward.* SNOWBOY *straightens up and meekly returns to his place.* RIFF *steps forward and beckons to his girl,* VELMA. *She is terribly young, sexy, lost in a world of jive. She slithers forward to take her place with* RIFF. *The challenge is met by* BERNARDO, *who steps forward, leading* ANITA *as though he were presenting the most magnificent lady in all the world. The other kids follow, forming the two circles* GLAD HAND *requested*)

GLAD HAND: That's it, kids. Keep the ball rolling. Round she goes and where she stops, nobody knows. All right: here we go!

(*Promenade music starts and the circles start revolving.* GLAD HAND, *whistle to his mouth, is in the center with* KRUPKE. *He blows the whistle and the music stops, leaving Jet boys opposite Shark girls, and vice versa. There is a moment of tenseness, then* BERNARDO *reaches across the Jet girl opposite for* ANITA'S *hand, and she comes to him.* RIFF *reaches for* VELMA; *and the kids of both gangs follow suit. The "get-together" has failed, and each gang is on its own side of the hall as a mambo starts. This turns into a challenge dance between* BERNARDO *and* ANITA *—cheered on by the Sharks—and* RIFF *and* VELMA*—cheered on by the Jets. During it,* TONY *enters and is momentarily embraced by* RIFF, *who is delighted that his best friend did turn up. The dance builds wilder and wilder, until, at the peak, everybody is dancing and shouting, "Go, Mambo!" It is at this moment that* TONY *and* MARIA*—at opposite sides of the hall—see each other. They have been cheering on their respective friends, clapping in rhythm. Now, as they see each other, their voices die, their smiles fade, their hands slowly go to their sides. The lights fade on the others, who disappear into the haze of the background as a delicate cha-cha begins and* TONY *and* MARIA *slowly walk forward to meet each other. Slowly, as though in a dream, they drift into the steps of the dance, always looking at each other, completely lost in each other; unaware of anyone, any place, any time, anything but one another*)

TONY: You're not thinking I'm someone else?

MARIA: I know you are not.

TONY: Or that we have met before?

MARIA: I know we have not.

TONY: I felt, I *knew* something-never-before was going to happen, had to happen. But this is—

MARIA: (*Interrupting*) My hands are cold. (*He takes them in his*) Yours, too. (*He moves her hands to his face*) So warm. (*She moves his hands to her face*)

TONY: Yours, too.

MARIA: But of course. They are the same.

TONY: It's so much to believe—you're not joking me?

MARIA: I have not yet learned how to joke that way. I think now I never will.

(*Impulsively, he stops to kiss her hands; then tenderly, in-*

nocently, her lips. The music bursts out, the lights flare up, and BERNARDO *is upon them in an icy rage*)

BERNARDO: Go home, "*American.*"

TONY: Slow down, Bernardo.

BERNARDO: Stay away from my sister!

TONY: . . . Sister? (RIFF *steps up*)

BERNARDO: (*To* MARIA) Couldn't you see he's one of them?

MARIA: No; I saw only him.

BERNARDO: (*As* CHINO *comes up*) I told you: there's only one thing they want from a Puerto Rican girl!

TONY: That's a lie!

RIFF: Cool, boy.

CHINO: (*To* TONY) Get away.

TONY: You keep out, Chino. (*To* MARIA) Don't listen to them!

BERNARDO: She will listen to her brother before–

RIFF: (*Overlapping*) If you characters want to settle–

GLAD HAND: Please! Everything was going so well! Do you fellows get pleasure out of making trouble? Now come on–it won't hurt you to have a good time.

(*Music starts again.* BERNARDO *is on one side with* MARIA *and* CHINO; ANITA *joins them.* TONY *is on the other with* RIFF *and* DIESEL. *Light emphasizes the first group*)

BERNARDO: I warned you–

CHINO: Do not yell at her, 'Nardo.

BERNARDO: You yell at babies.

ANITA: And put ideas in the baby's head.

BERNARDO: Take her home, Chino.

MARIA: 'Nardo, it is my first dance.

BERNARDO: Please. We are family, Maria. Go.

(MARIA *hesitates, then starts out with* CHINO *as the light follows her to the other group, which she passes*)

RIFF: (*To* DIESEL, *indicating* TONY *happily*) I guess the kid's with us for sure now.

(TONY *doesn't even hear; he is staring at* MARIA, *who stops for a moment*)

CHINO: Come, Maria. (*They continue out*)

TONY: Maria . . .

(*He is unaware that* BERNARDO *is crossing toward him, but* RIFF *intercepts*)

BERNARDO: I don't want you.

RIFF: I want you, though. For a war council–Jets and Sharks.

BERNARDO: The pleasure is mine.

RIFF: Let's go outside.

BERNARDO: I would not leave the ladies here alone. We will meet you in half an hour.

RIFF: Doc's drugstore? (BERNARDO *nods*) And no jazz before then.

BERNARDO: I understand the rules—Native Boy.

(*The light is fading on them, on everyone but* TONY)

RIFF: Spread the word, Diesel.

DIESEL: Right, Daddy-o.

RIFF: Let's get the chicks and kick it. Tony?

TONY: Maria . . .

(*Music starts*)

RIFF: (*In darkness*) Tony!

DIESEL: (*In darkness*) Ah, we'll see him at Doc's.

TONY: (*Speaking dreamily over the music—he is now standing alone in the light*) Maria . . .

(*Singing softly*)
The most beautiful sound I ever heard.

VOICES: (*Offstage*)
Maria, Maria, Maria, Maria . . .

TONY:
All the beautiful sounds of the world in a single word:

VOICES: (*Offstage*)
Maria, Maria, Maria, Maria . . .
(*Swelling in intensity*)
Maria, Maria . . .

TONY:
Maria!
I've just met a girl named Maria,
And suddenly that name
Will never be the same
To me.
Maria!
I've just kissed a girl named Maria,
And suddenly I've found
How wonderful a sound
Can be!
Maria!
Say it loud and there's music playing—
Say it soft and it's almost like praying—

Maria . . .
I'll never stop saying
Maria!

CHORUS: (*Offstage, against* TONY'S *obbligato*)
I've just met a girl named Maria,
And suddenly that name
Will never be the same
To me.
Maria–
I've just kissed a girl named Maria,
And suddenly I've found
How wonderful a sound
Can be!

TONY:
Maria–
Say it loud and there's music playing–
Say it soft and it's almost like praying–
Maria–
I'll never stop saying Maria!
The most beautiful sound I ever heard–
Maria.

(*During the song, the stage behind* TONY *has gone dark; by the time he has finished, it is set for the next scene*)

SCENE 5

11:00 P.M. A back alley.

A suggestion of buildings; a fire escape climbing to the rear window of an unseen flat.

As TONY *sings, he looks for where* MARIA *lives, wishing for her. And she does appear, at the window above him, which opens onto the fire escape. Music stays beneath most of the scene.*

TONY: (*Sings*)
Maria, Maria . . .

MARIA: Ssh!
TONY: Maria!!
MARIA: Quiet!
TONY: Come down.
MARIA: No.
TONY: Maria . . .

MARIA: Please. If Bernardo—

TONY: He's at the dance. Come down.

MARIA: He will soon bring Anita home.

TONY: Just for a minute.

MARIA: (*Smiles*) A minute is not enough.

TONY: (*Smiles*) For an hour, then.

MARIA: I cannot.

TONY: Forever!

MARIA: Ssh!

TONY: Then I'm coming up.

WOMAN'S VOICE: (*From the offstage apartment*) Maria!

MARIA: *Momentito,* Mama . . .

TONY: (*Climbing up*) Maria, Maria—

MARIA: *Cállate!* (*Reaching her hand out to stop him*) Ssh!

TONY: (*Grabbing her hand*) Ssh!

MARIA: It is dangerous.

TONY: I'm *not* "one of them."

MARIA: You are; but to me, you are not. Just as I am one of them— (*She gestures toward the apartment*)

TONY: To me, you are all the—

(*She covers his mouth with her hand*)

MAN'S VOICE: (*From the unseen apartment*) Maruca!

MARIA: *Sí, ya vengo,* Papa.

TONY: Maruca?

MARIA: His pet name for me.

TONY: I like him. He will like me.

MARIA: No. He is like Bernardo: afraid. (*Suddenly laughing*) Imagine being afraid of you!

TONY: You see?

MARIA: (*Touching his face*) I see you.

TONY: See only me.

MARIA: (*Sings*)

Only you, you're the only thing I'll see forever.
In my eyes, in my words and in everything I do,
Nothing else but you
Ever!

TONY:

And there's nothing for me but Maria,
Every sight that I see is Maria.

MARIA:

Tony, Tony . . .

TONY:

Always you, every thought I'll ever know,
Everywhere I go, you'll be.

MARIA:

All the world is only you and me!
(*And now the buildings, the world fade away, leaving them suspended in space*)
Tonight, tonight,
It all began tonight,
I saw you and the world went away.
Tonight, tonight,
There's only you tonight,
What you are, what you do, what you say.

TONY:

Today, all day I had the feeling
A miracle would happen–
I know now I was right.
For here you are
And what was just a world is a star
Tonight!

BOTH:

Tonight, tonight,
The world is full of light,
With suns and moons all over the place.
Tonight, tonight,
The world is wild and bright,
Going mad, shooting sparks into space.
Today the world was just an address,
A place for me to live in,
No better than all right,
But here you are
And what was just a world is a star
Tonight!

MAN'S VOICE: (*Offstage*) Maruca!

MARIA: Wait for me! (*She goes inside as the buildings begin to come back into place*)

TONY: (*Sings*)

Tonight, tonight,
It all began tonight,
I saw you and the world went away.

MARIA: (*Returning*) I cannot stay. Go quickly!

TONY: I'm not afraid.

MARIA: They are strict with me. Please.

TONY: (*Kissing her*) Good night.

MARIA: *Buenas noches.*

TONY: I love you.

MARIA: Yes, yes. Hurry. (*He climbs down*) Wait! When will I see you? (*He starts back up*) No!

TONY: Tomorrow.

MARIA: I work at the bridal shop. Come there.

TONY: At sundown.

MARIA: Yes. Good night.

TONY: Good night. (*He starts off*)

MARIA: Tony!

TONY: Ssh!

MARIA: Come to the back door.

TONY: *Sí.* (*Again, he starts out*)

MARIA: Tony! (*He stops. A pause*) What does Tony stand for?

TONY: Anton.

MARIA: *Te adoro,* Anton.

TONY: *Te adoro,* Maria.

BOTH: (*Sing as music starts again*)
Good night, good night,
Sleep well and when you dream,
Dream of me
Tonight.

(*She goes inside; he ducks out into the shadows just as* BERNARDO *and* ANITA *enter, followed by* INDIO, *and* PEPE *and their girls. One is a bleached-blond, bangled beauty:* CONSUELO. *The other, more quietly dressed, is* ROSALIA. *She is not too bright*)

BERNARDO: (*Looking up to the window*) Maria?

ANITA: She *has* a mother. Also a father.

BERNARDO: They do not know this country any better than she does.

ANITA: You do not know it at all! Girls here are free to have fun. She-is-in-America-now.

BERNARDO: (*Exaggerated*) But Puerto-Rico-is-in-America-now!

ANITA: (*In disgust*) Ai!

BERNARDO: (*Cooing*) Anita Josefina Teresita—

ANITA: It's plain Anita now—

BERNARDO: (*Continuing through*)—Beatriz del Carmen Margarita, etcetera, etcetera—

ANITA: Immigrant!

BERNARDO: (*Pulling her to him*) Thank God, you can't change your hair!

PEPE: (*Fondling* CONSUELO'S *bleached mop*) Is that possible?

CONSUELO: In the U.S.A., everything is real.

BERNARDO: (*To* CHINO, *who enters*) Chino, how was she when you took her home?

CHINO: All right. 'Nardo, she was only dancing.

BERNARDO: With an "*American*." Who is really a Polack.

ANITA: Says the Spic.

BERNARDO: You are not so cute.

ANITA: That Tony is.

ROSALIA: And he works.

CHINO: A delivery boy.

ANITA: And what are you?

CHINO: An assistant.

BERNARDO: *Sí!* And Chino makes half what the Polack makes—the Polack is American!

ANITA: Ai! Here comes the whole commercial! (*A burlesque oration in mock Puerto Rican accent.* BERNARDO *starts the first line with her*) The mother of Tony was born in Poland; the father still goes to night school. Tony was born in America, so that makes him an American. But us? Foreigners!

PEPE and CONSUELO: Lice!

PEPE, CONSUELO, ANITA: Cockroaches!

BERNARDO: Well, it is true! You remember how we were when we first came! Did we even think of going back?

BERNARDO and ANITA: No! We came ready, eager—

ANITA: (*Mocking*) With our hearts open—

CONSUELO: Our arms open—

PEPE: You came with your pants open.

CONSUELO: *You* did, pig! (*Slaps him*) You'll go back with handcuffs!

BERNARDO: I am going back with a Cadillac!

CHINO: Air-conditioned!

BERNARDO: Built-in bar!

CHINO: Telephone!

BERNARDO: Television!

CHINO: Compatible color!

BERNARDO: And a king-sized bed. (*Grabs* ANITA) Come on.

ANITA: (*Mimicking*) Come on.

BERNARDO: Well, are you or aren't you?

ANITA: Well, are you or aren't you?

BERNARDO: Well, are you?

ANITA: You have your big, important war council. The council or me?

BERNARDO: First one, then the other.

ANITA: (*Breaking away from him*) I am an American girl now. I don't wait.

BERNARDO: (*To* CHINO) Back home, women know their place.

ANITA: Back home, little boys don't have war councils.

BERNARDO: You want me to be an American? (*To the boys*) *Vámonos, chicos, Es tarde.* (*A mock bow*) *Buenas noches,* Anita Josefina del Carmen, etcetera, etcetera, etcetera. (*He exits with the boys*)

ROSALIA: That's a very pretty name: Etcetera.

ANITA: Ai!

CONSUELO: She means well.

ROSALIA: We have many pretty names at home.

ANITA: (*Mimicking*) At home, at home. If it's so nice "at home," why don't you go back there?

ROSALIA: I would like to—(*A look from* ANITA)—just for a successful visit.

(*She sings nostalgically*)
Puerto Rico . . .
You lovely island . . .
Island of tropical breezes.
Always the pineapples growing,
Always the coffee blossoms blowing . . .

ANITA: (*Sings sarcastically*)
Puerto Rico . . .
You ugly island . . .
Island of tropic diseases.
Always the hurricanes blowing,
Always the population growing . . .
And the money owing,
And the babies crying,
And the bullets flying.
I like the island Manhattan—
Smoke on your pipe and put that in!

ALL: (*Except* ROSALIA)
I like to be in America!
O.K. by me in America!
Everything free in America
For a small fee in America!

ROSALIA:
I like the city of San Juan—

ANITA:
I know a boat you can get on.

ROSALIA:
Hundreds of flowers in full bloom—

ANITA:
Hundreds of people in each room!

ALL: (*Except* ROSALIA)
Automobile in America,
Chromium steel in America,
Wire-spoke wheel in America—
Very big deal in America!

ROSALIA:
I'll drive a Buick through San Juan—

ANITA:
If there's a road you can drive on.

ROSALIA:
I'll give my cousins a free ride—

ANITA:
How you get all of them inside?

ALL: (*Except* ROSALIA)
Immigrant goes to America,
Many hellos in America;
Nobody knows in America
Puerto Rico's in America.
(*The girls whistle and dance*)

ROSALIA:
When I will go back to San Juan—

ANITA:
When you will shut up and get gone!

ROSALIA:
I'll give them new washing machine—

ANITA:
What have they got there to keep clean?

ALL: (*Except* ROSALIA)
I like the shores of America!
Comfort is yours in America!
Knobs on the doors in America,
Wall-to-wall floors in America!
(*They whistle and dance*)

ROSALIA:
I'll bring a TV to San Juan—

ANITA:
If there's a current to turn on.

ROSALIA:
Everyone there will give big cheer!

ANITA:
Everyone there will have moved here!
(*The song ends in a joyous dance*)

The Lights Black Out

SCENE 6

Midnight. The drugstore.

A suggestion of a run-down, musty general store which, in cities, is called a drugstore. A door leading to the street outside; another leading to the cellar below.

BABY JOHN *is reading a comic book;* A-RAB *is playing solitaire;* ANYBODYS *is huddled by the juke box;* ACTION *is watching the street door. The atmosphere is tense, jumpy.* ACTION *slams the door and strides to the dart board.*

ACTION: Where the devil are they? Are we havin' a war council tonight or ain't we? (*He throws a dart savagely*)

BABY JOHN: He don't use knives. He don't even use an atomic ray gun.

A-RAB: Who don't?

BABY JOHN: Superman. Gee, I love him.

A-RAB: So marry him.

ANYBODYS: I ain't never gonna get married: too noisy.

A-RAB: You ain't never gonna get married: too ugly.

ANYBODYS: (*"Shooting" him*) Pow pow!

A-RAB: Cracko, jacko! (*Clutching his belly, he spins to the floor*) Down goes a teen-age hoodlum.

BABY JOHN: Could a zip gun make you do like that?

(*A second of silence. Then* SNOWBOY *slams into the room and they all jump*)

ACTION: What the hell's a matter with you?

SNOWBOY: I got caught sneakin' outa the movies.

A-RAB: Sneakin' *out?* Wadd'ya do that for?

SNOWBOY: I sneaked in.

ACTION: A war council comin' up and he goes to the movies.

ANYBODYS: And you let him be a Jet!

BABY JOHN: Ah, go walk the streets like ya sister.

ANYBODYS: (*Jumping him*) Lissen, jail bait, I licked you twice and I can do it again.

(*From the doorway behind the counter a little middle-aged man enters:* DOC)

DOC: Curfew, gentlemen. And lady. Baby John, you should be home in bed.

BABY JOHN: We're gonna have a war council here, Doc.

DOC: A who?

A-RAB: To decide on weapons for a big-time rumble!

SNOWBOY: We're gonna mix with the PRs.

DOC: Weapons. You couldn't play basketball?

ANYBODYS: Get with it, buddy boy.

DOC: War councils–

ACTION: Don't start, Doc.

DOC: Rumbles . . .

ACTION: Doc–

DOC: Why, when I was your age–

ACTION: When you was my age; when my old man was my age; when my brother was my age! *You was never my age, none a you!* The sooner you creeps get hip to that, the sooner you'll dig us.

DOC: I'll dig your early graves, that's what I'll dig.

A-RAB: Dig, dig, dig–

DOC: What're you gonna be when you grow up?

ANYBODYS: (*Wistfully*) A telephone call girl!

(*The store doorbell tinkles as* RIFF *enters with* VELMA)

SNOWBOY: Riff, hey!

ACTION: Are they comin'?

RIFF: Unwind, Action. Hey, Doc, Tony here?

DOC: No, Riff, it's closing time.

ACTION: (*To* RIFF) What d'ya think they're gonna ask for?

A-RAB: Just rubber hoses, maybe, huh?

RIFF: Cool, little men. Easy, freezy cool.

VELMA: Oo, oo, ooblee–oo.

(DIESEL *enters with a would-be grand number:* GRAZIELLA)

DIESEL: They're comin' any minute now!

ACTION: Chung chung!

A-RAB: Cracko, jacko!

VELMA: Ooblee-oo.

RIFF: (*Sharply*) Cool!

ANYBODYS: Riff—in a tight spot you need every man you can—

RIFF: No.

GRAZIELLA: (*Indicating* ANYBODYS *to* VELMA) An American tragedy.

ANYBODYS: (*"Shooting" her*) Pow.

GRAZIELLA: Poo.

VELMA: Ooblee-pooh.

(*They giggle*)

RIFF: Now when the victims come in, you chicks cut out.

GRAZIELLA: We might, and then again we might not.

DIESEL: This ain't kid stuff, Graziella.

GRAZIELLA: I and Velma ain't kid stuff, neither. Are we, Vel?

VELMA: No thank you-oo, ooblee-oo.

GRAZIELLA: And you can punctuate it!

VELMA: Ooo!

(*They giggle again*)

ACTION: (*To* RIFF) What're we poopin' around with dumb broads?

GRAZIELLA: (*Enraged*) I and Velma ain't dumb!

ACTION: We got important business comin'.

DOC: Makin' trouble for the Puerto Ricans?

SNOWBOY: They make trouble for us.

DOC: Look! He almost laughs when he says it. For you, trouble is a relief.

RIFF: We've got to stand up to the PRs, Doc. It's important.

DOC: Fighting over a little piece of the street is so important?

ACTION: To us, it is.

DOC: To hoodlums, it is. (*He goes out through the cellar doorway as* ACTION *lunges for him*)

ACTION: Don't you call me hoodlum!

RIFF: (*Holding him*) Easy, Action! Save your steam for the rumble.

A-RAB: He don't want what we want, so we're hoodlums!

BABY JOHN: I wear a jacket like my buddies, so my teacher calls me hoodlum!

ACTION: I swear the next creep who calls me hoodlum—

RIFF: *You'll laugh!* Yeah. Now you all better dig this and dig it the most. No matter who or what is eatin' at you, you show it, buddy boys, and *you are dead*. You are cuttin' a hole in yourselves for them to stick in a red hot umbrella and open it. Wide. You wanna live? You play it cool.

(*Music starts*)

ACTION: I wanna get even!

RIFF: Get cool.

A-RAB: I wanna bust!

RIFF: Bust cool.

BABY JOHN: I wanna go!

RIFF: *Go cool!*

(*He sings*)

Boy, boy, crazy boy—Get cool, boy!
Got a rocket in your pocket—Keep coolly cool, boy!
Don't get hot,
'Cause, man, you got
Some high times ahead.
Take it slow and, Daddy-o, You can live it up and die in bed!
Boy, boy, crazy boy—Stay loose, boy!
Breeze it, buzz it, easy does it—Turn off the juice, boy!
Go man, go,
But not like a yo-
Yo school boy—
Just play it cool, boy,
Real cool!

Easy, Action. Easy.

(*This leads into a frenetic dance in which the boys and girls release their emotions and get "cool." It finishes, starts again when a Jet bounces in with the gang whistle. Everyone but* RIFF *and* VELMA *stops dancing. A moment, then* BERNARDO, CHINO, PEPE *and* INDIO *enter. The tinkle of the doorbell brings a worried* DOC *back in. Tension—but* RIFF *dances a moment longer. Then he pats* VELMA *on her behind. Followed by* GRAZIELLA, *she runs out, slithering past the Sharks.* ANYBODYS *is back, huddled by the juke box, but* RIFF *spots her. She gives him a pleading let-me-stay look, but he gestures for her to go. Unlike the other girls, as she exits,* ANYBODYS *shoves the Sharks like a big tough man*)

RIFF: Set 'em up, Doc. Cokes all around.

BERNARDO: Let's get down to business.

RIFF: Bernardo hasn't learned the procedures of gracious livin'.

BERNARDO: I don't like you, either. So cut it.

RIFF: Kick it, Doc.

DOC: Boys, couldn't you maybe all talk it—

RIFF: Kick it!

(DOC *goes out. The two gangs take places behind their leaders*)

RIFF: We challenge you to a rumble. All out, once and for all. Accept?

BERNARDO: On what terms?

RIFF: Whatever terms you're callin', buddy boy. You crossed the line once too often.

BERNARDO: You started it.

RIFF: Who jumped A-rab this afternoon?

BERNARDO: Who jumped me the first day I moved here?

ACTION: Who asked you to move here?

PEPE: Who asked you?

SNOWBOY: Move where you're wanted!

A-RAB: Back where ya came from!

ACTION: Spics!

PEPE: Micks!

INDIO: Wop!

BERNARDO: *We accept!*

RIFF: Time:

BERNARDO: Tomorrow?

RIFF: After dark. (*They shake*) Place:

BERNARDO: The park.

RIFF: The river.

BERNARDO: Under the highway. (*They shake*)

RIFF: Weapons:

(*The doorbell tinkles as* TONY *bursts in, yelling*)

TONY: Hey, Doc! (*He stops as he sees them. Silence. Then he comes forward*)

RIFF: Weapons!

(DOC *enters*)

BERNARDO: Weapons . . .

RIFF: You call.

BERNARDO: Your challenge.

RIFF: Afraid to call?

BERNARDO: . . . . Sticks.

RIFF: . . . . Rocks.

BERNARDO: . . . Poles.

RIFF: . . . Cans.

BERNARDO: . . Bricks.

RIFF: . . Bats.

BERNARDO: . Clubs.

RIFF: Chains.

TONY: Bottles, knives, guns! (*They stare*) What a coop full of chickens!

ACTION: Who you callin' chicken?

BERNARDO: Every dog knows his own.

TONY: I'm callin' all of you chicken. The big tough buddy boys have to throw bricks! Afraid to get close in? Afraid to slug it out? Afraid to use plain skin?

BABY JOHN: Not even garbage?

ACTION: That ain't a rumble.

RIFF: Who says?

BERNARDO: You said call weapons.

TONY: A rumble can be clinched by a fair fight. If you have the guts to risk that. Best man from each gang to slug it out.

BERNARDO: (*Looking at* TONY) I'd enjoy to risk that. O.K.! Fair fight!

PEPE: What?

ACTION: (*Simultaneously*) No!

RIFF: The commanders say yes or no. (*To* BERNARDO) Fair fight. (*They shake*)

BERNARDO: (*To* TONY) In two minutes you will be like a fish after skinnin'.

RIFF: Your best man fights our best man—and we pick him. (*Claps* DIESEL *on the shoulder*)

BERNARDO: But I thought I would be—

RIFF: We shook on it, Bernardo.

BERNARDO: Yes. I shook on it.

ACTION: (*Quickly*) Look, Bernardo, if you wanna change your mind, maybe we could all—

(*One of the Jets near the door suddenly whistles. Instantly, they shift positions so they are mixed up: no segregation. Silence; then in comes* SCHRANK. *During the following, the gangs are absolutely silent and motionless, unless otherwise indicated*)

DOC: (*Unhappily*) Good evening, Lieutenant Schrank. I and Tony was just closing up.

SCHRANK: (*Lifting a pack of cigarettes*) Mind?

DOC: I have no mind. I am the village idiot.

SCHRANK: (*Lighting a cigarette*) I always make it a rule to smoke in the can. And what else is a room with half-breeds in it, eh, Riff? (BERNARDO'S *move is checked by* RIFF. SCHRANK *speaks again, pleasantly*) Clear out, Spics. Sure; it's a free country and I ain't got the right. But it's a country with laws: and I can find the right. I got the badge, you got the skin. It's tough all over. Beat it! (*A second. Then* RIFF *nods once to* BERNARDO, *who nods to his gang. Slowly, they file out.* BERNARDO *starts to whistle "My Country 'Tis of Thee" as he exits proudly. His gang joins in, finishing a sardonic jazz lick offstage.* SCHRANK, *still pleasant*) From their angle, sure. Say, where's the rumble gonna be? Ah, look: I know regular Americans don't rub with the gold-teeth otherwise. The river? The park? (*Silence*) I'm for *you*. I want this beat cleaned up and you can do it for me. I'll even lend a hand if it gets rough. Where ya gonna rumble? The playground? Sweeney's lot? (*Angered by the silence*) Ya think I'm a lousy stool pigeon? I wanna help ya get rid of them! Come on! Where's it gonna be? . . . Get smart, you stupid hoodlums! I oughta fine ya for litterin' the streets. You oughta be taken down the station house and have your skulls mashed to a pulp! You and the tinhorn immigrant scum you come from! How's your old man's d.t.'s, A-rab? How's the action on your mother's mattress, Action? (ACTION *lunges for him but is tripped up by* RIFF. SCHRANK *crouches low, ready for him. Quiet now*) Let him go, buddy boy, just let him go. (ACTION *starts to his feet but* DIESEL *holds him*) One of these days there won't be nobody to hold you. (RIFF *deliberately starts for the door, followed by the others, except* TONY) I'll find out where ya gonna rumble. But be sure to finish each other off. Because if you don't, I will! (RIFF *has stayed at the door until the others have passed through. Now he just looks at* SCHRANK *and cockily saunters out. Silence.* SCHRANK *looks at* DOC) Well, you try keepin' hoodlums in line and see what it does to you. (*He exits*)

DOC: (*Indicating* SCHRANK) It wouldn't give me a mouth like his.

TONY: Forget him. From here on in, everything goes my way. (*He starts to clean up, to turn out the lights*)

DOC: You think it'll really be a fair fight.

TONY: Yeah.

DOC: What have you been takin' tonight?

TONY: A trip to the moon. And I'll tell you a secret. It isn't a man that's up there, Doc. It's a girl, a lady. (*Opens the door*) *Buenas noches, señor.*

DOC: *Buenas noches?!* So that's why you made it a fair fight. (TONY *smiles*) . . . Tony . . . things aren't tough enough?

TONY: Tough? Doc, I'm in love.

DOC: How do you know?

TONY: Because . . . there isn't any other way I could feel.

DOC: And you're not frightened?

TONY: Should I be? (*He opens door, exits*)

DOC: Why? I'm frightened enough for both of you. (*He turns out the last light*)

The Stage Is Dark

SCENE 7

5:30 P.M. The next day. The bridal shop.

Hot late-afternoon sun coloring the workroom. One or two sewing machines. Several dressmaker dummies, male and female, in bridal-party garb.

MARIA, *in a smock, is hand-sewing a wedding veil as* ANITA *whirls in whipping off her smock.*

ANITA: She's gone! That old bag of a *bruja* has gone!

MARIA: *Bravo!*

ANITA: The day is over, the jail is open, home we go!

MARIA: You go, *querida.* I will lock up.

ANITA: Finish tomorrow. Come!

MARIA: But I am in no hurry.

ANITA: I am. I'm going to take a bubble bath all during supper: Black Orchid.

MARIA: You will not eat?

ANITA: After the rumble–with 'Nardo.

MARIA: (*Sewing, angrily*) That rumble, why do they have it?

ANITA: You saw how they dance: like they have to get rid of something, quick. That's how they fight.

MARIA: To get rid of what?

ANITA: Too much feeling. And they get rid of it: after a fight, that brother of yours is so healthy! Definitely: Black Orchid. (*There is a knock at rear door, and* TONY *enters*)

TONY: *Buenas noches!*

ANITA: (*Sarcastically, to* MARIA) "You go, *querida*. I will lock up." (*To* TONY) It's too early for *noches*. *Buenas tardes*.

TONY: (*Bows*) *Gracias. Buenas tardes.*

MARIA: He just came to deliver aspirin.

ANITA: You'll need it.

TONY: No, we're out of the world.

ANITA: You're out of your heads.

TONY: We're twelve feet in the air.

MARIA: (*Gently taking his hand*) Anita can see all that. (*To* ANITA) You will not tell?

ANITA: Tell what? How can I hear what goes on twelve feet over my head? (*Opens door. To* MARIA) You better be home in fifteen minutes. (*She goes out*)

TONY: Don't worry. She likes us!

MARIA: But she is worried.

TONY: She's foolish. We're untouchable; we *are* in the air; we have magic!

MARIA: Magic is also evil and black. Are you going to that rumble?

TONY: No.

MARIA: Yes.

TONY: Why??

MARIA: You must go and stop it.

TONY: I have stopped it! It's only a fist fight. 'Nardo won't get—

MARIA: *Any* fight is not good for us.

TONY: Everything is good for us and we are good for everything.

MARIA: Listen and *hear* me. You must go and stop it.

TONY: Then I will.

MARIA: (*Surprised*) Can you?

TONY: You don't want even a fist fight? There won't be any fight.

MARIA: I believe you! You *do* have magic.

TONY: Of course, I have you. You go home and dress up. Then tonight, I will come by for you.

MARIA: You cannot come by. My mama . . .

TONY: (*After a pause*) Then I will take you to my house—

MARIA: (*Shaking her head*) *Your* mama . . .

(*Another awkward pause. Then he sees a female dummy and pushes it forward*)

TONY: She will come running from the kitchen to welcome you. She lives in the kitchen.

MARIA: Dressed so elegant?

TONY: I told her you were coming. She will look at your face and try not to smile. And she will say: Skinny—but pretty.

MARIA: She is plump, no doubt.

TONY: (*Holding out the waist of dummy's dress*) Fat!

MARIA: (*Indicating another female dummy*) I take after my mama; delicate-boned. (*He kisses her*) Not in front of Mama! (*He turns the dummy around as she goes to a male dummy*) Oh, I would like to see Papa in this! Mama will make him ask about your prospects, if you go to church. But Papa—Papa *might* like you.

TONY: (*Kneeling to the "father" dummy*) May I have your daughter's hand?

MARIA: He says yes.

TONY: *Gracias!*

MARIA: And your mama?

TONY: I'm afraid to ask her.

MARIA: Tell her she's not getting a daughter; she's getting rid of a son!

TONY: She says yes.

MARIA: She has good taste. (*She grabs up the wedding veil and puts it on as* TONY *arranges the dummies*)

TONY: Maid of honor!

MARIA: That color is bad for Anita.

TONY: Best man!

MARIA: That is my Papa!

TONY: Sorry, Papa. Here we go, Riff: Womb to Tomb! (*He takes hat off dummy*)

MARIA: Now you see, Anita, I told you there was nothing to worry about.

(*Music starts as she leaves the dummy and walks up to* TONY. *They look at each other—and the play acting vanishes. Slowly, seriously, they turn front, and together kneel as before an altar.*)

TONY: I, Anton, take thee, Maria . . .

MARIA: I, Maria, take thee, Anton . . .

TONY: For richer, for poorer . . .

MARIA: In sickness and in health . . .

TONY: To love and to honor . . .

MARIA: To hold and to keep . . .
TONY: From each sun to each moon . . .
MARIA: From tomorrow to tomorrow . . .
TONY: From now to forever . . .
MARIA: Till death do us part.
TONY: With this ring, I thee wed.
MARIA: With this ring, I thee wed.

TONY: (*Sings*)
Make of our hands one hand,
Make of our hearts one heart,
Make of our vows one last vow:
Only death will part us now.

MARIA:
Make of our lives one life,
Day after day, one life.

BOTH:
Now it begins, now we start
One hand, one heart–
Even death won't part us now.

(*They look at each other, then at the reality of their "game." They smile tenderly, ruefully, and slowly put the dummies back into position. Though brought back to earth, they continue to sing*)

Make of our lives one life,
Day after day, one life.
Now it begins, now we start
One hand, one heart–
Even death won't part us now.
(*Very gently, he kisses her hand*)

The Lights Fade Out

SCENE 8

6:00 to 9:00 P.M. The neighborhood.

Spotlights pick out RIFF *and the Jets,* BERNARDO *and the Sharks,* ANITA, MARIA *and* TONY *against small sets representing different places in the neighborhood. All are waiting expectantly for the coming of night, but for very different reasons.*

JETS: (*Sing*)
The Jets are gonna have their day
Tonight.

SHARKS:

The Sharks are gonna have their way
Tonight.

JETS:

The Puerto Ricans grumble,
"Fair fight."
But if they start a rumble,
We'll rumble 'em right.

SHARKS:

We're gonna hand 'em a surprise
Tonight.

JETS:

We're gonna cut 'em down to size
Tonight.

SHARKS:

We said, "O.K., no rumpus,
No tricks"—
But just in case they jump us,
We're ready to mix
Tonight!

BOTH GANGS:

We're gonna rock it tonight,
We're gonna jazz it up and have us a ball.
They're gonna get it tonight;
The more they turn it on, the harder they'll fall!

JETS:

Well, they began it—

SHARKS:

Well, they began it—

BOTH GANGS:

And we're the ones to stop 'em once and for all,
Tonight!

ANITA:

Anita's gonna get her kicks
Tonight.
We'll have our private little mix
Tonight.
He'll walk in hot and tired,
So what?

Don't matter if he's tired,
As long as he's hot
Tonight!

TONY:

Tonight, tonight
Won't be just any night,
Tonight there will be no morning star.

Tonight, tonight,
I'll see my love tonight.
And for us, stars will stop where they are.

Today
The minutes seem like hours,
The hours go so slowly,
And still the sky is light . . .

Oh moon, grow bright,
And make this endless day endless night!

RIFF: (*To* TONY)

I'm counting on you to be there
Tonight.
When Diesel wins it fair and square
Tonight.

That Puerto Rican punk'll
Go down.
And when he's hollered Uncle
We'll tear up the town
Tonight!

MARIA:

Tonight, tonight
Won't be just any night . . .
(*She reprises the same chorus* TONY *has just sung*)

RIFF:

So I can count on you, boy?

TONY:

All right.

RIFF:

We're gonna have us a ball.

TONY:

All right . . .

(*Regretting his impatience*)
Womb to tomb!

RIFF:
Sperm to worm!
I'll see you there about eight . . .

TONY:
Tonight . . .

BERNARDO and SHARKS:
We're gonna rock it tonight!!!

ANITA:
Tonight . . .
(*All have been singing at once, reprising the choruses they sang before*)

BERNARDO and SHARKS:
We're gonna jazz it tonight
They're gonna get it tonight–tonight.
They began it–they began it
And we're the ones
To stop 'em once and for all!
The Sharks are gonna have their way,
The Sharks are gonna have their day,
We're gonna rock it tonight–
Tonight!

ANITA:
Tonight,
Late tonight,
We're gonna mix it tonight.
Anita's gonna have her day,
Anita's gonna have her day,
Bernardo's gonna have his way
Tonight–tonight.
Tonight–this very night,
We're gonna rock it tonight,
Tonight!

RIFF and JETS:
They began it.
They began it.
We'll stop 'em once and for all
The Jets are gonna have their day,

The Jets are gonna have their way,
We're gonna rock it tonight.
Tonight!

MARIA:

Tonight there will be no morning star.
Tonight, tonight, I'll see my love tonight.
When we kiss, stars will stop where they are.

TONY and MARIA:

Today the minutes seem like hours.
The hours go so slowly,
And still the sky is light.
Oh moon, grow bright,
And make this endless day endless night,
Tonight!

(*The lights build with the music to the climax, and then blackout at the final exultant note*)

SCENE 9

9:00 P.M. Under the highway.

A dead end: rotting plaster-and-brick walls and mesh wire fences. A street lamp.

It is nightfall. The almost-silhouetted gangs come in from separate sides: climbing over the fences or crawling through holes in the walls. There is silence as they fan out on opposite sides of the cleared space. Then BERNARDO *and* DIESEL *remove their jackets, handing them to their seconds:* CHINO *and* RIFF.

BERNARDO: Ready.

CHINO: Ready!

DIESEL: Ready.

RIFF: Ready! Come center and shake hands.

BERNARDO: For what?

RIFF: That's how it's done, buddy boy.

BERNARDO: More gracious living? Look: I don't go for that pretend crap you all go for in this country. Every one of you hates every one of us, and we hate you right back. I don't drink with nobody I hate, I don't shake hands with nobody I hatc. Let's get at it.

RIFF: O.K.

BERNARDO: (*Moving toward center*) Here we go.

(DIESEL *begins to move toward him. There are encourage-*

ments called from each side. The "fair fight" is just beginning when there is an interruption)

TONY: Hold it! (*He leaps over a fence and starts toward* BERNARDO)

RIFF: Get with the gang.

TONY: No.

RIFF: What're you doin'?

BERNARDO: Maybe he has found the guts to fight his own battles.

TONY: (*Smiling*) It doesn't take guts if you *have* a battle. But we haven't got one, 'Nardo. (*He extends his hand for* BERNARDO *to shake it.* BERNARDO *knocks the hand away and gives* TONY *a shove that sends him sprawling*)

BERNARDO: *Bernardo.*

RIFF: (*Quiet, strong*) The deal is a fair fight between you and Diesel. (*To* TONY, *who has gotten up*) Get with the gang.

(*During the following,* BERNARDO *flicks* TONY'S *shirt, pushes his shoulder, pinches his cheek*)

BERNARDO: (*To* TONY) I'll give you a battle, Kiddando.

DIESEL: You've got one.

BERNARDO: I'll take pretty boy on as a warm-up. Afraid, pretty boy? Afraid, chicken? Afraid, gutless?

RIFF: Cut that–

TONY: I don't want to, Bernardo . . .

BERNARDO: I'm sure.

TONY: Bernardo, you've got it wrong.

BERNARDO: Are you chicken?

TONY: You *won't* understand!

BERNARDO: What d'ya say, chicken?

ACTION: Get him, Tony!

BERNARDO: He *is* chicken.

DIESEL: Tony–

A-RAB: Get him!

TONY: Bernardo, *don't.*

BERNARDO: Don't what, pretty little chicken?

RIFF: Tony, don't just stand–

BERNARDO: Yellow-bellied chicken–

RIFF: TONY!

ACTION: Murder him!

SNOWBOY: Kill him!

TONY: DON'T PUSH ME!

BERNARDO: Come on, you yellow-bellied Polack bas–

(He never finishes, for RIFF *hauls off and hits him. Immediately, the two gangs alert, and the following action takes on the form of a dance. As* BERNARDO *reels back to his feet, he reaches for his back pocket.* RIFF *reaches for his back pocket, and at the same instant each brings forth a gleaming knife. They jockey for position, feinting, dueling; the two gangs shift position, now and again temporarily obscuring the fighters.* TONY *tries to get between them)*

RIFF: Hold him!

(DIESEL *and* ACTION *grab* TONY *and hold him back. The fight continues.* RIFF *loses his knife, is passed another by a Jet. At last, he has* BERNARDO *in a position where it seems that he will be able to run him through.* TONY *breaks from* DIESEL *and, crying out, moves to stop* RIFF)

TONY: Riff, don't!

(RIFF *hesitates a moment; the moment is enough for* BERNARDO*—whose hand goes forward with a driving motion, running his knife into* RIFF. TONY *leaps forward to catch* RIFF. *He breaks his fall, then takes the knife from his hand. A free-for-all has broken out as* TONY, RIFF'S *knife in hand, leaps at the triumphant* BERNARDO. *All this happens terribly fast; and* TONY *rams his knife into* BERNARDO. *The free-for-all continues a moment longer. Then there is a sharp police whistle. Everything comes to a dead stop—dead silence. Then a distant police siren: the kids waver, run one way, another, in panic, confusion. As the stage is cleared,* TONY *stands, horrified, over the still bodies of* RIFF *and* BERNARDO. *He bends over* RIFF'S *body; then he rolls* BERNARDO'S *body over—and stares. Then* TONY *raises his voice in an anguished cry)*

TONY: MARIA!

(Another police whistle, closer now, but he doesn't move. From the shadows, ANYBODYS *appears. She scurries to* TONY *and tugs at his arm. A siren, another whistle, then a searchlight cuts across the playground.* ANYBODYS' *insistent tugging brings* TONY *to the realization of the danger. He crouches, starts to run with her to one escapeway. She reaches it first, goes out—but the searchlight hits it just as he would go through. He stops, runs the other way. He darts here, there, and finally gets away as a distant clock begins to boom)*

The Curtain Falls

ACT TWO

SCENE 1

9:15 P.M. A bedroom.

Part of a parlor is also visible. The bedroom has a window opening onto the fire escape, a bed on a wall, a small shrine to the Virgin, and a curtained doorway, rear. There is a door between bedroom and the parlor.

Gay music for CONSUELO, *who is examining herself in the mirror, and for* ROSALIA, *who is on the bed, finishing her nails.*

CONSUELO: This is my last night as a blonde.

ROSALIA: No loss.

CONSUELO: A gain! The fortune teller told Pepe a dark lady was coming into his life.

ROSALIA: So that's why he's not taking you out after the rumble!

(*The music becomes festively, humorously Spanish as* MARIA *enters through the curtained doorway. She is finishing getting very dressed up*)

MARIA: There is not going to be a rumble.

ROSALIA: Another fortune teller.

CONSUELO: Where is Chino escorting you after the rumble-that-is-not-going-to-be-a-rumble?

MARIA: Chino is escorting me no place.

ROSALIA: She is just dolling up for us. *Gracias, querida.*

MARIA: No, not for you. Can you keep a secret?

CONSUELO: I'm hot for secrets!

MARIA: Tonight is my wedding night!

CONSUELO: The poor thing is out of her mind.

MARIA: I am: crazy!

ROSALIA: She might be at that. She looks somehow different.

MARIA: I do?

ROSALIA: And I think she is up to something tonight.

MARIA: I am?

CONSUELO: "I do?" "I am?" What is going on with you?

MARIA: (*Sings*)

I feel pretty,
Oh, so pretty,
I feel pretty, and witty and bright,
And I pity
Any girl who isn't me tonight.

I feel charming,
Oh, so charming–

It's alarming how charming I feel,
And so pretty
That I hardly can believe I'm real.

See the pretty girl in that mirror there:
Who can that attractive girl be?
Such a pretty face,
Such a pretty dress,
Such a pretty smile,
Such a pretty me!

I feel stunning
And entrancing—
Feel like running and dancing for joy,
For I'm loved
By a pretty wonderful boy!

ROSALIA and CONSUELO:

Have you met my good friend Maria,
The craziest girl on the block?
You'll know her the minute you see her—
She's the one who is in an advanced state of shock.

She thinks she's in love.
She thinks she's in Spain.
She isn't in love,
She's merely insane.

It must be the heat
Or some rare disease
Or too much to eat,
Or maybe it's fleas.

Keep away from her—
Send for Chino!
This is not the Mar-
Ia we know!

Modest and pure,
Polite and refined,
Well-bred and mature
And out of her mind!

MARIA:

I feel pretty,
Oh, so pretty,
That the city should give me its key.

A committee
Should be organized to honor me.

I feel dizzy,
I feel sunny,
I feel fizzy and funny and fine,
And so pretty,
Miss America can just resign!
See the pretty girl in that mirror there:

ROSALIA and CONSUELO:
What mirror where?

MARIA:
Who can that attractive girl be?

ROSALIA and CONSUELO:
Which? What? Where? Whom?

MARIA:
Such a pretty face,
Such a pretty dress,
Such a pretty smile,
Such a pretty me!

ALL:
I feel stunning
And entrancing–
Feel like running and dancing for joy,
For I'm loved
By a pretty wonderful boy!

CHINO: (*Offstage*) Maria!
CONSUELO: It's Chino.
ROSALIA: The happy bridegroom.
CHINO: (*Closer*) Maria!
MARIA: Please–
CONSUELO: Yes, little bride, we're going. (*She exits*)
ROSALIA: They have a quaint old-fashioned custom in this country, Maria: they get married here *before* the wedding night. (*She follows* CONSUELO *out as* CHINO *enters from offstage. His clothes are dirty and torn from the fight; his face is smeared. They shake their heads at him and flounce out. He closes the outer door*)
CHINO: Maria? . . .
MARIA: I'm in here. I was just getting ready to– (*She is hurriedly*

trying to put a bathrobe over her dress. CHINO *comes in before she can finish, so that she leaves it over her shoulders, holding it closed with her hand*)

CHINO: Where are your parents?

MARIA: At the store. If I had known you were– You have been fighting, Chino.

CHINO: Yes. I am sorry.

MARIA: That is not like you.

CHINO: No.

MARIA: Why, Chino?

CHINO: I don't know why. It happened so fast.

MARIA: You must wash up.

CHINO: Maria–

MARIA: You can go in there.

CHINO: In a minute. Maria . . . at the rumble–

MARIA: There was no rumble.

CHINO: There was.

MARIA: You are wrong.

CHINO: No; there was. Nobody meant for it to happen . . .

MARIA: . . . Tell me.

CHINO: It's bad.

MARIA: Very bad?

CHINO: (*Nods*) You see . . . (*He moves closer to her, helplessly*)

MARIA: It will be easier if you say it very fast.

CHINO: (*Nods*) There was a fight–(*She nods*) And 'Nardo–(*She nods*) And somehow a knife–and 'Nardo and someone –(*He takes her hand*)

MARIA: Tony. What happened to Tony? (*The name stops* CHINO. *He drops her hand: the robe opens*) Tell me! (*Crudely,* CHINO *yanks off the robe, revealing that she is dressed to go out*) Chino, is Tony all right?!

CHINO: He killed your brother. (*He walks into the parlor, slamming the door behind him. A pause*)

MARIA: You are lying! (CHINO *has started to leave the parlor, but turns back now. Swiftly searching behind furniture, he comes up with an object wrapped in material the same color as Bernardo's shirt. From the bedroom,* MARIA'S *voice calls out, louder*) You are lying, Chino! (*Coldly,* CHINO *unwraps a gun which he puts in his pocket. There is the sound of a police siren at a distance. He goes out. During this,* MARIA *has knelt before the shrine on the wall. She rocks back and forth in prayer, some of it in Spanish, some of it in English*) Make it not be true . . . please make it not be true . . . I will do anything: make *me* die . . . Only, please—make it not be true. (*As she prays,* TONY *appears at the fire-escape window and quietly climbs in. His shirt is ripped, half-torn off. He stands still, limp, watching her. Aware that someone is in the room, she stops her prayers. Slowly, her head turns; she looks at him for a long moment. Then, almost in one spring, she is on him, her fists beating his chest*) Killer killer killer killer killer—

(*But her voice breaks with tears, her arms go about him, and she buries her face in his chest, kissing him. She begins to slide down his body. He supports her as, together, they go to the floor, he cradling her body in his arms. He pushes her hair back from her face; kisses her hair, her face, between the words that tumble out*)

TONY: I tried to stop it; I did try. I don't know how it went wrong. . . . I didn't mean to hurt him; I didn't want to; I didn't know I had. But Riff . . . Riff was like my brother. So when Bernardo killed him—(*She lifts her head*) 'Nardo didn't mean it, either. Oh, I know he didn't! Oh, no. I didn't come to tell you. Just for you to forgive me so I could go to the police—

MARIA: No!

TONY: It's easy now—

MARIA: No . . .

TONY: Whatever you want, I'll do—

MARIA: Stay. Stay with me.

TONY: I love you so much.

MARIA: Tighter.

(*Music starts*)

TONY: We'll be all right. I know it. We're really together now.

MARIA: But it's not us! It's everything around us!

TONY: Then we'll find some place where nothing can get to us; not one of them, not anything. And—

(*He sings*)

I'll take you away, take you far far away out of here,
Far far away till the walls and the streets disappear,
Somewhere there must be a place we can feel we're free,
Somewhere there's got to be some place for you and for me.

(As he sings, the walls of the apartment begin to move off, and the city walls surrounding them begin to close in on them. Then the apartment itself goes, and the two lovers begin to run, battering against the walls of the city, beginning to break through as chaotic figures of the gangs, of violence, flail around them. But they do break through, and suddenly—they are in a world of space and air and sun. They stop, looking at it, pleased, startled, as boys and girls from both sides come on. And they, too, stop and stare, happy, pleased. Their clothes are soft pastel versions of what they have worn before. They begin to dance, to play: no sides, no hostility now; just joy and pleasure and warmth. More and more join, making a world that TONY *and* MARIA *want to be in, belong to, share their love with. As they go into the steps of a gentle love dance, a voice is heard singing)*

OFFSTAGE VOICE: (*Sings*)

There's a place for us,
Somewhere a place for us.
Peace and quiet and room and air
Wait for us
Somewhere.

There's a time for us,
Someday a time for us,
Time together with time to spare,
Time to learn, time to care
Someday!

Somewhere
We'll find a new way of living,
We'll find a way of forgiving
Somewhere,
Somewhere . . .

There's a place for us,
A time and place for us.
Hold my hand and we're halfway there.
Hold my hand and I'll take you there
Someday,
Somehow,
Somewhere!

(The lovers hold out their hands to each other; the others follow suit: Jets to Sharks; Sharks to Jets. And they form what is almost a procession winding its triumphant way through this

would-be world, as they sing the words of the song with wonderment. Then, suddenly, there is a dead stop. The harsh shadows, the fire escapes of the real, tenement world cloud the sky, and the figures of RIFF *and* BERNARDO *slowly walk on. The dream becomes a nightmare: as the city returns, there are brief re-enactments of the knife fight, of the deaths.* MARIA *and* TONY *are once again separated from each other by the violent warring of the two sides.* MARIA *tries to reach* BERNARDO, TONY *tries to stop* RIFF; *the lovers try to reach each other, but they cannot. Chaotic confusion and blackness, after which they find themselves back in the bedroom, clinging to each other desperately. With a blind refusal to face what they know must be, they reassure each other desperately as they sing)*

TONY and MARIA:

Hold my hand and we're halfway there.
Hold my hand and I'll take you there
Someday,
Somehow,
Somewhere!
(*As the lights fade, together they sink back on the bed*)

SCENE 2

10:00 P.M. Another alley.

A fence with loose boards; angles between buildings.

Softly, from behind the fence, the Jet gang whistle. A pause, then the answering whistle, softly, from offstage or around a corner. Now a loose board flips up and BABY JOHN *wriggles through the fence. He whistles again, timidly, and* A-RAB *comes on.*

A-RAB: They get you yet?
BABY JOHN: No. You?
A-RAB: Hell, no.
BABY JOHN: You seen Tony?
A-RAB: Nobody has.
BABY JOHN: Geez . . .
A-RAB: You been home yet?
BABY JOHN: Uh uh.
A-RAB: Me, either.
BABY JOHN: Just hidin' around?
A-RAB: Uh huh.
BABY JOHN: A-rab . . . did you get a look at 'em?
A-RAB: Look at who?

BABY JOHN: Ya know. At the rumble. Riff and Bernardo. (*Pause*)

A-RAB: I wish it was yesterday.

BABY JOHN: Wadaya say we run away?

A-RAB: What's a matter? You scared?

BABY JOHN: . . . Yeah.

A-RAB: You cut it out, ya hear? You're only makin' me scared and that scares me! (*Police whistle. He grabs* BABY JOHN) Last thing ever is to let a cop know you're scared or anythin'.

KRUPKE: (*Offstage*) Hey, you two!

A-RAB: Play it big with the baby blues.

BABY JOHN: (*Scared*) O.K.

A-RAB: (*Gripping him*) Big, not scared, big!

(*Again a whistle. Elaborately casual, they start sauntering off as* KRUPKE *appears*)

KRUPKE: Yeah, you. (*They stop, so surprised*)

A-RAB: Why, it *is* Officer Krupke, Baby John.

BABY JOHN: (*Quaking*) Top of the evening, Officer Krupke.

KRUPKE: I'll crack the top of your skulls if you punks don't stop when I whistle.

A-RAB: But we stopped the very moment we heard.

BABY JOHN: We got twenty-twenty hearing.

KRUPKE: You wanna get hauled down to the station house?

BABY JOHN: Indeed not, sir.

KRUPKE: I'll make a little deal. I know you was rumblin' under the highway–

BABY JOHN: We was at the playground, sir.

A-RAB: We like the playground. It keeps us deprived kids off the foul streets.

BABY JOHN: It gives us comradeship–

A-RAB: A place for pleasant pastimes– And for us, born like we was on the hot pavements–

KRUPKE: O.K., wise apples, down to the station house.

BABY JOHN: Which way?

A-RAB: This way! (*He gets down on all fours,* BABY JOHN *pushes* KRUPKE, *so that he tumbles over* A-RAB. BABY JOHN *starts off one way,* A-RAB *the other.* KRUPKE *hesitates, then runs after one of them, blowing his whistle like mad. The moment he is off,* A-RAB *and* BABY JOHN *appear through the fence, followed by the other Jets*) Look at the brass-ass run!

BABY JOHN: I hope he breaks it!

ACTION: Get the lead out, fat boy!

DIESEL: Easy. He'll come back and drag us down the station house.

ACTION: I already been.

SNOWBOY: We both already been.

A-RAB: What happened?

SNOWBOY: A big fat nuthin'!

A-RAB: How come?

SNOWBOY: Cops believe everythin' they read in the papers.

ACTION: To them we ain't human. We're cruddy juvenile delinquents. So that's what we give 'em.

SNOWBOY: (*Imitating* KRUPKE) Hey, you!

ACTION: Me, Officer Krupke?

SNOWBOY: Yeah, you! Gimme one good reason for not draggin' ya down the station house, ya punk.

ACTION: (*Sings*)

Dear kindly Sergeant Krupke,
You gotta understand–
It's just our bringin' upke
That gets us out of hand,
Our mothers all are junkies,
Our fathers all are drunks.

ALL:

Golly Moses–natcherly we're punks!

Gee, Officer Krupke, we're very upset;
We never had the love that every child oughta get.
We ain't no delinquents,
We're misunderstood.
Deep down inside us there is good!

ACTION:

There is good!

ALL:

There is good, there is good,
There is untapped good.
Like inside, the worst of us is good.

SNOWBOY: (*Imitating* KRUPKE)

That's a touchin' good story.

ACTION:

Lemme tell it to the world!

SNOWBOY: (*Imitating* KRUPKE)
Just tell it to the judge.

ACTION: (*To* DIESEL)
Dear kindly Judge, your Honor,
My parents treat me rough.
With all their marijuana,
They won't give me a puff.
They didn't wanna have me,
But somehow I was had.
Leapin' lizards—that's why I'm so bad!

DIESEL: (*Imitating a judge*)
Right!
Officer Krupke, you're really a square;
This boy don't need a judge, he needs a analyst's care!
It's just his neurosis that oughta be curbed—
He's psychologically disturbed!

ACTION:
I'm disturbed!

ALL:
We're disturbed, we're disturbed,
We're the most disturbed.
Like we're psychologically disturbed.

DIESEL: (*Speaks, still acting part of judge*) Hear ye, Hear ye! In the opinion of this court, this child is depraved on account he ain't had a normal home.
ACTION: Hey, I'm depraved on account I'm deprived!
DIESEL: (*As judge*) So take him to a headshrinker.

ACTION: (*To* A-RAB)
My father is a bastard,
My ma's an S.O.B.
My grandpa's always plastered,
My grandma pushes tea.
My sister wears a mustache,
My brother wears a dress.
Goodness gracious, that's why I'm a mess!

A-RAB: (*As psychiatrist*)
Yes!
Officer Krupke, you're really a slob.
This boy don't need a dotor, just a good honest job.

Society's played him a terrible trick,
And sociologically he's sick!

ACTION:
I am sick!

ALL:
We are sick, we are sick,
We are sick sick sick,
Like we're sociologically sick!

A-RAB: (*Speaks as psychiatrist*) In my opinion, this child don't need to have his head shrunk at all. Juvenile delinquency is purely a social disease.

ACTION: Hcy, I got a social disease!

A-RAB: (*As psychiatrist*) So take him to a social worker!

ACTION: (*To* BABY JOHN)
Dear kindly social worker,
They say go earn a buck,
Like be a soda jerker,
Which means like be a schmuck.
It's not I'm antisocial,
I'm only antiwork.
Glory Osky, that's why I'm a jerk!

BABY JOHN: (*As female social worker*)
Eek!
Officer Krupke, you've done it again.
This boy don't need a job, he needs a year in the pen.
It ain't just a question of misunderstood;
Deep down inside him, he's no good!

ACTION:
I'm no good!

ALL:
We're no good, we're no good,
We're no earthly good,
Like the best of us is no damn good!

DIESEL: (*As judge*)
The trouble is he's crazy,

A-RAB: (*As psychiatrist*)
The trouble is he drinks.

BABY JOHN: (*As social worker*)
The trouble is he's lazy.

DIESEL: (*As judge*)
The trouble is he stinks.

A-RAB: (*As psychiatrist*)
The trouble is he's growing.

BABY JOHN: (*As social worker*)
The trouble is he's grown!

ALL:
Krupke, we got troubles of our own!

Gee, Officer Krupke,
We're down on our knees,
'Cause no one wants a fella with a social disease.
Gee, Officer Krupke,
What are we to do?
Gee, Officer Krupke–
Krup you!

(*At the end of the song,* ANYBODYS *appears over the fence*)

ANYBODYS: Buddy boys!

ACTION: Ah! Go wear a skirt.

ANYBODYS: I got scabby knees. Listen–

ACTION: (*To the gang*) Come on, we gotta make sure those PRs know we're on top.

DIESEL: Geez, Action, ain't we had enough?

ANYBODYS: (*Going after them*) Wotta buncha Old Man Rivers: they don't know nuthin' and they don't say nuthin'.

ACTION: Diesel, the question ain't whether we had enough–

ANYBODYS: The question is: Where's Tony and what party is lookin' for him.

ACTION: What do you know?

ANYBODYS: I know I gotta get a skirt. (*She starts off, but* DIESEL *stops her*)

DIESEL: Come on, Anybodys, tell me.

SNOWBOY: Ah, what's that freak know?

ANYBODYS: Plenty. I figgered somebody oughta infiltrate PR territory and spy around. I'm very big with shadows, ya know. I can slip in and out of 'em like wind through a fence.

SNOWBOY: Boy, is she ever makin' the most of it!

ANYBODYS: You bet your fat A, I am!

ACTION: Go on. Wadd'ya hear?

ANYBODYS: I heard Chino tellin' the Sharks somethin' about Tony and Bernardo's sister. And then Chino said, "If it's the last thing I do, I'm going to get Tony."

ACTION: What'd I tell ya? Them PRs won't stop!
SNOWBOY: Easy, Action!
DIESEL: It's bad enough now—
BABY JOHN: Yeah!
ACTION: You forgettin'? Tony came through for us Jets. We gotta find him and protect him from Chino.
A-RAB: Right!
ACTION: O.K. then! Snowboy—cover the river! (SNOWBOY *runs off*) A-rab—get over to Doc's.
BABY JOHN: I'll take the back alleys.
ACTION: Diesel?
DIESEL: I'll cover the park.
ACTION: Good boy! (*He begins to run off*)
ANYBODYS: What about me?
ACTION: You? You get a hold of the girls and send 'em out as liaison runners so we'll know who's found Tony where.
ANYBODYS: Right! (*She starts to run off*)
ACTION: Hey! (*She stops*) You done good, buddy boy.
ANYBODYS: (*She has fallen in love*) Thanks, Daddy-o. (*They both run off*)

The Lights Black Out

SCENE 3

11:30 P.M. The bedroom.

The light is, at first, a vague glow on the lovers, who are asleep on the bed. From offstage, faint at first, there is the sound of knocking. It gets louder; TONY *stirs. At a distance a police siren sounds, and the knocking is now very loud.* TONY *bolts upright.* ANITA *comes in from outside and goes to the bedroom door—which is locked—tries the knob.*

ANITA: (*Holding back tears*) Maria? . . . Maria? (TONY *is reaching for his shirt when* MARIA *sits up. Quickly, he puts his hand, then his lips, on her lips*) Maria, it's Anita. Why are you locked in?
MARIA: I didn't know it was locked.
ANITA: Open the door. I need you.
(MARIA *reaches for the knob,* TONY *stops her*)
MARIA: (*A whisper*) Now you are afraid, too.
ANITA: What?
MARIA: (*Loud*) One moment.
TONY: (*Whispering*) Doc'll help. I'll get money from him. You meet me at his drugstore.

(*In the other room,* ANITA *is aware of voices but unsure of what they are saying*)

MARIA: At Doc's, yes. (*Aloud*) Coming, Anita!

TONY: (*Kisses her*) Hurry!

(*He scrambles out the window as* MARIA *hastily puts a bathrobe on over her slip. In the other room* ANITA *has stiffened and moved away from the door. She stands staring at it coldly as* MARIA *prattles to her through the door*)

MARIA: Did you see Chino? He was here before, but he left so angry I think maybe he . . . (*She opens the door and sees* ANITA'*s look. A moment, then* ANITA *pushes her aside: looks at the bed, at the window, then turns accusingly to* MARIA) All right: now you know.

ANITA: (*Savagely*) And you still don't know: *Tony is one of them!*

(*She sings bitterly*)

A boy like that who'd kill your brother,
Forget that boy and find another!
One of your own kind–
Stick to your own kind!

A boy like that will give you sorrow–
You'll meet another boy tomorrow!
One of your own kind,
Stick to your own kind!

A boy who kills cannot love,
A boy who kills has no heart.
And he's the boy who gets your love
And gets your heart–
Very smart, Maria, very smart!

A boy like that wants one thing only,
And when he's done he'll leave you lonely.
He'll murder your love; he murdered mine.
Just wait and see–
Just wait, Maria,
Just wait and see!

MARIA: (*Sings*)

Oh no, Anita, no–
Anita, no!
It isn't true, not for me,
It's true for you, not for me,

I hear your words—
And in my head
I know they're smart,
But my heart, Anita,
But my heart
Knows they're wrong

(ANITA *reprises the chorus she has just sung, as* MARIA *continues her song*)

MARIA:

And my heart
Is too strong,
For I belong
To him alone, to him alone,
One thing I know:
I am his,
I don't care what he is.
I don't know why it's so,
I don't want to know.
Oh no, Anita, no—you should know better!
You were in love—or you said.
You should know better . . .

I have a love, and it's all that I have.
Right or wrong, what else can I do?
I love him; I'm his,
And everything he is
I am, too.
I have a love and it's all that I need,
Right or wrong, and he needs me too.
I love him, we're one;
There's nothing to be done,
Not a thing I can do
But hold him, hold him forever,
Be with him now, tomorrow
And all of my life!

BOTH:

When love comes so strong,
There is no right or wrong,
Your love is your life!

ANITA: (*Quietly*) Chino has a gun . . . He is sending the boys out to hunt for Tony—

MARIA: (*Tears off her bathrobe*) If he hurts Tony— If he touches him—I swear to you, I'll—

ANITA: (*Sharply*) You'll do what Tony did to Bernardo?

MARIA: I love Tony.

ANITA: I know. I loved Bernardo.

(SCHRANK *comes into the outer room*)

SCHRANK: Anybody home? (*Goes to bedroom door. Pleasantly*) Sorry to disturb you. Guess you're disturbed enough.

MARIA: (*Gathering her robe*) Yes. You will excuse me, please. I must go to my brother.

SCHRANK: There are just a coupla questions—

MARIA: Afterwards, please. Later.

SCHRANK: It'll only take a minute.

ANITA: Couldn't you wait until—

SCHRANK: (*Sharply*) No! (*A smile to* MARIA) You were at the dance at the gym last night.

MARIA: Yes.

SCHRANK: Your brother got in a heavy argument because you danced with the wrong boy.

MARIA: Oh?

SCHRANK: Who was the boy?

MARIA: Excuse me. Anita, my head is worse. Will you go to the drugstore and tell them what I need?

SCHRANK: Don't you keep aspirin around?

MARIA: This is something special. Will you go for me, Anita?

ANITA: (*Hesitates, looks at* MARIA, *then nods*) Shall I tell him to hold it for you till you come?

MARIA: (*To* SCHRANK) Will I be long?

SCHRANK: As long as it takes.

MARIA: (*To* ANITA) Yes. Tell him I will pick it up myself. (ANITA *goes out*) I'm sorry. Now you asked?

SCHRANK: (*As the lights dim*) I didn't ask, I told you. There was an argument over a boy. Who was that boy?

MARIA: Another from my country.

SCHRANK: And his name?

MARIA: José.

The Lights Are Out

SCENE 4

11:40 P.M. The drugstore.

A-RAB *and some of the Jets are there as* ANYBODYS *and other Jets run in.*

ACTION: Where's Tony?

A-RAB: Down in the cellar with Doc.

DIESEL: Ya warn him about Chino?

A-RAB: Doc said he'd tell him.

BABY JOHN: What's he hidin' in the cellar from?

SNOWBOY: Maybe he can't run as fast as you.

ACTION: Cut the frabbajabba.

ANYBODYS: Yeah! The cops'll get hip, if Chino and the PRs don't.

ACTION: Grab some readin' matter; play the juke. Some of ya get outside and if ya see Chino or any PR—

(*The shop doorbell tinkles as* ANITA *enters. Cold silence, then slowly she comes down to the counter. They all stare at her. A long moment. Someone turns on the juke box; a mambo comes on softly*)

ANITA: I'd like to see Doc.

ACTION: He ain't here.

ANITA: Where is he?

A-RAB: He's gone to the bank. There was an error in his favor.

ANITA: The banks are closed at night. Where is he?

A-RAB: You know how skinny Doc is. He slipped in through the night-deposit slot.

ANYBODYS: And got stuck halfway in.

ACTION: Which indicates there's no tellin' when he'll be back. *Buenas noches, señorita.*

(ANITA *starts to go toward the cellar door*)

DIESEL: Where you goin'?

ANITA: Downstairs—to see Doc.

ACTION: Didn't I tell ya he ain't here?

ANITA: I'd like to see for myself.

ACTION: (*Nastily*) Please.

ANITA: (*Controlling herself*) . . . Please.

ACTION: *Por favor.*

ANITA: Will you let me pass?

SNOWBOY: She's too dark to pass.

ANITA: (*Low*) Don't.

ACTION: *Please* don't.

SNOWBOY: *Por favor.*

DIESEL: *Non comprende.*

A-RAB: *Gracias.*

BABY JOHN: *Di nada.*

ANYBODYS: Ai! Mambo! Ai!

ANITA: Listen, you– (*She controls herself*)

ACTION: We're listenin'.

ANITA: I've got to give a friend of yours a message. I've got to tell Tony–

DIESEL: He ain't here.

ANITA: I know he is.

ACTION: Who says he is?

A-RAB: Who's the message from?

ANITA: Never mind.

ACTION: Couldn't be from Chino, could it?

ANITA: I want to stop Chino! I want to help!

ANYBODYS: Bernardo's girl wants ta help?

ACTION: Even a greaseball's got feelings.

ANYBODYS: But she wants to help get Tony!

ANITA: No!

ACTION: Not much–Bernardo's tramp!

SNOWBOY: Bernardo's pig!

ACTION: Ya lyin' Spic–!

ANITA: Don't do that!

BABY JOHN: Gold tooth!

DIESEL: Pierced ear!

A-RAB: Garlic mouth!

ACTION: Spic! Lyin' Spic!

(*The taunting breaks out into a wild, savage dance, with epithets hurled at* ANITA, *who is encircled and driven by the whole pack. At the peak, she is shoved so that she falls in a corner.* BABY JOHN *is lifted up high and dropped on her as* DOC *enters from the cellar door and yells*)

DOC: *Stop it!* . . . What've you been doing now?

(*Dead silence.* ANITA *gets up and looks at them*)

ANITA: (*Trying not to cry*) Bernardo was right . . . If one of you was bleeding in the street, I'd walk by and spit on you. (*She flicks herself off and makes her way toward the door*)

ACTION: Don't let her go!

DIESEL: She'll tell Chino that Tony–

(SNOWBOY *grabs her; she shakes loose*)

ANITA: Let go! (*Facing them*) I'll give you a message for your American buddy! Tell the murderer Maria's *never* going to meet him! Tell him Chino found out and–and shot her! (*She slams out. There is a stunned silence*)

DOC: What does it take to get through to you? When do you stop? *You make this world lousy!*

ACTION: That's the way we found it, Doc.

DOC: Get out of here!

(*Slowly, they start to file out*)

The Lights Fade

SCENE 5

11:50 P.M. The cellar.

Cramped: a box or crate; stairs leading to the drugstore above; a door to the outside.

TONY *is sitting on a crate, whistling "Maria" as* DOC *comes down the stairs, some bills in his hand.*

TONY: Make a big sale?

DOC: No.

TONY: (*Taking the money that* DOC *is holding*) Thanks. I'll pay you back as soon as I can.

DOC: Forget that.

TONY: I won't; I couldn't. Doc, you know what we're going to do in the country, Maria and me? We're going to have kids and we'll name them all after you, even the girls. Then when you come to visit–

DOC: (*Slapping him*) *Wake up!* (*Raging*) Is that the only way to get through to you? Do just what you all do? Bust like a hot-water pipe?

TONY: Doc, what's gotten–

DOC: (*Overriding angrily*) Why do you live like there's a war on? (*Low*) Why do you kill?

TONY: I told you how it happened, Doc. Maria understands. Why can't you?

DOC: I never had a Maria.

TONY: (*Gently*) I have, and I'll tell you one thing, Doc. Even if it only lasts from one night to the next, it's worth the world.

DOC: That's all it did last.

TONY: What?

DOC: That was no customer upstairs, just now. That was Anita. (*Pause*) Maria is dead. Chino found out about you and her– and shot her.

(*A brief moment.* TONY *looks at* DOC, *stunned, numb. He shakes his head, as though he cannot believe this.* DOC *holds out his hands to him, but* TONY *backs away, then suddenly turns and runs out the door. As he does, the set flies away and the stage goes dark. In the darkness, we hear* TONY'S *voice*)

TONY: Chino? *Chino?* Come and get me, too, Chino.

SCENE 6

Midnight. The street.

The lights come up to reveal the same set we saw at the beginning of Act One—but it is now jagged with shadows. TONY *stands in the emptiness, calling, whirling around as a figure darts out of the shadows and then runs off again.*

TONY: Chino? . . . COME ON: GET ME, TOO!

ANYBODYS: (*A whisper from the dark*) Tony . . .

TONY: (*Swings around*) Who's that?

ANYBODYS: (*Darting on*) Me: Anybodys.

TONY: Get outa here. HEY, CHINO! COME GET ME, DAMN YOU!

ANYBODYS: What're you doin', Tony?

TONY: I said get outa here! CHINO!

ANYBODYS: Look, maybe if you and me just—

TONY: (*Savagely*) It's not playing any more! Can't any of you get that?

ANYBODYS: But the gang—

TONY: You're a girl: *be a girl!* Beat it. (*She retreats*) CHINO, I'M CALLING FOR YOU, CHINO! HURRY! IT'S CLEAR NOW. THERE'S NOBODY BUT ME. COME ON! Will you, please. I'm waiting for you. I want you to— (*Suddenly, all the way across the stage from him, a figure steps out of the dark. He stops and peers as light starts to glow on it. He utters an unbelieving whisper*) Maria . . . Maria?

MARIA: Tony . . . (*As she holds out her arms toward him, another figure appears:* CHINO)

TONY: MARIA! (*As they run to each other, there is a gun shot.* TONY *stumbles, as though he has tripped.* MARIA *catches him and cradles him in her arms as he falters to the ground. During this* BABY JOHN *and* A-RAB *run on; then* PEPE *and* INDIO *and other Sharks.* CHINO *stands very still, bewildered by the gun dangling from his hand. More Jets and Sharks, some girls run on, and* DOC *comes out to stare with them*) I didn't believe hard enough.

MARIA: Loving is enough.

TONY: Not here. They won't let us be.

MARIA: Then we'll get away.

TONY: Yes, we can. We *will.* (*He shivers, as though a pain went through him. She holds him closer and begins to sing—without orchestra*)

MARIA:

Hold my hand and we're halfway there.
Hold my hand and I'll take you there,
Someday,
Somehow . . .

(*He has started to join in on the second line. She sings harder, as though to urge him back to life, but his voice falters and he barely finishes the line. She sings on, a phrase or two more, then stops, his body quiet in her arms. A moment, and then, as she gently rests* TONY *on the floor, the orchestra finishes the last bars of the song. Lightly, she brushes* TONY'S *lips with her fingers. Behind her,* ACTION, *in front of a group of Jets, moves to lead them toward* CHINO. MARIA *speaks, her voice cold, sharp*)

MARIA: *Stay back.* (*The shawl she has had around her shoulders slips to the ground as she gets up, walks to* CHINO *and holds out her hand. He hands her the gun. She speaks again, in a flat, hard voice*) How do you fire this gun, Chino? Just by pulling this little trigger? (*She points it at him suddenly; he draws back. She has all of them in front of her now, as she holds the gun out and her voice gets stronger with anger and savage rage*) How many bullets are left, Chino? Enough for you? (*Pointing at another*) And you? (*At* ACTION) All of you? WE ALL KILLED HIM; and my brother and Riff. I, too. I CAN KILL NOW BECAUSE *I* HATE NOW. (*She has been pointing the gun wildly, and they have all been drawing back. Now, again, she holds it straight out at* ACTION) How many can I kill, Chino? How many—and still have one bullet left for me? (*Both hands on the gun, she pushes it forward at* ACTION. *But she cannot fire, and she breaks into tears, hurls the gun away and sinks to the ground.* SCHRANK *walks on, looks around and starts toward* TONY'S *body. Like a madwoman,* MARIA *races to the body and puts her arms around it, all-embracing, protecting, as she cries out*) DON'T YOU TOUCH HIM! (SCHRANK *steps back.* KRUPKE *and* GLAD HAND *have appeared in the shadows behind him.* MARIA *now turns and looks at* CHINO, *holds her hand out to him. Slowly he comes and stands by the body. Now she looks at* ACTION, *holds out her hand to him. He, too, comes forward, with* DIESEL, *to stand by the body.* PEPE *joins* CHINO. *Then* MARIA *leans low over* TONY'S *face. Softly, privately*) Te adoro, Anton.

(She kisses him gently. Music starts as the two Jets and two Sharks lift up TONY'S *body and start to carry him out. The others, boys and girls, fall in behind to make a procession, the same procession they made in the dream ballet, as* BABY JOHN *comes forward to pick up* MARIA'S *shawl and put it over her head. She sits quietly, like a woman in mourning, as the music builds, the lights start to come up and the procession makes its way across the stage. At last, she gets up and, despite the tears on her face, lifts her head proudly, and triumphantly turns to follow the others. The adults—*DOC, SCHRANK, KRUPKE, GLAD HAND*—are left bowed, alone, useless)*

The Curtain Falls

GYPSY

Book by Arthur Laurents
Music by Jule Styne
Lyrics by Stephen Sondheim

(Suggested by the memoirs of Gypsy Rose Lee)

Production Notes

Gypsy was first presented by David Merrick and Leland Hayward at the Broadway Theatre, New York, on May 21, 1959. The cast was as follows:

Uncle Jocko, *Mort Marshall*
George, *Willy Sumner*
Arnold (and his accordion), *Johnny Borden*
Balloon Girl, *Jody Lane*
Baby Louise, *Karen Moore*
Baby June, *Jacqueline Mayro*
Rose, *Ethel Merman*
Pop, *Erv Harmon*
Newsboys: *Bobby Brownell, Gene Castle, Steve Curry, Billy Harris*
Weber, *Joe Silver*
Herbie, *Jack Klugman*
Louise, *Sandra Church*
June, *Lane Bradbury*
Tulsa, *Paul Wallace*
Yonkers, *David Winters*
L.A., *Michael Parks*
Angie, *Ian Tucker*
Kringelein, *Loney Lewis*
Mr. Goldstone, *Mort Marshall*
Miss Cratchitt, *Peg Murray*
Farmboys: *Marvin Arnold, Ricky Coll, Don Emmons, Michael Parks, Ian Tucker, Paul Wallace, David Winters*
Cow, *Willy Sumner and George Zima*
Pastey, *Richard Porter*
Tessie Tura, *Maria Karnilova*
Mazeppa, *Faith Dane*
Cigar, *Loney Lewis*
Electra, *Chotzi Foley*
Showgirls: *Kathryn Albertson, Denise McLaglen, Barbara London, Theda Nelson, Carroll Jo Towers, Marie Wallace*
Renée, *Marsha Rivers*
Phil, *Joe Silver*
Bougeron-Cochon, *George Zima*

HOLLYWOOD BLONDES

Agnes, *Marilyn Cooper*
Marjorie May, *Patsy Bruder*
Dolores, *Marilyn D'Honau*
Thelma, *Merle Letowt*
Edna, *Joan Petlak*
Gail, *Linda Donovan*

Entire production directed and choreographed by *Jerome Robbins*
Settings and lighting by *Jo Mielziner*
Costumes designed by *Raoul Pène du Bois*
Musical direction by *Milton Rosenstock*
Orchestrations by *Sid Ramin* with *Robert Ginzler*
Dance music arranged by *John Kander*
Additional dance music by *Betty Walberg*

The action of the play covers a period from the early twenties to the early thirties, and takes place in various cities throughout the country.

Musical Numbers

Act One

May We Entertain You	Baby June and Baby Louise
Some People	Rose
Traveling	
Small World	Rose and Herbie
Baby June and Her Newsboys	
Mr. Goldstone, I Love You	Rose and Ensemble
Little Lamb	Louise
You'll Never Get Away from Me	Rose and Herbie
Dainty June and Her Farmboys	
If Momma Was Married	Louise and June
All I Need Is the Girl	Tulsa and Louise
Everything's Coming Up Roses	Rose

Act Two

Madame Rose's Toreadorables	Louise and the Hollywood Blondes
Together, Wherever We Go	Rose, Louise and Herbie
You Gotta Get a Gimmick	Tessie, Mazeppa and Electra
Small World (Reprise)	Rose
Let Me Entertain You	Louise and Company
Rose's Turn	Rose

ACT ONE

SCENE 1

On either side of the proscenium, there are illuminated placards—as in the days of vaudeville. After the overture, the placards light up to read:

UNCLE JOCKO'S KIDDIE SHOW
SEATTLE

The light illuminating the placards fades slowly as the curtain rises on the stage of a tacky vaudeville theatre.

The stage is half-set for the rehearsal of a kiddie show. "UNCLE JOCKO"*—the nervous, oily master of ceremonies—is sur-*

rounded by a pack of babbling kids and their tigress mothers. The kids are in horrible, homemade costumes; the mothers wear clothes of the very early twenties; JOCKO *wears a tartan cap and fake horn-rimmed glasses as a concession to his name.*

JOCKO: Everybody–SHUT UP! . . . All mothers–*out.* (*To his assistant*) Georgie, I don't want them in the wings, I don't want them in the theatre, I want them OUT!

GEORGIE: It's a pleasure. O.K., mothers–this way. Move. (*He herds them out as–*)

JOCKO: All right, kids, get in a straight line along here and come forward one at a time. The doors open at seven and Uncle Jocko doesn't have enough time to rehearse your darlin' acts. (*He takes a simpering little girl completely covered with balloons out of line and moves her down, apart from the others*) You wait here, girly-girl. (*Calling out front to the* SPOT MAN) Oh, Gus! Hit this doll with a surprise pink when she does her turn. (*To the girl*) Uncle Jocko promised the wee bairn would be a winner and she will. (*The kid kisses him coyly. To* GEORGIE) Chip off her sister's block. And you ought to see them balloons! O.K. Let's have the first wee laddie in Uncle Jocko's Kiddie Show. (*As a little boy with a big accordion comes forward,* JOCKO *speaks to the actual* CONDUCTOR *in the pit*) Take each of them from the top and then cut to the last eight. Every Friday night, ya ta ta, ya ta ta, Uncle Jocko dinna ken there were so many talented bairns right here in Seattle and the rest of the crap–ARNOLD AND HIS ACCORDION! (*As* ARNOLD *plays–indicating the kid*) Georgie, that's what's gonna kill vaudeville. All right, Arnold, cut to the end. The end, kiddo. (*He signals the* CONDUCTOR *for a sick chord;* GEORGIE *pushes* ARNOLD *off.* JOCKO *speaks to two little girls dressed as a Dutch boy and girl*) And who does Uncle Jocko have here? Who the hell does he–BABY JUNE AND COMPANY? . . . (*To the* CONDUCTOR) Half of the song, half of the dance, and off.

CONDUCTOR: Got ya.

(*A small band starts the introduction*)

JUNE: (*Singing*)

May we entertain you?
May we see you smile?
I will do some kicks–

LOUISE: (*Singing*)
I will do some tricks.

ROSE: (*From out front*) Sing out, Louise—sing out!

JOCKO: Who said that?

JUNE: (*Singing*)
I'll tell you a story.

LOUISE: (*Singing*)
I'll dance when she's done.

ROSE: (*From front*) You're behind, Louise! Catch up, honey, catch up!

JOCKO: Who let in one of them mothers?

JUNE and LOUISE:
By the time we're through entertaining you—

(*Coming down the aisle and onto the stage, carrying a little dog and a big handbag is—momma!*)

ROSE: Hold it, please, hold it! Save your strength, June. Louise, dear, if you don't count—

JOCKO: Madam, do you realize you are absolutely—

ROSE: I do, Uncle Jocko, but I want to save your very valuable time for you.

JOCKO: In that case—

ROSE: When I saw your sensitive face at the Odd Fellows Hall —my first husband was an Odd Fellow—

JOCKO: I am not an Odd Fellow!

ROSE: I meant a Knight of Pythias. My second husband was—

JOCKO: I'm not a Knight of Pythias!

ROSE: Then where *did* you catch our act?

JOCKO: At the Elks.

ROSE: My father is an Elk! I have his tooth here someplace. (*She dumps the dog into* JOCKO's *arms as she rummages in her handbag*) If you'll just hold Chowsie for me—that's short for chow mein. (*Baby talk*) Mommy just loves chow mein, doesn't she, Chowsie Wowsie? Stop sucking your thumb, Louise. (*To the* CONDUCTOR) Professor, I just marvel how you can make a performer into an artist.

JOCKO: (*Following her as she gads about*) What is going on here??

ROSE: Now if you could help my little girls by giving them a good loud la da *da* de da da *da*—(*To* JOCKO, *whom she delicately shoves back as he moves to intervene*) God helps him who helps himself. (*To the* DRUMMER) Mr. Zipser–when the girls do their specialty would you please ad lick it? Show him, girls.

JOCKO: Is this really happening? !

ROSE: Oh, Gus? Gus, would you please slap Baby June with something pink? She's the star. Smile, Baby dear!

JOCKO: I have seen all kinds of mothers–

ROSE: Do you know of a really good agent–don't hang on the baby, Louise, you're rumpling her dress–who could book a professional act like ours?

JOCKO: A professional act! Hey, Georgie! Get a load of this crazy–

ROSE: (*Suddenly grabbing him*) Don't you laugh! *Don't you dare laugh!* . . . That child is going to be a star.

JOCKO: That's what they all say. All right– (*He shoves the dog back into her arms*)

ROSE: But we're not finished!

JOCKO: You are as far as I'm concerned.

ROSE: Because you're trying to play favorites!

JOCKO: (*Stops*) What?

ROSE: How dare you let that rotten, untalented fat balloon block up my babies? I won't leave this stage till she does!

JOCKO: That child–

ROSE: Have you no loyalty to the Elks?

JOCKO: I'm not an Elk!

ROSE: Well, the editor of the *Gazette is!* I happen to know because at the last meeting he showed my father a letter he got –complaining some contest was fixed . . . I guess desperate people do desperate things. (JOCKO *stares at her, then motions the* BALLOON GIRL *to go.* ROSE *looks at the* CONDUCTOR, *and signals him as before*) La da *da* de da *da!* (*Music starts and the girls begin their act*) Thank you, Professor. Thank you, Uncle Jocko. (*She gives him the dog*) Thank you, Gus! Thank you, Mr. Zipser! Smile, girls, smile!

(*She is singing along with her girls when she sees the* BALLOON GIRL, *who has edged out from the wings. Still singing gaily,* ROSE *removes her hatpin. The* BALLOON GIRL *backs into the wings as* ROSE *marches after her, the hatpin extended like Joan of Arc's sword. Her dancing daughters watch, grin, and finish to a blare of music*)

The Lights Black Out

SCENE 2

The illuminated placards change to read:

"HOME SWEET HOME"
SEATTLE

The scene is the kitchen of a frame house. Later that night.

We see an icebox, a sink overflowing with dishes; calendars and timetables on the walls, a rocker, etc.

LOUISE *and* JUNE *enter yawning, and take off the coats they wear over their costumes as* ROSE *slams in, throws her coat on a chair and heads for the icebox. She gives Chowsie, the little dog, to* LOUISE *as she gets a plate of food from the icebox. As usual, she is talking all the time.*

ROSE: That rotten little Uncle Jocko! He's as cheap as your grandpa. (*To* JUNE) Ten bucks for a talent like yours! Well, we're through with Kiddie Shows. *And* with your grandpa's lodge hall. It's time we moved on anyway! I'm gonna get us an agent to book the act on the Orpheum Circuit.

LOUISE: That's dog food, Momma.

ROSE: That's what she thinks. I'm hungry.

LOUISE: Then why didn't you eat some of our chow mein after the show?

ROSE: Because you two did the work and we gotta save every cent. (*To* JUNE, *who brings her a hair brush—as she brushes* JUNE'*s hair*) I had a dream last night: a whole new act for you! Baby June and Her Newsboys!

LOUISE: Momma, do we have to stay in show business?

JUNE: Honest, Louise! How are you going to get the boys, Momma?

ROSE: Louise can be a boy—(LOUISE *exits*)—and I'll find three others.

JUNE: How are you going to pay them?

ROSE: The experience'll be their pay. I've got just enough saved up for scenery and costumes. If I can squeeze a few bucks out of Grandpa, we can head for Los Angeles and the Orpheum Circuit . . .

(POP *enters. He is a crusty old man, holding the Bible he is eternally reading. A short pause*)

JUNE: (*Tactfully*) Good night, Momma. Good night, Grandpa. (*She exits*)

POP: You oughta be ashamed: fooling your kids with those dreams!

ROSE: They're real dreams and I'm gonna make 'em *come* real for my kids!

POP: What are you, Rose, a crazy woman?! God put you down right here because He meant for you to stay right here!

ROSE: God's like me, Pop: we both need outside assistance.

POP: You've squeezed the last penny outa me that you're ever gonna get!

ROSE: It ain't for me! It's for my girls. It's too late for me.

POP: It ain't too late for you to get a husband to support you.

ROSE: After three husbands, I'm through with marriage. I want to enjoy myself. I want my girls to enjoy themselves and travel like Momma does!

POP: And you'll leave them just like your mother left you!

ROSE: Never! (*She turns to see* LOUISE, *who has entered behind her*) Why aren't you ready for bed, Louise?

LOUISE: June says you said she can sleep with you tonight.

ROSE: You know how high-strung the baby is after a performance.

LOUISE: I performed.

ROSE: It ain't the same. Now say good night and go to bed.

LOUISE: Good night, Grandpa. (*She kisses him*)

POP: Good night, Plug. You're a good girl.

ROSE: You *are* a good girl and I was proud of you tonight. (LOUISE *runs to her and hugs her*)

LOUISE: Momma, how come I have three fathers?

ROSE: Because you're lucky . . . You were born with a caul. That means you got powers to read palms and tell fortunes and wonderful things are going to happen for you! (LOUISE *goes*)

POP: Why do you fill her with such bunk?

ROSE: It ain't bunk!

POP: Nothin' wonderful is going to happen to her or June—or to you.

ROSE: Maybe not to me, but they're gonna have a marvelous time! I'll be damned if I'm gonna let them sit away their lives like I did. And like you do—with only that calendar to tell you one day is different from the next! And that plaque— (*Pointing to a gold plaque on the wall*)—from your rotten railroad company to say congratulations: for fifty years, you did the same dull thing every dull day!

POP: That plaque is a great tribute! It's solid gold!

ROSE: How much could you get for it?

POP: Rose, if you–
ROSE: What good's it doin' sittin' there?!
POP: That plaque belongs there like you belong home–instead of running around the country like a Gypsy!
ROSE: Anybody that stays home is dead! If I die, it won't be from sittin'! It'll be from fightin' to get up and get out! (*She sings*)

Some people can get a thrill
Knitting sweaters and sitting still–
  That's okay for some people who don't know they're alive;

Some people can thrive and bloom,
Living life in a living room–
  That's perfect for some people of one hundred and five!

But I
At least gotta try,
When I think of all the sights that I gotta see yet,
All the places I gotta play,
All the things that I gotta be yet–
  Come on, Poppa, whaddaya say?

Some people can be content
Playing bingo and paying rent–
  That's peachy for some people,
  For some humdrum people
To be,
But some people ain't me!

I had a dream,
A wonderful dream, Poppa,
  All about June and the Orpheum Circuit–
  Give me a chance and I know I can work it!
I had a dream,
Just as real as can be, Poppa–
There I was in Mr. Orpheum's office
And he was saying to me,
"Rose!
Get yourself some new orchestrations,
New routines and red velvet curtains,
Get a feathered hat for the Baby,
Photographs in front of the theatre,
Get an agent–and in jig time
You'll be being booked in the big time!"

Oh, what a dream,
A wonderful dream, Poppa,
And all that I need
Is eighty-eight bucks, Poppa!
That's what he said, Poppa,
Only eighty-eight bucks, Poppa . . .

POP: You ain't gettin' eight cents from me, Rose! (*He goes*)

ROSE: (*Shouting after him*) Then I'll get it someplace else—but I'll get it and get my kids out! (ROSE *sings*)

Good-bye
To blueberry pie!
Good riddance to all the socials I had to go to,
All the lodges I had to play,
All the Shriners I said hello to—
Hey, L.A., I'm coming your way!
Some people sit on their butts,
Got the dream—yeah, but not the guts!
That's living for some people,
For some humdrum people,
I suppose.
Well, they can stay and rot—

(*She starts out, comes back to take the plaque from the wall, dumps it in her purse, then finishes her song*)

But not
Rose!

(*And she strides out*)

The Lights Black Out

SCENE 3

A road.

In front of the curtain, JUNE *and* LOUISE*—wearing their coats and hats and carrying suitcases—stand trying to thumb a ride. The music of "Some People" is continuous underneath. The cutout of a fancy old touring car "driven" by a rich man and his little son comes on and stops to pick up the children. But as they get in,* JUNE *signals—and* ROSE *comes running out carrying a suitcase and Chowsie.*

She sings as the car "drives" across. Behind it, boys cross carrying signs indicating the lessening distance between Seattle and ROSE'S *goal: Los Angeles.*

They pass an urchin tap dancing, his hat held out for money.

ROSE *puts some pennies in his cap, then, impressed by his dancing, she yanks him into the car and they move on.*

A troop of boy scouts passes, singing. ROSE *hears the last little boy hold a good high note—and yanks him into the car.*

At last, they reach a welcome banner: LOS ANGELES. *The car stops.* ROSE *gets out with her daughters and the dog and the suitcases and the two stolen boys. The car drives away and as the little band marches off gaily,* ROSE *brings up the rear—with the rich man's tearful little boy, whom she has also stolen.*

SCENE 4

The illuminated placards change to read:

"DON'T CALL US"
LOS ANGELES

The backstage of a vaudeville house. There are odds and ends of scenery, crates, trunks, lights, etc.

MR. WEBER, *the theatre manager, rushes on, followed by* ROSE *and her exhausted brood, who collapse near the wings.*

WEBER: No, Madam Rose, no!

ROSE: Now listen, Mr. Weber, I did not come all the way from Seattle to Los Angeles to take "No" for an answer.

WEBER: You'll take it from me.

ROSE: Because you don't know how to run your theatre. Your business is slipping. You need youth, fresh young talent.

WEBER: Madam Rose, I told you this morning, I told you this afternoon and I am telling you now: if there is anything I hate worse than kids, it's kids on stage!

ROSE: Children, go play in the alley. (*As they go*) Mr. Weber, that was a rotten remark. If you were a gentleman, you'd apologize and book my act.

WEBER: I am not a gentleman.

(*A nice-looking man carrying a suitcase enters. He has a sweetly sad, tired quality*)

ROSE: Oh, deep down, you are. And if you—

WEBER: (*To the man*) Herbie! I been looking for you to get your opinion of the show.

HERBIE: I doubled your crackerjack order, Ed.

WEBER: That bad?

HERBIE: Except for a coupla acts. I left a memo on your desk.

ROSE: Mr. Weber, you left me right in the middle of a sentence.

WEBER: Madam Rose, you're always in the middle of a sentence.

ROSE: But if your show is as bad as this intelligent gentleman says, you could certainly try my act for a few nights. (*To* HERBIE) Couldn't he?

HERBIE: Yeah, he could. You could, Ed.

WEBER: What? ?

HERBIE: Your theatre gets a family audience. They love kids.

ROSE: And my kids are great!

HERBIE: They sure are.

(ROSE *and* WEBER *gape*)

WEBER: How do you know?

HERBIE: I've seen 'em.

WEBER: Where?

HERBIE: In–Seattle. They'd give your show a lift, Ed.

WEBER: Well . . .

ROSE: Listen–

WEBER: Stop pushing. Let me think it over. (*He goes*)

ROSE: (*Pumps* HERBIE'S *hand several times*) Gee–it's hard for me to say thanks!

HERBIE: You just said it.

ROSE: Why'd he listen to you?

HERBIE: Everybody in show business listens to anybody. Besides, I used to book acts into this theatre.

ROSE: Are you an agent?

HERBIE: I was but I'm in the candy business now: I sell to vaudeville houses all over the West.

ROSE: How could you ever leave show business?

HERBIE: When the acts I handled had too little talent, I got sick to my stomach. Ulcers.

ROSE: You're too sympathetic.

HERBIE: Also I went bust. I was always giving them my commission and telling them they got a raise.

ROSE: The good Lord says charity begins at home.

HERBIE: I don't have a home.

ROSE: (*Eyes him*) You're not married?

HERBIE: I had five sisters, and the ugly one didn't get married until a year ago.

ROSE: . . . Why'd you help me just now?

HERBIE: I love kids.

ROSE: Oh.

HERBIE: Also–I saw you before.

ROSE: Where?

HERBIE: Waiting outside Weber's office. You looked like a pioneer woman without a frontier.

ROSE: I don't suppose you'd consider being an agent again.

HERBIE: Would you consider marrying again?

ROSE: How do you know I'm not married now?

HERBIE: I asked your kids about you.

ROSE: Oh. Well, after three husbands, it takes a lot of butter to get you back in the frying pan.

HERBIE: After twenty years of show business—(*Picks up bag*)—you kinda breathe better in the real world.

ROSE: Funny.

(*Music starts*)

HERBIE: What?

ROSE: Us. I like you—but I don't want marriage. You like me—but you don't want show business.

HERBIE: That seems to leave you there—and me here.

ROSE: Oh, that depends on how you look at it. You look at what we don't have, I look at what we do have. (ROSE *sings*)

Funny, you're a stranger who's come here,
  Come from another town.
Funny, I'm a stranger myself here—
Small world, isn't it?
Funny, you're a man who goes traveling
  Rather than settling down.
Funny, 'cause I'd love to go traveling—
Small world, isn't it?

We have so much in common,
  It's a phenomenon.
We could pool our resources
By joining forces
  From now on.
Lucky, you're a man who likes children—
  That's an important sign.
Lucky, I'm a woman with children—
Small world, isn't it?
Funny, isn't it?
  Small, and funny, and fine.

(*Music continues as* WEBER *returns*)

WEBER: Well, I'm not gonna pay you much money.

ROSE: Oh, you'll have to talk about money to Herbie.

WEBER: You handling her act?!

HERBIE: Well–no, I–(*Looks at her. She smiles in appeal and he laughs*)–yeah, I guess I am.

WEBER: (*As he goes*) I'll be in the office.

ROSE: (*Singing happily*)
We have so much in common,
It's a phenomenon.
We could pool our resources
By joining forces
From now on.

HERBIE: Rose . . . is that act of yours any good?

ROSE: Good? It's great–and June is absolutely sensational! Wait till you see it! (*Singing*)
Lucky, you're a man who likes children–
That's an important sign.
Lucky, I'm a woman with children–
Small world, isn't it?
Funny, isn't it?
Small, and funny, and fine.

The Lights Fade Out

SCENE 5

The illuminated placards change to read:

BABY JUNE AND HER NEWSBOYS
LOS ANGELES

The curtains part to show a street drop typical of vaudeville; before it, a newspaper kiosk. The orchestra is a tacky, rickety vaudeville combination that tears into the screeching musical introduction for BABY JUNE AND HER NEWSBOYS. *The* BOYS, *of course, are* LOUISE *and the three little kids* ROSE *stole en route to L.A. Their costumes are cheap representations of newsboy outfits, and they wave papers wildly as they sing.*

NEWSBOYS: (*Singing*)
Extra! Extra! Hey, look at the headline!
Historical news is being made!
Extra! Extra! They're drawing a red line
Around the biggest scoop of the decade!
A barrel of charm, a fabulous thrill!
The biggest little headline in vaud-e-ville:

(*Spoken—to ecstatic drum rolls*)
Presenting—in person—that three-foot-three bundle of dynamite: BABY JUNE!

(*There is the greatest drum roll of them all, and crashing through the "front page" plastered across the kiosk comes* JUNE, *wearing the gaudiest, fanciest, richest costume* ROSE *has been able to whip up. She whirls madly to the footlights, does a split and coyly screeches—*)

JUNE: Hello, everybody! My name is June. What's yours?
(*Then, assisted by the* NEWSBOYS, JUNE *sings a ragtime version of "Let Me Entertain You"*)

Let me entertain you,
Let me make you smile.
  Let me do a few tricks,
  Some old and then some new tricks—
I'm very versatile!
  And if you're real good,
  I'll make you feel good—
I want your spirits to climb.
So let me entertain you
And we'll have a real good time—yessir!
We'll have a real good time!

(*After that, she tap dances wildly about the stage and does every trick* ROSE *has been able to teach, steal and think up. She has a big finish—with the* BOYS *offstage, of course. She does high kicks for her bows and then, breathing as though each gasp were her last, she trips daintily to the footlights and says—*) Thank you so much, ladies and gentlemen. You're *very* kind . . . You know, everybody has someone to thank for their success. Usually, it's their mother; sometimes, it's their father. But tonight, I'd like you all to join me in giving thanks to an uncle of mine—and an uncle of yours. The Greatest Uncle of Them All: OUR—UNCLE—SAM! (*A crash from the orchestra and, as* JUNE *darts behind the kiosk to change her costume, the* NEWSBOYS *and* LOUISE *return—in military costumes. Each of the three* BOYS *represents a wing of our armed forces;* LOUISE *is Uncle Sam. Each child does whatever he can for a specialty;* LOUISE *does a trick step—which she also did in the opening. The* pièce de résistance *is, naturally,* JUNE. *This time she is dressed like a red, white, and blue Statue of Liberty and she is on point, twirling batons for all she is worth. Behind her, the American Eagle pops up over the kiosk; the band plays "The Stars and Stripes." But* ROSE *takes no chances. As* JUNE *twirls herself into a split,* LOUISE *and the* BOYS *fire the rifles they are carrying–and American flags pop up. Wild applause, stopped by* JUNE, *breathing harder than ever*) Mr. Conductor, if you please.

(*The orchestra strikes up again and* JUNE *and her* NEWSBOYS *start a traveling step. As the music builds and gets faster, the name of the city on the illuminated placard changes. It goes from one town to another, finally winding up with* AKRON. *During this, however, the lights on the performers begin to flicker faster and faster–and as* JUNE *and her* BOYS *seem to dance faster and faster, they appear to be flying through space and growing. Actually through the flickering dissolve, they are replaced by another* JUNE, *another* LOUISE, *and other* BOYS–*all in the same costumes as the originals, but all older and bigger. Time has passed. The act is the same, but the cast is older and the placard has changed to read:*

DAINTY JUNE AND HER NEWSBOYS
AKRON

The music ends with a flourish. The older JUNE *blows the same coy kiss and does the same high-kick bow that the* BABY JUNE *did, and–thank heaven–*)

The Lights Black Out

SCENE 6

The placards read:

"HAPPY BIRTHDAY"
AKRON

Two plaster-cracked hotel rooms.

An alarm clock is ringing wildly as the light comes up on the smaller room. It is festooned with clotheslines hung with winter underwear, costumes, etc. On the bare bedsprings of the one bed lies LOUISE, *wrapped up in a blanket of a very distinct pattern. The mattress has been put on the floor and on it, wrapped in another blanket of the same pattern, are three of the* BOYS *in the act. Asleep on two chairs pushed together is the oldest, best-looking and brightest boy in the act:* TULSA. *He is also wrapped in one of the blankets. There is one small window with the shade down.*

As the alarm keeps ringing, LOUISE *reaches out and shuts it off. A moment, then she bolts upright and looks around. Carefully then, she reaches out, sets the alarm off again and lies back quickly.*

YONKERS: (*From the floor. A wiseguy*) Awright, awright!

L.A.: (*Sweet-ass*) We're up, Madam Rose!

YONKERS: (*Looks at clock*) Hey, it ain't even ten o'clock! Turn it off!

L.A.: *Louise!*

TULSA: (*Quietly*) Turn it off, Plug.

LOUISE: (*Sits up and turns off the alarm. Yawns elaborately*) Was that the alarm?

YONKERS: No, it was your mother singing! Shut up!

LOUISE: I was having the loveliest dream. About a special day— My dream book says you dream about a day like that because it maybe really is your—

ANGIE: We wanna sleep!

LOUISE: I just wanted to say—(*She catches* TULSA's *eye. He shakes his head*) I'm sorry. (*Silence. She watches them return to sleep. Then she gets out of bed with a great clomping. No reaction. She goes to the window and considers the shade, finally yanking it up quickly. It rolls up with a tremendous clatter—but not a drop of light comes in: the window is smack up against a brick wall. She sticks her head out, craning her neck like mad to see the sky*) How can you all sleep on such a beautiful day!!

YONKERS: Easy—if you shut up.

LOUISE: Do you suppose the sun is so bright because—(JUNE *enters from the other room. Her hair is in curlers; she wears a frilly nightgown and robe*)

JUNE: You woke up Mother.

LOUISE: (*Whispering*) I didn't mean to, June. But today is . . . well, you know.

JUNE: Today is one day we don't have to travel and we don't have to rehearse.

YONKERS: Which means we could sleep!

LOUISE: Is Momma mad?

JUNE: She's in the bathroom—making coffee. (*To the* BOYS) She says as long as *she's* up, everybody come have breakfast.

LOUISE: June—

JUNE: Honest, Louise! (*She goes out as the* BOYS *groan.* LOUISE *groans back at them*)

LOUISE: I said I was sorry! (*A moment, then she timidly goes into the other room. The light comes up just a trifle as she enters, but the room is very dim. It is much larger than the other room.* LOUISE *speaks, wistfully*) Momma? . . . Momma?

ROSE: (*Calling*) Happy Birthday! (*The bathroom door bursts open and out comes* ROSE *in a battered bathrobe, carrying a small birthday cake with lighted candles. She,* JUNE *and the* BOYS*–who pop up and come crashing through the doorway –sing "Happy Birthday" to* LOUISE*, who is startled and cries happily. One of the boys turns on the lights and the room is bright and gay. There is a big bed and a table near it. Little dogs run about yapping; there are* JUNE'S *cat, a monkey chained to the bed, and bird cages suspended from the chandelier, etc. There are yells of "Surprise! Surprise!" "Blow out the candles," "Make a wish," hugs and kisses, etc.*) Make a wish!

LOUISE: I wish . . . oh, Momma, I wish–

ROSE: Oh! That rotten monkey ate a piece outa the cake! (*Going to the monkey*) Gigolo! Bad, Gigolo, bad bad! (*Then, looking at the blanket* LOUISE *has draped over her pajamas*) Say, that would make a good coat.

(LOUISE *blows out the candles*)

YONKERS: Hey, there's only ten candles on this cake!

ROSE: What do you care? You ain't gonna eat candles.

YONKERS: But she only had ten candles last year.

L.A.: And the year before that.

YONKERS: Come to think of it, she's had ten candles for the last–

ROSE: STOP RIGHT THERE! As long as we have this act, nobody is over twelve and you all know it! Excepting of course me and–where's Herbie? I had a dream–Tulsa, go across the hall and see what's keeping Herbie. The rest of you can give Louise her presents while I see if the chow mein is warmed up.

YONKERS: Chow mein?

LOUISE: It's my birthday!

YONKERS: But chow mein for breakfast??

ROSE: Why not? There's egg roll, ain't there? (*She exits into the bathroom*)

YONKERS: If Madam Rose paid us a salary, we coulda *bought* you presents, Louise–(*He has picked up a box from under the bed*) But it's more fun to clip from the five and dime anyway. (*Hands her the box proudly*) It's a catcher's mitt and a big-league baseball.

LOUISE: Thank you, Yonkers.

L.A.: Here's a real stuffed cat.

ANGIE: I clipped a bowl of goldfish. But they caught me, so I drew a fish instead.

LOUISE: I love it. Oh, June, what a beautiful package!

JUNE: It's a complete sewing set in a velvet-lined basket.

(*They embrace.* TULSA, *who has come back into the room, picks up his present—three second-hand books tied with cord—and puts it into* LOUISE'S *hands*)

TULSA: I should have wrapped them.

LOUISE: (*Very touched*) You don't have to wrap books.

TULSA: Well—happy birthday, Plug.

LOUISE: Happy birthday, Tulsa. I mean, you're welcome.

(ROSE *comes out of the bathroom carrying food. During the following, the others help by arranging the plates and food*)

ROSE: All right, one egg roll apiece and no more.

TULSA: Herbie wasn't in his room, Madam Rose.

ROSE: (*Stops dead*) . . . He wasn't?

TULSA: No.

ROSE: Where could he be?

LOUISE: Momma, can I see my present from you, please?

ROSE: It's from Herbie and me.

LOUISE: It's not from Herbie. He's an agent. It's from *you.*

ROSE: Well, I picked it out, but Herbie paid for it—with his commission for a whole month.

YONKERS: Old Herb makes the same salary we do!

ROSE: Inside, you, and get the coffee! (*Serving food*) Here I am, busting to tell Herbie the dream I had—

LOUISE: Momma—

ROSE: It's really in your honor, coming on the very evening of your birthday. (*To* JUNE) Oh, Baby! You'll love it. You all will. It's—(*Looks toward door, then makes a gesture of dismissal*)—children, it's a *new act!*

YONKERS: That ain't a dream, it's a miracle!

ROSE: In this dream, I saw June singing a song in like a barnyard. And then—a cow came on stage.

TULSA: A cow??

YONKERS: That's pretty sexy.

ROSE: Not a real cow. Sort of a dancing cow—with a great big smile. And that cow—that cow leaned right over my bed and spoke to me!

JUNE: (*Fascinated*) What did the cow say?

(*A knocking on the door*)

KRINGELEIN: (*Offstage*) Madam Rose—

ROSE: I am *not* cooking in here, Mr. Kringelein. That cow—

KRINGELEIN: Open this door!

ROSE: I'm dressing. That cow—

KRINGELEIN: Madam Rose—

ROSE: I'll call you tomorrow when I'm finished. That dear fat cow looked me right in the eye and said: "Rose, if you want to get on the Orpheum Circuit, put *me* in your act." Children, you know what I'm going to do?

YONKERS: You're going to pay that crummy cow and not us!

ROSE: I'm not paying anybody but I'm going to take that cow's advice! I'm going to call the new act: Dainty June and Her Farmboys. I'm going to get more boys. I'm going to put that cow in the act—(KRINGELEIN—*a pompous hotel manager—quietly opens the door of the other room, shuts it behind him and tiptoes to the doorway between the two rooms*)—and Chowsie and the monkey. And Louise's present—if you don't mind, honey—

LOUISE: But, Momma, I don't even know what it is!

KRINGELEIN: (*Coming into the room. Haughtily*) No cooking, Madam Rose?

ROSE: How dare you enter a lady's boudoir without knocking?

KRINGELEIN: (*Advancing*) Where's your hot plate?

ROSE: Where's your search warrant?

KRINGELEIN: (*Heading toward the bathroom*) In all the years I have been running a theatrical hotel—

ROSE: (*Opening the corridor door*) If you don't leave, I'm going to scream!

(*One of the boys darts to block the bathroom door*)

KRINGELEIN: (*Pointing toward a sign*) You know the rules. No cooking. No electrical appliances. No—no pets other than small—(*Pushes the kid out of the way*)—dogs or—(*He opens the bathroom door. A little lamb in rubber drawers runs out between his legs and over to* LOUISE)

ROSE: Happy birthday, darling!

KRINGELEIN: It's a GODDAM ZOO!

ROSE: Profanity in front of my babies! June, get the Bible! Get the Bible!

(*People in bathrobes and wrappers begin to appear in the doorway, flowing into the room*)

KRINGELEIN: You pack up this dirty menagerie and get out!

ROSE: You'll have to throw me out, you rotten ANIMAL-HATER! (*To the others*) That's what he is! Send for the SPCA!

KRINGELEIN: Send for the police! I rented these two rooms to one adult and three children! Now I see one adult! Five pets and one, two, three, four–

ROSE: (*Points to one of the boys*) You counted him twice! (*The kids are running in and out. She turns to the others*) It's a simple little birthday party for my baby–

KRINGELEIN: One, two, three, four–STAND STILL!

ROSE: Chow mein. I'd offer you some but there's only one egg roll–

KRINGELEIN: One, two, three, four, five–how many are sleeping in that room?

ROSE: What room?

KRINGELEIN: (*In the doorway between the two rooms*) THIS room, madam, THIS room!

ROSE: (*Pushing him in*) There isn't a soul in this room.

KRINGELEIN: Now you know what I–

ROSE: (*Closing the door behind them*) Except you and me. (*She lets out a scream as she shoves him down onto the mattress on the floor*) Mr. Kringelein, what are you trying to do?!! (*Throws pillows and blankets on him*) Mr. Kringelein! Stop! Help! Help! (*She wrenches her robe open and staggers back into the other room, where the people get a chair for her and ad lib their concern as* ROSE *continues*) My babies! My babies! *MONSTER!* Thank you, Gladys. A little birthday party–chow mein–a tiny little cake–

(LOUISE, *with her lamb, goes into other room during this.* KRINGELEIN *gets out of the snarl of blankets and exits*)

HERBIE'S VOICE: (*From the hall*) Rose! Rose! Are you all right? (*He enters the room and pushes his way to* ROSE'S *side*) Rose! What's happened? Are you O.K., honey?

ROSE: (*Straightening herself*) Sure! Where have you–(*Then, remembering*) Herbie. Mr. Kringelein, the hotel manager, he –he tried to–to–

HERBIE: (*A cynical eye*) Again? (*He starts for the other room*)

ROSE: Well, I had to do something, Herbie, don't you dare apologize to him!

HERBIE: Where's Louise?

ROSE: A fat lot you care. The child has a birthday–

HERBIE: Does she like her present?

ROSE: I'm surprised you remembered, where've you been? That's what I want to know.

HERBIE: (*Bringing forward a mild little man*) Rose, this is Mr. Goldstone.

ROSE: I ask you, Mr. Goldstone. The child has a birthday once a year. We plan a little party–I'm sorry it's such a small cake and–

HERBIE: Mr. Goldstone is from the Orpheum Circuit.

ROSE: There's only one egg roll and some fried . . . rice . . . and sub . . . gum . . . chow . . .

HERBIE: The act is booked on the Orpheum Circuit.

(*A long pause.* ROSE *stares, numb with a growing happiness. Mechanically, she picks up a plate from the trunk and holds it out*)

ROSE: (*Singing*)
Have an egg roll, Mr. Goldstone,
Have a napkin, have a chopstick, have a chair!
Have a sparerib, Mr. Goldstone–
Any sparerib that I can spare, I'd be glad to share!
Have a dish, have a fork,
Have a fish, have a pork,
Put your feet up, feel at home.
Have a smoke, have a coke,
Would you like to hear a joke?
I'll have June recite a poem!
Have a lichee, Mr. Goldstone,
Tell me any little thing that I can do.
Ginger-peachy, Mr. Goldstone,
Have a kumquat–have two!
Everybody give a cheer–
Santa Claus is sittin' here–
Mr. Goldstone, I love you!
(*Hysterical with excitement*)

Have a goldstone, Mr. Egg Roll,
Tell me any little thing that I can do.
Have some fried rice, Mr. Soy Sauce,
Have a cookie, have a few!
What's the matter, Mr. G.?

Have another pot of tea!
Mr. Goldstone, I love you!
There are good stones and bad stones
And curbstones and Gladstones
And touchstones and such stones as them!
There are big stones and small stones
And grindstones and gallstones,
But Goldstone is a gem.

There are milestones, there are millstones,
There's a cherry, there's a yellow, there's a blue!
But we don't want any old stone,
Only Goldstone will do!

ALL: (*Singing*)
Moonstone, sunstone–we all scream for one stone!
Mervyn Goldstone, we love you!
Goldstone!

(*The lights black out in the larger bedroom and fade in slowly on the small room, where a forgotten* LOUISE *sits with the lamb*)

LOUISE: (*Singing softly*)
Little lamb, little lamb,
My birthday is here at last.
Little lamb, little lamb,
A birthday goes by so fast.
Little bear, little bear,
You sit on my right, right there.
Little hen, little hen,
What game shall we play, and when?
Little cat, little cat,
Ah, why do you look so blue?
Did somebody paint you like that,
Or is it your birthday, too?
Little fish, little fish,
Do you think I'll get my wish?
Little lamb, little lamb,
I wonder how old I am.
I wonder how old I am . . .

The Lights Dim Out

SCENE 7

The placards change to read:

"TABLE FOR TWO"
NEW YORK

The scene is a section of a gaudy Chinese restaurant. HERBIE, *puffing away at a cigarette, sits at a table slightly detached from* ROSE *and* JUNE, *who are wearing coats made of the hotel blankets.* ROSE *is scraping leftovers from the plates into cartons which she eventually gathers into a paper sack. She hums happily.*

ROSE: Hand me Louise's plate.

JUNE: (*Embarrassed*) Mother–

ROSE: We're paying for it, ain't we? You'll get an ulcer like Herbie. Besides, what the dogs don't eat, we will.

HERBIE: Rose, did it ever occur to you there might be somebody in this world who *doesn't* like Chinese food?

ROSE: Don't be silly. Who? (*Hums, scrapes; then softly*) Don't you like it, Herbie?

HERBIE: (*A beat, then he smiles*) Sure, Rose. I love it.

(LOUISE *enters wearing a blanket-coat and holding a little dog that is also wearing a blanket-coat*)

ROSE: Did she?

LOUISE: Yes.

ROSE: (*Baby talk to the dog*) 'Atsa healthy-wealthy lady-wadie.

HERBIE: Oh, God!

JUNE: Herbie's angry: he's chain smoking.

ROSE: Herbie's never angry; it's bad for his stomach. Come on, girls, beddie-bye.

JUNE: It's so early!

ROSE: You're going to audition for Mr. T. T. Grantziger and his Palace Theatre tomorrow and you have to look *young*.

LOUISE: Can I wear a dress?

ROSE: You'd look old in a dress. Besides, you haven't got one.

JUNE: Good night, Uncle Herbie. (*She kisses him*)

HERBIE: Good night, June. (*Stands up to kiss* LOUISE, *who stiff-arms him*) Good night, Louise.

LOUISE: Good night, Herbie. (*She exits with* JUNE)

ROSE: I'll cold-cream their faces and be right back.

HERBIE: The hotel is two doors away! Honestly, you behave as though those girls–Rose! (*This because she is collecting silverware and is about to put it in her bag*)

ROSE: We need new silverware. (*Stops, then puts down the silver. Quietly*) Herbie, how long is it going to take you to get used to me?

HERBIE: How long did it take me to get used to those coats?

ROSE: What's the matter with them? They're real stylish! Louise is very talented with a needle. Herbie, as the good Lord says: an eye for an eye, a tooth for a tooth–(*On this, she sweeps the silver into her bag*) And it serves them right for overcharging. (*Starts to go.* HERBIE *hands her a knife, which she also takes. But then she stops and returns*) They can skip the cold cream for one night. (*Automatically, he gets up and helps her off with her coat.* ROSE, *admiringly*) All this time we've been together, and you still stand up for me!

HERBIE: It's instead of standing up *to* you.

ROSE: O.K., you say we're never alone. I wanted to have dinner tonight, just the two of us, but what was I going to do with the girls? They're babies.

HERBIE: Rose, no matter how you dress 'em, no matter how you smother 'em, they're big girls. They're almost young women–

ROSE: They're not and they never will be!

HERBIE: I'm embarrassed in front of them! When are you going to marry me, Rose?

ROSE: Don't forget to take our scrapbooks to Mr. Grantziger's tomorrow.

HERBIE: When are you going to quit stalling?

ROSE: We got to show him proof that we headlined on the Orpheum.

HERBIE: Rose–

ROSE: All right: so it was a long time ago.

HERBIE: (*Gets up*) Rose, if I walk out, you'll be stuck with the check! (ROSE *pulls* HERBIE *back into the chair*) Honey, don't you know there's a depression?

ROSE: Of course I know! I read *Variety*.

HERBIE: Don't you know what it's doing to vaudeville? Don't you know what the talkies are doing to vaudeville? Don't you know I love you?

ROSE: You think I'd be unfaithful to my husbands if you didn't? But I have to think of my girls and their happiness.

HERBIE: Louise is very happy being the front end of a cow!

ROSE: It's better than being the rear end! Anyway, she loves animals.

HERBIE: She and June should both be in school–

ROSE: And be just like other girls; cook and clean and sit and die! (*To a passing waitress, sweetly*) Honey, could I have a spoon to stir my tea? . . . Herbie, I promised June I'd make her a star and I will. I promised I'd get her on the Pantages Circuit and I did. I promised I'd get her on the Orpheum Circuit and I did.

HERBIE: *I* did! And you promised me that after I did, you'd marry me.

ROSE: I promised her she'd headline on Broadway and–

HERBIE: Didn't you hear what I said?

ROSE: Yes, but I'm ignoring it. (*To the waitress, for the spoon*) Thanks, honey. Herbie, it isn't very polite for a gentleman to remind a lady that she welched. There was no date on that promise–

HERBIE: ROSE, STOP HANDING ME–

ROSE: Your stomach! (*Quickly handing him a pill*) Herbie, why don't you get angry outside, instead of letting it settle in your stomach?

HERBIE: I'm afraid.

ROSE: Of me?

HERBIE: Of me.

ROSE: What do you mean?

HERBIE: If I ever let loose, it'll end with me picking up and walking.

ROSE: Only around the block.

HERBIE: No.

ROSE: Don't say that. (*Sings*)

You'll never get away from me.
You can climb the tallest tree,
  I'll be there somehow.
True, you could say, "Hey, here's your hat,"
But a little thing like that
  Couldn't stop me now.
I couldn't get away from you
Even if you told me to,
  So go on and try!
Just try,

And you're gonna see
How you're gonna not at all get away from me!

HERBIE: What is it? What do you want? There are better agents.

ROSE: Not for me.

HERBIE: And even weaker men.

ROSE: Not for me.

HERBIE: Then what?

ROSE: You. Oh, Herbie, just help me like you been helping. Just let me get June's name up in lights so big, they'll last my whole life.

HERBIE: Rose, what you expect—

ROSE: I'll *get!* And after I get it, I promise I'll marry you. (HERBIE *moves away from the table*) I even promise to keep my promise. (*Silence*) Please, Herbie. I don't want to upset anything before the audition tomorrow. Including your stomach.

HERBIE: (*Singing*)
Rose, I love you,
But don't count your chickens.

ROSE: (*Singing*)
Come dance with me.

HERBIE:
I warn you
That I'm no Boy Scout.

ROSE:
Relax a while—come dance with me.

HERBIE:
So don't think
That I'm easy pickin's—

ROSE:
The music's so nice—

HERBIE:
Rose!
'Cause I just may
Some day
Pick up and pack out.

ROSE:
Oh no, you won't,
No, not a chance.

No arguments,
Shut up and dance.

You'll never get away from me,
You can climb the tallest tree—
I'll be there somehow!

True, you could say "Hey, here's your hat,"
But a little thing like that
Couldn't stop me now.

BOTH:
I couldn't get away from you
Even if I wanted to—

ROSE:
Well, go on and try!
Just try—

HERBIE:
Ah, Rose—

ROSE:
And you're gonna see—

HERBIE:
Ah, Rose—

ROSE:
How you're gonna not at all
Get away from me!

The Lights Fade

SCENE 8

The placards change to read:

GRANTZIGER'S PALACE
NEW YORK

The scene is the stage of a good theatre.

A telephone is ringing as the lights come up on the gold theatre curtains. An attractive, smartly groomed secretary— CRATCHITT—*hurries on, signals toward the top of the theatre, pulls out a telephone attached on a bracket to the proscenium and answers.*

CRATCHITT: Yes, Mr. Grantziger . . . I know, but they're having a little difficulty with their scenery. Well, wait till you see it . . . I am trying, Mr. Grantziger.
(*Rose appears wearing a hat and coat*)

ROSE: (*To the* CONDUCTOR) Now keep the tempo bright. Keep it up.

CRATCHITT: (*On phone*) That's the mother . . . I *have* told her!

ROSE: (*Peering out front*) Hello, Mr. Grantziger. Where is he?

CRATCHITT: (*Pointing*) In his office at the top of the theatre.

ROSE: (*Waving–neighborly*) Hi!

HERBIE: (*Runs on to try to get* ROSE *off*) It's a privilege to audition for you, Mr. Grantziger!

ROSE: (*Just before* HERBIE *drags her off*) You're going to love us! (*They exit*)

CRATCHITT: (*Into the phone*) That's the agent. *He's* nice.

HERBIE: (*Returning*) We're ready now.

CRATCHITT: (*Into the phone*) They're ready now, Mr. Grantziger. (*To* HERBIE) Good luck.

HERBIE: Thank you.

(*They both go off, the lights dim and the curtains part to reveal a corny set of a vaudeville barnyard, complete with haystack.* ROSE'S NEWSBOYS *are now* FARMBOYS, *and they stand with rakes, hoes, etc., in a picturesque tableau* (*!*) *as birds and music twitter the approach of dawn–which comes up violently. The music crashes into the introduction for the* NEWSBOYS' *song –sung, this time, by the* FARMBOYS*–and on cue, the haystack parts for* DAINTY JUNE *to whirl out and down front, where she ends in that same split. This time, she sings and dances with a* COW, *however. During the dance, the front end of the* COW *does a familiar trick step:* LOUISE *is still doing her big specialty*)

FARMBOYS: (*Singing*)

Extra! Extra! Hey, look at the headline!
Historical news is being made!
Extra! Extra! They're drawing a red line
Around the biggest scoop of the decade!
A barrel of charm, a fabulous thrill!
The biggest little headline in vaud-e-ville!
(*Spoken*)
Presenting–in person–that five-foot-two bundle of dynamite:
DAINTY JUNE!

JUNE: Hello, everybody! My name is June. What's yours? (*She sings*)

I have a moo cow, a new cow, a true cow
Named Caroline.

COW: Moo moo moo moo–

JUNE:
She's an extra special friend of mine.

COW: Moo moo moo moo–

JUNE:
I like everything about her fine.

COW: Moo moo moo moo–

JUNE:
She likes to moo in the moonlight
When the moody moon appears.
And when she moos in the moonlight,
Gosh, it's moosic to my ears!
She's so moosical . . .
She loves a man cow, a tan cow who can cow
Her with a glance.

(*The* COW *recites, "Moo moo moo moo," following this and the next two lines*)

When he winks at her, she starts to dance,
It's what grownups call a real romance,
But if we moved to the city
Or we settled by the shore,
She'd make the mooooooooove,
'Cause she loves me more!

(JUNE *and the* COW *continue the dance to the end and exit. The phone rings.* CRATCHITT *comes on to answer*)

CRATCHITT: (*Into the phone*) Yes, Mr. Grantziger. Dainty June, will you come out please? (JUNE *comes on*) Face front, dear. Profile. (ROSE *appears in the other wing*) Yes, Mr. Grantziger. Thank you. That's all.

ROSE: But we have a great dramatic finale!

CRATCHITT: I'm sure. But he's seen quite enough.

ROSE: (*To the* CONDUCTOR) Hit it!

CRATCHITT: But Mr. Grantziger does not want to see any–

(*But even while she is talking, the music crashes in and the* FARMBOYS*–directed by* ROSE*–dance on in Eton suits with high hats and canes, frightening* CRATCHITT *off. They launch into the song and tap dance that always built up to the entrance of the blonde star. And it does this time, for* JUNE *comes on, dazzling, glamorous, singing and dancing for all she–and* ROSE*–are worth.*

During the BOYS' *number, one of the high hats falls off, and* ROSE *dashes out from the wings to retrieve and replace it. At the end of* JUNE'S *song-and-dance with the* BOYS, ROSE *helps the stagehands get the haystack offstage. Behind it is the front of a train which puffs smoke*)

FARMBOYS: (*Singing*)
Broadway, Broadway! We've missed it so!
We're going soon and taking June
To star her in a show!
Bright lights! White lights!
Rhythm and romance!
The train is late so while we wait
We're gonna do a little dance!

(*And they do—as a prelude to* JUNE'S *song*)

JUNE: (*Singing*)
Broadway! Broadway! How great you are!
I'll leave the farm with all its charm
To be a Broadway star!
Bright lights! White lights!
Where the neons glow!
My bag is packed, I've got my act.
So all aboard, come on, let's go!

YONKERS: (*Calls*) All aboard!

ROSE: Woo woo . . . Watch this! It's a train.

FARMBOYS: Let's go!

(*Waving and "good-byes" from everybody. A train effect; the* COW *tries to run after the train*)

JUNE: (*To the* COW) Good-bye, Caroline. I'll write to you.

COW: Moo!

JUNE: Good-bye, Caroline—take care. Don't forget to write! . . . Wait! Stop the train! (*A chord*) Stop everything! I can't go to Broadway with you!

TULSA: Why not, Dainty June?

JUNE: (*To soupy music*) Because everything in life that really matters is right here! What care I for tinsel and glamour when I have friendship and true love? I'm staying here with Caroline!

(*She runs off the train platform and embraces the* COW *to general cheering. A chord from the orchestra—which launches once again into "The Stars and Stripes"; this time the American*

Eagle—and a big one—pops up over the train; JUNE *grabs batons from the platform and twirls them madly as she marches downstage to end in a triumphant split while the* FARMBOYS *fire American flags from their canes.* ROSE *has done it again. The gold curtain closes on this heart-rending sight and the phone is ringing loudly.* CRATCHITT *comes out to answer it.* ROSE *and* HERBIE *come out from the opposite wing to hear the verdict*)

CRATCHITT: Yes, Mr. Grantziger . . . What?? (*To* ROSE *and* HERBIE, *in astonishment*) He liked it! (*On the phone again*) Yes, sir. Yes, sir, if that's what you want. (*Hangs up and turns to* ROSE) If you and your tribe will come up to the office—I'll make out the contracts. (*She shoots a peculiar look up to Mr. Grantziger's office and exits as* ROSE *shouts up*)

ROSE: You won't be sorry, Mr. Grantziger! (HERBIE *yanks her off, but she is right back to add*) This is gonna make ya!

The Lights Black Out

SCENE 9

An ornately Gothic office with two doors. JUNE *is playing the piano madly while* LOUISE *hurls herself around the room in an improvised "interpretive" dance, possibly explaining it to* JUNE *in a phrase or two. The ringing of the telephone does not stop them. Then through one of the doors comes* CRATCHITT. *The girls stop their artistic efforts, embarrassed, but the piano keeps playing: it is electric.* CRATCHITT *turns it off and answers the phone.*

CRATCHITT: Yes? . . . No. Mr. Grantziger's busy. He's gone down to the stage. (*Hangs up*) Your mother and her friend are just reading over the contract. They won't be much longer. She's gotta eat *some*time . . . Say, woman to woman, how old are you?

JUNE: Nine.

CRATCHITT: Nine *what?*

JUNE: Nine going on ten.

CRATCHITT: How long has that been going on?

(HERBIE *comes in carrying a contract, followed by* ROSE)

HERBIE: Miss Cratchitt, I think Mr. Grantziger made a mistake in this contract.

CRATCHITT: (*Gaily*) So do I. (*The phone rings.* CRATCHITT *picks it up*) Yes?

ROSE: You happy, girls?

LOUISE: Yes, Momma.

CRATCHITT: No. (*She hangs up*)

HERBIE: Miss Cratchitt, we were auditoning for Grantziger's Palace. This contract is for Grantziger's Variety.

CRATCHITT: That's right.

HERBIE: But the Variety is way down on Twelfth Street.

CRATCHITT: He'll give you a visa to get there. (*The phone rings again*) Yes?

HERBIE: I'd like to talk to Mr. Grantziger.

CRATCHITT: (*Hangs up quickly*) No. Listen, I told you: he's down on the stage.

HERBIE: (*Going toward the second door*) This the way?

CRATCHITT: You can't disturb him. He's still holding auditions.

HERBIE: Then I'll wait.

CRATCHITT: Look, friend. Strictly between us, if I were you I'd sign that contract. There's only one item in that act of yours that the Boss likes: Dainty Little June. He thinks she can be an actress.

ROSE: (*As* JUNE *stands up*) He's right.

CRATCHITT: Can be–*if*.

HERBIE: If what?

CRATCHITT: If she goes to school for a solid year and takes lessons. He's ready to pay for everything–on one condition. (*To* ROSE) You stay away.

ROSE: Stay away? I'm her mother!

CRATCHITT: You said it, I didn't.

HERBIE: What about the act?

CRATCHITT: (*Shrugs*) One week at the Variety.

ROSE: But June *is* the act! How is it supposed to go on without her?

HERBIE: Rose, we could–

ROSE: (*To* CRATCHITT) How are Louise and I supposed to live?

CRATCHITT: You might get a job, dear.

ROSE: I have a job, dear, and I do it damn well! My daughters are my job and I have two of them!

LOUISE: Momma, if June–

ROSE: June is my baby! I'm her mother!

(*The phone rings*)

CRATCHITT: (*Answering*) Yes–

ROSE: (*Taking it away and putting the receiver down on the table*) Don't you dare answer the phone when I'm yelling at you! Nobody knows June like I do and nobody can do for her what I can!

JUNE: Momma, this is my chance to be an actress. Mr. Grantziger can make me a star!

ROSE: You *are* a star! And I made you one! Who's got clippings like she has? Look at 'em! Books full of 'em! She don't need lessons any more than she needs Mr. T. T. Grantziger!

CRATCHITT: There isn't a person in show business who doesn't need Mr. Grantziger!

ROSE: Take a good look at *this* person!

HERBIE: Rose—

ROSE: They're so smart in New York!

CRATCHITT: New York is the center of everything.

ROSE: New York is the center of New York! There's a whole country full of people who *know* people!—who know what a mother means to her daughter! It's hicks like you who don't know! And you want to know something else? Grantziger's a hick! He'll get no place!

HERBIE: Rose—

ROSE: He's trying to take my baby away from me, that's what he's trying to do! Well, over my dead body, he will! (*And she storms out the door to the "stage," with* HERBIE *and* CRATCHITT *calling and running out after her. A pause, then* LOUISE *picks up the phone left off the hook*)

LOUISE: (*Quietly*) No. (*Hangs up*) Momma's just talking big, June. She won't really—

JUNE: Yes, she will.

LOUISE: Maybe Mr. Grantziger will—

JUNE: No, he won't . . . Well, that's show business.

LOUISE: Aren't you happy someone like Mr. T. T. Grantziger thinks you can be a star?

JUNE: You're funny.

LOUISE: Why?

JUNE: You're never jealous.

LOUISE: Oh. Well, I don't have any talent. I don't really mind—except Momma would like it better if I did.

JUNE: I guess that's what she likes about me. Momma's no fool. I'm not a star.

LOUISE: You are.

JUNE: *I'm not!* Mr. Grantziger could make me one if she only didn't— (*Her voice cracks.* LOUISE *puts an arm around her*)

LOUISE: Momma can make you a star, too.

JUNE: (*In control again, moves away*) Momma can do one thing: she can make herself believe anything she makes up. Like with that rhinestone finale dress *you* sewed for me. Momma wants publicity so she makes up a story that three nuns went blind sewing it! Now she believes it. She even believes the act is good.

LOUISE: Isn't it?

JUNE: (*Cold anger*) It's a terrible act and I hate it! I've hated it from the beginning and I hate it more now! I hate pretending I'm two years old. I hate singing those same awful songs, doing those same awful dances, wearing those same awful costumes—I didn't mean it about the costumes.

LOUISE: No. You just meant you're too big for them now.

JUNE: Do you ever feel like you didn't have a sister?

LOUISE: . . . Sometimes.

JUNE: It's Momma's fault.

LOUISE: You can't blame everything on Momma.

JUNE: *You* can't maybe. I wish she'd marry Herbie and let me alone.

LOUISE: Herbie doesn't want to marry her. All he cares about is the act.

JUNE: Honest, Louise.

LOUISE: Well, he's an agent!

HERBIE: (*Enters and tosses the contract back on the desk*) Your mother isn't feeling well. I'm going to take her back to the hotel . . . Don't worry, I'll get you a good booking. (*He exits*)

LOUISE: I wish Momma would marry a plain man . . . so we'd all be together.

(*She sings*)

If Momma was married we'd live in a house,
As private as private can be:
Just Momma, three ducks, five canaries, a mouse,
Two monkeys, one father, six turtles and me . . .
If Momma was married.

JUNE: (*Singing*)

If Momma was married, I'd jump in the air
And give all my toeshoes to you.
I'd get all these hair ribbons out of my hair,
And once and for all, I'd get Momma out, too . . .
If Momma was married.

LOUISE:

Momma, get out your white dress!
You've done it before—

JUNE:

Without much success—

BOTH:

Momma, God speed and God bless,
We're not keeping score—
What's one more or less?
Oh, Momma, say yes
And waltz down the aisle while you may.

LOUISE:

I'll gladly support you,
I'll even escort you—

JUNE:

And I'll gladly give you away!

BOTH:

Oh, Momma, get married today!

JUNE:

If Momma was married there wouldn't be any more—
"Let me entertain you,
Let me make you smile.
I will do some kicks."

LOUISE:

"I will do some tricks."

JUNE:

Sing out, Louise!

LOUISE:

Smile, baby!
Momma, please take our advice:
We aren't the Lunts.

JUNE:

I'm not Fanny Brice.
Momma, we'll buy you the rice,
If only this once

BOTH:

You wouldn't think twice!

It could be so nice
If Momma got married to stay.

LOUISE:
But Momma gets married–

JUNE:
And–

LOUISE:
Married–

JUNE:
And–

LOUISE:
Married

BOTH:
And never gets carried away.
Oh, Momma,
Oh, Momma,
Oh, Momma, get married today!

The Lights Dim Out

SCENE 10

The placards change to read:

"DREAMS OF GLORY"
BUFFALO

A theatre alley, with steps that lead up to the stage door.

Without music, TULSA *is dancing, rehearsing a routine with a broom for a partner.* HERBIE *comes out the stage door and watches until* TULSA *sees him and stops in embarrassment.*

HERBIE: That's pretty fancy footwork, Tulsa. Why don't you show it to Madam Rose?

TULSA: I'm not that good, Herbie. It's just foolin' around.

HERBIE: (*As, unseen by him,* LOUISE *enters*) You started "foolin' around" about three months ago. Just after Mr. Grantziger canceled our booking.

TULSA: Well . . .

HERBIE: Why, Tulsa?

LOUISE: He's just had more time, that's all. Like that two-week layoff in Albany.

TULSA: And the layoff in Rochester.

LOUISE: And the layoff in Niagara Falls.

HERBIE: Oh. I thought you were maybe worried about the act.

TULSA: Oh, no, Herbie.

HERBIE: Because the way things are pickin' up—why, I wouldn't be surprised if you kids got paid! (*To* LOUISE) Matter of fact, they're good enough right now for me to treat you to an ice cream soda.

LOUISE: No, thank you.

HERBIE: Chow mein?

LOUISE: Momma doesn't like us to eat just before a show.

HERBIE: (*After a moment, gently*) Louise—there's one thing your momma knows that I wish you did: I like her. (*He starts toward the stage door*)

LOUISE: Herbie . . . (*He stops. A moment, then she shakes her head*) Nothing.

HERBIE: Tulsa, if you or any of the boys have any problems, you bring 'em to me.

TULSA: Sure, Herbie. (HERBIE *exits*)

LOUISE: You didn't tell him, did you? I mean that you're rehearsing a dance team act?

TULSA: How'd you know I was?

LOUISE: I saw you practicing Monday after the matinée, with your broom for a partner. I was up in the flies.

TULSA: Louise—

LOUISE: Oh, I won't tell anybody, Tulsa! I'm very secretive. Just like you. (*Takes his hand*) See? That's what this means in your palm. And this means you make up dreams—just like me.

TULSA: (*Moves away*) What do you make up dreams about, Louise?

LOUISE: . . . People.

TULSA: Oh, I do that too.

LOUISE: Yes, but yours are about a partner for your act.

TULSA: She's gonna be more than a partner, I hope. I mean I dream . . . well, you know . . . (*He starts to dance around*)

LOUISE: What would she have to be like, Tulsa? A wonderful singer and dancer, I guess.

TULSA: No. I'm going to do most of that. I don't mean I'm going to hog it but—they always look at the girl . . . in a dance team. Especially if she's pretty.

LOUISE: Makeup can help. And costumes.

TULSA: I've got the costumes all figured out. A blue satin tux for me—

LOUISE: With rhinestone lapels—

TULSA: You think?

LOUISE: I'll sew them on.

(*Music*)

TULSA: (*As the music starts*) O.K. Thanks. Well, I pretend I'm home getting ready for a date. I'm combing my hair. I take a flower. Put it in my lapel. Then I spot the audience. (*He sings*)

Once my clothes were shabby,
Tailors called me "Cabbie,"
So I took a vow,
Said "This bum'll
  Be Beau Brummel."
Now I'm smooth and snappy,
Now my tailor's happy.
  I'm the cat's meow,
  My wardrobe is a wow:
Paris silk, Harris tweed,
There's only one thing I need.
Got my tweed pressed,
Got my best vest,
  All I need now is the girl!
Got my striped tie,
Got my hopes high,
  Got the time and the place, and I got rhythm—
  Now all I need's the girl to go with 'em!
If she'll
Just appear, we'll
  Take this big town for a whirl,
And if she'll say, "My
Darling, I'm yours," I'll throw away my
  Striped tie and my best-pressed tweed—
  All I really need
  Is the girl!

(LOUISE *has been watching with yearning and now, as* TULSA *begins to dance, the yearning increases. He explains his dance to her as he goes along*)

TULSA: I start easy . . . Now I'm more—debonair . . . Break! And I sell it here . . . I start this step—double it—and she appears! All in white! (*He reaches out his hand to the invisible partner, and* LOUISE–*who has gotten up–holds out her hand, tentatively. He is unaware of her, unaware of her hopes, unaware she is following him about, visualizing herself as the partner for him*) I take her hand–kiss it–and lead her out on the floor . . . This step is good for the costumes . . . Now we waltz. Strings come in. And I lift her! . . . Again! . . . Once more! . . . Now the tempo changes; all the lights come up; and I build for the finale! (*At last, he starts a step that* LOUISE *knows, and, clumsily, she starts to do it with him. At last, he notices and shouts*) That's it, Louise! But do it over here! Give me your hand! Faster! Now Charleston right! Again! Again! Turn!

(*She is dancing joyously, her happiness making up for her awkwardness. They end together–in triumph.* L.A. *runs in from the stage door in costume for the Cow Act and whistles to them. They get up and race into the theatre*)

The Lights Dim Out

SCENE 11

The placards change to read:

"TERMINAL"
OMAHA

The scene is a railroad platform. It is a misty night. Baggage is piled near ROSE *and* HERBIE. YONKERS *and* ANGIE *are there.*

ROSE: Don't lower yourself to argue, Herbie. If those rats want to quit the act, let them quit. If they want their train tickets home, give them their bus tickets home. (*Crossing*) What's keeping those girls?

HERBIE: There's plenty of time, Rose.

ROSE: (*Going to the end of the platform, peering out*) And you say they're big enough to take care of themselves.

HERBIE: Look, fellas, I know we've had a couple of layoffs in the–

YONKERS: It ain't that, Herbie.

HERBIE: Then what is it?

YONKERS: We're–too old.

HERBIE: (*Sotto voce*) Would you be too old if Madam Rose and I could see our way clear to increasing your salary?

ROSE: (*A bellow from clear across the stage*) Increase what salary?!

ANGIE: Herbie's been paying us–

YONKERS: (*Kicks him*) Moron!

ROSE: (*Coming back*) Herbie . . .

HERBIE: How long is it going to take you to get used to me, Rose?

ROSE: (*Gently*) Button your coat. (*To the* BOYS) Ingrates! You take the bread out of that man's mouth and spit it in his face! Well, as the good Lord says, "Good riddance to bad rubbish." Give 'em their tickets, Herbie. They were both rotten in the act anyway.

HERBIE: O.K. (*He takes out tickets as she peers out for the girls*)

YONKERS: Thanks, Herbie. Only we'd like tickets for all the fellows.

HERBIE: . . . All the fellows?

YONKERS: Well, they asked us.

HERBIE: You're all leaving?

ANGIE: Yes, sir, Herbie.

ROSE: Something's funny. Something's very funny here.

HERBIE: Why, Angie? (*Silence*)

ROSE: What's this all about? (*Silence*)

HERBIE: O.K. If you're all going, you're all going. But why, Yonkers–

(LOUISE *runs on, a note in her hand*)

ROSE: Where've you been? Where's June? (*Silence*) Louise, where's June? (LOUISE *holds out the note*) Don't give me any of your poems to read now. Answer me!

LOUISE: June wrote this. To you.

ROSE: Wrote what? What's she writing me for?

LOUISE: Momma, *read it!*

(ROSE *looks at her, then takes the letter. She reads it, then sits and stares at it, not moving, looking like a dead woman through the following*)

ANGIE: (*To* HERBIE) She eloped.

YONKERS: She didn't elope, stupid. They got married three weeks ago.

HERBIE: Who got married?

YONKERS: June and Tulsa. Only they hadda wait till their act was ready before they took off.

ANGIE: It's a keen act. Ain't it, Louise?

LOUISE: I didn't see it.

YONKERS: We ain't rats, Herbie. We just knew that without June–

HERBIE: Where'd they go?

ANGIE: Well, first they got a club date in Kansas City . . .

YONKERS: (*Kicks him*) Big mouth! Could we have the tickets now, please, Herbie? We gotta get moving. See, we fixed up an act of our own and–

HERBIE: (*Suddenly, looking at* ROSE) Get moving!

L.A.: Don't be sore, Herbie. Geez, it ain't our fault the act's washed up. (*He and* ANGIE *start off*)

HERBIE: Hey, fellas. Good luck!

YONKERS: (*Brightens*) Thanks. Good luck to you, Herbie.

ANGIE: Good luck, Louise.

LOUISE: Good luck.

YONKERS: Good luck, Madam Rose. (*Silence*) Come on, Angie.

(*They go off.* LOUISE *stands a good distance from* ROSE, *who has not moved.* HERBIE *goes to* ROSE *and speaks softly, tenderly*)

HERBIE: Rose . . . Honey, listen. I can go back in the candy business. It's steady: fifty-two weeks all year every year. I'll work my fingers to the bone; I'll do twice what I did before and that was pretty fair. Rose, I could be a district manager and we could stay put in one place. We could have our own house. Louise could go to school. Rose? Rose, honey, you still got Herbie. You can marry me and I promise you, you won't have one single worry the rest of your life. Rose, don't you want that?

LOUISE: (*A burst*) *Yes! Momma, say yes!*

(HERBIE *turns and looks at her. A moment, then she runs across the platform into his arms. He holds her tight and rocks her*)

LOUISE: Herbie . . .

HERBIE: You read palms, I read minds. It's O.K. (*Going back to* ROSE, *brighter*) It's going to be fine now, honey. Everything happens for the best. O.K., the act's finished. But you and me and our daughter, we're going to have a home–say, we got a cow for the backyard! Why, we are going to be the best damn–

(*During the last,* ROSE *slowly gets up and brushes* HERBIE *aside as though she has not heard a word. The letter hangs from her hand as she walks–as though in a trance–to* LOUISE. *Her voice is flat and deadly calm*)

ROSE: I'm used to people walking out. When my own mother did it, I cried for a week. Your father did it, and then the man I married after him did it, and now—(*Unaware, she tears the letter in half*) Well this time, I'm not crying. This time, I'm apologizing. To you. I pushed you aside for her. I made everything only for her.

LOUISE: No, Momma.

ROSE: (*Looks at the torn letter*) But she says I can't make her an actress like she wants to be. (*Puts torn letter in her dress. Her voice gets stronger, takes on color*) The boys walk because they think the act's finished. They think we're nothing without her. (*Now beginning to build in volume and strength and passion*) Well, she's nothing without me! I'm her mother and I made her! And I can make you now! And I will, my baby, I swear I will! I'm going to *make* you a star! (*She is so carried away now by her own determination and emotion that she does not see the look that has come over* LOUISE'S *face. With enthusiasm—*) I'm going to build a whole new act—all around you! It's going to be better than anything we ever did before! Better than anything we even dreamed!

HERBIE: Rose!

ROSE: (*Like a gallant, joyous express train*) You're right, Herbie! It *is* for the best! The old act was getting stale and tired! But the new one?! Look at the new star, Herbie! She's going to be beautiful! She *is* beautiful! Finished?! We're just beginning and there's no stopping us this time! (*Her face alive with fight and plans and happiness, she roars into a violently joyous song about how great everything is going to be*)

I had a dream,
A dream about you, Baby!
It's gonna come true, Baby!
They think that we're through,
But,
Baby,
You'll be swell, you'll be great,
Gonna have the whole world on a plate!
Starting here, starting now.
  Honey, everything's coming up roses!
Clear the decks, clear the tracks,
You got nothing to do but relax!
Blow a kiss, take a bow—
  Honey, everything's coming up roses!
Now's your inning—

Stand the world on its ear!
Set it spinning,
'N that'll be just the beginning!
Curtain up, light the lights,
You got nothing to hit but the heights!
You'll be swell,
You'll be great,
I can tell—
Just you wait!
That lucky star I talk about is due!
Honey, everything's coming up roses for me and for you!

You can do it,
All you need is a hand.
We can do it,
Momma is gonna see to it!
Curtain up, light the lights,
We got nothing to hit but the heights!
I can tell,
Wait and see!
There's the bell,
Follow me,
And nothing's gonna stop us till we're through!
Honey, everything's coming up roses and daffodils,
Everything's coming up sunshine and Santa Claus,
Everything's gonna be bright lights and lollipops,
Everything's coming up roses for me and for you!

(HERBIE *and* LOUISE *stand silent, numb, as she plows on, singing triumphantly*)

The Curtain Falls

ACT TWO

SCENE 1

Before the curtain, the illuminated placards read:

MME. ROSE'S TOREADORABLES
TEXAS

It is desert country. Late afternoon. The rear end of a touring car sticks out from one side. From the other, part of a tent.

ROSE: (*Calling*) Are you ready, Louise?

LOUISE: (*Off*) Yes, Momma.

ROSE: Ready, girls?

GIRLS: (*Off*) Yes, Madam Rose.

ROSE: Now don't let the past discourage you. Remember: you're artists of the theatre! (*She imitates a trumpet call*) Madam Rose's Toreadorables!

(*A crash of Spanish-type music and an assortment of* GIRLS *lurches on in ghastly, homemade señorita costumes. What they lack in talent—everything—they make up for in enthusiasm. And what do they sing? The same opening as the* NEWSBOYS *and* FARMBOYS, *their predecessors*)

GIRLS: (*As* ROSE *yells for them to "Sing out!"*)

Extra! Extra! Hey, look at the headline!
Historical news is being made!
Extra! Extra! They're drawing a red line
Around the biggest scoop of the decade!
A barrel of charm, a fabulous thrill!
The biggest little headline in vaud-e-ville!

ROSE: Now sell it! Sell it! And give it atmosphere!

GIRLS: Presenting—in person—that five-foot-four bundle of dynamite: SEÑORITA LOUISE!

ROSE: Come on, Louise, come on!

(LOUISE *comes on in a glittering, gaudy toreador costume—and a blonde wig. She makes a pathetic attempt to twirl and do a split like* JUNE *before saying—*)

LOUISE: Olé, everybody! My name's Louise. What's yours? (*She looks up at* ROSE *in appeal. A pause. Then—*)

ROSE: Well—it's coming along.

LOUISE: Momma, I'm just no good at it.

ROSE: Don't be silly. Let's try the finale. After all, if you have a good strong finish, they'll forgive anything! (*The* COW *runs on*) You're late . . . Now, girls, make it stirring! (*She again imitates a trumpet call—and the music launches into—surprise—"The Stars and Stripes."* LOUISE *tries vainly to twirl that same baton*) Pick your feet up, Louise, pick 'em up! (HERBIE *strolls on wearily in time for the finale: the* GIRLS *remove their Spanish shawls and turn them around to form an American flag. But the stars are on bottom, there is much switching and when the last note is ended, the stars are in place but some of the stripes go the wrong way.* ROSE *looks at* HERBIE'S *face*) I guess they're tired. Up to your tent, girls. Get ready for bed.

AGNES: (*One of the girls*) Good night, Madam Rose.

ROSE: Good night, Louise. (ROSE *takes the blonde wig from* LOUISE *and kisses her good night. Then she calls to the others*) Don't forget to write your mothers. For money! (*To* HERBIE) How'd you make out in town?

HERBIE: Not even a lodge hall.

ROSE: They're too damn un-American down here, that's the trouble. (*Starts to brush the wig*) We better talk about heading up north after I tell the girls their bedtime story.

HERBIE: Once upon a time, there was a prince named Ziegfeld–

ROSE: It could happen! . . . Anyway, everybody needs something impossible to hope for.

HERBIE: Rose . . . Why do you make Louise wear that wig in the act?

ROSE: It makes her look more like–a star.

HERBIE: And why do you keep that cow?

ROSE: Herbie, if that cow goes, I go! (*As* LOUISE *enters behind them in pajamas*) The act can be fixed. If I was doing it for June, I'd have it all set.

LOUISE: But you're not, and I'm not June.

HERBIE: Now, Plug, nobody expects you to–

LOUISE: (*Quietly*) Herbie, I love you very much but you always let everything slide.

ROSE: He does not!

LOUISE: (*Quietly*) Momma, I love you so much I've tried hard as I could. The act is rotten and I'm rotten in it.

ROSE: How do you like that? Typical of a kid!

LOUISE: I've been wanting to say this–

ROSE: Always impatient!

LOUISE: Momma–

ROSE: A few break-in dates don't go too hot so she–

LOUISE: (*Grabs the wig out of* ROSE'S *hand and throws it away*) Momma, I am not June! I am not a blonde! I can't do what she did!

HERBIE: She's not asking you to.

LOUISE: Maybe you want to stay in show business–

ROSE: Maybe??

LOUISE: Well, I thought–

ROSE: That's our whole life! What've we been working for ever since you were a baby? . . . Maybe I've been on the wrong track with you and the material, but like the good Lord says, you gotta take the rough with the smooth, Baby. And like

I always said, you're lucky—because you don't have to take it alone. Right, Herbie?

HERBIE: Right.

ROSE: You got Herbie for brains; we got you for talent; and you both got me—to yell at. (*She sings*)

Wherever we go,
Whatever we do,
We're gonna go through it together.
We may not go far.
But sure as a star,
Wherever we are, it's together!

Wherever I go, I know he goes.
Wherever I go, I know she goes.
No fits, no fights, no feuds and no egos—
Amigos, together!

Through thick and through thin,
All out or all in,
And whether it's win, place or show,
With you for me and me for you
We'll muddle through whatever we do
Together, wherever we go!

(ROSE *holds out her hands to them. They start to sway together*)

ALL:

Wherever we go,
Whatever we do,
We're gonna go through it together.

ROSE:

Wherever we sleep—

LOUISE:

If prices are steep—

HERBIE:

We'll always sleep cheaper together.

ROSE:

Whatever the boat I row, you row—

HERBIE:

A duo!

ROSE:
Whatever the row I hoe, you hoe—

LOUISE:
A trio!

ROSE:
And any IOU I owe, you owe—

HERBIE:
Who, me? Oh,
No, you owe!

LOUISE:
No, we owe—

ALL:
Together!
We all take the bow,

ROSE:
Including the cow,

ALL:
Though business is lousy and slow.

ROSE:
With Herbie's vim, Louise's verve—

HERBIE and LOUISE:
Now all we need is someone with nerve—

ROSE: (*Giving them a look*)
Together—

HERBIE and LOUISE:
Together—

ROSE:
Wherever—

HERBIE and LOUISE:
Wherever—

ALL:
Together wherever we go!

ROSE:
If I start to dance,

HERBIE and LOUISE:
We both start to dance,

ALL:

And sometimes by chance we're together.

ROSE:

If I sing B flat–ohhhh–

LOUISE:

We both sing B flat–ohhhh–

HERBIE:

We all can be flat–ohhhh–

ALL:

Together!

HERBIE: (*Twirling a pie plate*)

Whatever the trick, we can do it!

LOUISE: (*Twirling a pie plate*)

With teamwork we're bound to get through it!

ROSE: (*Twirling a third pie plate*)

There really isn't anything to it–

You do it.

(*They toss the plates in the air as if to catch them–the trick is a disaster*)

I knew it–

ALL:

We blew it–

Together!

We go in a group,

We tour in a troupe,

We land in the soup

But we know:

The things we do, we do by threes,

A perfect team–

(LOUISE *heads off in the wrong direction*)

ROSE:

No, this way, Louise!

Together–

HERBIE and LOUISE:

Wherever–

ALL:

Together wherever we go!

(AGNES *enters with letters*)

AGNES: Here are the letters, Madam Rose.

ROSE: That's a good girl. Now go to bed, Agnes.

AGNES: Now that I'm an actress, it's Amanda.

ROSE: Whatever it is, go to bed.

AGNES: Could I please ask Herbie a question first?

HERBIE: Sure.

AGNES: Herbie . . . do you think we'll ever work again?

ROSE: Of course we will!

HERBIE: I'll get us a booking, Amanda.

AGNES: Thank you, Herbert. (*Turns to go, then sees the wig*) Oh, Louise, your hair!

LOUISE: It's yours if you want it.

AGNES: Gee, I always wanted to be a blonde!

ROSE: (*Taking the wig from her*) Then get some peroxide and a toothbrush. Wigs are expensive. (AGNES *goes off.* ROSE *looks at the wig*) You know, we could get a nice refund on this—if we'd ever paid for it.

HERBIE: How about getting a gallon of peroxide and a carton of toothbrushes?

ROSE: What for?

HERBIE: Make 'em all blondes!

ROSE: I was only joking, Herbie.

HERBIE: So was I, honey.

LOUISE: But why not do it?

ROSE: They're children, Louise!

LOUISE: They're young girls, Momma. With blonde hair, they could be pretty young girls.

HERBIE: With a stretch of imagination, they might be. It'd sure jazz up the act and make it easier to sell. We could call it, Madam Rose's Blonde Babies.

ROSE: Baby Blondes!

LOUISE: Nothing with babies.

HERBIE: Hollywood Blondes.

LOUISE: Yes!

ROSE: All blondes except you—because you're the star!

LOUISE: If I'm the star, it should be: *Louise* and Her Hollywood Blondes.

ROSE: (*Looks at her—then*) *Rose* Louise and Her Hollywood Blondes.

LOUISE: O.K.

ALL: (*Singing*)
Through thick and through thin,

All out or all in
And whether it's win, place or show,
With you for me and me for you
We'll muddle through whatever we do
Together, wherever we go!

The Lights Dim Out

SCENE 2

The placards change to read:

"THE BOTTOM"
WICHITA

Backstage. At one side, there is a large theatre dressing room. A long corridor leads to the "stage" (presumably on the opposite side, offstage). The corridor continues (unseen) behind the dressing room, thus leading to other, unseen dressing rooms. A large door opens into the theatre alley.

During the scene, snatches of brassy music come from the "stage." Right now, there is silence as the alley door opens and AGNES *and three or four other* GIRLS *in the act come in. Each is awed; each carries bags, props, part of the* COW; *and each has hair of the same, exact hideous shrieking shade of white blonde.*

AGNES: (*In happy awe*) It's a real live theatre!

MAN'S VOICE: (*Off*) Let in the traveler!

MARJORIE MAY: (*Looking off*) With a real live stage! Don't you love it?

AGNES: Oh, Marjorie May, we've arrived at last!

(*They squeal and hug each other as* LOUISE*—in slacks—enters from the alley, also carrying bags, props and the* COW'S *head*)

DOLORES: Louise, look!

AGNES: A real live theatre!

MAN: (*Off*) Will you kill them floods?

LOUISE: (*Happily*) It's just like opening day rehearsals used to be! Oh, Momma's going to love it!

MAN: (*Off*) Will you kill them floods?

PASTEY: (*Off*) Will you shut your hole?

AGNES: (*Shocked*) She isn't going to love that!

MARJORIE MAY: (*Pointing to the "stage"*) Or *that!*

AGNES: What kind of a act is that?

PASTEY: (*Off*) O.K., jailbait! (*He enters: a young snot, with clipboard and pencil*) You the Hollywood Blondes?

LOUISE: Yes. I'm—

PASTEY: You're late.

LOUISE: Well, our car broke down and—

PASTEY: Skip it. Some of you dogs can use this dressing room, and the rest of you the one past it. The first one you share with Tessie Tura, the Texas Twirler—

LOUISE: My mother doesn't—

PASTEY: The second with Mazeppa, Revolution in Dance. Shake it up. (*Starts to go, then turns back*) So you're the act that's supposed to keep the cops out. Boy, you must be lousy! (*He exits. A moment of deflation. Then—*)

LOUISE: It's a real live theatre, all right.

AGNES: He reminds me of my brother.

LOUISE: Don't start sniveling, Amanda. Take the cow and anything else you can carry in there. Marjorie May, you take the other girls into the second room and start unpacking. (*She starts with props and bags for the big dressing room. The others pick up their stuff and start after her. Thus, all their backs are turned and they do not see two girls who enter from the "stage" to get a gilded spear from a stack leaning against the corridor wall. Each of these bored females wears a gladiator helmet, gladiator boots and carries a large shield in front of her. As they return to the "stage," we see that the shield is the only thing that covers them. They are nude. In the dressing room,* LOUISE *and* AGNES *have started to hang up costumes*)

AGNES: Oooh, look at this! (*She is holding up a jeweled G-string, which she proceeds to try on as a necklace*) That Tessie Tura must be a very fancy lady!

LOUISE: (*Trying to clean a messy dressing table*) She must also be a pig!

(ROSE *enters through the alley door, carrying more bags and props*)

ROSE: Louise?

LOUISE: In here, Momma. (*Goes to the door*) Let me help you.

ROSE: (*Looking around*) Baby, we're back in a theatre! We're back in a real theatre!

LOUISE: Momma, where's Herbie?

ROSE: He went around front to check our billing. Louise, I need you here to help me with the rest of the things. (*To the* STAGEHAND, *who crosses*) Good morning! (*As she turns back, she stops dead and her mouth drops open.* LOUISE *turns and she gapes too. One hand on the curtain at the edge of the "stage," throwing wild bumps savagely, is* TESSIE TURA, *a blowsy stripper wearing almost nothing besides a G-string, which does not bump with her. She looks up, during her exercises*)

TESSIE: It ain't weighted right, goddamit. (MAZEPPA—*a pseudo-exotic grand stripper dressed as Queen of the Gladiators—writhes past* TESSIE *to get her spear from the wall*) It scratches hell outa me and it just don't bump when I do.

MAZEPPA: Maybe there's something wrong with your bumper. (*She exits*)

TESSIE: Big joke. (*To* ROSE) I'm out there bumpin' my brains off with no action and she's bein' witty! (*To* AGNES, *who is gaping at her from the dressing room doorway*) Hey you with the neck! I paid six bucks for that G-string. Back where you found it!

AGNES: Yes, ma'am. (*She curtsies and scurries back in as* TESSIE *goes off.* ROSE *looks at* LOUISE)

ROSE: (*Low*) Get the bags. Get the cow. Get the props.

LOUISE: Now, Momma—

ROSE: You don't know what kind of people are out there on that stage. You don't know what kind of a theatre this is.

LOUISE: Yes I do. It's a house of burlesque.

ROSE: A house of burlesque. Do you know what that is? Filth, that's what! I tell you, when your friend Herbie shows his face—

LOUISE: Momma, I'm sure Herbie didn't know—

ROSE: (*Picking up the props, etc., which keep dropping*) Not much, he didn't know! Agnes!

LOUISE: He got the booking over the telephone—

ROSE: Agnes!

LOUISE: We were all so happy—

ROSE: (*Storming to the dressing room door*) AGNES, DAMMIT!

AGNES: Madam Rose, you know my name is—

ROSE: Your name is Agnes and I want you and the other girls out of this hell hole in two seconds flat.

AGNES: But, Madam—

ROSE: March!

AGNES: Yes, ma'am. (*She comes out.* ROSE *goes inside and starts to pack up what has been unpacked*)

LOUISE: (*To* AGNES) Wait in the other room. (AGNES *disappears behind the dressing room as* LOUISE *goes in*)

ROSE: You take the rear end of the cow, I'll take the front and what bags we can't carry, your friend Herbie can damn well pick up and carry himself. (LOUISE *shuts the door.* ROSE *turns and looks at* LOUISE *leaning against it. Her voice is low and cold*) Now you listen to me, Louise. Just because you think your friend Herbie can do no wrong—

LOUISE: This has nothing to do with Herbie.

ROSE: You don't know what burlesque is.

LOUISE: Yes I—

ROSE: NO YOU DON'T. No daughter of mine is going to work in burlesque. And no daughter of any woman I know—

LOUISE: Then where *are* we going to work?

ROSE: I'd rather starve!

LOUISE: Momma, how much money do we have? Including what's left of their allowances, how much money do we have?

ROSE: Something'll turn up.

LOUISE: It *has* turned up and *this is it!* We're flat broke, Momma. We've *got* to take this job . . . Even if you wanted to quit and go home, we'd have to take it.

(ROSE *stops in the act of taking a costume off a hook. A pause. Then abruptly, heavily, she sits*)

ROSE: I had a dream . . .

LOUISE: Momma . . .

ROSE: You'll like this one. I had it over a week ago, only I didn't want to tell. I was home in Seattle, and the Cow came into my room. But she wasn't dancing and smiling this time. She was wheezing and sad-like. She came over to the bed and looked at me and she said: "Rose, move over."

LOUISE: I'm sorry, Momma.

ROSE: (*Smiles*) Why? She didn't ask you to move over.

LOUISE: I mean I'm sorry I'm not good enough. In the act.

ROSE: Oh, it's the act that ain't good enough, Baby. Or something.

(HERBIE *hurries in through the alley door*)

HERBIE: Rose?

LOUISE: (*Opens the dressing room door*) In here, Herbie.

HERBIE: (*Runs in*) Rose, I didn't know, believe me.

ROSE: I do, honey. What the hell! The money's good, it's only two weeks, and maybe by that time, something'll turn up. Right?

LOUISE: Right.

HERBIE: You're a nice girl, Rose. Thank you.

ROSE: Well—that's show business. (*She starts to unpack again*)

LOUISE: One good thing: I'll bet we got top billing.

HERBIE: Well—actually, they kind of had us lost in the middle. I thought last was better, so it says: "*And* Rose Louise and Her Hollywood Blondes." And I'm making them put a box around it.

ROSE: Forget the box, Herbie.

LOUISE: But, Momma, if—

ROSE: You don't know what they say in the business. But Herbie does. They say when a vaudeville act plays in burlesque, that means it's all washed up. (*Pause*) Herbie . . . nothin's gonna turn up for us, is it?

HERBIE: No.

ROSE: I guess it is a pretty rotten act.

HERBIE: It ain't the act, honey. I been telling you, vaudeville's dead . . . stone cold dead.

ROSE: Well—we sure as hell tried!

HERBIE: You sure as hell did. Right?

LOUISE: Right.

HERBIE: Well, I better get the cues ready. (*He goes to the door*)

ROSE: Herbie—how about marrying me?

HERBIE: (*Turns around. A moment. Then, casually*) Sure!

ROSE: I love you, you know.

HERBIE: I know.

LOUISE: Do it today!

ROSE: Not while we're in burlesque!

HERBIE: The day we close.

ROSE: It's a deal. (*They shake hands and suddenly kiss*) I do, Herbie, I do.

HERBIE: So do I, Rose.

(PASTEY *barges in. During the following,* TESSIE *appears in the corridor*)

PASTEY: Hey, Rose Louise, where the hell's your music and light cues?

HERBIE: I'll be right with you.

PASTEY: (*Snotty*) You Rose Louise?

HERBIE: Yeah, I'm Rose Louise.

PASTEY: Things're looking up. Well, I got a show to open, Rose Louise, so move your ass.

(*Before* PASTEY *can get out,* HERBIE *has grabbed him, whirled him around and cracked him in the face. Then, holding him by the scruff of his neck—*)

HERBIE: Listen, you little punk. For the next two weeks, you're gonna speak like a Sunday School teacher. You have something in this theatre you probably never saw before. A lady. (*Points him toward* ROSE) Look at her. That is a lady. (*Points him toward* LOUISE) That is also a lady. Every girl in this damn act is a lady, you understand?

PASTEY: Yes, sir.

HERBIE: Now get on stage and I'll give you those cues when I'm ready.

PASTEY: Yes, sir. Excuse me, ma'am. (*He goes out and off.* ROSE *kisses* HERBIE. *He goes out but is stopped in the corridor by* TESSIE)

TESSIE: Oh, sir? Won't you give *me* your protection? I'm a lady, too! (*On the last, a vivacious grind and bump. The bumper flips*) Hey! The goddam thing worked! (*She goes into the dressing room as* HERBIE *goes off to the "stage"*) If you ladies will excuse me—

ROSE: We're very busy.

TESSIE: In *my* dressing room.

ROSE: In *your* dress—

LOUISE: (*Overlapping*) Momma—

TESSIE: You're damn right. And I don't like sharing it any more than you do. Particularly with a troupe of professional virgins.

ROSE: We are not—

TESSIE: All right, so you're acrobats.

ROSE: We happen to be headliners from the Orpheum Circuit. We were booked into this theatre by mistake.

TESSIE: Weren't we all! (*Reaching for a costume* ROSE *has unpacked*) Say! Who made that?

LOUISE: I did. I make all our costumes.

TESSIE: My! Look at them ladylike little stitches! That miserable broad who makes my gowns must be usin' a fish hook!

LOUISE: What do you pay her?

TESSIE: Twenty-five bucks a gown and I provide the material.

ROSE: Thirty.

TESSIE: She's new in the business!

ROSE: Thirty.

TESSIE: Who're you? Her mother?

ROSE: Yes.

TESSIE: Thirty. I'll get the material after the matinée.

ROSE: It's a deal. (*To* LOUISE) Where's your toreador costume?

LOUISE: The girls must have it in the dressing room with them.

ROSE: God knows what else they've got in there with them! (*She exits*)

TESSIE: You know, from the way that dame walks, she would have made a damn good stripper in her day.

(*A burly man,* CIGAR, *the manager enters*)

CIGAR: Hey, Tessie, I'm short a talking woman.

TESSIE: Tough titty.

CIGAR: The new comic won't use a chorus girl.

TESSIE: Then let him use Mazeppa. (*To* LOUISE) Everyone else has. (*She laughs at her joke*)

CIGAR: Now you know Mazeppa's got her Gladiator Ballet just before his spot.

TESSIE: Cut the ballet. It stinks anyway.

CIGAR: Be a sport. I'm in a bind.

TESSIE: You're always in a bind in this flea-bitten trap. I'm a strip woman, slob. I don't do no scenes. Now screw! (*To* LOUISE) You ever hear of a strip woman playing scenes? Well, you play stock in a dump like this, you gotta expect to be insulted.

CIGAR: The work is steady, ain't it?

TESSIE: But you bring in a new star for each show, don't you?

CIGAR: Tessie, it's just a few lines—

TESSIE: Fat boy, save your bad breath.

CIGAR: I'll give you ten bucks extra.

TESSIE: Nah.

LOUISE: (*As* ROSE *returns*) I can read lines.

CIGAR: Who're you?

LOUISE: Rose Louise. Of Rose Louise and Her Hollywood Blondes.

ROSE: Wait a minute. What kind of lines?

CIGAR: You in her act?

ROSE: Well, not exactly.

CIGAR: Shut up. (*To* LOUISE) How are your legs?

TESSIE: Great! And I'll learn her the scenes.

CIGAR: O.K. Ten bucks. (*He goes*)

LOUISE: It's money, Momma.

ROSE: (*Going to* TESSIE) What is she going to be saying out there on that stage?

TESSIE: The same burlesque junk that's been said since the Year One. Say, where you been all your life?

ROSE: (*Proudly*) Playing vaudeville.

TESSIE: Where? In the Vatican?

ROSE: You name a big city and we've played it!

LOUISE: My grandpa says we've covered the country like Gypsies!

TESSIE: Yeah? Well, you may be a Gypsy, Rose Louise—say, that ain't a bad name if you ever take up stripping—

ROSE: She won't!

TESSIE: No! But you'll let her feed lines to a bum comic for a lousy ten bucks a week!

ROSE: That's training: she's going to be an actress! This is only temporary! After we finish here, she goes right back to vaudeville! (*She turns away—and sees* LOUISE's *look. Embarrassed, she sits*)

TESSIE: (*Quietly*) Back to vaudeville, my eye. There ain't any vaudeville left except burlesque.

LOUISE: We know.

TESSIE: *You* know. You better wise *her* up.

LOUISE: (*Sudden burst*) She's wise! (*Holding* ROSE) She's a damn sight wiser than any of you!

TESSIE: (*Shrugs*) Like mother, like daughter. O.K. (ROSE *exits with the makeup kit and heads for the other dressing room.* TESSIE *turns to* LOUISE, *perplexed*) Say, whose feelings did I hurt? Yours or hers?

LOUISE: (*Smiles*) Neither. We'll both be fine.

TESSIE: I hope so, because sharing a dressing room is like sleeping together. And if you don't get along with—

(MAZEPPA *comes storming in with* ELECTRA, *another stripper*)

MAZEPPA: Miss Tura, I'll thank you not to give the boss any notion that I would ever play scenes. And one more disparaging remark about my ballet will find this bugle right up your—

TESSIE: Please: there's a lady present!

MAZEPPA: Where?

TESSIE: Open your eyes instead of your mouth. Gypsy, meet Miss Mazeppa—and Miss Electra.

ELECTRA: Say, you're even younger than I was when I began stripping.

LOUISE: I'm not going to strip.

MAZEPPA: (*Belligerent*) Something wrong with stripping?

LOUISE: No. I just meant I don't have any talent.

TESSIE: You think they have? I myself of course was a ballerina. But take it from me, to be a stripper all you need to have is no talent.

MAZEPPA: You'll pardon me, but to have no talent is not enough. What you need is an idea that makes your strip special.

(*During the following number, each of the three strippers demonstrates the gimmick that has made her a "star"*)

MAZEPPA: (*Sings*)

You can pull all the stops out
Till they call the cops out,
Grind your behind till you're banned,
But you gotta get a gimmick
If you wanna get a hand.

You can sacrifice your sacro
Workin' in the back row,
Bump in a dump till you're dead.
Kid, you gotta get a gimmick
If you wanna get ahead.

You can—!, you can—!, you can—!!!
That's how burlesque was born.
So I—! and I—! and I—!!!
But I do it with a horn!

(*She demonstrates: bumping and grinding like mad while she blows army calls on her bugle*)

Once I was a schlepper,
Now I'm Miss Mazeppa
With my Revolution in Dance.
You gotta have a gimmick
If you wanna have a chance!!

ELECTRA: (*Singing*)

She can—!, she can—!, she can—!!!
They'll never make her rich.
Me, I—! and I—! and I—!!!
But I do it with a switch!

(*She demonstrates: punctuating* her *bumps and grinds with electric lights which illuminate her strategic points*)

I'm electrifying,
And I'm not even trying.
I never have to sweat to get paid.
'Cause if you got a gimmick,
Gypsy girl, you've got it made.

TESSIE: (*Singing*)

All them—!s and them—!s and them—!!!s

Ain't gonna spell success.
Me, I—! and I—! and I—!!!
But I do it with finesse!
(*And she demonstrates: a broken-down version of ballet climaxed with the same eternal bumps and grinds*)
Dressy Tessie Tura
Is so much demurer
Than all them other ladies because
You gotta get a gimmick
If you wanna get applause!

ALL:
Do somethin' special;
Anything that's fresh'll
Earn you a big fat cigar.
You're more than just a mimic
When you got a gimmick—
Take a look how different we are!
(*They bump and grind: what else?*)

ELECTRA:
If you wanna make it,
Shake it till you break it.

TESSIE:
If you wanna grind it,
Wait till you've refined it.

MAZEPPA:
If you wanna bump it,
Bump it with a trumpet!

ALL:
Get yourself a gimmick
And you too
Can be a star!

The Lights Black Out

SCENE 3

The scene is the backstage corridor.

STAGEHAND: (*To* PASTEY, *who is crossing*) Kill the floods and bring in number four!

PASTEY: I tole ya we ain't usin' number four this show, ya pinhead!

HERBIE: (*Runs on with a little bouquet*) Hey, you seen Amanda?

PASTEY: She must be packin'. Ain't your act through today?

HERBIE: (*Joyously*) You bet it is! Through–finished–over!

(AGNES *comes on with a suitcase.* HERBIE *crosses to her*)

PASTEY: (*To the* STAGEHAND) Will you kill number four? (*He exits*)

HERBIE: (*To* AGNES) I've been hunting for you. Here. (*He gives her the bouquet*)

AGNES: Oh, Herbie, it's like for a funeral!

HERBIE: It's for the wedding! Madam Rose and I want you to be bridesmaid, Amanda.

AGNES: It's Agnes again.

HERBIE: (*Hugs her*) You'll be happier as Agnes, Amanda. (*Dashing off*) See you out front.

TESSIE: (*Runs on*) Oh, you're leaving and I didn't get you a memento!

AGNES: My career as an actress is over. I have to go home and let my hair grow out.

TESSIE: Ya poor kid.

PASTEY: (*Off*) Tessie!

TESSIE: Well–for the last time: (*Doing a grind*) Meet ya round the corner (AGNES *joins in*) in a half-hour.

(AGNES *breaks down on* TESSIE'S *bosom*)

PASTEY: TESSIE!

TESSIE: TESSIE! I'm coming, ya creep!

(*She hurries to the wings leading to the "stage." A farewell wave to* AGNES, *a lift to her sagging bosoms–and she floats off like a ballerina*)

The Lights Black Out

SCENE 4

The dressing room looks emptier. Most of ROSE'S *belongings have been packed.*

The lights are different. The corridor is darker but streaked with colored light coming from the "stage," where the show is on: a production number, to judge from the music which is continuous under the scene. HERBIE*–in a different suit–*ROSE *and* LOUISE*–in coats–are finishing packing.* ROSE *is very subdued;* HERBIE *is very up;* LOUISE *keeps watching* ROSE.

HERBIE: (*To* ROSE) Why aren't you nervous? I've never been so nervous in my whole life!

LOUISE: (*Hands* ROSE *a baton*) You've never been married before.

HERBIE: Well, your mother's never been married like she's going to be this time. For keeps and forever—to me! Ain't you a *little* nervous, honey!

ROSE: Sure.

LOUISE: She's a little sad, too. About the girls.

HERBIE: (*Admiring the marriage license*) Say, the minister doesn't keep this, does he? I want to have it framed. Framed and hanging in our living room.

LOUISE: (*Holding the* COW *head*) What about this, Momma?

ROSE: Take it.

HERBIE: Rose—

LOUISE: (*Putting the* COW *head on the suitcase*) We can hang her up in the living room, too, Herbie. Over the mantelpiece.

HERBIE: Rose honey, it ain't that I don't know what you're feeling. Or that I don't know I oughta shut up. But I'm so goddamn happy, I can't! (CIGAR *and* PASTEY *enter the corridor from the "stage." Their dialogue and* HERBIE'S *are simultaneous.* ROSE *listens to* HERBIE) I'm finally getting everything I wanted! Even a fancy ceremony with bridesmaids. Of course, what the minister's going to say when he gets a load of all that hair, I don't know. But the hell with him! (ROSE'S *attention shifts to the hall*) All he's gotta say is, Do you, Rose, take him, Herbie?

CIGAR: I don't know why the hell I stay in this business. If it ain't one damn headache, it's another!

PASTEY: Ssh! They'll hear you out front.

CIGAR: It's my theatre, ain't it? Let 'em! Last show, no talking woman. Show before that, no second banana. If that crazy broad wasn't here, why did you start the performance?

PASTEY: She don't go on till next to closing, and she said she was only goin' next door to the drugstore.

(HERBIE *and then* LOUISE *become aware that* ROSE *is standing dead still, listening. They stand, watching her, tense, afraid*)

CIGAR: What'd they arrest her for? Shoplifting?

PASTEY: No, soliciting.

CIGAR: She always was greedy. Well, cut the spot.

HERBIE: Honey, do you think we can invite the minister for a drink after?

PASTEY: It's the star strip!

CIGAR: Cut it.

PASTEY: They'll yell murder if it's only the same bags they've been seeing the last eight weeks. The star's the novelty!

CIGAR: Whaddya want me to do? Let you strip?

(ROSE *throws down whatever she is holding and walks swiftly out of the dressing room into the corridor*)

ROSE: My daughter can do it. (*They look at her. She steps back, as though afraid of herself*) Rose Louise.

PASTEY: Since when?

ROSE: Since she's been here to see how little there is to it.

CIGAR: She didn't look bad in them scenes.

ROSE: She'll look great in her own gowns.

PASTEY: What's the gimmick?

CIGAR: She's young. And you got any better ideas?

PASTEY: (*As he exits*) Well, she better get ready right damn now.

ROSE: It's the star spot.

CIGAR: You telling me?

ROSE: That means the star salary.

CIGAR: If we keep her.

ROSE: You will. She's going to be wonderful! (CIGAR *goes off as* ROSE *runs excitedly into the dressing room and begins opening a suitcase.* HERBIE *and* LOUISE *stand dead still, watching*) I knew something would turn up! Where's that dress you were gonna make for Tessie? It'll work perfect for you! . . . (*Gets the dress out*) Well, get your makeup on, there ain't much time! . . . Oh, silly, you're not really gonna strip! All you'll do is walk around the stage in time to the music and drop a shoulder strap at the end. (*Takes out the makeup*) You're a lady–like Herbie says you are! You just parade so grand they'll think it's a favor if you even show them your knee–Louise, it's the star spot! I promised my daughter we'd be a star! (*Still,* LOUISE *just stands.* ROSE *speaks quietly now*) Baby, it's all right to walk out when they *want* you. But you can't walk out when after all these rotten years, we're still a flop. That's quitting. (*A brief burst*) We can't quit because we're a flop! Louise . . . don't be like June. Just do this, and then we can walk away proud because we made it! Maybe only in burlesque, maybe only in second-rate burlesque at that–but let's walk away a star! (LOUISE *unbuttons her coat.* ROSE *hugs her, helps her, then rummages for the dress as* LOUISE *begins quickly to get ready*) I guess there ain't time to finish the dress, but we can pin it easy. Hey, here's some material for extra panels! Didn't I always say you were born lucky? You can unpin the panels and drop 'em every once in a while so they'll think you're taking something off. (*Slowly,* HERBIE *folds up the license and puts it in his pocket as he walks out of the room, and disappears in the corridor.* LOUISE *is making up feverishly*) Not too much makeup, Baby. Young and girlish. Pure. Don't smear that junk all over your face like they do. You just keep your mouth the way the Lord made it . . . No rouge. No beauty marks. You be a lady: grand, elegant . . . with a classy, ladylike walk. My God! Shoes! . . . Well, we can use the old silver ones we borrowed from Tessie. (*She takes them from her own suitcase*) They'll do for this performance . . . Come on. Get into 'em. (*As* LOUISE *does*) Oh, no—your hair's wrong. You can't let it just hang like spaghetti. Put it up! Like Momma's! It's got to have class! Puff it out in front. Thank God, the Lord gave us good color—and that you washed it this morning . . . Say, do you think we should put a couple of feathers in? (*Tries some*) No, that's what they all do. (*Tosses them aside*) Jewelry? No. Let Tessie and the others wear all the vulgar junk they want.

PASTEY: (*Rushes in*) She almost ready? She goes on in five minutes.

ROSE: (*Pushing him out*) She'll be there—she'll be there! Come on, get into the dress. (LOUISE *exits through another door, presumably leading into a bathroom, to change into the strip dress.* ROSE *picks up a pair of long white gloves*) Whose are these? Oh—my wedding present from Tessie. Good for a lady. Wear 'em . . . Now, what else? . . . Music! (*Flips through sheet music in the suitcase*) "Spanish"—"Cow"—"Military"? (*Shakes her head*) No. Say, you can do June's "Let Me Entertain You" number! I'll mark it for the conductor to repeat two choruses slow—no, two and a half choruses, and sing out, Louise! You just walk and dip . . . you're a lady; you make 'em beg for more—and then *don't* give it to them! . . . Now—have I forgotten anything? Anything else? (*On this last,* HERBIE *enters the dressing room. He is almost shaking with anger and his effort to control it*) Where you been? Out front?

HERBIE: No, I got sick to my stomach, and threw up.

ROSE: But you feel better now.

HERBIE: No.

ROSE: Herbie—I just had to.

HERBIE: That's why I'm leaving.

ROSE: I apologize.

HERBIE: No, let me. For my resemblance to a mouse. No: to a worm–the way I've crawled after you. No more, Rose. I won't. I was even going to crawl away from you–because my stomach started to turn over at the idea of coming back and telling you we're finished.

ROSE: Tell me tomorrow–after we're married.

HERBIE: We're never getting married, Rose.

ROSE: We certainly are! First thing in the morning, we'll–

HERBIE: *Never,* Rose. Not if you went down on your knees and begged. I still love you–but all the vows from here to doomsday . . . they couldn't make you a wife. I want a wife, Rose. I'm going to be a man if it kills me.

ROSE: (*Angrily*) So you're killing *me!*

HERBIE: Nobody can kill you.

ROSE: You think I got a bullet-proof vest? You're jealous, that's what you are! Like every man I've ever known! Jealous–because my girls come first. Well, they always did and they always will!

HERBIE: Then why did June leave?

ROSE: I don't wanna hear her name!

HERBIE: She didn't want the act any more than Louise wants this!

ROSE: Louise does!

HERBIE: She'll leave like June did!

ROSE: Never! She's gonna be a star.

HERBIE: She's gonna be a star! If it kills *you and her,* she's gonna be a star *someplace! She's* gonna be a star. Where are *you* gonna be, Rose? Where are you gonna be when *she* gets married?

ROSE: She won't be getting married for years–she's a baby!

HERBIE: Sure!

ROSE: Anyway, her career will always come first. (*She sits, looks over the music defiantly*)

HERBIE: That's right. That-is-right. (*He picks up his suitcase, and starts out*)

ROSE: Herbie . . . why does everybody walk out?

HERBIE: Maybe Louise won't. (*He pats her shoulder. Without looking up, she reaches for his hand and holds it there*)

ROSE: Don't leave, Herbie . . . I need you.

HERBIE: . . . What for?

ROSE: A million things.

HERBIE: Just one would be better. Good-bye, honey. (*Silence. He kisses the top of her head*) Be a good girl. (*Quietly, he goes out the door. Music starts*)

ROSE: You go to hell! (ROSE *sits staring and* PASTEY *runs in*)

PASTEY: Get her music to the conductor and you better stand by me for the light cues. I just hope you know what you're doing. (PASTEY *races out.* ROSE *touches the place where* HERBIE *kissed her*)

ROSE: (*Singing*)

Lucky, you're a man who likes children–
That's an important sign.
Lucky, I'm a woman with children–
Funny,
Small and funny–

(ROSE *gets up and slowly walks to the white gloves. She has them in her hand, and is staring at them as* LOUISE *comes out and takes the gloves from her.* ROSE *watches her start to put them on, then speaks quietly, as though dazed*)

ROSE: I'll get the music to the conductor. Just remember–you're a lady. (*With anguished determination*) And you-are-going-to-be-a-star!

(*Music in hand, she walks out, leaving* LOUISE *alone before a long mirror in the dressing room. As she draws on the white gloves, the music ends and the light in the corridor goes very dark. There is a soft glow on the mirror as dark figures scurry through the corridor outside saying: "Let's watch from the wings." "No, I'm going out front." "What's she gonna do?" "She isn't the type." "She'll quit halfway through." "How do you know?" "She'll never make it." "Come on, let's get a good place." "I'm scared for her." During this, the dressing room has been rolling off, leaving only the mirror. The only light on the stage is the glow of the mirror bulbs; the only figure is* LOUISE. *She looks at herself, goes close to the mirror to check her makeup, then suddenly stops. She touches her body lightly, moves back, straightens up and stares at her reflection. Very softly–*)

LOUISE: Momma . . . I'm pretty . . . I'm a pretty girl, Momma! (*Very grand, very proud, very beautiful, she turns from the mirror and begins to walk away from it, as though she were going in the direction of the "stage." The mirror moves off, the lights come up and we are "on the stage." The curtain is upstage; strip music can be heard, a dim stripper can be seen through the curtain.* ROSE, *who is peering through, turns around and sees* LOUISE)

ROSE: (*Softly*) You look beautiful!

TESSIE: (*Runs on with an old fur stole which she wraps around* LOUISE) For luck, honey!

ROSE: Are you nervous, Baby?

LOUISE: . . . What?

ROSE: I said, Are you nervous?

LOUISE: No, Mother.

(*The offstage music ends; there is applause as the weary stripper comes on from behind the curtain, looks at* LOUISE *and goes off.* PASTEY *grabs a microphone*)

PASTEY: Wichita's one and only Burlesque Theatre presents–

LOUISE: (*Nervous after all*) Momma–

PASTEY: Miss–Gypsy–Rose–Lee!

TESSIE: (*Correcting him angrily*) Louise!

(*But he shrugs. Everyone exits but* LOUISE, *who stands alone before the curtain. A roll of the drum and lights reveal the curtain as a scrim. Through it, we can see the glow of the strippers' runway. Another drum roll: the curtains part and* LOUISE *steps forward. Another drum roll: a spotlight hits her and her head goes back as though she has been blinded. Blinding floodlights then shine directly into the eyes of the audience; then a total blackout. When the lights go on again,* LOUISE *is downstage, facing the audience before a curtain the exact replica of the one upstage. Her head is back a bit, her eyes closed, the spotlight bright on her. The small burlesque band in the pit begins "Let Me Entertain You."* LOUISE *can barely start singing.* ROSE, *from the wings, calls out*)

ROSE: Sing out, Louise!

(*As* LOUISE *sings she seems to get more confidence, even to begin to enjoy herself. And her voice finally rings out true and clear. And then, unsure of exactly what to do, she begins to walk*)

CIGAR: (*From the wings*) Don't just walk! Do something!

ROSE: Dip! Just dip!

(LOUISE *does. After a moment*)

CIGAR: Take something off!

ROSE: A glove! Give 'em a glove!

(*And* LOUISE *does take off a glove. As she walks more, she begins to relax, to grow, to enjoy—until just before she exits, she looks at the audience humorously, and lowers one shoulder strap. The lights on the curtains change; the placards roll to read:*

DETROIT
GYPSY ROSE LEE

And an ANNOUNCER'S *voice comes over the speaker*)

ANNOUNCER: The Alhambra Theatre of Detroit is happy to present that lovely newcomer, Miss Gypsy Rose Lee!

(*And out she comes, in another dress, with one glove off, one shoulder strap down, as though the strip were continuous. But now she is more poised, more glinting with humor—but always, a lady. Again, the curtain lights change; again the placards roll, to read this time:*

PHILADELPHIA
GYPSY ROSE LEE

And we hear an ANNOUNCER'S *voice*)

ANNOUNCER: Philadelphia's Diamond Burlesque takes pleasure in presenting that lovely new star, Miss Gypsy Rose Lee!

(*The strip continues in another gown, with a big feather hat added this time.* LOUISE *has grown again and no matter what she does, is, as always, the lady. And one never seen in the nude. A great drum roll; the lights on the curtains change; the placards now read:*

GYPSY ROSE LEE
MINSKY'S

And another ANNOUNCER'S *voice*)

ANNOUNCER: Minsky's World Famous Burlesque takes great pride and pleasure in presenting the Queen of the Strip Tease, the Incomparable Miss Gypsy Rose Lee—in our Salute To Xmas!

(*And the curtains open for a brief flash of a garish, loud, corny production number with nudes on a Christmas tree and slithering show girls. The* pièce de résistance *is a Christmas present brought on by comics dressed as Santa Claus. They open it—and out comes* GYPSY*—glittering like a diamond in a sewer. Her head high, she somehow has elegance as she reprises her song. At the end, she pulls the curtain across the* *stage with her, shutting out the production, shutting out everything but The Lady of the Strip Tease,* MISS GYPSY ROSE LEE)

The Lights Fade

SCENE 5

The placards change to read:

"MOTHER'S DAY"
MINSKY'S

A dressing room.

The basic crumminess of the room is all but hidden by the trappings its occupant has installed: gleaming bottles; a nude statue festooned with feathers and a rhinestone G-string; souvenirs; costumes, etc.

ROSE *is hammering a spike into the wall, as she talks to* RENÉE, *the maid, who barely listens. During the following,* ROSE *hangs the* COW'S *head up on the spike.*

ROSE: Sure I saw that sign! If I can read the fine print in our contracts, I can certainly read letters two feet high: "THE MOTHER OF MISS GYPSY ROSE LEE IS NOT ALLOWED BACKSTAGE AT THIS THEATRE." You know what I did with that sign? (*Puts a string of beads on the* COW'S *horn*) I tore it off the wall, spread it on the floor, and set Chowsie III down on it. That dog's a trouper: *she* knew what to do! . . . It'll take more than signs to keep me out of a theatre!

(*The door opens and* LOUISE *enters in her strip costume. She is singing until she sees* ROSE. *And the* COW *head*)

LOUISE: (*Angrily*) Now look, Mother—(RENÉE *quickly comes with a negligee and a calming look.* LOUISE *points to the* COW) Renée, that comes down. (*She sits at the dressing table and swiftly sets about repairing her makeup*)

ROSE: You need *something* to remind you your goal was to be a great actress, not a cheap stripper.

LOUISE: June's the actress, Mother. And I'm not a cheap stripper. I'm the highest paid in the business.

ROSE: You won't be ready when vaudeville comes back.

LOUISE: No, I'll be dead. (*Then, indicating the furs she has thrown on a chair*) Renée, tell Sam he can lock up the animals for the night.

ROSE: I'll do it.

LOUISE: Mother, please. (*To* RENÉE) And bring my press agent in as soon as he gets here.

RENÉE: O.K. (*She goes out with the furs and the* COW *head*)

ROSE: Since when do you fix your face before you take your bath?

LOUISE: A photographer's coming.

ROSE: Where's he going to photograph you? In the tub?

LOUISE: Eventually.

ROSE: (*Shocked*) Louise!

LOUISE: It's for *Vogue*.

ROSE: (*Elated*) Louise!! Think I ought to freshen up?

LOUISE: They only want me in the tub, Mother. (*The telephone rings*)

ROSE: I've got it.

LOUISE: (*Beating* ROSE *to it*) Hello? . . . (*Intimately*) Hello. No, it's difficult right now.

ROSE: I'm not leaving.

LOUISE: Let's meet at the party . . . Yes, I promise. *À bientôt*. (*She hangs up*)

ROSE: *À bien* what?

LOUISE: I guess I am being a little much–but, Momma, I love it.

ROSE: . . . Who's giving the party?

LOUISE: Some friends.

ROSE: In the old days, I was always invited first.

LOUISE: Mother–

ROSE: (*Very grandly*) I wouldn't go even if I *did* have something to wear. I got more important things to do–like thinking up an idea for a new strip for us.

LOUISE: Mother, we're still stuck with that wind machine you bought to *blow* my clothes off . . . Actually–I'm putting in a new number on Saturday.

ROSE: . . . What is it?

LOUISE: You'll see.

ROSE: I'll see.

LOUISE: Let me surprise you.

ROSE: These days, you're just one big surprise after another . . . Well, we better go shopping tomorrow for the material for the gown.

LOUISE: I've got a French lesson tomorrow.

ROSE: Oh. Well, I'll go alone. Got any particular color in mind?

LOUISE: Mother–I've already started to make the gown.

ROSE: Oh . . . Well, I better run your bath for you.

LOUISE: You don't have to. That's what I've got a maid for.

ROSE: LET ME DO SOMETHING, DAMMIT!

LOUISE: (*Very quietly*) What, Mother?

ROSE: A million things. I'm not a baby.

LOUISE: Neither am I.

ROSE: Don't you take that tone to me. Your sister used to get that edge to her voice—

LOUISE: I am not June!

ROSE: You're not Louise, either!

LOUISE: And neither are you!

ROSE: Oh, yes I am! More than you, Miss Gypsy Rose Lee—with your dirty pictures for *Vogue!*

LOUISE: Mother—

ROSE: And your maids and your press agents and your fancy friends with their fancy parties!

LOUISE: They happen—

ROSE: Your loud-mouth mother ain't invited to those goddam parties. They laugh at her!

LOUISE: They don't—

ROSE: THEY DO! And don't think I don't know that's one reason why you don't want me backstage: so I won't hear 'em laugh. Well, it's *them* you oughta keep out, not me! Because they're laughing at you, too! The burlesque queen who speaks lousy French and reads book reviews like they was books!

LOUISE: Turn it off, Mother.

ROSE: You know what you are to them? A circus freak! This year's novelty act! And when the bill is changed—

LOUISE: I SAID TURN IT OFF! *Nobody laughs at me*—because I laugh first! *At* me! ME—from Seattle; me—with no education; me, with no talent—as you've kept reminding me my whole life. Look at me now: a star! Look how I live! Look at my friends! Look where I'm going! I'm not staying in burlesque. I'm moving—maybe up, maybe down—but wherever it is, I'm *enjoying* it! I'm having the time of my life because for the first time, it *is* my life! I love it! I love every second of it and I'll be damned if you're going to take it away from me! I *am* Gypsy Rose Lee! I love her—and if you don't, you can clear out *now!*

(*A moment:* ROSE *stares at her, stunned. Then a knocking on the door and* RENÉE *enters*)

RENÉE: Your press agent is here with the photographer.

LOUISE: Tell him I'll be ready in a minute. (*Softly*) Momma, we can't go shouting seven performances of this a week.

ROSE: The whole family shouts: it comes from our living so near the railroad tracks.

LOUISE: I'm getting an ulcer.

ROSE: (*She is trying to make peace*) You think I'm not?

LOUISE: Yes, I think you're not. And if you want an ulcer, Momma, get one of your own. You can't have mine.

ROSE: Let's forget it.

LOUISE: No, let's finish it.

ROSE: I should go feed Chowsie.

LOUISE: Mother, you fought your whole life. I wish you could relax now—

ROSE: You need more mascara on your left eye.

LOUISE: *Momma, you have got to let go of me!*

ROSE: Let go?

LOUISE: I'll give you anything you want—

ROSE: You *need* me!

LOUISE: A house, a farm, a school—a dramatic school for kids? You were always great with kids!

ROSE: (*Cutting in*) *I'm a pro!* Not an old workhorse you can turn out to pasture just because you think you're riding high on your own!

LOUISE: Momma, no kid does it all on his own but *I am not a kid any more!* From now on, even if I flop, I flop on my own! (*A knock on the door*)

PHIL: (*Off*) Hey, Gyps, what do you say?

ROSE: "So long, Rose," that's what she says. "Don't slam the door as you leave." (*She starts to go, but is pushed aside by the press agent and photographer who come in. She stands watching*)

PHIL: (*As he enters*) Hi, Rose. Gyps, baby, may I present Monsieur Bougeron-Cochon.

LOUISE: *Enchanté, monsieur.*

BOUGERON-COCHON: *Enchanté.*

PHIL: Let's make with the *oiseau* kiddies. One before you take the plunge, Gyps. All set . . . (LOUISE *takes a cheesecake pose*) Fine!

ROSE: All right, miss. But just one thing I want to know. All the working and pushing and fenagling . . . All the scheming and scrimping and lying awake nights figuring: how do we get from one town to the next? How do we all eat on a buck?

How do I make an act out of nothing? What'd I do it for? You say I fought my whole life. I fought *your* whole life. So now tell me: *what'd I do it for?*

LOUISE: (*Quietly, after a long moment*) I thought you did it for me, Momma.

(ROSE *stares. Her hands drop to her sides. She turns and quietly goes out*)

PHIL: Come on, smile, Gyps. Show us your talent! (*She poses*) That's it!

(*The flashbulb explodes*)

The Lights Black Out

SCENE 6

A lone spot picks up ROSE *as she moves down front.*

ROSE: "I thought you did it for me, Momma." "I thought you did it for me, Momma . . ." I thought you made a no-talent ox into a star because you like doing things the hard way, Momma. (*Louder*) And you *haven't* got any talent!—not what *I* call talent, Miss Gypsy Rose Lee! (*The lights now begin to come up, showing the whole stage, bare except for a few stacked flats of scenery used earlier in the big production number.* ROSE *shouts defiantly*) I made you!—and you wanna know why? You wanna know what I did it for?! (*Louder*) *Because I was born too soon and started too late, that's why!* With what I have in me, I could've been better than ANY OF YOU! What I got in me—what I been holding down inside of me—if I ever let it out, there wouldn't be signs big enough! There wouldn't be lights bright enough! (*Shouting right out to everyone now*) HERE SHE IS, BOYS! HERE SHE IS, WORLD! HERE'S ROSE!! (*She sings*)

CURTAIN UP!!!
LIGHT THE LIGHTS!!!
(*Speaking*)
Play it, boys.
(*Singing*)
You either got it,
or you ain't—
And, boys, I got it!
You like it?

ORCHESTRA: Yeah!

ROSE:

Well, I got it!
Some people got it
  And make it pay,
Some people can't even
  Give it away.
This people's got it
  And this people's spreadin' it around.
You either have it
  Or you've had it.
(*Speaking*)
Hello, everybody! My name's Rose. What's yours? (*Bumps*)
How d'ya like them egg rolls, Mr. Goldstone?
(*Singing*)
Hold your hats,
  And hallelujah,
Momma's gonna show it to ya!
(*Speaking*)
Ready or not, here comes Momma!
(*Singing*)
Momma's talkin' loud,
Momma's doin' fine,
Momma's gettin' hot,
Momma's goin' strong,
Momma's movin' on,
Momma's all alone,
Momma doesn't care,
Momma's lettin' loose,
Momma's got the stuff,
Momma's lettin' go–
(*Stopping dead as the words hit her*)
Momma–
Momma's–
(*Shaking off the mood*)
Momma's got the stuff,
Momma's got to move,
Momma's got to go–
(*Stopping dead again, trying to recover*)
Momma–
Momma's–
Momma's gotta let go!
(*Stops; after a moment she begins to pace*)

Why did I do it?
  What did it get me?
Scrapbooks full of me in the background.
Give 'em love and what does it get you?
What does it get you?
One quick look as each of 'em leaves you.
All your life and what does it get you?
Thanks a lot—and out with the garbage.
They take bows and you're battin' zero.
I had a dream—
I dreamed it for you,
  June,
It wasn't for me, Herbie.
And if it wasn't for me
Then where would you be,
Miss Gypsy Rose Lee!
Well, someone tell me, when is it my turn?
Don't I get a dream for myself?
Startin' now it's gonna be my turn!
Gangway, world,
  Get offa my runway!
Startin' now I bat a thousand.
This time, boys, I'm takin' the bows and
Everything's coming up Rose—
Everything's coming up Roses—
Everything's coming up Roses
This time for me!
For me—
For me—
For me—
For me—
FOR ME!

(LOUISE *comes on quietly and stands tall and beautiful in a mink coat over a perfect evening gown.* ROSE *turns, and with an embarrassed smile says—*)

ROSE: Just trying out a few ideas you might want to use . . .

LOUISE: (*Quietly*) You'd really have been something, Mother.

ROSE: Think so?

LOUISE: If you had had someone to push you like I had . . .

ROSE: (*Tough with herself, too, she shakes her head*) If I could've been, I would've been. And *that's* show business

. . . About that school—for kids, like you said. I could open one. Only—kids grow up. And twice is enough . . . I guess I did do it for me.

LOUISE: Why, Mother?

ROSE: Just wanted to be noticed.

LOUISE: Like I wanted you to notice me. (ROSE *turns and looks at her*) I still do, Momma. (*She holds out her arms to* ROSE, *who hesitates, then comes running to* LOUISE *like a child.* LOUISE *pats her, kisses her hair as she says*) O.K., Momma . . . O.K., Rose.

(ROSE *clutches her, then moves away. She forces a smile as she turns back*)

ROSE: Say, you look like you should speak French!

LOUISE: You're coming to that party with me.

ROSE: No.

LOUISE: Come on.

ROSE: Like this?

LOUISE: Here. You wear my mink. I've got a stole in the box office.

ROSE: Well—just for an hour or two. Say, this looks better on me than on you! . . . Funny how we can wear the same size.

LOUISE: (*A knowing look*) Especially in mink.

ROSE: You know, I had a dream last night. (*She links her arm through* LOUISE'S *as they start slowly across the stage*) It was a big poster of a mother and daughter—you know, like the cover of that ladies' magazine.

LOUISE: (*Warningly*) Yes, Mother?

ROSE: (*Stops moving*) Only it was you and me, wearing exactly the same gown. It was an ad for Minsky—and the headline said: (*She traces the name in the air*) MADAM ROSE— (LOUISE *gives her a look;* ROSE *catches it and, moving her hand up to give* LOUISE *top billing, says*) AND HER DAUGHTER, GYPSY! (*They both begin to laugh as they walk off*)

The Curtain Falls

FIDDLER ON THE ROOF

Book by Joseph Stein
Music by Jerry Bock
Lyrics by Sheldon Harnick

Based on Sholom Aleichem's stories

Production Notes

Fiddler on the Roof was first presented by Harold Prince at the Imperial Theatre, New York, on September 22, 1964. The cast was as follows:

Tevye, a dairyman, *Zero Mostel*
Golde, his wife, *Maria Karnilova*
Their Daughters
Tzeitel, *Joanna Merlin*
Hodel, *Julia Migenes*
Chava, *Tanya Everett*
Shprintze, *Marilyn Rogers*
Bielke, *Linda Ross*
Yente, a matchmaker, *Beatrice Arthur*
Motel Kamzoil, a tailor, *Austin Pendelton*
Shandel, his mother, *Helen Verbit*
Perchik, a student, *Bert Convy*
Lazar Wolf, a butcher, *Michael Granger*
Mordcha, an innkeeper, *Zvee Scooler*
Rabbi, *Gluck Sandor*
Mendel, his son, *Leonard Frey*
Avram, a bookseller, *Paul Lipson*
Nahum, a beggar, *Maurice Edwards*
Grandma Tzeitel, Golde's grandmother, *Sue Babel*
Fruma-Sarah, Lazar Wolf's first wife, *Carol Sawyer*
Yussel, a hatter, *Mitch Thomas*
Constable, *Joseph Sullivan*
Fyedka, a young man, *Joe Ponazecki*
Sasha, his friend, *Robert Berdeen*
and
The Fiddler, *Gino Conforti*
Villagers: *Tom Abbott, John C. Attle, Sue Babel, Sammy Bayes, Robert Berdeen, Lorenzo Bianco, Duane Bodin, Robert Currie, Sarah Felcher, Tony Gardell, Louis Genevrino, Ross Gifford, Dan Jasin, Sandra Kazan, Thom Koutsoukos, Sharon Lerit, Sylvia Mann, Peff Modelski, Irene Paris, Charles Rule, Carol Sawyer, Roberta Senn, Mitch Thomas, Helen Verbit*

Entire production directed and choreographed by *Jerome Robbins*
Settings by *Boris Aronson*
Costumes by *Patricia Zipprodt*
Lighting by *Jean Rosenthal*
Orchestrations by *Don Walker*
Musical Direction and Vocal Arrangements by *Milton Greene*
Dance Music arranged by *Betty Walberg*
Production Stage Manager, *Ruth Mitchell*
Produced by special permission of the *Estate of Olga Rabinowitz, Arnold Perl,* and *Crown Publishers, Inc.*

The Place: Anatevka, a village in Russia.
The Time: 1905, on the eve of the revolutionary period.

Musical Numbers

Act One

Tradition	Tevye and the Villagers
Matchmaker, Matchmaker	Tzeitel, Hodel, and Chava
If I Were a Rich Man	Tevye
Sabbath Prayer	Tevye, Golde, and the Villagers
To Life	Tevye, Lazar, and Men
Miracle of Miracles	Motel
The Tailor, Motel Kamzoil	Tevye, Golde, Grandma Tzeitel Fruma-Sarah and the Villagers
Sunrise, Sunset	Tevye, Golde, and the Villagers
Bottle Dance	Yussel, Hershel, Shloime and Duvidel
Wedding Dance	The Villagers

Act Two

Now I Have Everything	Perchik and Hodel
Do You Love Me?	Tevye and Golde
I Just Heard	Yente and the Villagers
Far From the Home I Love	Hodel
Chavaleh	Tevye
Anatevka	Tevye, Golde, Yente, Lazar, Mendel and Avram
Epilogue	The Entire Company

ACT ONE

Prologue

The exterior of TEVYE'S *house. A* FIDDLER *is seated on the roof, playing.* TEVYE *is outside the house.*

TEVYE: A fiddler on the roof. Sounds crazy, no? But in our little village of Anatevka, you might say every one of us is a fiddler on the roof, trying to scratch out a pleasant, simple tune without breaking his neck. It isn't easy. You may ask, why do we stay up here if it's so dangerous? We stay because Anatevka is our home. And how do we keep our balance? That I can tell you in a word—tradition!

VILLAGERS: (*Enter, singing*)
Tradition, tradition–Tradition.
Tradition, tradition–Tradition.

TEVYE: Because of our traditions, we've kept our balance for many, many years. Here in Anatevka we have traditions for everything–how to eat, how to sleep, how to wear clothes. For instance, we always keep our heads covered and always wear a little prayer shawl. This shows our constant devotion to God. You may ask, how did this tradition start? I'll tell you–I don't know! But it's a tradition. Because of our traditions, everyone knows who he is and what God expects him to do.

TEVYE and PAPAS: (*Sing "Tradition"*)
Who, day and night,
Must scramble for a living,
Feed a wife and children,
Say his daily prayers?
And who has the right,
As master of the house,
To have the final word at home?

ALL:
The papa, the papa–Tradition.
The papa, the papa–Tradition.

GOLDE and MAMAS:
Who must know the way to make a proper home,
A quiet home, a kosher home?
Who must raise a family and run the home
So Papa's free to read the Holy Book?

ALL:
The mama, the mama–Tradition.
The mama, the mama–Tradition.

SONS:
At three I started Hebrew school,
At ten I learned a trade.
I hear they picked a bride for me.
I hope she's pretty.

ALL:
The sons, the sons–Tradition.
The sons, the sons–Tradition.

DAUGHTERS:

And who does Mama teach
To mend and tend and fix,
Preparing me to marry
Whoever Papa picks?

ALL:

The daughters, the daughters—Tradition.
The daughters, the daughters—Tradition.

(*They repeat the song as a round*)

PAPAS:

The papas.

MAMAS:

The mamas.

SONS:

The sons.

DAUGHTERS:

The daughters.

ALL:

Tradition.

PAPAS:

The papas.

MAMAS:

The mamas.

SONS:

The sons.

DAUGHTERS:

The daughters.

ALL:

Tradition.

TEVYE: And in the circle of our little village, we have always had our special types. For instance, Yente, the matchmaker . . .

YENTE: Avram, I have a perfect match for your son. A wonderful girl.

AVRAM: Who is it?

YENTE: Ruchel, the shoemaker's daughter.

AVRAM: Ruchel? But she can hardly see. She's almost blind.

YENTE: Tell the truth, Avram, is your son so much to look at? The way she sees and the way he looks, it's a perfect match.

(*All dance*)

TEVYE: And Reb Nahum, the beggar . . .

NAHUM: Alms for the poor, alms for the poor.

LAZAR: Here, Reb Nahum, is one kopek.

NAHUM: One kopek? Last week you gave me two kopeks.

LAZAR: I had a bad week.

NAHUM: So if you had a bad week, why should I suffer?

(*All dance*)

TEVYE: And, most important, our beloved rabbi . . .

MENDEL: Rabbi, may I ask you a question?

RABBI: Certainly, my son.

MENDEL: Is there a proper blessing for the Tsar?

RABBI: A blessing for the Tsar? Of course. May God bless and keep the Tsar—far away from us!

(*All dance*)

TEVYE: Then, there are the others in our village. They make a much bigger circle.

(*The* PRIEST, *the* CONSTABLE, *and other* RUSSIANS *cross the stage. The two groups nod to each other*)

TEVYE: His Honor the Constable, his Honor the Priest, and his Honor—many others. We don't bother them, and, so far, they don't bother us. And among ourselves we get along perfectly well. Of course, there was the time (*Pointing to the* TWO MEN) when he sold him a horse and he delivered a mule, but that's all settled now. Now we live in simple peace and harmony and—

(*The* TWO MEN *begin an argument, which is taken up by the entire group*)

FIRST MAN: It was a horse.

SECOND MAN: It was a mule.

FIRST MAN: It was a horse!

SECOND MAN: It was a mule, I tell you!

VILLAGERS: Horse!

VILLAGERS: Mule!

VILLAGERS: Horse!

VILLAGERS: Mule!

VILLAGERS: Horse!

VILLAGERS: Mule!

VILLAGERS: Horse!

VILLAGERS: Mule!

EVERYONE:

Tradition, tradition—Tradition.
Tradition, tradition—Tradition.

TEVYE: (*Quieting them*) Tradition. Without our traditions, our lives would be as shaky as—as a fiddler on the roof!

(*The* VILLAGERS *exit, and the house opens to show its interior*)

SCENE 1

The kitchen of TEVYE'S *house.* GOLDE, TZEITEL, *and* HODEL *are preparing for the Sabbath.* SHPRINTZE *and* BIELKE *enter from outside, carrying logs.*

SHPRINTZE: Mama, where should we put these?

GOLDE: Put them on my head! By the stove, foolish girl. Where is Chava?

HODEL: She's in the barn, milking.

BIELKE: When will Papa be home?

GOLDE: It's almost Sabbath and he worries a lot when he'll be home! All day long riding on top of his wagon like a prince.

TZEITEL: Mama, you know that Papa works hard.

GOLDE: His horse works harder! And you don't have to defend your papa to me. I know him a little longer than you. He could drive a person crazy. (*Under her breath*) He should only live and be well. (*Out loud*) Shprintze, bring me some more potatoes.

(CHAVA *enters, carrying a basket, with a book under her apron*)

GOLDE: Chava, did you finish milking?

CHAVA: Yes, Mama. (*She drops the book*)

GOLDE: You were reading again? Why does a girl have to read? Will it get her a better husband? Here. (*Hands* CHAVA *the book*)

(CHAVA *exits into the house.* SHPRINTZE *enters with basket of potatoes*)

SHPRINTZE: Mama, Yente's coming. She's down the road.

HODEL: Maybe she's finally found a good match for you, Tzeitel.

GOLDE: From your mouth to God's ears.

TZEITEL: Why does she have to come now? It's almost Sabbath.

GOLDE: Go finish in the barn. I want to talk to Yente alone.

SHPRINTZE: Mama, can I go out and play?

GOLDE: You have feet? Go.

BIELKE: Can I go too?

GOLDE: Go too.

(SHPRINTZE *and* BIELKE *exit*)

TZEITEL: But Mama, the men she finds. The last one was so old and he was bald. He had no hair.

GOLDE: A poor girl without a dowry can't be so particular. You want hair, marry a monkey.

TZEITEL: After all, Mama, I'm not yet twenty years old, and—

GOLDE: Shah! (*Spits between her fingers*) Do you have to boast about your age? Do you want to tempt the Evil Eye? Inside.

(TZEITEL *leaves the kitchen as* YENTE *enters from outside*)

YENTE: Golde darling, I had to see you because I have such news for you. And not just every-day-in-the-week news—once-in-a-lifetime news. And where are your daughters? Outside, no? Good. Such diamonds, such jewels. You'll see, Golde, I'll find every one of them a husband. But you shouldn't be so picky. Even the worst husband, God forbid, is better than no husband, God forbid. And who should know better than me? Ever since my husband died I've been a poor widow, alone, nobody to talk to, nothing to say to anyone. It's no life. All I do at night is think of him, and even thinking of him gives me no pleasure, because you know as well as I, he was not much of a person. Never made a living, everything he touched turned to mud, but better than nothing.

MOTEL: (*Entering*) Good evening. Is Tzeitel in the house?

GOLDE: But she's busy. You can come back later.

MOTEL: There's something I'd like to tell her.

GOLDE: Later.

TZEITEL: (*Entering*) Oh, Motel, I thought I heard you.

GOLDE: Finish what you were doing. (TZEITEL *goes out. To* MOTEL) I said later.

MOTEL: (*Exiting*) All right!

YENTE: What does that poor little tailor, Motel, want with Tzeitel?

GOLDE: They have been friends since they were babies together. They talk, they play . . .

YENTE: (*Suspiciously*) They play? What do they play?

GOLDE: Who knows? They're just children.

YENTE: From such children, come other children.

GOLDE: Motel, he's a nothing. Yente, you said—

YENTE: Ah, children, children! They are your blessing in your old age. But my Aaron, may he rest in peace, couldn't give me children. Believe me, he was good as gold, never raised his voice to me, but otherwise he was not much of a man, so what good is it if he never raised his voice? But what's the use complaining. Other women enjoy complaining, but not Yente. Not every woman in the world is a Yente. Well, I must prepare my poor Sabbath table, so goodbye, Golde, and it was a pleasure talking our hearts out to each other. (*She starts to exit*)

GOLDE: Yente, you said you had news for me.

YENTE: (*Returning*) Oh, I'm losing my head. One day it will fall off altogether, and a horse will kick it into the mud, and goodbye, Yente. Of course, the news. It's about Lazar Wolf, the butcher. A good man, a fine man. And I don't have to tell you that he's well off. But he's lonely, the poor man. After all, a widower . . . You understand? Of course you do. To make it short, out of the whole town, he's cast his eye on Tzeitel.

GOLDE: My Tzeitel?

YENTE: No, the Tsar's Tzeitel! Of course your Tzeitel.

GOLDE: Such a match, for my Tzeitel. But Tevye wants a learned man. He doesn't like Lazar.

YENTE: Fine. So he won't marry him. Lazar wants the daughter, not the father. Listen to me, Golde, send Tevye to him. Don't tell him what it's about. Let Lazar discuss it himself. He'll win him over. He's a good man, a wealthy man–true? Of course true! So you'll tell me how it went, and you don't have to thank me, Golde, because aside from my fee–which anyway Lazar will pay–it gives me satisfaction to make people happy–what better satisfaction is there? So goodbye, Golde, and you're welcome. (*She goes out. Enter* TZEITEL)

TZEITEL: What did she want, Mama?

GOLDE: When I want you to know, I'll tell you. Finish washing the floor.

(*She exits.* HODEL *and* CHAVA *enter with wash mop and bucket*)

HODEL: I wonder if Yente found a husband for you?

TZEITEL: I'm not anxious for Yente to find me a husband.

CHAVA: (*Teasing*) Not unless it's Motel, the tailor.

TZEITEL: I didn't ask you.

HODEL: Tzeitel, you're the oldest. They have to make a match for you before they can make one for me.

CHAVA: And then after her, one for me.

HODEL: So if Yente brings–

TZEITEL: Oh, Yente! Yente!

HODEL: Well, somebody has to arrange the matches. Young people can't decide these things for themselves.

CHAVA: She might bring someone wonderful–

HODEL: Someone interesting–

CHAVA: And well off–

HODEL: And important–(*Sings "Matchmaker, Matchmaker"*)

Matchmaker, Matchmaker,
Make me a match,
Find me a find.
Catch me a catch.
Matchmaker, Matchmaker,
Look through your book
And make me a perfect match.

CHAVA:

Matchmaker, Matchmaker,
I'll bring the veil,
You bring the groom,
Slender and pale.
Bring me a ring for I'm longing to be
The envy of all I see.

HODEL:

For Papa,
Make him a scholar.

CHAVA:

For Mama,
Make him rich as a king.

CHAVA and HODEL:

For me, well,
I wouldn't holler
If he were as handsome as anything.
Matchmaker, Matchmaker,
Make me a match,
Find me a find,
Catch me a catch.
Night after night in the dark I'm alone,
So find me a match
Of my own.

TZEITEL: Since when are you interested in a match, Chava? I thought you just had your eye on your books. (HODEL *chuckles*) And you have your eye on the rabbi's son.

HODEL: Why not? We only have one rabbi and he only has one son. Why shouldn't I want the best?

TZEITEL: Because you're a girl from a poor family. So whatever Yente brings, you'll take. Right? Of course right. (*Sings*)

Hodel, oh Hodel,
Have I made a match for you!
He's handsome, he's young!
All right, he's sixty-two,
But he's a nice man, a good catch–true? True.

I promise you'll be happy.
And even if you're not,
There's more to life than that–
Don't ask me what.

Chava, I found him.
Will you be a lucky bride!
He's handsome, he's tall–
That is, from side to side.
But he's a nice man, a good catch–right? Right.

You heard he has a temper.
He'll beat you every night,
But only when he's sober,
So you're all right.
Did you think you'd get a prince?
Well, I do the best I can.
With no dowry, no money, no family background
Be glad you got a man.

CHAVA:
Matchmaker, Matchmaker,
You know that I'm
Still very young.
Please, take your time.

HODEL:
Up to this minute
I misunderstood
That I could get stuck for good.

CHAVA and HODEL:
Dear Yente,
See that he's gentle.
Remember,
You were also a bride.

It's not that
I'm sentimental.

CHAVA, HODEL, and TZEITEL:
It's just that I'm terrified!
Matchmaker, Matchmaker,
Plan me no plans,
I'm in no rush.
Maybe I've learned
Playing with matches
A girl can get burned.
So,
Bring me no ring,
Groom me no groom,
Find me no find,
Catch me no catch,
Unless he's a matchless match.

SCENE 2

The exterior of TEVYE'S *house.* TEVYE *enters, pulling his cart. He stops, and sits on the wagon seat, exhausted.*

TEVYE: Today I am a horse. Dear God, did You have to make my poor old horse lose his shoe just before the Sabbath? That wasn't nice. It's enough You pick on me, Tevye, bless me with five daughters, a life of poverty. What have You got against my horse? Sometimes I think when things are too quiet up there, You say to Yourself: "Let's see, what kind of mischief can I play on my friend Tevye?"

GOLDE: (*Entering from house*) You're finally here, my bread-winner.

TEVYE: (*To heaven*) I'll talk to You later.

GOLDE: Where's your horse?

TEVYE: He was invited to the blacksmith's for the Sabbath.

GOLDE: Hurry up, the sun won't wait for you. I have something to say to you. (*Exits into the house*)

TEVYE: As the Good Book says, "Heal us, O Lord, and we shall be healed." In other words, send us the cure, we've got the sickness already. (*Gestures to the door*) I'm not really complaining—after all, with Your help, I'm starving to death. You made many, many poor people. I realize, of course, that it's no shame to be poor, but it's no great honor either. So what would have been so terrible if I had a small fortune? (*Sings "If I Were a Rich Man"*)

If I were a rich man,
Daidle deedle daidle
Digguh digguh deedle daidle dum,
All day long I'd biddy biddy bum,
If I were a wealthy man.

Wouldn't have to work hard,
Daidle deedle daidle
Digguh digguh deedle daidle dum,
If I were a biddy biddy rich
Digguh digguh deedle daidle man.

I'd build a big, tall house with rooms by the dozen
Right in the middle of the town,
A fine tin roof and real wooden floors below.
There would be one long staircase just going up,
And one even longer coming down,
And one more leading nowhere just for show.

I'd fill my yard with chicks and turkeys and geese
And ducks for the town to see and hear,
Squawking just as noisily as they can.
And each loud quack and cluck and gobble and honk
Will land like a trumpet on the ear,
As if to say, here lives a wealthy man.

(*Sighs*)
If I were a rich man,
Daidle deedle daidle
Digguh digguh deedle daidle dum,
All day long I'd biddy biddy bum,
If I were a wealthy man.

Wouldn't have to work hard,
Daidle deedle daidle
Digguh digguh deedle daidle dum,
If I were a biddy biddy rich
Digguh digguh deedle daidle man.

I see my wife, my Golde, looking like a rich man's wife,
With a proper double chin,
Supervising meals to her heart's delight.
I see her putting on airs and strutting like a peacock,
Oi! what a happy mood she's in,
Screaming at the servants day and night.

The most important men in town will come to fawn on me.
They will ask me to advise them like a Solomon the Wise,
"If you please, Reb Tevye. Pardon me, Reb Tevye,"
Posing problems that would cross a rabbi's eyes.

(*He chants*)
And it won't make one bit of diff'rence
If I answer right or wrong.
When you're rich they think you really know!

If I were rich I'd have the time that I lack
To sit in the synagogue and pray,
And maybe have a seat by the eastern wall,
And I'd discuss the Holy Books with the learned men
Seven hours every day.
That would be the sweetest thing of all.

(*Sighs*)
If I were a rich man,
Daidle deedle daidle
Digguh digguh deedle daidle dum,
All day long I'd biddy biddy bum,
If I were a wealthy man.

Wouldn't have to work hard,
Daidle deedle daidle
Digguh digguh deedle daidle dum,
Lord, who made the lion and the lamb,
You decreed I should be what I am,
Would it spoil some vast, eternal plan—
If I were a wealthy man?

(*As the song ends,* MORDCHA, MENDEL, PERCHIK, AVRAM, *and other* TOWNSPEOPLE *enter*)

MORDCHA: There he is! You forgot my order for the Sabbath!
TEVYE: Reb Mordcha, I had a little accident with my horse.
MENDEL: Tevye, you didn't bring the rabbi's order.
TEVYE: I know, Reb Mendel.
AVRAM: Tevye, you forgot my order for the Sabbath.
TEVYE: This is bigger news than the plague in Odessa.
AVRAM: (*Waving the newspaper that he holds*) Talking about news, terrible news in the outside world—terrible!
MORDCHA: What is it?
MENDEL: What does it say?

AVRAM: In a village called Rajanka, all the Jews were evicted, forced to leave their homes.
(*They all look at each other*)

MENDEL: For what reason?

AVRAM: It doesn't say. Maybe the Tsar wanted their land. Maybe a plague . . .

MORDCHA: May the Tsar have his own personal plague.

ALL: Amen.

MENDEL: (*To* AVRAM) Why don't you ever bring us some good news?

AVRAM: I only read it. It was an edict from the authorities.

MORDCHA: May the authorities start itching in places that they can't reach.

ALL: Amen.

PERCHIK: (*Has quietly entered during above and sat down to rest*) Why do you curse them? What good does your cursing do? You stand around and curse and chatter and don't do anything. You'll all chatter your way into the grave.

MENDEL: Excuse me, you're not from this village.

PERCHIK: No.

MENDEL: And where are you from?

PERCHIK: Kiev. I was a student in the university there.

MORDCHA: Aha! The university. Is that where you learned to criticize your elders?

PERCHIK: That's where I learned that there is more to life than talk. You should know what's going on in the outside world.

MORDCHA: Why should I break my head about the outside world? Let them break their own heads.

TEVYE: He's right. As the Good Book says, "If you spit in the air, it lands in your face."

PERCHIK: That's nonsense. You can't close your eyes to what's happening in the world.

TEVYE: He's right.

AVRAM: He's right and he's right? How can they both be right?

TEVYE: You know, you're also right.

MORDCHA: He's right! He's still wet behind the ears! Good Sabbath, Tevye.

VILLAGERS: Good Sabbath, Tevye. (*They take their orders and leave.* MENDEL *remains*)

MENDEL: Tevye, the rabbi's order. My cheese!

TEVYE: Of course. So you're from Kiev, Reb . . .

PERCHIK: Perchik.

TEVYE: Perchik. So, you're a newcomer here. As Abraham said, "I am a stranger in a strange land."

MENDEL: Moses said that.

TEVYE: (*To* MENDEL) Forgive me. As King David put it, "I am slow of speech and slow of tongue."

MENDEL: That was also Moses.

TEVYE: For a man with a slow tongue, he talked a lot.

MENDEL: And the cheese!

(TEVYE *notices that* PERCHIK *is eying the cheese hungrily*)

TEVYE: Here, have a piece.

PERCHIK: I have no money. And I am not a beggar.

TEVYE: Here—it's a blessing for me to give.

PERCHIK: Very well—for your sake! (*He takes the cheese and devours it*)

TEVYE: Thank you. You know, it's no crime to be poor.

PERCHIK: In this world, it's the rich who are the criminals. Some day their wealth will be ours.

TEVYE: That would be nice. If they would agree, I would agree.

MENDEL: And who will make this miracle come to pass?

PERCHIK: People. Ordinary people.

MENDEL: Like you?

PERCHIK: Like me.

MENDEL: Nonsense!

TEVYE: And until your golden day comes, Reb Perchik, how will you live?

PERCHIK: By giving lessons to children. Do you have children?

TEVYE: I have five daughters.

PERCHIK: Five?

TEVYE: Daughters.

PERCHIK: Girls should learn too. Girls are people.

MENDEL: A radical!

PERCHIK: I would be willing to teach them. Open their minds to great thoughts.

TEVYE: What great thoughts?

PERCHIK: Well, the Bible has many lessons for our times.

TEVYE: I am a very poor man. Food for lessons? (PERCHIK *nods*) Good. Stay with us for the Sabbath. Of course, we don't eat like kings, but we don't starve, either. As the Good Book says, "When a poor man eats a chicken, one of them is sick."

MENDEL: Where does the Book say that?

TEVYE: Well, it doesn't exactly say that, but someplace it has something about a chicken. Good Sabbath.

MENDEL: Good Sabbath.

PERCHIK: Good Sabbath.

(MENDEL *exits as* TEVYE *and* PERCHIK *enter the house*)

SCENE 3

The interior of TEVYE'S *house.* TEVYE'S *daughters are there.* TEVYE *and* PERCHIK *enter.*

TEVYE: Good Sabbath, children.

DAUGHTERS: (*Running to him*) Good Sabbath, Papa.

TEVYE: Children! (*They all stop*) This is Perchik. Perchik, this is my oldest daughter.

PERCHIK: Good Sabbath.

TZEITEL: Good Sabbath.

PERCHIK: You have a pleasant daughter.

TEVYE: I have five pleasant daughters. (*He beckons to the girls, and they run into his arms, eagerly, and* TEVYE *kisses each*) This is mine . . . this is mine . . . this is mine . . . this is mine . . . this is mine . . .

(MOTEL *enters.* TEVYE *almost kisses him in sequence*)

TEVYE: This is not mine. Perchik, this is Motel Kamzoil and he is–

GOLDE: (*Entering*) So you did me a favor and came in.

TEVYE: This is also mine. Golde, this is Perchik, from Kiev, and he is staying the Sabbath with us. He is a teacher. (*To* SHPRINTZE *and* BIELKE) Would you like to take lessons from him? (*They giggle*)

PERCHIK: I am really a good teacher, a very good teacher.

HODEL: I heard once, the rabbi who must praise himself has a congregation of one.

PERCHIK: Your daughter has a quick and witty tongue.

TEVYE: The wit she gets from me. As the Good Book says–

GOLDE: The Good Book can wait. Get washed!

TEVYE: The tongue she gets from her mother.

GOLDE: Motel, you're also eating with us? (MOTEL *gestures, "Yes, if I may"*) Of course, another blessing. Tzeitel, two more. Shprintze, Bielke, get washed. Get the table.

TZEITEL: Motel can help me.

GOLDE: All right. Chava, you go too. (*To* PERCHIK) You can wash outside at the well.

(*Exit the* DAUGHTERS, PERCHIK, *and* MOTEL)

GOLDE: Tevye, I have something to say to you.

TEVYE: Why should today be different? (*He starts to pray*)

GOLDE: Tevye, I have to tell you—

TEVYE: Shhh. I'm praying. (*Prays*)

GOLDE: (*Having waited a moment*) Lazar Wolf wants to see you.

(TEVYE *begins praying again, stopping only to respond to* GOLDE, *then returning to prayer*)

TEVYE: The butcher? About what? (*Prays*)

GOLDE: I don't know. Only that he says it is important.

TEVYE: What can be important? I have nothing for him to slaughter. (*Prays*)

GOLDE: After the Sabbath, see him and talk to him.

TEVYE: Talk to him about what? If he is thinking about buying my new milk cow (*Prays*) he can forget it. (*Prays*)

GOLDE: Tevye, don't be an ox. A man sends an important message, at least you can talk to him.

TEVYE: Talk about what? He wants my new milk cow! (*Prays*)

GOLDE: (*Insisting*) Talk to him!

TEVYE: All right. After the Sabbath, I'll talk to him.

(TEVYE *and* GOLDE *exit. He is still praying.* MOTEL, TZEITEL, *and* CHAVA *bring in the table.* CHAVA *exits*)

TZEITEL: Motel, Yente was here.

MOTEL: I saw her.

TZEITEL: If they agree on someone, there will be a match and then it will be too late for us.

MOTEL: Don't worry, Tzeitel. I have found someone who will sell me his used sewing machine, so in a few weeks I'll have saved up enough to buy it, and then your father will be impressed with me and . . .

TZEITEL: But, Motel, a few weeks may be too late.

MOTEL: But what else can we do?

TZEITEL: You could ask my father for my hand tonight. Now!

MOTEL: Why should he consider me now? I'm only a poor tailor.

TZEITEL: And I'm only the daughter of a poor milkman. Just talk to him.

MOTEL: Tzeitel, if your father says no, that's it, it's final. He'll yell at me.

TZEITEL: Motel!

MOTEL: I'm just a poor tailor.

TZEITEL: Motel, even a poor tailor is entitled to some happiness.

MOTEL: That's true.

TZEITEL: (*Urgently*) Will you talk to him? Will you talk to him?

MOTEL: All right, I'll talk to him.

TEVYE: (*Entering*) It's late! Where is everybody? Late.

MOTEL: (*Following him*) Reb Tevye–

TEVYE: (*Disregarding him*) Come in, children, we're lighting the candles.

MOTEL: Reb Tevye. (*Summoning courage*) Reb Tevye, Reb Tevye.

TEVYE: Yes? What is it? (*Loudly*) Well, Motel, what is it?

MOTEL: (*Taken aback*) Good Sabbath, Reb Tevye.

TEVYE: (*Irritated with him*) Good Sabbath, Good Sabbath. Come, children, come.

(TEVYE'S *family,* PERCHIK, *and* MOTEL *gather around the table.* GOLDE *lights the candles and says a prayer under her breath*)

TEVYE and GOLDE: (*Sing to* DAUGHTERS *"Sabbath Prayer"*)

May the Lord protect and defend you,
May He always shield you from shame,
May you come to be
In Yisroel a shining name.

May you be like Ruth and like Esther,
May you be deserving of praise.
Strengthen them, O Lord,
And keep them from the stranger's ways.

May God bless you
And grant you long lives.

(*The lights go up behind them, showing other families, behind a transparent curtain, singing over Sabbath candles*)

GOLDE:

May the Lord fulfill our Sabbath prayer for you.

TEVYE and GOLDE:

May God make you
Good mothers and wives.

TEVYE:

May He send you husbands who will care for you.

TEVYE and GOLDE:

May the Lord protect and defend you
May the Lord preserve you from pain.
Favor them, O Lord,

With happiness and peace.
O hear our Sabbath prayer.
Amen.

SCENE 4

The Inn, the following evening. AVRAM, LAZAR, MENDEL, *and several other people are sitting at tables.* LAZAR *is waiting impatiently drumming on the tabletop, watching the door.*

LAZAR: Reb Mordcha.

MORDCHA: Yes, Lazar Wolf.

LAZAR: Please bring me a bottle of your best brandy and two glasses.

AVRAM: "Your best brandy," Reb Lazar?

MORDCHA: What's the occasion? Are you getting ready for a party?

LAZAR: There might be a party. Maybe even a wedding.

MORDCHA: A wedding? Wonderful. And I'll be happy to make the wedding merry, lead the dancing, and so forth. For a little fee, naturally.

LAZAR: Naturally, a wedding is no wedding without you—and your fee.

(FYEDKA *enters with several other* RUSSIANS)

FIRST RUSSIAN: Good evening, Innkeeper.

MORDCHA: Good evening.

FIRST RUSSIAN: We'd like a drink. Sit down, Fyedka.

MORDCHA: Vodka? Schnapps?

FYEDKA: Vodka.

MORDCHA: Right away.

(TEVYE *enters.* LAZAR, *who has been watching the door, turns away, pretending not to be concerned*)

TEVYE: Good evening.

MORDCHA: Good evening, Tevye.

MENDEL: What are you doing here so early?

TEVYE: (*Aside to* MENDEL) He wants to buy my new milk cow. Good evening, Reb Lazar.

LAZAR: Ah, Tevye. Sit down. Have a drink. (*Pours a drink*)

TEVYE: I won't insult you by saying no. (*Drinks*)

LAZAR: How goes it with you, Tevye?

TEVYE: How should it go?

LAZAR: You're right.

TEVYE: And you?

LAZAR: The same.

TEVYE: I'm sorry to hear that.

LAZAR: (*Pours a drink*) So how's your brother-in-law in America?

TEVYE: I believe he is doing very well.

LAZAR: He wrote you?

TEVYE: Not lately.

LAZAR: Then how do you know?

TEVYE: If he was doing badly, he would write. May I? (*Pours himself another drink*)

LAZAR: Tevye, I suppose you know why I wanted to see you.

TEVYE: (*Drinks*) Yes, I do, Reb Lazar, but there is no use talking about it.

LAZAR: (*Upset*) Why not?

TEVYE: Why yes? Why should I get rid of her?

LAZAR: Well, you have a few more without her.

TEVYE: I see! Today you want one. Tomorrow you may want two.

LAZAR: (*Startled*) Two? What would I do with two?

TEVYE: The same as you do with one!

LAZAR: (*Shocked*) Tevye! This is very important to me.

TEVYE: Why is it so important to you?

LAZAR: Frankly, because I am lonesome.

TEVYE: (*Startled*) Lonesome? What are you talking about?

LAZAR: You don't know?

TEVYE: We're talking about my new cow. The one you want to buy from me.

LAZAR: (*Stares at* TEVYE, *then bursts into laughter*) A milk cow! So I won't be lonesome! (*He howls with laughter.* TEVYE *stares at him*)

TEVYE: What's so funny?

LAZAR: I was talking about your daughter. Your daughter, Tzeitel! (*Bursts into laughter.* TEVYE *stares at him, upset*)

TEVYE: My daughter, Tzeitel?

LAZAR: Of course, your daughter, Tzeitel! I see her in my butcher shop every Thursday. She's made a good impression on me. I like her. And as for me, Tevye, as you know, I'm pretty well off. I have my own house, a good store, a servant. Look, Tevye, why do we have to try to impress each other? Let's shake hands and call it a match. And you won't need a dowry for her. And maybe you'll find something in your own purse, too.

TEVYE: (*Shouting*) Shame on you! Shame! (*Hiccups*) What do you mean, my purse? My Tzeitel is not the sort that I would sell for money!

LAZAR: (*Calming him*) All right! Just as you say. We won't talk about money. The main thing is, let's get it done with. And I will be good to her, Tevye. (*Slightly embarrassed*) I like her. What do you think?

TEVYE: (*To the audience*) What do I think? What do I think? I never liked him! Why should I? You can have a fine conversation with him, if you talk about kidneys and livers. On the other hand, not everybody has to be a scholar. If you're wealthy enough, no one will call you stupid. And with a butcher, my daughter will surely never know hunger. Of course, he has a problem—he's much older than her. That's her problem. But she's younger. That's his problem. I always thought of him as a butcher, but I misjudged him. He is a good man. He likes her. He will try to make her happy. (*Turns to* LAZAR) What do I think? It's a match!

LAZAR: (*Delighted*) You agree?

TEVYE: I agree.

LAZAR: Oh, Tevye, that's wonderful. Let's drink on it.

TEVYE: Why not? To you.

LAZAR: No, my friend, to you.

TEVYE: To the both of us.

LAZAR: To our agreement.

TEVYE: To our agreement. To our prosperity. To good health and happiness. (*Enter* FIDDLER) And, most important—(*Sings "To Life"*)

To Life, to Life, L'Chaim.

TEVYE and LAZAR:

L'Chaim, L'Chaim, to Life.

TEVYE:

Here's to the father I've tried to be.

LAZAR:

Here's to my bride to be.

TEVYE and LAZAR:

Drink, L'Chaim,
To Life, to Life, L'Chaim.
L'Chaim, L'Chaim, to Life.

TEVYE:

Life has a way of confusing us,

LAZAR:
Blessing and bruising us,

TEVYE and LAZAR:
Drink, L'Chaim, to Life.

TEVYE:
God would like us to be joyful,
Even when our hearts lie panting on the floor.

LAZAR:
How much more can we be joyful
When there's really something
To be joyful for!

TEVYE and LAZAR:
To Life, to Life, L'Chaim.

TEVYE:
To Tzeitel, my daughter.

LAZAR:
My wife. It gives you something to think about,

TEVYE:
Something to drink about,

TEVYE and LAZAR:
Drink, L'Chaim, to Life.

LAZAR: Reb Mordcha.
MORDCHA: Yes, Lazar Wolf.
LAZAR: Drinks for everybody.
MENDEL: What's the occasion?
LAZAR: I'm taking myself a bride.
VILLAGERS: Who? Who?
LAZAR: Tevye's eldest, Tzeitel.
VILLAGERS: Mazeltov. . . . Wonderful. . . . Congratulations . . . (*Sing*)
To Lazar Wolf.

TEVYE:
To Tevye.

VILLAGERS:
To Tzeitel, your daughter.

LAZAR:
My wife.

ALL:

May all your futures be pleasant ones,
Not like our present ones.
Drink, L'Chaim, to Life,
To Life, L'Chaim,
L'Chaim, L'Chaim, to Life.
It takes a wedding to make us say,
"Let's live another day,"
Drink, L'Chaim, to Life.

We'll raise a glass and sip a drop of schnapps
In honor of the great good luck
That favored you.
We know that
When good fortune favors two such men
It stands to reason we deserve it, too.
To us and our good fortune.
Be happy, be healthy, long life!
And if our good fortune never comes,
Here's to whatever comes.
Drink, L'Chaim, to Life.
Dai-dai-dai-dai-dai-dai-dai.

(*They begin to dance. A* RUSSIAN *starts to sing, and they stop, uncomfortable*)

RUSSIAN:

Za va sha, Zdarovia,
Heaven bless you both, Nazdrovia,
To your health, and may we live together in peace.

Za va sha, Zdarovia,
Heaven bless you both, Nazdrovia,
To your health, and may we live together in peace.

OTHER RUSSIANS:

May you both be favored with the future of your choice.
May you live to see a thousand reasons to rejoice

Za va sha, Zdarovia,
Heaven bless you both, Nazdrovia,
To your health, and may wc live together in peace.
Hey!

(*The* RUSSIANS *begin to dance, the* OTHERS *join in and they dance to a wild finale pileup on the bar*)

TEVYE: (*From the pileup*)
To Life!

Blackout

SCENE 5

The street outside the Inn. Entering through the inn door are the FIDDLER, LAZAR, TEVYE, *the other* VILLAGERS, *and the* RUSSIANS, *singing "To Life."*

LAZAR: You know, Tevye, after the marriage, we will be related. You will be my papa.

TEVYE: Your papa! I always wanted a son, but I wanted one a little younger than myself.

(*The* CONSTABLE *enters*)

CONSTABLE: Good evening.

FIRST RUSSIAN: Good evening Constable.

CONSTABLE: What's the celebration?

FIRST RUSSIAN: Tevye is marrying off his oldest daughter.

CONSTABLE: May I offer my congratulations, Tevye?

TEVYE: Thank you, your Honor.

(*All but* TEVYE *and the* CONSTABLE *exit*)

CONSTABLE: Oh, Tevye, I have a piece of news that I think I should tell you, as a friend.

TEVYE: Yes, your Honor?

CONSTABLE: And I'm giving you this news because I like you. You are a decent, honest person, even though you are a Jewish dog.

TEVYE: How often does a man get a compliment like that? And your news?

CONSTABLE: We have received orders that sometime soon this district is to have a little unofficial demonstration.

TEVYE: (*Shocked*) A pogrom? Here?

CONSTABLE: No—just a little unofficial demonstration.

TEVYE: How little?

CONSTABLE: Not too serious—just some mischief, so that if an inspector comes through, he will see that we have done our duty. Personally, I don't know why there has to be this trouble between people, but I thought I should tell you, and you can tell the others.

TEVYE: Thank you, your Honor. You're a good man. If I may say so, it's too bad you're not a Jew.

CONSTABLE: (*Amused*) That's what I like about you, Tevye, always joking. And congratulations again, for your daughter.

TEVYE: Thank you, your Honor. Goodbye. (*The* CONSTABLE *exits.* TEVYE *turns to heaven*) Dear God, did You have to send me news like that, today of all days? It's true that we are the Chosen People. But once in a while can't You choose someone else? Anyway, thank You for sending a husband for my Tzeitel. L'Chaim.

(*The* FIDDLER *enters, he circles* TEVYE, *and they dance off together*)

SCENE 6

Outside TEVYE'S *house,* PERCHIK *is teaching* SHPRINTZE *and* BIELKE *while they peel potatoes at a bench.* HODEL *is cleaning pails at the pump.*

PERCHIK: Now, children, I will tell you the story from the Bible, of Laban and Jacob, and then we will discuss it together. All right? (*They nod*) Good. Now Laban had two daughters, Leah and the beautiful Rachel. And Jacob loved the younger, Rachel, and he asked Laban for her hand. Laban agreed, if Jacob would work for him for seven years.

SHPRINTZE: Was Laban a mean man?

PERCHIK: (*Dryly*) He was an employer! Now, after Jacob worked seven years, do you know what happened? Laban fooled him, and gave him his ugly daughter, Leah. So, to marry Rachel, Jacob was forced to work another seven years. You see, children, the Bible clearly teaches us, you must never trust an employer. Do you understand?

SHPRINTZE: Yes, Perchik.

BIELKE: Yes, Perchik.

PERCHIK: Good, now—

GOLDE: (*Entering from the barn*) Papa isn't up yet?

HODEL: No, Mama.

GOLDE: Then enough lessons. We have to do Papa's work today. How long can he sleep? He staggered home last night and fell into bed like a dead man. I couldn't get a word out of him. Put that away and clean the barn. (SHPRINTZE *and* BIELKE *exit into the barn. To* HODEL) Call me when Papa gets up. (GOLDE *exits.* HODEL *pumps a bucket of water*)

HODEL: That was a very interesting lesson, Perchik.

PERCHIK: Do you think so?

HODEL: Although I don't know if the rabbi would agree with your interpretation.

PERCHIK: And neither, I suppose, would the rabbi's son.

HODEL: My little sisters have big tongues.

PERCHIK: And what do you know about him, except that he is the rabbi's son? Would you be interested in him if he were the shoemaker's son, or the tinsmith's son?

HODEL: At least I know this, he does not have any strange ideas about turning the world upside down.

PERCHIK: Certainly. Any new idea would be strange to you. Remember the Lord said, "Let there be light."

HODEL: Yes, but He was not talking to you personally. Good day. (*Starts off*)

PERCHIK: You have spirit. Even a little intelligence, perhaps.

HODEL: Thank you.

PERCHIK: But what good is your brain? Without curiosity it is a rusty tool. Good day, Hodel.

HODEL: We have an old custom here. A boy acts respectfully to a girl. But, of course, that is too traditional for an advanced thinker like you.

PERCHIK: Our traditions! Nothing must change! Everything is perfect exactly the way it is!

HODEL: We like our ways.

PERCHIK: Our ways are changing all over but here. Here men and women must keep apart. Men study. Women in the kitchen. Boys and girls must not touch, should not even look at each other.

HODEL: I am looking at you!

PERCHIK: You are very brave! Do you know that in the city boys and girls can be affectionate without permission of a matchmaker? They hold hands together, they even dance together—new dances—like this. (*He seizes her and starts dancing, humming*) I learned it in Kiev. Do you like it?

HODEL: (*Startled*) It's very nice.

PERCHIK: (*Stops dancing*) There. We've just changed an old custom.

HODEL: (*Bewildered*) Yes. Well, you're welcome—I mean, thank you—I mean, good day.

PERCHIK: Good day!

(TEVYE *enters, suffering from a headache*)

TEVYE: Bielke, Shprintze, what's your name?

HODEL: Hodel, Papa.

TEVYE: Where is Tzeitel?

HODEL: She's in the barn.

TEVYE: Call her out. (HODEL *exits into the barn*) Reb Perchik. How did the lesson go today?

PERCHIK: (*Watching* HODEL'S *exit*) I think we made a good beginning.

(*Enter* GOLDE)

GOLDE: Ah, he's finally up. What happened last night, besides your drinking like a peasant? Did you see Lazar Wolf? What did he say? What did you say? Do you have news?

TEVYE: Patience, woman. As the Good Book says, "Good news will stay and bad news will refuse to leave." And there's another saying that goes–

GOLDE: (*Exasperated*) You can die from such a man!

(TZEITEL *enters from the barn.* HODEL *and* CHAVA *follow her*)

TEVYE: Ah, Tzeitel, my lamb, come here. Tzeitel, you are to be congratulated. You are going to be married!

GOLDE: Married!

TZEITEL: What do you mean, Papa?

TEVYE: Lazar Wolf has asked for your hand.

GOLDE: (*Thrilled*) I knew it!

TZEITEL: (*Bewildered*) The butcher?

GOLDE: (*Enraptured*) My heart told me this was our lucky day. O dear God, I thank Thee, I thank Thee.

TEVYE: And what do you say, Tzeitel?

GOLDE: What can she say? My first-born, a bride! May you grow old with him in fortune and honor, not like Fruma-Sarah, that first wife of his. She was a bitter woman, may she rest in peace. Not like my Tzeitel. And now I must thank Yente. My Tzeitel, a bride! (*She hurries off*)

HODEL and CHAVA: (*Subdued*) Mazeltov, Tzeitel.

TEVYE: You call that a Mazeltov? (HODEL *and* CHAVA *exit*) And you, Reb Perchik, aren't you going to congratulate her?

PERCHIK: (*Sarcastic*) Congratulations, Tzeitel, for getting a rich man.

TEVYE: Again with the rich! What's wrong with being rich?

PERCHIK: It is no reason to marry. Money is the world's curse.

TEVYE: May the Lord smite me with it! And may I never recover! Tzeitel knows I mean only her welfare. Am I right, Tzeitel?

TZEITEL: Yes, Papa.

TEVYE: You see.

PERCHIK: I see. I see very well. (*He exits*)

TEVYE: Well, Tzeitel, my child, why are you so silent? Aren't you happy with this blessing?

TZEITEL: (*Bursts into tears*) Oh, Papa, Papa.

TEVYE: What is it? Tell me.

TZEITEL: Papa, I don't want to marry him. I can't marry him. I can't–

TEVYE: What do you mean, you can't? If I say you will, you will.

TZEITEL: Papa, if it's a matter of money, I'll do anything. I'll hire myself out as a servant. I'll dig ditches, I'll haul rocks, only don't make me marry him, Papa, please.

TEVYE: What's wrong with Lazar? He likes you.

TZEITEL: Papa, I will be unhappy with him. All my life will be unhappy. I'll dig ditches, I'll haul rocks.

TEVYE: But we made an agreement. With us an agreement is an agreement.

TZEITEL: (*Simply*) Is that more important than I am, Papa? Papa, don't force me. I'll be unhappy all my days.

TEVYE: All right. I won't force you.

TZEITEL: Oh, thank you, Papa.

TEVYE: It seems it was not ordained that you should have all the comforts of life, or that we should have a little joy in our old age after all our hard work.

(*Enter* MOTEL, *breathless*)

MOTEL: Reb Tevye, may I speak to you?

TEVYE: Later, Motel. Later.

MOTEL: I would like to speak to you.

TEVYE: Not now, Motel. I have problems.

MOTEL: That's what I want to speak to you about. I think I can help.

TEVYE: Certainly. Like a bandage can help a corpse. Goodbye, Motel. Goodbye.

TZEITEL: At least listen to him, Papa.

TEVYE: All right. You have a tongue, talk.

MOTEL: Reb Tevye, I hear you are arranging a match for Tzeitel.

TEVYE: He also has ears.

MOTEL: I have a match for Tzeitel.

TEVYE: What kind of match?

MOTEL: A perfect fit.

TEVYE: A perfect fit.

MOTEL: Like a glove.

TEVYE: Like a glove.

MOTEL: This match was made exactly to measure.

TEVYE: A perfect fit. Made to measure. Stop talking like a tailor and tell me who it is.

MOTEL: Please, don't shout at me.

TEVYE: All right. Who is it?

MOTEL: Who is it?

TEVYE: (*Pauses*) Who is it?

MOTEL: Who is it?

TEVYE: Who is it?

MOTEL: It's me—myself.

TEVYE: (*Stares at him, then turns to the audience, startled and amused*) Him? Himself? (*To* MOTEL) Either you're completely out of your mind or you're crazy. (*To the audience*) He must be crazy. (*To* MOTEL) Arranging a match for yourself. What are you, everything? The bridegroom, the matchmaker, the guests all rolled into one? I suppose you'll even perform the ceremony. You must be crazy!

MOTEL: Please don't shout at me, Reb Tevye. As for being my own matchmaker, I know it's a little unusual.

TEVYE: Unusual? It's crazy.

MOTEL: Times are changing, Reb Tevye. The thing is, your daughter Tzeitel and I gave each other our pledge more than a year ago that we would marry.

TEVYE: (*Stunned*) You gave each other your pledge?

TZEITEL: Yes, Papa, we gave each other our pledge.

TEVYE: (*Looks at them, turns to the audience. Sings "Tradition" reprise*)

They gave each other a pledge.
Unheard of, absurd.
You gave each other a pledge?
Unthinkable.
Where do you think you are?
In Moscow?
In Paris?
Where do they think they are?
America?
What do you think you're doing?
You stitcher, you nothing!
Who do you think you are?
King Solomon?

This isn't the way it's done,
Not here, not now.
Some things I will not, I cannot, allow.
Tradition—
Marriages must be arranged by the papa.
This should never be changed.
One little time you pull out a prop,
And where does it stop?
Where does it stop?

(*Speaks*)
Where does it stop? Do I still have something to say about my daughter, or doesn't anyone have to ask a father anymore?

MOTEL: I have wanted to ask you for some time, Reb Tevye, but first I wanted to save up for my own sewing machine.

TEVYE: Stop talking nonsense. You're just a poor tailor.

MOTEL: (*Bravely*) That's true, Reb Tevye, but even a poor tailor is entitled to some happiness. (*Looks at* TZEITEL, *triumphantly*) I promise you, Reb Tevye, your daughter will not starve.

TEVYE: (*Impressed, turns to the audience*) He's beginning to talk like a man. On the other hand, what kind of match would that be, with a poor tailor? On the other hand, he's an honest, hard worker. On the other hand, he has absolutely nothing. On the other hand, things could never get worse for him, they could only get better. (*Sings*)

They gave each other a pledge—
Unheard of, absurd.
They gave each other a pledge—
Unthinkable.
But look at my daughter's face—
She loves him, she wants him—
And look at my daughter's eyes,
So hopeful.

(*Shrugs. To the audience*)
Tradition!

(*To* TZEITEL *and* MOTEL)
Well, children, when shall we make the wedding?

TZEITEL: Thank you, Papa.

MOTEL: Reb Tevye, you won't be sorry.

TEVYE: I won't be sorry? I'm sorry already!

TZEITEL: Thank you, Papa.

MOTEL: Thank you, Papa.

TEVYE: Thank you, Papa! They pledged their troth! (*Starts to exit, then looks back at them*) Modern children! (*Has a sudden thought*) Golde! What will I tell Golde? What am I going to do about Golde? (*To heaven*) Help! (*Exits*)

TZEITEL: Motel, you were wonderful!

MOTEL: It was a miracle! It was a miracle. (*Sings "Miracle of Miracles"*)

Wonder of wonders, miracle of miracles,
God took a Daniel once again,
Stood by his side, and miracle of miracles,
Walked him through the lion's den.

Wonder of wonders, miracle of miracles,
I was afraid that God would frown.
But, like He did so long ago in Jericho,
God just made a wall fall down.

When Moses softened Pharaoh's heart,
That was a miracle.
When God made the waters of the Red Sea part,
That was a miracle, too.

But of all God's miracles large and small,
The most miraculous one of all
Is that out of a worthless lump of clay
God has made a man today.

Wonder of wonders, miracle of miracles,
God took a tailor by the hand,
Turned him around, and, miracle of miracles,
Led him to the Promised Land.

When David slew Goliath, yes!
That was a miracle.
When God gave us manna in the wilderness,
That was a miracle, too.

But of all God's miracles, large and small,
The most miraculous one of all
Is the one I thought could never be—
God has given you to me.

SCENE 7

TEVYE'S *bedroom. The room is in complete darkness. A groan is heard, then another, then a scream.*

TEVYE: Aagh! Lazar! Motel! Tzeitel!

GOLDE: What is it? What?

TEVYE: Help! Help! Help!

GOLDE: Tevye, wake up! (GOLDE *lights the lamp. The light reveals* TEVYE *asleep in bed*)

TEVYE: (*In his sleep*) Help! Help!

GOLDE: (*Shaking him*) Tevye! What's the matter with you? Why are you howling like that?

TEVYE: (*Opening his eyes, frightened*) Where is she? Where is she?

GOLDE: Where is who? What are you talking about?

TEVYE: Fruma-Sarah. Lazar Wolf's first wife, Fruma-Sarah. She was standing here a minute ago.

GOLDE: What's the matter with you, Tevye? Fruma-Sarah has been dead for years. You must have been dreaming. Tell me what you dreamt, and I'll tell you what it meant.

TEVYE: It was terrible.

GOLDE: Tell me.

TEVYE: All right—only don't be frightened!

GOLDE: (*Impatiently*) Tell me!

TEVYE: All right, this was my dream. In the beginning I dreamt that we were having a celebration of some kind. Everybody we knew was there, and musicians too.

(*As he speaks,* MEN, *including a* RABBI, WOMEN *and* MUSICIANS *enter the bedroom.* TEVYE, *wearing a nightshirt, starts to get out of bed to join the dream*)

TEVYE: In the middle of the dream, in walks your Grandmother Tzeitel, may she rest in peace.

GOLDE: (*Alarmed*) Grandmother Tzeitel? How did she look?

TEVYE: For a woman who is dead thirty years, she looked very good. Naturally, I went up to greet her. She said to me—

(GRANDMA TZEITEL *enters, and* TEVYE *approaches her and greets her in pantomime*)

GRANDMA TZEITEL: (*Sings "The Tailor, Motel Kamzoil"*)

A blessing on your head,

RABBI:

Mazeltov, Mazeltov.

GRANDMA TZEITEL:
To see a daughter wed.

RABBI:
Mazeltov, Mazeltov.

GRANDMA TZEITEL:
And such a son-in-law,
Like no one ever saw,
The tailor Motel Kamzoil.

GOLDE: (*Bewildered*) Motel?

GRANDMA TZEITEL:
A worthy boy is he,

RABBI:
Mazeltov, Mazeltov.

GRANDMA TZEITEL:
Of pious family.

RABBI:
Mazeltov, Mazeltov.

GRANDMA TZEITEL:
They named him after my
Dear Uncle Mordecai,
The tailor Motel Kamzoil.

GOLDE: A tailor! She must have heard wrong. She meant a butcher.

(TEVYE, *who has returned to* GOLDE, *listens to this, then runs back to* GRANDMA TZEITEL)

TEVYE:
You must have heard wrong, Grandma,
There's no tailor,
You mean a butcher, Grandma,
By the name of Lazar Wolf.

GRANDMA TZEITEL: (*Flies into the air, screaming angrily*) No!!
(*Sings*)
I mean a tailor, Tevye.
My little Tzeitel, who you named for me,
Motel's bride was meant to be.
For such a match I prayed.

CHORUS:
Mazeltov, Mazeltov,

GRANDMA TZEITEL:
In heaven it was made.

CHORUS:
Mazeltov, Mazeltov,

GRANDMA TZEITEL:
A fine upstanding boy,
A comfort and a joy,
The tailor Motel Kamzoil.

GOLDE: (*From bed*) But we announced it already. We made a bargain with the butcher.

TEVYE:
But we announced it, Grandma,
To our neighbors.
We made a bargain, Grandma,
With the butcher, Lazar Wolf.

GRANDMA TZEITEL: (*Again flies into the air, screaming angrily*) No!! (*Sings*)

So you announced it, Tevye,
That's your headache.
But as for Lazar Wolf, I say to you,
Tevye, that's your headache, too.

CHORUS:
A blessing on your house, Mazeltov, Mazeltov,
Imagine such a spouse, Mazeltov, Mazeltov,
And such a son-in-law,
Like no one ever saw,
The tailor Motel Kamzoil.

TEVYE: (*Speaks*) It was a butcher!

CHORUS:
The tailor Motel Kamzoil.

TEVYE: (*Speaks*) It was Lazar Wolf! (*Sings*)

The tailor Motel Kam . . .

CHORUS:
Shah! shah!
Look!
Who is this?
Who is this?
Who comes here?

Who? who? who? who? who?
What woman is this
By righteous anger shaken?

SOLO VOICES:
Could it be?
Sure!
Yes, it could!
Why not?
Who could be mistaken?

CHORUS:
It's the butcher's wife come from beyond the grave.
It's the butcher's dear, darling, departed wife,
Fruma-Sarah, Fruma-Sarah
Fruma-Sarah, Fruma-Sarah, Fruma-Sarah.

FRUMA-SARAH:
Tevye! Tevye!
What is this about your daughter marrying my husband?

CHORUS:
Yes, her husband.

FRUMA-SARAH:
Would you do this to your friend and neighbor,
Fruma-Sarah?

CHORUS:
Fruma-Sarah.

FRUMA-SARAH:
Have you no consideration for a woman's feelings?

CHORUS:
Woman's feelings.

FRUMA-SARAH:
Handing over my belongings to a total stranger.

CHORUS:
Total stranger.

FRUMA-SARAH:
How can you allow it, how?
How can you let your daughter take my place?
Live in my house, carry my keys,
And wear my clothes, pearls–how?

CHORUS:

How can you allow your daughter
To take her place?

FRUMA-SARAH:

Pearls!

CHORUS:

House!

FRUMA-SARAH:

Pearls!

CHORUS:

Keys!

FRUMA-SARAH:

Pearls!

CHORUS:

Clothes!

FRUMA-SARAH:

Pearls!

CHORUS:

How?

FRUMA-SARAH:

Tevye!

CHORUS:

Tevye!

FRUMA-SARAH:

Such a learned man as Tevye wouldn't let it happen.

CHORUS:

Let it happen.

FRUMA-SARAH:

Tell me that it isn't true, and then I wouldn't worry.

CHORUS:

Wouldn't worry.

FRUMA-SARAH:

Say you didn't give your blessing to your daughter's marriage.

CHORUS:

Daughter's marriage.

FRUMA-SARAH:
Let me tell you what would follow such a fatal wedding.

CHORUS:
Fatal wedding. Shh!

FRUMA-SARAH:
If Tzeitel marries Lazar Wolf,
I pity them both.
She'll live with him three weeks,
And when three weeks are up,
I'll come to her by night,
I'll take her by the throat, and . . .
This I'll give your Tzeitel,
That I'll give your Tzeitel,
This I'll give your Tzeitel,
(*Laughs wildly*)

Here's my wedding present if she marries Lazar Wolf!
(*She starts choking* TEVYE. *The* CHORUS *exits screaming*)

GOLDE: (*While* TEVYE *is being choked*) It's an evil spirit; may it fall into the river; may it sink into the earth. Such a dark and horrible dream! And to think it was brought on by that butcher. If my Grandmother Tzeitel, may she rest in peace, took the trouble to come all the way from the other world to tell us about the tailor, all we can say is that it is all for the best, and it couldn't possibly be any better. Amen.

TEVYE: Amen.

GOLDE: (*Sings*)
A blessing on my head, Mazeltov, Mazeltov,
Like Grandma Tzeitel said, Mazeltov, Mazeltov,
We'll have a son-in-law,
Like no one ever saw,
The tailor Motel Kamzoil.

TEVYE:
We haven't got the man,

GOLDE:
Mazeltov, Mazeltov.

TEVYE:
We had when we began.

GOLDE:
Mazeltov, Mazeltov.

TEVYE:

But since your Grandma came,
She'll marry what's his name?

GOLDE:

The tailor Motel Kamzoil.

TEVYE and GOLDE:

The tailor Motel Kamzoil,
The tailor Motel Kamzoil,
The tailor Motel Kamzoil.

(GOLDE *goes back to sleep.* TEVYE *mouths the words "Thank You" to God, and goes to sleep*)

SCENE 8

The village street and the interior of MOTEL'S *tailor shop.* MOTEL *and* CHAVA *are in the shop.* VILLAGERS *pass by.*

MAN: Bagels, fresh bagels.

WOMAN: (*Excited*) Did you hear? Did you hear? Tevye's Tzeitel is marrying Motel, not Lazar Wolf.

VILLAGERS: No!

WOMAN: Yes.

MENDEL: Tzeitel is marrying Motel?

WOMAN: Yes!

VILLAGERS: No! (*They rush into the shop and surround* MOTEL. MORDCHA *enters the street*) Mazeltov, Motel. Congratulations.

MORDCHA: What's all the excitement?

AVRAM: Tevye's Tzeitel is going to marry—

MORDCHA: I know. Lazar Wolf, the butcher. It's wonderful.

AVRAM: No. Motel, the tailor.

MORDCHA: Motel, the tailor, that's terrible! (*Rushes into the shop*) Mazeltov, Motel.

WOMAN: (*To* SHANDEL, *exiting from the shop*) Imagine! Tzeitel is marrying Motel. I can't believe it!

SHANDEL: (*Outraged*) What's wrong with my son, Motel?

WOMAN: Oh, excuse me, Shandel. Mazeltov.

VILLAGERS: (*Inside the shop*) Mazeltov, Mazeltov.

MOTEL: Yussel, do you have a wedding hat for me?

YUSSEL: Lazar Wolf ordered a hat but it's not cheap.

MOTEL: I got his bride, I can get his hat!

YUSSEL: Then come, Motel, come.

MOTEL: Chava, can you watch the shop for a few minutes? I'll be back soon.

CHAVA: Of course.

MOTEL: Thank you, Chava. (*They all exit from the shop, calling Mazeltovs*)

VILLAGERS: (*To* CHAVA) We just heard about your sister . . . Mazeltov, Chava . . . Mazeltov, Chava.

CHAVA: Thanks—thank you very much.

(*All but* CHAVA *exit.* FYEDKA, SASHA *and another* RUSSIAN *enter at the same time. They cross to* CHAVA, *blocking her way into the shop*)

SASHA and RUSSIAN: (*Mockingly, imitating others, with a slight mispronunciation*) Mazeltov, Chava, Mazeltov, Chava.

CHAVA: Please may I pass.

SASHA: (*Getting in her way*) Why? We're congratulating you.

RUSSIAN: Mazeltov, Chava.

FYEDKA: (*Calmly*) All right, stop it.

SASHA: What's wrong with you?

FYEDKA: Just stop it.

SASHA: Now listen here, Fyedka—

FYEDKA: Goodbye, Sasha. (SASHA *and the* RUSSIAN *hesitate*) I said goodbye! (*They look at* FYEDKA *curiously, then exit*) I'm sorry about that. They mean no harm.

CHAVA: Don't they? (*She enters shop. He follows her*) Is there something you want?

FYEDKA: Yes, I'd like to talk to you.

CHAVA: I'd rather not. (*She hesitates*)

FYEDKA: I've often noticed you at the bookseller's. Not many girls in this village like to read. (*A sudden thought strikes him. He extends the book he is holding*) Would you like to borrow this book? It's very good.

CHAVA: No, thank you.

FYEDKA: Why? Because I'm not Jewish? Do you feel about us the way they feel about you? I didn't think you would. And what do you know about me? Let me tell you about myself. I'm a pleasant fellow, charming, honest, ambitious, quite bright, and very modest.

CHAVA: I don't think we should be talking this way.

FYEDKA: I often do things I shouldn't. Go ahead, take the book. It's by Heinrich Heine. Happens to be Jewish, I believe.

CHAVA: That doesn't matter.

FYEDKA: You're quite right. (*She takes the book*) Good. After you return it, I'll ask you how you like it, and we'll talk about it for a while. Then we'll talk about life, how we feel about things, and it can all turn out quite pleasant.

(CHAVA *puts the book on the table as* MOTEL *enters*)

MOTEL: Oh, Fyedka! Can I do something for you?

FYEDKA: No, thank you. (*Starts to leave*)

MOTEL: Oh, you forgot your book.

CHAVA: No, it's mine.

MOTEL: Thank you, Chava. (CHAVA *takes the book and leaves the shop with* FYEDKA)

FYEDKA: (*Outside*) Good day, Chava.

CHAVA: Good day.

FYEDKA: (*Pleasantly*) Fyedka.

CHAVA: Good day, Fyedka. (*They exit,* MOTEL *puts on his wedding hat*)

SCENE 9

Part of TEVYE'S *yard. Night.* TZEITEL, *in a bridal gown, enters, followed by* TEVYE, GOLDE, HODEL, BIELKE, CHAVA, SHPRINTZE, *and* RELATIONS. MOTEL *enters, followed by his* PARENTS *and* RELATIONS. *Many* GUESTS *enter, carrying lit candles. The men take their places on the right, as a group, the women on the left;* TZEITEL *and* MOTEL *stand in the center.* MOTEL *places a veil over* TZEITEL'S *head.* FOUR MEN *enter, carrying a canopy. They are followed by the* RABBI. *The canopy is placed over* MOTEL *and* TZEITEL. GUESTS *start singing.*

TEVYE: (*Sings "Sunrise, Sunset"*)

Is this the little girl I carried?
Is this the little boy at play?

GOLDE:

I don't remember growing older.
When did they?

TEVYE:

When did she get to be a beauty?
When did he grow to be so tall?

GOLDE:

Wasn't it yesterday, when they were small?

MEN:

Sunrise, sunset,
Sunrise, sunset,

Swiftly flow the days.
Seedlings turn overnight to sunflowers,
Blossoming even as we gaze.

WOMEN:

Sunrise, sunset,
Sunrise, sunset,
Swiftly fly the years.
One season following another,
Laden with happiness and tears.

TEVYE:

What words of wisdom can I give them?
How can I help to ease their way?

GOLDE:

Now they must learn from one another
Day to day.

PERCHIK:

They look so natural together.

HODEL:

Just like two newlyweds should be.

PERCHIK and HODEL:

Is there a canopy in store for me?

ALL:

Sunrise, sunset,
Sunrise, sunset,
Swiftly fly the years.
One season following another,
Laden with happiness and tears.

(*During the song, the following mime is performed. The* RABBI *lifts* TZEITEL'S *veil. He prays over a goblet of wine and hands it to the bride and groom. They each sip from it.* TZEITEL *slowly walks in a circle around* MOTEL. MOTEL *places a ring on* TZEITEL'S *finger. The* RABBI *places a wineglass on the floor. The song ends. A moment's pause.* MOTEL *treads on the glass*)

ALL: (*At the moment the glass breaks*) Mazeltov!

SCENE 10

The set opens to show the entire yard of TEVYE'S *house. Part of it is divided down the center by a short partition. Several tables are set up at the rear of each section. The* MUSICIANS *play, and all dance and then seat themselves on benches at the tables. The women are on the left, the men on the right. As the dance concludes,* MORDCHA *mounts a stool and signals for silence. The noise subsides.*

ALL: Shah. Shah. Quiet. Reb Mordcha. Shah. Shah.

MORDCHA: My friends, we are gathered here to share the joy of the newlyweds, Motel and Tzeitel. May they live together in peace to a ripe old age. Amen.

ALL: Amen.

(*The* RABBI *slowly makes his way to the table, assisted by* MENDEL)

MORDCHA: Ah, here comes our beloved rabbi. May he be with us for many, many years.

RABBI: (*Ahead of the others*) Amen.

ALL: Amen.

MORDCHA: I want to announce that the bride's parents are giving the newlyweds the following: a new featherbed, a pair of pillows—

GOLDE: (*Shouting from the women's side*) *Goose* pillows.

MORDCHA: Goose pillows. And this pair of candlesticks.

ALL: Mazeltov!

MORDCHA: Now let us not in our joy tonight forget those who are no longer with us, our dear departed, who lived in pain and poverty and hardship and who died in pain and poverty and hardship. (*All sob. He pauses a moment*) But enough tears. (*The mourning stops immediately*) Let's be merry and content, like our good friend, Lazar Wolf, who has everything in the world, except a bride. (*Laughter*) But Lazar has no ill feelings. In fact, he has a gift for the newlyweds that he wants to announce himself. Come, Lazar Wolf.

LAZAR: (*Rising*) Like he said, I have no ill feelings. What's done is done. I am giving the newlyweds five chickens, one for each of the first five Sabbaths of their wedded life. (*Murmurs of appreciation from all*)

TEVYE: (*Rising*) Reb Lazar, you are a decent man. In the name of my daughter and her new husband, I accept your gift. There is a famous saying that—

LAZAR: Reb Tevye, I'm not marrying your daughter. I don't have to listen to your sayings.

TEVYE: If you would listen a second, I was only going to say—

LAZAR: Why should I listen to you? A man who breaks an agreement!

(*Murmurs by the assemblage*)

MENDEL: Not now, Lazar, in the middle of a wedding.

LAZAR: I have a right to talk.

TEVYE: (*Angry*) What right? This is not your wedding.

LAZAR: It should have been!

(*Murmurs by the assemblage*)

MENDEL: Reb Lazar, don't shame Reb Tevye at his daughter's wedding.

LAZAR: But he shamed me in front of the whole village!

(*An argument breaks out. Everyone takes sides*)

ALL: That's true . . . The rabbi said . . . It was a shame . . . He has no feelings . . . This is not the place–

MENDEL: Shah. Shah. Quiet. The rabbi. The rabbi, the rabbi.

RABBI: (*Rising, as the noise subsides*) I say–Let's sit down. (*Sits*)

TEVYE: We all heard the wise words of the rabbi.

(*Everyone returns to his seat*)

MORDCHA: Now, I'd like to sing a little song that–

TEVYE: (*Bursting out*) You can keep your diseased chickens!

LAZAR: Leave my chickens out of this. We made a bargain.

TEVYE: The terms weren't settled.

LAZAR: We drank on it–

FIRST MAN: I saw them, they drank on it.

SECOND MAN: But the terms weren't settled.

SHANDEL: What's done is done.

TEVYE: Once a butcher, always a butcher.

GOLDE: I had a sign. My own grandmother came to us from the grave.

YENTE: What sign? What grandmother? My grandfather came to me from the grave and told me that her grandmother was a big liar.

LAZAR: We drank on it.

(*Bedlam.* MORDCHA *tries to quiet the guests.* PERCHIK *climbs onto a stool, banging two tin plates together*)

MORDCHA: Quiet, I'm singing.

TEVYE: The terms weren't settled.

GOLDE: I had a sign.

YENTE: An agreement is an agreement.

PERCHIK: (*Silences them*) Quiet! Quiet! What's all the screaming about? "They drank on it–" "An agreement–" "A sign." It's all nonsense. Tzeitel wanted to marry Motel and not Lazar.

MENDEL: A young girl decides for herself?
PERCHIK: Why not? Yes! They love each other.
AVRAM: Love!
LAZAR: Terrible!
MENDEL: He's a radical!
YENTE: What happens to the matchmaker?
(*Another violent argument breaks out*)
RABBI: I say—I say—(*They all turn to him*)
TEVYE: Let's sit down? (RABBI *nods*)
MORDCHA: Musicians, play. A dance, a dance! (*The music starts, but no one dances*) Come on, dance. It's a wedding.
YENTE: Some wedding!
(PERCHIK *crosses to the women's side*)
AVRAM: What's he doing?
TEVYE: Perchik!
FIRST MAN: Stop him!
PERCHIK: (*To* HODEL) Who will dance with me?
MENDEL: That's a sin!
PERCHIK: It's no sin to dance at a wedding.
AVRAM: But with a girl?
LAZAR: That's what comes from bringing a wild man into your house.
TEVYE: (*Signaling* PERCHIK *to return to the men's side*) He's not a wild man. His ideas are a little different, but—
MENDEL: It's a sin.
PERCHIK: It's no sin. Ask the rabbi. Ask him. (*They all gather around the* RABBI)
TEVYE: Well, Rabbi?
RABBI: (*Thumbs through a book, finds the place*) Dancing—Well, it's not exactly forbidden, but—
TEVYE: There, you see? It's not forbidden.
PERCHIK: (*To* HODEL) And it's no sin. Now will someone dance with me? (HODEL *rises to dance*)
GOLDE: Hodel!
HODEL: It's only a dance, Mama.
PERCHIK: Play! (PERCHIK *and* HODEL *dance*)
LAZAR: Look at Tevye's daughter.
MENDEL: She's dancing with a man.
TEVYE: I can see she's dancing. (*Starts toward them as if to stop them. Changes his mind*) And I'm going to dance with my wife. Golde! (GOLDE *hesitates, then dances with him*)
SHANDEL: Golde! (MOTEL *crosses to* TZEITEL) Motel!

(TZEITEL *dances with* MOTEL. *Others join them. They all dance, except for* LAZAR *and* YENTE, *who storm off. As the dance reaches a wild climax, the* CONSTABLE *and his* MEN *enter, carrying clubs. The dancers see them and slowly stop*)

CONSTABLE: I see we came at a bad time, Tevye. I'm sorry, but the orders are for tonight. For the whole village. (*To the* MUSICIANS) Go on, play, play. All right, men.

(*The* RUSSIANS *begin their destruction, turning over tables, throwing pillows, smashing dishes and the window of the house. One of them throws the wedding-gift candlesticks to the ground, and* PERCHIK *grapples with him. But he is hit with a club and falls to the ground. The* GUESTS *leave*)

HODEL: (*Rushes to* PERCHIK) No, Perchik!

(*The* GUESTS *have left during the above action*)

CONSTABLE: (*To his* MEN) All right, enough! (*To* TEVYE) I am genuinely sorry. You understand. (TEVYE *does not answer. To his* MEN) Come. (*The* CONSTABLE *and his* MEN *exit*)

GOLDE: Take him in the house. (HODEL *helps* PERCHIK *into the house*)

TEVYE: (*Quietly*) What are you standing around for? Clean up. Clean up.

(*They start straightening up, picking up broken dishes, bringing bedding back to the house.* TZEITEL *picks up the candlesticks, one of which is broken. They freeze at sudden sounds of destruction in a nearby house, then continue straightening up as:*)

The Curtain Falls

ACT TWO

Prologue

The exterior of TEVYE'S *house.* TEVYE *is sitting on a bench.*

TEVYE: (*To heaven*) That was quite a dowry You gave my daughter Tzeitel at her wedding. Was that necessary? Anyway, Tzeitel and Motel have been married almost two months now. They work very hard, they are as poor as squirrels in winter. But they are both so happy they don't know how miserable they are. Motel keeps talking about a sewing machine. I know You're very busy—wars and revolutions, floods, plagues, all those little things that bring people to You—

couldn't You take a second away from Your catastrophes and get it for him? How much trouble would it be? Oh, and while You're in the neighborhood, my horse's left leg—Am I bothering You too much? I'm sorry. As the Good Book says—Why should I tell You what the Good Book says? (*Exits*)

SCENE 1

The exterior of TEVYE'S *house. Afternoon.* HODEL *enters, petulantly, followed by* PERCHIK.

PERCHIK: Please don't be upset, Hodel.

HODEL: Why should I be upset? If you must leave, you must.

PERCHIK: I do have to. They expect me in Kiev tomorrow morning.

HODEL: So you told me. Then goodbye.

PERCHIK: Great changes are about to take place in this country. Tremendous changes. But they can't happen by themselves.

HODEL: So naturally you feel that you personally have to—

PERCHIK: Not only me. Many people. Jews, Gentiles, many people hate what is going on. Don't you understand?

HODEL: I understand, of course. You want to leave. Then goodbye.

PERCHIK: Hodel, your father, the others here, think what happened at Tzeitel's wedding was a little cloudburst and it's over and everything will now be peaceful again. It won't. Horrible things are happening all over the land—pogroms, violence—whole villages are being emptied of their people. And it's reaching everywhere, and it will reach here. You understand?

HODEL: Yes, I—I suppose I do.

PERCHIK: I have work to do. The greatest work a man can do.

HODEL: Then goodbye, Perchik.

PERCHIK: Before I go (*He hesitates, then summons up courage*), there is a certain question I wish to discuss with you.

HODEL: Yes?

PERCHIK: A political question.

HODEL: What is it?

PERCHIK: The question of marriage.

HODEL: This is a political question?

PERCHIK: (*Awkwardly*) In a theoretical sense, yes. The relationship between a man and woman known as marriage is based on mutual beliefs, a common attitude and philosophy towards society—

HODEL: And affection.

PERCHIK: And affection. This relationship has positive social values. It reflects a unity and solidarity—

HODEL: And affection.

PERCHIK: Yes. And I personally am in favor of it. Do you understand?

HODEL: I think you are asking me to marry you.

PERCHIK: In a theoretical sense, yes, I am.

HODEL: I was hoping you were.

PERCHIK: Then I take it you approve? And we can consider ourselves engaged, even though I am going away? (*She nods*) I am very happy, Hodel. Very happy.

HODEL: So am I, Perchik.

PERCHIK: (*Sings "Now I Have Everything"*)

I used to tell myself
That I had everything,
But that was only half true.
I had an aim in life,
And that was everything,
But now I even have you.

I have something that I would die for,
Someone that I can live for, too.

Yes, now I have everything—
Not only everything,
I have a little bit more—
Besides having everything,
I know what everything's for.

I used to wonder,
Could there be a wife
To share such a difficult, wand'ring kind of life.

HODEL:

I was only out of sight,
Waiting right here.

PERCHIK:

Who knows tomorrow
Where our home will be?

HODEL:

I'll be with you and that's
Home enough for me.

PERCHIK:
Everything is right at hand.

HODEL and PERCHIK:
Simple and clear.

PERCHIK:
I have something that I would die for,
Someone that I can live for, too.

Yes, now I have everything—
Not only everything,
I have a little bit more—
Besides having everything,
I know what everything's for.

HODEL: And when will we be married, Perchik?

PERCHIK: I will send for you as soon as I can. It will be a hard life, Hodel.

HODEL: But it will be less hard if we live it together.

PERCHIK: Yes.
(TEVYE *enters*)

TEVYE: Good evening.

PERCHIK: Good evening. Reb Tevye, I have some bad news. I must leave this place.

TEVYE: When?

PERCHIK: Right away.

TEVYE: I'm sorry, Perchik. We will all miss you.

PERCHIK: But I also have some good news. You can congratulate me.

TEVYE: Congratulations. What for?

PERCHIK: We're engaged.

TEVYE: Engaged?

HODEL: Yes, Papa, we're engaged. (*Takes* PERCHIK'S *hand*)

TEVYE: (*Pleasantly, separating them*) No, you're not. I know, you like him, and he likes you, but you're going away, and you're staying here, so have a nice trip, Perchik. I hope you'll be very happy, and my answer is no.

HODEL: Please, Papa, you don't understand.

TEVYE: I understand. I gave my permission to Motel and Tzeitel, so you feel that you also have a right. I'm sorry, Perchik. I like you, but you're going away, so go in good health and my answer is still no.

HODEL: You don't understand, Papa.

TEVYE: (*Patiently*) You're not listening. I say no. I'm sorry, Hodel, but we'll find someone else for you, here in Anatevka.

PERCHIK: Reb Tevye.

TEVYE: What is it?

PERCHIK: We are not asking for your permission, only for your blessing. We are going to get married.

TEVYE: (*To* HODEL) You're not asking for my permission?

HODEL: But we would like your blessing, Papa.

TEVYE: (*"Tradition" Reprise*)

I can't believe my own ears. My blessing? For What?
For going over my head? Impossible.
At least with Tzeitel and Motel, they asked me,
They begged me.
But now, if I like it or not,
She'll marry him.
So what do you want from me? Go on, be wed.
And tear out my beard and uncover my head.
Tradition!
They're not even asking permission
From the papa.
What's happening to the tradition?
One little time I pulled out a thread
And where has it led? Where has it led?

Where has it led? To this! A man tells me he is getting married.
He doesn't ask me, he tells me. But first, he abandons her.

HODEL: He is not abandoning me, Papa.

PERCHIK: As soon as I can, I will send for her and marry her. I love her.

TEVYE: (*Mimicking him*) "I love her." Love. It's a new style. On the other hand, our old ways were once new, weren't they? On the other hand, they decided without parents, without a matchmaker. On the other hand, did Adam and Eve have a matchmaker? Yes, they did. Then it seems these two have the same matchmaker. (*Sings*)

They're going over my head—
Unheard of, absurd.
For this they want to be blessed?—
Unthinkable.
I'll lock her up in her room.
I couldn't—I should!—

But look at my daughter's eyes.
She loves him.
Tradition!

(*Shrugs*)
Very well, children, you have my blessing and my permission.

HODEL: Oh, thank you, Papa. You don't know how happy that makes me.

TEVYE: (*To the audience*) What else could I do?

PERCHIK: Thank you, Papa.

TEVYE: (*Worried*) "Thank you, Papa." What will I tell your mother? Another dream?

PERCHIK: Perhaps if you tell her something—that I am going to visit a rich uncle—something like that.

TEVYE: Please, Perchik. I can handle my own wife. (PERCHIK *and* HODEL *exit. He calls aggressively*) Golde! Golde! (*She enters from the house. He speaks timidly*) Hello, Golde. I've just been talking to Perchik and Hodel.

GOLDE: Well?

TEVYE: They seem to be very fond of each other—

GOLDE: Well?

TEVYE: Well, I have decided to give them my permission to become engaged. (*Starts into the house*)

GOLDE: (*Stopping him*) What? Just like this? Without even asking me?

TEVYE: (*Roaring*) Who asks you? I'm the father.

GOLDE: And who is he? A pauper. He has nothing, absolutely nothing!

TEVYE: (*Hesitating*) I wouldn't say that. I hear he has a rich uncle, a very rich uncle. (*Changes the subject*) He is a good man, Golde. I like him. He is a little crazy, but I like him. And what's more important, Hodel likes him. Hodel loves him. So what can we do? It's a new world, a new world. Love. (*Starts to go, then has a sudden thought*) Golde— (*Sings "Do You Love Me?"*)

Do you love me?

GOLDE: Do I what?

TEVYE:

Do you love me?

GOLDE:

Do I love you?

With our daughters getting married
And this trouble in the town,
You're upset, you're worn out,
Go inside, go lie down.
Maybe it's indigestion.

TEVYE: Golde, I'm asking you a question—

Do you love me?

GOLDE: You're a fool.

TEVYE: I know—

But do you love me?

GOLDE:

Do I love you?
For twenty-five years I've washed your clothes,
Cooked your meals, cleaned your house,
Given you children, milked the cow.
After twenty-five years, why talk about
Love right now?

TEVYE:

Golde, the first time I met you
Was on our wedding day.
I was scared.

GOLDE:

I was shy.

TEVYE:

I was nervous.

GOLDE:

So was I.

TEVYE:

But my father and my mother
Said we'd learn to love each other.
And now I'm asking, Golde,
Do you love me?

GOLDE:

I'm your wife.

TEVYE: I know—

But do you love me?

(*Above*) Anita (Chita Rivera) being taunted by members of The Jets in the drug-store. (*Below*) The Dance at the Gym. *Pictures, Fred Fehl*

(*Above*) The Jets and The Sharks rumble under the shadows of the highway. *Theatre Collection, New York Public Library*. (*Opposite*) Tony (Larry Kert) and Maria (Carol Lawrence) exchange vows in the bridal shop. *Fred Fehl*

(*Above*) Rose (Ethel Merman) storms the backstage bastion of daughter Gypsy Rose Lee (Sandra Church) at Minsky's burlesque theatre. (*Opposite, top*) Rose (Ethel Merman), Herbie (Jack Klugman), Louise (Sandra Church) and Chowsie. (*Opposite, below*) The dressing room in Wichita where Rose (Ethel Merman) and Louise (Sandra Church) encounter stripper Tessie Tura (Maria Karnilova). *Pictures, Friedman-Abeles*

5
INTERNATIONAL
CUISINE

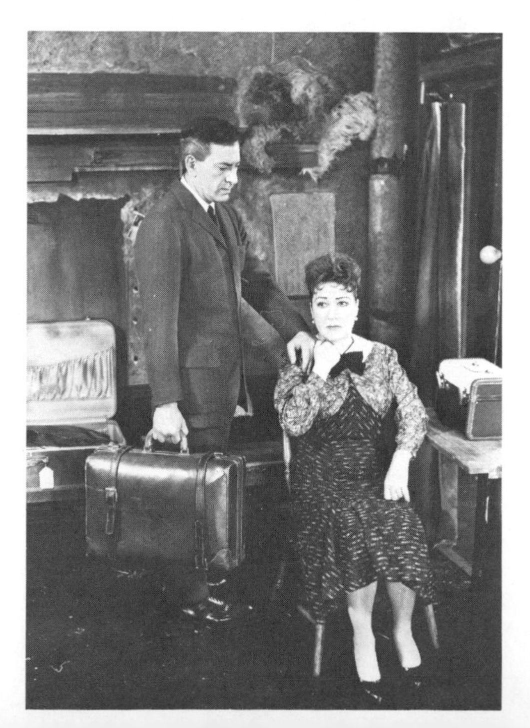

Herbie (Jack Klugman) bids farewell to Rose (Ethel Merman). *Friedman-Abeles*

(*Above*) Tevye (Zero Mostel), Anatevka's celebrated dairyman, seated on his cart, exploring the possibilities of "If I Were a Rich Man." (*Opposite, top*) The wedding of Tzeitel (Joanna Merlin) to Motel, the Tailor (Austin Pendleton). *Pictures, Friedman-Abeles*

(*Above*) Golde (Maria Karnilova) preparing to leave Anatevka. (*Below*) Tevye (Zero Mostel) celebrating "To Life." *Pictures, Friedman-Abeles*

GOLDE:

Do I love him?
For twenty-five years I've lived with him,
Fought with him, starved with him.
Twenty-five years my bed is his.
If that's not love, what is?

TEVYE:

Then you love me?

GOLDE:

I suppose I do.

TEVYE:

And I suppose I love you, too.

TEVYE and GOLDE:

It doesn't change a thing,
But even so,
After twenty-five years,
It's nice to know.

SCENE 2

The village street. YENTE, TZEITEL, *and other* VILLAGERS *cross.* YENTE *and* TZEITEL *meet.*

FISH SELLER: Fish! Fresh fish!

YENTE: Oh, Tzeitel, Tzeitel darling. Guess who I just saw! Your sister Chava with that Fyedka! And it's not the first time I've seen them together.

TZEITEL: You saw Chava with Fyedka?

YENTE: Would I make it up? Oh, and Tzeitel, I happened to be at the post office today and the postman told me there was a letter there for your sister Hodel.

TZEITEL: Wonderful, I'll go get it. (*Starts off*)

YENTE: I got it! It's from her intended, Perchik. (*Hands letter to* TZEITEL)

TZEITEL: Hodel will be so happy, she's been waiting–But it's open.

YENTE: It happened to be open. (TZEITEL *exits.* YENTE *watches her leave, then turns to a group of* VILLAGERS) Rifka, I have such news for you. (*Sings "I Just Heard"*)

Remember Perchik, that crazy student?
Remember at the wedding,
When Tzeitel married Motel

And Perchik started dancing
With Tevye's daughter Hodel?
Well, I just learned
That Perchik's been arrested, in Kiev.

VILLAGERS: No!

YENTE: Yes! (YENTE *and the* FIRST GROUP *exit. A* WOMAN *crosses to a* SECOND GROUP)

FIRST WOMAN:

Shandel, Shandel! Wait till I tell you—
Remember Perchik, that crazy student?
Remember at the wedding,
He danced with Tevye's Hodel?
Well,
I just heard
That Hodel's been arrested, in Kiev.

VILLAGERS: No! Terrible, terrible! (*The* SECOND GROUP *exits. A* SECOND WOMAN *crosses to a* THIRD GROUP)

SECOND WOMAN:

Mirila!
Do you remember Perchik,
That student, from Kiev?
Remember how he acted
When Tzeitel married Motel?
Well, I just heard
That Motel's been arrested
For dancing at the wedding.

VILLAGERS: No!

SECOND WOMAN: In Kiev!

(*The* THIRD GROUP *exits.* MENDEL *crosses to a* FOURTH GROUP)

MENDEL:

Rabbi! Rabbi!
Remember Perchik, with all his strange ideas?
Remember Tzeitel's wedding
Where Tevye danced with Golde?
Well, I just heard
That Tevye's been arrested
And Golde's gone to Kiev.

VILLAGERS: No!

MENDEL: God forbid.

VILLAGERS: She didn't.

MENDEL: She did.

(*The* FOURTH GROUP *exits.* AVRAM *crosses to the* FIFTH GROUP. YENTE *enters and stands at the edge of the* GROUP *to listen*)

AVRAM:

Listen, everybody, terrible news—terrible—
Remember Perchik,
Who started all the trouble?
Well, I just heard, from someone who should know,
That Golde's been arrested,
And Hodel's gone to Kiev.
Motel studies dancing,
And Tevye's acting strange.
Shprintze has the measles,
And Bielke has the mumps.

YENTE:

And that's what comes from men and women dancing!

SCENE 3

The exterior of the railroad station. Morning. HODEL *enters and walks over to a bench.* TEVYE *follows, carrying her suitcase.*

HODEL: You don't have to wait for the train, Papa. You'll be late for your customers.

TEVYE: Just a few more minutes. Is he in bad trouble, that hero of yours? (*She nods*) Arrested? (*She nods*) And convicted?

HODEL: Yes, but he did nothing wrong. He cares nothing for himself. Everything he does is for humanity.

TEVYE: But if he did nothing wrong, he wouldn't be in trouble.

HODEL: Papa, how can you say that, a learned man like you? What wrongs did Joseph do, and Abraham, and Moses? And they had troubles.

TEVYE: But why won't you tell me where he is now, this Joseph of yours?

HODEL: It is far, Papa, terribly far. He is in a settlement in Siberia.

TEVYE: Siberia! And he asks you to leave your father and mother and join him in that frozen wasteland, and marry him there?

HODEL: No, Papa, he did not ask me to go. I *want* to go. I don't want him to be alone. I want to help him in his work. It is the greatest work a man can do.

TEVYE: But, Hodel, baby—

HODEL: Papa—(*Sings "Far From the Home I Love"*)

How can I hope to make you understand
Why I do what I do,
Why I must travel to a distant land
Far from the home I love?

Once I was happily content to be
As I was, where I was,
Close to the people who are close to me
Here in the home I love.

Who could see that a man would come
Who would change the shape of my dreams?
Helpless, now, I stand with him
Watching older dreams grow dim.

Oh, what a melancholy choice this is,
Wanting home, wanting him,
Closing my heart to every hope but his,
Leaving the home I love.

There where my heart has settled long ago
I must go, I must go.
Who could imagine I'd be wand'ring so
Far from the home I love?
Yet, there with my love, I'm home.

TEVYE: And who, my child, will there be to perform a marriage, there in the wilderness?

HODEL: Papa, I promise you, we will be married under a canopy.

TEVYE: No doubt a rabbi or two was also arrested. Well, give him my regards, this Moses of yours. I always thought he was a good man. Tell him I rely on his honor to treat my daughter well. Tell him that.

HODEL: Papa, God alone knows when we shall see each other again.

TEVYE: Then we will leave it in His hands. (*He kisses* HODEL, *starts to go, stops, looks back, then looks to heaven*) Take care of her. See that she dresses warm. (*He exits, leaving* HODEL *seated on the station platform*)

SCENE 4

The village street, some months later. The VILLAGERS *enter.*

AVRAM: Reb Mordcha, did you hear the news? A new arrival at Motel and Tzeitel's.

MORDCHA: A new arrival at Motel and Tzeitel's? I must congratulate him.

AVRAM: Rabbi, did you hear the news? A new arrival at Motel and Tzeitel's.

RABBI: Really?

MENDEL: Mazeltov.

FIRST MAN: Mazeltov.

SECOND MAN: Mazeltov.

(SHANDEL *crosses quickly, meeting a* WOMAN)

WOMAN: Shandel, where are you running?

SHANDEL: To my boy, Motel. There's a new arrival there.

VILLAGERS: Mazeltov, Mazeltov, Mazeltov, Shandel.

SCENE 5

MOTEL'S *tailor shop.* MOTEL *and* CHAVA *are in the shop.* GOLDE *and the* VILLAGERS *crowd around* MOTEL, *congratulating him. They fall back, revealing a used sewing machine.*

VILLAGERS: Mazeltov, Motel. We just heard. Congratulations. Wonderful.

MOTEL: Thank you, thank you, very much.

(TZEITEL *enters*)

AVRAM: Mazeltov, Tzeitel.

TZEITEL: (*Ecstatic*) You got it!

MOTEL: I got it!

TZEITEL: It's beautiful.

MOTEL: I know!

TZEITEL: Have you tried it yet?

MOTEL: (*Holds up two different-colored pieces of cloth sewn together*) Look.

TZEITEL: Beautiful.

MOTEL: I know. And in less than a minute. And see how close and even the stitches are.

TZEITEL: Beautiful.

MOTEL: I know. From now on, my clothes will be perfect, made by machine. No more handmade clothes.

(*The* RABBI *enters*)

MORDCHA: The rabbi, the rabbi.

MOTEL: Look, Rabbi, my new sewing machine.

RABBI: Mazeltov.

TZEITEL: Rabbi, is there a blessing for a sewing machine?

RABBI: There is a blessing for everything. (*Prays*) Amen.

VILLAGERS: Amen . . . Mazeltov. (VILLAGERS, RABBI *exit*)

GOLDE: And the baby? How is the baby?

TZEITEL: He's wonderful, Mama.

(FYEDKA *enters. There is an awkward pause*)

FYEDKA: Good afternoon.

MOTEL: Good afternoon, Fyedka.

FYEDKA: I came for the shirt.

MOTEL: It's ready.

TZEITEL: See, it's my new sewing machine.

FYEDKA: I see. Congratulations.

MOTEL: Thank you.

FYEDKA: (*After another awkward moment*) Good day. (*Leaves the shop*)

MOTEL: Good day.

GOLDE: How does it work?

MOTEL: See, it's an amazing thing. You work it with your foot and your hand.

(CHAVA *exits from the shop and meets* FYEDKA *outside*)

FYEDKA: They still don't know about us? (*She shakes her head*) You must tell them.

CHAVA: I will, but I'm afraid.

FYEDKA: Chava, let me talk to your father.

CHAVA: No, that would be the worst thing, I'm sure of it.

FYEDKA: Let me try.

CHAVA: No, I'll talk to him. I promise.

(TEVYE *enters*)

FYEDKA: (*Extending his hand*) Good afternoon.

TEVYE: (*Takes the hand limply*) Good afternoon.

FYEDKA: (*Looks at* CHAVA) Good day. (*Exits*)

TEVYE: Good day. What were you and he talking about?

CHAVA: Nothing, we were just talking. (TEVYE *turns to go into* MOTEL'S *shop*) Papa, Fyedka and I have known each other for a long time and and—

TEVYE: (*Turning back*) Chava, I would be much happier if you would remain friends from a distance. You must not forget who you are and who that man is.

CHAVA: He has a name, Papa.

TEVYE: Of course. All creatures on earth have a name.

CHAVA: Fyedka is not a creature, Papa. Fyedka is a man.

TEVYE: Who says that he isn't? It's just that he is a different kind of man. As the Good Book says, "Each shall seek his own kind." Which, translated, means, "A bird may love a fish, but where would they build a home together?" (*He starts toward the shop, but* CHAVA *seizes his arm*)

CHAVA: The world is changing, Papa.

TEVYE: No. Some things do not change for us. Some things will never change.

CHAVA: We don't feel that way.

TEVYE: We?

CHAVA: Fyedka and I. We want to be married.

TEVYE: Are you out of your mind? Don't you know what this means, marrying outside of the faith?

CHAVA: But, Papa—

TEVYE: No, Chava! I said no! Never talk about this again! Never mention his name again! Never see him again! Never! Do you understand me?

CHAVA: Yes, Papa. I understand you.

(GOLDE *enters from the shop, followed by* SHPRINTZE *and* BIELKE)

GOLDE: You're finally here? Let's go home. It's time for supper.

TEVYE: I want to see Motel's new machine.

GOLDE: You'll see it some other time. It's late.

TEVYE: Quiet, woman, before I get angry. And when I get angry, even flies don't dare to fly.

GOLDE: I'm very frightened of you. After we finish supper, I'll faint. Come home.

TEVYE: (*Sternly*) Golde. I am the man in the family. I am head of the house. I want to see Motel's new machine, now! (*Strides to the door of the shop, opens it, looks in, closes the door, turns to* GOLDE) Now, let's go home! (*They exit.* CHAVA *remains looking after them*)

SCENE 6

A road. Late afternoon. TEVYE *is pushing his cart.*

TEVYE: (*Sinks down on the cart*) How long can that miserable horse of mine complain about his leg? (*Looks up*) Dear God, if I can walk on two legs, why can't he walk on three? I know I shouldn't be too upset with him. He is one of Your creatures and he has the same rights as I have: the right to be sick, the right to be hungry, the right to work like a horse. And, dear God, I'm sick and tired of pulling this cart. I know, I know, I should push it a while. (*He starts pushing the cart*)

GOLDE: (*Offstage*) Tevye! (*She enters, upset*) Tevye!

TEVYE: (*Struck by her manner*) What? What is it?

GOLDE: It's Chava. She left home this morning. With Fyedka.

TEVYE: What?

GOLDE: I looked all over for her. I even went to the priest. He told me—they were married.

TEVYE: Married! (*She nods*) Go home, Golde. We have other children at home. Go home, Golde. You have work to do. I have work to do.

GOLDE: But, Chava—

TEVYE: Chava is dead to us! We will forget her. Go home. (GOLDE *exits*)

TEVYE: (*Sings "Chavaleh"*)
Little bird, little Chavaleh,
I don't understand what's happening today.
Everything is all a blur.
All I can see is a happy child,
The sweet little bird you were,
Chavaleh, Chavaleh.
Little bird, little Chavaleh,
You were always such a pretty little thing.
Everybody's fav'rite child,
Gentle and kind and affectionate,
What a sweet little bird you were,
Chavaleh, Chavaleh.
(CHAVA *enters*)

CHAVA: Papa, I want to talk with you. Papa, stop. At least listen to me. Papa, I beg you to accept us.

TEVYE: (*To heaven*) Accept them? How can I accept them. Can I deny everything I believe in? On the other hand, can I deny my own child? On the other hand, how can I turn my back on my faith, my people? If I try to bend that far, I will break. On the other hand . . . there is no other hand. No, Chava. No—no—no!

CHAVA: Papa. Papa.

VILLAGERS: (*Seen behind a transparent curtain, sing as* CHAVA *exits slowly*)
Tradition. Tradition. Tradition.

SCENE 7

TEVYE'S *barn.* YENTE *enters with two* BOYS, *teenage students, who are obviously uncomfortable in the situation.*

YENTE: Golde, are you home? I've got the two boys, the boys I told you about.

(GOLDE *enters, followed by* SHPRINTZE *and* BIELKE)

YENTE: Golde darling, here they are, wonderful boys, both learned boys, Golde, from good families, each of them a prize, a jewel. You couldn't do better for your girls—just right. From the top of the tree.

GOLDE: I don't know, Yente. My girls are still so young.

YENTE: So what do *they* look like, grandfathers? Meanwhile they'll be engaged, nothing to worry about later, no looking around, their future all signed and sealed.

GOLDE: Which one for which one?

YENTE: What's the difference? Take your pick.

GOLDE: I don't know, Yente. I'll have to talk with—

(*Enter* LAZAR WOLF, AVRAM, MENDEL, MORDCHA, *and other* VILLAGERS)

AVRAM: Golde, is Reb Tevye home?

GOLDE: Yes, but he's in the house. Why, is there some trouble?

AVRAM: (*To* BIELKE *and* SHPRINTZE) Call your father. (*They exit*)

YENTE: (*To the* BOYS) Go home. Tell your parents I'll talk to them. (*They exit*)

GOLDE: What is it? Why are you all gathered together like a bunch of goats? What's—

(TEVYE *enters*)

AVRAM: Reb Tevye, have you seen the constable today?

TEVYE: No. Why?

LAZAR: There are some rumors in town. We thought because you knew him so well, maybe he told you what is true and what is not.

TEVYE: What rumors?

AVRAM: Someone from Zolodin told me that there was an edict issued in St. Petersburg that all—shh. Shh.

(*He stops as the* CONSTABLE *enters with* TWO MEN)

TEVYE: Welcome, your Honor. What's the good news in the world?

CONSTABLE: I see you have company.

TEVYE: They are my friends.

CONSTABLE: It's just as well. What I have to say is for their ears also. Tevye, how much time do you need to sell your house and all your household goods? (*There is a gasp from the* VILLAGERS. *They are stunned. They look to* TEVYE)

TEVYE: Why should I sell my house? Is it in anybody's way?

CONSTABLE: I came here to tell you that you are going to have to leave Anatevka.

TEVYE: And how did I come to deserve such an honor?

CONSTABLE: Not just you, of course, but all of you. At first I thought you might be spared, Tevye, because of your daughter Chava, who married—

TEVYE: My daughter is dead!

CONSTABLE: I understand. At any rate, it affects all of you. You have to leave.

TEVYE: But this corner of the world has always been our home. Why should we leave?

CONSTABLE: (*Irritated*) I don't know why. There's trouble in the world. Troublemakers.

TEVYE: (*Ironically*) Like us!

CONSTABLE: You aren't the only ones. Your people must leave all the villages—Zolodin, Rabalevka. The whole district must be emptied. (*Horrified and amazed exclamations from the* VILLAGERS) I have an order here, and it says that you must sell your homes and be out of here in three days.

VILLAGERS: Three days! . . . Out in three days!

TEVYE: And you who have known us all your life, you'd carry out this order?

CONSTABLE: I have nothing to do with it, don't you understand?

TEVYE: (*Bitterly*) We understand.

FIRST MAN: And what if we refuse to go?

CONSTABLE: You will be forced out.

LAZAR: We will defend ourselves.

VILLAGERS: Stay in our homes . . . Refuse to leave . . . Keep our land.

SECOND MAN: Fight!

CONSTABLE: Against our army? I wouldn't advise it!

TEVYE: I have some advice for you. Get off my land! (*The* VILLAGERS *crowd toward the* CONSTABLE *and his* MEN) This is still my home, my land. Get off my land! (*The* CONSTABLE *and his* MEN *start to go. The* CONSTABLE *turns*)

CONSTABLE: You have three days! (*Exits*)

FIRST MAN: After a lifetime, a piece of paper and get thee out.

MORDCHA: We should get together with the people of Zolodin. Maybe they have a plan.

FIRST MAN: We should defend ourselves. An eye for an eye, a tooth for a tooth.

TEVYE: Very good. And that way, the whole world will be blind and toothless.

MENDEL: Rabbi, we've been waiting for the Messiah all our lives. Wouldn't this be a good time for him to come?

RABBI: We'll have to wait for him someplace else. Meanwhile, let's start packing. (*The* VILLAGERS *start to go, talking together*)

VILLAGERS: He's right . . . I'll see you before I go.

FIRST MAN: Three days!

MORDCHA: How will I be able to sell my shop? My merchandise?

THIRD MAN: Where can I go with a wife, her parents, and three children?

(*Exits all but* YENTE, GOLDE, AVRAM, LAZAR, MENDEL, *and* TEVYE)

YENTE: Well, Anatevka hasn't been exactly the Garden of Eden.

AVRAM: That's true.

GOLDE: After all, what've we got here? (*Sings "Anatevka"*)

A little bit of this,
A little bit of that,

YENTE:

A pot,

LAZAR:

A pan,

MENDEL:

A broom,

AVRAM:

A hat.

TEVYE: (*Speaks*) Someone should have set a match to this place long ago.

MENDEL:

A bench,

AVRAM:

A tree,

GOLDE:

So what's a stove?

LAZAR:

Or a house?

MENDEL: (*Speaks*) People who pass through Anatevka don't even know they've been here.

GOLDE:
A stick of wood,

YENTE:
A piece of cloth.

ALL:
What do we leave?
Nothing much,
Only Anatevka . . .

Anatevka, Anatevka,
Underfed, overworked Anatevka,
Where else could Sabbath be so sweet?

Anatevka, Anatevka
Intimate, obstinate Anatevka,
Where I know everyone I meet.

Soon I'll be a stranger in a strange new place,
Searching for an old familiar face
From Anatevka.

I belong in Anatevka,
Tumbledown, workaday Anatevka,
Dear little village, little town of mine.

GOLDE: Eh, it's just a place.
MENDEL: And our forefathers have been forced out of many, many places at a moment's notice.
TEVYE: (*Shrugs*) Maybe that's why we always wear our hats.

SCENE 8

Outside TEVYE'S *house.* MOTEL *and* TZEITEL *are packing baggage into a cart and a wagon.* SHPRINTZE *and* BIELKE *enter with bundles.*

SHPRINTZE: Where will we live in America?
MOTEL: With Uncle Abram, but he doesn't know it yet.
SHPRINTZE: I wish you and the baby were coming with us.
TZEITEL: We'll be staying in Warsaw until we have enough money to join you.
GOLDE: (*Entering, with goblets*) Motel, be careful with these. My mother and father, may they rest in peace, gave them to us on our wedding day.
TZEITEL: (*To* BIELKE *and* SHPRINTZE) Come, children, help me pack the rest of the clothes. (*They exit into house*)
YENTE: (*Enters*) Golde darling, I had to see you before I left

because I have such news for you. Golde darling, you remember I told you yesterday I didn't know where to go, what to do with these old bones? Now I know! You want to hear? I'll tell you. Golde darling, all my life I've dreamed of going to one place and now I'll walk, I'll crawl, I'll get there. Guess where. You'll never guess. Every year at Passover, what do we say? "Next year in Jerusalem, next year in the Holy Land."

GOLDE: You're going to the Holy Land!

YENTE: You guessed! And you know why? In my sleep, my husband, my Aaron, came to me and said, "Yente, go to the Holy Land." Usually, of course, I wouldn't listen to him, because, good as he was, too much brains he wasn't blessed with. But in my sleep it's a sign. Right? So, somehow or other, I'll get to the Holy Land. And you want to know what I'll do there? I'm a matchmaker, no? I'll arrange marriages, yes? Children come from marriages, no? So I'm going to the Holy Land to help our people increase and multiply. It's my mission. So goodbye, Golde.

GOLDE: Goodbye, Yente. Be well and go in peace. (*They embrace*)

YENTE: (*Exiting*) Maybe next time, Golde, we will meet on happier occasions. Meanwhile, we suffer, we suffer, we suffer in silence! Right? Of course, right. (*She exits.* GOLDE *sits on a large straw trunk, sadly wrapping a pair of silver goblets.* TEVYE *enters, carrying a bundle of books, and puts them on the wagon*)

TEVYE: We'll have to hurry, Golde. (*She is looking at the goblets*) Come, Golde, we have to leave soon.

GOLDE: Leave. It sounds so easy.

TEVYE: We'll all be together soon. Motel, Tzeitel and the baby, they'll come too, you'll see. That Motel is a person.

GOLDE: And Hodel and Perchik? When will we ever see them?

TEVYE: Do they come visiting us from Siberia every Sabbath? You know what she writes. He sits in prison, and she works, and soon he will be set free and together they will turn the world upside down. She couldn't be happier. And the other children will be with us.

GOLDE: (*Quietly*) Not all.

TEVYE: (*Sharply*) All. Come, Golde, we have to get finished.

GOLDE: I still have to sweep the floor.

TEVYE: Sweep the floor?

GOLDE: I don't want to leave a dirty house. (*She exits behind the house as* LAZAR *enters, carrying a large suitcase*)

LAZAR: Well, Tevye, I'm on my way.

TEVYE: Where are you going?

LAZAR: Chicago. In America. My wife, Fruma-Sarah, may she rest in peace, has a brother there.

TEVYE: That's nice.

LAZAR: I hate him, but a relative is a relative! (*They embrace*) Goodbye, Tevye. (LAZAR *exits.* TEVYE *enters the house, passing* TZEITEL, *who enters with a blanket and a small bundle*)

TEVYE: Tzeitel, are they finished inside?

TZEITEL: Almost, Papa. (TZEITEL *puts the blanket on* MOTEL'S *wagon, kneels down, and begins rummaging in the bundle.* CHAVA *and* FYEDKA *enter.* TZEITEL *turns to enter the house, and sees them*) CHAVA! (CHAVA *runs to her. They embrace.* TZEITEL *looks toward the house*) Papa will see you.

CHAVA: I want him to. I want to say goodbye to him.

TZEITEL: He will not listen.

CHAVA: But at least he will hear.

TZEITEL: Maybe it would be better if I went inside and told Mama that—

(GOLDE *comes round the side of the house*)

GOLDE: Chava!

(*She starts toward her as* TEVYE *enters from the house with a length of rope. He sees them, turns, re-enters house, returns, and bends down to tie up the straw trunk, his back to* CHAVA *and* FYEDKA)

CHAVA: Papa, we came to say goodbye. (TEVYE *does not respond, but goes on working*) We are also leaving this place. We are going to Cracow.

FYEDKA: We cannot stay among people who can do such things to others.

CHAVA: We wanted you to know that. Goodbye, Papa, Mama. (*She waits for an answer, gets none, and turns to go*)

FYEDKA: Yes, we are also moving. Some are driven away by edicts, others by silence. Come, Chava.

TZEITEL: Goodbye, Chava, Fyedka.

TEVYE: (*To* TZEITEL, *prompting her under his breath as he turns to another box*) God be with you!

TZEITEL: (*Looks at him, then speaks to* CHAVA, *gently*) God be with you!

CHAVA: We will write to you in America. If you like.

GOLDE: We will be staying with Uncle Abram.

CHAVA: Yes, Mama. (CHAVA *and* FYEDKA *exit.* TEVYE *turns and watches them leave. There is a moment of silence; then he turns on* GOLDE)

TEVYE: (*With mock irritation*) We will be staying with Uncle Abram! We will be staying with Uncle Abram! The whole world has to know our business!

GOLDE: Stop yelling and finish packing. We have a train to catch. (MOTEL, SHPRINTZE, *and* BIELKE *enter from the house*)

TEVYE: I don't need your advice, Golde. Tzeitel, don't forget the baby. We have to catch a train, and a boat. Bielke, Shprintze, put the bundles on the wagon.

(TEVYE *moves the wagon to the center of the stage, and* MOTEL *puts the trunk on it.* TZEITEL *brings the baby out of the house. They turn to one another for goodbyes*)

TZEITEL: Goodbye, Papa. (*They embrace*)

GOLDE: Goodbye, Motel.

MOTEL: Goodbye, Mama.

(TZEITEL *and* GOLDE *embrace*)

TEVYE: Work hard, Motel. Come to us soon.

MOTEL: I will, Reb Tevye. I'll work hard. (TEVYE *takes one last look at the baby, then* TZEITEL *and* MOTEL *exit with their cart. When they are gone,* TEVYE *turns to the wagon*)

TEVYE: (*Picking up pots*) Come, children. Golde, we can leave these pots.

GOLDE: No, we can't.

TEVYE: All right, we'll take them. (*Puts them back*)

BIELKE: (*Childishly, swinging around with* SHPRINTZE) We're going on a train and a boat. We're going on a—

GOLDE: (*Sharply*) Stop that! Behave yourself! We're not in America yet!

TEVYE: Come, children. Let's go.

(*The stage begins to revolve, and* TEVYE *begins to pull the wagon in the opposite direction. The other* VILLAGERS, *including the* FIDDLER, *join the circle. The revolve stops. There is a last moment together, and the* VILLAGERS *exit, at different times and in opposite directions, leaving the family on stage.* TEVYE *begins to pull his wagon upstage, revealing the* FIDDLER, *playing his theme.* TEVYE *stops, turns, beckons to him. The* FIDDLER *tucks his violin under his arm and follows the family upstage as:*)

The Curtain Falls

1776

Book by Peter Stone
Music and Lyrics by Sherman Edwards

(Based on a conception of Sherman Edwards)

Production Notes

1776 was first presented by Stuart Ostrow at the Forty-Sixth Street Theatre, New York, on March 16, 1969. The cast was as follows:

Members of the Continental Congress

President
John Hancock, *David Ford*

New Hampshire
Dr. Josiah Bartlett, *Paul-David Richards*

Massachusetts
John Adams, *William Daniels*

Rhode Island
Stephen Hopkins, *Roy Poole*

Connecticut
Roger Sherman, *David Vosburgh*

New York
Lewis Morris, *Ronald Kross*
Robert Livingston, *Henry Le Clair*

New Jersey
Reverend John Witherspoon, *Edmund Lyndeck*

Pennsylvania
Benjamin Franklin, *Howard Da Silva*
John Dickinson, *Paul Hecht*
James Wilson, *Emory Bass*

Delaware
Caesar Rodney, *Robert Gaus*
Colonel Thomas McKean, *Bruce MacKay*
George Read, *Duane Bodin*

Maryland
Samuel Chase, *Philip Polito*

Virginia
Richard Henry Lee, *Ronald Holgate*
Thomas Jefferson, *Ken Howard*

North Carolina
Joseph Hewes, *Charles Rule*

South Carolina
Edward Rutledge, *Clifford David*

Georgia
Dr. Lyman Hall, *Jonathan Moore*

Secretary
Charles Thomson, *Ralston Hill*

Custodian and bell-ringer
Andrew McNair, *William Duell*

Abigail Adams, *Virginia Vestoff*
Martha Jefferson, *Betty Buckley*
A Leather Apron, *B. J. Slater*
A Painter, *William Duell*
A Courier, *Scott Jarvis*

Directed by *Peter Hunt*
Musical numbers staged by *Onna White*
Scenery and lighting by *Jo Mielziner*
Costumes by *Patricia Zipprodt*
Musical direction and dance arrangements by *Peter Howard*
Orchestrations by *Eddie Sauter*
Vocal arrangements by *Elise Bretton*

The Place

A single setting representing the Chamber and an Anteroom of the Continental Congress; a Mall, High Street, and Thomas Jefferson's room, in Philadelphia; and certain reaches of John Adams' mind.

The Time

May, June, and July, 1776.

The Scenes

1 The Chamber of the Continental Congress
2 The Mall
3 The Chamber
4 Thomas Jefferson's room and High Street
5 The Chamber
6 A Congressional Anteroom
7 The Chamber

The action is continuous, without intermission.

Musical Numbers

Scene 1.

Sit Down, John — John Adams and the Congress
Piddle, Twiddle, and Resolve — Adams
Till Then — John and Abigail Adams

Scene 2.

The Lees of Old Virginia — Lee, Franklin, and Adams

Scene 3.

But, Mr. Adams– — Adams, Franklin, Jefferson, Sherman, and Livingston

Scene 4.

Yours, Yours, Yours — John and Abigail Adams
He Plays the Violin — Martha Jefferson, Franklin, and Adams

Scene 5.

Cool, Cool Considerate Men — Dickinson and the Conservatives
Momma, Look Sharp — Courier, McNair, and Leather Apron

Scene 6.

The Egg — Franklin, Adams, and Jefferson

Scene 7.

Molasses to Rum — Rutledge
Yours, Yours, Yours (Reprise) — Abigail Adams
Is Anybody There? — Adams

SCENE 1

In front of the curtain.

JOHN ADAMS: I have come to the conclusion that one useless man is called a disgrace, that two are called a law firm, and that three or more become a Congress. And by God, I have had *this* Congress! For ten years King George and his Parliament have gulled, cullied, and diddled these Colonies with their illegal taxes—Stamp Acts, Townshend Acts, Sugar Acts, *Tea* Acts—and when we *dared* to stand up like men they stopped our trade, seized our ships, blockaded our ports, burned our towns, *and* spilled our blood—and still this Congress won't grant any of my proposals on Independence even so much as the courtesy of open debate! Good God, what in hell are they waiting for?

The curtain flies up to reveal the Chamber of the Second Continental Congress in Philadelphia. At rise, Congress is in session, sweltering in the heat of a premature summer's evening. A large day-by-day wall calendar reads: "MAY 8."

CONGRESS: (*Singing*)
Sit down, John!
Sit down, John!
For God's sake, John,
Sit down!

Sit down, John!
Sit down, John!
For God's sake, John,
Sit down!

VOICE:
Someone ought to open up a window!

CONGRESS:
It's ninety degrees!
Have mercy, John, please!
It's hot as Hell in
Philadel-phia!

TWO VOICES:
Someone ought to open up a window!

JOHN:
I say "Vote Yes!
Vote Yes!"
Vote for independency!

CONGRESS A:

Someone ought to open up a window!

JOHN:

I say "Vote Yes!"

CONGRESS:

Sit down, John!

JOHN:

Vote for independency!

VOICE FROM CONGRESS B:

Someone ought to open up a window!

CONGRESS B:

No! No! No!
Too many flies!
Too many flies!

CONGRESS A:

But it's hot as Hell in
Philadel-phia!

VOICES FROM CONGRESS A:

Are you going to open up a window?

CONGRESS A:

Can't we
Compromise here?

JOHN:

Vote Yes!

CONGRESS B:

No, too many
Flies here!

JOHN:

Vote Yes!

CONGRESS: (*Full*)

Oh, for God's sake, John,
Sit down!

(*They freeze*)

JOHN: (*Speaks, roaring*) *Good God!!* Consider yourselves fortunate that you have John Adams to abuse, for no sane man would tolerate it!

CONGRESS: (*Resuming action, singing*)
John, you're a bore!
We've heard this before!
Now, for God's sake, John,
Sit down!

JOHN:
I say, "Vote Yes!"

SOME VOICES:
No!!

JOHN:
Vote Yes!

CONGRESS: (*Full*)
No!!

JOHN:
Vote for
Independency!

CONGRESS A:
Someone ought to open up a window!

JOHN:
I say "Vote Yes!"

CONGRESS: (*Full*)
Sit down, John!

JOHN:
Vote for independency!!!

VOICE:
Will someone shut that man up!!

JOHN: (*Speaking*) Never! Never! (*He storms from the Chamber, coming downstage, and looks to Heaven for guidance*) Dear God! For one solid year they have been sitting there—for *one year! Doing nothing!*

(*Singing*)
I do believe you've laid a curse on
North America!
A curse that we here now rehearse in
Philadelphia!
A second flood, a simple famine,
Plagues of locusts everywhere,
Or a cataclysmic earthquake,

I'd accept with some despair.
But, no, you've sent us Congress—
Good God, Sir, was that fair?
I say this with humility in
Philadelphia!
We're your responsibility in
Philadelphia!
If you don't want to see us hanging
On some far-off British hill,
If you don't want the voice of independency
Forever still,
Then, God, Sir, get Thee to it,
For Congress never will!

You see we
    Piddle, twiddle, and resolve.
    Not one damned thing do we solve.
    Piddle, twiddle, and resolve.
    Nothing's ever solved in
    Foul, fetid, fuming, foggy, filthy
Philadelphia!

(*From the Chamber, rear, a* CONGRESSIONAL VOICE *can be heard*)

VOICE:
Someone ought to open up a window!

JOHN: (*Speaking*) Oh, shut up!

JOHN HANCOCK: I now call the Congress' attention to the petition of Mr. Melchior Meng, who claims twenty dollars' compensation for his dead mule. It seems the animal was employed transporting luggage in the service of the Congress.

JAMES WILSON: The question, then, would appear to be one of occasion, for if the mule expired not while carrying, but after being unloaded, then surely the beast dropped dead on its own time!

JOHN: *Good God!!*

(*Singing*)
They may sit here for years and years in
Philadelphia!
These indecisive grenadiers of
Philadelphia!
They can't agree on what is right or wrong

Or what is good or bad.
I'm convinced the only purpose
This Congress ever had
Was to gather here, specifically,
To drive John Adams mad!

You see we
Piddle, twiddle, and resolve.
Not one damned thing do we solve.
Piddle, twiddle, and resolve
Nothing's ever solved in
Foul, fetid, fuming, foggy, filthy
Philadelphi—

(ABIGAIL ADAMS, JOHN'S *wife, a handsome woman of thirty-two, now appears in* JOHN'S *imagination and interrupts*)

ABIGAIL: John, John! Is that you carrying on, John?

JOHN: (*Speaking*) Oh, Abigail! Abigail—I have such a desire to knock heads together!

ABIGAIL: I know, my dearest. I know. But that's because you make everything so complicated. It's all quite simple, really:

(*Singing*)
Tell the Congress to declare
Independency!
Then sign your name, get out of there,
And hurry home to me!
Our children all have dysentery,
Little Tom keeps turning blue.
Little Abby has the measles
And I'm coming down with flu.
They say we may get smallpox—

JOHN: (*Speaking*) Madame, what else is new? (*Music under*) Abigail, in my last letter I told you that the King has collected twelve thousand German mercenaries to send against us. I asked you to organize the ladies and make saltpetre for gunpowder. Have you done as I asked?

ABIGAIL: No, John, I have not.

JOHN: Why have you not?

ABIGAIL: Because you neglected to tell us how saltpetre is made.

JOHN: (*Impatient*) By treating sodium nitrate with potassium chloride, of course!

ABIGAIL: (*A woman*) Oh, yes—of course.

JOHN: Will it be done, then?

ABIGAIL: I'm afraid we have a more urgent problem, John.

JOHN: *More* urgent, Madame?

ABIGAIL: (*Singing*)

There's one thing every woman's missed in
Massachusetts Bay–
Don't smirk at me, you egotist, pay
Heed to what I say!
We've gone from Framingham to Boston
And cannot find a pin.
"Don't you know there is a war on?"
Says each tradesman with a grin.
Well!
We will not make saltpetre
Until you send us pins!

JOHN:

Pins, Madame? Saltpetre!

ABIGAIL:

Pins!

JOHN and ABIGAIL: (*Alternating*)

Saltpetre!
    Pins!
Saltpetre!
    Pins!
Saltpetre!
    Pins!
'Petre!
    Pins!
'Petre!
    Pins!
'Petre!
    Pins!
'Petre!
    Pins!

JOHN: (*Speaking, beaten*) Done, Madame. Done.

ABIGAIL: Done, John. (*Smiling*) *Hurry home, John.*

JOHN: As soon as I'm able.

ABIGAIL: Don't stop writing–it's all I have.

JOHN: Every day, my dearest friend.

ABIGAIL: (*Singing*)
Till then . . .

ABIGAIL and JOHN:
Till then,
I am, as I ever was, and ever shall be–
Yours . . .
Yours . . .
Yours . . .
Yours . . .
Yours . . .

JOHN: Saltpetre. (*He throws a kiss*) John.

ABIGAIL: Pins. (*She throws a kiss*) Abigail. (*She goes*)

CONGRESS: (*Singing*)
For God's sake, John,
Sit down!

(JOHN *turns, waves them off in disgust, then crosses*)

JOHN: (*Calling*) Franklin!

SCENE 2

The Mall. Sunlight. BENJAMIN FRANKLIN *sits on a bench, having his portrait painted.* JOHN *discovers him.*

JOHN: Franklin! Where in God's name were you when I needed you?

FRANKLIN: Right here, John, being preserved for posterity. Do y'like it?

JOHN: (*After examining the painting carefully*) It stinks. (*The* PAINTER *goes*)

FRANKLIN: As ever, the soul of tact.

JOHN: The man's no Botticelli.

FRANKLIN: And the subject's no Venus.

JOHN: Franklin! You heard what I suffered in there?

FRANKLIN: Heard? Of course I heard–along with the rest of Philadelphia. Lord, your voice is piercing, John!

JOHN: I wish to heaven my arguments were. By God, Franklin, when will they make up their minds? With one hand they can raise an army, dispatch one of their own to lead it, and cheer the news from Bunker's Hill–while with the other they wave the olive branch, begging the King for a happy and permanent reconciliation. Why damn it, Fat George has declared us in rebellion–why in bloody hell can't *they?*

FRANKLIN: John, really! You talk as if independence were the rule! *It's never been done before!* No colony has ever broken from the parent stem in the history of the world!

JOHN: Dammit, Franklin, you make us sound treasonous!

FRANKLIN: Do I? (*Thinking*) Treason—"Treason is a charge invented by winners as an excuse for hanging the losers."

JOHN: I have more to do than stand here listening to you quote yourself.

FRANKLIN: No, that was a new one!

JOHN: Dammit, Franklin, we're at war!

FRANKLIN: To defend ourselves, nothing more. *We* expressed our displeasure, the English moved against us, and *we,* in turn, have resisted. Now our fellow Congressmen want to effect a reconciliation *before* it becomes a war.

JOHN: Reconciliation, my ass! The *people* want independence!

FRANKLIN: The people have read Mr. Paine's *Common Sense.* I doubt the Congress has. (*He studies him*) John, why don't you give it up? Nobody listens to you–you're obnoxious and disliked.

JOHN: I'm not promoting John Adams, I'm promoting independence.

FRANKLIN: Evidently they cannot help connecting the two.

JOHN: (*Suspicious*) What are you suggesting?

FRANKLIN: Let someone else in Congress propose.

JOHN: Never! (FRANKLIN *shrugs*) Who did you have in mind?

FRANKLIN: I don't know. I really haven't given it much thought.

(RICHARD HENRY LEE, *a tall, loose-jointed Virginia aristocrat of forty-five, enters*)

LEE: You sent for me, Benjamin?

JOHN: (*Looking at* LEE, *then at* FRANKLIN) *Never!!*

LEE: Halloo, Johnny.

JOHN: (*Nodding*) Richard.

FRANKLIN: Richard, John and I need some advice.

LEE: If it's mine t'give, it's yours, y'know that.

FRANKLIN: Thank you, Richard. As you know, the cause that we support has come to a complete standstill. Now, why do you suppose that is?

LEE: Simple! Johnny, here, is obnoxious and disliked.

FRANKLIN: Yes, that's true. What's the solution, I wonder?

LEE: (*It's obvious*) Get someone else in Congress to propose—

FRANKLIN: Richard, that's brilliant! Wasn't that brilliant, John?

JOHN: (*Dully*) Brilliant.

FRANKLIN: Yes. Now the question remains—who can it be? The man we need must belong to a delegation publicly committed to support independence, and at the present time only Massachusetts, New Hampshire, and Delaware have declared our way.

LEE: And Virginia, Benjy—don't forget Virginia.

FRANKLIN: Oh, I haven't, Richard—how could I? But strictly speaking, while Virginia's views on independence are well known, your legislature in Williamsburg has never formally authorized its delegation here in Congress to support the cause. Of course, if we could think of a Virginian with enough influence to go down there and persuade the House of Burgesses—

LEE: Damn me if *I* haven't thought of someone!

FRANKLIN and ADAMS: (*Together*) *Who?*

LEE: *Me!*

FRANKLIN: Why didn't I think of that!

LEE: I'll leave tonight—why, hell, right now, if y'like! I'll stop off at Stratford just long enough to refresh the missus, and then straight to the matter. Virginia, the land that gave us our glorious Commander-in-Chief—(*A short drum roll*)—George Washington, will now give the continent its proposal on independence! And when Virginia proposes, the South is bound to follow, and where the South goes the Middle Colonies go! Gentlemen, a salute! To Virginia, the Mother of American Independence!

JOHN: Incredible! We're free, and he hasn't even left yet! (*To* LEE) What makes you so sure you can do it?
(*Music begins*)

LEE: *Hah!!* (*Singing*)
My name is Richard Henry Lee!
Virginia is my home.
My name is Richard Henry Lee!
Virginia is my home,
And may my horses turn to glue
If I can't deliver up to you
A resolution—on independency!

For I am F.F.V.
The First Family
In the Sovereign Colony of Virginia.
The F.F.V.

The Oldest Family
In the oldest colony in America!

And may the British burn my land
If I can't deliver to your hand
A resolution—on independency!

Y'see it's—
Here a Lee
There a Lee
Everywhere a Lee, a Lee!

FRANKLIN and LEE: (*Alternating*)
Social—
LEE!
Political—
LEE!
Financial—
LEE!
Natural—
LEE!
*In*ternal—
LEE!
*Ex*ternal—
LEE!
*Fra*ternal—
LEE!
E-ternal—
LEE!

(*Together*)
The F.F.V.,
The First Family
In the Sovereign Colony of Virginia!

LEE:
And may my wife refuse my bed
If I can't deliver (as I said)
A resolution—on independency!

JOHN: (*Speaking*) Spoken modest-*Lee*. God help us!
FRANKLIN: He will, John! He will!

LEE: (*Singing*)
They say that God in Heaven
Is everybody's God.

FRANKLIN:
Amen!

LEE:
I'll admit that God in Heaven
Is everybody's God.
But I tell y', John, with pride,
God leans a little on the side
Of the Lees! The Lees of old Virginia!

Y'see it's
Here a Lee, there a Lee
Everywhere a Lee–a Lee!

FRANKLIN and LEE:
Here a Lee, there a Lee
Everywhere a Lee–

LEE:
Look out! There's
Arthur Lee!
"Bobby" Lee! . . . an'
General "Lighthorse" Harry Lee!
Jesse Lee!
Willie Lee!

FRANKLIN:
And Richard H.–

LEE:
That's me!!
And may my blood stop running blue
If I can't deliver up to you
A resolution–on independency!
(*He begins strutting, a military cakewalk*)
Yes sir, by God, it's
Here a Lee!
There a Lee!
Come on, boys, join in with me!
(*They do,* JOHN *reluctantly*)
Here a Lee! There a Lee!

FRANKLIN: (*Speaking*) When do y'leave?

LEE: (*Singing*)
Immediate-*Lee!*
Here a Lee! There a Lee!

FRANKLIN: (*Speaking*) When will you return?

LEE: (*Singing*)
Short-*Lee!*
Here a Lee! There a Lee!
And I'll come back
Triumphant-*Lee!*

FRANKLIN and JOHN:
Here a Lee! There a Lee!
Ev'rywhere a Lee! A Lee!

LEE:
Forrr-warrr . . .
Ho-ooo!
(LEE *struts off.* FRANKLIN *and* JOHN *follow him almost as far as the wings, then drop out and return, breathless but relieved*)

JOHN: (*Speaking*) That was the most revolting display I ever witnessed.

FRANKLIN: They're a warm-blooded people, Virginians!

JOHN: Not him, Franklin–*you!* You and your infernal obsession for deviousness! If you'd come right out and asked him straight, he'd've been gone a half hour ago!

FRANKLIN: Cheer up, John. At this very moment our cause is again riding high–sitting straight in the saddle and in full gallop for Virginia!
(LEE *suddenly reappears*)

LEE: (*Singing*)
–And our women are . . . serene . . .

JOHN: (*Speaking*) Oh, good God!

LEE:
Full-bosomed . . .

FRANKLIN: (*Perking up*) Full-bosomed?

LEE:
Full-bosomed, Benjy,
Every one a queen! Why, they are . . .
(*Music in, at tempo*)
–Lees! Dammit!
The Lees of old Virginia! Yes, sir! By God!

(*Waving his riding crop, he parades around, followed by* FRANKLIN *and* JOHN)

ALL:

It's here a Lee!
There a Lee!

LEE:

Come on, John,
Step live-a-*Lee!*

ALL:

Here a Lee!
There a Lee!
Everywhere a Lee–a Lee!

(*Again* LEE *starts off, strutting between, but ahead of,* JOHN *and* FRANKLIN, *who are halfheartedly marching after him. Suddenly* LEE *has still another afterthought and turns back to express it–but* JOHN *and* FRANKLIN *are ready for him this time, hooking his arms as he passes between them, and dragging the surprised and frustrated Virginian off backwards*)

SCENE 3

The Chamber.

Featured prominently, rear, is a tally board. Under three main headings (YEA, NAY, *and* ABSTAIN) *are thirteen slots, each with a shuttle containing the name of a single colony. This device, during a vote, is the province of the Secretary of the Congress.*

At rise, the Chamber is empty save for its aging custodian, ANDREW MC NAIR, *who is preparing the room for the day's session with the help of a* LEATHER APRON, *a working man. The wall calendar now reads:* "JUNE 7." *Then, as* MC NAIR *sets out quill pens and fills the several inkwells from a large jar, Georgia's* DR. LYMAN HALL, *fifty-five, enters and looks around, finally clearing his throat.* MC NAIR *looks up.*

MC NAIR: Yes?

HALL: I'm Dr. Lyman Hall, new delegate from Georgia.

MC NAIR: I'm Andrew McNair, Congressional Custodian. (*He goes back to work*) If you'll be wantin' anything at all just holler out, "McNair!" as you'll hear the others do, and there won't be too long to wait.

HALL: (*Looking around*) Where does the Georgia delegation belong?

MC NAIR: Oh, they mill about over in that corner–near the two Carolinas.

HALL: (*Checking his watch*) It's after ten. I was told the Congress convenes at ten.

MC NAIR: They'll be wanderin' in any time now, sir—with Old Grape 'n' Guts leadin' the pack.

HALL: Old *who?*

HOPKINS' VOICE: (*Offstage*) *McNair!!*

MC NAIR: Grape 'n' Guts.

(STEPHEN HOPKINS, *a thin round-shouldered man of seventy, wearing a black suit, black Quaker hat, his gray hair at shoulder length, enters*)

HOPKINS: Fetch me a mug o' rum!

MC NAIR: Mr. Hopkins, you'll be pleased to meet Dr. Lyman Hall—

HOPKINS: I don't need a doctor, dammit—

MC NAIR: —new delegate from Georgia—

HOPKINS: Why didn't you say so? (*To* HALL) I'm Stephen Hopkins, *old* delegate from Rhode Island. McNair! *Two* mugs o' rum!

HALL: I fear it's a little early in the day—

HOPKINS: Nonsense! It's a medicinal fact that rum gets a man's heart started in the morning—I'm surprised you didn't know it. And speaking as the oldest man in the Congress—

MC NAIR: Ben Franklin's older by almost a year—

HOPKINS: *Rum!!* (MC NAIR *scurries off*) Tell me, Dr. Hall, where does Georgia stand on the question of independence?

(EDWARD RUTLEDGE, *a young, handsome, dandified aristocrat of twenty-six, has entered*)

RUTLEDGE: With South Carolina, of course.

HOPKINS: (*Laughing*) Good morning, Neddy. Shake the hand of Dr. Lyman Hall from Georgia. Doctor, this here is Edward Rutledge from whichever Carolina he says he's from—God knows I can't keep 'em straight.

RUTLEDGE: A pleasure, Dr. Hall.

HALL: Your servant, Mr. Rutledge.

HOPKINS: You've met the long and short of it now, Doctor. Neddy here is only twenty-six; he's the *youngest* of us—

RUTLEDGE: Except for Ben Franklin—

HOPKINS: *McNair!!*

(MC NAIR *has returned and now stands at* HOPKINS' *elbow*)

MC NAIR: Your rum.

HOPKINS: Where'd y'go for it, man—Jamaica?

(RUTLEDGE *and* HALL *walk away*)

RUTLEDGE: Where *does* Georgia stand on independence at the present time, Dr. Hall?

HALL: I am here without instructions, able to vote my own personal convictions.

RUTLEDGE: And they are—?

HALL: (*A pause; he examines him*) Personal.

RUTLEDGE: Dr. Hall, the Deep South speaks with one voice. It is traditional—even more, it is historical.

(*They regard one another for a moment. Then the Delaware delegation enters:* CAESAR RODNEY, *forty-eight, thin and pale, wears a green scarf tied around his face, covering some infirmity;* GEORGE READ, *forty-three, small and round, speaks with a high voice; and* COLONEL THOMAS MC KEAN, *forty-two, tall and florid, has a booming voice decorated with a Scottish brogue. As always, the three are arguing*)

RUTLEDGE: Enter Delaware—*tria juncta in uno!*

MC KEAN: Speak plain, Rutledge, y'know I can't follow none o' y'r damn French!

RUTLEDGE: Latin, Colonel McKean—a tribute to the eternal peace and harmony of the Delaware delegation.

MC KEAN: What're y'sayin', man? Y'know perfectly well neither Rodney nor I can stand this little wart! (*He indicates* READ)

RUTLEDGE: Gentlemen, gentlemen, this is Dr. Lyman Hall of Georgia—Caesar Rodney, George Read, and Colonel Thomas McKean.

(HALL *shakes hands with each in turn and they exchange greetings*)

RODNEY: Where do you stand on independence, sir?

HALL: (*A look to* RUTLEDGE) With South Carolina, it seems.

RUTLEDGE: I leave the doctor in your excellent company, gentlemen. (*Smiling, he bows and walks away, joining another group*)

(*Slowly the Chamber has begun to fill with Congressmen:* LEWIS MORRIS *and* ROBERT LIVINGSTON *of New York;* ROGER SHERMAN *of Connecticut;* JOSEPH HEWES *of North Carolina; the portly* SAMUEL CHASE *of Maryland;* JOSIAH BARTLETT *of New Hampshire; others; and last to enter, unnoticed,* THOMAS JEFFERSON *of Virginia, thirty-three, six feet three, with copper-colored hair, carrying several books*)

RODNEY: (*Drawing* HALL *aside*) Tell me, sir, would you be a doctor of medicine or theology?

HALL: Both, Mr. Rodney. Which one can be of service?

RODNEY: (*Good-naturedly*) By all means the physician first! Then we shall see about the other.

HALL: (*Smiling*) I'll call at your convenience, sir.

(*They are joined by two members of the Pennsylvania delegation:* JOHN DICKINSON, *forty-four, a thin, hawkish man, not without elegance; and* JAMES WILSON, *thirty-three, a bespectacled, cautious little sycophant*)

DICKINSON: (*Pleasantly*) I trust, Caesar, when you're through converting the poor fellow to independency that you'll give the opposition a fair crack at him.

RODNEY: You're too late, John; once I get 'em they're got. Dr. Lyman Hall of Georgia—Mr. John Dickinson of Pennsylvania.

DICKINSON: An honor, sir.

HALL: Your servant.

WILSON: (*Waiting*) Ahem.

RODNEY: Ah, Judge Wilson, forgive me—but how can anyone see you if you insist on standing in Mr. Dickinson's shadow? (*To* HALL) James Wilson, also of Pennsylvania.

WILSON: Sir.

HALL: An honor, sir.

(FRANKLIN *enters, limping on a cane, one foot bandaged*)

FRANKLIN: Will you get out of my way, please? Good morning, all!

HALL: (*Recognizing him*) Good Lord, do you have the honor to be Dr. Franklin?

FRANKLIN: Yes, I have that honor—unfortunately the gout accompanies the honor.

HOPKINS: Been living too high again, eh, Pappy?

FRANKLIN: Stephen, I only wish King George felt like my big toe—all over!

HOPKINS: *McNair!!* Fetch a pillow—and two more mugs o' rum!

(*Now* JOHN *enters the Chamber and looks around, searching for someone.*

It is now evident that the colors and styles of the various costumes change gradually from colony to colony—from the fancy greens and golds of the Deep South to the somber blacks of New England)

FRANKLIN: Good morning, John!

JOHN: (*Joining him*) Well, Franklin? Where's that idiot Lee? Has he returned yet? I don't see him.

FRANKLIN: Softly, John—your voice is hurting my foot.

JOHN: One more day, Franklin—that's how long I'll remain silent, and not a minute longer! That strutting popinjay was so damned sure of himself. He's had time to bring back a *dozen* proposals by now!

(DICKINSON *turns to* WILSON *and addresses him in a loud voice, for all to hear*)

DICKINSON: Tell me, James, how do you explain the strange, monumental quietude that Congress has been treated to these past thirty days? (*Everyone, including* JOHN, *has turned to listen*) Has the ill wind of independence finally blown itself out?

WILSON: If you ask me–

DICKINSON: For myself, I must confess that a month free from New England noise is more therapeutic than a month in the country! Don't you agree, James?

WILSON: Well, I–

DICKINSON: (*Turning*) Mr. Adams, pray look for your voice, sir! It cannot be far, and God knows we need the entertainment in this Congress!

(*Laughter from his fellow conservatives. Everyone turns to* ADAMS, *who is trembling with rage*)

FRANKLIN: Congratulations, John, you've just made your greatest contribution to independence–you kept your flap shut!

JOHN: One more day . . . !

(JOHN HANCOCK, *forty, takes his place at the President's desk; he is followed by* CHARLES THOMSON, *forty-seven, the pedantic Secretary to the Congress.* HANCOCK *pounds his gavel*)

HANCOCK: Gentlemen, the usual morning festivities concluded, I will now call the Congress to order (*Gavel*) Mr. Thomson.

THOMSON: (*Rising and ringing a bell*) The Second Continental Congress, meeting in the city of Philadelphia, is now in session, seventh June, seventeen seventy-six, the three hundred eightieth meeting.

MC NAIR: Sweet Jesus!

THOMSON: The Honorable John Hancock of Massachusetts Bay, President. (*He rings the bell and sits*)

HANCOCK: Thank you, Mr. Thomson. (*He swats a fly*) Mr. McNair, the stores of rum and other drinking spirits are hereby closed to the colony of Rhode Island for a period of three days.

MC NAIR: Yes, sir.

HOPKINS: John, y'can't do that!

HANCOCK: Sit down, Mr. Hopkins. You've abused the privilege.

The Chair takes this opportunity to welcome Dr. Lyman Hall of Georgia to this Congress and hopes he will make the best of it. My God, it's hot! The Secretary will read the roll.

THOMSON: All members present with the following exceptions: Mr. Charles Carroll of Maryland; Mr. Samuel Adams of Massachusetts; Mr. Button Gwinnett of Georgia; Mr. George Wythe and Mr. Richard Henry Lee of Virginia; and the entire delegation of New Jersey.

HANCOCK: I'm concerned over the continued absence of one-thirteenth of this Congress. Where *is* New Jersey?

DICKINSON: Somewhere between New York and Pennsylvania.

HANCOCK: Thank you very much. Dr. Franklin, have *you* heard anything? Your son resides there.

FRANKLIN: Son, sir? What son?

HANCOCK: (*Sorry he brought it up*) The Royal Governor of New Jersey, sir.

FRANKLIN: As that title might suggest, sir, we are not in touch at the present time.

HANCOCK: Yes. Very well–uh–the weather report–Mr. Jefferson of Virginia. (*No reaction;* JEFFERSON *is reading a book*) Mr. Jefferson!

JEFFERSON: (*Jumping to his feet*) Present, sir!

HANCOCK: May we hear about the weather, as if it weren't speaking for itself.

JEFFERSON: (*Going to several gauges at the window*) Eighty-seven degrees of temperature, thirty-point-aught-six inches of mercury, wind from the southwest for the rest of the day, and tonight–(*He turns*)–tonight I'm leaving for home.

HANCOCK: On business?

JEFFERSON: Family business.

HOPKINS: Give her a good one for me, young feller!

JEFFERSON: (*Smiling*) Yes, sir, I will.

(*A uniformed* COURIER, *dusty from his long ride, enters and approaches* THOMSON *removing a communiqué from his pouch. He tosses it onto the Secretary's desk and leaves wearily*)

THOMSON: (*Ringing his bell*) From the Commander, Army of the United Colonies; in New York, dispatch number one thousand, one hundred and thirty-seven–

MC NAIR: Sweet Jesus!

THOMSON: (*Reading*) "To the Honorable Congress, John Hancock, President. Dear Sir: It is with grave apprehension that I have learned this day of the sailing, from Halifax, Nova

Scotia, of a considerable force of British troops in the company of foreign mercenaries and under the command of General Sir William Howe. There can be no doubt that their destination is New York, for to take and hold this city and the Hudson Valley beyond would serve to separate New England from the other colonies permitting both sections to be crushed in turn. Sadly, I see no way of stopping them at the present time as my army is absolutely falling apart, my military chest is totally exhausted, my Commissary General has strained his credit to the last, my Quartermaster has no food, no arms, no ammunition, and my troops are in a state of near mutiny! I pray God some relief arrives before the armada but fear it will not. Y'r ob'd't—"

(*Drum roll*)

"G. Washington."

(*During the brief silence that follows,* THOMSON *shrugs and files the dispatch*)

MC KEAN: Mr. President!

HANCOCK: (*Wearily; he knows what's coming*) Colonel McKean.

MC KEAN: Surely we've managed to promote the *gloomiest* man on this continent to the head of our troops. Those dispatches are the most depressing accumulation of disaster, doom, and despair in the entire annals of military history! And furthermore—

HANCOCK: (*Pounding his gavel*) Please, Colonel McKean—it's too hot.

MC KEAN: Oh. Yes. I suppose so.

HANCOCK: General Washington will continue wording his dispatches as he sees fit, and I'm sure we all pray that he finds happier thoughts to convey in the near—(*Swats a fly*)—future. Mr. Thomson, are there any resolutions?

THOMSON: Dr. Josiah Bartlett of New Hampshire.

BARTLETT: (*Rising and reading*) "Resolved: that for the duration of the present hostilities the Congress discourage every type of extravagance and dissipation, elaborate funerals and other expensive diversions, especially all horse-racing—"

(*He is shouted down by the entire Congress. Then the door bursts open and* LEE *sweeps in*)

LEE: Benjy, I'm back—I'm back, Johnny! (*He lets out a Southern war whoop*)

(*In a flash,* JOHN, JEFFERSON, MC KEAN, *and even the hobbling* FRANKLIN *crowd around him*)

MC KEAN: Richard, we're pleased t'see y'!

FRANKLIN: What news, Dickie boy, what news?

JOHN: Lee! Is it done?

LEE: First things first. (*Looking around*) Tom—where's Tom? (*Turning and seeing* JEFFERSON) Tom! Your little bride wants to know: "When's he coming home?"

JEFFERSON: I leave tonight!

JOHN: (*Grabbing* LEE'S *shoulders*) Never mind that—*is it done?*

LEE: Done? (*A pause*) Why, certain-*Lee!* (*Cheers from those for independence*) Mr. President, I have returned from Virginia with the followin' resolution. (*He produces a paper and reads*) "Resolved: that these united colonies are (and of a right ought to be) free and independent states, that they are absolved from all allegiance to the British Crown, and that all political connection between them and the state of Great Britain is (and ought to be) totally dissolved!"

JOHN: Mr. President, I second the proposal!

(*A silence; then* HANCOCK *swats a fly*)

HANCOCK: The resolution has been proposed and seconded. The Chair will now entertain debate.

DICKINSON: (*Rising, assuming weariness*) Mr. President, Pennsylvania moves, as always that the question of independence be postponed—indefinitely.

WILSON: I second the motion!

HANCOCK: Judge Wilson, in your eagerness to be loved you seem to have forgotten that Pennsylvania cannot second its own motion.

READ: Delaware seconds.

MC KEAN: You would, y'little weasel!

HANCOCK: The motion to postpone has been moved and seconded. Mr. Thomson.

(THOMSON *goes to the tally board. As each colony votes, he announces it and* MC NAIR, *in turn, mechanically records it on the board.* HOPKINS, *during this preparation, rises and leaves the Chamber*)

THOMSON: On the motion to postpone indefinitely the resolution of independency or proceed with the debate, all those in favor of debate say "Yea," all those for postponement say "Nay." (*Intoning*) New Hampshire—

BARTLETT: New Hampshire favors debate and says Yea.

THOMSON: New Hampshire says Yea. Massachusetts—

JOHN: Massachusetts, having borne the brunt of the King's tyranny—

THOSE AGAINST: *Shame!! Shame!!*

THOSE FOR: *Sit down, John!*

JOHN: Yes, I said *tyranny!* Massachusetts now and for all time says *Yea!*

THOMSON: (*Flatly*) Massachusetts says Yea. Rhode Island—Mr. Hopkins? Where's Rhode Island?

MC NAIR: Rhode Island is out visitin' the "necessary."

HANCOCK: After what Rhode Island's consumed, I can't say I'm surprised. We'll come back to him, Mr. Thomson.

THOMSON: Rhode Island passes. (*Laughter;* THOMSON *looks around, not understanding, then proceeds*) Connecticut—

SHERMAN: (*He holds, as he will throughout the entire play, a shallow bowl of coffee; he is never without it*) While Connecticut has, till now, been against this proposal, our legislature has instructed me that, in the event it is introduced by any colony *outside* of New England, Connecticut could not any longer withhold its support. Connecticut says Yea.

(FRANKLIN *and* JOHN *exchange satisfied looks*)

THOMSON: Connecticut says Yea. New York—

MORRIS: Mr. Secretary, New York abstains—courteously.

THOMSON: New York abstains—

MORRIS: —courteously.

THOMSON: New Jersey—

HANCOCK: Absent, Mr. Secretary.

THOMSON: New Jersey is absent. Pennsylvania—

DICKINSON: Pennsylvania, for the twenty-fourth time, says Nay.

THOMSON: Pennsylvania says Nay. Delaware—

RODNEY: Delaware, as ever for independence, says Yea.

THOMSON: Delaware says Yea. Mary-land—

CHASE: Mary-land would welcome independence if it were given but is highly skeptical that it can be taken. Mary-land says Nay.

THOMSON: Mary-land says Nay. Virginia—

LEE: Virginia, the First Colony, says Yea!

THOMSON: Virginia says Yea. North Carolina—

HEWES: North Carolina respectfully yields to *South* Carolina.

THOMSON: South Carolina—

RUTLEDGE: Mr. President, although we in South Carolina have never seriously considered the question of independence, when a *gentleman* proposes it, attention must be paid. However—we in the Deep South, unlike our friends in New England, have no cause for impatience at the present time. If, at some future date, it becomes the wish of *all* our sister colonies to effect a separation, we will not stand in the way. But for the time bein', South Carolina will wait—and watch. The vote is Nay.

THOMSON: South Carolina says Nay.

HEWES: (*Jumping up*) *North* Carolina—

THOMSON: —says Nay. Yes, Mr. Hewes, I know. Georgia—(HALL *rises, looks around, but says nothing, obviously in great uncertainty*) Georgia—

HALL: Mr. Secretary—(*His eyes meet* RUTLEDGE'S, *then quickly look away*) Georgia seems to be split right down the middle on this issue. The people are against it—and I'm for it. (*Understanding laughter*) But I'm afraid I'm not yet certain whether representing the people means relying on their judgment or on my own. So in all fairness, until I can figure it out, I'd better lean a little toward their side. Georgia says Nay.

THOMSON: Georgia says Nay. (*He checks the board*) Rhode Island. (*Calling off*) *Second call—Rhode Island!*

HOPKINS: (*Offstage*) *I'm comin'! I'm comin'!* (*Entering*) Hold y'r damn horses!

THOMSON: We're waiting on *you,* Mr. Hopkins.

HOPKINS: It won't kill you. You'd think the Congress would have its own pisser! All right, where does she stand?

THOMSON: Five for debate, five for postponement, one abstention, and one absence.

HOPKINS: So it's up to me, is it? Well, I'll tell y'—in all my years I never heard, seen, nor smelled an issue that was so dangerous it couldn't be talked about. Hell yes, I'm for debatin' anything—Rhode Island says Yea!

(*Cheers from those for, including another war whoop from* LEE, *as they crowd around* HOPKINS)

HANCOCK: McNair, get Mr. Hopkins a rum!

MC NAIR: But you said—

HANCOCK: Get him the whole damn barrel if he wants!

MC NAIR: Yes, sir!

HANCOCK: The Chair now declares this Congress a committee-of-the-whole for the purpose of debating Virginia's resolution of independence. Mr. Dickinson.

DICKINSON: Well, now. You've got your way at last, Mr. Adams —the matter may now be discussed. I confess I'm almost relieved. There's a question I've been fairly itching to ask you: Why?

JOHN: Why what, Mr. Dickinson?

DICKINSON: Why independence, Mr. Adams?

JOHN: For the obvious reason that our continued association with Great Britain has grown intolerable.

DICKINSON: To whom, Mr. Adams? To you? Then I suggest you sever your ties immediately. But please be kind enough to leave the rest of us where we are. Personally, I have no objections at all to being part of the greatest empire on earth, to enjoying its protection and sharing its benefits—

JOHN: Benefits? What benefits? Crippling taxes? Cruel repressions? Abolished rights?

DICKINSON: Is that all England means to you, sir? Is that *all* the affection and pride you can muster for the nation that bore you—for the noblest, most civilized nation on the face of this planet? Would you have us forsake Hastings and Magna Carta, Strongbow and Lionhearted, Drake and Marlborough, Tudors, Stuarts, and Plantagenets? For what, sir? Tell me for what? For *you?* (*He smiles, then turns*) Some men are patriots, like General Washington—some are anarchists, like Mr. Paine—some even are internationalists, like Dr. Franklin. But you, sir, you are merely an *a-gi-ta-tor,* disturbing the peace, creating disorder, endangering the public welfare—and for what? Your petty little personal complaints. Your taxes are too high. Well, sir, so are mine. Come, come, Mr. Adams, if you have grievances—and I'm sure you have—our present system must provide a gentler means of redressing them short of—(*Suddenly his manner changes as he brings his fist down on the desk with a crash*)*—revolution!!* (*Wheeling to the Congress*) That's what *he* wants—nothing less will satisfy him! Violence! Rebellion! *Treason!* Now, Mr. Adams, are these the acts of Englishmen?

JOHN: Not Englishmen, Dickinson—Americans!

DICKINSON: (*Again pounding the desk*) No, sir! *Englishmen!!*

FRANKLIN: (*He's been asleep, his chin on his chest; now an eye opens*) Please, Mr. Dickinson—but must you start banging? How is a man to sleep?

(*Laughter*)

DICKINSON: Forgive me, Dr. Franklin, but must you start speaking? How is a man to stay awake?

(*Laughter*)

DICKINSON: We'll promise to be quiet, sir. I'm sure everyone prefers that you remain asleep.

FRANKLIN: If I'm to hear myself called an Englishman, sir, then I assure you I'd prefer I'd remained asleep.

DICKINSON: What's so terrible about being called an Englishman? The English don't seem to mind.

FRANKLIN: Nor would I, were I given the full rights of an Englishman. But to call me one *without* those rights is like calling an ox a bull—he's thankful for the honor but he'd much rather have restored what's rightfully his.

(*Laughter,* FRANKLIN *laughing the longest*)

DICKINSON: (*Finally*) When did you first notice they were missing, sir?

(*Laughter*)

DICKINSON: Fortunately, Dr. Franklin, the people of these colonies maintain a higher regard for their mother country.

FRANKLIN: Higher, certainly, than she feels for them. Never was such a valuable possession so stupidly and recklessly managed than this entire continent by the British Crown. Our industry discouraged, our resources pillaged—and, worst of all, our very character stifled. We've spawned a new race here—rougher, simpler, more violent, more enterprising, and less refined. We're a new nationality, Mr. Dickinson—we require a new nation.

DICKINSON: That may be your opinion, Dr. Franklin, but as I said, the people feel quite differently.

JOHN: What do you know about the people, Dickinson? You don't speak for the people; you represent only yourself. And that precious "status quo" you keep imploring the people to preserve for *their* own good is nothing more than the eternal preservation of *your* own property!

DICKINSON: Mr. Adams, you have an annoying talent for making such delightful words as "property" sound quite distasteful. In Heaven's name, what's wrong with property? Perhaps you've forgotten that many of us first came to these shores in order to secure rights to property—and that we hold *those* rights no less dear than the rights you speak of.

JOHN: So safe, so fat, so comfortable in Pennsylvania—

DICKINSON: And what is this independence of yours except the private grievance of Massachusetts? Why, even your own cousin, so busy now with his seditious activities in Boston that he has no time to attend this Congress, is a fugitive with a price on his head!

HANCOCK: Slowly, Mr. Dickinson. I remind you that the same price that covers Sam Adams also covers me—we are wanted together.

DICKINSON: What did you expect? You both dress up like red savages in order to commit piracy against one of His Majesty's ships—an event so embarrassing to your sister colonies that even your good friend Dr. Franklin offered to pay for all that spilt tea from his own pocket!

FRANKLIN: I'm usually able to speak for myself, Mr. Dickinson.

DICKINSON: Then tell me this: what good can come from this radicalism and civil disorder? Where can it lead except to chaos, mob rule, and anarchy? And why in God's name is it always *Boston* that breaks the King's peace? (*To the Congress*) My dear Congress, you must not adopt this evil measure. It is the work of the devil. Leave it where it belongs—in New England.

SHERMAN: Brother Dickinson, New England has been fighting the devil for more than a hundred years.

DICKINSON: And as of now, "Brother" Sherman, the devil has been winning hands down! (*Indicating* JOHN) Why, at this very moment he is sitting here in this Congress! Don't let him deceive you—this proposal is entirely his doing! It may bear Virginia's name, but it reeks of Adams, Adams, and more Adams! Look at him—ready to lead this continent down the fiery path of total destruction!

JOHN: Good God! Why can't you acknowledge what already exists? It has been more than a year since Concord and Lexington. Dammit, man, we're at war right now!

DICKINSON: *You* may be at war—you: Boston and John Adams—but you will never speak for Pennsylvania!

READ: (*Jumping up*) Nor for Delaware!

RODNEY: Mr. Read, you represent only one-third of Delaware!

READ: The sensible third, Mr. Rodney!

MC KEAN: Sit down, y'little roach, or I'll knock y'down!

HANCOCK: Sit down, all three of you! *McNair!!* Do something about these damned flies!

HOPKINS: *McNair!!* Fetch me a rum!

HANCOCK: Get the flies first!

MC NAIR: I've only got two hands!

HANCOCK: (*Mopping his brow*) Christ, it's hot! Please do go on, gentlemen; you're making the only breeze in Philadelphia.

RUTLEDGE: Mr. Adams, perhaps you could clear something up for *me:* after we have achieved independence, who do you propose would govern in South Carolina?

JOHN: The people, of course.

RUTLEDGE: Which people, sir? The people of South Carolina? Or the people of Massachusetts?

HOPKINS: Why don't you admit it, Neddy? You're against independence now, and you always will be.

MC KEAN: Aye!

RUTLEDGE: You refuse to understand us, gentlemen! We desire independence, yes—for South Carolina. That is our country. And as such we don't wish it to belong to anyone—not to England, and not to you.

JOHN: We intend to be one nation, Rutledge.

RUTLEDGE: A nation of sovereign states, Mr. Adams, united for our mutual protection, but separate for our individual pursuits. That is what we have understood it to be, and that is what we will support—as soon as *every*one supports it.

WILSON: There you are, Mr. Adams, you must see that we need time to make certain who we are and where we stand in regard to one another—for if we do not determine the nature of the beast before we set it free, it will end by consuming us all.

JOHN: For once in your life, Wilson—take a chance. I say the time is now! It may never come again!

HEWES: Your clock is fast, Mr. Adams. I say we're not yet ripe for independence.

HOPKINS: Not ripe? Hell, we're *rotting* for want of it!

CHASE: Gentlemen, please. What in God's name is the infernal hurry? Why must this question be settled now?

RODNEY: What's wrong with now, Mr. Chase?

CHASE: General Washington is in the field. If he's defeated, as it now appears, we'll be inviting the hangman. But if, by some miracle, he should actually win, we can then declare anything we damn please!

HEWES: The sentiments of North Carolina precisely.

JOHN: Has it ever occurred to either of you that an army needs something to fight for in order *to* win—a cause, a purpose, a flag of its own?

CHASE: Mr. Adams, how can a nation of only two million souls stand up to an empire of ten million? Think of it—*ten million!* How do we *compensate* for that shortage?

FRANKLIN: It's simple, Mr. Chase—increase and multiply!

CHASE: How's that?

JOHN: We will more than compensate—with *spirit!* I tell you there's a spirit out there with the people that's sadly lacking in this Congress!

DICKINSON: Yes, of course—now it's *spirit!* Why didn't I think of that? No army, no navy, no arms, no ammunition, no treasury, no friends—but, bless our soul, *spirit!* (*Turning*) Mr. Lee, Mr. Hopkins, Mr. Rodney, Colonel McKean, Dr. Franklin, why have you joined this incendiary little man? This Boston radical, this *a-gi-ta-tor,* this demagogue—this *madman!*

JOHN: Are you calling me a madman, you—you—you—*fribble!!*

FRANKLIN: Easy, John!

JOHN: You and your Pennsylvania proprietors—you cool, considerate men! You keep to the rear of every issue so if we should go under you'll still remain afloat!

DICKINSON: Are you calling me a coward?

JOHN: Yes! *Coward!!*

DICKINSON: *Madman!!*

JOHN: *Landlord!!*

DICKINSON: *Lawyer!!*

(*The battle is joined. They begin whacking away at each other with their walking sticks. Congress is in an uproar*)

HOPKINS: Whack him, John!

FRANKLIN: Ho, Spartacus!

CONGRESS: Stop! Go! For shame! At Last! (*Et cetera*)

(RODNEY *now steps forward, between them, and pushes them apart*)

RODNEY: Stop it! *Stop it!!* This is the Congress! Stop it, I say! The enemy is out *there!*

DICKINSON: No, Mr. Rodney, the enemy is here!

RODNEY: No, no, I say he's out there—England, *England,* closing in, cutting off our air—there's no time—no air—(*He is stricken*) Thomas! (*He collapses into* MC KEAN'S *arms*)

MC KEAN: Cacsar—*Caesar!!* (*He looks around as the Congress falls silent and moves in*) Doctor Hall?

HALL: (*Kneeling beside* RODNEY *and looking under the green scarf; his expression reflects what he finds*) Colonel McKean—

MC KEAN: Aye, it's the cancer.
HALL: He should go home.
RODNEY: (*Disgusted with himself*) Yes, a man should die in his own bed. John–John Adams–
JOHN: I'm here, Caesar.
RODNEY: I leave you a divided Delaware. Forgive me.
MC KEAN: I'll take y'home, Caesar. (*He lifts* RODNEY *and turns to* JOHN) I'll be back within the week. (*He carries* RODNEY *out*)

(*There is a moment of silence; then* RUTLEDGE *steps forward*)

RUTLEDGE: Mr. President, South Carolina calls the question.
HANCOCK: (*Distracted*) What's that, Mr. Rutledge?
RUTLEDGE: (*Walking to the tally board*) I said, Mr. President, South Carolina desires to end the debate and–(*He moves the Delaware marker from the "Yea" to the "Nay" column*) –call the question of independence.
READ: (*Glowing*) Delaware seconds!

(*Again, bedlam, as everyone understands what has happened*)

CONGRESS: No! Yes! You can't do that! Call the question! (*Et cetera*)
HANCOCK: (*Pounding for order*) Gentlemen, *please!* The question has been called and seconded. Mr. Secretary, you will record the vote.
JOHN: (*To* FRANKLIN) Franklin, do something–*think!*
FRANKLIN: I'm thinking, I'm thinking–but nothing's coming!
THOMSON: All those in favor of the resolution on independence as proposed by the colony of Virginia signify by saying–
FRANKLIN: Mr. Secretary, would you read the resolution again? (*As everyone looks at him in surprise, he shrugs*) I've forgotten it.

(*Annoyed,* THOMSON *looks to* HANCOCK, *who nods; he sighs*)

THOMSON: "Resolved: That these United Colonies are (and of a right ought to be) free and independent–"

(*The* REVEREND JOHN WITHERSPOON, *a lean and ascetic clergyman of fifty-four, enters*)

WITHERSPOON: I beg your pardon, I'm the Reverend John Witherspoon, new delegate from New Jersey–? (*As everyone moves in expectantly, he draws back, then seeks out the only familiar face*) Dr. Franklin, I regret I must be the bearer of unhappy tidings, but your son, the Royal Governor of New

Jersey, is taken prisoner and has been moved under guard to the colony of Connecticut for safe-keeping.

FRANKLIN: Is he unharmed, sir?

WITHERSPOON: When last I heard, he was, yes, sir.

FRANKLIN: Then why the long face? I hear Connecticut is an excellent location. Why'd they arrest the little bastard?

WITHERSPOON: (*Rattled*) Our–uh–New Jersey legislature has recalled the old delegation to this Congress and has sent a new one.

JOHN: Quickly, man–where do y'stand on independence?

WITHERSPOON: Oh, haven't I made that clear? No, I s'pose I haven't. But that was the reason for the change–we've been instructed to vote *for* independence.

JOHN: (*Quickly*) Mr. President! (*He goes to the tally board*) Massachusetts is now ready for the vote on independence– (*He records New Jersey under the "Yea" column*)–and reminds the Chair of its privilege to decide all votes that are deadlocked!

HANCOCK: I won't forget, Mr. Adams. The Chair would like to welcome the Reverend Witherspoon and appoint him Congressional Chaplain if he will accept the post.

WITHERSPOON: With much pleasure, sir.

HANCOCK: Very well. Mr. Thomson, you may now–(*He swats a fly*)–proceed with the vote on independence.

THOMPSON: All in favor of the resolution on independence as proposed by the colony of Virginia signify by saying–

DICKINSON: (*Jumping up*) Mr. President, Pennsylvania moves that any vote in favor of independence must be unanimous!

JOHN: *What?*

WILSON: I second the motion!

HANCOCK: (*Admonishing*) Judge Wilson–

WILSON: (*Chagrined*) Oh my God.

READ: Delaware seconds, Mr. President.

JOHN: No vote's ever had to be unanimous, Dickinson, and you know it!

DICKINSON: Yes, but this one must be.

JOHN: On what grounds?

DICKINSON: That no colony be torn from its mother country without its own consent.

RUTLEDGE: Hear, hear!

JOHN: But it'll never be unanimous, dammit!

DICKINSON: If you say so, Mr. Adams.

THOMSON: It has been moved and seconded that the vote on independence must be unanimous in order to carry. All those in favor signify by saying "Yea." (DICKINSON, CHASE, READ, RUTLEDGE, HEWES, *and* HALL *say "Yea."*) Six colonies say "Yea." All those opposed signify by saying "Nay." (JOHN, BARTLETT, HOPKINS, SHERMAN, LEE, *and* WITHERSPOON *say "Nay."*) Six colonies say "Nay."

MORRIS: Mr. Secretary, New York abstains—courteously.

HANCOCK: Mr. Morris, why does New York constantly abstain? Why doesn't New York simply stay in New York? Very well, the vote is tied. (*He covers his eyes for a moment*) The principles of independence have no greater advocate in Congress than its President—and that is why I must join those who vote *for* unanimity.

JOHN: (*As the Congress reacts, stunned, he jumps up, horrified*) Good God! What're y'doing, John? You've sunk us!

HANCOCK: Hear me out. Don't you see that any colony who opposes independence will be forced to fight on the side of England—that we'll be setting brother against brother, that our new nation will carry as its emblem the mark of Cain? I can see no other way. Either we walk together or together we must stay where we are. (*A silence*) Very well. Proceed, Mr. Thomson.

THOMSON: A unanimous vote being necessary to carry, if any be opposed to the resolution on independence as proposed by the colony of Virginia, signify by saying—

JOHN: *Mr. President!!*

THOMSON: For heaven's sake, let me get through it *once!*

JOHN: Mr. President, I move for a postponement!

DICKINSON: *Ha!* I wish you the same luck *I* had with it!

FRANKLIN: Mr. Adams is right, we need a postponement!

DICKINSON: On what grounds?

FRANKLIN: (*To* JOHN) On what grounds?

JOHN: Mr. President, how can this Congress vote on independence without—uh—a written declaration of some sort defining it?

HANCOCK: What sort of declaration?

JOHN: Well, you know—uh—listing all the reasons for the separation and—uh—our goals and aims and so on and so forth, ditto, ditto, et cetera, et cetera.

HANCOCK: (*Not getting it*) We know those, don't we?

JOHN: Well, good God, yes, *we* know them, but what about the rest of the world? Certainly we require the aid of a powerful nation like France or Spain, and such a declaration would be consistent with European delicacy.

CHASE: Come, now, Mr. Adams, you'll have to do better than that! Answer straight—what would be its purpose?

(*A pause; for once* JOHN *is at a loss for words*)

JOHN: Yes, well—

JEFFERSON: (*Rising and speaking deliberately*) To place before mankind the common sense of the subject, in terms so plain and firm as to command their assent. (*Winking at* JOHN, *he sits. A moment of surprise; then* DICKINSON *laughs*)

DICKINSON: Mr. Jefferson, are you seriously suggesting that we publish a paper declaring to all the world that an illegal rebellion is, in reality, a legal one?

FRANKLIN: Why, Mr. Dickinson, I'm surprised at you! You should know that rebellion is *always* legal in the first person —such as "our" rebellion. It is only in the third person— "their" rebellion—that it is *il*legal. (*Laughter*) Mr. President, I second the motion to postpone the vote on independence for a period of time sufficient for the writing of a declaration.

HANCOCK: It has been moved and seconded. Mr. Secretary—

THOMSON: All those in favor of the motion to postpone signify by saying "Yea." (ADAMS, BARTLETT, HOPKINS, SHERMAN, WITHERSPOON, *and* LEE *say "Yea."*) Six colonies say "Yea." Against? (DICKINSON, CHASE, READ, RUTLEDGE, HEWES, *and* HALL *say "Nay."*) Six colonies say "Nay."

MORRIS: Mr. Secretary, New York abstains—courteously.

HANCOCK: (*Threatening him with his fly-swatter, then restraining himself*) Mr. Morris! What in hell goes on in New York?

MORRIS: I'm sorry, Mr. President, but the simple fact is that our legislature has never sent us explicit instructions on anything.

HANCOCK: *Never?* That's impossible!

MORRIS: Have you ever been present at a meeting of the New York legislature? They speak very fast and very loud and nobody pays any attention to anybody else, with the result that nothing ever gets done. I beg the Congress' pardon.

HANCOCK: My sympathies, Mr. Morris. The vote again being ticd, the Chair decides in favor of the postponement. (*His gavel*) So ruled. A committee will now be formed to manage the declaration, said document to be written, debated, and approved by the beginning of July, three weeks hence, at which time Virginia's resolution on independence will finally be voted. Is that clear? (*Meeting general agreement*) Very well. Will the following gentlemen serve on the Declaration Committee. Dr. Franklin, Mr. John Adams, Mr. Sherman, Mr. Livingston, and, of course, Mr. Lee.

LEE: Excuse me, but I must be returnin' to the sovereign country of Virginia as I have been asked to serve as governor. Therefore I must decline–respectful-*Lee*.

HANCOCK: Very well, Mr. Lee, you're excused. I suppose we could leave it a four-man committee.

JOHN: Just a moment. This business needs a Virginian. Therefore, I propose a replacement–Mr. Thomas Jefferson!

JEFFERSON: No, Mr. Adams, *no!*

HANCOCK: Very well, Mr. Adams, Mr. Jefferson will serve.

JEFFERSON: I'm going home too–to my wife!

JOHN: Move to adjourn!

JEFFERSON: No, wait–

FRANKLIN: *Second!!*

JEFFERSON: It's been six months since I've seen her!

HANCOCK: Moved and seconded–any objections?

JEFFERSON: Yes! I have objections!

HANCOCK: (*Gaveling*) So ruled, Congress stands adjourned!

JEFFERSON: (*On deaf ears*) I need to see my wife, I tell you!

(*Congress rises and goes as* JOHN, FRANKLIN, SHERMAN, *and* LIVINGSTON *move downstage, with* JEFFERSON *following, still protesting. Music begins*)

JOHN: All right, gentlemen! Let's get on with it. Which of us is going to write our declaration on independence?

FRANKLIN: (*Singing*)

Mr. Adams, I say you should write it,
To your legal mind and brilliance we defer.

JOHN:

Is that so!
Well, if I'm the one to do it,
They'll run their quill pens through it.
I'm obnoxious and disliked, you know that, sir!

FRANKLIN: (*Speaking*) Yes, I know.

JOHN: Then I say you should write it, Franklin, yes, you!

FRANKLIN: (*Singing*)

Hell, no!

JOHN:
Yes, you, Dr. Franklin, you!

FRANKLIN:
But–

JOHN:
You!

FRANKLIN:
But–

JOHN:
You!

FRANKLIN:
But–
Mr. Adams!
But–Mr. Adams!
The things I write
Are only light extemporanea.
I won't put politics on paper.
It's a mania.
So, I refuse to use the pen–in Pennsylvania!

(*A* GLEE CLUB *is formed by* SHERMAN, LIVINGSTON, *and* FRANKLIN)

GLEE CLUB:
Pennsylvania!
Pennsylvania!
Refuse
To use . . . the pen!
(JOHN *begins to pace, thinking*)

JOHN:
Mr. Sherman, I say you should write it.
You are never "controversial," as it were.

SHERMAN: (*Speaking*) That is true.

JOHN: (*Singing*)
Whereas, if I'm the one to do it
They'll run their quill pens through it.
I'm obnoxious and disliked, you know that, sir.

SHERMAN: (*Speaking*) Yes, I do.

JOHN: (*Singing*)
Then you should write it, Roger, you.

SHERMAN: (*Speaking*) Good heavens, no!

JOHN: (*Singing*)
Yes, you, Roger Sherman, you!

SHERMAN:
But–

JOHN:
You!

SHERMAN:
But–

JOHN:
You!

SHERMAN:
But–
Mr. Adams!
But–Mr. Adams!
I cannot write with any style
Or proper etiquette.
I don't know a preposition
From a predicate.
I am just a simple cobbler
From Connecticut!

GLEE CLUB:
Connecticut!
Connecticut!
A simple cobbler . . . he!
(JOHN *resumes his pacing*)

JOHN:
Mr. Livingston, maybe you should write it.
You have many friends, and you're a diplomat.

FRANKLIN: (*Speaking*) Oh, that word!

JOHN: (*Singing*)
Whereas, if I'm the one to do it,
They'll run their quill pens through it.

GLEE CLUB:
He's obnoxious and disliked, did you know that?

LIVINGSTON: (*Speaking*) I hadn't heard–

JOHN: (*Singing*)
Then I say you should write it, Robert! Yes, you!

LIVINGSTON: (*Speaking*) Not me, Johnny–

JOHN: (*Singing*)
Yes! You, Robert Livingston–you!

LIVINGSTON:
But–

JOHN:
You!

LIVINGSTON:
But–

JOHN:
You!

LIVINGSTON:
But–
Mr. Adams!
Dear Mr. Adams!
I've been presented with a new son
By the noble stork,
So I am going home to celebrate
And pop a cork
With all the Livingstons together,
Back in old New York!

GLEE CLUB:
New York!
New York!
Livingston's . . .
Going to pop . . . a cork!
(*Slowly, all eyes turn to* JEFFERSON)

JEFFERSON:
Mr. Adams!
Leave me Alone!!!

(*The* GLEE CLUB *sings a "La-la" theme, under*)

JOHN: (*Speaking firmly*) Mr. Jefferson–

JEFFERSON: (*Speaking*) Mr. Adams, I beg you! I've not seen my wife these six months!

JOHN: (*Quoting*) ". . . and we solemnly declare we will preserve our liberties, being with one mind resolved to die free men–rather than to live slaves!" (*The* GLEE CLUB *stops to listen*) Thomas Jefferson, on the "Necessity of Taking Up

Arms," seventeen seventy-five, magnificent! You write ten times better than any man in the Congress—including me! For a man of only thirty-three years you possess a happy talent for composition and a remarkable felicity of expression. Now! Will you be a patriot? Or a lover?

JEFFERSON: A lover!

JOHN: No!

JEFFERSON: (*Singing*)
But I burn, Mr. A.!

JOHN:
So do I, Mr. J.!

(*Everything stops*)

JEFFERSON: (*Speaking*) *You?*

SHERMAN: You do?

FRANKLIN: John!

LIVINGSTON: Who'd 'a' thought it?

JOHN: (*Singing*)
Mr. Jefferson,
Dear Mr. Jefferson,
I'm only forty-one,
I still have my virility!
And I can romp through Cupid's grove
With great agility!
But life is more than
Sexual combustibility!

GLEE CLUB:
Bust-a-bility!
Bust-a-bility!
Com-bust-a-bil-i—

JOHN: (*Shouting*) Quiet!

(*He sings*)
Now, you'll write it, Mr. J.!

JEFFERSON: (*Six feet three*)
Who will make me, Mr. A.?

JOHN: (*Five feet eight*)
I!

JEFFERSON:
You?

JOHN:

Yes!

JEFFERSON:

How?

JOHN: (*Speaking*) By—by physical force if necessary! It's your duty—*your duty, dammit!!*

JEFFERSON: (*Singing*)

Mr. Adams!
Damn you, Mr. Adams!
You're obnoxious and disliked,
That cannot be denied.
(*This is agreed to by all*)
Once again you stand between me
And my lovely bride!

GLEE CLUB:

Lovely bride!

JEFFERSON:

Oh, Mr. Adams, you are driving me . . . to
Homicide!!

GLEE CLUB:

Homicide!
Homicide!

JOHN: (*Roaring*) Quiet!! (*He is furious*) The choice is yours, Mr. Jefferson! (*He thrusts a large quill pen into* JEFFERSON'S *hand; evenly*) Do—as—you—like—with—it.

GLEE CLUB: (*Gleefully*)

We may see mur-der yet!!

(JOHN *goes, followed by the others.* JEFFERSON, *alone, studies the pen for a moment, then turns and heads for his lodgings, still regarding the pen as he goes*)

SCENE 4

JEFFERSON'S *room, above High Street. It is spare and unaffected, like the man, with a desk, a cupboard, a chair, a couch, and a music stand; a violin sits on the desk.*

JEFFERSON *mounts the steps and enters his apartment. He takes another look at the pen and throws it onto the desk angrily.*

JEFFERSON: Damn the man! (*He removes his coat; then he*

catches sight of the pen again) GOD damn the man! (*Then, resigned, he sits at the desk and writes a few words. Suddenly he crumples the page and throws it on the floor. He writes some more; but again he crumples the paper and throws it on the floor. Now, merely thinking some unacceptable words, he crumples still another sheet, this one blank. Discouraged, he sits back, picks up his violin to play.*)

(*Meanwhile,* JOHN *and* FRANKLIN *have appeared outside and now enter.* FRANKLIN *heads for the couch and stretches out, closing his eyes*)

JOHN: Jefferson, are y'finished? (*There is no answer*) You've had a whole week, man. Is it done? Can I see it? (JEFFERSON *points to all the crumpled paper on the floor.* JOHN *picks one at random and, flattening it out, reads it*)

JOHN: "There comes a time in the lives of men when it becomes necessary to advance from that subordination in which they have hitherto remained–" this is terrible. (*Looking up*) Where's the rest of it? (*Again* JEFFERSON *points to the floor*) Do you mean to say it's *not* finished?

JEFFERSON: No, sir–I mean to say it's not begun.

JOHN: Good God! A whole week! The entire earth was created in a week!

JEFFERSON: (*Fed up, turning to* JOHN) Some day you must tell me how you did it.

JOHN: Disgusting! Look at him, Franklin–Virginia's most famous lover–

JEFFERSON: Virginia abstains.

JOHN: Cheer up, Jefferson, get out of the dumps. It'll come out right, I promise you. Now get back to work. Franklin, tell him to get to work.

JEFFERSON: He's asleep.

(*Outside, a cloaked woman appears. She stops, looks around, then sees the door and enters. It is* MARTHA, JEFFERSON'S *wife, a lovely girl of twenty-seven*)

FRANKLIN: (*Sitting bolt upright on the couch*) View-hal-*loo*, and whose-little-girl are you?

(*But* JEFFERSON *and* MARTHA *are suddenly oblivious to everything but each other as they meet and embrace. They kiss, and kiss, and will continue kissing throughout the remainder of the scene*)

FRANKLIN: John, who is she?

JOHN: His wife–(*He studies them*)–I hope.

FRANKLIN: (*His eyes never leaving them*) What makes y'think so?

JOHN: Because I sent for her.

FRANKLIN: Y'*what?*

JOHN: It simply occurred to me that the sooner his problem was solved, the sooner *our* problem was solved.

FRANKLIN: Good thinking, John, good thinking!

JOHN: (*Stepping forward*) Madame, may I present myself? John Adams. (*No reaction*) Adams—*John Adams!* (*Nothing*) And Dr. Franklin. (*Nothing*) Inventor of the stove!! (*No luck*) Jefferson, would you kindly present me to your wife? (*No reaction*) She *is* your wife, isn't she?

FRANKLIN: Of course she is—look how they fit! (*Starting for the door*) Come along, John, come along.

JOHN: Come along where? There's work to be done!

FRANKLIN: (*With a look back over his shoulder*) Heh! Obviously!

(*Outside, on the street:*)

JOHN: Good God! Y'mean they—They're going to—(*He stops*) In the middle of the *afternoon?*

FRANKLIN: Not everybody's from Boston, John. (*He takes* JOHN'S *arm and leads him aside.* JOHN *keeps looking back, unable to get over it*)

JOHN: Incredible.

FRANKLIN: Well—good night, John.

JOHN: Have y'eaten, Franklin?

FRANKLIN: Not yet, but—

JOHN: I hear the turkey's fresh at the Bunch o' Grapes.

FRANKLIN: I have a rendezvous, John.

JOHN: Oh.

FRANKLIN: I'd ask you along, but talking makes her nervous.

JOHN: Yes, of course.

FRANKLIN: Good night, then.

JOHN: Good night. (FRANKLIN *goes. It has grown dark.* JOHN *stands for a moment, lost in thought. Then he turns and looks up at the lighted window, just as* JEFFERSON'S *violin is heard playing a lush arpeggio. An instant later the light goes out*) Incredible! (*Music begins*) Oh, Abigail—(ABIGAIL *appears, as before*) I'm very lonely, Abigail.

ABIGAIL: Are you, John? Then as long as you were sending for wives, why didn't you send for your own?

JOHN: Don't be unreasonable, Abigail.

ABIGAIL: Now I'm unreasonable–you must add that to your list.

JOHN: List?

ABIGAIL: The catalogue of my faults you included in your last letter.

JOHN: They were fondly intended, madame!

ABIGAIL: That I play at cards badly?

JOHN: A compliment!

ABIGAIL: That my posture is crooked?

JOHN: An endearment!

ABIGAIL: That I read, write, and think too much?

JOHN: An irony!

ABIGAIL: That I am *pigeon-toed?*

JOHN: Ah, well, there you have me, Abby–I'm afraid you *are* pigeon-toed. (*Smiling*) Come to Philadelphia, Abigail–please come.

ABIGAIL: Thank you, John, I do want to. But you know it's not possible now. The children have the measles.

JOHN: Yes, so you wrote–Tom and little Abby.

ABIGAIL: Only now it's Quincy and Charles. And it appears the farm here in Braintree is failing, John–the chickens and geese have all died and the apples never survived the late frost. How do you s'pose *she* managed to get away?

JOHN: (*With a glance to the shuttered window*) The winters are softer in Virginia.

ABIGAIL: And their women, John?

JOHN: Fit for Virginians, madame, but pale, puny things beside New England girls!

ABIGAIL: (*Pleased*) John! I thank you for that.

(*A pause*)

JOHN: How goes it with you, Abigail?

ABIGAIL: Not well, John–not at all well.

(*She sings*)
I live like a nun in a cloister,
Solitary, celibate, I hate it.
(And you, John?)

JOHN: (*Singing*)
Hm!
I live like a monk in an abbey,
Ditto, ditto, I hate it.

ABIGAIL:
Write to me with sentimental effusion,
Let me revel in romantic illusion.

JOHN:

Do y'still smell of vanilla and spring air?
And is my fav'rite lover's pillo' still firm and fair?

ABIGAIL:

What was there, John!
Still is there, John!

Come soon as you can to my cloister.
I've forgotten the feel of your hand.

JOHN:

Soon, madame, we shall walk in Cupid's grove together . . .

JOHN and ABIGAIL:

And we'll fondly survey that promised land!
Till then, till then,
I am, as I ever was, and ever shall be,
Yours . . .
Yours . . .
Yours . . .
Yours . . .
Yours . . .

ABIGAIL: (*Beating him to it*)
Saltpetre, John! (*And she goes*)

(JOHN *smiles. Now the daylight returns; it's the next morning.* FRANKLIN *enters*)

FRANKLIN: Sorry to be late, John—I was up till all hours. Have y'been here long?

JOHN: Not long.

FRANKLIN: And what're y'doing out here? I expected you'd be up there cracking the whip.

JOHN: The shutters are still closed.

FRANKLIN: My word, so they are! Well, as the French say—

JOHN: Oh, *please,* Franklin! Spare me your bawdy mind first thing in the morning! (*They regard the closed shutters*) Dare we call?

FRANKLIN: A Congressman dares anything. Go ahead.

JOHN: *Me?*

FRANKLIN: Your voice is more piercing.

JOHN: (*He starts, then hesitates*) This is positively indecent!

FRANKLIN: Oh, John, they're young and they're in love.

JOHN: Not them, Franklin—us! Standing out here—(*He gestures vaguely at the shuttered room*)—waiting for them to—I mean, what will people think?

FRANKLIN: Don't worry, John. The history books will clean it up.

JOHN: It doesn't matter. I won't appear in the history books, anyway—only you. (*He thinks about it*) Franklin did this, Franklin did that, Franklin did some other damned thing. Franklin smote the ground, and out sprang George Washington, fully grown and on his horse. Franklin then electrified him with his miraculous lightning rod, and the three of them—Franklin, Washington, *and* the horse—conducted the entire Revolution all by themselves.

(*A pause*)

FRANKLIN: I like it!

(*Now the shutter opens and* MARTHA *appears, dressed and radiant. She is humming a tune*)

FRANKLIN: Look at her, John—just look at her!

JOHN: (*Hypnotized*) I am.

FRANKLIN: She's even more magnificent than I remember! Of course, we didn't see much of her front last night. (*Calling*) Good morrow, madame! (*She looks down at him blankly*)

JOHN: Good morrow!

MARTHA: Is it the habit in Philadelphia for strangers to shout at ladies from the street?

FRANKLIN: Not at all, madame, but we're not—

MARTHA: And from men of your age it is not only unseemly, it's unsightly.

JOHN: Excuse me, madame, but we met last evening.

MARTHA: I spoke to no one last evening.

FRANKLIN: Indeed you did not, madame, but nevertheless we presented ourselves. This is Mr. John Adams and I am Dr. Franklin. (*As she stares at them, dumfounded*) Inventor of the stove?

MARTHA: Oh please, I know your names very well. But you say you presented yourselves?

FRANKLIN: (*Smiling*) It's of no matter. Your thoughts were well taken elsewhere.

MARTHA: (*Turning to the room for a moment*) My husband is not yet up.

FRANKLIN: Shall we start over? Please join us, madame.

MARTHA: Yes, of course. (*She disappears from the window*)

FRANKLIN: No wonder the man couldn't write. Who could think of independence, married to her?

(*She appears, smiling*)

MARTHA: I beg you to forgive me. It is indeed an honor meeting the two greatest men in America.

FRANKLIN: (*Smiling back*) Certainly the greatest within earshot, anyway.

MARTHA: I am not an idle flatterer, Dr. Franklin. My husband admires you both greatly.

FRANKLIN: Then we are doubly flattered, for we admire very much that which your husband admires.

(*A pause as they regard each other warmly. They have hit it off*)

JOHN: (*Finally; the bull in the china shop*) Did you sleep well, madame? (FRANKLIN *nudges him with his elbow*) I mean, did you lie comfortably? Oh, damn! Y'know what I mean!

FRANKLIN: Yes, John, we do. Tell us about yourself, madame; we've had precious little information. What's your first name?

MARTHA: Martha.

FRANKLIN: Ah, Martha. He might at least have told us that. I'm afraid your husband doesn't say very much.

JOHN: He's the most silent man in Congress. I've never heard him utter three sentences together.

FRANKLIN: Not everyone's a talker, John.

MARTHA: It's true, you know. (*She turns to look at the window*) Tom is not—a talker.

(*She sings*)

Oh, he never speaks his passions,
He never speaks his views.
Whereas other men speak volumes,
The man I love is mute.

In truth
I can't recall
Being woo'd with words
At all.

Even now . . .
(*Music continues under*)

JOHN: (*Speaking*) Go on, madame.

FRANKLIN: How did he win you, Martha, and how does he hold onto a bounty such as you?

MARTHA: Surely you've noticed that Tom is a man of many accomplishments: author, lawyer, farmer, architect, statesman

—(*She hesitates*)—and still one more that I hesitate to mention.

JOHN: Don't hesitate, madame—don't hesitate!

FRANKLIN: Yes, what *else* can that redheaded tombstone do?

MARTHA: (*She looks at them for a moment, then leans in and sings, confidentially*)

He plays the violin
He tucks it right under his chin,
And he bows,
Oh, he bows,
For he knows,
Yes, he knows, that it's . . .

Heigh, heigh, heigh diddle-diddle,
'Twixt my heart, Tom, and his fiddle,
My strings are unstrung.
Heigh-heigh-heigh-heigh-igh-igh . . .
Heigh—I am undone!

(JOHN *and* FRANKLIN *look at one another, not at all sure if she's putting them on or not*)

FRANKLIN: (*Speaking*) The *violin,* madame?

MARTHA:

I hear his violin,
And I get that feeling within,
And I sigh . . .
Oh, I sigh . . .
He draws near,
Very near, and it's . . .

Heigh, heigh, heigh diddle-diddle, and . . .
Good-by to the fiddle!
My strings are unstrung.
Heigh-heigh-heigh-heigh-igh-igh . . .
Heigh—I'm always undone!

FRANKLIN: (*Speaking*) That settles it, John, we're taking up the violin!

JOHN: (*To* MARTHA) Very well, madame, you've got us playing the violin! What happens next?

MARTHA: Next, Mr. Adams?

JOHN: Yes! What does Tom do now?

MARTHA: (*Demurely*) Why, just what you'd expect.

(JOHN *and* FRANKLIN *exchange expectant looks*)

MARTHA: We dance!

JOHN and FRANKLIN: (*Together and to each other*) Dance?

FRANKLIN: Incredible!

MARTHA: One-two-three, one-two-three!

(*And in an instant she has swept* FRANKLIN *off into an energetic waltz.* JOHN *watches them for a moment, still trying to understand*)

JOHN: Who's playing the violin?

FRANKLIN: Oh, John—really!

(*And* MARTHA *leaves* FRANKLIN *to begin waltzing with* JOHN, *who, to* FRANKLIN'S *astonishment, turns out to dance expertly*)

FRANKLIN: John! You can dance!

JOHN: (*Executing an intricate step—he is having a grand time*) We still do a few things in Boston, Franklin! (*Finally they have twirled and spun and danced themselves out*)

MARTHA: (*Singing, as she catches her breath*)

When Heaven calls to me,
Sing me no sad elegy!
Say I died
Loving bride,
Loving wife,
Loving life. Oh, it was . . .

MARTHA, JOHN, and FRANKLIN:

Heigh, heigh, heigh diddle-diddle . . .

MARTHA:

'Twixt my heart, Tom, and his
Fiddle, and
Ever 'twill be
Heigh-heigh-heigh-heigh-igh-igh . . .
Heigh, through eternity.

FRANKLIN: (*In counterpoint*)

He plays the violin . . .

JOHN: (*In counterpoint*)

He plays the violin . . .

MARTHA: (*In counterpoint*)

He plays the violin!

(*They bow to her, and she curtsies. Now* JEFFERSON *appears, a fiddle under his arm, and stuck on the end of his bow is a paper. He collects his wife, and together they start back toward the room*)

JOHN: Franklin, look! He's written something—he's done it! (*He dashes after them, snatches the paper off the bow, and comes back to* FRANKLIN, *delighted, and reads it*) "Dear Mr. Adams: I am taking my wife back to bed. Kindly go away. Y'r ob'd't, T. Jefferson."

FRANKLIN: What, again?

JOHN: Incredible!

FRANKLIN: Perhaps I'm the one who should've written the declaration, after all. At my age there's little doubt that the pen is mightier than the sword.

(*He sings*)
For it's
Heigh, heigh, heigh diddle-diddle.
(*Enviously*)
And God bless the man who can fiddle . . .

JOHN: (*Ever the old warhorse*)
And independency!

JOHN and FRANKLIN: (*Regaining their energy*)
Heigh-heigh-heigh-heigh-igh-igh.
Yata-ta-ta-tah!
Through eternity!
(*And they exit arm in arm*)
He plays the violin! . . . Violin! . . . Violin! . . .

SCENE 5

The Chamber, as before.

At rise, Congress is in session, though in an exceedingly loose manner. While SECRETARY THOMSON *delivers a droning report, it is clear that no one is listening.* HANCOCK *sits at the President's table, but he is occupied reading the* Philadelphia Gazette, *his feet up on the desk; one group of Congressmen—*MORRIS, READ, WILSON, *and* DICKINSON*—sit with their heads together, talking; another group—*HOPKINS, BARTLETT, *and* SHERMAN*—stands in the rear, also conversing;* RUTLEDGE *and* HEWES *pace back and forth across the length of the Chamber as they talk;* MC KEAN *stands by the window, cleaning a long rifle;* CHASE, *a large napkin tied around his neck, sits eating a complete meal;* WITHERSPOON *is asleep at his desk, his head thrown back, his mouth open and snoring; and* MC NAIR *is kept hopping from one group to another on this errand and that. The wall calendar now reads:* "JUNE 22."

THOMSON: . . . and what follows is a complete and up-to-date list of the committees of this Congress now sitting, about to sit, or just having sat: A committee formed to investigate a complaint made against the quality of yeast manufactured at Mr. Henry Pendleton's mill, designated as the Yeast Committee; a committee formed to consider the most effective method of dealing with spies, designated as the Spies Committee; a committee formed to think, perhaps to do, but in any case to gather, to meet, to confer, to talk, and perhaps even to resolve that each rifle regiment be allowed at least one drum and one fife attached to each company, designated as the Drum and Fife Committee; a committee formed to . . .

(FRANKLIN *and* DR. HALL *have entered and now stand surveying the room*)

FRANKLIN: Look at it, doctor—democracy! What Plato called a "charming form of government, full of variety and disorder." I never knew Plato had been to Philadelphia.

HANCOCK: (*As he reads the newspaper*) *McNair!* Open that damn window!

HOPKINS: (*Joining* FRANKLIN *and* HALL, *a mug of rum in his hand*) Ben, I want y'to see some cards I've gone 'n' had printed up that ought t'save everybody here a whole lot of time 'n' effort, considering the epidemic of bad disposition that's been going around lately. (*He reads*) "Dear sir: You are without any doubt a rogue, a rascal, a villain, a thief, a scoundrel, and a mean, dirty, stinking, sniveling, sneaking, pimping, pocket-picking, thrice double-damned, no good son-of-a-bitch"—and y'sign y'r name. What do y'think?

FRANKLIN: (*Delighted*) Stephen, I'll take a dozen right now!

THOMSON: . . . a committee formed to answer all Congressional correspondence designated as the Congressional Correspondence Committee . . .

(JOHN *strides in and joins* FRANKLIN)

JOHN: All right, Franklin, enough socializing—there's work to be done!

FRANKLIN: (*Pointedly*) Good morning, John!

JOHN: What? Oh. (*Waving it aside*) Good morning, good morning. Now, then, let's get to it.

FRANKLIN: Let's get to what?

JOHN: (*Indicating the tally board*) Unanimity, of course. Look at that board—six Nays to win over in little more than a week!

THOMSON: . . . a committee formed to consider the problem of counterfeit money, designated as the Counterfeit Money Committee . . .

FRANKLIN: All right, John, where do we start?

JOHN: How about Delaware? It's a sad thing to find her on the wrong side after all this time. Is there any news of Rodney?

FRANKLIN: (*Pointing*) McKean's back.

JOHN: Thomas!

(*They go to him*)

THOMSON: . . . a committee formed to study the causes of our military defeat in Canada, designated as the Military Defeat Committee . . .

JOHN: How did you leave Caesar? Is he still alive?

MC KEAN: Aye, but the journey to Dover was fearful hard on him. He never complained, but I could see the poor man was sufferin'.

FRANKLIN: But you got him safely home.

MC KEAN: I did, but I doubt he'll ever set foot out of it again.

JOHN: That leaves you and Read split down the middle. Will he come over?

MC KEAN: I don't know. He's a stubborn little snot!

JOHN: Then work on him. Keep at him till you wear him down!

MC KEAN: Och, John, face facts, will y'? If it were just Read standin' in our way it wouldn't be so bad. But look for yourself, man—(*Indicating the tally board*)—Mary-land, Pennsylvania, the entire South—it's impossible!

JOHN: It's impossible if we all stand around complaining about it. To work, McKean—one foot in front of the other.

FRANKLIN: I believe I put it a better way: "Never leave off till tomorrow that which you can do—"

JOHN: Shut up, Franklin!

MC KEAN: But what good will it do? Y'know Dickinson—he'll never give in! And y'haven't heard the last of Rutledge yet, either.

JOHN: Never mind about them. Your job is George Read. Talk him deaf if you have to, but bring us back Delaware!

MC KEAN: There's a simpler way. (*He holds up his rifle*) This'll break the tie! (*He goes to talk to* READ)

FRANKLIN: All right, John, who's next?

(*Again they turn to study the board*)

THOMSON: . . . a committee formed to keep secrets, designated as the Secrets Committee . . .

JOHN: Pennsylvania and Mary-land. I suggest you try to put

your own house in order while I take a crack at Old Bacon Face—look at him stuff himself!—Mr. Chase! (*He goes to him*) How about it, Chase? When are you coming to your senses?

CHASE: (*Sourly*) Please, Mr. Adams—not while I'm eating!

FRANKLIN: (*Drawing* WILSON *aside*) Mr. Wilson, it's time to assert yourself. When you were a judge, how in hell did you ever make a decision?

WILSON: The decisions I made were all based on legality and precedence. But there is no legality here—and certainly no precedent.

FRANKLIN: Because it's a new idea, you clot! We'll be setting our own precedent!

READ: (*Arguing with* MC KEAN) No, Mr. McKean—no, no, *no!*

MC KEAN: Damn y'r eyes, Read, y'came into this world screamin' "no," and y're determined to leave it the same way, y'little worm!

JOHN: (*With* CHASE) The Congress is waiting on you, Chase—America's waiting—the whole *world* is waiting! What's that, kidney? (*He takes a morsel of food from* CHASE'S *plate with his fingers, but* CHASE *slaps his hand and he drops it*)

CHASE: Leave me alone, Mr. Adams, you're wasting your time. If I thought we could win this war I'd be at the front of your ranks. But you must know it's impossible! You've heard General Washington's dispatches. His army has fallen apart.

JOHN: Washington's exaggerating the situation in order to arouse this torpid Congress into action. Why, as Chairman of the War Committee I can tell you for a fact that the army has never been in better shape! Never have troops been so cheerful! Never have soldiers been more resolute! Never have discipline and training been more spirited!

(*The* COURIER *enters, dusty as ever.* JOHN *winces*)

JOHN: Good God!

(*The* COURIER *deposits his dispatch on* THOMSON'S *desk and goes.* HANCOCK *puts down his paper and pounds the gavel*)

HANCOCK: May we have your ears, gentlemen? Mr. Thomson has a dispatch.

(*Everyone turns to listen.* WITHERSPOON *is nudged awake*)

THOMPSON: (*Ringing his bell*) From the Commander, Army of the United Colonies; in New York, dispatch number one thousand, one hundred and fifty-seven. "To the honorable Congress, John Hancock, President. Dear Sir: It is with the utmost despair that I must report to you the confusion and disorder that reign in every department—"

MC NAIR: Sweet Jesus!

THOMSON: "The Continental soldier is as nothing ever seen in this, or any other, century; he is a misfit, ignorant of hygiene, destructive, disorderly and totally disrespectful of rank. Only this last is understandable as there is an incredible reek of stupidity amongst the officers. The situation is most desperate at the New Jersey Training Ground in New Brunswick where every able-bodied whore—*whore*—in the Colonies has assembled. There are constant reports of drunkenness, desertion, foul language, naked bathing in the Raritan River, and an epidemic of the French disease. I have declared the town 'off-limits' to all military personnel—with the exception of officers. I beseech the Congress to dispatch the War Committee to this place in the hope of restoring some of the order and discipline we need to survive. Y'r ob'd't—(*Drum roll*)—G. Washington."

MC KEAN: Och! That man would depress a hyena!

HANCOCK: Well, Mr. Adams, you're Chairman of the War Committee. Do y'feel up to whoring, drinking, deserting, and New Brunswick?

WITHERSPOON: There must be some mistake. I have an aunt who lives in New Brunswick!

(*Laughter*)

DICKINSON: You must tell her to keep up the good work!

(*Laughter*)

DICKINSON: Come, come, Mr. Adams, you must see that it's hopeless. Let us recall General Washington and disband the Continental Army before we are overwhelmed.

JOHN: Oh, yes, the English would like that, wouldn't they?

DICKINSON: Why not ask them yourself? They ought to be here any minute.

(*Laughter*)

RUTLEDGE: And when they hang you, Mr. Adams, I hope you will put in a good word for the rest of us.

(*A distressed silence*)

CHASE: Face facts, Mr. Adams—a handful of drunk and disorderly recruits against the entire British Army, the finest musketmen on earth. How can we win? How can we even hope to survive?

JOHN: Answer me straight, Chase. If you thought we *could* beat the redcoats, would Mary-land say "yea" to independence?

CHASE: Well, I suppose–

JOHN: No supposing, Chase–would you or wouldn't you?

CHASE: Very well, Mr. Adams–yes, we would.

JOHN: Then come with me to New Brunswick and see for yourself!

MC KEAN: John! Are y'mad?

BARTLETT: Y'heard what Washington said–it's a shambles!

HOPKINS: They're pushin' y'into it, Johnny!

JOHN: What do y'say, Chase?

MORRIS: Go ahead, Sam. It sounds lively as hell up there.

CHASE: All right–why not? And maybe it'll be John Adams who comes to his senses.

JOHN: Mr. President, the War Committee will heed General Washington's request! A party consisting of Mr. Chase, Dr. Franklin, and myself will leave immediately.

HANCOCK: Is that satisfactory with you, Dr. Franklin?

(*All eyes turn to* FRANKLIN, *who is asleep again.* HOPKINS *nudges him*)

JOHN: Wake up, Franklin, you're going to New Brunswick!

FRANKLIN: Like hell I am. What for?

HOPKINS: The whoring and the drinking.

FRANKLIN: (*Perking up*) Why didn't you say so?

(*They start out.* JOHN *driving them ahead of him like a sergeant-major*)

JOHN: Come on, Chase, move all that lard! We've no time to lose! Left-right, left-right, left-right–!

(*And they are gone. The other liberals then go, leaving only the conservatives.* DICKINSON *looks around, then rises*)

DICKINSON: Mr. McNair, all this talk of independence has left a certain foulness in the air.

(*Laughter from the conservatives*)

DICKINSON: My friends and I would appreciate it if you could open some windows.

MC NAIR: What about the flies?

DICKINSON: (*Smiling*) The windows, Mr. McNair.

(*As* MC NAIR *goes to the windows, the clock strikes four*)

DICKINSON: (*Takes a deep breath, surveys the Chamber, then sings*)

Oh, say, do you see what I see?

Congress sitting here in sweet serenity.
I could cheer.
The reason's clear:
For the first time in a year
Adams isn't here!
And, look!
The sun is in the sky,
The breeze is blowing by,
And there's not a single fly!

Oh, sing Hosanna, Hosanna!

CONSERVATIVES:
Hosanna, Hosanna!

DICKINSON:
And it's cool!

Oh, ye cool, cool conservative men,
Our like may never ever be seen again.
We have land,
Cash in hand,
Self-command,
Future planned.
Fortune thrives,
Society survives,
In neatly ordered lives
With well-endowered wives.

CONSERVATIVES:
Come sing Hosanna, Hosanna!

DICKINSON:
In our breeding and our manner . . .

CONSERVATIVES:
. . . We are cool!

(*The cool, cool conservative men*—RUTLEDGE, WILSON, READ, MORRIS, HALL, LIVINGSTON, *and* HEWES *among them—elegantly prepare to dance*)

DICKINSON:
Come, ye cool, cool considerate set,
We'll dance together to the same minuet,
To the right,
Ever to the right,
Never to the left,

Forever to the right,
Let our creed,
Be never to exceed,
Regulated speed,
No matter what the need!

CONSERVATIVES:
Come sing Hosanna, Hosanna!

DICKINSON:
Emblazoned on our banner
Is "Keep Cool!"

(*The Minuet is led by* DICKINSON *and* RUTLEDGE, *as the* CONSERVATIVES *dance. During this the* COURIER *re-enters and deposits his dispatch, as usual, on* THOMSON'S *desk.* MC NAIR *goes to him, offers him a rum, and he stays*)

CONSERVATIVES:
To the right,
Ever to the right,
Never to the left,
Forever to the right.

DICKINSON:
Hands attach,
Tightly latch,
Everybody match.

THOMSON: (*Singing*)
I have a new dispatch . . .

(*Music stops, but the Minuet continues silently*)

THOMSON: (*Speaking*) From the Commander, Army of the United Colonies; in New York, dispatch number one thousand, one hundred and fifty-eight. "To the honorable Congress, John Hancock, President. Dear Sir: I awoke this morning to find that Gen. Howe has landed twenty-five thousand British regulars and Hessian mercenaries on Staten Island and that the fleet, under the command of his brother, Admiral Lord Howe, controls not only the Hudson and East Rivers, but New York Harbour, which now looks like all of London afloat. I can no longer, in good conscience, withhold from the Congress my certainty that the British military object at this time is Philadelphia. Happy should I be if I could see the means of preventing them, but at present I confess I do not.

Oh, how I wish I had never seen the Continental Army. I would have done better to retire to the back country and live in a wigwam. Y'r ob'd't—
(*Drum roll*)—G. Washington."
(*A short pause; then music begins again and the song continues as if nothing had happened*)

CONSERVATIVES: (*Singing*)
What we do, we do rationally.

DICKINSON:
We never ever go off half
Cocked, not we.

CONSERVATIVES:
Why begin,
Till we know that we can win?
And if we cannot win,
Why bother to begin?

RUTLEDGE:
We say this game's not of our choosing,
Why should we risk losing?

CONSERVATIVES:
We cool, cool men.

DICKINSON: (*Speaking, still dancing*) Mr. Hancock, you're a man of property—one of us. Why don't you join us in our minuet? Why do you persist in dancing with John Adams? Good Lord, sir, you don't even like him!

HANCOCK: (*Singing*)
That is true,
He annoys me quite a lot,
But still I'd rather trot
To Mr. Adams' new gavotte.

DICKINSON: (*Speaking, continuing to dance*) But why? For personal glory? For a place in history? Be careful, sir. History will brand him and his followers as traitors!

HANCOCK: Traitors to what, Mr. Dickinson—the British Crown? Or the British *half*-crown? Fortunately, there are not enough men of property in America to dictate policy.

DICKINSON: Perhaps not, but don't forget that most men with nothing would rather protect the possibility of becoming rich than face the reality of being poor. And that is why they will follow us . . .

CONSERVATIVES:

. . . To the right,
Ever to the right,
Never to the left,
Forever to the right.
Where there's gold,
A market that will hold,
Tradition that is old,
A reluctance to be bold.

DICKINSON:

I sing Hosanna, Hosanna!
In a sane and lucid manner!

CONSERVATIVES:

We are cool!

We're the cool, cool considerate men,
Whose like may never ever be seen again!
With our land,
Cash in hand,
Self-command,
Future planned.

And we'll hold
To our gold,
Tradition that is old,
Reluctant to be bold!
We say this game's not of our choosing.
Why should we risk losing?

We Cool, Cool, Cool, Cool, Cool, Cool,
Cool, Cool, Cool, Cool, Cool, Cool,
Cool–!
Cool–!
Men!!

(*They turn and go, leaving only* MC NAIR, *the* LEATHER APRON, *and the* COURIER *in the Chamber. They are silent for a moment*)

MC NAIR: How'd you like to try 'n' borrow a dollar from one o' them? (*To the* COURIER) Want another rum, Gen'rul?

COURIER: Gen'rul? (*He grins*) Lord, I ain't even a *corp'l.*

MC NAIR: Yeah, well, what's the Army know? (*He pours the* COURIER *another drink, pours himself and the* LEATHER APRON *a pair, selects one of* HANCOCK'S *good clay pipes, lights it, then bangs with the gavel*) Sit down, gentlemen. The Chair rules it's too damn hot to work! (*He occupies one chair, the* COURIER *another, and the* LEATHER APRON *still a third*) What's it like out there, Gen'rul?

COURIER: You prob'ly know more'n me.

MC NAIR: Sittin' in here? Sweet Jesus! This is the *last* place to find out what's goin' on!

LEATHER APRON: (*To the* COURIER) I'm aimin' t'join up!

MC NAIR: What're you talkin' about? You don't have to join up —you're in the Congress!

LEATHER APRON: What's that got t'do with it?

MC NAIR: Y'don't see *them* rushin' off t'get killed, do you? But they sure are great ones f'r sendin' others, I'll tell you that.

COURIER: (*Indicating his chair*) Who sets here?

MC NAIR: Caesar Rodney of Delaware. Where *you* from, Gen'rul?

COURIER: Watertown.

MC NAIR: Where's that?

COURIER: Massachusetts.

MC NAIR: Well, then, you belong down there. (*He indicates* JOHN'S *chair*) But be careful; there's somethin' about that chair that makes a man awful noisy.

(*The* COURIER *goes to* ADAMS' *chair and touches it reverently before he sits*)

LEATHER APRON: You seed any fightin'?

COURIER: (*Proudly*) Sure did. I seed my two best friends git shot dead on the very same day! Right on the village green it was, too! (*The recollection takes hold*) An' when they didn't come home f'r supper, their mommas went down the hill lookin' for 'em. (*Music in, softly*) Miz Lowell, she foun' Tim'thy right off, but Miz Pickett, she looked near half the night f'r Will'm cuz he'd gone 'n' crawled off the green 'fore he died.

(*He is silent for a moment; then he sings*)

Momma, hey, Momma,
Come lookin' for me.
I'm here in the meadow
By the red maple tree.
Momma, hey, Momma,
Look sharp—here I be.
Hey, Hey—
Momma, look sharp!

Them so'jurs, they fired,
Oh, Ma, did we run.
But then we turned round
An' the battle begun.
Then I went under—
Oh, Ma, am I done?
Hey, Hey—
Momma, look sharp!

My eyes are wide open,
My face to the sky.
Is that you I'm hearin'
In the tall grass nearby?
Momma, come find me
Before I do die.
Hey, Hey—
Momma, look sharp!

COURIER, MC NAIR, *and* LEATHER APRON:
I'll close y'r eyes, my Billy,
Them eyes that cannot see,
An' I'll bury ya, my Billy,
Beneath the maple tree.

COURIER: (*As* MC NAIR *and* LEATHER APRON *hum quietly*)
An' never ag'in
Will y'whisper t'me,
"Hey, Hey—"
Oh, Momma, look sharp!

The Lights Fade

SCENE 6

An anteroom off the main Congressional Chamber.

At rise, the stage remains dark from the previous scene as the sounds of Congress in session are heard: first, THOMSON'S *bell, asking for attention.*

HANCOCK: The Secretary will now read the report of the Declaration Committee. Mr. Thomson.

THOMSON: "A Declaration by the Representatives of the United States of America in General Congress assembled."

(*Lights come up on the anteroom. It is deserted save for* JEFFERSON, *who stands by the door into the Chamber, holding it ajar so he can listen to* THOMSON *read his Declaration*)

THOMSON: "When in the Course of Human Events, it becomes necessary for one People to dissolve the Political Bands which have connected them with another, and to assume among the Powers of the Earth, the separate and equal Station to which the Laws of Nature and of Nature's God entitle them, a decent Respect to the Opinions of Mankind requires that they should declare the causes which impel them to the Separation. We hold these Truths to be self-evident, that all Men are created equal, that they are endowed by their Creator with certain inalienable Rights–"

(JEFFERSON, *having heard a sound offstage, closes the door, silencing* THOMSON'S *voice.* JOHN *and* FRANKLIN *enter from the wings, wearing capes and hats*)

JOHN: Jefferson! We're back and we've got Mary-land–that is, we *will,* soon as Chase gets through telling the Mary-land Assembly what we saw in New Brunswick!

FRANKLIN: He's in Annapolis right now, describing a ragtag collection of provincial militiamen who couldn't train together, drill together, or march together–but when a flock of ducks flew by and they saw their first dinner in three full days, sweet Jesus! Could they *shoot* together! It was a slaughter!

JEFFERSON: (*Not listening*) They're reading the Declaration.

JOHN: What? How far have they got?

JEFFERSON: ". . . to render the Military independent of and superior to the Civil Power."

(JOHN *opens the door to the Chamber*)

THOMSON: ". . . independent of and superior to–"

(JOHN *closes the door. The three men pace for a moment*)

JOHN: Well, there's nothing to fear. It's a masterpiece! I'm to be congratulated.

FRANKLIN: *You?*

JOHN: For making him write it.

FRANKLIN: Ah, yes–of course.

(*They are silent for a moment; then* . . .)

JOHN: (*Singing*)

It's a masterpiece, I say.
They will cheer ev'ry word,
Ev'ry letter!

JEFFERSON:

I wish I felt that way.

FRANKLIN:
I believe I can put it better!
Now then, attend,
As friend to friend,
Our Declaration Committee—
For us I see
Immortality . . .

ALL:
In Philadelphia city.

FRANKLIN:
A farmer,
A lawyer,
And a sage!—
A bit gouty in the leg.
You know, it's quite bizarre
To think that here we are,
Playing midwives to
An egg.

JOHN: (*Speaking*) Egg? What egg?
FRANKLIN: America—the birth of a new nation!
JEFFERSON: If only we could be sure of what kind of a bird it's going to be.
FRANKLIN: Tom's got a point. What sort of a bird should we choose as the symbol of our new America?
JOHN: The eagle.
JEFFERSON: The dove.
FRANKLIN: The turkey.
(JOHN *and* JEFFERSON *look at* FRANKLIN *in surprise, then at each other*)
JOHN: The eagle.
JEFFERSON: The dove.
JOHN: The *eagle!*
JEFFERSON: (*Shrugging*) The eagle. (*A pause*)
FRANKLIN: The turkey.
JOHN: The eagle is a majestic bird.
FRANKLIN: The eagle is a scavenger, a thief, a coward, and the symbol of more than ten centuries of European mischief.
JOHN: And the turkey?
FRANKLIN: A truly noble bird, a native of America, a source of sustenance to our settlers, and an incredibly brave fellow (*Kettle drums*) who would not flinch from attacking an entire

regiment of Englishmen singlehandedly! Therefore the national bird of America is going to be (*Drums out*)—

JOHN: The eagle.

FRANKLIN and JEFFERSON: (*Shrugging*) The eagle. (*A pause*)

JOHN: (*Singing*)
We're waiting for the . . .

ALL:
Chirp! chirp! chirp!
Of an eaglet being born,
Waiting for the
Chirp! chirp! chirp!
On this humid Monday morning in this
—Congressional incubator!

FRANKLIN:
God knows, the temp'rature's hot enough
To hatch a stone,
Let alone
An egg!

JOHN:
We're waiting for the . . .

ALL:
Scratch! scratch! scratch!
Of that tiny little fellow,
Waiting for the egg to hatch,
On this humid Monday morning in this
—Congressional incubator!

JOHN:
God knows the temp'rature's hot enough
To hatch a stone!

JEFFERSON:
But will it hatch
An egg?

JOHN: (*Speaking*) The Declaration will be a triumph, I tell you —a triumph! If I was ever sure of anything I'm sure of that— a triumph! (*A pause*) And if it isn't, we've still got four days left to think of something else.

(*He sings*)
The eagle's going to

Crack the shell
Of the egg that England laid!

ALL:
Yessir! We can
Tell! tell! tell!
On this humid Monday morning in this
–Congressional incubator!

FRANKLIN:
And just as Tom, here, has written,
Though the shell may belong to Great Britain,
The eagle inside
Belongs to us!

ALL:
And just as Tom, here, has written,
We say "To hell with Great Britain!"
The eagle inside
Belongs to us!!!
(*They turn and go confidently into the Chamber*)

SCENE 7

The Chamber. Congress is in session–HANCOCK, BARTLETT, HOPKINS, SHERMAN, MORRIS, LIVINGSTON, WITHERSPOON, DICKINSON, WILSON, MC KEAN, READ, HEWES, RUTLEDGE, *and* HALL *being present–and now* JOHN, FRANKLIN, *and* JEFFERSON *take their places, this action continuing from the previous scene, as* THOMSON *completes his reading of the Declaration. The calendar on the wall now reads:* "JUNE 28."

THOMSON: "–and that as Free and Independent States, they have full Power to levy War, conclude Peace, contract Alliances, establish Commerce, and to do all other Acts and Things which Independent States may of right do. And for the support of this Declaration we mutually pledge to each other our Lives, our Fortunes, and our sacred Honor." (*Finished, he looks up. Nobody moves, nobody speaks, nobody reacts; the silence is complete and prolonged*)

HANCOCK: (*Finally*) Very well. Thank you, Mr. Thomson. The Congress has heard the report of the Declaration Committee. Are there any who wish to offer amendments, deletions, or alterations to the Declaration?

(*Suddenly every hand but* JOHN'S, FRANKLIN'S, *and* HOPKINS' *shoots up*)

CONGRESS: Mr. President! . . . Hear me, Mr. President! . . . I've got one! . . . Over here! . . . (*Et cetera*)

HANCOCK: (*Pounding the gavel for order*) Gentlemen, *please!* McNair, you'd better open the window. Colonel McKean, I saw your hand first.

MC KEAN: Mr. Jefferson, it's a bonny paper y've written, but somewhere in it y've mentioned "Scottish and foreign mercenaries sent t'destroy us." *Scottish,* Tom?

JOHN: It's in reference to a Highland regiment which stood against us at Boston.

MC KEAN: Och, it was more like Germans wearin' kilts to disguise their bein' there. I ask y'to remove the word and avoid givin' offense to a good people.

THOMSON: Mr. Jefferson?

(JEFFERSON *nods and* THOMSON *scratches his quill pen through the word. The many hands go up again*)

HANCOCK: The Reverend Witherspoon?

WITHERSPOON: Mr. Jefferson, nowhere do you mention the Supreme Being. Certainly this was an oversight, for how could we hope to achieve a victory without His help? Therefore I must humbly suggest the following addition to your final sentence: "With a firm reliance on the protection of Divine Providence."

(*Again* THOMSON *looks at* JEFFERSON, *who in turn looks at* JOHN; *the two patriots shrug, then* JEFFERSON *turns back to* THOMSON *and nods; the phrase is added. More hands*)

HANCOCK: Mr. Read?

READ: Among your charges against the King, Mr. Jefferson, you accuse him of depriving us of the benefits of trial by jury. This is untrue, sir. In Delaware we have always had trial by jury.

JOHN: In Massachusetts we have not.

READ: Oh. Then I suggest that the words "in many cases" be added.

THOMSON: Mr. Jefferson?

(*And again* JEFFERSON *nods; the words are added*)

MC KEAN: "In many cases!"—och, brilliant! I s'pose every time y'see those three words y'r puny little chest'll swell up wi' pride over y'r great historical contribution!

READ: It's more memorable than your unprincipled whitewash of that race of barbarians!

HANCOCK: (*Pounding the gavel*) Mr. Read, Colonel McKean—that's enough! (*The hands are raised, this time* HOPKINS' *among them*) Mr. Hopkins?

HOPKINS: No objections, Johnny, I'm just trying to get a drink.

HANCOCK: I should've known. McNair, get him a rum.

(*Again the hands go up.* MC NAIR *crosses to the wall calendar and removes a leaf, uncovering* "JUNE 29")

HANCOCK: Mr. Bartlett?

BARTLETT: Mr. Jefferson, I beg you to remember that we still have friends in England. I see no purpose in antagonizing them with such phrases as "unfeeling brethren" and "enemies in war." Our quarrel is with the British King, not the British people.

JOHN: Be sensible, Bartlett. Remove those phrases, and the entire paragraph becomes meaningless. And it so happens it's among the most stirring and poetic of any passage in the entire document. (*He picks up the Declaration from* THOMSON'S *desk, preparing to read*)

BARTLETT: We're a Congress, Mr. Adams, not a literary society. I ask that the entire paragraph be stricken.

THOMSON: Mr. Jefferson?

(*And again, after some thought this time, and with some sadness,* JEFFERSON *nods*)

JOHN: Good God, Jefferson! Don't you ever intend to speak up for your own work?

JEFFERSON: I had hoped that the work would speak for itself.

(THOMSON *scratches out the paragraph*)

MC NAIR: Mr. Hancock.

HANCOCK: What is it, Mr. McNair?

MC NAIR: I can't say I'm very fond of the United States of America as a name for a new country.

HANCOCK: I don't care *what* you're fond of, Mr. McNair. You're not a member of this Congress! Mr. Sherman?

SHERMAN: (*Coffee in hand, as usual*) Brother Jefferson, I noted at least two distinct and direct references to the British Parliament in your Declaration. Do you think it's wise to alienate that august body in light of our contention that they have never had any direct authority over us anyway?

JOHN: This is a revolution, dammit! We're going to have to offend *some*body!

FRANKLIN: John. (*He leads* JOHN *downstage as the debate in the Chamber continues silently behind them*) John, you'll have an attack of apoplexy if you're not careful.

JOHN: Have you heard what they're doing to it? Have *you heard?*

FRANKLIN: Yes, John, I've heard, but–

JOHN: And so far it's only been our friends! Can you imagine what our enemies will do?

HANCOCK: The word "Parliament" will be removed wherever it occurs.

JOHN: They won't be satisfied until they remove one of the Fs from Jefferson's name.

FRANKLIN: Courage, John! It won't last much longer.

(*They start back toward their seats as the hands go up again. And again* MC NAIR *goes to the calendar and removes another page; it now reads:* "JUNE 30")

HANCOCK: Mr. Dickinson?

DICKINSON: Mr. Jefferson, I have very little interest in your paper, as there is no doubt in my mind that we have all but heard the last of it. But I am curious about one thing: why do you refer to King George as a tyrant?

JEFFERSON: Because he is a tyrant.

DICKINSON: I remind you, Mr. Jefferson, that this "tyrant" is still your King.

JEFFERSON: When a king becomes a tyrant he thereby breaks the contract binding his subjects to him.

DICKINSON: How so?

JEFFERSON: By taking away their rights.

DICKINSON: Rights that came from him in the first place.

JEFFERSON: All except one–the right to be free comes from nature.

DICKINSON: Mr. Wilson, do we in Pennsylvania consider King George a tyrant?

WILSON: Hmm? Well–I don't know. (*As he meets* DICKINSON'S *stony stare*) Oh. No–no, we don't. He's not a tyrant–in Pennsylvania.

DICKINSON: There you are, Mr. Jefferson. Your Declaration does not speak for us all. I demand the word "tyrant" be removed! (THOMSON *begins scratching it out*)

JEFFERSON: Just a moment, Mr. Thomson, I do not consent. The King is a tyrant whether we say so or not. We might as well say so.

THOMSON: But I already scratched it out.

JEFFERSON: (*Forcefully*) Then scratch it back in!

(*A surprised silence*)

HANCOCK: (*Finally*) Put it back, Mr. Thomson. The King will remain a tyrant.

(*Once more* MC NAIR *goes to the calendar and changes the date—to* "JULY 1")

HANCOCK: Mr. Hewes?

HEWES: Mr. Jefferson, nowhere do you mention deep-sea fishin' rights. We in North Carolina—

(*Everyone throws up his hands in disgust and impatience*)

JOHN: Good God! *Fishing* rights! How long is this piddling to go on? We have been sitting here for three full days. We have endured, by my count, eighty-five separate changes and the removal of close to four hundred words. Would you whip it and beat it till you break its spirit? I tell you this document is a masterful expression of the American mind!

(*There is a silence*)

HANCOCK: If there are no more changes, then, I can assume that the report of the Declaration Committee has been—

RUTLEDGE: (*Deliberately*) Just a moment, Mr. President.

FRANKLIN: (*To* JOHN) Look out.

RUTLEDGE: I wonder if we could prevail upon Mr. Thomson to read again a small portion of Mr. Jefferson's Declaration—the one beginnin' "He has waged cruel war—"?

HANCOCK: Mr. Thomson?

THOMSON: (*Reading back rapidly to himself*) ". . . He has affected . . . He has combined . . . He has abdicated . . . He has plundered . . . He has constrained . . . He has excited . . . He has *in*cited . . . He has waged cruel war!" Ah. (*He looks up*) Here it is. (*He clears his throat and reads*) "He has waged cruel war against human nature itself, in the persons of a distant people who never offended him, captivating and carrying them into slavery in another hemisphere. Determined to keep open a market where men should be bought and sold, he has prostituted—"

RUTLEDGE: That will suffice, Mr. Thomson, I thank you. Mr. Jefferson, I can't quite make out what it is you're talkin' about.

JEFFERSON: Slavery, Mr. Rutledge.

RUTLEDGE: Ah, yes. You're referrin' to us as slaves of the King.

JEFFERSON: No, sir, I'm referring to *our* slaves. Black slaves.

RUTLEDGE: Ah! Black slaves. Why didn't you say so, sir? Were you tryin' to hide your meanin'?

JEFFERSON: No, sir.

RUTLEDGE: Just another literary license, then.

JEFFERSON: If you like.

RUTLEDGE: I don't like at all, Mr. Jefferson. To us in South Carolina, black slavery is our peculiar institution and a cherished way of life.

JEFFERSON: Nevertheless, we must abolish it. Nothing is more certainly written in the Book of Fate than that this people shall be free.

RUTLEDGE: I am not concerned with the Book of Fate right now, sir. I am more concerned with what's written in your little paper there.

JOHN: That "little paper there" deals with freedom for Americans!

RUTLEDGE: Oh, really! Mr. Adams is now callin' our black slaves Americans. Are-they-now?

JOHN: They are! They're people and they're here—if there is any other requirement, I've never heard of it.

RUTLEDGE: They are here, yes, but they are not people, sir, they are *property*.

JEFFERSON: No, sir! They are people who are being treated as property. I tell you the rights of human nature are deeply wounded by this infamous practice!

RUTLEDGE: (*Shouting*) Then see to your own wounds, Mr. Jefferson, for you are a—*practitioner,* are you not? (*A pause.* RUTLEDGE *has found the mark*)

JEFFERSON: I have already resolved to release my slaves.

RUTLEDGE: Then I'm sorry, for you have also resolved the ruination of your personal economy.

JOHN: Economy. Always economy. There's more to this than a filthy purse-string, Rutledge. It's an offense against man and God.

HOPKINS: It's a stinking business, Mr. Rutledge—a stinking business!

RUTLEDGE: Is it really, Mr. Hopkins? Then what's that I smell floatin' down from the North—could it be the aroma of *hypocrisy*? For who holds the other end of that filthy purse-string, Mr. Adams? (*To everyone*) Our northern brethren are feelin' a bit tender toward our slaves. They don't keep slaves, no-o, but they're willin' to be considerable carriers of slaves

—to others! They are willin', for the shillin'—(*Rubbing his thumb and forefinger together*)—or haven't y'heard, Mr. Adams? Clink! Clink!

(*He sings*)
Molasses to
Rum to
Slaves!
Oh, what a beautiful waltz!

You dance with us,
We dance with you, in
Molasses and
Rum and
Slaves!
(*Afro-rhythm*)

Who sail the ships out of Boston,
Laden with Bibles and Rum?
Who drinks a toast
To the Ivory Coast,
"Hail, Africa! The slavers have come."
New England, with Bibles and Rum!

Then,
It's off with the Rum and the Bibles
Take on the Slaves, clink! clink!
Then,
Hail and farewell!
To the smell of the African
Coast!

Molasses to
Rum to
Slaves!
'Tisn't morals, 'tis money that saves!
Shall we dance to the sound
Of the profitable pound, in
Molasses and
Rum and
Slaves!

Who sail the ships out of Guinea,
Laden with Bibles and Slaves?
'Tis Boston can boast
To the West Indies coast:

"Jamaica! We brung what y'craves!
Antigua! Barbados!
We brung Bibles
And Slaves!"

(*He speaks. Afro-rhythm continues*)

Gentlemen! You mustn't think our northern friends merely see our slaves as figures on a ledger. Oh, no, sir! They see them as figures on the block! Notice the faces at the auctions, gentlemen—white faces on the African wharves—New England faces, seafaring faces: "Put them in the ships, cram them in the ships, *stuff* them in the ships!" Hurry, gentlemen, let the auction begin!

(*He sings*)

Ya-ha . . .
Ya-ha . . . ha-ma-ha-cundahhh!
Gentlemen, do y'hear?
That's the cry of the auctioneer!

Ya-ha . . .
Ya-ha . . . ha-ma-ha-cundahhh!
Slaves, gentlemen! Black gold, livin' gold—gold!
From:
Annn-go-laah!
Guinea-Guinea-Guinea!
Blackbirds for sale!
Aaa-shan-tiiii!
Ibo! Ibo! Ibo! Ibo!
Blackbirds for sale!
Handle them!
Fondle them!
But don't finger them!
They're prime, they're prime!

Ya-ha . . .
Ya-ha . . . ha-ma-ha-cundahhh!
(*Music stops*)

BARTLETT: (*Pleading*) For the love of God, Mr. Rutledge, *please!*
(*Music resumes*)

RUTLEDGE:
Molasses to

Rum to
Slaves!

Who sail the ships back to Boston,
Laden with gold, see it gleam?
Whose fortunes are made
In the triangle trade?
Hail, Slavery, the New England
Dream!

Mr. Adams, I give you a toast!
Hail, Boston!
Hail, Charleston!
Who *stinketh* the most?!

(*He turns and walks straight out of the Chamber.* HEWES *of North Carolina follows, and* HALL *of Georgia is right behind them*)

JOHN: (*Desperate*) Mr. Rutledge! Mr. Hewes! Dr. Hall!

(HALL, *the last, hesitates at the door as his name is called. He turns, looks at* JOHN, *starts to say something, then turns and goes after the others*)

WITHERSPOON: Don't worry, they'll be back.

MC KEAN: Aye–t'vote us down.

(*There is a silence. Then* CHASE *bursts into the Chamber*)

CHASE: (*Elated*) It's done! Adams, Franklin–I have it! And the Maryland Assembly's approved it! I told them about one of the greatest military engagements in history, against a flock of–(*He runs down as the news is greeted with less enthusiasm than expected, and he sees the glum faces*) What's wrong? I thought–

DICKINSON: (*Cordially*) You'll have to forgive them, Mr. Chase, they've just suffered a slight setback. And after all, what is a man profited, if he shall gain Mary-land, and lose the entire South? (*Smiling as he goes*) Matthew, chapter sixteen, verse twenty-six.

(WILSON, READ, LIVINGSTON, *and* MORRIS *follow him out.* CHASE *joins the ranks of the depressed as* THOMSON *moves Maryland into the "Yea" column*)

HANCOCK: (*Lifelessly*) Mr. McNair–

MC NAIR: I know, the flies.

HANCOCK: No–a rum.

JOHN: (*Surveying the sorry sight*) Well? What're you all sitting around for? We're wasting time–precious time! (*To* MC-

KEAN) Thomas! I want you to ride down into Delaware and fetch back Caesar Rodney!

MC KEAN: John! Are y'mad? It's eighty miles on horseback, an' he's a dyin' man!

JOHN: No! He's a patriot!

MC KEAN: Och, John, what good'll it do? The South's done us in.

JOHN: And suppose they change their minds—can we get Delaware without Rodney?

MC KEAN: (*Shaking his head*) God! What a bastardly bunch we are! (*He goes*)

JOHN: (*Turning to* HOPKINS) Stephen—

HOPKINS: I'm goin' to the tavern, Johnny. If there's anything I can do for y'there, let me know. (*He goes*)

JOHN: Chase, Bartlett—

BARTLETT: What's the use, John? The vote's tomorrow morning.

CHASE: There's less than a full day left!

(*They go*)

JOHN: Roger!

SHERMAN: Face facts, John—it's finished!

WITHERSPOON: I'm sorry, John.

(*And they go.* JOHN *looks around, stunned by the defection. Only* FRANKLIN, JEFFERSON, HANCOCK, *and* THOMSON *remain*)

FRANKLIN: We've no other choice, John. The slavery clause has to go.

JOHN: Franklin, what are y'saying?

FRANKLIN: It's a luxury we can't afford.

JOHN: A luxury? A half-million souls in chains, and Dr. Franklin calls it a luxury! Maybe you should've walked out with the South!

FRANKLIN: You forget yourself, sir! I founded the first anti-slavery society on this continent!

JOHN: Don't wave your credentials at me! Perhaps it's time you had them renewed!

FRANKLIN: (*Angrily*) The issue here is independence! Maybe you've lost sight of that fact, but I have not! How dare you jeopardize our cause when we've come so far? These men, no matter how much we disagree with them, are not ribbon clerks to be ordered about; they're proud, accomplished men, the cream of their colonies—and whether you like it or not, they and the people they represent will be a part of the new country you'd hope to create! Either start learning how to live with them or pack up and go home—but in any case, stop acting like a Boston fishwife!

(*And he leaves* JOHN *alone, returning upstage to join* JEFFERSON. JOHN *turns and comes downstage*)

JOHN: Good God, what's happened to me? John Adams, the great John Adams, Wise Man of the East—what have I come to? My law practice down the pipe, my farm mortgaged to the hilt—at a stage in life when other men prosper I'm reduced to living in Philadelphia.

(ABIGAIL *appears, as before*)

JOHN: Oh, Abigail, what am I going to do?

ABIGAIL: Do, John?

JOHN: I need your help.

ABIGAIL: You don't usually ask my advice.

JOHN: Yes—well, there doesn't appear to be anyone else right now.

ABIGAIL: (*Sighing*) Very well, John, what is it?

JOHN: The entire South has walked out of this Congress, George Washington is on the verge of total annihilation, the precious cause for which I've labored these several years has come to nothing, and it seems—(*A pause*)—it seems I am obnoxious and disliked.

ABIGAIL: Nonsense, John.

JOHN: That I am unwilling to face reality.

ABIGAIL: Foolishness, John.

JOHN: That I am pig-headed.

ABIGAIL: (*Smiling*) Ah, well, there you have me, John. I'm afraid you *are* pig-headed.

(*He smiles; a pause*)

JOHN: Has it been any kind of life for you, Abby? God knows I haven't given you much.

ABIGAIL: I never asked for more. After all, I am Mrs. John Adams—that's quite a lot for one lifetime.

JOHN: (*Bitterly*) Is it, Abby?

ABIGAIL: Think of it, John! To be married to the man who is always first in line to be hanged!

JOHN: Yes. The ag-i-ta-tor. (*Turning to her*) Why, Abby? You must tell me what it is! I've always been dissatisfied, I know that; but lately I find that I *reek* of discontentment! It fills my throat and floods my brain, and sometimes—sometimes I fear that there is no longer a dream, but only the discontentment.

ABIGAIL: Oh, John, can you really know so little about yourself? And can you think so little of me that you'd believe I married the man you've described? Have you forgotten what you used to say to me? I haven't. "Commitment, Abby–commitment! There are only two creatures of value on the face of this earth: those with a commitment, and those who require the commitment of others." (*A pause*) Do you remember, John?

JOHN: (*Nodding*) I remember.

(MC NAIR *enters, carrying two gaily beribboned kegs, and thumps them down in front of* JOHN)

MC NAIR: Mr. Adams–

JOHN: What?

MC NAIR: These're for you.

JOHN: Just a minute–what are they? What's in them? Who sent them?

(*Music in, glissando*)

ABIGAIL: (*Singing*)
Compliments of the Concord Ladies' Coffee Club,
And the Sisterhood of the Truro Synagogue,
And the Friday Evening Baptist Sewing Circle,
And the Holy Christian Sisters of Saint Clare–
All for you, John!
I am, as I ever was, and ever shall be . . .
Yours . . .
Yours . . .
Yours . . .
Yours–

JOHN: (*Speaking*) Just a moment, Abigail–what's in those kegs?

ABIGAIL: (*Singing triumphantly*)
Saltpetre, John! (*She blows a kiss and goes*)

(JOHN *turns back to the Chamber*)

JOHN: McNair! Go out and buy every damned pin in Philadelphia!

MC NAIR: Pin? What sort of pin?

JOHN: I don't know–whatever ladies use with their sewing! And take these kegs to the armory–hurry, man! (*Turning as* MC-NAIR *goes*) Franklin, Jefferson, what are you just sitting around for?

FRANKLIN: John, didn't you hear a word that I said before?

JOHN: Never mind that. Here's what you've got to do—

FRANKLIN: John! I'm not even speaking to you!

JOHN: It's too late for that, dammit! (*Music in, vigorously*) There's work to be done!

(*He sings*)

Time's running out!
Get up!
Get out of your chair!
Tomorrow is here.
Too late,
Too late to despair!

Jefferson! Talk to Rutledge, talk!
If it takes all night,
Keep talking.

JOHN and JEFFERSON:

Talk and talk and talk!

JOHN: (*Speaking*) You're both Southern aristocrats—gentlemen. If he'll listen to anybody, he'll listen to you!

(*He sings*)

Franklin!
Time's running out!

FRANKLIN:

I know. Get out of my chair!
Do I have to talk to Wilson?

JOHN:

Yes, yes, you do!
If it takes all night,
Keep talking!

JOHN, FRANKLIN, and JEFFERSON:

Talk and talk and talk!

JOHN: (*Speaking*) Get him away from Dickinson, that's the only way to do it!

(FRANKLIN *and* JEFFERSON *go. Music under*)

HANCOCK: (*Coming forward*) I'm still from Massachusetts, John; you know where I stand. I'll do whatever you say.

JOHN: (*Considering*) No, you're the President of Congress. You're a fair man, Hancock—stay that way.

(*The* COURIER *enters and stops short as he comes face to*

face with JOHN, *who takes his dispatch and crosses up to* THOMSON'S *desk, where he hands it to the Secretary*)

JOHN: Tell me, Mr. Thomson, out of curiosity, do you stand with Mr. Dickinson, or do you stand with me?

THOMSON: (*Holding up the dispatch*) I stand with the General. Lately–I've had the oddest feeling that he's been–writing to *me.*

(*He reads, singing*)
"I have been in expectation
Of receiving a reply
On the subject of my last fifteen dispatches.
Is anybody there?
Does anybody care?
Does anybody care?
Y'r humble and ob'd't–"

(*Drum roll; then it runs down as* THOMSON, *unable to read the signature, rises and goes, thoroughly discouraged.*

It is growing dark outside. HANCOCK *stands by the door, watching* JOHN, *concerned*)

HANCOCK: Are y'hungry, John?

JOHN: No, I think I'll stay.

HANCOCK: G'night, then. (*He goes*)

(JOHN *looks around the Chamber, then goes to* THOMSON'S *desk and picks up the dispatch*)

JOHN: (*Singing*)
"Is anybody there?
Does anybody care?"
(*He drops the dispatch*)
Does anybody see what I see?

They want me to quit,
They say, "John, give up the fight!"
Still to England I say:
"Good night forever, good night!"

For I have crossed the Rubicon,
Let the bridge be burn'd behind me!
Come what may, come what may . . .
Commitment!

The croakers all say
We'll rue the day,

There'll be hell to pay in
Fiery Purgatory!

Through all the gloom,
Through all the gloom, I can
See the rays of ravishing light and
Glory!

Is anybody there?!
Does anybody care?!
Does anybody see
What I see?!

I see
Fireworks!
I see the Pageant and Pomp and Parade!
I hear the bells ringing out!
I hear the cannons' roar!

I see Americans, *all* Americans,
Free! For evermore!
(*He "comes to" and looks around, realizing that it's dark and that he's alone*)
How quiet . . .
How quiet the Chamber is . . .
How silent . . .
How silent the Chamber is . . .

Is anybody there—?
(*He waits for an answer; there is none*)
Does anybody care—?
(*Again, nothing*)
Does anybody see—what I see?
(*Music out*)

HALL: (*Speaking*) Yes, Mr. Adams, I do.
(JOHN *turns and discovers the Georgia delegate standing by the door, in the shadows*)
JOHN: Dr. Hall, I didn't know anyone was—
HALL: I'm sorry if I startled you. I couldn't sleep. In trying to resolve my dilemma I remembered something I'd once read—"that a representative owes the People not only his industry, but his judgment, and he betrays them if he sacrifices it to their opinion." (*He smiles*) It was written by Edmund Burke, a member of the British Parliament.
(*He walks to the tally board and moves the name of Georgia

from the "Nay" to the "Yea" column. The two men regard each other for a moment.

It has been growing light outside and now the clock, offstage, chimes ten and the men of the Congress return silently, in single file, each with his own private thoughts, MC KEAN *supporting* RODNEY *at the end.*

Then HANCOCK *pounds the gavel*)

HANCOCK: Very well. The Congress will now vote on Virginia's resolution on independence. (*To* RODNEY) Thank you for coming, Caesar. And God bless you, sir. (*Foot-stamping and other signs of approval from all*) Call the roll, Mr. Thomson. And I'd remind you, gentlemen, that a single "Nay" vote will defeat the motion. Mr. Thomson?

(THOMSON *goes to the tally board. During the following,* FRANKLIN *is deeply engaged in silent argument with* DICKINSON *and* WILSON, *their heads remaining together*)

THOMSON: (*Droning*) New Hampshire–

BARTLETT: New Hampshire says "Yea."

THOMSON: New Hampshire says "Yea." Massachusetts–

JOHN: Massachusetts says "Yea."

THOMSON: Massachusetts says "Yea." Rhode Island–

HOPKINS: Rhode Island says "Yea."

THOMSON: Rhode Island says "Yea." Connecticut–

SHERMAN: Connecticut says "Yea."

THOMSON: Connecticut says "Yea." New York–

MORRIS: New York abstains–courteously.

THOMSON: New York abstains.

MORRIS: (*Disgusted and ashamed*) Courteously.

THOMSON: New Jersey–

WITHERSPOON: New Jersey says "Yea."

THOMSON: New Jersey says "Yea." Pennsylvania–(*As no one responds*) Pennsylvania?

FRANKLIN: Mr. Secretary, Pennsylvania isn't ready yet. Come back to us later.

(*He returns to the argument*)

THOMSON: Pennsylvania passes. Delaware–

RODNEY: (*As* MC KEAN *helps him to his feet*) Delaware, by majority vote–

MC KEAN: Aye!

RODNEY: –says "Yea."

FRANKLIN: Well done, sir.

THOMSON: Delaware says "Yea."

(*And Delaware's marker on the tally board is moved into the "Yea" column*)

THOMSON: Mary-land—

CHASE: Mary-land says "Yea."

THOMSON: Mary-land says "Yea." Virginia—

JEFFERSON: Virginia says "Yea."

THOMSON: Virginia says "Yea." North Carolina—

HEWES: North Carolina yields to South Carolina!

THOMSON: South Carolina—

RUTLEDGE: (*Rising, then turning to* JOHN) Well, Mr. Adams?

JOHN: (*Returning his stare*) Well, Mr. Rutledge?

RUTLEDGE: Mr. Adams, you must believe that I will do what I have promised to do.
(*A pause*)

JOHN: What do y'want, Rutledge?

RUTLEDGE: Remove the offendin' passage from your Declaration.

JOHN: If we did that we'd be guilty of what we ourselves are rebelling against.

RUTLEDGE: Nevertheless, remove it or South Carolina will bury now and forever your dream of independence.

FRANKLIN: (*Imploring*) John, I *beg* you to consider what you're doing.

JOHN: Mark me, Franklin, if we give in on this issue, posterity will never forgive us.

FRANKLIN: That's probably true. But we won't hear a thing, John—we'll be long gone. And besides, what will posterity think we were—demigods? We're men—no more, no less—trying to get a nation started against greater odds than a more generous God would have allowed. John, first things first! Independence! America! For if we don't secure that, what difference will the rest make?

JOHN: (*Looking around, uncertain*) Jefferson, say something.

JEFFERSON: What else is there to do?

JOHN: Well, man, you're the one who wrote it!

JEFFERSON: I wrote *all* of it, Mr. Adams! (*He goes to* THOMSON'S *table, takes up the quill pen, and scratches the passage from the Declaration. Then he returns to his seat.* JOHN *snatches up the Declaration, goes to* RUTLEDGE, *and waves it under his nose*)

JOHN: There! There it is, Rutledge! You've got your slavery, and little good may it do you! Now vote, damn you!

RUTLEDGE: (*Unruffled*) Mr. Secretary, the fair colony of South Carolina says "Yea."

THOMSON: South Carolina says "Yea."

HEWES: (*Jumping up*) North Carolina says "Yea!"

THOMSON: North Carolina says "Yea."

(*The two markers on the tally board are moved out of the "Nay" column. Only Pennsylvania remains there*)

THOMSON: Georgia.

HALL: Georgia says "Yea."

THOMSON: Georgia says "Yea." Pennsylvania, second call–

DICKINSON: (*Rising*) Mr. President, Pennsylvania regrets all of the inconvenience that such distinguished men as Adams, Franklin, and Jefferson were put to just now. They might have kept their document intact, for all the difference it will make. Mr. President, Pennsylvania says–

FRANKLIN: Just a moment! I ask that the delegation be polled.

DICKINSON: Dr. Franklin, don't be absurd!

FRANKLIN: A poll, Mr. President. It's a proper request.

HANCOCK: Yes, it is. Poll the delegation, Mr. Thomson.

THOMSON: Dr. Benjamin Franklin–

FRANKLIN: Yea!

THOMSON: Mr. John Dickinson–

DICKINSON: Nay!

THOMSON: Mr. James Wilson–(*As there is no response*) Judge Wilson?

(*All eyes turn to* WILSON)

FRANKLIN: There it is, Mr. Wilson, it's up to you now–the whole question of American independence rests squarely on your shoulders. An entirely new nation, Mr. Wilson, waiting to be born or to die in birth, all on your say-so. Which will it be, Mr. Wilson? Every map-maker in the world is waiting for your decision!

DICKINSON: Come now, James, nothing has changed. We mustn't let Dr. Franklin create one of his confusions. The question is clear.

FRANKLIN: Most questions are clear when someone else has to decide them.

JOHN: (*Quietly, turning the screw*) It would be a pity for a man who handed down hundreds of wise decisions from the bench to be remembered only for the one unwise decision he made in Congress.

DICKINSON: James, you're keeping everybody waiting. The Secretary has called for your vote.

WILSON: (*To* DICKINSON) Please don't push me, John, I know what you want me to do. But Mr. Adams is correct about one thing. *I'm* the one who'll be remembered for it.

DICKINSON: What do you mean?

WILSON: I'm different from you, John. I'm different from most of the men here. I don't want to be remembered. I just don't want the responsibility!

DICKINSON: Yes, well, whether you want it or not, James, there's no way of avoiding it.

WILSON: Not necessarily. If I go with them, I'll only be one among dozens; no one will ever remember the name of James Wilson. But if I vote with you, I'll be the man who prevented American independence. I'm sorry, John—I just didn't bargain for that.

DICKINSON: And is that how new nations are formed—by a nonentity trying to preserve the anonymity he so richly deserves?

FRANKLIN: Revolutions come into this world like bastard children, Mr. Dickinson—half improvised and half compromised. Our side has provided the compromise; now Judge Wilson is supplying the rest.

WILSON: (*To* DICKINSON) I'm sorry, John. My vote is "Yea."

FRANKLIN: Mr. Secretary, Pennsylvania says "Yea."

THOMSON: Pennsylvania says "Yea."

(*There is a stunned silence as all eyes go to the tally board and Pennsylvania's marker is moved into the "Yea" column*)

THOMSON: The count being twelve to none with one abstention, the resolution on independence—(*Surprised*)—is adopted.

JOHN: It's done. It's done.

(*A pause*)

HANCOCK: Mr. Thomson, is the Declaration ready to be signed?

THOMSON: It is.

HANCOCK: Then I suggest we do so. And the Chair further proposes, for our mutual security and protection, that no man be allowed to sit in this Congress without attaching his name to it.

(*All eyes now go to* DICKINSON)

DICKINSON: I'm sorry, Mr. President, I cannot, in good conscience, sign such a document. I will never stop hoping for our eventual reconciliation with England. But because, in my own way, I regard America no less than does Mr. Adams,

I will join the Army and fight in her defense—even though I believe that fight to be hopeless. Good-by, gentlemen. (*He starts out*)

JOHN: Gentlemen of the Congress, I say ye John Dickinson!

(DICKINSON *stops as the members of Congress express their admiration for him by stamping their feet and banging their walking sticks on the floor. Then he goes and* HANCOCK *pounds the gavel*)

HANCOCK: Gentlemen, are there any objections to the Declaration being approved as it now stands?

JOHN: I have one, Mr. Hancock.

HANCOCK: *You,* Mr. Adams?

JOHN: Yes. Mr. Jefferson, it so happens the word is *un*alienable, not *in*alienable.

JEFFERSON: I'm sorry, Mr. Adams, *in*alienable is correct.

JOHN: (*His voice rising*) I happen to be a Harvard graduate—

JEFFERSON: (*His voice also rising*) And *I* attended William and Mary—

HANCOCK: (*Pounding the gavel*) Gentlemen, please! Mr. Jefferson, will you yield to Mr. Adams' request?

(*A pause*)

JEFFERSON: No, sir, I will not.

JOHN: Oh, very well, I'll withdraw it.

FRANKLIN: Good for you, John!

JOHN: (*Privately*) I'll speak to the printer about it later.

HANCOCK: Very well, gentlemen. (*He goes to* THOMSON'S *desk and picks up the quill*) We are about to brave the storm in a skiff made of paper, and how it will end, God only knows. (*He signs with a flourish*)

HOPKINS: That's a pretty large signature, Johnny.

HANCOCK: So Fat George in London can read it without his glasses!

(*Laughter*)

HANCOCK: All right, gentlemen, step right up, don't miss your chance to commit treason!

(*Laughter*)

FRANKLIN: Hancock's right. This paper is our passport to the gallows. But there's no backing out now. If we don't hang together, we shall most assuredly hang separately.

(*Laughter*)

MC KEAN: (*Patting his ample middle*) In any case hanging won't be so bad—one snap and it'll be over—(*Snap!*)—just like that!

But look at Read, there—he'll be dancing a jig long after I'm gone!

(*Laughter*)

HANCOCK: Gentlemen, forgive me if I don't join in the merriment, but if we're arrested now—my name is still the only one *on* the damn thing!

(*More laughter, which subsides slowly as the* COURIER *enters, deposits his dispatch on* THOMSON'S *desk, and departs, turning to glance at* JOHN *as he goes*)

THOMSON: From the Commander, Army of the United Colonies —(*He stops, looks up*)—Army of the United States—in New York, dispatch number one thousand, two hundred and nine. "To the Hon. Congress, John Hancock, President. Dear Sir: I can now report with some certainty that the eve of battle is near at hand. Toward this end I have ordered the evacuation of Manhattan and directed our defenses to take up stronger positions on the Brooklyn Heights. At the present time my forces consist entirely of Haslet's Delaware Militia and Smallwood's Mary-landers, a total of five thousand troops to stand against—(*He hesitates in horrified astonishment*)—twenty-five thousand of the enemy—and I begin to notice that many of them are lads under fifteen and old men, none of whom could truly be called soldiers. One personal note to Mr. Lewis Morris of New York—I must regretfully report that his estates have been totally destroyed but that I have taken the liberty of transporting Mrs. Morris and eight of the children to Connecticut and safety. The four older boys are now enlisted in the Continental Army. As I write these words, the enemy is plainly in sight beyond the river. How it will end only Providence can direct—but dear God! what brave men—I shall lose—before this business ends. Y'r ob'd't—(*Drum roll*) —G. Washington."

(*There is a silence, during which* MC NAIR *goes to the calendar and removes the final leaf, revealing:* "JULY 4."

The light outside has dimmed; it is becoming evening)

HANCOCK: (*Finally*) Very well, gentlemen. McNair, go ring the bell.

(MC NAIR *goes*)

MORRIS: (*Rising*) Mr. President!

HANCOCK: Mr. Morris?

MORRIS: To hell with New York—I'll sign it anyway.

HANCOCK: Thank you, Mr. Morris. Stephen, sit down.

HOPKINS: (*Who has been standing next to the Declaration on* THOMSON'S *desk*) No–I want t'remember each man's face as he signs.

HANCOCK: Very well. Mr. Thomson–

(*As each name is called, the signer rises, comes to the Secretary's desk, signs, then stands to one side. The tolling Liberty Bell begins, offstage*)

THOMSON: (*In measured tones*)
New Hampshire, Dr. Josiah Bartlett.
Massachusetts, Mr. John Adams.
Rhode Island, Mr. Stephen Hopkins.
Connecticut, Mr. Roger Sherman.
New York, Mr. Lewis Morris.
New Jersey, the Reverend John Witherspoon.
Pennsylvania, Dr. Benjamin Franklin.
Delaware, Mr. Caesar Rodney.

(HANCOCK *takes the Declaration to the infirm* RODNEY, *then returns it to the table*)

Mary-land, Mr. Samuel Chase.
Virginia, Mr. Thomas Jefferson.
North Carolina, Mr. Joseph Hewes.
South Carolina, Mr. Edward Rutledge.
Georgia, Dr. Lyman Hall.

(*As the last man signs, the sound of the tolling Liberty Bell in the belfry above becomes almost deafening.*

Then the scene freezes for a brief instant, and the pose of the familiar Pine-Savage engraving of this occasion has been captured.

A scrim curtain falls, the scene visible through it. Then as the back-light dims and the curtain is lit from the front, it becomes opaque and reveals the lower half of the Declaration, featuring the signatures)

Curtain

COMPANY

Book by George Furth
Music and Lyrics by Stephen Sondheim

Production Notes

Company was first presented by Harold Prince, in association with Ruth Mitchell, at the Alvin Theatre, New York, on April 26, 1970. The cast was as follows:

Robert, *Dean Jones*
Sarah, *Barbara Barrie*
Harry, *Charles Kimbrough*
Susan, *Merle Louise*
Peter, *John Cunningham*
Jenny, *Teri Ralston*
David, *George Coe*
Amy, *Beth Howland*
Paul, *Steve Elmore*
Joanne, *Elaine Stritch*
Larry, *Charles Braswell*
Marta, *Pamela Myers*
Kathy, *Donna McKechnie*
April, *Susan Browning*
The Vocal Minority, *Cathy Corkill*
Carol Gelfand
Marilyn Saunders
Dona D. Vaughn

There is no singing or dancing ensemble. Only the members of the cast become the choir, waiters, patrons, etc.

Directed by *Harold Prince*
Musical numbers staged by *Michael Bennett*
Sets and projections designed by *Boris Aronson*
Costumes by *D. D. Ryan*
Lighting by *Robert Ornbo*
Orchestrations by *Jonathan Tunick*
Dance music arrangements by *Wally Harper*
Musical Director: *Harold Hastings*

THE SCENE: New York City, NOW

Musical Numbers

Act One

Company	Robert and Company
The Little Things You Do Together	Joanne and Company
Sorry-Grateful	Harry, David and Larry
You Could Drive a Person Crazy	Kathy, April and Marta
Have I Got a Girl for You?	Larry, Peter, Paul, David and Harry
Someone Is Waiting	Robert
Another Hundred People	Marta
Getting Married Today	Amy, Paul, Jenny and Company

ACT ONE

SCENE 1

The curtain rises on a multi-leveled steel structure indicating various high-rise Manhattan apartments. Two elevators and stairs link the different levels. There are five empty living areas on the various levels of the raised structure. Each of the areas is to denote the apartment of one couple, and it is that same area to which the couple will always return at various points during the action. When cleared, the stage level belongs to ROBERT. *For reasons of vision and space, most of the longer scenes are played in this stage-level area, with sections containing furniture moved on. As the scenes change, rear and frontal projections are used to indicate different skylines and city sights.*

As the lights come up slowly, ROBERT'S *apartment slides in on stage level. The five couples are sitting at or standing around a dining room table. Each of the wives is carrying a gaily wrapped gift box.* JOANNE *goes to the center of the room and places her present on a coffee table. She is followed by* SUSAN, *who puts her gift down and smiles at* JOANNE, *who tokenly smiles back and moves away.* JOANNE *puts a cigarette in her mouth.* LARRY *crosses to her, lights his lighter and holds it up.* JOANNE *chooses to ignore it, lighting her own cigarette. She moves around* LARRY *and returns to the dining room table.*

We hear footsteps in the distance growing louder, and the sound of a key in the lock. At this point the couples scramble for positions around the table and the lights are turned out.

ALL: Shhhh!

(*The door opens and* ROBERT *enters. A glaring spotlight hits his face. He jumps*)

ROBERT: (*Shielding his face*) What's this? What the hell is going on around here? Huh? Who is it? Who is that?

ALL: (*Intoning*) Surprise.

ROBERT: My birthday. It's my birthday. Do you know you had me scared to death. I was just about to run out of this place like nobody's business. I *was*. I mean, I didn't know—I mean, what kind of friends would surprise you on your thirty-fifth birthday? (*He pauses*) Mine. Then again, how many times do you get to be thirty-five? Eleven? (*He pauses*) Okay, come on. Say it and get it over with. It's embarrassing. Quick. I can't stand it.

ALL: (*Intoning*) Happy birthday, Robert.

ROBERT: I stood it. Thank you for including me in your thoughts, your lives, your families. Yes, thank you for remembering. Thank you.

ALL: (*Intoning*) You don't look it.

ROBERT: (*Laughs*) Well, I feel it.

ALL: (*Intoning*) It's the birthday boy!

ROBERT: Now, you've rehearsed. Very good. I am touched.

SUSAN: (*Breaking intonation. Excitedly*) I love it when people are really surprised.

PETER: She loves it when people are really surprised.

SARAH: (*Handing him her gift*) If you don't like it, you can take it back.

ROBERT: Well, I haven't even seen it yet.

SARAH: I mean, though, if you don't like it—

HARRY: Why don't you wait until the man looks at the thing?

ROBERT: I know I'll like it.

SARAH: Why don't you just take it back?

HARRY: For God's sake, he just said he likes it.

SARAH: Pretend not to notice Harry, Robert. I think I'll leave. (*She starts to move away*)

HARRY: I was being funny, Sarah. We could stay a little longer.

(*They both come eye to eye, and slowly, very slowly, sink stiffly, simultaneously, into two chairs as the action continues*)

PETER: (*Throwing his present to* ROBERT) Hey, Bobby, take ours back too.

AMY: (*Bringing hers to* ROBERT) Here's from Paul and me. If I were you, I would take it back and get the money. It cost so much I fainted.

PAUL: It did not, Robert. It's a sweater.

AMY: You told him what it was! (*To* ROBERT) Well, when I saw the price tag, I thought it was a house.

JOANNE: (*As* JENNY *starts toward* ROBERT) Miss, Miss. YOU! Yes, you! Tell him to take yours back and get the money. It's not the gift, it's the cost that counts.

JENNY: (*Handing her present to* ROBERT) Who *is* that?

JOANNE: That is I, Miss. I am very rich and I am married to him (*Indicates her husband*) and I'd introduce him, but I forgot his name.

ROBERT: (*Quickly*) Haven't you two met?

JOANNE: Pass, baby. Pass. There's no one here I want to meet. Except her. She's crazy. (*Points to* AMY) And him. He's a looker. (*Points to* PETER, *going over to him*) The rest are Lois and Larry Loser— (*She takes* PETER'S *drink from him*) Here's to you, winner. (*She downs the drink*)

PETER: (*Smiling, flattered, to* JOANNE) I find you quite fascinating. Quite delightful. Quite—

JOANNE: You just blew it. (*She puts the empty glass back in* PETER'S *hand and moves away from him*)

LARRY: Many happy returns of the day, old man.

JENNY: (*Breaking the tension. Gaily*) David is now going to deliver *our* greeting. Go on, sweetheart.

DAVID: (*Looks at her, stunned. A moment; then*) Robert, happy birthday from us. (*An awkward salute and smile to* ROBERT)

PETER: (*Giving him that friendly punch on the arm*) And may this year bring you fame, fortune, and your first wife.

ALL: Hear, hear!

ROBERT: Listen, I'm fine without the three.

JOANNE: You bet your ass, baby.

(AMY *slips out*)

SUSAN: (*To* JOANNE) He might have meant that superciliously.

JOANNE: (*A "what-do-you-know" look to* SUSAN) Oooo, isn't she darling with all that free help.

SUSAN: (*In a whimpering tone*) I meant he could have been being funny, is all I meant. (*She sits down*)

JOANNE: (*Sitting down, across from* SUSAN) Now, don't cry. Don't cry or I'll push your chair over.

LARRY: (*Crosses behind* JOANNE'S *chair*) She's kidding ya. She's a great kidder.

ROBERT: (*Nervously*) All right. Let's cut out the many happy returns, and that is about enough about me. I am just indeed lucky to have all of you. I mean, when you've got friends like mine . . .

AMY: (*Enters, with a lighted cake*) Well, our blessings, Robert.

(JENNY *starts the group singing "Happy Birthday," which comes out in monotone*)

AMY: (*Interrupting the song*) Blow out your candles and get your wish.

JENNY: Don't tell your wish, Bobby, or it won't come true.

SUSAN: You have to close your eyes and blow them all out.

JOANNE: SHUT–UP!

LARRY: (*Laughing*) That's just her way of fooling. (JOANNE *laughs*) See what I mean?

PETER: Talk about your sense of humor! Terrific!

AMY: Be sure you make it a good one, Robert.

(*He closes his eyes, wishes and blows, but only half the candles go out. The wives hurriedly blow out the rest. As the following lines are spoken, each couple picks up a piece of* ROBERT'S *furniture and carries it out*)

JENNY: You still get your wish. He still gets his wish!

SUSAN: He does? It must be a new rule!

AMY: Sure you do.

JOANNE: (*Moving away*) Don't believe a word of it.

(*Music begins under, sounding like a busy signal*)

SARAH: Of course you do.

ROBERT: Oh, I know it. I will. Actually, I didn't wish for anything.

LARRY: He's kidding. You gotta be kidding.

DAVID: Anyway, don't tell it.

PETER: Tell it if it's dirty.

PAUL: They say you're not supposed to tell it.

AMY: Paul's right. Don't tell.

HARRY: Anyway, Robert, you're in your prime—thirty-five.

SARAH: Harry, hush! You don't tell a person's age at our ages.

(*Now* ROBERT *stands alone in a completely denuded room, his friends now watching from their living areas above. He faces front, listening*)

JENNY: (*Sings*)

Bobby . . .

PETER:
Bobby . . .

AMY:
Bobby baby . . .

PAUL:
Bobby bubi . . .

JOANNE:
Robby . . .

SUSAN:
Robert darling . . .

DAVID:
Bobby, we've been trying to call you.

JENNY:
Bobby . . .

LARRY:
Bobby . . .

AMY:
Bobby baby . . .

PAUL:
Bobby bubi . . .

SARAH:
Angel, I've got something to tell you.

HARRY:
Bob . . .

LARRY:
Rob-o . . .

JOANNE:
Bobby love . . .

SUSAN:
Bobby honey . . .

AMY and PAUL:
Bobby, we've been trying to reach you all day.

LARRY:
Bobby . . .

HARRY:
Bobby . . .

PETER:
Bobby baby . . .

SARAH:
Angel . . .

JOANNE:
Darling . . .

DAVID and JENNY:
The kids were asking, Bobby . . .

HARRY:
Bobby . . .

SUSAN:
Robert . . .

JOANNE:
Robby . . .

PETER:
Bob-o . . .

LARRY and JOANNE:
Bobby, there was something we wanted to say.

SARAH and HARRY:
Bobby . . .

PAUL:
Bobby bubi . . .

AMY:
Sweetheart . . .

SUSAN:
Sugar . . .

DAVID and JENNY:
Your line was busy.

PETER:
What have you been up to, kiddo?

AMY and PAUL:
Bobby, Bobby, how have you been?

HARRY:
Fella . . .

SARAH:
Sweetie . . .

HARRY and SARAH:
  How have you been?

PETER and SUSAN:
  Bobby, Bobby, how have you been?

DAVID, JENNY, JOANNE and LARRY:
  Stop by on your way home–

AMY and PAUL:
  Seems like weeks since we talked to you!

HARRY and SARAH:
  Bobby, we've been thinking of you!

PETER and SUSAN:
  Bobby, we've been thinking of you!

DAVID, JENNY, JOANNE and LARRY:
  Drop by anytime.

AMY and PAUL:
  Bobby, there's a concert on Tuesday.

DAVID and JENNY:
  Hank and Mary get into town tomorrow.

PETER and SUSAN:
  How about some scrabble on Sunday?

SARAH and HARRY:
  Why don't we all go to the beach?

JOANNE and LARRY:
  Bob, we're having people in Saturday night.

HARRY and SARAH:
  Next weekend?

JENNY:
  Bobby . . .

PETER:
  Bobby . . .

AMY:
  Bobby, baby . . .

DAVID and JENNY:
  Whatcha doing Thursday?

HARRY:
  Bobby . . .

SARAH:
Angel . . .

PAUL:
Bobby bubi . . .

SARAH and HARRY:
Time we got together, is Wednesday all right?

AMY:
Bobby . . .

LARRY:
Rob-o . . .

SUSAN:
Bobby honey . . .

AMY and PAUL:
Eight o'clock on Monday.

JOANNE:
Robby darling . . .

PETER:
Bobby fella . . .

PETER and JOANNE:
Bobby baby . . .

ALL:
Bobby, come on over for dinner!
We'll be so glad to see you!
Bobby, come on over for dinner!
Just be the three of us,
Only the three of us,
We loooooove you!

ROBERT:
Phone rings, door chimes, in comes company!
No strings, good times, room hums, company!
Late nights, quick bites, party games,
Deep talks, long walks, telephone calls,
Thoughts shared, souls bared, private names,
All those photos up on the walls
"With love,"
With love filling the days,
With love seventy ways,
"To Bobby, with love"

From all
Those
Good and crazy people, my friends,
Those
Good and crazy people, my married friends!
And that's what it's all about, isn't it?
That's what it's really about,
Really about!

(*The three girlfriends,* APRIL, KATHY *and* MARTA, *enter*)

APRIL:
Bobby . . .

KATHY:
Bobby . . .

MARTA:
Bobby baby . . .

PAUL:
Bobby bubi . . .

JOANNE:
Robby . . .

SUSAN:
Robert darling . . .

SARAH:
Angel, will you do me a favor?

LARRY:
Bobby . . .

AMY:
Bobby . . .

ROBERT:
Name it, Sarah.

JENNY:
Bobby baby . . .

PAUL:
Bobby bubi . . .

PETER:
Listen, pal, I'd like your opinion . . .

HARRY:
Bob . . .

LARRY:
Rob-o . . .

ROBERT:
Try me, Peter.

KATHY:
Bobby love . . .

MARTA:
Bobby honey . . .

LARRY and AMY:
Bobby, there's a problem—I need your advice . . .

APRIL and PAUL:
Bobby . . .

MARTA and HARRY:
Bobby . . .

KATHY and PETER:
Bobby baby . . .

SARAH:
Angel . . .

JOANNE:
Darling . . .

APRIL, MARTA and KATHY:
Just half an hour . . .

ROBERT:
Amy, can I call you back tomorrow?

DAVID and JENNY:
Honey, if you'd visit the kids once or twice . . .

SARAH and PETER:
Bobby . . .

JOANNE and HARRY:
Bobby . . .

PAUL and MARTA:
Bobby bubi . . .

AMY:
Sweetheart . . .

SUSAN:
Sugar . . .

APRIL, MARTA and KATHY:
What's happened to you?

ROBERT:
Jenny, I could take them to the zoo on Friday.

WIVES:
Bobby . . . Bobby, where have you been?

HUSBANDS:
Fella . . . kiddo, where have you been?

GIRLS:
Bobby . . . Bobby, how have you been?

HARRY, SARAH, PETER and SUSAN:
Stop by on your way home . . .

ROBERT:
Susan, love, I'll make it after seven if I can.

WIVES:
Bobby, dear, I don't mean to pry.

HUSBANDS:
Bobby, we've been thinking of you!

GIRLS:
Bobby, we've been thinking of you!

PAUL, AMY, JOANNE, LARRY, DAVID and JENNY:
Drop by anytime . . .

ROBERT:
Sorry, Paul, I made a date with Larry and Joanne.

WIVES:
Bobby, dear, it's none of my business . . .

HUSBANDS:
Lookit, pal, I have to work Thursday evening . . .

WIVES:
Darling, you've been looking peculiar . . .

HUSBANDS:
Bobby boy, you know how I hate the opera . . .

WIVES:
Funny thing, your name came up only last night.

ROBERT:
Harry . . . David . . . Kathy, I . . .

GIRLS:

I shouldn't say this but . . .

ROBERT:

April . . . Marta . . . Listen, people . . .

WIVES:

Bobby, we've been worried, you sure you're all right?

HUSBANDS:

Bobby . . . Bobby . . . Bobby baby . . .

GIRLS:

Did I do something wrong?

HUSBANDS:

Bobby bubi, Bobby fella, Bobby, Bobby,

ALL:

Bobby, come on over for dinner!
We'll be so glad to see you!
Bobby, come on over for dinner!
Just be the three of us,
Only the three of us,
We LOOOOOOOOOOOOOVE you!

Phone rings, door chimes, in comes company!
No strings, good times, just chums, company!
Late nights, quick bites, party games,
Deep talks, long walks, telephone calls,
Thoughts shared, souls bared, private names,
All those photos up on the walls
"With love,"
With love filling the days,
With love seventy ways,
"To Bobby, with love"
From all
Those
Good and crazy people, my friends,
Those good and crazy people, my married friends!
And that's what it's all about, isn't it?
That's what it's really about, isn't it?
That's what it's really about, really about!

HUSBANDS:

Isn't it? Isn't it? Isn't it? Isn't it?

WIVES and GIRLS:

LOOOOOOVE

HUSBANDS:

Isn't it? Isn't it? Isn't it? Isn't it?

ROBERT:

You I love and you I love and you and you I love
And you I love and you I love and you and you I love,
I love you!

ALL:

Company! Company! Company, lots of company!
Years of company! Love is company!
Company!

(*The ringing of telephones and doorbells and city sounds are heard. The following lines are spoken simultaneously as the company moves and exits in the frantic pace of New York streets and lives*)

JOANNE: What time was that?

LARRY: Five o'clock, I think, Joanne.

JOANNE: Thank God, cocktail hour!

APRIL: Final departure call for NSEW Airlines Flight One-nineteen. Will the passengers that have not boarded please do so.

SARAH: Harry, it's the door. I'll get it.

HARRY: I've got it.

SARAH: *I'll* get it. I always do.

PETER: What the hell is that noise?

SUSAN: They're cleaning the building next door, or tearing it down.

KATHY: Taxi! Taxi! Oh, please, please!

MARTA: Will you stop blowing that horn, you dodo!

AMY: Paul, what is that noise?

PAUL: I don't hear anything.

JENNY: Oh, David, the phone!

DAVID: I'll get it.

JENNY: Oh, the kids. It's gonna wake up the kids.

(*They have all exited*)

SCENE 2

The scene is SARAH *and* HARRY'S *living room on the ground floor of a garden apartment. Chic. Classy. There is much laughing, giggling, smiling and affection.*

ROBERT *is their dinner guest. He tries to maintain this atmosphere of conviviality, even when he's not sure of what is happening. The three have finished a long dinner and are seated, having coffee in the living room.*

SARAH: (*Pouring coffee*) There's cinnamon in the coffee, Robert . . . The odd taste is cinnamon. Sugar and cream?

ROBERT: Both. May I have lots of both?

SARAH: Of course you may.

HARRY: Do you want some brandy in it, Robert? Or do you just want some brandy?

ROBERT: You having some?

SARAH: We don't drink, but you have some, you darling. Go ahead.

HARRY: Or do you want a real drink? We have anything you want.

ROBERT: Well, Harry, if you don't mind, could I have some bourbon?

HARRY: Right. (*He goes to the bar and begins the elaborate preparation of* ROBERT'S *drink*)

SARAH: Sweetheart!

HARRY: Okay, darling.

ROBERT: (*As* HARRY *gets the bourbon*) Are you both on the wagon? Sarah? You're not on the wagon?

SARAH: Goodness, Robert, all the questions! Or do you just collect trivia like some old quiz kid? We spend half of our lives with you and now you notice Harry's on the wagon?

HARRY: A year and a half.

SARAH: No, love. Just a year.

HARRY: It was a year in February. It's a year and a half now.

SARAH: I know for a fact next month it will be a year.

HARRY: And a half.

SARAH: One year. Count it, one! Harry got arrested for being drunk, and quit out of some kind of humiliation.

HARRY: I quit to see if I could is actually what happened. C'mon, I must have told you about all that.

ROBERT: Never. You never mentioned it or I never would have brought you the bourbon. How were you arrested?

SARAH: Another question! Here, why don't you have one of these brownies you brought?

HARRY: I was in California on business and I really got soused one night and these guys drove me back to my hotel, but instead of going in, I walked down to the corner to get something to eat to sober up. (*He has poured the bourbon into* ROBERT'S *glass, and sniffs it longingly*)

SARAH: (*Interrupting*) You said it was three blocks away.

HARRY: No, just the corner.

SARAH: (*In a stage whisper to* ROBERT) Three blocks away.

HARRY: Anyway, this patrol car stopped me and said, "You're drunk." I said, "Drunk? I'm clobbered." He said, "I'm taking you in." "Take me to my hotel, for God's sake," I said. "It's just on the corner." (*He cracks the ice and adds the soda*)

SARAH: Three blocks away.

(ROBERT *moves to the bar and reaches for his drink, but is stopped by* HARRY, *who indicates that the lemon peel has not yet been added*)

HARRY: Anyway, they mugged me and booked me for being drunk. Unbelievable. California is a police state, though. And then, Robert, the very next time I was out there, I got arrested all over again—drunk driving. I only had wine—

SARAH: Only five bottles . . .

HARRY: And I *insisted* on taking a drunk test. I flunked it by one point. (*He adds lemon peel to the drink with a flourish*)

SARAH: And that is when you quit, precious. He always thinks it was the first arrest, but it was the second. We never told you that? Curious, I thought Harry had told *everybody*.

HARRY: (*His gaze fixed on* ROBERT'S *drink*) Anyway, I quit to see if I really had a drinking problem, and I don't.

SARAH: Just a problem drinking.

(ROBERT *finally takes the drink from* HARRY, *breaking* HARRY'S *"trance"*)

ROBERT: Do you miss it?

SARAH: See how you talk in questions! Harry, do you miss it?

HARRY: No. No, I really don't.

SARAH: (*Loud whisper to* ROBERT) Yes. Yes, he really does. (*Full voice, and a wave to* HARRY) Hi, darling.

HARRY: Anyway, I stopped. Haven't had a drink since.

SARAH: Whoops.

HARRY: What's whoops? I haven't had a drink since.

SARAH: (*She sings this*)
At Evelyn and George's wedding.

HARRY: A toast, for God's sake. Sorry, Robert, you must have noticed how staggering falling-down drunk I got on one swallow of champagne.

SARAH: I *never* said you got drunk, but you did have the champagne.

HARRY: A swallow. One swallow.

SARAH: And it was gone. An elephant's swallow.

ROBERT: I'd like to ask for another bourbon, but I'm terrified.

(HARRY *grabs the glass and runs back to the bar*)

SARAH: Darling Robert, put a nipple on the bottle for all we care. Don't you want a brownie?

ROBERT: God, no. I'll bust.

SARAH: Bust? *You* bust! You skinny thing. Just look at you. Bones. You're skin and bones. I bet when you get on a scale it goes the other way—minus.

ROBERT: Well, thank you, Sarah. I am touched and honored. And I think I was just insulted.

SARAH: (*Takes a brownie from the box*) Oh, Robert, I was praying that you'd eat just one so I could watch.

ROBERT: Sarah! Is it possible you've become a food voyeur?

SARAH: Mexican food. What I crave without cease is Mexican food. With all the Tabasco sauce in the world.

HARRY: (*With his back to* SARAH, *but knowing what she's up to*) Don't eat that brownie!

SARAH: I'm not. I'm just smelling it. Oh, Robert, you eat one!

ROBERT: Not with bourbon. (*Takes his second drink*) Thank you, Harry.

(HARRY *looks upset, as he hasn't the lemon nor his other "extras"*)

SARAH: And chocolate. I'd kill for chocolate. Or a baked potato with sour cream and chives. Doesn't that just make you writhe? Or hot sourdough bread and all the butter there is.

HARRY: Chili.

SARAH: Oh, chili, dear God, yes, chili!

HARRY: Manicotti.

SARAH: Manicotti. One teaspoon of manicotti.

HARRY: Sara Lee cake.

SARAH: Sara Lee cake! Sara Lee is the most phenomenal woman since Mary Baker Eddy.

HARRY: How about sweet and sour shrimp?

SARAH: How about sweet and sour pork?

(*She pretends to pass out by falling behind the sofa, but* ROBERT *has seen her stick a brownie in her mouth on the way down. She eats it, hidden from their sight behind the sofa.* ROBERT *watches this, and turns in time to see* HARRY *stealing one swallow of bourbon*)

ROBERT: (*Crosses to the sofa and calls to the hidden* SARAH) I get the impression you guys are on diets.

HARRY: Not me. Sarah.

SARAH: (*Rises and crosses from behind the sofa, still chewing*) Look at these pants. You can put your fist in there. That's how much weight I've lost.

HARRY: She always does that. Look, I can put my fist in my pants too, you know. She thinks I buy that.

SARAH: Darling, I've lost eight pounds already.

HARRY: It's the magazines, Robert. Did you ever look at any of those women's magazines? Pages and pages of cakes and pies and roasts and potatoes. I bet Sarah subscribes to about forty magazines. It's a sickness. We're up to our ass in magazines.

SARAH: I read them all.

HARRY: Don't.

SARAH: Do.

HARRY: Look at this, Robert. Wrestling. She even subscribes to a magazine on wrestling.

SARAH: Karate, not wrestling. It's karate.

HARRY: Wouldn't you like to see it? All those fat broads in her gym learning karate. What wouldn't you give to see that?

SARAH: Strangely enough, darling, I'm terribly good at it.

ROBERT: How long have you been studying it?

SARAH: (*To* ROBERT, *in a mock-scolding tone*) Who asked that question? Oh, Robert! Seven months.

HARRY: Show us some karate.

SARAH: No. Robert, would you like some more coffee, love? You, Harry?

HARRY: No. I want some karate. I want to see how my money is being wasted.

SARAH: No.

ROBERT: Do one thing.

SARAH: No.

ROBERT: (*Flirtatiously*) Come on, Sarah, I really would give anything to see you do just one. I bet you are *excellent*. Hey, I'll be your partner.

SARAH: (*Responding girlishly*) No. Oh, Harry, this is embarrassing.

HARRY: Aw, come on.

SARAH: My God—all right.

HARRY: Hooray!

SARAH: One throw!

HARRY: Hooray!

SARAH: Harry, do you want to stand there?

HARRY: Where?

SARAH: There.

HARRY: All right. I'm standing here. Now what?

(SARAH, *with intense concentration, goes into her karate preparation ritual, complete with kneebends, deep-breathing, grunts and a variety of chops and holds*)

SARAH: Okay. Now just come at me.

HARRY: Okay.

(*He does, and she lets out a piercing samurai sound, "Hyieeeee," flipping him spread-eagle to the floor.* SARAH *does a Japanese bow to* HARRY, *and does a feminine tiptoe dance to the sofa, where she lies majestically and adorably, looking at her fingernails*)

ROBERT: Fantastic. That's hysterical.

HARRY: (*Gets up and moves away, doing some sort of twist to loosen his back from the impact of the fall*) Actually, I could have prevented that.

SARAH: How?

HARRY: By blocking it.

SARAH: No, that can't be blocked.

HARRY: It certainly can. I just didn't do it.

SARAH: Anyway, Robert, that can't be blocked.

HARRY: Let's do it again.

SARAH: All right, darling. (*She is the sweet killer, arranging herself*)

HARRY: I'll come at you again.

SARAH: Okay. (*He goes at her. She attempts the same thing and he blocks it by lifting her and putting her over his shoulder. Taken by surprise,* SARAH *quickly reworks the movement in her mind and comes up with her mistake*) Oh, I see. Put me down. Okay, do it again.

(*He does it again and she overcomes his block, throwing him again. She then gives a karate scream and jumps on top of him, pinning him down.* ROBERT, HARRY *and* SARAH *freeze in their positions.* JOANNE *appears and looks for a moment with wry detachment at the pair on the floor. She sings "The Little Things You Do Together"*)

JOANNE:

It's the little things you do together,
Do together,
Do together,
That make perfect relationships.
The hobbies you pursue together,
Savings you accrue together,
Looks you misconstrue together
That make marriage a joy.
Mm-hm . . .

(*They break the freeze*)

ROBERT: (*To break the tension, forcing a laugh*) That's very good.

HARRY: Once more. Do it once more.

ROBERT: Harry, could I have another bourbon?

(*There is a much more serious look on both of their faces now . . .* HARRY *lunges at her. They block each other and are caught in a power struggle*)

HARRY: Give up?

SARAH: Do you?

HARRY: I've got you.

SARAH: I've got *you.*

HARRY: Do you want to do it again?

SARAH: All right. You break first.

HARRY: Uh-uh. You break first.

SARAH: We can just stay here.

HARRY: All right with me. Fine with me.

ROBERT: You're both very good.

HARRY: I could get out of this, you know.

SARAH: Try it.

(HARRY *kicks a foot behind her two feet, knocking her to the floor. He's on top of her, pinning her down*)

HARRY: Okay, I tried it.

(SARAH *grabs* HARRY *by his shirt and somersaults him over her head, so that he ends up flat on his back on the floor. She quickly stands up, grabs* HARRY'S *arm and pins him down with her foot, holding him in place with an arm pull. Groaning loudly in agony,* HARRY *beats on the floor with his free hand*)

SARAH: Uncle?

HARRY: Uncle, your ass!

(HARRY, SARAH *and* ROBERT *freeze*)

JOANNE:

It's the little things you share together,
Swear together,
Wear together,
That make perfect relationships.
The concerts you enjoy together,
Neighbors you annoy together,
Children you destroy together,
That keep marriage intact.

It's not so hard to be married
When two maneuver as one,
It's not so hard to be married
And, Jesus Christ, is it fun.

It's sharing little winks together,
Drinks together,
Kinks together,
That make marriage a joy.

It's bargains that you shop together,
Cigarettes you stop together,
Clothing that you swap together,
That make perfect relationships.

Uh-huh . . .
Mm-hm . . .

(*They break the freeze, and* SARAH *and* HARRY *prepare for a third fall.* ROBERT *gets up from his chair with his empty glass and tries to cross the room to get a refill*)

ROBERT: Could I have another bourbon?

(*Inadvertently he finds himself between* SARAH *and* HARRY, *and suddenly he is hit from the front by* HARRY *and from the rear by* SARAH. *All three go down to the floor with much noise. Intertwined, the three freeze. The other married couples enter and sing with* JOANNE)

ALL:

It's not talk of God and the decade ahead that
Allow you to get through the worst.
It's "I do" and "You don't" and "Nobody said that"
And "Who brought the subject up first?"
It's the little things, the little things, the little things . . .
It's the little things, the little things, the little things . . .
The little ways you try together,

Cry together,
Lie together,
That make perfect relationships.
Becoming a cliché together,
Growing old and gray together

JOANNE:
Withering away together

ALL:
That makes marriage a joy.

MEN:
It's not so hard to be married,

WOMEN:
It's much the simplest of crimes.

MEN:
It's not so hard to be married,

JOANNE:
I've done it three or four times.

JENNY:
It's people that you hate together,

PAUL and AMY:
Bait together,

PETER and SUSAN:
Date together,

ALL:
That make marriage a joy.

DAVID:
It's things like using force together,

LARRY:
Shouting till you're hoarse together,

JOANNE:
Getting a divorce together,

ALL:
That make perfect relationships.
Uh-huh . . .
Kiss, kiss . . .
Mm-hm.

(JOANNE *and the others leave. Finally* ROBERT, SARAH *and* HARRY *break at the same time; all are panting for air*)

ROBERT: My . . . wow . . . How 'bout that? Huh?

HARRY: (*Laughing*) I had you there . . .

SARAH: (*Laughing*) I had *you* there . . .

(*They start for each other again, but* ROBERT *steps between them*)

ROBERT: I'd say it was a draw. (*They say nothing, trying to pull themselves together*) Wow. Look at the time. I've got to get going.

SARAH and HARRY: Awww!

ROBERT: Wow. Listen, I had a great time.

SARAH: (*Still panting hard*) So did we.

HARRY: (*Panting*) Great to see you. Sure you wouldn't care for a nightcap?

ROBERT: Right! (HARRY *starts for the bar*) I mean, no! I mean, will I see you soon?

SARAH: (*With a slight smile*) Don't answer that, Harry. He gets no more questions, that sneaky Pete. (*Gives* ROBERT *an affectionate peck on the cheek*)

ROBERT: (*Still panting*) Wow. (*The music of "Bobby Baby" is heard in the orchestra; there is a slight and self-conscious pause*) Thanks again.

(*He leaves the scene slowly, utterly bewildered.* HARRY *heads for the bar. With his fingertip he catches a drop of liquor from the spout of each bottle on the bar.* SARAH *has headed for the coffee table, where she pops a brownie into her mouth*)

HARRY: I'll turn out the lights.

SARAH: (*With mouth very full*) I will! (HARRY *points and gives her that "I-caught-you" look*) I always do.

HARRY: No, you don't.

SARAH: Oh, Harry, I love you.

(*She leaves.* HARRY *goes over to steal a drink out of* ROBERT'S *old glass*)

ROBERT: (*From the other side of the stage, having observed the previous scene*) Harry? (HARRY *looks up*) You ever sorry you got married?

HARRY: (*Sings "Sorry-Grateful"*)

You're always sorry,
You're always grateful
You're always wondering what might have been.

Then she walks in.
(SARAH *has entered to clear the coffee table*)
And still you're sorry,
And still you're grateful,
And still you wonder and still you doubt,
And she goes out.
(SARAH *leaves with the coffee service*)
Everything's different,
Nothing's changed,
Only maybe slightly
Rearranged.
You're sorry-grateful,
Regretful-happy.
Why look for answers where none occur?
You always are what you always were,
Which has nothing to do with,
All to do with her.

SARAH: (*Offstage*) Harry, darling, come to bed.
HARRY: Coming, darling.

(*He stands still.* ROBERT *looks up as* DAVID *appears in his apartment and begins to sing*)

DAVID:
You're always sorry,
You're always grateful,
You hold her thinking, "I'm not alone."
You're still alone.
You don't live for her,
You do live with her,
You're scared she's starting to drift away
And scared she'll stay.

LARRY: (*Appears in his apartment and sings*)
Good things get better,
Bad get worse.
Wait–I think I meant that in reverse.

HARRY, DAVID and LARRY:
You're sorry-grateful,
Regretful-happy,
Why look for answers where none occur?
You'll always be what you always were,
Which has nothing to do with,
All to do with her.

(DAVID *leaves*)

HARRY and LARRY:

You'll always be what you always were,
Which has nothing to do with,
All to do with her.

(LARRY *leaves*)

HARRY:

Nothing to do with,
All to do with her.

(*The lights fade on him.* ROBERT *takes an elevator to a terrace overlooking the city*)

SCENE 3

The scene is PETER *and* SUSAN'S *terrace. He is an Ivy League fellow, and she is a pretty, wide-eyed Southern lady.*

PETER: (*Offstage*) Bob, Bob, where are you? (*Finding* ROBERT *on the terrace, and joining him*) What are you doing out here?

ROBERT: It is so great to have a terrace. Wow.

SUSAN: (*Coming out on the terrace; stepping over the clutter*) We never use it. We keep things like old sleds and stuff out here.

ROBERT: You don't ever just sit out here?

PETER: I hate it. And the kids are impossible out here. And everyone can hear everything you say. (*Yelling up to the floors above*) Are you listening? And it's dirty all the time. And look at all the bird-do. (*He points to the railing where* ROBERT *has put his coat.* ROBERT *quickly removes it*)

SUSAN: And noisy. Oo, that traffic. You can't even hear yourself think. And what can you see? It's not like you see something. You just see the building across the street.

PETER: Well, if you lean way out and look over there you can see the East River.

(*All three lean over the railing*)

SUSAN: (*Nervously pulling them back*) Exccpt we decided you really can't. Peter almost met his Maker one night trying to see that old East River. He did.

ROBERT: You saved him?

SUSAN: Me? No. Well—in a way.

PETER: She fainted. So I got down.

SUSAN: Peter just is not afraid of anything at all. Unfortunately, I was not made that way. One day Peter fell off the ladder when he was putting up my curio cabinet and he split his head right open. Well, I fainted. I came to, I looked at his head and I fainted again. Four times I fainted that night.

ROBERT: (*Laughing*) Well, that is sweet. I mean you're a woman. I think that is very charming. Very. I do. In fact she is, without a doubt, the most charming woman I have ever, ever met. You are a lucky guy, Peter. (*Gives her a little hug*) I mean, that kind of—oh, Southern graciousness—there just ain't no more of that around. You two are beautiful together. Really. And Peter—if you ever decide to leave her I want to be the first to know.

SUSAN: (*Smiles at* PETER) Well . . .

PETER: You're the first to know.

ROBERT: What?

SUSAN: (*Excitedly*) We're getting divorced.

PETER: We haven't told anyone yet.

ROBERT: (*Stunned; pauses*) Oh! (*The music of "Bobby Baby" is heard in the orchestra*) I'm—uh—so surprised. (*They just smile at him. They don't speak*) Maybe you'll work it out. (*He gets no reaction. The music of "Bobby Baby" is heard again*) Don't think so, huh? Well, I know how hard it is for you and how you must feel . . .

(*The lights fade on the terrace as* ROBERT *takes the elevator down to* DAVID *and* JENNY'S *apartment*)

SCENE 4

JENNY *and* DAVID, *staring straight ahead, are seated in their den, which also seems to serve as their children's playroom.* ROBERT *enters and sits near* JENNY. JENNY *directs much of this opening conversation to* DAVID, *who doesn't respond, but smiles increasingly.*

JENNY: (*Very rapidly, answering* ROBERT'S *last line from the previous scene*) Feel? I just don't feel anything. David, I don't care for any more. (*Hands him the butt of a joint.* DAVID, *staring straight ahead, caught up in his own euphoria, takes the butt and, as if by rote, extinguishes it in an ashtray*) It's too small. That's too small. It probably just doesn't work on me. Do you feel anything, David? Do you, honey? Because I don't.

ROBERT: You will.

JENNY: *When?* I mean, we've had *two,* for heavensake. I think maybe it depends on the person's constitution. Don't you, Dave? Well, listen, it's always good to try everything once.

(DAVID *doesn't respond*)

ROBERT: Just wait!

JENNY: I'm not planning to go anywhere. Maybe I'm just too dumb or square, but I honestly don't feel anything. Do you, Dave? Because I don't. Absolutely nothing. Honestly, not a thing. I mean, I *wish* I did. I just don't. Maybe they gave you *real* grass, right off the front lawn. I knew I wouldn't feel anything, though. I don't have that kind of constitution. Why am I talking so much?

ROBERT: You're stoned.

JENNY: Am I? Am I? I am not.

DAVID: (*Gives a short chortle; then*) I am.

JENNY: Are you? You are not. I'm so dry!

ROBERT: You're stoned.

JENNY: Is that part of it?

ROBERT: You'll probably get hungry, too.

JENNY: Yes? Should I feel *that,* too?

ROBERT: You don't have to feel anything.

JENNY: Are you hungry, Dave?

DAVID: No. I'd like some water, though.

JENNY: Me, too. (*She gets up to get a pitcher of water*) Do you want some, Robert?

ROBERT: No, thank you.

JENNY: (*She stops and turns back to* ROBERT) What?

ROBERT: I don't want any, Jenny, thank you.

JENNY: Any what, Robert?

DAVID: You asked him, honey. Water!

JENNY: Oh, water . . . I could not remember what we were talking about.

ROBERT: See, you forget when you're high!

JENNY: Ohhh, God, do you. Wow. Are you high, Dave?

DAVID: I'm potted.

JENNY: (*Sits down again, laughing*) Potted. That is beautiful. Jesus!

ROBERT: You're really high now, huh?

JENNY: Jesus!

DAVID: That's twice you said "Jesus."

JENNY: You're kidding.

DAVID: No. You said it two times. She never swears.

JENNY: I didn't even know I said it once.

DAVID: Say "son-of-a-bitch."

JENNY: Son-of-a-bitch.

(*They all laugh so riotously that* DAVID *falls out of his chair*)

DAVID: (*From the floor*) Say "Kiss my ass."

JENNY: Kiss my ass. (*They roar at this, and* JENNY *tumbles to the floor near* DAVID *and they hug each other*) Kiss my ass, you son-of-a-bitch. (*They all scream with laughter. Now* ROBERT *falls to the floor*) Oh, Jesus. (*She yells*) That's three!

A VOICE: (*Offstage*) Will you shut up—down there! It's two o'clock, for Chrissakes!

JENNY: Shhh, oh, shhh. Laugh to yourselves. (*She quiets them down and almost tiptoes to the direction of the voice. Then she loudly yells in the same direction*) IT'S ALL RIGHT, NOW!

DAVID: Shhh, Jenny, for God's sake.

(ROBERT *starts laughing again*)

JENNY: (*Comes back to them*) Bobby, stop! We'll get evicted.

ROBERT: Jenny, you're terrific. You're the girl I should have married.

(*The laughter subsides a bit*)

JENNY: Listen, I know a darling girl in this building you'll just love.

ROBERT: What?

JENNY: When are you going to get married?

DAVID: What?

JENNY: I mean it. To me a person's not complete until he's married.

ROBERT: Oh, I will. It's not like I'm avoiding marriage. It's avoiding me, if anything. I'm ready.

JENNY: Actually, you're not. But listen, not everybody should be married, I guess.

DAVID: I don't know. See, to me, a man should be married. Your life has a—what? What am I trying to say? A point to it—a bottom, you know what I'm saying? I have everything, but freedom. Which is everything, huh? No. (*Takes* JENNY'S *hand*) *This* is everything. I got my wife, my kids, a home. I feel that —uh—well, you gotta give up to get. Know what I'm saying?

ROBERT: Listen, I agree. But you know what bothers me—is, if you marry, then you've got another person *there* all the time. Plus you can't get out of it, whenever you just might want to get out of it. You are caught! See? And even if you do get out of it, what do you have to show for it? Not to mention the fact that—then—you've always been married. I mean, you can never not have been married again.

JENNY: I don't feel you're really ready. Do you think, just maybe, I mean, subconsciously—you might be resisting it?

ROBERT: No. Negative. Absolutely not! I meet girls all the time. All over the place. All you have to do is live in New York and you meet a girl a minute. Right now, I date this stewardess, cute, original . . . (APRIL *appears with the "Bobby Baby" music*) . . . odd. And Kathy, you never met Kathy, did you? Well, she's the best . . . (KATHY *appears*) . . . just the best! And then there's Marta. (MARTA *appears*) God, she's fun! I'm certainly not resisting marriage! (*The three girls react to this in absolute disbelief*) My life is totally prepared for a gigantic change right now. I'm ready to be married.

DAVID: Right. Then, why aren't you?

ROBERT: Right.

MARTA: Right.

APRIL: Right.

KATHY: Right.

APRIL, KATHY and MARTA: (*Sing "You Could Drive a Person Crazy"*)

Doo-doo-doo-doo
Doo-doo-doo-doo
Doo-doo-doo-doo-doo-doo
You could drive a person crazy,
You could drive a person mad.
Doo-doo doo-doo doo
First you make a person hazy
So a person could be had.
Doo-doo doo-doo doo
Then you leave a person dangling sadly
Outside your door.
Which it only makes a person gladly
Want you even more,
I could understand a person
If it's not a person's bag.
Doo-doo doo-doo doo
I could understand a person
If a person was a fag.

Doo-doo doo-doo doo
Boo-boo-boo-boo
But worse'n that,
A person that
Titillates a person and then leaves her flat
Is crazy,
He's a troubled person,
He's a truly crazy person
Himself!

You crummy bastard! You son-of-a-bitch!

Bobby is my hobby and I'm giving it up.

KATHY:

When a person's personality is personable,
He shouldn't oughta sit like a lump.
It's harder than a matador coercin' a bull
To try to get you off-a your rump.
So single and attentive and attractive a man
Is everything a person could wish,
But turning off a person is the act of a man
Who likes to pull the hooks out of fish.

APRIL, KATHY and MARTA:

Knock, knock, is anybody there?
Knock, knock, it really isn't fair.
Knock, knock, I'm working all my charms.
Knock, knock, a zombie's in my arms.
All that sweet affection,
What is wrong?
Where's the loose connection?
How long, oh Lord, how long?
Bobby baby, Bobby bubi, Bobby,

You could drive a person buggy,
You could blow a person's cool.
Doo-doo doo-doo doo
Like you make a person feel all huggy
While you make her feel a fool.
Doo-doo doo-doo doo
When a person says that you've upset her
That's when you're good.
You impersonate a person better
Than a zombie should.

I could understand a person
If he wasn't good in bed.
Doo-doo-doo-doo doo
I could understand a person
If he actually was dead.
Doo-doo-doo-doo
Exclusive you,
Elusive you,
Will any person ever get the juice of you?
You're crazy,
You're a lovely person,
You're a moving, deeply maladjusted,
Never to be trusted
Crazy person
Yourself.

(*After a bow to the audience, they exit*)

JENNY: I'm starving. I'll get us something to eat. (*Gets up*) Do one of you sons-of-bitches want to help? Then kiss my ass. (*She laughs*)

DAVID: (*Strangely serious, not looking at* JENNY) Oh, boy. (*He lights a cigarette and moves away*)

JENNY: Did you light another one?

DAVID: Just a cigarette.

ROBERT: Shall I roll another one?

JENNY: Maybe one.

DAVID: No.

ROBERT: I can roll another one in a second.

DAVID: No.

JENNY: No more?

DAVID: (*A moment. Then looks at* JENNY) I don't think so.

JENNY: (*After a pause*) I don't think so either.

ROBERT: It'll just take a second to make another one.

(*There is a long pause*)

DAVID: Listen, you two have one.

JENNY: I don't want one.

DAVID: Have one if you want one.

JENNY: But I don't. (*A pause*) I'll get some food. (*She embraces* DAVID) Isn't he a marvelous man?

DAVID: (*Lovingly*) I married a square. A confessed square.

JENNY: (*She starts to go, then turns seriously to* ROBERT) Bobby, we're just too old! We were all—trying to keep up with the kids tonight. Goodness, we've *been* there already. Who wants to go back? But, anyway, what do I know?

DAVID: Hey, screwball. I'm starving.

JENNY: I love you . . . so much.

DAVID: Food!

JENNY: And, Bobby–put that stuff away. C'mon, put it in your pocket. Take it home. Comc on. (ROBERT *does so*) Thank you. I don't know. Maybe you're right. Who ever knows? (*She smiles and goes out*)

ROBERT: (*Not happy*) What was all that?

DAVID: She doesn't go for it. I thought she wouldn't go for it.

ROBERT: (*Cold*) She was stoned.

DAVID: Not really. She doesn't get things like that. I mean, she'll go along with it, but that's about it.

ROBERT: (*Colder*) She didn't like it?

DAVID: I know her. She didn't.

ROBERT: (*Pauses*) You want me to get *you* some?

DAVID: She'd have a fit. I'm really surprised she did it tonight.

ROBERT: She loved it.

DAVID: (*Correcting* ROBERT) For *me*. She loved it for me. She didn't really love it. I know her. She's what she said . . . square . . . dumb . . .

ROBERT: Like a fox.

(*The music of "Bobby Baby" is heard in the orchestra*)

DAVID: (*After a pause of staring at each other*) I'll go see if I can give her a hand. What do you say? (*He exits*)

ROBERT: (*Watching him go*) Wow! Oh, wow! (*He starts to leave but is stopped by all the couples, who begin to appear in their apartments, as in the opening number*)

ALL:

Bobby, Bobby, Bobby baby,
Bobby bubi, Robby, Robert darling,
Bobby, we've been trying to reach you.
Angel, I've got something to tell you . . .
Bobby, it's important or I wouldn't call . . .
Whatcha doing Thursday?
Bobby, look, I know how you hate it and all . . .
But this is something special.
Bobby, come on over for dinner.
There's someone we want you to meet.
Bobby, come on over for dinner . . .

This girl from the office . . .
My niece from Ohio . . .
It'll just be the four of us . . .
You'lll looooooooooooove her!

(*The wives exit and the husbands now sing "Have I Got a Girl for You?"*)

LARRY:
Have I got a girl for you? Wait till you meet her!
Have I got a girl for you, boy? Hoo, boy!
Dumb!—and with a weakness for Sazerac slings—
You give her even the fruit and she swings.
The kind of girl you can't send through the mails—
Call me tomorrow, I want the details.

PETER:
Have I got a chick for you? Wait till you meet her!
Have I got a chick for you, boy? Hoo, boy!
Smart!—She's into all those exotic mystiques:
The Kamasutra and Chinese techniques—
I hear she knows more than seventy-five . . .
Call me tomorrow if you're still alive.

HUSBANDS: (*In canon*)
Have I got a girl for you? Wait till you meet her!
Have I got a girl for you, boy? Hoo, boy!
Boy, to be in your shoes what I wouldn't give.
I mean the freedom to go out and live . . .
And as for settling down and all that . . .
Marriage may be where it's been, but it's not where it's at!

Whaddaya like, you like coming home to a kiss?
Somebody with a smile at the door?
Whaddaya like, you like indescribable bliss?
Then whaddaya wanna get married for?

Whaddaya like, you like an excursion to Rome,
Suddenly taking off to explore?
Whaddaya like, you like having meals cooked at home?
Then whaddaya wanna get married for?
Whaddaya wanna get married for?
Whaddaya wanna get married for?
Whaddaya wanna get married for?

(*The husbands exit, leaving* ROBERT *alone onstage. He now sings "Someone Is Waiting." Throughout the song as each wife is mentioned, she appears with her husband, intimately in their own apartment*)

ROBERT:

Someone is waiting,
Cool as Sarah,
Easy and loving as Susan—
Jenny.
Someone is waiting,
Warm as Susan,
Frantic and touching as Amy—
Joanne.

Would I know her even if I met her?
Have I missed her? Did I let her go?
A Susan sort of Sarah,
A Jennyish Joanne,
Wait for me, I'm ready now,
I'll find you if I can!

Someone will hold me,
Soft as Jenny,
Skinny and blue-eyed as Amy—
Susan.
Someone will wake me,
Sweet as Amy,
Tender and foolish as Sarah—
Joanne.

Did I know her? Have I waited too long?
Maybe so, but maybe so has she,
My blue-eyed Sarah
Warm Joanne
Sweet Jenny
Loving Susan
Crazy Amy,
Wait for me,
I'll hurry, wait for me.
Hurry.
Wait for me.
Hurry.
Wait for me.

(*The lights dim on the couples.* ROBERT *is left standing alone*)

SCENE 5

The lights come up on a girl, MARTA, *who is seated on a park bench on stage level.* ROBERT *sits on the other end of the bench. She sings "Another Hundred People."*

MARTA:

Another hundred people just got off of the train
And came up through the ground
While another hundred people just got off of the bus
And are looking around
At another hundred people who got off of the plane
And are looking at us
Who got off of the train
And the plane and the bus
Maybe yesterday.

It's a city of strangers—
Some come to work, some to play—
A city of strangers—
Some come to stare, some to stay,
And every day
The ones who stay
Can find each other in the crowded streets and the guarded parks,
By the rusty fountains and the dusty trees with the battered barks,
And they walk together past the postered walls with the crude remarks,
And they meet at parties through the friends of friends who they never know.
Will you pick me up or do I meet you there or shall we let it go?
Did you get my message? 'Cause I looked in vain.
Can we see each other Tuesday if it doesn't rain?
Look, I'll call you in the morning or my service will explain . . .

And another hundred people just got off of the train.

(APRIL, *in an airline stewardess' uniform, enters and sits next to* ROBERT. MARTA, *although she is not included, listens to the scene*)

APRIL: I didn't come right to New York. I went to Northwestern University for two years, but it was a pitiful mistake. I was on probation the whole two years. I was getting ready to go back to Shaker Heights when I decided where I really wanted to live more than any other place was—Radio City. I thought it was a wonderful little city near New York. So I came here. I'm very dumb.

ROBERT: You're not dumb, April.

APRIL: To me I am. Even the reason I stayed in New York was because I just cannot get interested in myself—I'm so boring.

ROBERT: I find you very interesting.

APRIL: Well, I'm just not. I used to think I was so odd. But my roommate is the same way. He's also very dumb.

ROBERT: Oh, you never mentioned him. Is he—your lover?

APRIL: Oh, no. We just share this great big apartment on West End Avenue. We have our own rooms and everything. I'd show it to you but we've never had company. He's the sweetest thing, actually. I think he likes the arrangement. I don't know, though—we never discuss it. He was born in New York, so *nothing* really interests him. I don't have anything more to say. (*She exits*)

MARTA: (*Sings*)

And they find each other in the crowded streets and the guarded parks,
By the rusty fountains and the dusty trees with the battered barks,
And they walk together past the postered walls with the crude remarks,
And they meet at parties through the friends of friends who they never know.
Will you pick me up or do I meet you there or shall we let it go?
Did you get my message? 'Cause I looked in vain.
Can we see each other Tuesday if it doesn't rain?
Look, I'll call you in the morning or my service will explain . . .
And another hundred people just got off of the train.

(*Now* KATHY *enters and sits next to* ROBERT *on the bench*)

KATHY: See, Bobby, some people have to know when to come to New York, and some people have to know when to leave. I always thought I'd just naturally come here and spend the rest of my life here. I wanted to have two terrific affairs and then get married. I always knew I was meant to be a wife.

ROBERT: You should have asked me.

KATHY: Wanna marry me?

ROBERT: I did. I honestly did . . . in the beginning. But I . . . I don't know. I never thought that you ever would.

KATHY: I would. I never understood why you'd never ask me.

ROBERT: (*Puts his arm around her*) You wanted to marry me? And I wanted to marry you. Well then, how the hell did we ever end up such good friends?

KATHY: Bobby, I'm moving to Vermont.

ROBERT: Vermont? Why Vermont?

KATHY: That's where *he* lives. I'm getting married.

ROBERT: (*A pause; takes his arm away*) What?

KATHY: Some people still get married, you know.

ROBERT: Do you love him?

KATHY: I'll be a good wife. I just don't want to run around this city any more like I'm having a life. (*She pauses*) As I said before, some people have to know when to come to New York and some people have to know when to leave.

(*And she's gone.* MARTA *continues singing*)

MARTA:

Another hundred people just got off of the train
And came up through the ground
While another hundred people just got off of the bus
And are looking around
At another hundred people who got off of the plane
And are looking at us
Who got off of the train
And the plane and the bus
Maybe yesterday.

It's a city of strangers—
Some come to work, some to play—
A city of strangers—
Some come to stare, some to stay,
And every day
Some go away.
(*She looks off in the direction in which* KATHY *has gone*)
Or they find each other in the crowded streets and the guarded parks,
By the rusty fountains and the dusty trees with the battered barks,

And they walk together past the postered walls with the crude remarks,
And they meet at parties through the friends of friends who they never know.
Will you pick me up or do I meet you there or shall we let it go?
Did you get my message? 'Cause I looked in vain.
Can we see each other Tuesday if it doesn't rain?
Look, I'll call you in the morning or my service will explain . . .
And another hundred people just got off of the train.
And another hundred people just got off of the train.
And another hundred people just got off of the train.
And another hundred people just got off of the train.
And another hundred people just got off of the train.

(*She turns to* ROBERT)

You wanna know why I came to New York? I came because New York is the center of the world and that's where I want to be. You know what the pulse of this city is?

ROBERT: A busy signal?

MARTA: The pulse of this city, kiddo, is *me*. This city is for the me's of this world. People that want to be right in the heart of it. *I* am the soul of New York.

ROBERT: How 'bout that.

MARTA: See, smart remarks do not a person make. How many Puerto Ricans do you know?

ROBERT: I'm not sure.

MARTA: How many blacks?

ROBERT: Well, very few, actually. I seem to meet people only like myself.

MARTA: (*Gives* ROBERT *a look*) Talk about your weirdos . . . *I* pass people on the streets and I know them. Every son-of-a-bitch is my friend. I go uptown to the dentist or something, and I suddenly want to cry because I think, "Oh my God, I'm *up*town." And Fourteenth Street. Well, nobody knows it, but *that* is the center of the universe.

ROBERT: Fourteenth Street?

MARTA: That's humanity, Fourteenth Street. That's everything. And if you don't like it there they got every subway you can name to take you where you like it better.

ROBERT: God bless Fourteenth Street.

MARTA: This city—I kiss the ground of it. Someday, you know what I want to do? I want to get all dressed up in black—black dress, black shoes, hat, everything black, and go sit in some bar, at the end of the counter, and drink and cry. That is my idea of honest-to-God sophistication. I mean, *that's* New York. (*Pauses*) You always make me feel like I got the next line. What is it with you?

ROBERT: I just never met anybody like you.

MARTA: Me neither. You know what this city is? Where a person can feel it? It's in a person's ass. If you're really part of this city, relaxed, cool and in the whole flow of it, your ass is like this. (*She makes a large round circle with her forefinger and thumb*) If you're just living here, running around uptight, not really part of this city, your ass is like this. (*She tightens the circle to nothing*)

ROBERT: I . . . hesitate to ask. (*She holds up the "tight" sign high and abruptly. As the lights start to dim we hear*) That's a fascinating theory. Indeed fascinating. And at this moment, extraordinarily accurate.

(*The lights fade to a blackout*)

SCENE 6

A GIRL *in a white choir robe appears on an upper level as* AMY'S *kitchen comes into view on stage level.* AMY, *in a white wedding dress, is seated at the counter, nervously shining a pair of black men's shoes. There are coats and umbrellas hanging on a wall rack.*

CHOIRGIRL: (*Sings softly to organ accompaniment*)

Bless this day, pinnacle of life,
Husband joined to wife,
The heart leaps up to behold
This golden day.

PAUL: (*Appears in a dress shirt, shorts and socks*) Amy, I can't find my shoes any . . . (*Sees* AMY *with his shoes, stops and sings to her adoringly*)

Today is for Amy,
Amy, I give you the rest of my life.
To cherish and to keep you,
To honor you forever,
Today is for Amy,
My happily soon-to-be wife.

Amy, we're really getting married! (*He goes out. She shakes her head "yes" and it becomes "no"*)

AMY: (*Looking at the audience, sings*)

Pardon me, is everybody there?
Because if everybody's
There, I want to thank you all for coming to the wedding. I'd ap-
Preciate your going even more, I mean, you must have lots of
Better things to do. And not a word of it to Paul. Remember
Paul? You know, the man I'm gonna marry, but I'm not be-cause I
Wouldn't ruin anyone as wonderful as he is—

Thank you all
For the gifts and the flowers.
Thank you all,
Now it's back to the showers.
Don't tell Paul,
But I'm not getting married today.

(*In choir robes, members of the company join the* CHOIRGIRL *on the upper level and hum*)

CHOIRGIRL:

Bless this day, tragedy of life,
Husband joined to wife.
The heart sinks down and feels dead
This dreadful day.

ROBERT: (*Enters, dressed as the best man*) Amy, Paul can't find his good cuff links.

AMY: On the dresser! Right next to my suicide note.

(ROBERT *leaves*)

Listen everybody, look, I don't know what you're waiting for—a
Wedding, what's a wedding? It's a prehistoric ritual where
Everybody promises fidelity forever, which is
Maybe the most horrifying word I ever heard, and which is
Followed by a honeymoon, where suddenly he'll realize he's
Saddled with a nut and wanna kill me and he should.

Thanks a bunch,
But I'm not getting married.
Go have lunch,
'Cause I'm not getting married.

You've been grand,
But I'm not getting married.
Don't just stand there,
I'm not getting married.
And don't tell Paul
But I'm not getting married today!

Go! Can't you go?
Why is nobody listening?
Goodbye! Go and cry
At another person's wake.
If you're quick, for a kick
You could pick up a christening,
But please, on my knees,
There's a human life at stake.

Listen everybody, I'm afraid you didn't hear, or do you
Want to see a crazy lady fall apart in front of you? It
Isn't only Paul who may be ruining his life, you know, we'll
Both of us be losing our identities—I telephoned my
Analyst about it but he said to see him Monday, and by
Monday I'll be floating in the Hudson, with the other garbage.

I'm not well,
So I'm not getting married.
You've been swell,
But I'm not getting married.
Clear the hall
'Cause I'm not getting married.
Thank you all
But I'm not getting married.
And don't tell Paul,
But I'm not getting married today!

(*More members of the company, dressed in choir robes, enter in a wedding march, now forming a complete choir*)

CHOIRGIRL:
Bless this bride, totally insane,
Slipping down the drain,
(*Sound of thunder*)
And bless this day in our hearts—
(*Sound of rain*)
As it starts to rain . . .

John Adams (William Daniels) and Benjamin Franklin (Howard Da Silva). *Martha Swope*

(*Above*) The Continental Congress in Philadelphia on the eve of American Independence. (*Opposite, below*) John Dickinson (Paul Hecht) debates John Adams (William Daniels). *Pictures, Martha Swope*

Richard Henry Lee (Ronald Holgate) reads Virginia's proposal on independence to the Continental Congress. *Martha Swope*

Company

(*Opposite, bottom*) While her husband Larry (Charles Braswell) looks on, Joanne (Elaine Stritch) begins to contemplate "The Ladies Who Lunch." (*This page, above*) Paul (Steve Elmore) and Amy (Beth Howland) deliberate about "Getting Married Today" as Robert (Dean Jones) stands by. (*Below*) After a romantic night with Robert (Dean Jones), airline stewardess April (Susan Browning) is—or should be—on her way to "Barcelona." *Pictures, Friedman-Abeles*

Robert (Larry Kert, who had taken over this role when Dean Jones became ill) and his cheerfully solicitous married friends engaged in a musical number. *Friedman-Abeles*

Robert (Dean Jones) and friends in bas-relief. *Friedman-Abeles*

(*Members of the* CHOIR *open up umbrellas of different colors.* PAUL *reenters, fully dressed in his tuxedo now*)

PAUL:

Today is for Amy.
Amy–
I give you
The rest of my life,
To cherish
And to keep
You,
To honor you
Forever.
Today is for
Amy,
My happily
Soon-to-be
Wife.

AMY:

Go, can't you go?
Look, you know
I adore you all,
But why watch me die
Like Eliza on the ice?
Look, perhaps
I'll collapse
In the apse right
Before you all,
So take back the cake,
Burn the shoes and boil the rice.
Look, I didn't want to have to tell you,
But I may be coming down with hepatitis
And I think I'm gonna faint,
So if you wanna see me faint,
I'll do it happily,
But wouldn't it be funnier
To go and watch a funeral?
So thank you for the
Twenty-seven dinner plates and
Thirty-seven butter knives and
Forty-seven paperweights and

PAUL:
My Adorable Wife–

AMY:
Fifty-seven candleholders . . .

PAUL:
One more thing,

AMY:
I am not getting married

CHOIR:
Amen.

PAUL:
Softly said,

AMY:
But I'm not getting married

CHOIR:
Amen.

PAUL:
"With this ring"

AMY:
Still I'm not getting married

CHOIR:
Amen.

PAUL:
"I thee wed."

AMY:
See, I'm not getting married

CHOIR:
Amen.

PAUL:
Let us pray,

AMY:
Let us pray,

CHOIR:
Amen.

PAUL:
And we are

AMY:

That I'm not

CHOIR:

Amen.

PAUL:

Getting married today!

AMY:

Getting married today!

(ROBERT *enters with the ring.* AMY *gets very busy preparing breakfast with toast, dishes, glasses, etc.*)

PAUL: Amy?

AMY: You're starting! (*He begins to speak*) Don't talk, please! Why don't the two of you sit down and talk to each other? I can't think with the two of you following me–every place I go–from the bedroom to the bathroom to the kitchen . . . I feel like I'm leading a parade. (*The two men sit down at the counter*) Paul, stop staring! I feel it–like bullets–right through my back. (*Without stopping*) No, Paul, please! (*Pouring orange juice*) I'm so crazy I left the refrigerator door open last night, so the orange juice is hot. (*Hands* PAUL *his juice*) Here, and if you say "thank you" I will go running right out of this apartment and move into the Hopeless Cases Section at Bellevue, where they'll understand me. Don't talk, please. (*Suddenly, from behind his chair, she throws her arms around his neck and kisses him all over his head, finally pressing her face against his*) Oh, Paul. I apologize. Oh, Paul, you say whatever you want to say. Whatever you like. Who am *I* telling *you* what to do? Oh, Paul.

PAUL: (*Pauses*) The orange juice is hot. But thanks.

AMY: Paul, see! You don't thank a person for hot orange juice! You slug 'em. (*Smoke is billowing out of the toaster*) The toast! Now I blew the toast. (*She flips up two charred pieces of toast*)

PAUL: That's okay.

AMY: I can't stand it! (*Scraping the burned toast*) IT'S NOT OKAY, PAUL. NOTHING ABOUT IT EVEN REMOTELY RESEMBLES OKAY. IT IS THE OPPOSITE OF OKAY. Oh, Robert, this is the real me. Crazed!

ROBERT: (*Teasing, hesitantly*) I was just thinking that this is probably a much more interesting wedding breakfast than most. And—uh—that the bride certainly has a lot of energy! The groom is abnormally quiet. But yet a festive atmosphere pervades the room—I guess it's the best man, smiling, even as he dies from drinking boiled orange juice. (*He holds up his orange juice in a mock toast*)

AMY: I would laugh, Robert, if it weren't all so tragic. (*To* PAUL) How do I look? Funny?

PAUL: Yeah, that's a funny dress. (*He starts pouring the coffee*)

AMY: That dumb hairdresser straightened my hair like he was on withdrawal. Paul, what are you so happy about all the time?

PAUL: You. (*He hands her a cup and saucer*)

AMY: This is the most neurotic . . . insane . . . it is . . . so *crazy* having this enormous wedding and everything after we've been living together all these years! It's embarrassing, Paul. People will think I'm pregnant.

PAUL: That's next year. Listen, if we hurry we're late.

AMY: What am I doing? I'm thirty-one.

PAUL: And perfect.

AMY: Oh, an oldie but a goodie, huh? It's just incredible. Two years with a psychiatrist . . . and look where it leads. I am just so glad we're not having a Catholic wedding because next year when I get the divorce I won't be a sinner. Whoever would have thought I'd *marry* someone Jewish? Jewish! I mean I didn't even *know* anybody who was Jewish. See, Robert. That was probably my main attraction. Look what a little Catholic rebellion will lead to! The very first moment I met Paul, I said to myself, "That's what I really like—that Jew!" Oh, he was so beautiful . . . inside and out beautiful. Paul would kiss me and I would think, "Oh, I got my very own Jew!"

PAUL: What is all this about me being Jewish today? About three-quarters of your friends are Jewish. Hurry.

AMY: Did I ever say I like my friends? I do not. I much prefer my gentile enemies—at least they leave you alone. And I need to be left alone. I'm just like Robert.

ROBERT: (*Outraged*) I'm not like *that!* What the hell are you talking about? But don't answer, because we don't have time.

PAUL: Amy. After all these years, don't you know we fit?

AMY: The higher you go, the harder you hurt when you fall.

PAUL: (*So gentle*) I never dropped you yet.

(*About to cry, she goes to take a sip of coffee, sees a note in the saucer, looks to* PAUL, *and then shows the saucer to* ROBERT. ROBERT *opens the note*)

ROBERT: "Whoever reads this . . . I love you." Well, thank you, I love *you.*

AMY: Thank *him.* The phantom. He leaves notes like that all over the place. A person can't stand all that sweetness, Paul. Nobody human can stand all that everlasting affection.

PAUL: Amy, don't you think we should go?

AMY: (*There is nothing more for her to do*) I can't.

PAUL: Amy, if anybody should be married, it's you. Tell her, Robert.

AMY: Robert tell me? Who's going to tell Robert?

ROBERT: (*He pauses; then, right at* PAUL) Paul, I can't tell anybody anything like that. I guess whatever is right will happen.

PAUL: (*Pauses*) I see.

ROBERT: Listen, I'm going to call and say that, ah . . . that . . . that we'll be late. That we'll be a little late. The people will be getting there, don't you think? (ROBERT *goes out*)

PAUL: Amy, do you see what you're doing to yourself? Do you know if other people did to you what you do to yourself, they could be put in jail? C'mon. (*Thunder is heard*)

AMY: Oh, Paul, look . . . oh, look . . . it's starting to rain.

ROBERT: (*Entering*) It's starting to rain. The line's busy. (*He tries to be light*) Oh, guess who I ran into coming over here today. Helen Kincaid. Remember Helen Kincaid? I brought her around a few times. Well, she's married now. I almost didn't recognize her, all fat and blowzy and . . . (*He realizes what he is saying*)

PAUL: (*Softly*) Amy, c'mon. We're late.

AMY: I can't do it, Paul. I don't understand how I ever let it get this far. (*Thunder is heard again*) Oh, look, will you look at that, now it's really starting to rain . . . Look at it . . . It's a flood, it's a sign—thank you, God, now explain it to him!

PAUL: (*Quietly*) Amy, let's go. All our friends are waiting.

AMY: That's no reason, Paul. I just can't. I'm so afraid.

PAUL: Of what?

AMY: (*She is crying*) I don't know. I don't know. I just think you're really not for me, Paul. I just think maybe nobody's for me. I never saw one good marriage. Never. Not in my entire life.

PAUL: You just see what you look for, you know. I've seen

a lot. Listen, Amy, married people are no more *marriage* than . . . oh . . . musicians are music. Just because some of the people might be wrong doesn't matter . . . *it* is still *right*.

AMY: Yes, well, I'll put that on a sampler, Paul. (*She looks up–right at* PAUL) Please. I'm not being emotional. I'm as sane as can be. Paul? I'm sorry. I don't love you enough.

(*There is a very long pause as they stare at each other*)

PAUL: (*He fights for control. He speaks hesitantly, yet his voice still trembles*) Robert . . . would you . . . call and, ah, explain and . . . I'm . . . I, ah, I . . . (*He goes out quickly*)

AMY: (*She doesn't move; drained of emotion, really asking . . .*) What did I just do?

ROBERT: (*Reflectively*) You did . . . what you had to do, I guess . . . If it was right, you would have gone through with it. That's what I think, anyway . . . (*A pause*) Amy, marry *me*.

AMY: What?

ROBERT: Marry me.

(*The music of "Bobby Baby" is heard in the orchestra*)

AMY: *Huh?*

ROBERT: You said it before—we're just alike. Why don't we, Amy?

AMY: Why don't we, Robert?

VOICES: (*Offstage*)

Bobby, Bobby,
Bobby baby, Bobby bubi,
Robby . . .

ROBERT: Marry me! And everybody'll leave us alone!

VOICES: (*Offstage*)

Bobby . . . Bobby . . . How have you been?
Stop by on your way home . . .
Bobby, we've been thinking of you!

AMY: Isn't this some world? I'm afraid to get married, and you're afraid not to. Thank you, Robert. I'm really . . . it's just that you have to want to marry *some*body, not just some*body*. (*She hugs him*)

VOICES: (*Offstage*)

Bobby, come on over for dinner!
Just be the three of us,

Only the three of us,
We LOOOOOOOOOOOOVE . . .

(*Thunder interrupts the voices.* AMY *notices the raincoats*)

AMY: Oh! Would you look at that! He went out without an umbrella or anything. (*She puts on a raincoat, and grabs another coat and umbrella for* PAUL) He'll get pneumonia. I've got to catch him. I'm getting married. Oh, and he's so good, isn't he? So good. (*She starts to leave*)

ROBERT: Amy! (*He picks up the bouquet and throws it to her*)

AMY: I'm the next bride. (*She leaves. The kitchen slides off*)

VOICES: (*Offstage*)
Bobby, Bobby,
Bobby baby, Bobby bubi,
Robby!

(*The lights come up on* ROBERT'S *apartment. All the birthday guests are looking at him as in Act One, Scene 1.* ROBERT *stares at* AMY *as she enters with the cake and the music builds*)

Curtain

ACT TWO

SCENE 1

ROBERT *is about to blow out the candles at the table, with all five couples standing there. As the scene progresses we find it to be more accelerated, isolating* ROBERT *at the end.*

AMY: Well, our blessings, Robert.

JENNY: Don't tell your wish, Bobby, or it won't come true.

(ROBERT *blows out most of the candles. The others blow out the rest hurriedly*)

JOANNE: You just blew it.

AMY: It probably was a wish you wouldn't have got anyway, Robert.

LARRY: You wish for a wife, Robert?

PETER: Don't. You're a lucky son-of-a-gun now. Hang in there.

SARAH: Stay exactly the same. You may be the one constant in this world of variables.

HARRY: I don't know, Sarah, you can't stay in your thirties forever.

JENNY: You'll still get your wish, Bobby.

JOANNE: Won't. I say he won't.

LARRY: Joanne, come on. See, when she and Robert get together . . .

JOANNE: Larry, I'm telling you, if you do not blow out all the candles on the cake, you do not get your wish. I know all the rules for birthday-candle blowing out. I've had enough for a wax museum.

ROBERT: All right, all right! Actually, I didn't wish for anything.

(*Again, each of the couples carries out a piece of* ROBERT'S *furniture as the following lines are spoken*)

DAVID: What do you mean you didn't wish for . . .

SUSAN: Oh, tell, everybody's so curious.

PETER: Tell, but lie.

ROBERT: Thank you for including me in your thoughts, your lives . . .

HARRY: Stay exactly as you are, Robert.

SARAH: That's right, you sweet thing, you stay exactly as you are.

(*The music of "Bobby Baby" is heard from the orchestra*)

JOANNE: Everyone adores you. What an awful thing. I'd kiss you good night, Robby, but Larry gets jealous.

AMY: Things always happen for the best. I don't even believe that myself.

(*All have exited on their final lines, leaving* ROBERT *alone*)

ROBERT: (*Shouting after them*) I mean, when you've got friends like mine . . . (*The music for "Side by Side by Side" begins*) I mean, when you've got friends like mine . . . (*He sings "Side by Side by Side"*)

Isn't it warm,
Isn't it rosy,
Side by side . . .

(*The couples appear in their living areas and look at* ROBERT)

SARAH: He's such a cutie.

ROBERT:

. . . by side?

SARAH: Isn't he a cutie?

ROBERT:

Ports in a storm,
Comfy and cozy,
Side by side . . .

PETER: He never loses his cool.

ROBERT:

. . . by side . . .

HARRY: I envy that.

(ROBERT *starts up the stairs. Throughout the following lines, he wanders through each couple's living area, while the couples continue to refer to* ROBERT *as if he were still standing center stage*)

ROBERT:

Everything shines,
How sweet . . .

ROBERT, SARAH and HARRY:

Side by side . . .

SUSAN: We're just so fond of him.

ROBERT:

. . . by side,
Parallel lines
Who meet . . .

AMY, PAUL, PETER and SUSAN:

Love him–
Can't get enough of him.

ROBERT:

Everyone winks,
Nobody's nosy,
Side by side . . .

JOANNE: He's just crazy about me.

ROBERT:

. . . by side.

PAUL: He's a very tender guy.

ROBERT:

You bring the drinks and
I'll bring the posy . . .

ROBERT, LARRY and JOANNE:

Side by side . . .

LARRY: He's always there when you need him.

ROBERT:

. . . by side.
One is lonely and two is boring,

Think what you can keep ignoring,
Side . . .

AMY: He's my best friend.

ROBERT:
. . . by side . . .

AMY: (*Touching* PAUL) Second best.

ROBERT:
. . . by side.

ALL: (*Except* ROBERT)
Never a bother,
Seven times a godfather.

ROBERT, AMY and PAUL:
Year after year,
Older and older . . .

LARRY: It's amazing. We've gotten older every year and he seems to stay exactly the same.

ALL:
Sharing a tear,
Lending a shoulder . . .

DAVID: You know what comes to my mind when I see him? The Seagram Building. Isn't that funny?

ROBERT, PETER, SUSAN, SARAH and HARRY:
Ain't we got fun?
No strain . . .

JOANNE: Sometimes I catch him looking and looking. And I just look right back.
(ROBERT *takes an elevator back to stage level*)

ALL:
Permanent sun, no rain . . .
We're so crazy, he's so sane.

Friendship forbids
Anything bitter . . .

PAUL: A person like Bob doesn't have the good things and he doesn't have the bad things. But he doesn't have the good things. Either . . .

ALL:
Being the kids
As well as the sitter . . .

HARRY: Let me make him a drink. He's the only guy I know, I feel should drink more.

ROBERT:
One's impossible, two is dreary,
Three is company, safe and cheery,

ALL: (*But* ROBERT *and* SARAH)
Side . . .

(*The couples leave their living areas.* ROBERT *is alone on-stage*)

SARAH: He always looks like he's keeping score.

ALL:
. . . by side . . .

SARAH: Who's winning, Robert?

ALL:
. . . by side.

ROBERT:
Here is the church,
Here is the steeple,
Open the doors and
See all the crazy married people.

(*The couples burst in all at once on stage level. The music continues directly into "What Would We Do Without You?"*)

ALL: (*Except* ROBERT)
What would we do without you?
How would we ever get through?
Who would I complain to for hours?
Who'd bring me the flowers
When I have the flu?
Who'd finish yesterday's stew?
Who'd take the kids to the zoo?
Who is so dear?
And who is so deep?
And who would keep her/him occupied
When I want to sleep?
How would we ever get through?
What would we do without you?

What would we do without you?
How would we ever get through?

Should there be a marital squabble,
Available Bob'll
Be there with the glue.
Who could we open up to,
Secrets we keep from guess-who?
Who is so safe and who is so sound?
You never need an analyst with Bobby around.
How could we ever get through?
What would we do without you?

What would we do without you?
How would we ever get through?
Who sends anniversary wishes?
Who helps with the dishes
And never says boo?
Who changes subjects on cue?
Who cheers us up when we're blue?
Who is a flirt but never a threat,
Reminds us of our birthdays, which we always forget?
How would we ever get through?
What would we do without you?

What would we do without you?
How would we ever get
How would we ever get
How would we ever get
How would we ever get . . . through?
What would we do without you?

ROBERT:

Just what you usually do!

ALL: (*Except* ROBERT)

Right!

You who sit with us,
You who share with us,
You who fit with us,
You who bear with us,
You-hoo, you-hoo, you-hoo,
You-hoo, you-hoo . . .

ROBERT: (*In a vaudeville call*) Okay, now everybody!

ALL:

Isn't it warm, isn't it rosy,

Side by side?
Ports in a storm, comfy and cozy,
Side by side,
Everything shines, how sweet,
Side by side,
Parallel lines who meet
Side by side.
Year after year, older and older,
Side by side,
Sharing a tear and lending a shoulder,
Side by side.
Two's impossible, two is gloomy,
Give another number to me.
Side by side,
By side, by side, by side, by side,
By side, by side, by side, by side,
By side!

(*All the couples exit, leaving* ROBERT *alone onstage*)

SCENE 2

The scene is ROBERT'S *apartment.* APRIL *enters. She is wearing her stewardess' uniform and appears self-conscious; this is her first visit. The stage level is completely cleared.* APRIL *and* ROBERT *refer to furnishings that aren't there.*

APRIL: Oh! It's a darling apartment.

ROBERT: Thank you.

APRIL: Just darling. Did you do it yourself?

ROBERT: Me? Yes, I did, yes.

APRIL: Yourself?

ROBERT: Yes.

APRIL: Really?

ROBERT: Yes.

APRIL: Well, it's darling—Did you really do it all yourself?

ROBERT: (*Getting tired of this*) Yes! Why? Did you hear I didn't?

APRIL: No, but look—this! This is just precious.

ROBERT: It is, isn't it? I never really look at it. I just—live here.

APRIL: Oh, it's terribly clever. See how nicely all the furniture is placed in areas to make it so warm and sweet and tucked in.

ROBERT: (*Amazed*) How about that?

APRIL: And the choice of colors is so relaxing and simple and masculine.

ROBERT: (*Still surprised, nodding his head in agreement*) See that!

APRIL: Isn't that tasteful and interesting?

ROBERT: Yes. I'll take it. (*They smile*) I mean I've always liked my apartment, but I'm never really in it. I just seem to pass through the living room on my way to the bedroom to get to the bathroom to get ready to go out again.

APRIL: You never really spend any time in here? And it's so dear . . . But maybe that's why you like it so much. If you don't spend much time in it, it keeps it special and important.

ROBERT: (*Amazed; slowly. He looks around*) Yes. (*The bed appears and moves downstage to its place opposite them*) And this is the bedroom over here. (*She slowly crosses to it apprehensively*) You love it, I can tell. Well, I can always look for another place.

(ROBERT *and* APRIL *begin to touch, embrace and then to kiss, all in very slow motion, as the lights come up on* SARAH *and* HARRY, *in their own apartment. They begin to sing "Poor Baby"*)

SARAH:
Darling—

HARRY:
Yes?

SARAH:
Robert—

HARRY:
What?

SARAH:
I worry—

HARRY:
Why?

SARAH:
He's all alone.
(HARRY *grunts*)
There's no one—

HARRY:
Where?

SARAH:

In his life.

HARRY:

Oh.

SARAH:

Robert ought to have a woman.
Poor baby, all alone,
Evening after evening by the telephone—
We're the only tenderness he's ever known.
Poor baby . . .

(*The lights come up on* JENNY *and* DAVID, *in their apartment*)

JENNY:

David—

DAVID:

Yes?

JENNY:

Bobby—

DAVID:

What?

JENNY:

I worry.

DAVID:

Why?

JENNY:

It's such a waste.

(DAVID *grunts*)

There's no one.

DAVID:

Where?

JENNY:

In his life.

DAVID:

Oh.

JENNY:

Bobby ought to have a woman.
Poor baby, sitting there,

Staring at the walls and playing solitaire,
Making conversation with the empty air—
Poor baby.

(*The lights go down on the couples*)

APRIL: Right after I became an airline stewardess, a friend of mine who had a garden apartment gave me a cocoon for my bedroom. He collects things like that, insects and caterpillars and all that . . . It was attached to a twig, and he said one morning I'd wake up to a beautiful butterfly in *my* bedroom—when it hatched. He told me that when they come out they're soaking wet, and there is a drop of blood there too—isn't that fascinating?—but within an hour they dry off and then they begin to fly. Well, I told him I had a cat. I had a cat then, but he said just put the cocoon somewhere where the cat couldn't get at it—which is impossible, but what can you do? So I put it up high on a ledge where the cat never went, and the next morning it was still there, at least, so it seemed safe to leave it. Well, anyway, almost a week later very, very early this one morning the guy calls me, and he said, "April, do you have a butterfly this morning?" I told him to hold on, and managed to get up and look, and there on the ledge I saw this wet spot and a little speck of blood but no butterfly, and I thought "Oh, dear God in Heaven, the cat got it." I picked up the phone to tell this guy and just then suddenly I spotted it under the dressing table—it was moving one wing. The cat had got at it, but it was still alive. So I told the guy, and he got so upset, and he said "Oh no! Oh, God, no! Don't you see that's a life—a living thing?" Well, I got dressed and took it to the park and put it on a rose—it was summer then—and it looked like it was going to be all right—I think, anyway. But that man . . . I really felt damaged by him—awful—that was just cruel. I got home and I called him back and said, "Listen, I'm a living thing too, you shithead!" (*A pause*) I never saw him again.

ROBERT: (*He stands staring—too stunned to move. They are both standing in the bedroom doorway. There is a pause*) That reminds me of something I did to someone once . . . in Miami. I mean . . . it's not really the same, but in a way. Well, you'll see. I met a girl, a lovely girl, at a party one night and, well, it was like you and me, April. We just—connected. You don't mind my telling this, do you?

APRIL: No.

ROBERT: It just . . . came to my mind. Anyway, we just connected, in such a beautiful way . . . exactly like tonight. Except we couldn't even contain ourselves. It was incredible. We were talking and suddenly we realized we just couldn't talk any more. No sounds came. We stood looking at each other and we were both bathed in perspiration. Our breathing was so short and our legs were trembling and we just left. We drove to one of those strips there where they have all those motels, and we didn't even say anything. She just sat so close to me. So close. We got inside that room and we started touching and kissing and laughing and holding, and suddenly she said I should go get lots of champagne and some baby oil and we should get beautifully high and then rub . . . well, you know. She said she'd be in bed waiting for me. (APRIL *is visibly turned on by this story*) I rushed out of there and I drove around until I could find a liquor store and a drugstore open, and I got all this champagne and the oil and finally I started back to the motel and–I–could not–find–it. (APRIL *almost faints*) I looked for over three hours. I never found it. And I never saw her again either.

APRIL: (*Her breathing is heavy and raspy–she has identified totally with "the girl"*) Oh. That is the most extraordinary story I have ever heard. (ROBERT *slowly helps her out of her jacket and starts unzipping her blouse. She is almost mesmerized*) That poor girl. (ROBERT *kneels and takes off one of her shoes; she immediately offers her foot*) And you drove around for three hours?

ROBERT: More!

(*Now they both start undressing rapidly, dropping or tossing their clothes anywhere. He pulls back the bedspread on both sides.* APRIL *sits on it and unrolls her stockings*)

ROBERT: All night I tried to find that motel. All night. With the oil and all that champagne and my hands trembling and sweat running down my face.

(*She has begun to cry a little bit for "the girl"–she is under the covers now, doing the last of her undressing under the covers*)

APRIL: Oh, that girl. She never knew. Oh. Well, I just don't know what to say or do. That's so sad!

ROBERT: I know. It is. Very.

APRIL: But, Robert, those stories don't really follow. I don't see the connection. (ROBERT *gives an "Oh, my God, caught" look*) Unless . . . oh . . . you must have thought of that poor girl as the wounded butterfly . . .

ROBERT: (*Takes out champagne, glasses and baby oil*) Yes, that's it!

(*The lights go down on the bedroom and come up on* SARAH *and* JENNY, *together. They sing*)

SARAH:

Robert.

JENNY:

Bobby.

SARAH:

Robert angel . . .

JENNY:

Bobby honey . . .

SARAH:

You know, no one
Wants you to be happy
More than I do.
No one, but
Isn't she a little bit, well,
You know,
Face it. Why her?
Better, no one . . .

JENNY:

. . . wants you to be happy
More than I do.
No one, but . . .

SARAH and JENNY:

. . . isn't she a little bit,
Well, you know, face it.

(SUSAN *joins them*)

SUSAN:

You know, no one
Wants you to be happy
More than I do.

(AMY *and* JOANNE *join them*)

AMY and JOANNE:

You know, no one
Wants you to be happy
More than I do. No one, but . . .

ALL:

Isn't she a little bit, well . . .

SARAH:

Dumb? Where is she from?

AMY:

Tacky? Neurotic? She seems so dead.

SUSAN:

Vulgar? Aggressive? Peculiar?

JENNY:

Old? And cheap and

JOANNE:

Tall? She's tall enough to be your mother.

SARAH:

She's very weird . . .

JENNY:

Gross and . . .

SUSAN:

Depressing, and . . .

AMY:

And immature . . .

JOANNE:

Goliath,

ALL:

Poor baby,
All alone,
Throw a lonely dog a bone,
It's still a bone.
We're the only tenderness
He's ever known.
Poor baby.

(*The lights go down on the women and the bedroom disappears. Now* KATHY *appears and begins to dance. Throughout the number* ROBERT *and* APRIL'S *voices are heard.* KATHY'S *dance expresses the difference between having sex and making love. During the dialogue between* ROBERT *and* APRIL, *she dances the "having sex"; during the rest of the sequence, the "making love")*

ROBERT: Oh, this is sensational . . .

APRIL: Oh, I think he really likes me.

(KATHY *changes her dance step and/or movement*)

ROBERT: Wow, she's nice.

APRIL: He's so nice.

ROBERT: Oh, God.

APRIL: Oh, dear.

ROBERT: Oh.

APRIL: Oh.

ROBERT: I like that.

APRIL: I love that.

(KATHY *changes her dance step and/or movement*)

ROBERT: Oh, she has such a smooth body.

APRIL: What is he doing?

(KATHY *changes her dance step and/or movement*)

ROBERT: With all that long hair I can't even find her head.

APRIL: He really likes me. (KATHY *changes her dance step and/or movement*) It's poetry.

ROBERT: It's beautiful.

APRIL: I think I could love him.

ROBERT: If only I could remember her name.

(KATHY *changes her dance step and/or movement*)

APRIL: He smells so good.

ROBERT: She tastes so good.

APRIL: He feels so good.

ROBERT: What is her name?

(KATHY *changes her dance step and/or movement. We hear the voices of the married couples*)

APRIL: I love you, I love you . . .

ROBERT: I . . . I . . .

(KATHY *changes her dance step and/or movement*)

SARAH: I love you, Harry.

HARRY: I love you, Sarah.

JENNY: I love you, David.

DAVID: I love you, Jenny.

ALL: I love you, I love you, I love you . . .

(*After the dance, the lights come up on the bedroom as before.* ROBERT *has his hand over his eyes; both he and* APRIL *are completely exhausted. The alarm clock goes off.* APRIL *shuts off the clock and turns on a light. She begins gathering her clothes. They sing)*

ROBERT:
Where you going?

APRIL:
Barcelona.

ROBERT:
. . . oh . . .

APRIL:
Don't get up.

ROBERT:
Do you have to?

APRIL:
Yes, I have to.

ROBERT:
. . . oh . . .

APRIL:
Don't get up.
(*Pauses*)
Now you're angry.

ROBERT:
No, I'm not.

APRIL:
Yes, you are.

ROBERT:
No, I'm not.
Put your things down.

APRIL:
See, you're angry.

ROBERT:
No, I'm not.

APRIL:
Yes, you are.

ROBERT:
No, I'm not.
Put your wings down
And stay.

APRIL:
I'm leaving.

ROBERT:
Why?

APRIL:
To go to–

ROBERT:
Stay–

APRIL:
I have to–

APRIL and ROBERT:
Fly–

ROBERT:
I know–

APRIL and ROBERT:
To Barcelona.

ROBERT:
Look,
You're a very special girl,
Not just overnight.
No, you're a very special girl,
And not because you're bright–
Not *just* because you're bright.
(*Yawning*)
You're just a very special girl,
June!

APRIL:
April . . .

ROBERT:
April . . .
(*There is a pause*)

APRIL:
Thank you.

ROBERT:
Whatcha thinking?

APRIL:
Barcelona.

ROBERT:
. . . oh . . .

APRIL:
Flight Eighteen.

ROBERT:
Stay a minute.

APRIL:
I would like to.

ROBERT:
. . . so? . . .

APRIL:
Don't be mean.

ROBERT:
Stay a minute.

APRIL:
No, I can't.

ROBERT:
Yes, you can.

APRIL:
No, I can't.

ROBERT:
Where you going?

APRIL:
Barcelona.

ROBERT:
So you said—

APRIL:
And Madrid.

ROBERT:
Bon voyage.

APRIL:
On a Boeing.

ROBERT:
Good night.

APRIL:
You're angry.

ROBERT:
No.

APRIL:
I've got to–

ROBERT:
Right.

APRIL:
Report to–

ROBERT:
Go.

APRIL:
That's not to
Say
That if I had my way . . .
Oh well, I guess okay.

ROBERT:
What?

APRIL:
I'll stay.

ROBERT:
But . . .
(*As she snuggles down*)
Oh, God!

Blackout

SCENE 3

(*The scene is* PETER *and* SUSAN'S *terrace.* ROBERT *and* MARTA *come up in the elevator.* PETER *and* SUSAN *are basking in the sun on the terrace.*

SUSAN: Oh, Peter, look who's here. It's Robert. And you must be Marta.

MARTA: (*Leans over the railing*) Oh, God, look! You can see the East River.

ROBERT: I'm surprised to find you out on the terrace. It's terrific.

SUSAN: Peter fixed it all up. Oh, Marta, I'm so glad Robert brought you by. You are just what he said . . . so pretty and original and pecul– I mean . . .

MARTA: Right!

SUSAN: Well, now, Robert, how have *you* been?

ROBERT: You know me. I'm always happy. (*All heads turn and stare at him, astonished. He is taken aback*) What did I say?

PETER: (*After an awkward moment*) Hey, Bob, did Susan show you the pictures I took in Mexico when I went down to get the divorce?

ROBERT: Divorce? You're not married now?

SUSAN: Not since the divorce.

ROBERT: Oh.

PETER: I flew down to Mexico. It is absolutely sensational down there. It is so terrific, I phoned Susan to come down and join me.

SUSAN: It's so pretty down there.

ROBERT: Where are you living now, Peter?

PETER: Well, here at home. I mean I've got responsibilities . . . Susan and the kids to take care of. I certainly wouldn't leave them.

ROBERT: It sure seems to be working.

SUSAN: Well, my goodness! We're all four single. It's nicer, I think. Especially if you have somebody. (SUSAN *and* PETER *embrace*)

MARTA: Now *this* is what I call New York!

Blackout

SCENE 4

The stage is alive with the activity of a private nightclub. There are running waiters and, in a cage to one side, a go-go girl.

JOANNE *and* ROBERT *are seated at a table on stage level, watching* JOANNE'S *husband,* LARRY, *dance with one of the patrons.* JOANNE *and* ROBERT *grow increasingly drunk as the scene progresses. She is an acerbic drunk.* ROBERT *laughs and gets silly, but never really loses himself.* LARRY *is quite decent and quite sober, but having a wonderful time.*

ROBERT: I think they're going to hurt themselves.

JOANNE: What if their mothers came in and saw them up there doing that? Think of their poor mothers. He's embarrassing.

ROBERT: Anyway, those people that laugh and carry on and dance like that–they're not happy.

JOANNE: (*She yells in* LARRY'S *direction*) Think of your poor mother!

ROBERT: He's not what you'd call self-conscious.

JOANNE: He's not what you'd call! Big show-off. It really shocks me to see a grown man dance like that! (*Yelling to* LARRY *again*) I am shocked, you hear, shocked! (*To* ROBERT) Where was I? Oh—my first husband. He is so difficult to remember. Even when you're with him. We got married here in New York. See, he was here on some business deal, but he owned a big meat-packing company in Chicago. Attractive? Well, we lived in New York for almost a year and then one day he had to go back to Chicago. And, you know, he was actually surprised when I told him I would just wait here for him. I mean, I still really don't know quite where Chicago is. It's over there somewhere. (*She points vaguely*) He said he didn't really plan to come back . . . So I knew we were in a tiny dilemma—or at least he was. I was still too young. But I was old enough to know where I was living, and I had no intention of leaving New York. I have never left New York. Never have, never will. And least of all would I ever want to go to a place where they actually feel honored being called "hog butcher for the world." I said, "Kiss off, Rodney," but I said it nicer. Well, we got a divorce. A divorce. Huh! One word means all of that. Another drink, guy . . . sir. *Oh, sir!*

(*The waiters are too busy and ignore her. The dance ends; everyone applauds.* LARRY *and his partner say goodbye, and he crosses to* JOANNE'S *table and stands there catching his breath.* LARRY *has a red flower in his lapel*)

LARRY: Whew!

JOANNE: (*Looking up at him and away*) We already gave.

LARRY: (*Sits; looks at* ROBERT) You all had a few while I was dancing, huh?

JOANNE: Larry, what the hell was all that carrying on? What was that? Shocking. (*Yells to passing waiters*) SIR! SIR! *TROIS ENCORE, S'IL VOUS PLAÎT!*

LARRY: (*Looks at* JOANNE) I asked you to dance.

JOANNE: I only dance when you can touch. I don't think standing bumping around and making an ass out of oneself is a dance. I find it unbelievably humiliating watching my own husband flouncing around the dance floor, jerking and sashaying all over the place like Ann Miller. Take off the red shoes, Larry. Off.

LARRY: (*To* ROBERT) Was I that good?

ROBERT: Very. Excellent. Amazingly good.

LARRY: (*Laughing*) Joanne, I love you when you're jealous. Kiss me.

JOANNE: I hated dinner. I hated the opera, and I hate it here. What I need is more to drink—and look at Bobby, how desperately he needs another drink. (*The waiters enter again. The female patrons are seen seated at various tables*) Here they come again. SIR! DRINKS HERE—TWO MORE BOURBONS AND A VODKA STINGER! Do you know that we are suddenly at an age where we find ourselves too young for the old people and too old for the young ones? We're nowhere. I think we better drink to us. To us—the generation gap. WE ARE THE GENERATION GAP! (*The other women in the club turn and stare at her*) Are they staring at me? Let 'em stare—let 'em, those broads. What else have they got to do—all dressed up with no place to go.

LARRY: What time is it?

JOANNE: In real life? Will somebody get us another drink! (*At this point each of the four waiters delivers a round of drinks to the table*) Oh, you did. So aggressive. (*To the other women*) STOP STARING! (*There is a blackout on the nightclub, leaving her alone in a spotlight; she turns to the audience*) I'd like to propose a toast. (*She sings*)

Here's to the ladies who lunch—
Everybody laugh.
Lounging in their caftans and planning a brunch
On their own behalf.
Off to the gym,
Then to a fitting,
Claiming they're fat.
And looking grim
'Cause they've been sitting
Choosing a hat—
(*She stands*)
Does anyone still wear a hat?
I'll drink to that.

Here's to the girls who stay smart—
Aren't they a gas?
Rushing to their classes in optical art,
Wishing it would pass.
Another long exhausting day,
Another thousand dollars,

A matinée, a Pinter play,
Perhaps a piece of Mahler's–
I'll drink to that.
And one for Mahler.

Here's to the girls who play wife–
Aren't they too much?
Keeping house but clutching a copy of *Life*
Just to keep in touch.
The ones who follow the rules,
And meet themselves at the schools,
Too busy to know that they're fools–
Aren't they a gem?
I'll drink to them.
Let's all drink to them.

And here's to the girls who just watch–
Aren't they the best?
When they get depressed, it's a bottle of Scotch
Plus a little jest.
Another chance to disapprove,
Another brilliant zinger,
Another reason not to move,
Another vodka stinger–
Aaaahh–I'll drink to that.

So here's to the girls on the go–
Everybody tries.
Look into their eyes and you'll see what they know:
Everybody dies.
A toast to that invincible bunch–
The dinosaurs surviving the crunch–
Let's hear it for the ladies who lunch–
Everybody rise! Rise!
Rise! Rise! Rise! Rise! Rise! Rise!
(*She sits as the lights come up on the nightclub again*)

I would like a cigarette, Larry. (*He gives her one and lights it*) Remember when everyone used to smoke? How it was more–uh–festive, happier or something. Now every place is not unlike an operating room, for Chrissake. (*Pokes* ROBERT) Huh?

ROBERT: I never smoked.

JOANNE: Why?

ROBERT: I don't know. I meant to. Does that count?

JOANNE: Meant to! Meant to! Story of your life. Meant to! Jesus, you are lifted right out of a Krafft-Ebing case history. You were always outside looking in the window while everybody was inside dancing at the party. Now I insist you smoke. Your first compromise. (*Shouts at the waiters again*) OH, SIR, MORE CIGARETTES PLEASE! THESE ARE FINE. LETHAL. (*She tears the package open completely*) Here, Rob! Smoke!

ROBERT: No, thank you.

LARRY: Joanne, honey, c'mon–he doesn't.

ROBERT: You smoke. I'll watch.

JOANNE: Watch? Did you hear yourself? Huh? Hear what you just said, kiddo? Watch. I am offering you . . .

ROBERT: (*Interrupting*) I don't want one.

JOANNE: (*Angry*) Because you're weak . . . (*Throws the pack down*) I hate people who are weak! (*Takes a deep drag and exhales*) That's the best. Better than Librium. Smoking may be the only thing that separates us from the lower forms.

LARRY: You wanna split?

JOANNE: Of what?

LARRY: We don't act like this when you're not here, Robby. I wish you could meet Joanne sometime. She's really great. In fact, when you marry, be sure you marry a girl just like her . . .

JOANNE: (*Sarcastically, really putting* ROBERT *down*) Don't ever get married, Robby. Never. Why should you?

ROBERT: For company, I don't know. Like everybody else.

JOANNE: Who else?

ROBERT: Everybody that ever fell in love and got married.

JOANNE: I know both couples and they're both divorced. Oh, Larry, you interrupted me before. See what happens when you rush me. I wanted to toast my second husband.

LARRY: (*Getting up*) I'm going to the john. And when I come back, we'll be leaving shortly. The holiday is ending. Okay? (*He goes out*)

ROBERT: (*Calling after* LARRY) I got the check. Damn. I know he's off to pay the check. (JOANNE *sits with a drink in one hand and a cigarette in the other and doesn't take her eyes off* ROBERT) Or maybe buy the place. It is a comfort to have rich friends. But I do like to pay some of the time. Oh, well, you talked me into it! (*Pauses. He becomes increasingly uncomfortable*) You have a good third husband, Joanne. He's a good man. Anyway, thank you for the evening. I'm glad I joined you. I was really feeling low . . . really depressed. I drank, but you really put it away tonight. The last several times you and I got together, I've had shameful hangovers—abominable. We may be doing permanent damage—think of that! I don't know what to think of the fact that you only drink with me . . . I guess, that is not unflattering. No! I hope I don't depress you! We have good times and it's a hoot, yes? Whatever you say! (*Pauses*) No. I don't care for a cigarette if that is what you're trying to stare me into. Even though I am a product of my generation, I still do not smoke. My age group is a very uptight age group. Middle age is breaking up that old gang of mine. Whew! It's very drunk out tonight. What are you looking at, Joanne? It's my charisma, huh? Well, stop looking at my charisma!

JOANNE: (*Still staring; no change in position or voice*) When are we gonna make it?

ROBERT: (*A pause*) I beg your pardon?

JOANNE: When're we gonna make it?

ROBERT: (*Making light of it*) What's wrong with now?

JOANNE: (*Slowly, directly, sultrily, quietly and evenly*) There's my place. It's free tomorrow at two. Larry goes to his gym then. Don't talk. Don't do your folksy Harold Teen with me. You're a terribly attractive man. The kind of a man most women want and never seem to get. I'll—take care of you.

ROBERT: (*A pause. He's been looking down; he looks up*) But who will I take care of?

JOANNE: (*A big smile*) Well, did you hear yourself? Did you hear what you just said, kiddo?

(*The discotheque music begins again*)

LARRY: (*Reenters*) Well, the check is paid and . . . (*Looks at a stunned* ROBERT) What's wrong?

ROBERT: I didn't mean that.

LARRY: What's wrong?

ROBERT: (*Getting angry*) I've looked at all that—marriages and all that—and what do you get for it? What do you get? (ROBERT *leaves the table. The music of "Bobby Baby" is heard in the orchestra*)

LARRY: What happened?

JOANNE: I just did someone a big favor. C'mon, Larry, let's go home.

(*The music of "Bobby Baby" is heard in the orchestra.* JO-

ANNE *and* LARRY *leave the nightclub table and return to their living area above. The husbands enter and join their wives—who were already seated in the living areas as the female patrons in the nightclub scene. The stage is cleared.* ROBERT *is center stage*)

ROBERT: What do you get?

JENNY: (*Sings*)
Bobby . . .

PETER:
Bobby . . .

AMY:
Bobby baby . . .

PAUL:
Bobby bubi . . .

HARRY:
Robby . . .

SARAH:
Robert darling . . .

DAVID:
Bobby, we've been trying to call you.

JENNY:
Bobby . . .

LARRY:
Bobby . . .

AMY:
Bobby baby . . .

PAUL:
Bobby bubi . . .

SARAH:
Angel, I've got something to tell you.

HARRY:
Bob . . .

LARRY:
Rob-o . . .

JOANNE:
Bobby love . . .

SUSAN:
Bobby honey . . .

AMY and PAUL:
Bobby, we've been trying to reach you all day.

LARRY:
Bobby . . .

HARRY:
Bobby . . .

PETER:
Bobby baby . . .

SARAH:
Angel . . .

JOANNE:
Darling . . .

DAVID and JENNY:
The kids were asking, Bobby . . .

HARRY:
Bobby . . .

SUSAN:
Robert . . .

JOANNE:
Robby . . .

PETER:
Bob-o . . .

LARRY and JOANNE:
Bobby, there was something we wanted to say.

SARAH and HARRY:
Bobby . . .

PAUL:
Bobby bubi . . .

AMY:
Sweetheart . . .

SUSAN:
Sugar . . .

DAVID and JENNY:
Your line was busy.

ALL:

Bobby . . .

ROBERT: (*Shouts; angry*) Stop! What do you get? (*He sings "Being Alive"*)

Someone to hold you too close,
Someone to hurt you too deep,
Someone to sit in your chair,
To ruin your sleep . . .

PAUL: That's true, but there's more than that.

SARAH: Is that all you think there is to it?

HARRY: You've got so many reasons for not being with someone, but Robert, you haven't got one good reason for being alone.

LARRY: Come on. You're on to something, Bobby. You're on to something.

ROBERT:

Someone to need you too much,
Someone to know you too well,
Someone to pull you up short
And put you through hell . . .

DAVID: You see what you look for, you know.

JOANNE: You're not a kid any more, Robby, and I don't think you'll ever be a kid again, kiddo.

PETER: Hey, buddy, don't be afraid it won't be perfect . . . The only thing to be afraid of really is that it won't *be!*

JENNY: Don't stop now! Keep going!

ROBERT:

Someone you have to let in,
Someone whose feelings you spare,
Someone who, like it or not, will want you to share
A little, a lot . . .

SUSAN: And what does all that mean?

LARRY: Robert, how do you know so much about it when you've never been there?

HARRY: It's all much better living it than looking at it, Robert.

PETER: Add 'em up, Bobby, add 'em up.

ROBERT:

Someone to crowd you with love,
Someone to force you to care,
Someone to make you come through,

Who'll always be there, as frightened as you,
Of being alive,
Being alive, being alive, being alive.

AMY: Blow out the candles, Robert, and make a wish. *Want* something! Want *something!*

(ROBERT, *touched and hurting, closes his eyes and clenches his fists*)

ROBERT:

Somebody hold me too close,
Somebody hurt me too deep,
Somebody sit in my chair
And ruin my sleep and make me aware
Of being alive, being alive.

(*The lights go down on the couples, leaving* ROBERT *alone on stage.* ROBERT *opens his eyes*)

Somebody need me too much,
Somebody know me too well,
Somebody pull me up short
And put me through hell and give me support
For being alive.
Make me alive.
Make me confused, mock me with praise,
Let me be used, vary my days.
But alone is alone, not alive.

Somebody crowd me with love,
Somebody force me to care,
Somebody make me come through.
I'll always be there, as frightened as you,
To help us survive
Being alive, being alive, being alive.

(*The lights come up on the birthday party in* ROBERT'S *apartment again*)

SCENE 5

The scene is ROBERT'S *apartment. There is an atmosphere of apprehension this time.*

We hear footsteps in the distance, growing louder. The lights are turned down, a key is heard in a lock—but it is another door that opens and closes. There are a few seconds of silence.

LARRY: (*More seriously than we're used to*) Must have been the apartment across the hall.

HARRY: (*A pause*) This is the craziest thing . . . huh?

AMY: Do you think something's wrong?

PAUL: No.

AMY: Neither do I.

PETER: I do. I've called every joint in town.

SUSAN: It *has* been over two hours now. Maybe he forgot.

SARAH: How can anyone forget a surprise birthday?

JOANNE: Or . . . maybe the surprise is on us. I think I got the message. C'mon, Larry, let's go home.

LARRY: Yeah. I think we should.

AMY: (*A pause*) Let's go, Paul.

PAUL: Yes, I think we can now.

SARAH: (*Quietly*) Maybe we should leave him a note.

HARRY: (*Gently, to* SARAH) Maybe we ought to leave him be.

SUSAN: I'll call him tomorrow.

PETER: (*In deep thought*) Don't.

SUSAN: (*Very quietly*) I won't.

JENNY: David?

DAVID: What?

JENNY: Nothing.

JOANNE: (*Gathering all around the table*) Okay. All together, everybody.

ALL: Happy birthday, Robert!

(*They blow out the candles and the lights go out in the apartment. Throughout this scene,* ROBERT *has stood center stage, listening; now he smiles*)

Curtain

EDITOR'S NOTES
The Musicals and Their Creators

OF THEE I SING

The first truly significant musical comedy of the thirties—and, indeed, one of the most influential in the history of the American musical theatre—*Of Thee I Sing* opened in New York on December 26, 1931, and critical superlatives were flung about as copiously and lavishly as campaign speeches. Brooks Atkinson declared in *The New York Times* that it was "funnier than the Government and not nearly so dangerous," while the reviewer for the *New York Herald Tribune* reported that "it says the most outrageous things in the most outrageous and funniest way." Even the haughty self-styled "dean" of Manhattan's drama critics, George Jean Nathan, succumbed: "In *Of Thee I Sing,* I believe that we discover the happiest and most successful native music-stage lampoon that has thus far come the way of the American theatre. With it, further, I believe that American musical comedy enters at length upon a new, original and independent lease of life."

With its witty, irreverent and satirical commentary on American politics in the depression year of 1931 and its integral use of music as a structural constituent rather than as an assortment of loosely inserted numbers, *Of Thee I Sing* brought a new and fresh approach to the musical stage. As Mr. Atkinson wrote four decades later, "*Of Thee I Sing* broke with stale musical comedy formula completely. It had a contemporary theme. It burlesqued the kind of sentiment that the musical comedy embraced. It had a stinging point of view. It had a score that gave the theme pace, wit and gusto. In the depths of the depression, when everything else seemed to be falling apart, it made the musical stage part of the culture of America."

With the opening and eager acceptance of this musical, it was clearly evident that progress in our musical theatre was no longer waiting in the wings; it palpably had arrived, triumphantly, on stage. Yet, the show was destined for further historic achievements; most notably, it was the very first musical ever to be awarded the Pulitzer Prize (1932). (The anticipated winner had been Eugene O'Neill's

Mourning Becomes Electra but *Of Thee I Sing* joyously walked off with the distinguished award.) In announcing their selection, the Pulitzer judges said, "This award may seem unusual, but the play is unusual. Not only is it coherent and well-knit enough to classify as a play, aside from the music, but it is a biting and true satire on American politics and the public attitude toward them. Its effect on the stage promises to be very considerable because musical plays are always popular and by injecting genuine satire and point into them, a very large public is reached. The spirit and style of the play are topical and popular, but of course the work is all the more spontaneous for that and has a freshness and vitality which are both unusual and admirable. The play is genuine, and it is felt the prize could not serve a better purpose than to recognize such work."

All the creators were cited for their contributions but, ironically, the Pulitzer committee did not name the composer George Gershwin (whose finest and most integrated score it was up to that date), in the official citation because of the technicality that the award was for "dramatic literature" and music did not qualify in that category. (Since 1932, only three other musicals have been accorded the Pulitzer Prize: *South Pacific,* 1950; *Fiorello!,* 1960; and *How to Succeed in Business Without Really Trying,* 1962).

Of Thee I Sing ran for 441 performances and it also has the distinction of being the first American musical comedy libretto to be published in book form.

In 1952, it was revived at the Ziegfeld Theatre, New York, with Jack Carson and Paul Hartman in the roles created by William Gaxton and Victor Moore.

The quartet of creators responsible for the show's enormous success fashioned a sequel (utilizing the same principal characters) in *Let 'Em Eat Cake*. Presented at the Imperial Theatre on October 21, 1933, the enterprise lasted for only ninety performances. As with most sequels, its occasional brightness was dimmed by the overall brilliance of the original.

George S. Kaufman (1889–1961), coauthor of the book with Morrie Ryskind, was one of the leading figures in the modern theatre. Born in Pittsburgh, Pennsylvania, he began his professional writing career by conducting a daily humorous column for the *Washington Times.* This was followed by a stint on the *New York Evening Mail,* and from there he moved on to the dramatic staff of the *New York Tribune* and, subsequently, *The New York Times.*

His first Broadway success came in 1921 with the comedy *Dulcy,* written in collaboration with Marc Connelly. It ran for 246 performances and established not only the reputations of the authors, but also that of its leading lady, Lynn Fontanne.

Known as "the great collaborator" during his long career in the theatre, Kaufman coauthored (along with Marc Connelly, Ring Lardner, Edna Ferber, Alexander Woollcott, Katherine Dayton and John P. Marquand) dozens of plays and musicals. These include: *Merton of the Movies; To the Ladies; Minick; The Royal Family; Beggar on Horseback; Animal Crackers; The Cocoanuts; June Moon; The Band Wagon; Dinner at Eight; First Lady; Stage Door; The Land Is Bright;* and *The Late George Apley.*

His most convivial writing partnership began in 1930 when he worked with Moss Hart on a devastating satire of Hollywood, *Once in a Lifetime.* It entertained audiences for 406 performances and later was made into a film, one of the first lampoons of itself produced by the industry. Thereafter, the team was to enliven the Broadway sector with *You Can't Take It With You* (which won the Pulitzer Prize in 1937), the musical *I'd Rather Be Right, The Fabulous Invalid, The American Way, Merrily We Roll Along, George Washington Slept Here* and *The Man Who Came to Dinner.*

As Brooks Atkinson has written about Kaufman and Hart: "They presided over an era and pioneered the darting, withering, iconoclastic play that made routine comedy obsolete."

Kaufman's final two Broadway successes as a dramatist were *The Solid Gold Cadillac* (written with Howard Teichmann, 1953) and the book for the 1955 Cole Porter musical, *Silk Stockings* (coauthored with Leueen McGrath and Abe Burrows).

Oddly enough, he only wrote one play without a collaborator during his more than thirty years in the theatre: *The Butter and Egg Man,* produced in 1925, which had an engagement of 243 performances.

Not only was George S. Kaufman a master of play construction and comic and biting satiric dialogue, but he also was a masterful director who piloted more than a score of plays and musicals to outstanding Broadway success.

Prior to their collaboration on *Of Thee I Sing,* Morrie Ryskind worked with Kaufman on the preparation of the script for the musical *The Cocoanuts* and as coauthor of *Animal Crackers,* both with the Marx Brothers as chief revelers.

In 1930, Ryskind was called in to revise the original Kaufman book for the musical *Strike Up the Band,* which had closed in Philadelphia during its 1927 pre-Broadway tour. This was something of a switch; for generally it was Kaufman who was summoned in to doctor an ailing show. A musical satire on war, international relations and American big business, *Strike Up the Band* was a hit in its new manifestation and, chronologically, the first musical success of the decade. It was also the precursor of *Of Thee I Sing* which felicitously reunited its four creators: Kaufman, Ryskind and the Gershwins.

Morrie Ryskind was born in New York City on October 20, 1895, and was educated at Columbia University. His initial entry into the theatre was in 1922 when he contributed sketches and lyrics to the revue *The Forty-Niners*. This was followed by material for the first *Garrick Gaieties* and for a number of other musicals of the period. After a long sojourn in Hollywood, he returned to the theatre in 1940 with the book for the Irving Berlin musical *Louisiana Purchase*.

During his tenure in Hollywood, he worked on numerous screenplays, among them: *The Cocoanuts; Animal Crackers; A Night at the Opera; Rhythm on the Range; Anything Goes; My Man Godfrey; Stage Door; Penny Serenade; Room Service; Claudia;* and *Where Do We Go From Here?*

His published works include *Unaccustomed As I Am*, a collection of light verse, and *The Diary of an Ex-President*.

(NOTE: George and Ira Gershwin, composer and lyricist of *Of Thee I Sing*, are discussed in the section devoted to *Porgy and Bess*.)

PORGY AND BESS

A towering work of the American musical theatre, *Porgy and Bess* had its premiere at the Alvin Theatre, New York, on October 10, 1935, and the occasion was a momentous one. Broadway had never seen or heard anything quite like it before; for here was an authentic folk opera produced by a Broadway management for a regular engagement in a standard playhouse. Even its press coverage was somewhat unique: each of the major metropolitan newspapers dispatched two critics, drama and music, to report on the event. By and large, the battery of drama observers offered their generous praise, but the music division was somewhat less enthusiastic. Yet, there was vindication ahead; for over the years (after the original production had closed following 124 performances), *Porgy and Bess* transcended its initial status as merely "a highly significant contribution to the American theatre" and became entrenched as a native cultural work of the first magnitude. With its eloquent score by George Gershwin, now considered by most music authorities as his masterwork, and its dramatic and moving legend of teeming Catfish Row, its people and a time past, *Porgy and Bess* now ranks with the major musical stage creations of the twentieth century.

It all began with the publication in 1925 of DuBose Heyward's novel, *Porgy*. Heyward, who was born in Charleston, South Carolina, was an accomplished poet and writer, known and admired for his sympathetic and perceptive interpretations of Southern Negro life. But long before he made up his mind to become a writer, Heyward had watched a crippled Negro beggar (named Samuel Smalls) who drove about the streets of Charleston behind an odoriferous billygoat. The beggar, the prototype of Porgy, set stirring in his mind the desire to put down on paper what he knew of the lives of Charleston's Negroes. This was to eventuate in *Porgy,* his novel of life on Catfish Row, and it was written with such "insight and understanding" that reviewers outdid each other in superlatives.

The inevitable next step was to dramatize *Porgy.* With his wife Dorothy (a playwright whom he married in 1923), Heyward fashioned the novel into stage terms. Produced by the Theatre Guild in 1927, it ran for 367 performances and was lauded as one of the first dramatic works of stature about American Negro life. (A year earlier, Paul Green's *In Abraham's Bosom* had also moved in this direction and was the recipient of a Pulitzer Prize.)

It has frequently been chronicled that George Gershwin first became interested in the property as a potential opera in 1926. Immediately after reading the novel, supposedly, he contacted DuBose Heyward and registered his proposal only to discover that the Heywards already had embarked on a dramatization. A musical version would have to wait. In the meantime, Gershwin proceeded to various other commitments. Finally, after word had leaked out that the Theatre Guild was interested in engaging Jerome Kern and Oscar Hammerstein II (who successfully had collaborated on *Show Boat*) to convert the play to the musical stage (as a vehicle for, of all people, Al Jolson), Gershwin agreed with Heyward to start immediate work on the project.

However, Norman Nadel, in his book *A Pictorial History of the Theatre Guild,* offers a different view of the evolution of the musical: "Not widely known is the fact that it was Warren P. Munsell, business manager of the Guild at the time, who conceived the idea of making *Porgy* into an opera and talked George Gershwin and his brother Ira into doing it." Whichever version one prefers, the historic fact remains that DuBose Heyward (librettist and co-lyricist), Ira Gershwin (co-lyricist) and George Gershwin (composer) ultimately were to unite to create *Porgy and Bess.*

The collaboration in itself was somewhat unusual; for it was largely done through the mail, with Heyward in South Carolina and the Gershwins ensconced in New York. Since the milieu of the play was rather remote from the environs of his accustomed Broadway, the composer did spend seven weeks on Folly Beach, off the coast of South Carolina, where he steeped himself in the life, lore and music of the Gullah Negroes.

It took Gershwin eleven months to compose the score, another nine months to do the orchestrations, a chore that he refused to entrust to a professional orchestrator, as invariably is done in the Broadway theatre.

After its New York engagement, *Porgy and Bess* toured for about three months; then the musical lithograph of life on Catfish Row seemed to have come to an end. But it was as irrepressible as its denizens and in 1942 it was resuscitated with enormous success. By this time, the music critics had changed their tune: this, they finally acknowledged, was "an American classic, a glorious achievement of our lyric theatre." The revival remained in New York for eight months, then made a tour of twenty-six cities. Subsequently, the folk opera was performed in many languages and in leading opera houses and theatres in other parts of the world, including Russia where it is said that the composer Dimitri Shostakovich called it "magnificent," comparing the work to "Borodin, Rimsky-Korsakov and Mussorgsky."

In 1952, a new production, brilliantly directed by Robert Breen and with Leontyne Price, LeVern Hutcherson and Cab Calloway among its principals, was sent by the U. S. Department of State on the first of several remarkably successful international goodwill tours. In 1953, between tours, the production settled in at the Ziegfeld Theatre, New York, for 312 performances.

A film version of *Porgy and Bess* was released in 1959. Produced by Samuel Goldwyn and directed by Otto Preminger, the protagonists of Catfish Row were portrayed by Sidney Poitier, Dorothy Dandridge, Sammy Davis, Jr., Pearl Bailey, and Diahann Carroll.

Curiously, though it toured extensively throughout the country and abroad, *Porgy and Bess* was not seen in Charleston, the city of its birth, until June 1970, when it was produced as the major event of South Carolina's tricentennial celebration. Presented under the auspices of the Charleston Symphony Association and directed by Ella Gerber (who had been associated with the 1952 Robert Breen production), *Porgy and Bess* was jubilantly embraced at its belated homecoming.

DuBose Heyward (1885–1940) attended public schools in Charleston, but left high school after one year in order to help support his family. One of the very first jobs he had, at an impressionable age, was checking cotton on the Charleston docks. It was here that he observed and learned to understand the waterfront Negroes, whom he later wrote about in *Porgy*.

By the early twenties, Heyward had become a successful insurance agent in Charleston. He spent his summers writing poetry and in 1922 helped to organize the Poetry Society of South Carolina. In the same year, he published a book of verse, *Carolina Chansons*, written with Hervey Allen who later gained fame as the author of *Anthony Adverse*. Shortly after his marriage to the former Dorothy

Kuhns, Heyward sold his insurance business and launched upon a full-time writing career.

Perhaps his most emphatic success after *Porgy* was the novel, *Mamba's Daughters*, which he later dramatized in collaboration with his wife. Presented at the Empire Theatre, New York, in 1939, it provided singer Ethel Waters with her first starring role in a drama.

Heyward's other published works include: *Skylines and Horizons; Half-Pint Flask; Jasbo Brown and Selected Poems; Peter Ashley;* and *Star Spangled Virgin*.

A titan among modern composers, *George Gershwin* was born in Brooklyn, New York, in 1898. He began playing the piano at a very early age and at fifteen took a job plugging songs for a Tin Pan Alley music publisher. He soon began to write popular songs and when he was eighteen one of his melodies was interpolated into the Sigmund Romberg score for *The Passing Show of 1916*.

Max Dreyfus, a partner in the influential music publishing house, T. B. Harms, became interested in the young Gershwin and engaged him as a staff composer. His songs now were being sung on stage with greater frequency; and in 1919, Al Jolson inserted Gershwin's "Swanee" into *Sinbad*, a musical comedy then running at the Winter Garden Theatre. The song (with lyrics by Irving Caesar) became an instantaneous hit and sold millions of copies of sheet music and phonograph records. It also became a permanent item in Jolson's lifelong repertoire.

During that same year, Gershwin composed his first complete score for a Broadway musical, *La La Lucille*. This was followed by his music for five sequential editions of *George White's Scandals*, beginning with the 1920 revue that entertained Broadway audiences for 318 performances.

From then on, Gershwin scores were in constant demand and his music was performed in a galaxy of Broadway shows, including, among others: *Lady, Be Good!* (1924); *Tip Toes* (1925); *Song of the Flame* (1925); *Oh, Kay!* (1926); *Funny Face* (1927); *Rosalie* (1928); *Show Girl* (1929); *Strike Up the Band* (1930); *Girl Crazy* (1930); *Of Thee I Sing* (1931); *Pardon My English* (1933); *Let 'Em Eat Cake* (1933); and his final show, *Porgy and Bess*.

Although he continued to write popular music, he became interested in serious composition and, after studying under Rubin Goldmark, began to produce works illustrating his belief in jazz "as an American folk music [that] can be made the basis of serious symphonic works of lasting value." A theory he was to put to practice when he revolutionized the concert field with *Rhapsody in Blue*, introduced by Paul Whiteman at Aeolian Hall, New York City, on February 12, 1924. It was the first of his several large instrumental works in the jazz idiom that were to be performed in international concert halls and brought him a new eminence as a composer. Others that followed: the tone poem, *An American in Paris; Concerto in F; Cuban Overture;* the *Piano Preludes;* and the *Second Rhapsody.*

Gershwin, who died in Hollywood in 1937, also composed for motion pictures; and two posthumous films celebrated his life (*Rhapsody in Blue*) and music (*An American in Paris,* winner of eight 1951 Academy Awards).

In 1973, to commemorate the seventy-fifth anniversary of the birth of the great composer, a postage stamp was issued bearing his likeness and the three characters immortalized in his masterwork: Porgy, Bess and Sportin' Life.

Ira Gershwin, the first lyricist ever to be awarded the Pulitzer Prize (*Of Thee I Sing,* 1932), was born in New York City on December 6, 1896. While attending the College of the City of New York, he began contributing "droll quatrains and comments" to several popular newspaper columns. Afterwards, he was to sell humorous pieces and verses to various periodicals.

Eventually, he was to turn to lyric writing, using the pseudonym of Arthur Francis so as not to capitalize on his brother's emerging fame in the theatre. As "Arthur Francis," he contributed lyrics to several musicals, the most successful being *Two Little Girls in Blue* (with music by Vincent Youmans) presented in 1921.

With the 1924 production of *Be Yourself,* he used his own name professionally for the first time. As he explains it in his book, *Lyrics on Several Occasions:* "In 1924, I dropped Arthur Francis. He was beginning to be confused with lyricist Arthur Jackson; also I'd been made aware that there was an English lyricist named Arthur Francis. Besides, all who knew me, knew me as a Gershwin anyway."

The famed Gershwin collaboration, which was to last until the composer's untimely death, officially began with a song written for Nora Bayes in *Ladies First,* but it wasn't really established until 1924 when they provided the words and music for *Lady, Be Good!* With Fred and Adele Astaire as stars, the show ran for 184 performances and was the Gershwins' first joint hit. Thereafter, Gershwin tunes always were embellished with Ira's lyrics, although the latter occasionally worked with other composers in the theatre or in films: Vernon Duke, Jerome Kern, Harold Arlen, Arthur Schwartz, among them.

Disconsolate after the death of his brother, he did not write for the theatre again until he was persuaded by producer Sam H. Harris and playwright Moss Hart to do the lyrics for the Kurt Weill score for *Lady in the Dark.* Opening on January 23, 1941 (with an exceptional cast headed by Gertrude Lawrence, Danny Kaye, Victor Mature, Macdonald Carey and Bert Lytell), it became one of the musical landmarks of the forties and reaffirmed Ira Gershwin's position as one of the most distinguished lyricists of his time.

Equally sought after by Hollywood, Ira Gershwin's lyrics have brightened almost a score of films, notably: *Shall We Dance; A Damsel in Distress; The Goldwyn Follies; Cover Girl; The Barkleys of Broadway; An American in Paris;* and *A Star Is Born.*

ONE TOUCH OF VENUS

By some measure of alchemy, the turbulent war years produced some of Broadway's brightest musicals and one of the most incandescent was *One Touch of Venus,* which opened at the Imperial Theatre on October 7, 1943. With book and lyrics by two of America's foremost humorists, S. J. Perelman and Ogden Nash, and an exceptional score by Kurt Weill, it was greeted as "a shining delight —a musical comedy hit of major proportions [that] comes at a time when something fresh and original is sorely needed in the theatre." It also was noted that "Kurt Weill has composed his finest score since *The Threepenny Opera,* [and] there is a Gilbert and Sullivan flavor to the libretto and the lyrics—all the collaborators have worked magnificently and imaginatively to give the season its first resounding hit." The show ran for 567 performances and over the years has enjoyed frequent revivals in summer theatres and musical tents.

One Touch of Venus also provided Mary Martin with her first starring role on Broadway and she was radiant as Venus. A native of Weatherford, Texas, Miss Martin had appeared on radio and in nightclubs before coming to Broadway in 1938 with a comparatively minor role in *Leave It To Me.* But it was her captivating rendition of Cole Porter's "My Heart Belongs to Daddy" that brought down the house and took center stage away from such musical stalwarts as William Gaxton, Victor Moore, Tamara and Sophie Tucker. After making one of the most dazzling debuts in Broadway history, she sped to Hollywood and films; but in 1943, she was lured back to the stage by *One Touch of Venus* and has remained ever since one of the theatre's most glowing stars.

S. J. Perelman was born in Brooklyn, New York, in 1904. After graduating from Brown University, he wrote for the magazine *Judge* and, later, *College Humor.* Since 1934, he has been a frequent contributor of humorous material to *The New Yorker* and other periodicals.

In 1931, Mr. Perelman provided sketches for the musical revue, *The Third Little Show,* which starred Beatrice Lillie and Ernest Truex. The following year, he collaborated with Robert MacGunigle on the sketches for *Walk a Little Faster,* once again with Miss Lillie at the helm of the comedy department, aided and abetted by the team of Bobby Clark and Paul McCullough.

Among his other works for the theatre are two plays written in collaboration with his wife, Laura Perelman: *All Good Americans* (1933) and *The Night Before Christmas* (1941). His impish comedy, *The Beauty Part,* with Bert Lahr, Alice Ghostley and other expert *farceurs* playing an assortment of roles, added to the merriment of the 1962–1963 Broadway season. He has authored many screenplays, most notably (with James Poe and John Farrow) *Around the World in Eighty Days,* for which he received the 1956 New York Film Critics Award and the Hollywood Academy Award. His humor also has brightened a number of television presentations, and he was the last librettist to work with Cole Porter, having written the book for the composer's final score, a musical version of *Aladdin,* televised nationally in 1958.

S. J. Perelman's published works include: *Dawn Ginsbergh's Revenge; Parlor, Bedlam, and Bath; Strictly from Hunger; Look Who's Talking!; Crazy Like a Fox; The Dream Department; Keep It Crisp; Acres and Pains; The Best of S. J. Perelman; Westward Ha!; Listen to the Mocking Bird; The Swiss Family Perelman; The Ill-Tempered Clavichord; Perelman's Home Companion; The Road to Miltown;* and *The Rising Gorge.*

Ogden Nash (1902–1971), whose droll verses with their unconventional rhymes made him the country's best-known creator of humorous poetry, was born in Rye, New York. He attended St. George's School in Newport, Rhode Island, and then spent one year at Harvard University before he had to drop out to earn a living. After coming to New York, he worked briefly on Wall Street as a bond salesman; but in two years, he said, he sold one bond—to his grandmother. He next wrote copy for an advertising agency, then gravitated to the advertising staff of a publishing house. On the side, he attempted to write serious poetry. He later declared, "I wrote sonnets about beauty and truth, eternity, poignant pain. That was what the people I read wrote about, too—Keats, Shelley, Byron, the classical English poets."

Finally, however, he decided that he had better "laugh at myself before anyone laughed at me," and with that he turned to humorous verse. As one critic observed after his death: "Much of Ogden Nash's reputation was based on his long, straggling lines of wildly irregular length, often capped with extravagantly misspelled words to create weird rhymes, but they were lines that, on close examination, revealed a carefully thought-out metrical scheme and a kind of relentless logic."

In addition to being a droll and witty versifier, Ogden Nash was "an ingenious critic of frailty and absurdity [and] a philosopher, albeit a laughing one, [who wrote of the] vicissitudes and eccentricities of domestic life as they affected an apparently gentle, somewhat bewildered man."

A prolific writer, Nash published numerous volumes of wit and satire and wrote regularly for *The New Yorker* and other publications. He also appeared frequently on television panel shows and authored the verses set to Saint-Saëns' *Carnival of the Animals,* Prokofiev's *Peter and the Wolf* and Dukas' *The Sorcerer's Apprentice.* In May 1973, *Nash at Nine,* described as a "wordsical" with verses and lyrics by Ogden Nash and music by Milton Rosenstock, was presented at the Helen Hayes Theatre, New York.

A virtuoso composer, *Kurt Weill* (1900–1950) was born in Dessau, Germany. Influenced by his father, a cantor, he began to compose while still in primary school. At the age of eighteen, he was sent to Berlin to study with Engelbert Humperdinck, the noted composer of *Hänsel und Gretel.* After serving as a director of a provincial opera company, he returned to Berlin, this time to study with the pianist-composer Ferruccio Busoni who would teach him "form, technique, classical tradition, but not formulate or influence his style." He continued his studies until 1924, meanwhile composing symphonies, operas and chamber music—music which, although in the classical tradition, was influenced occasionally by the American jazz idiom.

It was during this period that a Russian company visited Berlin and commissioned him to do a children's ballet; and it was in the composition of this work that he adapted his style to the theatre, the medium through which he was to attain eventual fame.

His first opera (with a text by Georg Kaiser) was *The Protagonist,* produced by the Dresden State Opera in 1926. After composing two other operas, *The Royal Palace* and *The Czar Has Himself Photographed,* Weill joined forces with Bertolt Brecht and together they created *The Threepenny Opera* (*Die Dreigroschenoper*). Adapted from John Gay's eighteenth century *The Beggar's Opera,* the Weill-Brecht collaboration opened in Berlin on August 28, 1928. It was an outstanding success; and before the Berlin run had ended, the work had been mounted in almost every major city in Germany as well as in many foreign countries. In 1933, it came to Broadway but apparently theatregoers were not quite prepared for the sardonic and trenchant musical, for it lasted a mere twelve performances. However, in a new English-language adaptation by Marc Blitzstein, *The Threepenny Opera* was to be an Off-Broadway sensation of the 1950s, playing at the Theatre de Lys for 2,611 performances.

Weill wrote several other theatre pieces with Brecht, including *The Rise and Fall of the City of Mahagonny.* In 1933, he collaborated again with Georg Kaiser on *The Silver Lake* and it incurred the wrath of the rising Nazi regime, prompting an official ban on all the composer's works in Germany. Soon after, he and his wife, singer-actress Lotte Lenya, left Germany and went to Paris, then London.

In 1935, the composer was brought to the United States by Max Reinhardt to write the music for his production of Franz Werfel's biblical spectacle, *The Eternal Road.* Due to production delays, however, his first American show was to be *Johnny Johnson,* presented by the Group Theatre in 1936.

Subsequently, he was to compose the scores for the following Broadway musicals: *Knickerbocker Holiday* (1938); *Lady in the Dark* (1941); *One Touch of Venus* (1943); *The Firebrand of Florence* (1945); *Street Scene* (1947); *Love Life* (1948); and *Lost in the Stars* (1949).

Among the distinguished authors who furnished the books and lyrics for the aforementioned productions are: Paul Green, Maxwell Anderson, Moss Hart, Ira Gershwin, Edwin Justus Mayer, Elmer Rice, Langston Hughes and Alan Jay Lerner.

Kurt Weill, who became an American citizen in 1943, also wrote music for several motion pictures and (with Arnold Sundgaard) the folk opera, *Down in the Valley.*

In 1941, the drama critic of *The New York Times* said of Weill: "He is not a song writer but a composer of organic music that can bind the separate elements of a production and turn the underlying motive into song."

BRIGADOON

A musical as enchanting as the village and people it celebrates in story and song, *Brigadoon* was one of the major successes of the 1940s. Opening on March 13, 1947, it was joyfully received by New York's leading drama critics. Howard Barnes wrote in the *New York Herald Tribune* that "it is a musical fantasy of rare delight and distinction, a jubilant and brilliantly integrated show." This was an opinion shared by Brooks Atkinson who stated that "all of the arts of the theatre have been woven into a single pattern of excitement." The peroration perhaps was delivered by Richard Watts, Jr., in his coverage in the *New York Post* of the Alan Jay Lerner–Frederick Loewe musical. "*Brigadoon* is a brilliant and beautiful show with imagination, taste, and distinction. . . . The treatment of the fable is sensitive, gracefully emotional and romantically effective in literate and intelligent fashion."

Brigadoon delighted Broadway theatregoers for 581 performances and was the second musical ever to win a New York Drama Critics'

Circle Award (1946–1947). (The first musical to win the critics' citation was the previous season's *Carousel.*)

The popularity of *Brigadoon* was not confined to the United States: a British production opened at His Majesty's Theatre on April 14, 1949, and held court there for 685 performances.

A film version of *Brigadoon* was released in 1954. It was directed by Vincente Minnelli and co-starred Gene Kelly, Van Johnson and Cyd Charisse.

Alan Jay Lerner, author of the book and lyrics, was born in New York City on August 31, 1918. He was educated in England and at Choate and Harvard University. While at Harvard, he contributed material to two Hasty Pudding Shows and after graduation wrote for radio.

His meeting with the Vienna-born composer, *Frederick Loewe,* proved to be a providential occasion; for they were destined to become one of the most renowned teams in the history of the American musical theatre.

Their first joint effort was *The Life of the Party,* presented in Detroit in 1942. In the following year, they made their Broadway debut as a team with the musical *What's Up?* Although its engagement was comparatively brief, it clearly indicated promise for Lerner and Loewe and they came to near-fulfillment with the charming but surprisingly underrated *The Day Before Spring* (1945).

True and unqualified success was to come in 1947 with the memorable production of *Brigadoon.* This was followed by *Paint Your Wagon* (1951); the record-breaking *My Fair Lady* (1956); and *Camelot* (1960).

In 1958, the magic of Lerner and Loewe was transferred to the screen with one of the most honored films of all time, *Gigi.* Named the best picture of the year, it received a total of nine Academy Awards, including one for Mr. Lerner's screenplay and for the team's title song.

In addition to his work with Frederick Loewe, Alan Jay Lerner wrote the book and lyrics for Kurt Weill's *Love Life* (1948); *On a Clear Day You Can See Forever* (with music by Burton Lane, 1965); and *Coco* (with music by André Previn). With the incantatory Katharine Hepburn making her musical stage debut as the legendary French *couturière,* Gabrielle Chanel, *Coco* was an outstanding success of the 1969–1970 Broadway season. Mr. Lerner also wrote the story and screenplay for *An American in Paris,* which brought him his first Hollywood Academy Award in 1951.

The team of Lerner and Loewe was recently reunited when the composer came out of retirement to provide the score for Lerner's lyrics and screenplay for a musical film based on Antoine de Saint-Exupéry's *The Little Prince.* And as this is being written, they are preparing a stage adaptation of their award-winning screen musical, *Gigi,* which is scheduled to open in Los Angeles in July 1973, to be followed by a tour and, subsequently, Broadway.

KISS ME, KATE

One of the most exquisitely crafted landmarks of the American musical theatre, *Kiss Me, Kate,* at its opening on December 30, 1948, was hailed by Brooks Atkinson of *The New York Times* as "a blissfully enjoyable musical show . . . the best musical comedy of the season." That judgment was amplified by other critics who found it a "triumphant [work] lavishly rich in entertainment [and] a smash hit of epic proportions." The latter was a prophetic statement: the gilt-edged musical ran for 1,077 performances on Broadway; won an Antoinette Perry (Tony) Award and a 1949 Page One Award of the American Newspaper Guild; toured nationally; and, since its original opening, has been frequently revived, probably more extensively (especially abroad) than any other American musical of the period.

Kiss Me, Kate not only was an outstanding box-office success, but it also represented the American musical stage in its most polished and glittering form. Yet, its appeal has been almost worldwide as indicated by the vast amount of foreign productions. In addition to a 400-performance engagement in London (Coliseum; March 8, 1951), it has brightened stages in dozens of countries, ranging from Japan to Poland, where it was the first American musical ever to be presented, achieving a record-breaking run of more than 200 performances. To this day, it remains a musical staple of both legitimate theatres and opera houses throughout Germany. In December 1970, it was a major presentation of England's celebrated Sadler's Wells Opera Company.

The passing decades have not dimmed its luster. As Howard Taubman wrote in his book, *The Making of the American Theatre:* "*Kiss Me, Kate* had an elegance, wit and distinction of style that no musical of its time matched. . . . Let us grant that Shakespeare is always a powerful asset, but let us credit Sam and Bella Spewack with making brilliant use of *The Taming of the Shrew* in their fable of actors on the road."

As for the score, it was best described by David Ewen in his entertaining account, *The Story of America's Musical Theatre:* "Cole Porter's lyrics and melodies are of the palpitant present, just as Shakespeare's humor and poetry belong to the past. But there is never a feeling of incongruity. The score—the best of Porter's Broadway career, one of the best, indeed, in all Broadway history—was in the composer's best sophisticated, satirical or sensual styles. . . ."

In their introduction to the original edition of *Kiss Me, Kate,* the coauthors of the book, Samuel and Bella Spewack, described it as "a musical love story of the eternal serio-comic battle of male and female played against the events of an opening night of the tryout of a musical version of Shakespeare's *The Taming of the Shrew* at Ford's Theatre in Baltimore. . . . The musical is a play within a play, the personal story paralleling Shakespeare's *Shrew,* and at certain points the action of one flows right into the action of the other."

To further quote from their enlightening introduction: "The writing of a musical comedy is a craft in itself, just as writing a play or a screenplay is. But they all have three things in common: situation, dialogue, and hard work." And unlike the earlier musical comedies with their banal books and stereotype characters, the modern musical cannot revolve around just anything. "It must not only be about something; it must also be entertaining. Unlike the straight play, this form is elastic—provided it can be made to serve the ear and the eye."

In *Kiss Me, Kate,* Cole Porter's songs handsomely served the story, especially in Shakespeare's *Shrew,* the play within the play. "We have always tried to let a song tell part of the story where it could do so, and we have always been willing to cut large passages of book, as certainly we did in *Kiss Me, Kate*. The spoken word in a musical comedy must compete with music, dance, color, and movement. When a spoken scene does compete successfully with these powerfully appealing elements, the writers can take pride in their craftsmanship. But anyone writing the book for a musical must be prepared to cut—and cut—and cut. There is no room for a writer's love of his own words. 'Love' lingers longest in lyrics."

As an example, "Lyrically the song 'Why Can't You Behave?' has tragic implications, but the scene that led to it was meant to be funny. By the time of the Philadelphia tryout, the parts of Lois and Bill contained only the essentials for plot and song cues. We could afford to be ruthless in cutting our own lines, but we hated to cut Shakespeare, and we hated to cut Porter.

"[Nonetheless,] in adapting *The Shrew* for the play within the play, it was necessary to drop the entire opening. From the body of the piece it was necessary to drop the servants of Lucentio's and Petruchio's ménage, as well as the scene with the Pedant. Here and there among the omitted passages were lines that we wanted to keep, and these we blithely distributed to the characters that remained. They came in handy when, during rehearsal, an actor would say: 'I feel here I need another line,' or 'I'd like a handle for this speech.'"

The writing team of *Samuel* and *Bella Spewack* was firmly established in 1932 with the successful production of *Clear All Wires.* How did their collaboration start? As Mrs. Spewack in a moving remembrance wrote to her husband published in the *Dramatists Guild Quarterly* after his death in 1971: "I suggested after a series of long walks that we be partners. We were then nineteen. For some reason, you misconstrued that and proposed marriage. All I had in mind was to start a magazine for the Pullman people to distribute free to its riders. We had railroads then.

"You had a steady job on the *New York World,* and I an unsteady and frequently payless job on the *New York Call.* I wrote short stories, all tragic or fantasy which sold from time to time but not enough to support my mother and half-brother. You always accused me of being stage-struck, Sam. I never wanted to act, but writing for the theatre was something else. I started writing one-act plays, and then three-acters later in Berlin.

"Our actual play collaboration didn't really take hold until after our return to the United States after four years of Moscow and Berlin. [NOTE: Mrs. Spewack was assistant to her husband who represented the *New York World* as foreign correspondent in Russia and Germany from 1922 to 1926.] We were broke. That's when you collaborated and took over with your brand of philosophical and political comedy, but it met with the same reaction as my unmitigated tragedies: not commercial, not box-office. So the various agents told us. That's when I picked up our plays and tackled theatrical offices myself."

Once Mrs. Spewack handled the reins, things began to happen and during the course of their collaboration they turned out a dozen plays. Among them: *Spring Song* (1934); *Boy Meets Girl* (which opened in November 1935, and ran for 669 performances); *Leave It To Me* (a 1938 musical based on their comedy, *Clear All Wires,* with a score by Cole Porter); *Miss Swan Expects* (1939); *Woman Bites Dog* (1946); and *My Three Angels* (from the French of Albert Husson, 1953).

The Spewacks also collaborated on a number of screenplays including: *My Favorite Wife; Weekend at the Waldorf; Three Loves Has Nancy; The Cat and the Fiddle;* as well as doing the screen versions of several of their plays. The musical film *Kiss Me, Kate* was released in 1954.

On his own, Mr. Spewack contributed to the theatre: *Two Blind Mice* (1949); *The Golden State* (1950); *Under the Sycamore Tree* (1952); and *Once There Was a Russian* (1961). He also published novels and short stories; and during World War II, he wrote and produced for the government the highly acclaimed, full-length documentary, *The World at War.*

One of the twentieth century's outstanding creators of words and music, *Cole Porter* was born in Peru, Indiana, on June 9, 1891. His grandfather was a wealthy lumber merchant and the young Cole grew up in an ambience of luxury. His mother, Kate, supervised his early musical training, having him study the violin and, later, the piano.

In 1909, he entered Yale and during his tenure there wrote a number of football songs, two of which were to become famous: "Bingo Eli Yale" and "Bull Dog." He also was president of the Yale Glee Club and created several successful campus shows. Following his graduation in 1913, he attended Harvard Law School, but after a year he abandoned the idea of pursuing law and transferred to the School of Music at Harvard.

His first Broadway musical was *See America First* which had a fleeting engagement in 1916. After an absence of several years, he was represented again on the New York stage with songs for the revue *Hitchy-Koo of 1919*. He next contributed material to the *Greenwich Village Follies of 1924*. But it was the 1928 musical, *Paris,* that firmly established him as the grand sophisticate of songwriters.

The Porter touch highlighted many shows after that significant year. In addition to *Kiss Me, Kate,* there were: *Fifty Million Frenchmen* (1929); *The New Yorkers* (1930); *Gay Divorcée* (1932); *Nymph Errant* (1933); *Anything Goes* (1934); *Jubilee* (1935); *Red, Hot and Blue!* (1936); *You Never Know* (1938); *Leave It To Me* (1938); *Panama Hattie* (1940); *Let's Face It* (1941); *Something for the Boys* (1943); *Mexican Hayride* (1944); *Seven Lively Arts* (1944); *Around the World in Eighty Days* (1946); *Can-Can* (1953); and *Silk Stockings* (1955).

Cole Porter also had the distinction of closing two successive decades with his musicals. *Wake Up and Dream* opened on December 30, 1929, and *Du Barry Was a Lady* was the final musical to be presented in the thirties (December 6, 1939).

He also contributed the scores to many films, notably: *Born to Dance; Rosalie; Broadway Melody of 1940; The Pirate; High Society;* and *Les Girls.*

His death in 1964 left an enormous void in the realm of the American musical theatre.

WEST SIDE STORY

Few musicals of the fifties created as much theatrical excitement as did *West Side Story* when it had its premiere at the Winter Garden Theatre, New York, on September 26, 1957. A timely and impassioned parallel of the Romeo and Juliet legend set to modern terms, "it came right out of urban America, out of the venom generated between races jammed festeringly together." As Brooks Atkinson described it: "Gang warfare is the material of *West Side Story,* and very little of the hideousness has been left out. But the author, composer and ballet designer are creative artists. Pooling imagination and virtuosity, they have written a profoundly moving show that is as ugly as the city jungles and also pathetic, tender and forgiving."

Richard Watts, Jr. (*New York Post*) offered the pronouncement that "*West Side Story* adds to the dramatic power of the American musical theatre," a view confirmed by other members of the press corps who added that "this was one of those rare occasions when the lyric stage has come graphically forward with a major work dealing vigorously with timely subject matters." A turbulent music drama, "Arthur Laurents' book provides an excellent framework for an extraordinary score by Leonard Bernstein, biting and tender lyrics by Stephen Sondheim, and magnificent staging by Jerome Robbins. It is a felicitous blending of all facets of the theatre." A striking collaboration, possessing a style entirely of its own, "all its elements are of the same exciting texture and unite in a really spectacular demonstration of that liveliest art, the American musical theatre."

West Side Story ran for 732 performances in New York; and in London, where it opened at Her Majesty's Theatre on December 12, 1958, it was seen for 1,040 performances.

It was the third Broadway musical to be developed from a concept by the celebrated choreographer and director Jerome Robbins. The first was *On the Town* (1944), a musical comedy expansion of his ballet, *Fancy Free;* then came *Look, Ma, I'm Dancin'!* (1948) with its cheerful satirization of some inhabitants of the ballet world. According to librettist Arthur Laurents, when Robbins initially broached the idea of a modern version of *Romeo and Juliet* to Bernstein and himself, "he envisioned Juliet as a Jewish girl, Romeo as an Italian Catholic." The locale was to be the lower East Side of Manhattan, "specifically, Allen Street for Juliet and the Capulets, Mulberry Street for Romeo and the Montagues." The original title was *East Side Story,* but as Mr. Laurents has noted: "The change represents more than a mere change in geographical direction or locale, it represents a basic change in the original conception." The final concept, with its topicality and urgency, proved to be a fortuitous one and in spite of its grim subject matter and background, *West Side Story* had a glowing lyricism that to this day remains undiminished.

A film version of *West Side Story* was released in 1961 and it was the recipient of ten Academy Awards, including the laurel for the best picture of the year.

Arthur Laurents, author of the book for *West Side Story,* was born in New York City on July 14, 1918. Educated at Cornell University, he first came to prominence in the theatre in 1945 with his provocative war drama, *Home of the Brave*. It won for him the Sidney Howard Award (shared with Garson Kanin for *Born Yesterday*) and later was made into a motion picture that received international acclaim.

This was followed by *Heartsong* (1947); *The Bird Cage* (starring Melvyn Douglas, 1950); and *The Time of the Cuckoo,* a leading success of the 1952–1953 Broadway season with Shirley Booth outstanding as a repressed American secretary who spends a somewhat eventful holiday at a *pensione* in Venice. The play subsequently was filmed as *Summertime,* starring Katharine Hepburn and Rossano Brazzi.

Mr. Laurents' other Broadway plays include *A Clearing in the Woods* (1957) and *Invitation to a March,* which he also directed. Presented by the Theatre Guild on October 29, 1960, it had in its cast: Celeste Holm, Eileen Heckart, Jane Fonda, James MacArthur and Richard Derr.

West Side Story represents Mr. Laurents' first musical. Thereafter, he authored the books for *Gypsy* (reuniting him with lyricist Stephen Sondheim and director-choreographer Jerome Robbins, 1959); *Anyone Can Whistle* (with music and lyrics by Mr. Sondheim, 1964); and *Do I Hear a Waltz?* (based on *The Time of the Cuckoo,* with music by Richard Rodgers, lyrics by Mr. Sondheim, 1965); and *Hallelujah, Baby!* (music by Jule Styne, lyrics by Betty Comden and Adolph Green: winner of the Antoinette Perry [Tony] Award for best musical of the 1967–1968 season).

In 1962, Mr. Laurents handled the direction for *I Can Get It for You Wholesale,* the Jerome Weidman–Harold Rome musical that served as a springboard to stardom for two little-known performers, Barbra Streisand and Elliott Gould.

In addition to his work for the theatre, Arthur Laurents is the author of a number of screenplays, particularly, *Rope; Caught; Bonjour Tristesse;* and *Anastasia.*

Described by *Time* magazine as a "Renaissance Man [who] in an age of specialization refuses to stay put in any cultural pigeonhole," *Leonard Bernstein* is one of the world's most eminent conductors, a front-rank composer of serious music, pianist, author, lecturer, teacher, television personality and the creator of the scores for four Broadway musicals: *On the Town; Wonderful Town* (1953); *Candide* (1956); and *West Side Story.*

Leonard Bernstein was born in Lawrence, Massachusetts, on August 25, 1918. From the Boston Latin School, he went on to Harvard, where he majored in music. At the suggestion of Dimitri Mitropoulos, he turned to the study of conducting, first with Fritz Reiner at the Curtis Institute of Music in Philadelphia, then with Serge Koussevitzky at the Berkshire Music Center, Tanglewood, Massachusetts.

In 1943, he rocketed to fame, when as an assistant conductor of the New York Philharmonic, he was called in at short notice to take over for the ailing conductor Bruno Walter. His performance electrified the audience and the next day's press coverage exceeded that bestowed on most musical events.

His growing renown as guest conductor of some of the nation's finest orchestras brought him offers from abroad; and in 1946, he began the first of a series of many international tours. In 1958, he was appointed Music Director of the New York Philharmonic, serving in this post until 1969 when he was given the lifetime title of Laureate Conductor.

In 1953, he made his operatic debut as the first American-born conductor to conduct at La Scala in Milan, Italy. Since then, he frequently has appeared at other leading opera houses of the world and in 1972 conducted the premiere performance of the Metropolitan Opera's widely acclaimed new production of *Carmen,* with Marilyn Horne in the title role.

As a composer, Bernstein has been successful in ballet, in symphonic composition (*Jeremiah; The Age of Anxiety;* and the *Kaddish Symphony*), in songs, choral and chamber works and, of course, in the musical theatre.

In addition to the aforementioned Broadway musicals, he also composed the incidental music for *Peter Pan* (1950); *The Lark* (1955); and Katharine Cornell's 1958 production of *The First-born.* For films, he did the score for the Academy Award winning *On the Waterfront.*

Mass, one of the composer's most recent works, was specially commissioned for the opening of the John F. Kennedy Center for the Performing Arts, Washington, D.C. (September 1971).

Charismatic as well as supremely talented, Leonard Bernstein has made more than one hundred recordings of classical music, has won countless awards and has been decorated by at least a half-dozen foreign countries.

Since 1957, when he wrote the lyrics for *West Side Story, Stephen Sondheim* has become one of the foremost figures in the American musical theatre and details of his career are given in the passage devoted to *Company.*

GYPSY

Gypsy, the musical celebration of the early life of Gypsy Rose Lee, from small-time vaudeville performer to her accession as Queen of Burlesque, opened at the Broadway Theatre, New York, on May

21, 1959, and promptly became the season's most sought-after ticket. Based on the memoirs of Gypsy Rose Lee, it reunited three of the gifted craftsmen who created *West Side Story;* Arthur Laurents (book), Stephen Sondheim (lyrics) and Jerome Robbins, whose staging and choreography once again vividly demonstrated his extraordinary versatility. Set to one of Jule Styne's finest theatre scores, *Gypsy* was lauded by Walter Kerr as, "The best damn musical I've seen in years!" Additional praise flowed from other journalistic quarters: "Delightfully entertaining;" a musical play that is both "touching and wonderfully funny [and certain to be] a walloping smash hit." That it was; and *Gypsy* continued to entertain Broadway audiences for 702 performances.

With its sharp and incisive book by Laurents and synchronous songs by Sondheim and Styne, *Gypsy* furnished Ethel Merman with her strongest and most provocative role of a remarkable career that extended back to 1930 when she first mesmerized Broadway with her stentorian voice and winningly forthright personality in the Gershwin musical, *Girl Crazy*. It was written of her performance: "Miss Merman, in the part of Madame Rose, mother of Gypsy, not only lines out her songs with that magnetism and splendid clarion voice that are hers alone, she moreover gives startling realism to a character that is both engaging and terrifying, a kind of archetypical stage mother. One moment Miss Merman is charming the audience with robust good humor, the next she is chilling it with the accuracy of her portrait, and her final number [the soliloquy, 'Rose's Turn'] will long be remembered as a climax unique in the theatre."

A film version of *Gypsy* was released in 1962. It was directed by Mervyn LeRoy and co-starred Rosalind Russell, Natalie Wood and Karl Malden.

After more than a decade, *Gypsy* remains as vibrant and entertaining a musical as ever; and as this is being written, it is about to conquer the stage again: this time in London (May 1973), with Angela Lansbury as the indomitable Madame Rose.

Composer *Jule Styne* was born in London on December 31, 1905. His family came to the United States and settled in Chicago, where he began his musical training at an early age. A scholarship brought him to the Chicago College of Music and there he specialized in piano study. Eschewing serious music, he later organized a dance band that performed in various Chicago night spots and eventually brought him to the attention of Hollywood, where in the ensuing years he was to write the scores and collaborate on songs for more than twenty-five motion pictures. During his tenure in Hollywood, he also accumulated six Academy Award nominations and finally, in 1954, the coveted prize itself for the title song from *Three Coins in the Fountain* (lyrics by Sammy Cahn).

Mr. Styne's first sortie in the Broadway theatre took place in 1947 with the music for *High Button Shoes*. With a book by Stephen Longstreet and lyrics by Sammy Cahn, it ran for 727 performances. His success as a composer for the musical theatre assured, he thereafter returned to Broadway at frequent intervals. Succeeding productions that carried his musical imprint include: *Gentlemen Prefer Blondes* (1949); *Two on the Aisle* (1951); *Hazel Flagg* (1953); *Peter Pan* (for which he composed additional music, 1954); *Bells Are Ringing* (1956); *Say, Darling* (1958); *Gypsy* (1959); *Do Re Mi* (1960); *Subways Are for Sleeping* (1961); *Fade Out–Fade In* (1964); *Funny Girl* (1964); and the Antoinette Perry (Tony) Award winner, *Hallelujah, Baby!* (1967).

He also has functioned as a producer or co-producer for a number of Broadway presentations, among these: *Make a Wish* (1951); *Pal Joey* (1952); *In Any Language* (1952); *Will Success Spoil Rock Hunter?* (1955); and *Mr. Wonderful* (1956).

(NOTE: For comments on Arthur Laurents, see *West Side Story;* Stephen Sondheim, *Company*.)

FIDDLER ON THE ROOF

A luminous musical, *Fiddler on the Roof* not only added to the canon of great works of the American musical stage, but it also became the longest-running show in Broadway history when it played its 3,225th performance on June 17, 1972, thereby surpassing the record of the previous title-holder, *Life With Father* (3,224 performances). Based on the stories of Sholom Aleichem—the most beloved and perhaps the greatest Jewish writer and humorist of modern times—the Joseph Stein–Jerry Bock–Sheldon Harnick musical play transcended areal and language differentiations and impressively traveled its way to worldwide success. It was performed in dozens of foreign countries, recorded on forty-three different record albums in various languages and was seen by an estimated 37,500,000 people.

At its opening in 1964, *Fiddler on the Roof* was lavishly hailed by most of the press. Henry Hewes, writing in the *Saturday Review*, described it as "a remarkably effective mixture that thoroughly entertains without ever losing a sense of connection with the more painful realities that underlie its humor, its beauty, and its ritual celebrations." John Chapman, then first-night arbiter for the New York *Daily News*, termed it "one of the great works of the American musical theatre"; while his colleague Howard Taubman of *The New York Times* joyously reported that "it catches the essence of a moment in history with sentiment and radiance . . . an exceptional accomplishment."

The acclaimed presentation won innumerable awards, including the New York Drama Critics' Circle Award as best musical of 1964–1965; the Page One Award of the American Newspaper Guild; and nine Antoinette Perry (Tony) Awards, notably the citation for best musical of the year. The production also scored "bests" in four leading categories in *Variety*'s annual Poll of New York's Drama Critics; and in London, where it ran for 2,030 performances, sixteen critics named *Fiddler on the Roof* the best foreign musical of the season.

In transmitting the Sholom Aleichem stories from the printed page to the musical stage, Joseph Stein noted that ". . . the problem of adaptation was to remain true to the spirit, the feeling of Sholom Aleichem and transmute it for a contemporary audience . . . to tell the story of Tevye, his family and his community in terms which would have meaning for today."

Utilizing some of the important episodes and, of course, certain of the main characters from the progenitor's works, Mr. Stein created a fresh story that dealt with "the gradual breakdown of the traditional cultural forms and beliefs of the *shtetl,* the village community, under the buffeting of social change and hostile forces, finally leading to disintegration of that society. We decided to make this crumbling of tradition, illustrated by the daughters' love stories and other developments, the theme of our play."

To endow the story with a further significance for our times, Mr. Stein and his collaborators "brought to the foreground an element implicit in the Tevye tales . . . the hostility, the violence, the injustice practiced by a ruling majority against a weak minority. We wanted, in this, to point up the internal strength, the dignity, the humor of that people and, like minorities today, their unique talent for survival."

A film version of *Fiddler on the Roof* was released in 1971 and the original stage production closed at the Broadway Theatre on July 2, 1972, after its 3,242nd performance.

Joseph Stein (book) was born in New York City and educated at James Monroe High School, City College and Columbia University's School of Social Work. He was employed as a psychiatric social worker when he wrote his first material, in 1946, for radio's "Chamber Music Society of Lower Basin Street." Subsequent writing assignments began to crowd his slate and he was compelled to relinquish social work. In the two years that followed, Mr. Stein became a leading writer in radio and, later, television. In 1948, he began writing for the theatre, contributing sketches (written in collaboration with Will Glickman) to various revues, principally *Inside*

U.S.A. and *Lend an Ear*. Between sketches, the coauthors fashioned a comedy, *Mrs. Gibbon's Boys,* produced by George Abbott in 1949. With that fleeting experience behind them, the Messrs. Stein and Glickman rejoined the world of revue by providing material for *Alive and Kicking,* which tarried rather briefly at the Winter Garden Theatre.

In 1955, however, the team surfaced to substantial success with the book for the musical *Plain and Fancy*. This was followed by the Sammy Davis, Jr. vehicle *Mr. Wonderful* (1956) and *The Body Beautiful* (1958).

In 1959, Mr. Stein coadapted (with Robert Russell) the musical book for *Take Me Along* (from Eugene O'Neill's nostalgic comedy, *Ah, Wilderness!*) and, individually, *Juno* (derived from Sean O'Casey's modern classic, *Juno and the Paycock*). And in 1963, his comedy, *Enter Laughing* (based on Carl Reiner's autobiographical novel), established a Broadway run of 419 performances.

During the 1968–1969 season, Joseph Stein was represented on the New York stage by the book for *Zorbá* and as a co-producer of Joseph Heller's drama, *We Bombed in New Haven*.

Jerry Bock (music) and Sheldon Harnick (lyrics) first came into joint view with the 1958 production of the aforementioned *The Body Beautiful*. Although that musical hardly could be classified as a success, it was an important (and catalytical) event for the songwriting duo; for their work so impressed producer Harold Prince, his late partner, Robert Griffith, and the doyen director George Abbott that they commissioned the collaborators to take on the assignment of creating the songs and musical numbers for *Fiorello!* The 1959 presentation ran for 795 performances, garnered a New York Drama Critics' Circle Award and the Pulitzer Prize and propelled the team of Bock and Harnick to the forefront of the American musical theatre. It also was the harbinger of their most celebrated success, *Fiddler on the Roof,* and the start of their long and successful association with Harold Prince under whose managerial banner they also collaborated on *Tenderloin* (1960) and *She Loves Me* (1963).

With their 1966 Broadway musical, *The Apple Tree* (based on stories by Mark Twain, Frank R. Stockton and Jules Feiffer), Bock and Harnick entered a new phase of collaboration: in addition to creating the words and music, they also functioned as coauthors of the book.

Jerry Bock was born in New Haven, Connecticut, in 1928, raised in Flushing, New York, and attended Flushing High School (where he began his composing career) and the University of Wisconsin. He received his baptism as a "professional" composer at Camp Tamiment in the Poconos, later wrote much of the music for television's *Your Show of Shows*. He also contributed songs (with Larry

Holofcener as lyricist) to the revue *Catch a Star* and an edition of the *Ziegfeld Follies*. His first full Broadway score was written for *Mr. Wonderful* (1956).

Born in Chicago in 1924, *Sheldon Harnick* was inspired by his mother's passion for commemorating all occasions in verse and while still at grammar school picked up the thread and commenced to write poems himself, "mostly doggerel and mostly nonsense." In 1943, he entered the army and it was while in service that he first started seriously to write songs which he performed at various USO shows, sandwiching them in between his violin solos.

In 1946, he returned to Chicago and enrolled at Northwestern University where he contributed songs to the annual student musicals and doubled as a fiddle player with the show's orchestra. After graduation from Northwestern, he worked with the Compass, an improvisational group and, for a while, as a violinist with Xavier Cugat's orchestra. Then after being fired for "swaying to the left instead of the right," he headed for New York and a career as a songwriter.

Prior to teaming up with Jerry Bock, Mr. Harnick contributed his talents to *New Faces of 1952* (notably, with the number "Boston Beguine"). During this period (the 1950s), some of his other works were included in revues: *Two's Company; The Littlest Revue; Take Five; Kaleidoscope;* and *John Murray Anderson's Almanac.*

In 1970, Bock and Harnick had another Broadway success with *The Rothschilds* (based on Frederic Morton's book and with a libretto by Sherman Yellen); it ran for 507 performances.

1776

A superb musical play that depicts, in richly human terms, the men and events involved in the writing and signing of the Declaration of Independence, *1776* opened to rousing acclaim at the Forty-Sixth Street Theatre, New York, on March 16, 1969. Clive Barnes of *The New York Times* termed it "a most striking, most gripping musical [that had] style, humanity, wit and compassion." *Variety* reviewer Hobe Morrison reported: "The novel and daring idea of taking the birth of American freedom as the basis for a musical—a serious and entertaining musical—has been happily carried out in *1776*. . . . Not only in its subject matter, but in its form and technique, *1776* is unusual. It is an original, engrossing, inspiring, and frequently touching show." John Chapman proclaimed to readers of the New York *Daily News:* "This is by no means a historical tract or a sermon on the birth of this nation. It is warm, with life of its own; it is funny, it is moving . . . a libretto which works perfectly on a musical stage."

The critical verdict would have gladdened the hearts of our

Founding Fathers, particularly George Oppenheimer's statement in *Newsday:* "With *1776,* the American musical takes on new luster. This should be not only a smash hit, but in my opinion, something of an American musical milestone." He was quite right; for *1776* had 1,217 performances in New York, several national tours and won both the New York Drama Critics' Circle Award and the Antoinette Perry (Tony) Award as the season's best musical. It also garnered a Drama Desk citation for best musical book. And in London, where it opened on June 16, 1970, it received the *Plays and Players* Award as the year's best new musical.

A film version of *1776* (with virtually all of the Broadway players re-creating their original roles) was produced by Jack L. Warner and released in 1972.

Sherman Edwards, who conceived the idea for *1776,* had reportedly worked for almost a decade on the project. After he had completed his work, he met with a number of managerial rejections until it came into the hands of producer Stuart Ostrow. According to a published account: "Ostrow bought the concept for *1776.* He agreed that nothing would be done to alter the aim. But he didn't like the (original) book. Mr. Edwards agreed to call in Peter Stone, a successful screenwriter."

Mr. Stone was urged to listen "not only to the songs Edwards had written, but to a detailed account of this historical occasion and the events leading to it as Edwards had researched it." In an introduction written specially for *The Best Plays of 1968–1969,* the librettist recalls: "I was enthralled. The suspense, intrigue, the courage and compromise, the richness of the men, their vagaries, vanities and fears, the issues and convictions motivating the thirteen colonies, the factions within them, the differences between them, their individual pride and their collective heritage–all of it held me spellbound for over three hours."

Mr. Stone continues: *"1776* was conceived as entertainment. But if it is indeed entertaining, it is, I believe, more than the songs and the jokes and the theatricality that make it so–it is the surprise of discovering that our Founding Fathers were men of flesh and blood and not cardboard, that our history is fascinating–and that the events of July 4, 1776, mean more to us during these troubled times than most of us could ever imagine."

In a comprehensive historical note published in the original edition of *1776,* the authors related: "The first question we are asked by those who have seen–or read–*1776* is invariably: 'Is it true? Did it really happen that way?'

"The answer is: Yes.

"Certainly a few changes have been made in order to fulfill basic dramatic tenets. To quote a European dramatist friend of ours, 'God writes lousy theatre.' In other words, reality is seldom artistic, orderly, or dramatically satisfying: life rarely provides a sound second act, and its climaxes usually have not been adequately prepared for. Therefore, in historical drama, a number of small licenses are almost always taken with strictest fact. . . . But none of them, either separately or in accumulation, has done anything to alter the historical truth of the characters, the times, or the events of American independence."

Peter Stone (book) was born in Los Angeles, California, on February 27, 1930. He took his B.A. degree at Bard College and his M.F.A. at Yale University. His first play produced was *Friend of the Family*, presented in 1958 at the Crystal Palace, St. Louis, Missouri.

In 1961, Mr. Stone made his New York debut as a dramatist with the libretto for the musical *Kean*, with Alfred Drake as the volatile nineteenth century actor, Edmund Kean. He next provided the book for *Skyscraper* (1965) which marked the musical comedy debut of Julie Harris. Then came *1776;* and following this memorable success, he fashioned the book for the 1970 Richard Rodgers musical *Two by Two* (based on the Clifford Odets play, *The Flowering Peach*). With Danny Kaye cavorting about the ark as Noah, the presentation entertained Broadway audiences for 351 performances.

His first Hollywood screenplay was *Charade*, produced and directed by Stanley Donen (who, incidentally, began his career as a dancer in the 1940 Broadway musical *Pal Joey*). The film had Cary Grant, Audrey Hepburn and Walter Matthau in the principal roles; and it won for Mr. Stone a 1964 Mystery Writers of America Award for best suspense picture of the year. His other works for the screen include: *Mirage; Arabesque; Sweet Charity; Skin Game;* and *Father Goose*, for which he received (with Frank Tarloff) the 1964 Academy Award for the year's best screenplay.

Mr. Stone also has written extensively for television and was the recipient of an Emmy Award for one of his scripts for *The Defenders*.

The author's most recent work for the theatre was the book for the 1972 Broadway musical *Sugar*.

Sherman Edwards, whose music and lyrics glowingly add to the emotional depth and dramatic turning points of *1776,* was born in New York City on April 3, 1919. He was educated at New York University and Cornell University, where he majored in history. His original interest was in ancient and Mediterranean history, but as he later declared in an interview: "I gravitated to American history and I was grabbed by this thing, this story of the Declaration of Independence. It excited me and I wanted to do it." Eventually, both of his major interests (history and music) were to culminate in *1776*.

A distinguished songwriter with a long list of successful credits, he also worked as a musician with such bandleaders as Benny Goodman, Tommy Dorsey and Louis Armstrong. Additionally, he has composed the scores for numerous Hollywood films, including several popular Elvis Presley vehicles.

COMPANY

One of the most strikingly innovative musicals of the present decade, *Company* opened on April 26, 1970 to a concordance of rare critical praise. It was described as "a consistently dazzling, brilliant, completely unconventional new musical [that] explodes like a final burst of rockets at a Fourth of July fireworks display. [It is] so extraordinary in execution that it defies comparison with any musical that has come before it; [here is] an original piece of work that joyously breaks new ground, delights and astonishes [and without hesitation] one must call *Company* a landmark musical." These lavish tributes were echoed by Brooks Atkinson who added that *Company* was "a brilliant musical drama that looks and sounds like 1970—witty, taut, wary and also explosive." The verdict was in and the public responded to the tune of 705 performances.

Not only was *Company* a major success, but it also acquired some of the theatre's most cherished prizes, notably the 1970 New York Drama Critics' Circle Award and the Antoinette Perry (Tony) Award for the season's best musical. Additional personal honors were bestowed upon Stephen Sondheim when he was named the year's best composer and lyricist in *Variety*'s annual poll of New York's drama critics.

Featuring a number of members from the Broadway cast (including Larry Kert, who replaced Dean Jones in the role of Robert shortly after the New York premiere), *Company* opened in London at Her Majesty's Theatre on January 18, 1972. An immediate success there as well, the reviewer for the London *Times* opined that, "it looks as if we will be having the pleasure of this *Company* for some time," as indeed it did. It also won the 1972 *Plays and Players* Award as the year's best new musical.

Stephen Sondheim is, indisputably, the reigning composer-lyricist of the contemporary American musical theatre. Beginning the decade with the prize-winning *Company*, his musicals have since won two additional New York Drama Critics' Circle Awards—for *Follies* (book by James Goldman, 1971) and *A Little Night Music* (book by Hugh Wheeler, 1973).

Mr. Sondheim was born in New York City on March 22, 1930. He attended Williams College, where he majored in music, and as an undergraduate gained a certain celebrity on campus by writing the book, lyrics and music for two college shows. Winner of the Hutchinson Prize for Musical Composition, after graduation he studied theory and composition with Milton Babbitt.

His first professional writing was done in 1953 when he authored scripts for the *Topper* television series. In 1956, he came to the Broadway theatre with the incidental music for *Girls of Summer;* but it was in the following year that he first commanded major attention with his lyrics for *West Side Story* and, after that, *Gypsy*.

It was in 1962, however, that Stephen Sondheim came full sail into the theatre as both composer and lyricist for *A Funny Thing Happened on the Way to the Forum.* Subsequent productions that were highlighted by Sondheim scores and lyrics include: *Anyone Can Whistle* (1964); *Company* (1970); *Follies* (1971); and *A Little Night Music* (1973).

In addition to the aforementioned, Mr. Sondheim (who is the incumbent president of The Dramatists Guild) served as lyricist for *Do I Hear a Waltz?* (book by Arthur Laurents, music by Richard Rodgers, 1965) and as the composer of incidental music for Mr. Laurents' 1960 comedy, *Invitation to a March.*

George Furth, author of the book for *Company,* was born on December 14, 1932, in Chicago, Illinois. After graduating from Northwestern University, he came to New York to get a Master's Degree at Columbia. In 1961, he entered the theatre as an actor in *A Cook for Mr. General.* Spotted by Hollywood, he was offered a film contract and thereafter appeared in a score of films, including: *The Best Man; The Boston Strangler; Myra Breckinridge;* and *Butch Cassidy and the Sundance Kid.*

Company was Mr. Furth's initial attempt at writing and it was followed by a second Broadway success, *Twigs,* which had 312 performances during the 1971–1972 season.

It seems most fitting at this junction to acknowledge producer-director Harold Prince, a creative Solon who inspired and helped fashion such distinguished American musicals as: *The Pajama Game; Damn Yankees; New Girl In Town; West Side Story; Fiorello!; A Funny Thing Happened on the Way to the Forum; She Loves Me; Fiddler on the Roof; Cabaret; Zorbá; Follies; A Little Night Music;* and, of course, *Company.*

STANLEY RICHARDS

Since the publication of his first collection in 1968, Stanley Richards has become one of our leading editors and play anthologists, earning rare encomiums from the nation's press and the admiration of a multitude of devoted readers.

In addition to *Ten Great Musicals of the American Theatre*, Mr. Richards has edited the following anthologies and series: *The Best Short Plays 1973; The Best Short Plays 1972; The Best Short Plays 1971; The Best Short Plays 1970; The Best Short Plays 1969; The Best Short Plays 1968; Ten Classic Mystery and Suspense Plays of the Modern Theatre; Best Mystery and Suspense Plays of the Modern Theatre; Best Plays of the Sixties* (the latter three, *The Fireside Theatre–Literary Guild* selections); *Best Short Plays of the World Theatre: 1968–1973; Best Short Plays of the World Theatre: 1958–1967; Modern Short Comedies from Broadway and London;* and *Canada on Stage.*

An established playwright as well, he has written twenty-five plays, twelve of which (including *Through a Glass, Darkly; Tunnel of Love; August Heat; Sun Deck; O Distant Land;* and *District of Columbia*) were originally published in earlier volumes of *The Best One-Act Plays* and *The Best Short Plays* annuals.

Journey to Bahia, which he adapted from a prize-winning Brazilian play and film, *O Pagador de Promessas,* premiered at The Berkshire Playhouse, Massachusetts, and later was produced in Washington, D.C., under the auspices of the Brazilian Ambassador and the Brazilian American Cultural Institute. The play also had a successful engagement Off-Broadway during the 1970–1971 season; and in September 1972, it was performed in a Spanish translation at Lincoln Center.

Mr. Richards' plays have been translated for production and publication abroad into Portuguese, Afrikaans, Dutch, Tagalog, French, German, Korean, Italian and Spanish.

He also has been the New York theatre critic for *Players Magazine* and a frequent contributor to *Playbill, Theatre Arts, The Theatre* and *Actors' Equity Magazine,* among other periodicals.

As an American Theatre Specialist, Mr. Richards was awarded three successive grants by the U. S. Department of State's International Cultural Exchange Program to teach playwriting and directing in Chile and Brazil. He taught playwriting in Canada for over ten years and in 1966 was appointed Visiting Professor of Drama at the University of Guelph, Ontario. He has produced and directed plays and has lectured extensively on theatre at universities in the United States, Canada and South America.

Mr. Richards, a New York City resident, is now at work on *The Best Short Plays 1974*.